Microsoft Exam Objectives
Exam 70-210: Installing, Configuring, and Administering Windows 2000 Professional

S0-BWV-698

Installing Windows 2000 Professional	Chapter(s):
Perform attended and unattended installations of Windows 2000 Professional.	2
Install Windows 2000 Professional by using either Windows 2000 Server Remote Installation Services (RIS) or the System Preparation Tool.	2
Create unattended answer files by using Setup Manager to automate Windows 2000 Professional installation.	2
Upgrade from previous Windows versions to Windows 2000 Professional.	2
Apply or deploy update and service packs to installed software applications.	2
Prepare a computer to meet upgrade requirements and troubleshoot failed installations.	2

Implementing and Conducting Administration of Resources	Chapter(s):
Monitor, manage, troubleshoot, and optimize access to files and folders.	6
Configure, manage, and troubleshoot file compression.	6
Control access to files, folders, and printers by using permissions.	6, 7
Create, remove, manage, control, and troubleshoot access to shared folders.	6
Connect to local and network print devices and manage printers and print jobs.	7
Connect to an Internet printer and to a local print device.	7
Configure and manage file systems.	4
Convert from one file system to another file system and configure file systems by using NTFS, FAT32, or FAT.	4

Implementing, Managing, and Troubleshooting Hardware Devices and Drivers	Chapter(s):
Implement, manage, and troubleshoot disk, DVD, and CD-ROM devices.	4
Monitor and configure disks and removable media, such as tape devices.	4
Monitor, configure, and troubleshoot volumes.	4
Implement, manage, and troubleshoot display devices and configure multiple-display support.	9
Install, configure, and troubleshoot a video adapter and Advanced Power Management (APM).	9, 12
Implement, manage, and troubleshoot mobile computer hardware and configure and manage card services.	12
Implement, configure, manage, and troubleshoot input and output (I/O) devices, such as printers, scanners, multimedia devices, mouse, keyboard, and smart card reader.	9
Monitor, configure, and troubleshoot multimedia hardware, such as cameras.	9
Install, configure, and manage modems, Infrared Data Association (IrDA) devices, network adapters, and USB devices.	9
Monitor and configure multiple processing units and update drivers.	9

Monitoring and Optimizing System Performance and Reliability	Chapter(s):
Manage and troubleshoot driver signing the use and synchronization of offline files.	14
Configure, manage, and troubleshoot the Task Scheduler.	14
Optimize and troubleshoot performance of the Windows 2000 Professional desktop, memory performance, processor usage, disk performance, and network and application performance.	5, 9, 14
Manage hardware profiles.	9
Recover systems and user data by using Windows Backup and by using the Recovery Console.	15
Troubleshoot system restoration by using Safe Mode.	15

Configuring and Troubleshooting the Desktop Environment	Chapter(s):
Configure and manage user profiles.	5
Configure support for multiple languages or multiple locations.	5
Enable and configure multiple-language support for users.	5
Configure local settings.	5
Configure Windows 2000 Professional for multiple locations.	5
Install applications by using Windows Installer packages.	5
Configure and troubleshoot desktop settings, fax support, and accessibility services.	5

Implementing, Managing, and Troubleshooting Network Protocols and Services	Chapter(s):
Configure and troubleshoot the TCP/IP protocol and Internet Connection Sharing.	10, 11
Connect to computers by using dial-up networking and virtual private network (VPN) connections.	10
Create a dial-up connection to connect to a remote access server and to the Internet.	10
Connect to shared resources on a Microsoft network.	16

Implementing, Monitoring, and Troubleshooting Security	Chapter(s):
Encrypt data on a hard disk by using Encrypting File System (EFS).	13
Implement, configure, manage, and troubleshoot local Group Policy, local user accounts, auditing, account settings, and account policy.	13,14
Create and manage local users and groups.	13
Implement, configure, manage, and troubleshoot user rights, local user authentication, and a security configuration.	13
Configure and troubleshoot local user and domain user accounts.	13

MCSE™
Windows® 2000
Professional

Michael D. Stewart

Neall Alcott

James Bloomingdale

MCSE™ Windows® 2000 Professional Exam Prep

Limits of Liability and Disclaimer of Warranty

The author and publisher of this book have used their best efforts in preparing the book and the programs contained in it. These efforts include the development, research, and testing of the theories and programs to determine their effectiveness. The author and publisher make no warranty of any kind, expressed or implied, with regard to these programs or the documentation contained in this book.

The author and publisher shall not be liable in the event of incidental or consequential damages in connection with, or arising out of, the furnishing, performance, or use of the programs, associated instructions, and/or claims of productivity gains.

Trademarks

Trademarked names appear throughout this book. Rather than list the names and entities that own the trademarks or insert a trademark symbol with each mention of the trademarked name, the publisher states that it is using the names for editorial purposes only and to the benefit of the trademark owner, with no intention of infringing upon that trademark.

The Coriolis Group, LLC
14455 N. Hayden Road, Suite 220
Scottsdale, Arizona 85260

(480)483-0192
FAX (480)483-0193
www.coriolis.com

Library of Congress Cataloging-in-Publication Data
Stewart, Michael (Michael DeJean)
    MCSE Windows 2000 Professional exam prep / by Michael Steward, James Bloomingdale, and Neall Alcott.
        p.   cm.
    Includes index.
    ISBN 1-57610-703-5
    1. Electronic data processing personnel--Certification.   2. Microsoft software--Examinations--Study guides.   3. Microsoft Windows (Computer file)   I. Bloomingdale, James.   II. Alcott, Neall.   III. Title.
QA76.3. S4965 2000
005.4'4769--dc21
                                                    00-043138
                                                    CIP

President and CEO
Keith Weiskamp

Publisher
Steve Sayre

Acquisitions Editor
Shari Jo Hehr

Marketing Specialist
Cynthia Caldwell

Project Editor
Don Eamon

Technical Reviewer
Rick Gross

Production Coordinator
Todd Halvorsen

Cover Designer
Jesse Dunn

Layout Designer
April Nielsen

CD-ROM Developer
Michelle McConnell

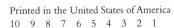
Printed in the United States of America
10 9 8 7 6 5 4 3 2 1

The Coriolis Group, LLC • 14455 North Hayden Road, Suite 220 • Scottsdale, Arizona 85260

ExamCram.com Connects You to the Ultimate Study Center!

Our goal has always been to provide you with the best study tools on the planet to help you achieve your certification in record time. Time is so valuable these days that none of us can afford to waste a second of it, especially when it comes to exam preparation.

Over the past few years, we've created an extensive line of *Exam Cram* and *Exam Prep* study guides, practice exams, and interactive training. To help you study even better, we have now created an e-learning and certification destination called **ExamCram.com**. (You can access the site at **www.examcram.com**.) Now, with every study product you purchase from us, you'll be connected to a large community of people like yourself who are actively studying for their certifications, developing their careers, seeking advice, and sharing their insights and stories.

I believe that the future is all about collaborative learning. Our **ExamCram.com** destination is our approach to creating a highly interactive, easily accessible collaborative environment, where you can take practice exams and discuss your experiences with others, sign up for features like "Questions of the Day," plan your certifications using our interactive planners, create your own personal study pages, and keep up with all of the latest study tips and techniques.

I hope that whatever study products you purchase from us—*Exam Cram* or *Exam Prep* study guides, *Personal Trainers*, *Personal Test Centers*, or one of our interactive Web courses—will make your studying fun and productive. Our commitment is to build the kind of learning tools that will allow you to study the way you want to, whenever you want to.

Visit ExamCram.com now to enhance your study program.

Help us continue to provide the very best certification study materials possible. Write us or email us at **learn@examcram.com** and let us know how our study products have helped you study. Tell us about new features that you'd like us to add. Send us a story about how we've helped you. We're listening!

Good luck with your certification exam and your career. Thank you for allowing us to help you achieve your goals.

Keith Weiskamp
President and CEO

Look for these other products from The Coriolis Group:

MCSE Windows 2000 Accelerated Exam Prep
By Lance Cockcroft, Erik Eckel, and Ron Kauffman

MCSE Windows 2000 Server Exam Prep
By David Johnson and Dawn Rader

MCSE Windows 2000 Network Exam Prep
By Tammy Smith and Sandra Smeeton

MCSE Windows 2000 Directory Services Exam Prep
By David V. Watts, Will Willis, and Tillman Strahan

MCSE Windows 2000 Security Design Exam Prep
By Richard Alan McMahon and Glen Bicking

MCSE Windows 2000 Network Design Exam Prep
By Geoffrey Alexander, Anoop Jalan, and Joseph Alexander

MCSE Migrating from NT 4 to Windows 2000 Exam Prep
By Glen Bergen, Graham Leach, and David Baldwin

MCSE Windows 2000 Directory Services Design Exam Prep
By J. Peter Bruzzese and Wayne Dipchan

MCSE Windows 2000 Core Four Exam Prep Pack

MCSE Windows 2000 Server Exam Cram
By Natasha Knight

MCSE Windows 2000 Professional Exam Cram
By Dan Balter, Dan Holme, Todd Logan, and Laurie Salmon

MCSE Windows 2000 Network Exam Cram
By Hank Carbeck, Derek Melber, and Richard Taylor

MCSE Windows 2000 Directory Services Exam Cram
By David V. Watts, Will Willis, and J. Peter Bruzzese

MCSE Windows 2000 Security Design Exam Cram
By Phillip G. Schein

MCSE Windows 2000 Network Design Exam Cram
By Kim Simmons, Jarret W. Buse, and Todd Halping

MCSE Windows 2000 Directory Services Design Exam Cram
By Dennis Scheil and Diana Bartley

MCSE Windows 2000 Core Four Exam Cram Pack

and...

MCSE Windows 2000 Foundations
By James Michael Stewart and Lee Scales

This book is dedicated to the four most important people in my life: Mom, Dad, Lynn, and Trice. Without your support, none of this would have been possible. Thanks for always being there.
—Michael D. Stewart
(P.S. Puppy, you too!)
❧

This book is dedicated to Murphy and Myles. You will be sorely missed.
—James Bloomingdale
❧

This book is dedicated to Ginny. You are my best friend and my foundation. Your support gives me the strength to accomplish any goal. I love ya, Jake!
—Neall Alcott
❧

About the Authors

Michael D. Stewart works is a consultant and is based in the Raleigh/Durham area of North Carolina. His certifications include MCSE, MCP+I, and CNA. Michael is also a MCT and has been providing computer training for over 12 years. In addition to his regular job assignments, Michael teaches the MCSE certification track at a local Microsoft ATTP (Authorized Academic Training Provider).

James Bloomingdale, MCSE+I, MCT, MCDBA, MCNE, has been a working Network Administrator and Consultant for the last five years and a Microsoft Trainer for the last two. He currently is an Independent Consultant based in Milwaukee, Wisconsin, providing design and installation services along with training.

Neall Alcott has been designing, building, and managing networks for the past eight years. He is also an MCT who has been training students in the Delaware Valley for the past four years. Currently, he is an Advisory System Engineer for Visalign LLC, a professional services firm specializing in Web solutions, Web infrastructure, and managed services for enterprise-wide clients in the pharmaceutical, financial services, power/utility, entertainment and media, emerging technology/growth, and state and local government industries. At Visalign, Neall is responsible for overseeing the Intel platform infrastructure at one client's North American headquarters, as well as 16 remote sites across the United States.

Acknowledgments

I would like to thank the Coriolis group—specifically, Shari Jo Hehr and Don Eamon. Thanks, Shari, for giving me the opportunity to take things to another level. Don, thanks for the guidance you provided during the process and for keeping the group on schedule.

I want to give special thanks to my two co-authors, James Bloomingdale and Neall Alcott. Without Jim and Neall, this would have been just a dream. I felt that we worked well as a team, and I appreciate all the effort each of you put forward to make this a reality. From our initial contact, we worked as a team, and I commend you both on the jobs you have done. I look forward to working with both of you in the near future again.

Also thanks to all my family members, friends, and students who put up with my crazy schedule during the writing of this book.
—*Michael D. Stewart*

First, I want to thank all the people at Coriolis who got this project complete and answered all of my questions. Don Eamon, the project editor, was very patient and never gave me a hard time. Shari Jo Hehr, who got the project going in the first place, and Wendy Cutts who always answered my questions. I especially want to thank Michael D. Stewart and Neall Alcott. It was a real pleasure working with both of you; you were always very professional and dedicated to making sure that this book was not only done, but was done well.

I also want to thank all the people that supported me through this project and gave me the time and encouragement to keep going. You know who you are. Thank you.
—*James Bloomingdale*

A special thanks to the team at Coriolis who helped get this project started and completed. To Don Eamon, our project editor, who worked with the three of us, coordinating all of our work, and keeping our eyes on the ball. To Shari Jo Hehr, our acquisitions editor, who had the foresight to bring us all together as a team. I would like to thank Neil Salkind and everyone at Studio B for all of their assistance.

I would also like to thank my co-authors, Michael Stewart and James Bloomingdale. It has been an honor working with the two of you. From the first conference call, I felt as though we were a team. I look forward to the possibility of future projects!

Acknowledgments

Of course, I must thank everyone at AZ. Call me. OK, thanks. Are we at JeffCon 5? Back to one.

The greatest thanks goes to my wife, Ginny, for her patience during this project, and my daughters, Lauren and Lindsey. Yes, Daddy can play now. Hey Jake! Remember me?
—*Neall Alcott*

Contents at a Glance

Table of Contents

Chapter 2
Installing and Deploying
Windows 2000 Professional 27

Chapter 5
Customizing Windows 2000 Professional 111

Chapter 7
Printing 177

Chapter 10
Networking 251

Exam Insights

Welcome to *MCSE Windows 2000 Professional Exam Prep*! This comprehensive study guide aims to help you get ready to take—and pass—Microsoft certification Exam 70-210, titled "Installing, Configuring, and Administering Microsoft Windows 2000 Professional." This Exam Insights section discusses exam preparation resources, the testing situation, Microsoft's certification programs in general, and how this book can help you prepare for Microsoft's Windows 2000 certification exams.

Exam Prep study guides help you understand and appreciate the subjects and materials you need to pass Microsoft certification exams. We've worked from Microsoft's curriculum objectives to ensure that all key topics are clearly explained. Our aim is to bring together as much information as possible about Microsoft certification exams.

Nevertheless, to completely prepare yourself for any Microsoft test, we recommend that you begin by taking the Self-Assessment included in this book immediately following this Exam Insights section. This tool will help you evaluate your knowledge base against the requirements for an MCSE under both ideal and real circumstances.

Based on what you learn from that exercise, you might decide to begin your studies with some classroom training or some background reading. You might decide to read The Coriolis Group's *Exam Prep* book that you have in hand first, or you might decide to start with another study approach. You may also want to refer to one of a number of study guides available from Microsoft or third-party vendors. We also recommend that you supplement your study program with visits to **ExamCram.com** to receive additional practice questions, get advice, and track the Windows 2000 MCSE program.

We also strongly recommend that you install, configure, and fool around with the software that you'll be tested on, because nothing beats hands-on experience and familiarity when it comes to understanding the questions you're likely to encounter on a certification test. Book learning is essential, but hands-on experience is the best teacher of all!

How to Prepare for an Exam

Preparing for any Windows 2000 Server-related test (including "Installing, Configuring, and Administering Microsoft Windows 2000 Professional") requires that you obtain and study materials designed to provide comprehensive information a bout the product and its capabilities that will appear on the specific exam for which you are preparing. The following list of materials will help you study and prepare:

➤ The Windows 2000 Professional product CD includes comprehensive online documentation and related materials; it should be a primary resource when you are preparing for the test.

➤ The exam preparation materials, practice tests, and self-assessment exams on the Microsoft Training And Certification Download page (**www.microsoft. com/train_cert/download/downld.htm**). Find the materials, download them, and use them!

➤ The exam preparation advice, practice tests, questions of the day, and discussion groups on the **ExamCram.com** e-learning and certification destination Web site (**www.examcram.com**).

In addition, you'll probably find any or all of the following materials useful in your quest for Windows 2000 Professional expertise:

➤ *Microsoft training kits*—Microsoft Press offers a training kit that specifically targets Exam 70-210. For more information, visit: **http://mspress. microsoft.com/books/1963.htm.** Here, you'll find more information about the *MCSE Training Kit—Microsoft Windows 2000 Professional* This training kit contains information that you will find useful in preparing for the test.

➤ *Microsoft TechNet CD*—This monthly CD-ROM-based publication delivers numerous electronic titles that include coverage of Windows 2000 Professional and related topics on the Technical Information (TechNet) CD. Its offerings include product facts, technical notes, tools and utilities, and information on how to access the Seminars Online training materials for Windows 2000 Professional. A subscription to TechNet costs $299 per year, but it is well worth the price. Visit **www.microsoft.com/technet/** and check out the information under the "TechNet Subscription" menu entry for more details.

➤ *Study guides*—Several publishers—including The Coriolis Group—offer Windows 2000 titles. The Coriolis Group series includes the following:

➤ *The Exam Cram series*—These books give you information about the material you need to know to pass the tests.

➤ *The Exam Prep series*—These books provide a greater level of detail than the *Exam Cram* books and are designed to teach you everything you need to know from an exam perspective. Each book comes with a CD that contains interactive practice exams in a variety of testing formats.

Together, the two series make a perfect pair.

➤ *Multimedia*—These Coriolis Group materials are designed to support learners of all types—whether you learn best by, reading or doing:

    ➤ *The Exam Cram Personal Trainer*—Offers a unique, personalized self-paced training course based on the exam.

    ➤ *The Exam Cram Personal Test Center*—Features multiple test options that simulate the actual exam, including Fixed-Length, Random, Review, and Test All. Explanations of correct and incorrect answers reinforce concepts learned.

➤ *Classroom training*—CTECs, online partners, and third-party training companies (like Wave Technologies, Learning Tree, Data-Tech, and others) all offer classroom training on TCP/IP. These companies aim to help you prepare to pass the TCP/IP test. Although such training runs upwards of $350 per day in class, most of the individuals lucky enough to partake find them to be quite worthwhile.

➤ *Other publications*—There's no shortage of materials available about Windows 2000 Professional. The complete resource section in the back of the book should give you an idea of where we think you should look for further discussion.

By far, this set of required and recommended materials represents a nonpareil collection of sources and resources for Windows 2000 Professional and related topics. We anticipate that you'll find that this book belongs in this company.

Taking a Certification Exam

Once you've prepared for your exam, you need to register with a testing center. Each computer-based MCP exam costs $100, and if you don't pass, you may retest for an additional $100 for each additional try. In the United States and Canada, tests are administered by Prometric (formerly Sylvan Prometric) and by Virtual University Enterprises (VUE). Here's how you can contact them:

➤ *Prometric*—You can sign up for a test through the company's Web site at **www.prometric.com**. Or, you can register by phone at 800-755-3926 (within the United States or Canada) or at 410-843-8000 (outside the United States and Canada).

➤ *Virtual University Enterprises*—You can sign up for a test or get the phone numbers for local testing centers through the Web page at **www.microsoft.com/train_cert/mcp/vue_info.htm**.

To sign up for a test, you must possess a valid credit card, or contact either company for mailing instructions to send them a check (in the U.S.). Only when payment is verified, or a check has cleared, can you actually register for a test.

To schedule an exam, call the number or visit either of the Web pages at least one day in advance. To cancel or reschedule an exam, you must call before 7 P.M. pacific standard time the day before the scheduled test time (or you may be charged, even if you don't appear to take the test). When you want to schedule a test, have the following information ready:

➤ Your name, organization, and mailing address.

➤ Your Microsoft Test ID. (Inside the United States, this means your Social Security number; citizens of other nations should call ahead to find out what type of identification number is required to register for a test.)

➤ The name and number of the exam you wish to take.

➤ A method of payment. (As we've already mentioned, a credit card is the most convenient method, but alternate means can be arranged in advance, if necessary.)

Once you sign up for a test, you'll be informed as to when and where the test is scheduled. Try to arrive at least 15 minutes early.

The Exam Situation

When you arrive at the testing center where you scheduled your exam, you'll need to sign in with an exam coordinator. He or she will ask you to show two forms of identification, one of which must be a photo ID. After you've signed in and your time slot arrives, you'll be asked to deposit any books, bags, or other items you brought with you. Then, you'll be escorted into a closed room.

All exams are completely closed book. In fact, you will not be permitted to take anything with you into the testing area, but you will be furnished with a blank sheet of paper and a pen or, in some cases, an erasable plastic sheet and an erasable pen. Before the exam, you should memorize as much of the important material as you can, so you can write that information on the blank sheet as soon as you are seated in front of the computer. You can refer to this piece of paper anytime you like during the test, but you'll have to surrender the sheet when you leave the room.

You will have some time to compose yourself, to record this information, and to take a sample orientation exam before you begin the real thing. We suggest you take the orientation test before taking your first exam, but because they're all more or less identical in layout, behavior, and controls, you probably won't need to do this more than once.

Typically, the room will be furnished with anywhere from one to half a dozen computers, and each workstation will be separated from the others by dividers designed to keep you from seeing what's happening on someone else's computer. Most test rooms feature a wall with a large picture window. This permits the exam coordinator to monitor the room, to prevent exam-takers from talking to one another, and to observe anything out of the ordinary that might go on. The exam coordinator will have preloaded the appropriate Microsoft certification exam—for this book, that's Exam 70-210—and you'll be permitted to start as soon as you're seated in front of the computer.

All Microsoft certification exams allow a certain maximum amount of time in which to complete your work (this time is indicated on the exam by an on-screen counter/clock, so you can check the time remaining whenever you like). All Microsoft certification exams are computer generated. In addition to multiple choice, you'll encounter select and place (drag and drop), create a tree (categorization and prioritization), drag and connect, and (build list and reorder) on most exams. Although this may sound quite simple, the questions are constructed not only to check your mastery of basic facts and figures about Windows 2000 Professional, but they also require you to evaluate one or more sets of circumstances or requirements. Often, you'll be asked to give more than one answer to a question. Likewise, you might be asked to select the best or most effective solution to a problem from a range of choices, all of which technically are correct. Taking the exam is quite an adventure, and it involves real thinking. This book shows you what to expect and how to deal with the potential problems, puzzles, and predicaments.

When you complete a Microsoft certification exam, the software will tell you whether you've passed or failed. Results are broken into several topic areas. Even if you fail, we suggest you ask for—and keep—the detailed report that the test administrator should print for you. You can use this report to help you prepare for another go-round, if needed.

If you need to retake an exam, you'll have to schedule a new test with Prometric or VUE and pay another $100.

Note: *The first time you fail a test, you can retake the test the next day. However, if you fail a second time, you must wait 14 days before retaking that test. The 14-day waiting period remains in effect for all retakes after the second failure.*

In the next section, you'll learn more about how Microsoft test questions look and how they must be answered.

Exam Layout and Design

The format of Microsoft's Windows 2000 exams is different from that of its previous exams. For the design exams (70-219, 70-220, 70-221), each exam consists entirely of a series of case studies, and the questions can be of six types. For the

Core Four exams (70-210, 70-215, 70-216, 70-217), the same six types of questions can appear, but you are not likely to encounter complex multiquestion case studies. These case studies will provide you with the opportunity to experience this question type (which is encountered in many if not all of the elective exams) and to improve your test-taking skills by approaching the material in a new way.

For design exams, each case study or "testlet" presents a detailed problem that you must read and analyze. Figure 1 shows an example of what a case study looks like. You must select the different tabs in the case study to view the entire case.

Following each case study is a set of questions related to the case study; these questions can be one of six types (which are discussed next). Careful attention to details provided in the case study is the key to success. Be prepared to toggle frequently between the case study and the questions as you work. Some of the case studies also include diagrams, which are called *exhibits*, that you'll need to examine closely to understand how to answer the questions.

Once you complete a case study, you can review all the questions and your answers. However, once you move on to the next case study, you may not be able to return to the previous case study and make any changes.

The six types of question formats are:

➤ Multiple choice, single answer

➤ Multiple choice, multiple answers

➤ Build list and reorder (list prioritization)

➤ Create a tree

➤ Drag and connect

➤ Select and place (drag and drop)

Note: *Exam formats may vary by test center location. You may want to call the test center or visit **ExamCram.com** to see if you can find out which type of test you'll encounter.*

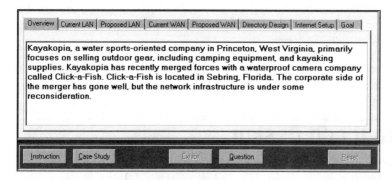

Figure 1 This is how case studies appear.

Multiple-Choice Question Format

Some exam questions require you to select a single answer, whereas others ask you to select multiple correct answers. The following multiple-choice question requires you to select a single correct answer. Following the question is a brief summary of each potential answer and why it is either right or wrong.

Question 1

What is the minimum amount of free disk space required to install Windows 2000 Professional?

○ a. 800MB

○ b. 2.2GB

○ c. 1.2GB

○ d. 128MB

Answer a is correct. Windows 2000 Professional requires 650MB of free disk space, although it is recommended that you have 1.2GB of free disk space.

This sample question format corresponds closely to the Microsoft certification exam format—the only difference on the exam is that questions are not followed by answer keys. To select an answer, you would position the cursor over the radio button next to the answer. Then, click the mouse button to select the answer.

Let's examine a question where one or more answers are possible. This type of question provides checkboxes rather than radio buttons for marking all appropriate selections.

Question 2

Mike is reviewing data that was created from a log file in system monitor. Mike would like to export this data to another program so he can present the data to people throughout his organization. What file types can be used to export this data? [Check all correct answers]

❑ a. .doc (Word)

❑ b. .html (Web)

❑ c. .xls (Excel)

❑ d. .tsv (Tab Delimited)

Answers b and d are correct. System Monitor can export files as either html or tsv. Html files can be viewed via a Web browser such as Internet Explorer. Tsv files can be imported into Microsoft Excel.

For this particular question, two answers are required. As far as the authors can tell (and Microsoft won't comment), such questions are scored as wrong unless all the required selections are chosen. In other words, a partially correct answer does not result in partial credit when the test is scored. For Question 2, you have to check the boxes next to items b and d to obtain credit for a correct answer. Notice that picking the right answers also means knowing why the other answers are wrong!

Build-List-and-Reorder Question Format

Questions in the build-list-and-reorder format present two lists of items—one on the left and one on the right. To answer the question, you must move items from the list on the right to the list on the left. The final list must then be reordered into a specific order.

These questions can best be characterized as "From the following list of choices, pick the choices that answer the question. Arrange the list in a certain order." To give you practice with this type of question, some questions of this type are included in this study guide. Here's an example of how they appear in this book; for a sample of how they appear on the test, see Figure 2.

Question 3

From the following list of famous people, pick those that have been elected President of the United States. Arrange the list in the order that they served.

Thomas Jefferson

Ben Franklin

Abe Lincoln

George Washington

Andrew Jackson

Paul Revere

The correct answer is:

George Washington
Thomas Jefferson
Andrew Jackson
Abe Lincoln

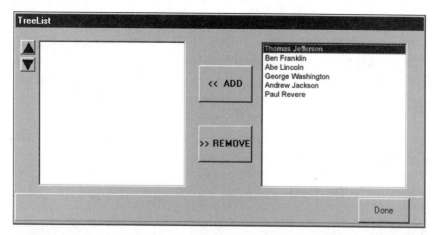

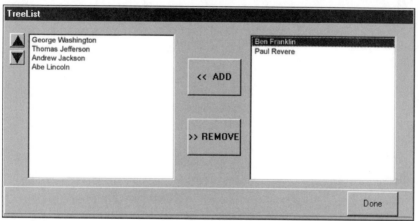

Figure 2   This is how build-list-and-reorder questions appear.

On an actual exam, the entire list of famous people would initially appear in the list on the right. You would move the four correct answers to the list on the left, and then reorder the list on the left. Notice that the answer to the question did not include all items from the initial list. However, this may not always be the case.

To move an item from the right list to the left list, first select the item by clicking on it, and then click on the Add button (left arrow). Once you move an item from one list to the other, you can move the item back by first selecting the item and then clicking on the appropriate button (either the Add button or the Remove button). Once items have been moved to the left list, you can reorder an item by selecting the item and clicking on the up or down button.

Create-a-Tree Question Format

Questions in the create-a-tree format also present two lists—one on the left side of the screen and one on the right side of the screen. The list on the right consists of individual items, and the list on the left consists of nodes in a tree. To answer the question, you must move items from the list on the right to the appropriate node in the tree.

These questions can best be characterized as simply a matching exercise. Items from the list on the right are placed under the appropriate category in the list on the left. Here's an example of how they appear in this book; for a sample of how they appear on the test, see Figure 3.

Question 4

The calendar year is divided into four seasons:

  Winter

  Spring

  Summer

  Fall

Identify the season when each of the following holidays occurs:

  Christmas

  Fourth of July

  Labor Day

  Flag Day

  Memorial Day

  Washington's Birthday

  Thanksgiving

  Easter

The correct answer is:

Winter
  Christmas
  Washington's Birthday

Spring
    Flag Day
    Memorial Day
    Easter
Summer
    Fourth of July
    Labor Day
Fall
    Thanksgiving

In this case, all the items in the list were used. However, this may not always be the case.

To move an item from the right list to its appropriate location in the tree, you must first select the appropriate tree node by clicking on it. Then, you select the item to be moved and click on the Add button. If one or more items have been added to a

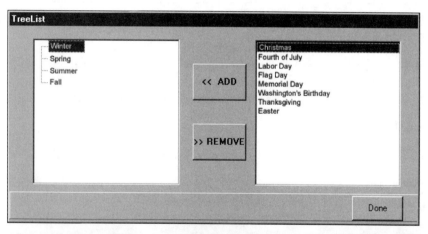

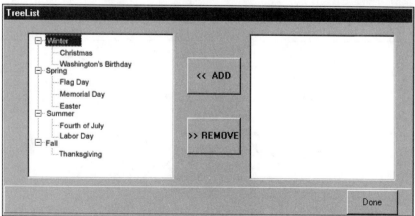

Figure 3 This is how create-a-tree questions appear.

tree node, the node will be displayed with a "+" icon to the left of the node name. You can click on this icon to expand the node and view the item(s) that have been added. If any item has been added to the wrong tree node, you can remove it by selecting it and clicking on the Remove button.

Drag-and-Connect Question Format

Questions in the drag-and-connect format present a group of objects and a list of "connections." To answer the question, you must move the appropriate connections between the objects.

This type of question is best described using graphics. Here's an example.

Question 5

The following objects represent the different states of water:

| Ice | Water Vapor | Water | Steam |

Use items from the following list to connect the objects so that they are scientifically correct.

Sublimates to form

Freezes to form

Evaporates to form

Boils to form

Condenses to form

Melts to form

The correct answer is:

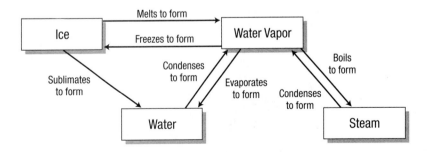

For this type of question, it's not necessary to use every object, and each connection can be used multiple times.

Select-and-Place Question Format

Questions in the select-and-place (drag-and-drop) format present a diagram with blank boxes, and a list of labels that need to be dragged to correctly fill in the blank boxes. To answer the question, you must move the labels to their appropriate positions on the diagram.

This type of question is best described using graphics. Here's an example.

Question 6

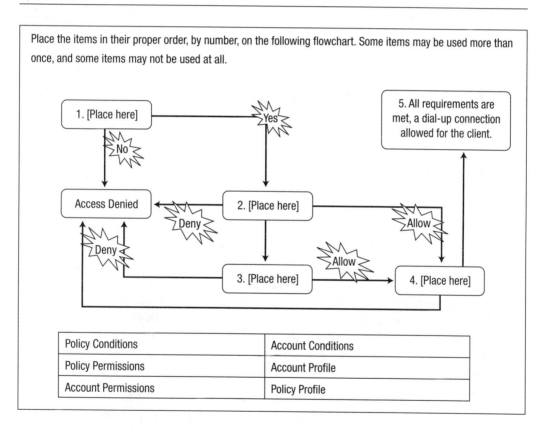

The correct answer is:

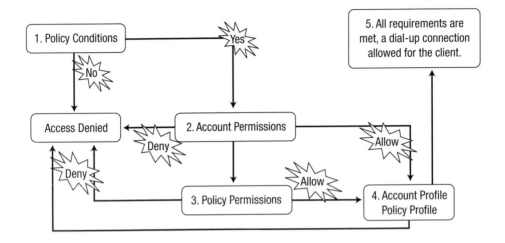

Microsoft's Testing Formats

Currently, Microsoft uses four different testing formats:

➤ Case study

➤ Fixed length

➤ Adaptive

➤ Short form

As we mentioned earlier, the case study approach is used with Microsoft's design exams, such as the one covered by this study guide. These exams consist of a set of case studies that you must analyze to enable you to answer questions related to the case studies. Such exams include one or more case studies (tabbed topic areas), each of which is followed by 4 to 10 questions. The question types for design exams and for Core Four Windows 2000 exams are multiple choice, build list and reorder, create a tree, drag and connect, and select and place. Depending on the test topic, some exams are totally case-based, whereas others are not.

Other Microsoft exams employ advanced testing capabilities that might not be immediately apparent. Although the questions that appear are primarily multiple choice, the logic that drives them is more complex than older Microsoft tests, which use a fixed sequence of questions, called a *fixed-length test*. Other exams employ a sophisticated user interface, which Microsoft calls a *simulation*, to test your knowledge of the software and systems under consideration in a more or less "live" environment that behaves just like the original.

For some exams, Microsoft has turned to a well-known technique, called *adaptive testing*, to establish a test-taker's level of knowledge and product competence. Adaptive exams look the same as fixed-length exams, but they discover the level of difficulty at which an individual test-taker can correctly answer questions. Test-takers with differing levels of knowledge or ability therefore see different sets of questions; individuals with high levels of knowledge or ability are presented with a smaller set of more difficult questions, whereas individuals with lower levels of knowledge are presented with a larger set of easier questions. Two individuals may answer the same percentage of questions correctly, but the test-taker with a higher knowledge or ability level will score higher because his or her questions are worth more.

Also, the lower-level test-taker will probably answer more questions than his or her more-knowledgeable colleague. This explains why adaptive tests use ranges of values to define the number of questions and the amount of time it takes to complete the test.

Adaptive tests work by evaluating the test-taker's most recent answer. A correct answer leads to a more difficult question (and the test software's estimate of the test-taker's knowledge and ability level is raised). An incorrect answer leads to a less difficult question (and the test software's estimate of the test-taker's knowledge and ability level is lowered). This process continues until the test targets the test-taker's true ability level. The exam ends when the test-taker's level of accuracy meets a statistically acceptable value (in other words, when his or her performance demonstrates an acceptable level of knowledge and ability), or when the maximum number of items has been presented (in which case, the test-taker is almost certain to fail).

Microsoft also introduced a short-form test for its most popular tests. This test delivers 30 questions to its takers, giving them exactly 60 minutes to complete the exam. This type of exam is similar to a fixed-length test, in that it allows readers to jump ahead or return to earlier questions, and to cycle through the questions until the test is done. Microsoft does not use adaptive logic in this test, but claims that statistical analysis of the question pool is such that the 30 questions delivered during a short-form exam conclusively measure a test-taker's knowledge of the subject matter in much the same way as an adaptive test. You can think of the short-form test as a kind of "greatest hits exam" (that is, the most important questions are covered) version of an adaptive exam on the same topic.

Note: *Several test-takers have reported that some of the Microsoft exams can appear as a combination of adaptive and fixed-length questions.*

Microsoft tests can come in any one of these forms. Whatever you encounter, you must take the test in whichever form it appears; you can't choose one form over another. If anything, it pays more to prepare thoroughly for an adaptive exam than for a fixed-length or a short-form exam: The penalties for answering incorrectly are built into the test itself on an adaptive exam, whereas the layout remains the same for a fixed-length or short-form test, no matter how many questions you answer incorrectly.

Tip: The biggest difference between an adaptive test and a fixed-length or short-form test is that on a fixed-length or short-form test, you can revisit questions after you've read them over one or more times. On an adaptive test, you must answer the question when it's presented and will have no opportunities to revisit that question thereafter.

Strategies for Different Testing Formats

Before you choose a test-taking strategy, you must know if your test is case study based, fixed length, short form, or adaptive. When you begin your exam, you'll know right away if the test is based on case studies. The interface will consist of a tabbed Window that allows you to easily navigate through the sections of the case.

If you are taking a test that is not based on case studies, the software will tell you that the test is adaptive, if in fact the version you're taking is an adaptive test. If your introductory materials fail to mention this, you're probably taking a fixed-length test (50 to 70 questions). If the total number of questions involved is 25 to 30, you're taking a short-form test. Some tests announce themselves by indicating that they will start with a set of adaptive questions, followed by fixed-length questions.

Tip: You'll be able to tell for sure if you are taking an adaptive, fixed-length, or short-form test by the first question. If it includes a checkbox that lets you mark the question for later review, you're taking a fixed-length or short-form test. If the total number of questions is 25 to 30, it's a short-form test; if more than 30, it's a fixed-length test. Adaptive test questions can be visited (and answered) only once, and they include no such checkbox.

The Case Study Exam Strategy

Most test-takers find that the case study type of test used for the design exams (70-219, 70-220, and 70-221) is the most difficult to master. When it comes to studying for a case study test, your best bet is to approach each case study as a standalone test. The biggest challenge you'll encounter is that you'll feel that you won't have enough time to get through all of the cases that are presented.

Tip: Each case provides a lot of material that you'll need to read and study before you can effectively answer the questions that follow. The trick to taking a case study exam is to first scan the case study to get the highlights. Make sure you read the overview section of the case so that you understand the context of the problem at hand. Then, quickly move on and scan the questions.

As you are scanning the questions, make mental notes to yourself so that you'll remember which sections of the case study you should focus on. Some case studies may provide a fair amount of extra information that you don't really need to answer the questions. The goal with our scanning approach is to avoid having to study and analyze material that is not completely relevant.

When studying a case, carefully read the tabbed information. It is important to answer each and every question. You will be able to toggle back and forth from case to questions, and from question to question within a case testlet. However, once you leave the case and move on, you may not be able to return to it. You may want to take notes while reading useful information so you can refer to them when you tackle the test questions. It's hard to go wrong with this strategy when taking any kind of Microsoft certification test.

The Fixed-Length and Short-Form Exam Strategy

A well-known principle when taking fixed-length or short-form exams is to first read over the entire exam from start to finish while answering only those questions you feel absolutely sure of. On subsequent passes, you can dive into more complex questions more deeply, knowing how many such questions you have left.

Fortunately, the Microsoft exam software for fixed-length and short-form tests makes the multiple-visit approach easy to implement. At the top-left corner of each question is a checkbox that permits you to mark that question for a later visit.

Note: Marking questions makes review easier, but you can return to any question by clicking the Forward or Back button repeatedly.

As you read each question, if you answer only those you're sure of and mark for review those that you're not sure of, you can keep working through a decreasing list of questions as you answer the trickier ones in order.

Tip: There's at least one potential benefit to reading the exam over completely before answering the trickier questions: Sometimes, information supplied in later questions sheds more light on earlier questions. At other times, information you read in later questions might jog your memory about Windows 2000 Professional facts, figures, or behavior that helps you answer earlier questions. Either way, you'll come out ahead if you defer those questions about which you're not absolutely sure.

Here are some question-handling strategies that apply to fixed-length and short-form tests. Use them if you have the chance:

➤ When returning to a question after your initial read-through, read every word again—otherwise, your mind can fall quickly into a rut. Sometimes, revisiting a question after turning your attention elsewhere lets you see something you missed, but the strong tendency is to see what you've seen before. Try to avoid that tendency at all costs.

➤ If you return to a question more than twice, try to articulate to yourself what you don't understand about the question, why answers don't appear to make sense, or what appears to be missing. If you chew on the subject awhile, your subconscious might provide the details you lack, or you might notice a "trick" that points to the right answer.

As you work your way through the exam, another counter that Microsoft provides will come in handy—the number of questions completed and questions outstanding. For fixed-length and short-form tests, it's wise to budget your time by making sure that you've completed one-quarter of the questions one-quarter of the way through the exam period, and three-quarters of the questions three-quarters of the way through.

If you're not finished when only five minutes remain, use that time to guess your way through any remaining questions. Remember, guessing is potentially more valuable than not answering, because blank answers are always wrong, but a guess may turn out to be right. If you don't have a clue about any of the remaining questions, pick answers at random, or choose all a's, b's, and so on. The important thing is to submit an exam for scoring that has an answer for every question.

Tip: At the very end of your exam period, you're better off guessing than leaving questions unanswered.

The Adaptive Exam Strategy

If there's one principle that applies to taking an adaptive test, it could be summed up as "Get it right the first time." You cannot elect to skip a question and move on to the next one when taking an adaptive test, because the testing software uses your answer to the current question to select whatever question it plans to present next. Nor can you return to a question once you've moved on, because the software gives you only one chance to answer the question. You can, however, take notes, because sometimes information supplied in earlier questions will shed more light on later questions.

Also, when you answer a question correctly, you are presented with a more difficult question next, to help the software gauge your level of skill and ability. When you answer a question incorrectly, you are presented with a less difficult question, and the software lowers its current estimate of your skill and ability. This continues until the program settles into a reasonably accurate estimate of what you know and can do, and takes you on average through somewhere between 15 and 30 questions as you complete the test.

The good news is that if you know your stuff, you'll probably finish most adaptive tests in 30 minutes or so. The bad news is that you must really, really know your stuff to do your best on an adaptive test. That's because some questions are so convoluted, complex, or hard to follow that you're bound to miss one or two, at a minimum, even if you do know your stuff. So the more you know, the better you'll do on an adaptive test, even accounting for the occasionally weird or unfathomable questions that appear on these exams.

Tip: Because you can't tell in advance if a test is fixed length, short form, or adaptive, you will be best served by preparing for the exam as if it were adaptive. That way, you should be prepared to pass no matter what kind of test you take. But if you do take a fixed-length or short-form test, remember our tips from the preceding section. They should help you improve on what you could do on an adaptive test.

If you encounter a question on an adaptive test that you can't answer, you must guess an answer immediately. Because of how the software works, you may suffer for your guess on the next question if you guess right, because you'll get a more difficult question next!

Question-Handling Strategies

Based on exams we have taken, some interesting trends have become apparent. For those questions that take only a single answer, usually two or three of the answers will be obviously incorrect, and two of the answers will be plausible—of course, only one can be correct. Unless the answer leaps out at you (if it does, reread the question to look for a trick; sometimes those are the ones you're most likely to get wrong), begin the process of answering by eliminating those answers that are most obviously wrong.

Almost always, at least one answer out of the possible choices for a question can be eliminated immediately because it matches one of these conditions:

➤ The answer does not apply to the situation.

➤ The answer describes a nonexistent issue, an invalid option, or an imaginary state.

After you eliminate all answers that are obviously wrong, you can apply your retained knowledge to eliminate further answers. Look for items that sound correct but refer to actions, commands, or features that are not present or not available in the situation that the question describes.

If you're still faced with a blind guess among two or more potentially correct answers, reread the question. Try to picture how each of the possible remaining answers would alter the situation. Be especially sensitive to terminology; sometimes the choice of words ("remove" instead of "disable") can make the difference between a right answer and a wrong one.

Only when you've exhausted your ability to eliminate answers, but remain unclear about which of the remaining possibilities is correct, should you guess at an answer. An unanswered question offers you no points, but guessing gives you at least some chance of getting a question right; just don't be too hasty when making a blind guess.

Note: If you're taking a fixed-length or a short-form test, you can wait until the last round of reviewing marked questions (just as you're about to run out of time, or out of unanswered questions) before you start making guesses. You will have the same option within each case study testlet (but once you leave a testlet, you may not be allowed to return to it). If you're taking an adaptive test, you'll have to guess to move on to the next question if you can't figure out an answer some other way. Either way, guessing should be your technique of last resort!

Numerous questions assume that the default behavior of a particular utility is in effect. If you know the defaults and understand what they mean, this knowledge will help you cut through many Gordian knots.

Mastering the Inner Game

In the final analysis, knowledge breeds confidence, and confidence breeds success. If you study the materials in this book carefully and review all the practice questions at the end of each chapter, you should become aware of those areas where additional learning and study are required.

After you've worked your way through the book, take the practice exam in the back of the book and the practice exams on the CD-ROM. Be sure to click on the Update button in our CD-ROM's testing engine to download 50 free questions from the Coriolis Web site! Taking tests will provide a reality check and help you identify areas to study further. Make sure you follow up and review materials related to the questions you miss on the practice exams before scheduling a real exam. Only when you've covered that ground and feel comfortable with the whole scope of the practice exams should you set an exam appointment. Only if you score 85 percent or better should you proceed to the real thing (otherwise, obtain some additional practice tests so you can keep trying until you hit this magic number).

Tip: If you take a practice exam and don't score at least 85 percent correct, you'll want to practice further. Microsoft provides a few free Personal Exam Prep (PEP) exams and also offers self-assessment exams from the Microsoft Certified Professional Web site's download page (**www.microsoft.com/train_cert/download/downld.htm**). You should also check out **ExamCram.com** for downloadable practice questions.

Armed with the information in this book and with the determination to augment your knowledge, you should be able to pass the certification exam. However, you need to work at it, or you'll spend the exam fee more than once before you finally pass. If you prepare seriously, you should do well. We are confident that you can do it!

The next section covers the exam requirements for the various Microsoft certifications.

The Microsoft Certified Professional (MCP) Program

The MCP Program currently includes the following separate tracks, each of which boasts its own special acronym (as a certification candidate, you need to have a high tolerance for alphabet soup of all kinds):

➤ *MCP (Microsoft Certified Professional)*—This is the least prestigious of all the certification tracks from Microsoft. Passing one of the major Microsoft exams qualifies an individual for the MCP credential. Individuals can demonstrate proficiency with additional Microsoft products by passing additional certification exams.

➤ *MCP+SB (Microsoft Certified Professional + Site Building)*—This certification program is designed for individuals who are planning, building, managing, and maintaining Web sites. Individuals with the MCP+SB credential will have demonstrated the ability to develop Web sites that include multimedia and searchable content and Web sites that connect to and communicate with a back-end database. It requires one MCP exam, plus two of these three exams: "70-055: Designing and Implementing Web Sites with Microsoft FrontPage 98," "70-057: Designing and Implementing Commerce Solutions with Microsoft Site Server, 3.0, Commerce Edition," and "70-152: Designing and Implementing Web Solutions with Microsoft Visual InterDev 6.0."

➤ *MCSE (Microsoft Certified Systems Engineer)*—Anyone who has a current MCSE is warranted to possess a high level of expertise with Windows 2000 and other Microsoft operating systems and products. This credential is designed to prepare individuals to plan, implement, maintain, and support information systems, networks, and internetworks built around Microsoft Windows 2000 and its BackOffice family of products.

To obtain an MCSE, an individual must pass four core operating system exams, plus two elective exams. The operating system exams require individuals to prove their competence with desktop and server operating systems and networking/internetworking components.

For Windows NT 4 MCSEs, the Accelerated exam, "70-240: Microsoft Windows 2000 Accelerated Exam for MCPs Certified on Microsoft Windows NT 4.0," is an option. This free exam covers all of the material tested in the Core Four exams. The hitch in this plan is that you can take the test only once. If you fail, you must take all four core exams to recertify. The Core Four exams are: "70-210: Installing, Configuring and Administering Microsoft Windows 2000 Professional," "70-215: Installing, Configuring and Administering Microsoft Windows 2000 Server," "70-216: Implementing and Administering a

Microsoft Windows 2000 Network Infrastructure," and "70-217: Implementing and Administering a Microsoft Windows 2000 Directory Services Infrastructure."

The two remaining exams are electives. An elective exam may fall in any number of subject or product areas, primarily BackOffice components. To fulfill the fifth core exam requirement, you can choose from three design exams: "70-219: Designing a Microsoft Windows 2000 Directory Services Infrastructure," "70-220: Designing Security for a Microsoft Windows 2000 Network," or "70-221: Designing a Microsoft Windows 2000 Network Infrastructure." The two design exams that you don't select as your fifth core exam also qualify as electives. If you are on your way to becoming an MCSE and have already taken some exams, visit **www.microsoft.com/mcp/certstep/mcse.htm** for information about how to complete your MCSE certification.

In September 1999, Microsoft announced its Windows 2000 track for MCSE and also announced retirement of Windows NT 4 MCSE core exams on 12/31/2000. Individuals who wish to remain certified MCSEs after 12/31/2001 must "upgrade" their certifications on or before 12/31/2001. The details are too complex to discuss here; to obtain those details, visit **www.microsoft.com/mcp/certstep/mcse.htm**.

New MCSE candidates must pass seven tests to meet the MCSE requirements. It's not uncommon for the entire process to take a year or so, and many individuals find that they must take a test more than once to pass. The primary goal of the *Exam Prep* series and the *Exam Cram* series, our test preparation books, is to make it possible, given proper study and preparation, to pass all Microsoft certification tests on the first try. Table 1 shows the required and elective exams for the Windows 2000 MCSE certification.

➤ *MCSD (Microsoft Certified Solution Developer)*—The MCSD credential reflects the skills required to create multi-tier, distributed, and COM-based solutions, in addition to desktop and Internet applications, using new technologies. To obtain an MCSD, an individual must demonstrate the ability to analyze and interpret user requirements; select and integrate products, platforms, tools, and technologies; design and implement code, and customize applications; and perform necessary software tests and quality assurance operations.

To become an MCSD, you must pass a total of four exams: three core exams and one elective exam. Each candidate must choose one of these three desktop application exams—"70-016: Designing and Implementing Desktop Applications with Microsoft Visual C++ 6.0," "70-156: Designing and Implementing Desktop Applications with Microsoft Visual FoxPro 6.0," or "70-176: Designing and Implementing Desktop Applications with Microsoft Visual Basic 6.0"—*plus* one of these three distributed application exams—"70-015: Designing and

Table 1   MCSE Windows 2000 Requirements

Core

If you have not passed these 3 Windows NT 4 exams	
Exam 70-067	Implementing and Supporting Microsoft Windows NT Server 4.0
Exam 70-068	Implementing and Supporting Microsoft Windows NT Server 4.0 in the Enterprise
Exam 70-073	Microsoft Windows NT Workstation 4.0
then you must take these 4 exams	
Exam 70-210	Installing, Configuring and Administering Microsoft Windows 2000 Professional
Exam 70-215	Installing, Configuring and Administering Microsoft Windows 2000 Server
Exam 70-216	Implementing and Administering a Microsoft Windows 2000 Network Infrastructure
Exam 70-217	Implementing and Administering a Microsoft Windows 2000 Directory Services Infrastructure
If you have already passed exams 70-067, 70-068, and 70-073, you may take this exam	
Exam 70-240	Microsoft Windows 2000 Accelerated Exam for MCPs Certified on Microsoft Windows NT 4.0

5th Core Option

Choose 1 from this group	
Exam 70-219*	Designing a Microsoft Windows 2000 Directory Services Infrastructure
Exam 70-220*	Designing Security for a Microsoft Windows 2000 Network
Exam 70-221*	Designing a Microsoft Windows 2000 Network Infrastructure

Elective

Choose 2 from this group	
Exam 70-019	Designing and Implementing Data Warehouse with Microsoft SQL Server 7.0
Exam 70-219*	Designing a Microsoft Windows 2000 Directory Services Infrastructure
Exam 70-220*	Designing Security for a Microsoft Windows 2000 Network
Exam 70-221*	Designing a Microsoft Windows 2000 Network Infrastructure
Exam 70-222	Migrating from Microsoft Windows NT 4.0 to Microsoft Windows 2000
Exam 70-028	Administering Microsoft SQL Server 7.0
Exam 70-029	Designing and Implementing Databases on Microsoft SQL Server 7.0
Exam 70-080	Implementing and Supporting Microsoft Internet Explorer 5.0 by Using the Internet Explorer Administration Kit
Exam 70-081	Implementing and Supporting Microsoft Exchange Server 5.5
Exam 70-085	Implementing and Supporting Microsoft SNA Server 4.0
Exam 70-086	Implementing and Supporting Microsoft Systems Management Server 2.0
Exam 70-088	Implementing and Supporting Microsoft Proxy Server 2.0

This is not a complete listing—you can still be tested on some earlier versions of these products. However, we have included mainly the most recent versions so that you may test on these versions and thus be certified longer. We have not included any tests that are scheduled to be retired.

* The 5th Core Option exam does not double as an elective.

Implementing Distributed Applications with Microsoft Visual C++ 6.0," "70-155: Designing and Implementing Desktop Applications with Microsoft Visual FoxPro 6.0," or "70-175: Designing and Implementing Desktop Applications with Microsoft Visual Basic 6.0." The third core exam is "70-100: Analyzing Requirements and Defining Solution Architectures." Elective exams cover specific Microsoft applications and languages, including Visual Basic, C++, the Microsoft Foundation Classes, Access, SQL Server, Excel, and more.

➤ *MCDBA (Microsoft Certified Database Administrator)*—The MCDBA credential reflects the skills required to implement and administer Microsoft SQL Server databases. To obtain an MCDBA, an individual must demonstrate the ability to derive physical database designs, develop logical data models, create physical databases, create data services by using Transact-SQL, manage and maintain databases, configure and manage security, monitor and optimize databases, and install and configure Microsoft SQL Server.

To become an MCDBA, you must pass a total of four exams and one elective exam. The required core exams are "70-028: Administering Microsoft SQL Server 7.0," "70-029: Designing and Implementing Databases with Microsoft SQL Server 7.0," and "70-215: Installing, Configuring and Administering Microsoft Windows 2000 Server."

The elective exams that you can choose from cover specific uses of SQL Server and include "70-015: Designing and Implementing Distributed Applications with Microsoft Visual C++ 6.0," "70-019: Designing and Implementing Data Warehouses with Microsoft SQL Server 7.0," "70-155: Designing and Implementing Distributed Applications with Visual FoxPro 6.0," "70-175: Designing and Implementing Distributed Applications with Visual Basic 6.0," and two exams that relate to Windows 2000: "70-216: Implementing and Administering Microsoft Windows 2000 Network Infrastructure," and "70-087: Implementing and Supporting Microsoft Internet Information Server 4.0."

If you have taken the three core Windows NT 4 exams on your path to becoming an MCSE, you qualify for the Accelerated exam (it replaces the Network Infrastructure exam requirement). The Accelerated exam covers the objectives of all four of the Windows 2000 core exams. In addition to taking the Accelerated exam, you must take only the two SQL exams—Administering and Database Design.

➤ *MCT (Microsoft Certified Trainer)*—Microsoft Certified Trainers are deemed able to deliver elements of the official Microsoft curriculum, based on technical knowledge and instructional ability. Thus, it is necessary for an individual seeking MCT credentials (which are granted on a course-by-course basis) to pass the related certification exam for a course and complete the official Microsoft training in the subject area, and to demonstrate an ability to teach. MCT candidates must also possess a current MCSE.

This teaching skill criterion may be satisfied by proving that one has already attained training certification from Novell, Banyan, Lotus, the Santa Cruz Operation, or Cisco, or by taking a Microsoft-sanctioned workshop on instruction. Microsoft makes it clear that MCTs are important cogs in the Microsoft training channels. Instructors must be MCTs before Microsoft will allow them to teach in any of its official training channels, including Microsoft's affiliated Certified Technical Education Centers (CTECs) and its online training partner network.

Microsoft has announced that the MCP+I and MCSE+I credentials will not be continued when the MCSE exams for Windows 2000 are in full swing because the skill set for the Internet portion of the program has been included in the new MCSE program. Therefore, details on these tracks are not provided here; go to **www.microsoft.com/train_cert/** if you need more information.

Once a Microsoft product becomes obsolete, MCPs typically have to recertify on current versions. (If individuals do not recertify, their certifications become invalid.) Because technology keeps changing and new products continually supplant old ones, this should come as no surprise. This explains why Microsoft has announced that MCSEs have 12 months past the scheduled retirement date for the Windows NT 4 exams to recertify on Windows 2000 topics. (Note that this means taking at least two exams, if not more.)

The best place to keep tabs on the MCP Program and its related certifications is on the Web. The URL for the MCP program is **www.microsoft.com/mcp/**. But Microsoft's Web site changes often, so if this URL doesn't work, try using the Search tool on Microsoft's site with either "MCP" or the quoted phrase "Microsoft Certified Professional Program" as a search string. This will help you find the latest and most accurate information about Microsoft's certification programs.

Tracking MCP Status

As soon as you pass any Microsoft exam, you'll attain Microsoft Certified Professional (MCP) status. Microsoft also generates transcripts that indicate which exams you have passed and your corresponding test scores. You can view a copy of your transcript at any time by going to the MCP secured site and selecting Transcript Tool. This tool will allow you to print a copy of your current transcript and confirm your certification status.

Once you pass the necessary set of exams, you'll be certified. Official certification normally takes anywhere from six to eight weeks, so don't expect to get your credentials overnight. When the package for a qualified certification arrives, it includes a Welcome Kit that contains a number of elements:

➤ An MCP, MCSE, or MCSD certificate, suitable for framing.

➤ A license to use the MCP logo, thereby allowing you to use the logo in advertisements, promotions, and documents, and on letterhead, business cards, and so on. Along with the license comes an MCP logo sheet, which includes camera-ready artwork. (Note: Before using any of the artwork, individuals must sign and return a licensing agreement that indicates they'll abide by its terms and conditions.)

➤ A subscription to *Microsoft Certified Professional Magazine*, which provides ongoing data about testing and certification activities, requirements, and changes to the program.

➤ A one-year subscription to the Microsoft Beta Evaluation program. This subscription will get you all beta products from Microsoft for the next year. (This does not include developer products. You must join the MSDN program or become an MCSD to qualify for developer beta products.)

In addition, a Professional Program Membership card and lapel pin will be shipped to you separately from the Welcome Kit.

Many people believe that the benefits of MCP certification go well beyond the perks that Microsoft provides to newly anointed members of this elite group. We're starting to see more job listings that request or require applicants to have an MCP, MCSE, and so on, and many individuals who complete the program can qualify for increases in pay and/or responsibility. As an official recognition of hard work and broad knowledge, one of the MCP credentials is a badge of honor in many IT organizations.

About the Book

Career opportunities abound for well-prepared network administrators. This book provides the knowledge you need to prepare for Microsoft's certification exam 70-210 "Installing, Configuring and Administering Microsoft Windows 2000 Professional." The exam is one of the core exams for the Windows 2000 MCSE track, and it is a crucial step in becoming a Microsoft Certified Systems Engineer.

The book is intended to provide you with knowledge that you can apply right away and a sound basis for understanding the changes that you will encounter in the future. It also is intended to give you the hands-on skills you need to be a valued professional in your organization.

The book is filled with real-world projects that cover every aspect of installing and managing Windows 2000 Professional. The projects are designed to make what you learn come alive through actually performing the tasks. Also, every chapter includes a range of practice questions to help prepare you for the Microsoft certification exam. All of these features are offered to reinforce your learning, so you'll feel confident in the knowledge you have gained from each chapter.

Features

To aid you in fully understanding Windows 2000 Professional, there are many features in this book designed to improve its value:

➤ *Chapter objectives*—Each chapter in this book begins with a detailed list of the topics to be mastered within that chapter. This list provides you with a quick reference to the contents of that chapter, as well as a useful study aid.

➤ *Illustrations and tables*—Numerous illustrations of screenshots and components aid you in the visualization of common setup steps, theories, and concepts. In addition, many tables provide details and comparisons of both practical and theoretical information.

➤ *Notes, tips, and warnings*—Notes present additional helpful material related to the subject being described. Tips from the author's experience provide extra information about how to attack a problem or what to do in certain real-world situations. Warnings are included to help you anticipate potential mistakes or problems so you can prevent them from happening.

➤ *Chapter summaries*—Each chapter's text is followed by a summary of the concepts it has introduced. These summaries provide a helpful way to recap and revisit the ideas covered in each chapter.

➤ *Review questions*—End-of-chapter assessment begins with a set of review questions that reinforce the ideas introduced in each chapter. These questions not only ensure that you have mastered the concepts, but are written to help prepare you for the Microsoft certification examination. Answers to these questions are found in Appendix A.

➤ *Real-world projects*—Although it is important to understand the theory behind Windows 2000 workstation, server, and networking technology, nothing can improve upon real-world experience. To this end, along with theoretical explanations, each chapter provides numerous hands-on projects aimed at providing you with real-world implementation experience.

➤ *Sample tests*—Use the sample test and answer key in Chapters 19 and 20 to test yourself. Then, move on to the interactive practice exams found on the CD-ROM. The testing engine offers a variety of testing formats to choose from.

Where Should You Start?

This book is intended to be read in sequence, from beginning to end. Each chapter builds upon those that precede it, to provide a solid understanding of the Windows 2000 Professional operating system. After completing the chapters, you may find it useful to go back through the book and use the review questions and projects to prepare for the Microsoft certification test for "Installing, Configuring, and Administering Microsoft Windows 2000 Professional" (Exam 70-210)". Readers are also encouraged to investigate the many pointers to online and printed sources of additional information that are cited throughout this book.

Please share your feedback on the book with us, especially if you have ideas about how we can improve it for future readers. We'll consider everything you say carefully, and we'll respond to all suggestions. Send your questions or comments to us at **learn@examcram.com**. Please remember to include the title of the book in your message; otherwise, we'll be forced to guess which book you're writing about. And we don't like to guess—we want to *know*! Also, be sure to check out the Web pages at **www.examcram.com**, where you'll find information updates, commentary, and certification information. Thanks, and enjoy the book!

Self-Assessment

The reason we included a Self-Assessment in this *Exam Prep* book is to help you evaluate your readiness to tackle MCSE certification. It should also help you understand what you need to know to master the topic of this book—namely, Exam 70-210, "Installing, Configuring, and Administering Microsoft Windows 2000 Professional." But before you tackle this Self-Assessment, let's talk about concerns you may face when pursuing an MCSE for Windows 2000, and what an ideal MCSE candidate might look like.

MCSEs in the Real World

In the next section, we describe an ideal MCSE candidate, knowing full well that only a few real candidates will meet this ideal. In fact, our description of that ideal candidate might seem downright scary, especially with the changes that have been made to the program to support Windows 2000. But take heart: Although the requirements to obtain an MCSE may seem formidable, they are by no means impossible to meet. However, be keenly aware that it does take time, involves some expense, and requires real effort to get through the process.

Increasing numbers of people are attaining Microsoft certifications, so the goal is within reach. You can get all the real-world motivation you need from knowing that many others have gone before, so you will be able to follow in their footsteps. If you're willing to tackle the process seriously and do what it takes to obtain the necessary experience and knowledge, you can take—and pass—all the certification tests involved in obtaining an MCSE. In fact, we've designed *Exam Preps*, the companion *Exam Crams*, *Exam Cram Personal Trainers*, and *Exam Cram Personal Test Centers* to make it as easy on you as possible to prepare for these exams. We've also greatly expanded our Web site, **www.examcram.com**, to provide a host of resources to help you prepare for the complexities of Windows 2000.

Besides MCSE, other Microsoft certifications include:

➤ MCSD, which is aimed at software developers and requires one specific exam, two more exams on client and distributed topics, plus a fourth elective exam drawn from a different, but limited, pool of options.

➤ Other Microsoft certifications, whose requirements range from one test (MCP) to several tests (MCP+SB, MCDBA).

The Ideal Windows 2000 MCSE Candidate

Just to give you some idea of what an ideal MCSE candidate is like, here are some relevant statistics about the background and experience such an individual might have. Don't worry if you don't meet these qualifications, or don't come that close—this is a far from ideal world, and where you fall short is simply where you'll have more work to do:

➤ Academic or professional training in network theory, concepts, and operations. This includes everything from networking media and transmission techniques through network operating systems, services, and applications.

➤ Three-plus years of professional networking experience, including experience with Ethernet, token ring, modems, and other networking media. This must include installation, configuration, upgrade, and troubleshooting experience.

Note: The Windows 2000 MCSE program is much more rigorous than the previous NT MCSE program; therefore, you'll really need some hands-on experience. Some of the exams require you to solve real-world case studies and network design issues, so the more hands-on experience you have, the better.

➤ Two-plus years in a networked environment that includes hands-on experience with Windows 2000 Server, Windows 2000 Professional, Windows NT Server, Windows NT Workstation, and Windows 95 or Windows 98. A solid understanding of each system's architecture, installation, configuration, maintenance, and troubleshooting is also essential.

➤ Knowledge of the various methods for installing Windows 2000, including manual and unattended installations.

➤ A thorough understanding of key networking protocols, addressing, and name resolution, including TCP/IP, IPX/SPX, and NetBEUI.

➤ A thorough understanding of NetBIOS naming, browsing, and file and print services.

➤ Familiarity with key Windows 2000-based TCP/IP-based services, including HTTP (Web servers), DHCP, WINS, DNS, plus familiarity with one or more of the following: Internet Information Server (IIS), Index Server, and Proxy Server.

➤ An understanding of how to implement security for key network data in a Windows 2000 environment.

➤ Working knowledge of NetWare 3.x and 4.x, including IPX/SPX frame formats, NetWare file, print, and directory services, and both Novell and Microsoft client software. Working knowledge of Microsoft's Client Service For NetWare (CSNW), Gateway Service For NetWare (GSNW), the NetWare Migration Tool (NWCONV), and the NetWare Client For Windows (NT, 95, and 98) is essential.

➤ A good working understanding of Active Directory. The more you work with Windows 2000, the more you'll realize how much this new operating system is differs from Windows NT. New technologies like Active Directory have really changed the way that Windows is configured and used. We recommend that you find out as much as you can about Active Directory and acquire as much experience using this technology as possible. The time you take learning about Active Directory will be time very well spent!

Fundamentally, this boils down to a bachelor's degree in computer science, plus three years' experience working in a position involving network design, installation, configuration, and maintenance. We believe that well under half of all certification candidates meet these requirements, and that, in fact, most meet less than half of these requirements—at least, when they begin the certification process. However, because all the people who already have been certified have survived this ordeal, you can survive it too—especially if you heed what our Self-Assessment can tell you about what you already know and what you need to learn.

Put Yourself to the Test

The following series of questions and observations is designed to help you figure out how much work you must do to pursue Microsoft certification and what kinds of resources you may consult on your quest. Be absolutely honest in your answers, or you'll end up wasting money on exams you're not yet ready to take. There are no right or wrong answers, only steps along the path to certification. Only you can decide where you really belong in the broad spectrum of aspiring candidates.

Two things should be clear from the outset, however:

➤ Even a modest background in computer science will be helpful.

➤ Hands-on experience with Microsoft products and technologies is an essential ingredient to certification success.

Educational Background

1. Have you ever taken any computer-related classes? [Yes or No]

   If Yes, proceed to question 2; if No, proceed to question 4.

2. Have you taken any classes on computer operating systems? [Yes or No]

If Yes, you will probably be able to handle Microsoft's architecture and system component discussions. If you're rusty, brush up on basic operating system concepts, especially virtual memory, multitasking regimes, user mode versus kernel mode operation, and general computer security topics.

If No, consider some basic reading in this area. We strongly recommend a good general operating systems book, such as *Operating System Concepts, 5th Edition*, by Abraham Silberschatz and Peter Baer Galvin (John Wiley & Sons, 1998, ISBN 0-471-36414-2). If this title doesn't appeal to you, check out reviews for other, similar titles at your favorite online bookstore.

3. Have you taken any networking concepts or technologies classes? [Yes or No]

If Yes, you will probably be able to handle Microsoft's networking terminology, concepts, and technologies (brace yourself for frequent departures from normal usage). If you're rusty, brush up on basic networking concepts and terminology, especially networking media, transmission types, the OSI Reference Model, and networking technologies such as Ethernet, token ring, FDDI, and WAN links.

If No, you might want to read one or two books in this topic area. The two best books that we know of are *Computer Networks, 3rd Edition*, by Andrew S. Tanenbaum (Prentice-Hall, 1996, ISBN 0-13-349945-6) and *Computer Networks and Internets, 2nd Edition*, by Douglas E. Comer (Prentice-Hall, 1998, ISBN 0-130-83617-6).

Skip to the next section, "Hands-on Experience."

4. Have you done any reading on operating systems or networks? [Yes or No]

If Yes, review the requirements stated in the first paragraphs after questions 2 and 3. If you meet those requirements, move on to the next section. If No, consult the recommended reading for both topics. A strong background will help you prepare for the Microsoft exams better than just about anything else.

Hands-on Experience

The most important key to success on all of the Microsoft tests is hands-on experience, especially with Windows 2000 Server and Professional, plus the many add-on services and BackOffice components around which so many of the Microsoft certification exams revolve. If we leave you with only one realization after taking this Self-Assessment, it should be that there's no substitute for time spent installing, configuring, and using the various Microsoft products upon which you'll be tested repeatedly and in depth.

5. Have you installed, configured, and worked with:

> ➤ Windows 2000 Server? [Yes or No]

If Yes, make sure that you understand basic concepts as covered in Exam 70-215. You should also study the TCP/IP interfaces, utilities, and services for Exam 70-216, plus implementing security features for Exam 70-220.

Tip: You can download objectives, practice exams, and other data about Microsoft exams from the Training and Certification page at **www.Microsoft.com/trainingandservices/default.asp?PageID=mcp/**. Use the " Exams" link to obtain specific exam information.

If you haven't worked with Windows 2000 Server, you must obtain one or two machines and a copy of Windows 2000 Server. Then, learn the operating system and whatever other software components on which you'll also be tested.

In fact, we recommend that you obtain two computers, each with a network interface, and set up a two-node network on which to practice. With decent Windows 2000-capable computers selling for about $500 to $600 apiece these days, this shouldn't be too much of a financial hardship. You may have to scrounge to come up with the necessary software, but if you scour the Microsoft Web site, you can usually find low-cost options to obtain evaluation copies of most of the software that you'll need.

> ➤ Windows 2000Professional? [Yes or No]

If Yes, make sure that you understand the concepts covered in Exam 70-210.

If No, you will want to obtain a copy of Windows 2000 Professional and learn how to install, configure, and maintain it. You can use *MCSE Windows 2000 Professional Exam Cram* to guide your activities and studies, or work straight from Microsoft's test objectives if you prefer.

Tip: For any and all of these Microsoft exams, the Resource Kits for the topics involved are a good study resource. You can purchase softcover Resource Kits from Microsoft Press (search for them at **http://mspress.microsoft.com/**), but they also appear on the TechNet CDs (**www.microsoft.com/technet**). Along with *Exam Crams* and *Exam Preps*, we believe that Resource Kits are among the best tools you can use to prepare for Microsoft exams.

---

6. For any specific Microsoft product that is not itself an operating system (for example, SQL Server), have you installed, configured, used, and upgraded this software? [Yes or No]

If the answer is Yes, skip to the next section. If it's No, you must get some experience. Read on for suggestions on how to do this.

Experience is a must with any Microsoft product exam, be it something as simple as FrontPage 2000 or as challenging as SQL Server 7. For trial copies of other software, search Microsoft's Web site using the name of the product as your search term. Also, search for bundles like "BackOffice" or "Small Business Server."

Tip: If you have the funds, or your employer will pay your way, consider taking a class at a Certified Training and Education Center (CTEC) or at an Authorized Academic Training Partner (AATP). In addition to classroom exposure to the topic of your choice, you get a copy of the software that is the focus of your course, along with a trial version of whatever operating system it needs, with the training materials for that class.

Before you even think about taking any Microsoft exam, make sure you've spent enough time with the related software to understand how it may be installed and configured, how to maintain such an installation, and how to troubleshoot that software when things go wrong. This will help you in the exam, and in real life!

Testing Your Exam-Readiness

Whether you attend a formal class on a specific topic to get ready for an exam or use written materials to study on your own, some preparation for the Microsoft certification exams is essential. At $100 a try, pass or fail, you want to do everything you can to pass on your first try. That's where studying comes in.

We have included a practice exam in this book, so if you don't score that well on the test, you can study more and then tackle the test again. We also have exams that you can take online through the **ExamCram.com** Web site at **www.examcram. com**. If you still don't hit a score of at least 70 percent after these tests, you'll want to investigate the other practice test resources we mention in this section.

For any given subject, consider taking a class if you've tackled self-study materials, taken the test, and failed anyway. The opportunity to interact with an instructor and fellow students can make all the difference in the world, if you can afford that privilege. For information about Microsoft classes, visit the Training and Certification page at **www.microsoft.com/education/partners/ctec.asp** for Microsoft Certified Education Centers or **www.microsoft.com/aatp/default.htm** for Microsoft Authorized Training Providers.

If you can't afford to take a class, visit the Training and Certification page anyway, because it also includes pointers to free practice exams and to Microsoft Certified Professional Approved Study Guides and other self-study tools. Even if you can't afford to spend much at all, you should still invest in some low-cost practice exams from commercial vendors.

7. Have you taken a practice exam on your chosen test subject? [Yes or No]

If Yes, and you scored 70 percent or better, you're probably ready to tackle the real thing. If your score isn't above that threshold, keep at it until you break that barrier.

If No, obtain all the free and low-budget practice tests you can find and get to work. Keep at it until you can break the passing threshold comfortably.

Tip: When it comes to assessing your test readiness, there is no better way than to take a good-quality practice exam and pass with a score of 70 percent or better. When we're preparing ourselves, we shoot for 80-plus percent, just to leave room for the "weirdness factor" that sometimes shows up on Microsoft exams.

Assessing Readiness for Exam 70-210

In addition to the general exam-readiness information in the previous section, there are several things you can do to prepare for the Installing, Configuring, and Administering Microsoft Windows 2000 Professional exam. As you're getting ready for Exam 70-210, visit the Exam Cram Windows 2000 Resource Center at **www.examcram.com/studyresource/w2kresource/**. Another valuable resource is the Exam Cram Insider newsletter. Sign up at **www.examcram.com** or send a blank email message to **subscribe-ec@mars.coriolis.com**. We also suggest that you join an active MCSE mailing list. One of the better ones is managed by Sunbelt Software. Sign up at **www.sunbelt-software.com** (look for the "Subscribe to…" button).

You can also cruise the Web looking for "braindumps" (recollections of test topics and experiences recorded by others) to help you anticipate topics you're likely to encounter on the test. The MCSE mailing list is a good place to ask where the useful braindumps are, or you can check Shawn Gamble's list at **www.command-central.com**.

Tip: You can't be sure that a braindump's author can provide correct answers. Thus, use the questions to guide your studies, but don't rely on the answers in a braindump to lead you to the truth. Double-check everything you find in any braindump.

Microsoft exam mavens also recommend checking the Microsoft Knowledge Base (available on its own CD-ROM as part of the TechNet collection, or on the Microsoft Web site at **http://support.microsoft.com/support/**) for "meaningful technical support issues" that relate to your exam's topics. Although we're not sure exactly what the quoted phrase means, we have also noticed some overlap between technical support questions on particular products and troubleshooting questions on the exams for those products.

Onward, through the Fog!

Once you've assessed your readiness, undertaken the right background studies, obtained the hands-on experience that will help you understand the products and technologies at work, and reviewed the many sources of information to help you prepare for a test, you'll be ready to take a round of practice tests. When your scores come back positive enough to get you through the exam, you're ready to go after the real thing. If you follow our assessment regime, you'll not only know what you need to study, but when you're ready to make a test date at Prometric or VUE. Good luck!

CHAPTER ONE

What's New in Windows 2000 Professional

After completing this chapter, you will be able to:

✓ Describe options available for users to personalize Windows 2000 Professional

✓ Explain why Windows 2000 Professional is easier to set up, configure, and administer

✓ Explain why Windows 2000 Professional is an operating system designed for mobile users

✓ Describe some of the new printing and imaging capabilities of Windows 2000 Professional

✓ Explain how Windows 2000 Professional has been integrated with Internet Explorer 5

✓ Explain why Windows 2000 Professional provides better performance

✓ Describe security features inherent in Windows 2000 Professional

Windows 2000 provides a user interface that is more customizable than what you may have encountered in Windows 95, 98, and NT 4. The following list present these changes:

➤ *Customizable Start Menu*—Users in Windows 2000 Professional are provided with more options to customize the Start and Program menus. Items can be easily dragged to the Start and Programs menus. Menu items can also be dragged from one submenu to another. Menu items can be sorted by dragging them into the appropriate sort order.

➤ *Personalized Menus*—A new feature of Windows 2000 Professional is Personalized Menus. The Personalized Menus feature is activated by selecting the Use Personalized Menus checkbox on the General tab of the Taskbar and Start Menu Properties dialog box. With the Personalized Menu feature, the operating system tracks the most frequently used programs and applications on the Program menu. The items that are accessed frequently are placed at the top of the Program menu. These items are launched quicker and the operating system continuously monitors how users launch programs and makes adjustments accordingly. The items that are used infrequently are hidden on the Program menu.

➤ *Customizable Taskbar*—The Taskbar can be customized to suit a user's specific needs. The Address, Links, and Desktop toolbars can be added to the Taskbar by right-clicking while on the Taskbar and selecting Toolbars. Users can create their own toolbars to add to the Taskbar by selecting Toolbars | New Toolbar. Users can also create toolbars by dragging files or folders onto the Taskbar.

➤ *Quick Launch Bar Revised*—The Quick Launch Bar, which was introduced with previous versions of Windows, is used to open frequently accessed programs and applications. Users can customize the Quick Launch Bar to make those programs that they use most accessible from the Taskbar.

➤ *Right-Clicking*—Users can open an item with a pop-up menu by right-clicking on the item.

➤ *Adding Folders To The Start Menu*—Users can specify Folders to add to the Start menu by using the Start Menu Settings on the Advanced tab in the Taskbar and Start Menu Properties dialog box. Windows 95 users had to use a Control Panel applet called Tweak UI (from the Power Toys collection) to perform this function.

➤ *Display Administrative Tools*—Administrative tools, such as Component Services, Computer Management, and Event Viewer, can be added to the Programs submenu by selecting the Display Administrative Tools checkbox.

➤ *Display Favorites*—Internet links stored in the Favorites folder in Internet Explorer can be added to the Favorites submenu of the Start menu. To do so, select the Display Favorites checkbox.

➤ *Display Logoff*—Users can add the Log Off Name button to the bottom of the Start menu by selecting the Display Logoff checkbox. Normally, users would have to press Ctrl+Alt+Del to display the Windows NT Security dialog box, and then press the Log Off button to perform this function.

➤ *Expand Control Panel*—Selecting the Expand Control Panel checkbox displays a submenu of the Settings menu that contains each Control Panel icon. Some of these submenus may have additional submenus.

➤ *Expand My Documents*—Selecting the Expand My Documents checkbox allows users to open all submenu files and folders in their My Documents folder.

➤ *Expand Network And Dial-Up Connections*—Selecting the Expand Network and Dial-Up Connections checkbox allows users to open a submenu that displays all their network and dial-up connections. Users can also access the Make New Connections wizard through this submenu.

➤ *Expand Printers*—Selecting the Expand Printers checkbox allows users to open a submenu that displays all printers installed on their computers. Users can also access Add Printer wizard through this submenu.

➤ *Scroll The Programs Menu*—Selecting the Scroll The Programs menu checkbox will scroll the Program's menu submenus that do not fit into a single column on the screen.

➤ *Customizable Toolbars*—Users can right-click anywhere on a toolbar to display the Customize Toolbar dialog box. Users can add or delete buttons, select the button size, and choose whether text labels are displayed.

➤ *Quick Launch Bars*—Easier access to programs, files, and folders is provided from the Quick Launch Bars. The Quick Launch Bar is located beside the Start menu on the Taskbar.

➤ *Show Display button*—The Show Display Button is a new button located on the Taskbar that allows you to switch between open windows and the desktop.

Quicker Access to Files

Windows 2000 provides more efficient file-handling options than were present in Windows 95, 98, and NT 4. The following list present these options:

➤ *Open With*—Although the Open With menu isn't new to Windows 2000, it has been improved to make its functionality easier. The Open With menu is always available when the user right-clicks on a file icon. The user can choose to open the file with the applications shown or select the Any Program options to display the Open With dialog box that was available in earlier versions of Windows.

➤ *Open And Save As*—The new Open And Save As dialog box has been changed to make it easier for users to locate folders. Icons are listed that represent the standard places where users save their files.

➤ *Most Frequent*—Windows 2000 Professional keeps a list of the most frequently used file names from every dialog box that prompts the user for a name. This list is continuously updated by the operating system.

➤ *AutoComplete*—AutoComplete makes locating files quicker for the user. When users type in a file name, they are given the option of choosing a matching file name from a list of suggestions. Users can continue typing the file name or choose from the list.

TIP: In Windows 2000 Professional, users can easily change the default programs that open a file. In previous versions of windows, users had to go to the File Types tab of the Folder Options dialog box to change the default program for a file type. With Windows 2000 Professional, users can choose Properties from the file's pop-up menu, and then select Change.

Easier to Find Files and Folders

Several items have been added to make it easier for users to find and organize files. These items are discussed in the following list:

➤ *My Network Places*—My Network Places replaces Network Neighborhood, which was in previous versions of Windows. This folder provides various views of the network. The Entire Network folder within the My Network Places folder contains a list of network clients in addition to each workgroup and domain. Under the workgroup and domain listing, each computer and the resources shared by each computer are displayed. Shortcuts to items in My Network can be placed at the top of the My Network Places folder for quicker access.

➤ *My Documents*—The My Documents folder is the default folder for saving documents. My Documents folder is displayed at the top of Windows Explorer, directly below the Desktop icon. This is a shortcut to the folder. The actual My Documents folder is located in the Documents and Settings\username folder. The content of the My Documents folder is saved on a per user basis.

➤ *My Pictures*—The My Pictures folder is the default folder for storing images. The My Pictures folder is a subfolder of the My Documents folder. Users can preview images in the My Pictures folder in Windows Explorer. The images can be viewed as thumbnails or full screen. Users can zoom in or out on an image, pan the image left, right, up, or down, and print the image. All of these functions can be accomplished without opening the file in an image editor.

➤ *Integrated Searching*—A Search tool has been integrated into Windows Explorer. A search can be activated by clicking on the Search button on the Windows Explorer's toolbar. Users can also activate a search by right-clicking on My Computer and selecting Search from the pop-up menu. Three types of searches can be performed. Users can search for files or folders, search on the Internet, or search for people. As in previous versions of Windows, users can choose a combination of more advanced search options by selecting the appropriate checkboxes including by date, by specific file type, by file size, and other advanced features. The integrated search feature included in Windows Explorer is all encompassing. Users can search the Internet, computers and printers on the network, and people in an organization in addition to Web pages and newsgroups.

Content indexing makes searching faster by creating a database that indexes keywords found in each file. This feature is not activated by default in Windows 2000 Professional. To enable content indexing, the user must click on the Indexing SŒrvice link under the Search Options in the Search bar.

➤ *Customizing Folders*—Windows 2000 Professional provides users with new options for viewing folders in Windows Explorer. Viewing options can be selected by using the Customize This Folder wizard or by choosing Folder Options from the Tools menu. Several templates are provided through the Customize This Folder Wizard, which the user can manipulate to personalize the appearance of the folder.

Better Guidance for Users

Windows 2000 contains new informational and help guidance to make it easier for users to find out what went wrong and, perhaps, easier ways to correct inefficiencies and errors. The new guidance items are discussed in the following sections.

Error Messages

Error messages in Windows 2000 Professional provide more information about the error that has occurred. More information is also provided on how to solve the problem. This is an improvement over previous versions of Windows, where error messages tended to be very terse and limited in helping to resolve problems. If the operating system is expecting a response from the user, and the user does not respond within a certain period, an appropriate response will be displayed.

HTML Help

Online help has been greatly improved over Windows NT 4. Troubleshooters have been added to aid users in solving their problems. The Troubleshooting guides the user through a series of questions. These questions provide a diagnosis and possible solution to the problem. Users access the interactive troubleshooters by choosing Troubleshooting and Maintenance from the Help menu, and then selecting Windows

2000 Troubleshooters. The following troubleshooters are provided in Windows 2000 Professional:

➤ Client Services for NetWare

➤ Displays

➤ Hardware

➤ Internet connections

➤ Modems

➤ MS-DOS programs

➤ Multimedia and games

➤ Networking and TCP/IP

➤ Printing

➤ Remote access to networks

➤ Sound

➤ System setup

➤ Windows 3.0 and Windows 3.1 programs

Additional troubleshooters are provided with Windows 2000 Server, which include Dynamic Host Configuration Protocol (DHCP), Directory Services, Domain Name Service (DNS), Policies, and so on.

Balloon Help

Windows 2000 Professional introduces Balloon Help, which is similar to tool tips in previous versions of Windows. Balloon Help is designed to help users discover many of the new enhancements included with Windows 2000 Professional.

Easier to Set Up, Configure, and Administer

Changes to Windows 2000 make setting up, configuring, and administering the OS easier than ever. These changes are discussed in the following sections.

More Comprehensive Setup Program

Migrating from previous versions of Windows is easier with Windows 2000. Migration paths are provided for Windows 95, 98, and NT. Enhancements included in the new operating system make it easier to deploy and automate the installation of this new operating system. Installing, configuring, and removing applications is easier with the Windows Installer Service. Removal of programs is more complete

1

than with previous versions of Windows when using the Windows Installer Service. Missing or damaged applications are self-repaired with minimal user intervention. Applications can also be installed directly from the Internet or from the network.

New Accessibility Options

Microsoft has worked to ensure that Windows 2000 Professional is accessible to everyone, including users with disabilities. Several Accessibility Options have been enhanced with Windows 2000 Professional to make access easier for users with disabilities. These features can be used to customize the computer to give users with disabilities better access to their programs and applications. The Accessibility wizard helps users turn these accessibility features on and off, as follows:

➤ *Accessibility Options for Users with Cognitive Disabilities*—Several built-in features are helpful to people with cognitive disabilities, such as Downs Syndrome, learning and developmental disabilities, memory loss, and perception difficulties. These include AutoCorrect, AutoComplete, Automatic Spell Checking, FilterKeys, Hot Keys, and Keyboard shortcuts.

➤ *Accessibility Options for Users with Hearing Impairments*—Users who are hard of hearing or deaf may find the Sound Schemes, Show Sounds, and Sound Sentry options beneficial.

➤ *Accessibility Options for Users with Physical Disabilities*—Users with physical impairments or disabilities can benefit from several options available for people with mobility impairments. These include the On-Screen Keyboard, the Dvorak Keyboard, Keyboard Shortcuts and Hot keys, StickKeys, and MouseKeys.

➤ *Accessibility Options for Users with Vision Impairments*—Users who are blind, have limited vision, suffer from colorblindness, or have other vision impairments may benefit from the Microsoft Narrator, the Microsoft Magnifier, Keyboard Audio Cues, and Color Schemes. The Magnifier utility is for users who need extra help reading the screen. Users can magnify a portion of the screen using the mouse pointer. The Narrator utility reads contents of the screen aloud.

Configuration Options

The configuration options in Windows 2000 Professional offers simpler installation, network and Internet configuration, and easier printer installation. The following list highlights these options:

➤ *Plug and Play hardware installation*—Windows 2000 Professional provides support for over 12,000 Plug and Play devices. These devices are automatically installed and only require minimal configuration by the user.

➤ *Simpler Dial-Up networking configuration*—Dial-Up Networking is much easier in Windows 2000 Professional than it was in Windows NT 4. Users no longer have to open separate windows to access Dial-Up Networking. Dial-Up Networking is integrated into the Windows Explorer hierarchy. The new Network Connection Wizard introduced in Windows 2000 Professional is much simpler to configure than its predecessor is. Users are asked to input only a phone number.

➤ *Connectivity to Virtual Private Networks (VPNs)*—Windows 2000 Professional allows users to connect to Virtual Private Networks, which can reduce the costs associated with connecting to remote offices. Creating and setting up a VPN connection is relatively simple. Users are asked if they want the networking connection wizard to have the VPN connection dial the Internet connection; they are then prompted for a host name or IP address. VPN connections are highly configurable, as are dial-up connections.

➤ *Support for multiple incoming connections*—The networking connection wizard can be used to create configurations for in-coming connections. Windows 2000 Professional supports three types of incoming connections: dial-up, VPNs, and direct. Anyone with administrative rights can configure Windows 2000 Professional as a remote access server. Support is provided for up to three incoming calls—one on a dial-up connection, one on a VPN connection, and one on a direct connection. Support is not provided for two connections of the same type. You cannot have two dial-up connections at the same time, but you can have a dial-up, VPN, and direct connection simultaneously.

➤ *Support for direct connections*—Windows 2000 Professional supports direct connections, which allow users to transfer data between two computers, for example, a desktop and a laptop. The two computers can be connected by any of the following methods: modems, ISDN devices, infrared ports, serial cables, and the new DirectParallel cables. Windows 2000 Professional computers can directly connect to Windows NT 4 computers.

➤ *Simpler printer installation*—Windows 2000 Professional has an improved printer installation wizard. Printers can be installed using the Uniform Naming Convention (UNC) path or the Uniform Resource Locator (URL). Users can also search the network to locate printers for installation. Windows 2000 Professional also introduces Internet printing for printing documents to remote printers via the Internet.

Centralized Computer Management

The Computer Management Console provides administrators with access to tools that were provided in Windows NT 4 and new tools introduced in Windows 2000 Professional, such as the Device Manager and the System Information tool. The Computer Management console is accessed through the Microsoft Management Console (MMC).

Windows Update

System updates, drivers, and service packs can be downloaded from the Windows Update Web Site. Users access The Windows Update Web Site by clicking on Windows Update from the Start menu. Users can have Windows Update scan their computers to give a list of updates specific to their hardware and software configuration.

Built for Mobile Users

Windows 2000 Professional is designed with mobile users in mind. Several new features have been added specifically for mobile users. Several features provided for mobile users in Windows NT and Windows 98 have been improved in Windows 2000 Professional. These new and improved features are discussed in the following list:

➤ *Hibernate*—Hibernate turns your computer off after a predetermined time. All information in memory is stored on your hard drive before the computer is powered down. Your desktop is retained and restored to its original configuration when you reactivate your notebook computer.

➤ *Offline files and folders*—The Briefcase in previous versions of Windows has been improved in Windows 2000 Professional. Users can make a network file or folder available offline. This is done by choosing Make Available from the file or folder's pop-up menu. Files are copied to the mobile computer and kept synchronized each time the user logs on or off a network connection. A wizard is started the first time a user makes a file available offline. The wizard walks the user through the process of configuring offline files and folders.

The Synchronization Manager allows users to synchronize files and folders from the network. Items can be synchronized when the system is idle or when users log on or off their computer. Only changes are copied, not the entire document.

➤ *Offline viewing*—Users can view entire Web pages on their notebook computer without an Internet connection. This includes any graphics associated with the Web page.

➤ *Enhanced security*—Security for mobile computers includes backing up files. Windows 2000 Professional includes a new Backup utility that allows users to back up files to the network before they pack their computers. If the mobile computer is part of a Windows 2000 net-work, files can be automatically mirrored on the server. This eliminates the need to manually back up the files.

➤ *Smart battery*—Smart Battery provides the user with an indication of the battery's life. This enables the user to reduce power to functions that are not needed.

➤ *Hot docking*—Support for docking stations has been improved through *hot docking*. Separate hard-ware profiles are provided for docked and undocked configurations. Notebook computers can be docked or undocked without having to reboot or change the hardware configuration.

➤ *Simpler dial-up connection configuration*—Dial-up connection support is designed with the same capabilities for users on a local area network (LAN), except for the slower speed connection.

Remote connections supported for mobile users are dial-up, Virtual Private Networks (VPNs), and direct connections. Multiple network configurations are supported for a single device. Each network connection maintains configuration information for each device that uses it. This includes scripts, passwords, and protocols. Users do not have to reconfigure the device for each computer connection. Every connection in the Network and Dial-Up Connections folders supports scripting, phone numbers and dial rules, dialing and redialing, security settings, and multilink.

➤ *PC Cards*—Support has been built-in for dynamic Plug and Play. PC Cards can be removed and installed without having to reboot. *Hot-swapping*, or dynamic Plug and Play support, is provided on ACPI (Advanced Configuration and Power Interface) computers only.

➤ *Power Management*—Windows 2000 Professional provides better power management for computers that have ACPI BIOS support. Users can now get longer life out of their computer batteries.

➤ *Hardware Profiles*—Hardware profiles are an important feature for portable computers that use docking stations. Drivers are automatically loaded when there are system hardware changes. Two profiles are automatically created: one for docked and one for undocked.

Multilanguage Support

Many users have a need to communicate on a global basis. Multilingual support provides users with the ability to read, create, and edit documents in over 60 languages. Users can switch on demand to a new user language interface as needed. There are three versions of Windows 2000 Professional that provide multilingual support: the English version, localized versions, and the new multilanguage version.

Enhanced Printing and Imaging Capabilities

Changes to Windows 2000 make installing, configuring, and administering printers easier than ever. These changes are discussed in the following list:

1

➤ *Effortless printer installation*—Printers can be installed in one of three ways—using the Add Printer wizard, letting Windows detect a Plug and Play printer, or using Point and Print.

➤ *The Add Printer Wizard*—The Add Printer wizard is similar to that in previous versions of Windows, except this version can connect to printers on the Internet.

➤ *Plug and Play printer detection*—Windows 2000 Professional includes Plug and Play printer detection. The Add Printer wizard is started automatically when a printer is attached to the computer.

➤ *Point and Print*—Point and Print is the easiest way to install a printer. Users select a printer using the My Network Places folder or Active Directory, and then choose Connect from the printer's pop-up menu. Users can also drag a printer from the My Network Places folder into the Printers folder. The operating system copies the appropriate drivers and adds an icon for the printer in the Printers folder.

➤ *Internet printing*—Internet printing is a new feature based on the Internet Printing Protocol (IIP). Internet Printing allows users to print to printers via the Internet. Users can send a document to an Internet printer just as they would to a local or network printer. To access printers on the Internet, the computer must be attached to a Windows 2000 server that is hosting IIS or a Peer Web Server.

➤ *Improved ways to find printers*—In previous versions of Windows, users had to browse each server on the network to locate the printer they wanted to print to. If Active Directory is installed, users can search for printers in two ways. They can choose Search from the Start menu, and then select Search For Printers, or they can click on the Search for Printers hyperlink at the bottom of Windows Explorer's Search bar. Users can also search for printers that meet specific criteria, such as a color printer or one that prints double-sided.

➤ *Image Color Management (ICM)*—ICM 2.0 is an API (Application Programming Interface) that ensures that colors are produced accurately across most output devices. It ensures consistent, high-quality images with little user intervention. ICM 2.0 support is provided for printers, scanners, and monitors.

➤ *Improved fonts*—Windows 2000 Professional adds support for OpenType fonts. OpenType is a new font format that is an extension of TrueType fonts. OpenType fonts support com-pression and public key signing. Compression results in faster downloading on the Internet. OpenType fonts are digitally signed, which ensures the integrity of the font.

Integrated Web and Desktop

The Windows 2000 Professional desktop contains fully integrated Web and desktop features. The new features are discussed in the following list:

➤ *Integrated Internet Explorer 5 (IE 5)*—IE 5 is integrated into the Windows 2000 Professional desktop. Users can utilize Windows Explorer to browse the Internet as they would their local computer, net-works, and intranets. Users can add Web browsing tools directly to the Taskbar. Web pages can be downloaded for offline viewing. Support is provided for Dynamic HTML (DHTML), HTML+Time, and Extensible Markup Language (XML).

➤ *Search Bar*—As a user, you can perform various types of searches from one location. You can even select the search engine you want to use to perform the search from the Search Bar. Customized searches and background searches can be performed using multiple search engines.

➤ *History Bar*—The History Bar tracks sites the user has viewed in the past. Not only does it include Web sites, but also intranet sites, network servers, and local folders. Users can view sites they have visited by Date, Site, Most Visited, and Order of Visit.

➤ *Internet Explorer Administration Kit (IEAK)*—The Internet Explorer Adminis-trator Kit provides administrators with the ability to control all aspects of IE 5. With the IE Administration Kit, administrators can customize IE 5 components to be installed, toolbars, and the Favorites list, as well as specify the installation folder. Users can be forced to a specific URL after a pre-determined time.

➤ *AutoComplete*—AutoComplete remembers where users have been and com-pletes the URL as they type. AutoComplete for forms automatically fills out forms on Web pages from pre-vious user input. This eliminates the need for users to reenter the same information.

➤ *Automated proxy*—Windows 2000 Professional automatically locates and config-ures IE 5 for a proxy server and allows it to connect through this proxy server.

➤ *Internet Connection Sharing (ICS)*—With ICS, users on a small network can access several computers on the network with only one computer physically connected via a dial-up connection. ICS provides IP address allocation, name resolution, and network address translation (NAT). Only one computer needs to be configured as a gateway to the Internet.

New Tools for HTML Developers

Windows 2000 Professional has support for the latest Internet standards. These include the following:

➤ Cascading style sheets (CSS)

> ➤ DHTML

> ➤ Dynamic Properties

> ➤ HTTP 1.1

> ➤ Platform for Internet Content Selection (PICS)

> ➤ Portable Network Graphics (PNG)

> ➤ XML

Better Overall Performance

Windows 2000's new performance features and enhanced utilities make it an all-around better performer than previous Windows versions. The new features and utilities are discussed in the following list:

> ➤ *Windows file protection*—Protection is provided to prevent core system files from being overwritten during software installation. If a core file is overwritten, Windows 2000 Professional auto-matically replaces the file with a correct version.

> ➤ *Reduced number of reboots*—Unlike previous versions of Windows, many software installations can be completed without having to reboot.

> ➤ *Microsoft Installer Service*—The Microsoft Installer Service provides users with an error free way to configure, upgrade, remove, and track software programs. If an application causes a problem, the Windows Installer Service fixes it.

> ➤ *Volume management*—The Logical Disk Manager (LDM) is introduced in Windows 2000 Professional. LDM manages dynamic disks. Dynamic disks contain dynamic volumes. They don't contain partitions or logical drives. Dynamic disks are created using the Disk Management Snap-in. Dynamic disks are used with Windows 2000 Professional if the user wants to take advantage of online volume extension, fault tolerance, and disk mirroring and striping. Dynamic disks can be created without having to reboot the operating system.

> ➤ *Upgraded NTFS*—NTFS is extended to version 5. NTFS 5 is the recommended version for use with Windows 2000 Professional. Version 5 supports version 4 in previous Windows NT systems, but has several enhancements. NTFS 5 supports striped partitions for high-speed data access. It has data encryption for protection of files. Partitions can be extended without restarting the computer. Disk quotas can be used to monitor and limit disk usage. Distributed Link Tracking can be utilized to preserve shortcuts when files are moved from one location on the hard drive to another. Mount points are supported to allow a volume to be grafted onto an NTFS folder. Faster retrieval of documents is provided through text and property indexing.

➤ *Disk quotas*—Administrators can allocate disk space to individual users. Quotas are allocated on a per user and per volume basis. Quotas cannot be administered for network shares or folders.

➤ *Disk Defragmenter Snap-In*—Windows NT did not have a disk defragmenter tool. If users wanted to defrag their hard drives in previous versions of Windows, they had to purchase a third-party utility. Windows 2000 includes a Disk Defragmenter tool that rearranges unused space on the hard drive. Performance of the computer is increased because fragmented files are stored in contiguous space on the hard drive. Disk Defragmenter can defrag FAT16, FAT32, and NTFS 5 volumes.

Disk Cleanup

Disk Cleanup is used to clear space on your hard drive. Disk Cleanup searches the hard drive for Internet cache files, temporary files, and unnecessary files that can be safely deleted. The Disk Cleanup wizard calculates the amount of free space it can free up by deleting the following files:

➤ Downloaded program files

➤ Files in the Recycle Bin

➤ Offline files

➤ Temporary files

➤ Temporary Internet files

➤ Temporary offline files

Additionally, unused Windows components and unused programs can be removed with Disk Cleanup.

Backup

The Backup tool is used to back up files to a variety of storage media. The Backup tool is greatly improved compared to previous versions of Windows. The Backup tool can be used to do these tasks:

➤ Back up files and folders on removable storage and mounted drives

➤ Back up files and folders on the computer's hard drive

➤ Back up Registry, system, and boot files

➤ Create an emergency repair disk (ERD)

➤ Restore files and folders to the computers hard drive

➤ Schedule backups

You can back up both FAT and NTFS volumes by using the Backup tool.

Enhanced Security

Microsoft has added new security features to Windows 2000 Professional. These include Encrypting File System (EFS), Internet Protocol Security (IPSec), Kerberos, and Smart Cards.

EFS

EFS is a new feature introduced with Windows 2000. EFS protects files by encrypting them with a randomly generated key. The encryption is transparent to the user. EFS is supported only on the NTFS version provided on Windows 2000.

IPSec

IPSec allows users to transmit data securely over the Internet. *IPSec* is a set of protocols that provides computers with the capability to communicate securely over an unsecured network.

Kerberos Support

Single Sign-On (SSO) allows users to access all network resources with a single logon authentication. SSO provides simpler administration, better administration control, improved user productivity, and better network security. Users of Windows 2000 Professional don't have to do anything to enable SSO. SSO administration is performed through Active Directory within Windows 2000 domains.

Smart Card Support

A Smart Card is the size of an ATM card and contains a chip that stores a digital certificate and the user's private key. Smart Cards allow the operating system to authenticate users with public and private keys that are stored on the card.

Public Key Security

Public Key Security is a prime component of Windows 2000 Professional security. It is different from Private key security, which is known as symmetric encryption or shared-secret encryption. With shared-secret encryption, the same secret key is used to encrypt and decrypt the data. With public key security or asymmetric encryption, two keys are used, one private and one public. The two keys are mathematically related to each other; what one key does, only the other can undo. To ensure the integrity of public key, users publish the keys with a public key certificate. The certificate contains information about the public key and is verified by a certificate authority, such as VeriSign (Certificate Server in IIS 4.0). Windows 2000 Professional provides the Certificate manager to manage certificates.

Best of Windows 2000

Windows 2000's best features and enhanced utilities are often the least intrusive. The new features and utilities are discussed in the following sections.

OnNow

OnNow is an initiative that makes computers instantly available after waking from a low power state. It isn't a technology; it's a standard for defining power-state definitions and power-management interfaces. OnNow comprises changes to hardware, software, and the operating system to allow them to operate together to manage the power of the computer.

Plug and Play

Plug and Play was introduced in Windows 95. It was improved upon in Windows 98, but not included in the Windows NT product line. Plug and Play is included in Windows 2000 Professional. It eliminates the need for user interaction when changes to the computer's hardware configuration are made. For full Plug and Play capability, users should use devices and drivers that comply with the OnNow design initiative.

Power Management

Windows 2000 Professional implements Advanced Configuration and Power Interface (ACPI), which is an open standard for power management. ACPI is a relatively new standard that is not supported by legacy systems. ACPI provides automatic detection of installed hardware, hardware resource allocation, and automatic loading of appropriate device drivers.

Computers with ACPI have the following features:

➤ Battery management

➤ Hibernation

➤ Hot and warm docking and undocking

➤ Hot-swapping of IDE, floppy devices, PC Cards, and CardBus cards

➤ Low-power processor states

➤ Low-power system states

Windows 2000 Professional includes support for computers that don't have ACPI support, but do have APM (Advanced Power Management) BIOS support. APM support must be enabled through the Power Options Properties dialog box in the Control Panel.

Win32 Driver Model

Windows 2000 Professional includes support for WDM (Win32 Driver Model). WDM enables vendors to develop drivers that are compatible with both Windows 98 and Windows 2000 Professional. It supports Plug and Play and power management.

Diagnostic Boot Options

As in previous versions of Windows, users can start the computer in Safe Mode if the operating system does not start properly. The following Safe Mode options are available in Windows 2000 Professional:

➤ *Enable Boot Logging*—Windows 2000 Professional is started normally, but logs all drivers and services that are loaded in systemroot\ntbtlog.txt.

➤ *Enable VGA Mode*—Windows 2000 Professional is started using the basic VGA driver.

➤ *Last Known Good Configuration*—Windows 2000 Professional is started using the configuration saved by the operating system before its last shut down.

➤ *Safe Mode*—Windows 2000 Professional is started with the minimum files and drivers.

➤ *Safe Mode with Command Prompt*—Windows 2000 Professional is started with the minimum number of files and drivers and displays the command prompt.

➤ *Safe Mode with Networking*—Windows 2000 Professional is started with the minimum files, drivers, and network connections.

More Powerful Search Capabilities

Locating files and folders is easier with Windows 2000 professional. Searches can be executed from the Start menu, My Computer, Windows NT Explorer, and IE 5. If Active Directory is installed, users can search for applications, people, and hardware resources throughout their organization.

Windows 2000 Professional has content-indexing capabilities. Content-Indexing creates keywords for each file. This makes searching and sorting much quicker.

If Active Directory is installed, users can

➤ Search for printers by attributes, such as color, double-sided printing, and so on

➤ Search for groups and individuals

➤ Search the Internet for information

Broader Hardware Support

Windows 2000 now has more comprehensive hardware support. The support features, including USB, IrDA, DVD, Plug and Play, and more, are discussed in the following list:

➤ *Universal Serial Bus (USB)*—USB is an external bus that supports Plug and Play installation. Microsoft introduced the use of USB with Windows 98. Users can connect or disconnect devices to the bus without having to reboot the computer. A single USB port supports the connection of 127 devices.

➤ *Infrared Data Association (IrDA) support*—IrDA provides computers with a way to exchange data using infrared transmissions. No cable connection is required. Windows 2000 Professional supports printing between two computers that use IrDA. IrDA is based on the TCP/IP protocol and WinSock APIs.

➤ *IEEE 1394*—Windows 2000 supports the IEEE 1394 bus standard, which is a serial protocol that supports high-bandwidth devices. These devices include digital cameras, camcorders, and VCRs. Speeds can range up to 400 Mbps. The need for peripheral devices to have their own power supply is eliminated with IEEE 1394. Up to 63 devices can be connected to one IEEE 1394 bus. Up to 1023 buses can be interconnected to form a network with a capacity of over 64,000 devices.

➤ *Digital Devices (DVD) support*—Digital Devices are designed for multimedia applications and storage of full-length movies. Audio, video, and data can be stored on DVD devices. Windows 2000 Professional supports DVD-Video, DVD-ROM, and DVD-RAM formats. DVDs can store over two hours of high-quality audio and video.

➤ *Plug and Play support*—Plug and Play support provides users with dynamic configuration of hardware devices and drivers. Resources are automatically allocated for needed resources. The operating system is notified when a new device is available for use.

➤ *Device Manager*—Information for devices configured in Windows 2000 Professional is provided in a device tree. The Device Manager is the tool used to access this tree. The Device Manager can be used to install and remove devices, update drivers, and troubleshoot problems associated with devices.

➤ *Human Interface Devices (HIDs)*—Windows 2000 Professional provides support for HIDs. These include a variety of devices including controls for vehicle simulators and virtual reality. Plug and Play support and power management are provided by Windows 2000 Professional for these devices.

Enhanced Multimedia and Graphics Support

1

Windows 2000 now has more complete multimedia and graphics support. This support is discussed in the following list:

➤ *Microsoft DirectX*—Windows 2000 supports Microsoft DirectX 7, which provides multimedia applications with the capability to run on Windows-based computers regardless of the hardware. Integration of multimedia tools is now easier for developers. DirectX 7.0 provides access to many peripheral devices including audio adapters, graphic cards, and input devices. DirectX provides improved 3-D graphics for easier deployment of 3-D sound algorithms.

➤ *OpenGL 1.2*—Open GL or Open Graphics Library provides developers with improved graphic capabilities for graphic applications and development.

➤ *Support for multiple display devices*—Windows 2000 Professional supports up to 10 monitors. Documents can be displayed across multiple monitors as a single image. For multiple monitors to be supported, the monitors must be an AGP (Accelerated Graphics Port) or PCI device. In a multiple display environment, only the primary monitor can run Microsoft DirectX applications in full-screen mode.

➤ *Accelerated Graphics Port*—AGP is a dedicated bus that provides improved video and graphics performance over PCI buses. AGP supports bandwidth that is up to four times larger than standard PCI buses. Graphics can be read directly from the system memory.

Advanced Networking Capabilities

Windows 2000 also comes with advanced networking, including TAPI 3, authentication and tunneling protocols, and more. These support features are discussed in the following sections.

Auto Private IP Addressing (APIPA)

APIPA is new feature of Windows 2000 TCP/IP. Users can create a single subnet TCP/IP network without having to set up a DHCP server or manually configuring the TCP/IP protocol. APIPA can assign an IP address and subnet mask, but not a default gateway. APIPA should be used only on a small network that has no routers.

Advanced Telephone Support

Windows 2000 Professional provides support for TAPI 3.0 for telephony providers and H.323 for conferencing and IP multicast conferences. TAPI 3.0 integrates into Active Directory.

Authentication Protocols

Windows 2000 Professional supports the following protocols, which were also supported in Windows NT 4:

➤ *CHAP (Challenge Handshake Authentication Protocol)*—A secure authentication protocol.

➤ *MS-CHAP (Microsoft Challenge Handshake Authentication Protocol)*—Similar to CHAP, but designed for Microsoft products.

➤ *PAP (Password Authentication Protocol)*—Uses clear-text passwords.

➤ *SPAP (Shiva Password Authentication Protocol)*—Allows Shiva clients to connect to Windows computers.

Windows 2000 Professional also supports the following new protocols:

➤ *Extensible Authentication Protocol (EAP)*—An extension of Point-to-Point Protocol (PPP) that provides remote authentication using third-party devices.

➤ *Layer 2 Tunneling Protocol (L2TP)*—An Internet tunneling protocol that, unlike Point-to-Point Tunneling Protocol (PPTP), needs no IP connectivity between the client workstation and the server.

➤ *RADIUS (Remote Authentication Dial-In User Service)*—Supports third-party accounting and auditing packages.

Tunneling Protocols

Windows 2000 Professional supports the following tunneling protocols.

➤ *Internet Protocol Security (IPSec)*—Can be used to tunnel through public and private networks.

➤ *Layer 2 Tunneling Protocol (L2TP)*—Provides client-to-server and server-to-server tunneling. Security is provided through IPSec.

➤ *PPTP (Point-to-Point Tunneling Protocol)*—Has been employed in Windows 95, 98, and NT.

Lower Costs of Ownership

Total Cost of Ownership is a growing concern for many organizations. Windows 2000 Professional addresses this concern.

Easier Deployment

Migration paths are provided for upgrading to Windows 2000 Professional from Windows 95, 98, and NT. Several tools make this migration easier. They include Setup Manager, Disk Image preparation, and Remote Windows installation.

➤ *Unattended installation*—Administrators are able to deploy Windows 2000 Professional through automatic and unattended methods. The Setup Manager is used to generate answer files, which automate the installation of Windows 2000 Professional (as with previous versions of Windows).

➤ *Disk image replication*—By utilizing the System Preparation tool (Sysprep.exe), administrators can deploy identical configurations of Windows 2000 Professional to multiple computers. The master and destination computers must have identical Hardware Abstraction Layers (HALs), ACPI support, and mass storage devices.

➤ *Remote installation*—Remote Installation Service (RIS) allows unattended installations of Windows 2000 Professional. Clients connect to a special Windows 2000-based server called a RIS server. RIS supports several installation methods including answer files and Sysprep imaging.

Better Management Tools

With the release of Windows 2000, you now have access to more powerful management tools. These tools are discussed in the following list:

➤ *Windows Update*—Windows Update provides users with the ability to update drivers from the Windows Update Web Site. Windows Update compares drivers on the user's computer with those available on the Web site to see if a new version needs to be installed.

➤ *MMC*—MMC is a console used to provide a common environment for Snap-ins. Many of the Windows 2000 Professional administrative tools are written as MMC Snap-ins. Snap-ins are the administrative tools written by Microsoft and independent software vendors (ISVs). These include Computer Management, Services, Disk Management, Event Viewer, and the new Device Manager. All management applications can be accessed through a single interface.

Chapter Summary

In this chapter, you learned that the Windows 2000 Professional interface is more customizable than previous versions of Windows, that searching for files and folders is easier because of the search tool now integrated into Windows Explorer, and that better guidance items were added to aid users in troubleshooting problems. You also read that online help has been improved with the addition of the newer troubleshooting feature.

You learned that Windows 2000 Professional includes a more comprehensive setup program that makes it easier to deploy and install the operating system and that new accessibility options were added to make it easier for people with disabilities to use. This chapter explained how dial-up networking configuration is easier than in previous versions of Windows and how support is now provided for VPNs and multiple incoming connections.

Several new features that were specifically added for mobile users were covered here, including hibernation, offline viewing, offline files and folders, and hot docking. Windows 2000 Professional also provides support for over 60 languages. Installing and administering printers is improved with the Add Printer wizard, Plug and Play detection, and Point and Print. Support is provided for printing to printers over the Internet. Internet Explorer 5 has been integrated into the Windows 2000 Professional desktop. Users can use Windows Explorer to browse the Internet as they would local computers or intranets.

You learned about improved performance of Windows 2000 Professional, how system files are protected with Windows File Protection, that the operating system requires fewer reboots when changing system configurations, and how the Microsoft Installer application allows users to track, configure, remove, and upgrade software programs.

This chapter also touched on some deeper changes. Dynamic disks were introduced. NTFS has been extended to version 5, and now Security has been enhanced using EFS, IPSec, smart card support, and public key security. Windows 2000 Professional includes support for new hardware devices such as DVDs, USB, HIDs, and Plug and Play compliant devices. Multimedia support is enhanced. Windows 2000 Professional has support up to 10 monitors (which must be AGP or PCI devices). Advanced net-working capabilities are provided in Windows 2000 Professional with support for APIPA, TAPI 3.0 and tunneling protocols.

Review Questions

1. What is the purpose of AutoComplete?

    a. It completes the Windows Setup installation.

    b. It completes words as a user types.

    c. It provides a list of the most frequently used files a user can choose from.

    d. It allows users to browse a network from a single location.

2. AGP stands for:

    a. Accessibility Graphics Port

    b. Access Graphics Port

    c. Accelerated Graphics Port

    d. Advanced Graphics Peripheral

3. ICM stands for:

   a. Internet Control Message

   b. Image Color Management

   c. Intermediate Certification Management

   d. Interdisciplinary Communication Medium

4. Internet Connection Sharing provides what function?

   a. It allows all computers on a local intranet to share the same external connection to the Internet.

   b. It provides message routing services.

   c. It provides individuals access to the Internet.

   d. It's a service that supports Web site creation.

5. Windows 2000 Professional supports which of the following developer tools? [Check all correct answers]

   a. DHTML

   b. XML

   c. PICS

   d. HTML+Time

6. Windows File Protection provides what function?

   a. It prevents system files from being deleted or altered by users.

   b. It allows the operating system to install and remove software from client computers.

   c. It provides a way for users to update drivers and download service packs.

   d. It is a software service that maps IP addresses to computer names.

7. Disk Quotas can be administered on network shares. True or false?

   a. True

   b. False

8. Disk Defragmenter can be used to defrag which of the following volumes? [Check all correct answers]

   a. NTFS 5

   b. NTFS 4

   c. FAT

   d. FAT32

9. Encrypting File System is supported by which file system(s) in Windows 2000 Professional?

   a. NTFS 5

   b. FAT16

   c. FAT32

   d. NTFS 4

10. My Network Places is a replacement for what in previous versions of Windows?

    a. My Computer

    b. Network Neighborhood

    c. My Briefcase

    d. My Documents

11. Where are files saved by default in Windows 2000 Professional?

    a. My Pictures folder

    b. My Documents Folder

    c. \winnt\System32\

    d. Documents and Settings

    e. Program Files

12. Which of the following is a not a troubleshooter provided with Windows 2000 Professional?

    a. Client Services for NetWare

    b. Directory Services

    c. Networking and TCP/IP

    d. Remote Access to Networks

13. Which of the following are examples of security in Windows 2000 Professional? [Check all correct answers]

    a. IPSec

    b. EFS

    c. OnNow

    d. Plug and Play

14. Dynamic disks

    a. Are physical disks that contain only dynamic volumes.

    b. Are the same as basic disks.

    c. Can be used on non–NTFS partitions.

    d. Can be on the same volume as a basic disk.

1

15. ACPI stands for:

   a. Advanced Configuration and Power Interface

   b. Accessible Configuration and Power Interface

   c. Access Code Power Interface

   d. Advanced Configuration and Power Interference

16. Windows 2000 Professional has support for which of the following hardware devices? [Check all correct answers]

   a. DVD

   b. Plug and Play

   c. USB

   d. HID

17. Windows 2000 Professional provides support for multiple display devices. True or false?

   a. True

   b. False

18. Which of the following authentication protocols are supported by Windows 2000 Professional? [Check all correct answers]

   a. EAP

   b. MS-CHAP

   c. SPAP

   d. PPTP

19. What is the purpose of the Windows Update utility?

   a. It provides a central location to find system files, product enhancements, and service packs.

   b. It's an interactive tool for setting up commonly used options.

   c. It automatically configures IP addresses for client computers.

   d. It specifies where an application should run on a client computer.

20. What does LDM stand for?

   a. Lightweight Directory Module

   b. Line Daemon Monitor

   c. Logical Disk Manager

   d. Logical Disk Module

CHAPTER TWO

Installing and Deploying Windows 2000 Professional

After completing this chapter, you will be able to:

✓ Install Windows 2000 Professional

✓ Automate the Installation with an answer file and Uniqueness Database File

✓ Deploy Windows 2000 with third-party imaging software

✓ Deploy Windows 2000 with the Remote Installation Service

✓ Upgrade your operating system to Windows 2000

✓ Apply update packs

✓ Apply service packs

Installing an operating system is no small task, especially when you decide to replace the operating system of all your client workstations in a networked environment. The operating system is the basis for everything you do with your computer. If you make the decision to upgrade or roll out Windows 2000, make sure that you do extensive testing before putting the new operating system into production. Windows 2000 does support far more hardware configurations than Windows NT; however, there is no guarantee that *your* computer hardware will be supported.

Windows NT had a major disadvantage in that you could not upgrade the operating system from Windows 95 or Windows 98. This made the task of adding a new operating system daunting. Windows 2000, however, allows for upgrades from Windows 95 and Windows 98, though you will need to check your software to make sure it will work after the upgrade, and you may need to obtain update packs for the software.

Windows 2000 has also made some great advances in the area of automation:

➤ The automated install is now much easier to set up and configure.

➤ Windows 2000 now fully supports the use of third-party drive imaging tools.

➤ Microsoft introduces a new technology called Remote Installation Service (RIS) in Windows 2000 Professional.

Checking the Hardware

Before deciding to install Windows 2000, make sure that your hardware supports the new operating system. Windows 2000 supports more hardware than any other Microsoft operating system. It is also a much larger operating system and thus requires more system resources than any other Microsoft operating system.

Windows 2000 Professional requires that you have at least a Pentium 133MHz processor. Note that this is a change from the Windows 2000 beta versions. During development, most of the documentation claimed that a Pentium 166MHz was going to be the minimum requirement. However, Microsoft does recommend that you have a faster processor than the minimum requirement. As is true of most operating systems, the faster the processor, the better. Windows 2000 Professional supports up to two processors on the same system.

Windows 2000 no longer has a build that works on the Alpha processor. Compaq made the decision to stop supporting Windows NT on the Alpha. They believed that the Intel machines they built with multiple processors were now fast enough to be equivalent to the Alpha processor. Although Microsoft is dedicated to supporting all current installs of their products on the Alpha processor, no new products have the Alpha build, including Windows 2000.

The minimum RAM that is required is 32MB; however, Microsoft recommends 64MB of RAM. Most of the time, Windows 2000 Professional uses about 62MB of RAM just for the operating system. This means that as you start running applications, you will see a considerable amount of paging to virtual memory. Although your system will still run, it is preferable, for better performance, to minimize the use of virtual memory. It is recommended, in a production environment, that you set a minimum level of memory to 128MB of RAM. Then monitor your systems to make sure that they don't need more memory allocation. Like Windows NT, Windows 2000 uses a great deal of memory, so the general rule is the more the better.

The minimum hard drive space required is 650MB of free space. If you are going to perform a network install, you will need more space.

You also need a VGA monitor or a monitor with higher resolution, a video card, a keyboard, and a mouse. If you install from a CD-ROM, you will need a CD-ROM drive or a DVD-ROM drive. If the CD-ROM drive doesn't support booting the system and starting the Setup program, you need a high-density 3.5" disk drive. If you are going to perform the install over a network, you will be required to have a Windows 2000 compatible network card, related cable, and access to the share point on the network that contains the installation files.

Microsoft only supports hardware that is listed in the Hardware Compatibility List (HCL). You can find this list on the Windows 2000 CD-ROM, in the support folder in a file called hcl.txt, which contains the hardware supported when the disc was burned. To find the most current listing of hardware, go to **www.microsoft.com/hcl**, which is updated often. If your hardware is not listed, it doesn't necessarily mean that it won't work. Many hardware vendors release their hardware and never get it certified, or they might be waiting for the process to be completed. It can take time for a piece of hardware to go through the process for listing in the HCL. If you have a problem with hardware that isn't listed, don't call Microsoft; call the manufacturer of the hardware.

Installing Windows 2000

The process of installing Windows 2000 is similar to the installation of Windows NT 4. If you have experience with Windows NT 4, you will see that most of the process is the same. Microsoft has added a few things to the installation procedure.

There are two choices of installation media. You can install Windows 2000 directly from the CD-ROM (the days of floppy disk installs are gone—you would need about 340 floppies to install Windows 2000), or you can install it from a network share. Regardless of the method you choose, the installation is the same. The highlights of some minor differences are discussed as we go through the procedure.

If you are going to install from the CD-ROM, you have two ways to access the procedure. The first, and probably the easiest, way is to boot directly from the disc. To do this, you must set your computer's BIOS to have the system boot from the CD-ROM, and your CD-ROM drive must support the El Torito No Emulation CD Boot standard. If both of these requirements are met, you can simply put the disc into the CD-ROM drive and reboot the computer. Make sure that you watch the system at this point because Microsoft has added a twist here. In Windows NT 4, if you had the CD-ROM in the drive, it would automatically boot to the install program. Windows 2000 gives you an option. You must press a key to actually start the install program. If you do not press a key, the install program waits a few seconds, and then boots from the hard drive.

Tip: If you are trying to boot from the floppy drive, make sure that you remove the disc from the CD-ROM drive. The CD's boot program tells the computer that, if you do not press a key, to then boot from the hard drive, which bypasses the floppy drive in the boot order.

If you do not have a bootable CD-ROM drive or if it doesn't seem to work properly, you do have another option. On the Windows 2000 CD-ROM, you will find a folder named *bootdisk*. In this folder, you will find a file named makeboot.exe. You can run this file in two ways. If you just run the makeboot file, it will ask in which drive you want to make the disks, or you can set this automatically by adding a drive letter after the executable by typing "makeboot.exe a:". You will need four blank formatted high-density disks. This program puts the proper files on the four disks for you to use to boot the system and load the proper drivers to access the CD-ROM. Although this is a helpful alternative, if your hardware doesn't support a bootable CD-ROM, it takes considerably longer to install with the boot disks.

If you plan to install from a network share point, you must first copy the contents of the i386 folder from the CD-ROM to a folder that is shared on the network. You need to have a boot disk that allows you to connect to the network server and the shared folder. If you are running Windows 95, 98, or Windows NT, run winnt32.exe. If you are running any other operating system, run winnt.exe.

Note: *For those of you familiar with Windows NT, recall that when performing an install, you ran winnt.exe if you were running an operating system other than Windows NT. With Windows 2000, Microsoft has changed the Winnt32 executable so that it runs under Windows 95 and Windows 98.*

Whichever way you decide to run the install, Windows 2000 starts the Setup wizard. After you confirm that you want to install Windows 2000, you are asked to choose a partition on which to install the operating system. You can delete and create partitions at this point. If the partition you choose to install on has not been formatted, you are asked whether you want to format the partition as FAT or NTFS. If you choose to format the partition as FAT, Windows 2000 formats the drive as FAT16 if it is smaller than 2GB or as FAT32 if the partition is larger than 2GB. After the partition is formatted, the Setup program starts copying files to the partition. The default location for the operating system is the \winnt folder. Once Setup has finished copying the files, the system automatically reboots.

After the system has rebooted, a GUI-based Setup wizard runs. This wizard takes you through the process of entering the proper information for your setup. You are required to enter your name and organization and set the date, time, and regional settings. You also need to enter a computer name and set a password for the administrator account. In the networking components section, you are required to verify that the proper network adapter was found by the system, and then select additional network components that you need to connect to your network. After you customize the install to your situation, Windows 2000 then copies the required files, saves all configuration information, and removes all temporary files that were needed by the Setup program. Now, the computer restarts, and you are ready to log in and customize your install.

The following is a list of the steps in the setup process:

1. Press a key to boot from the CD-ROM, or type "winnt.exe" or "winnt32.exe" for a network install.

2. Press Enter to set up Windows 2000, or press R to start the emergency repair process.

3. Press F8 to accept the Licensing agreement.

4. Configure the partitions on the hard drive and choose which partition will contain the system files. If you create a new partition, the Setup program asks whether you want to format the partition as FAT or NTFS.

5. Next, the Setup program copies some files to the hard drive and reboots the system, ending the text mode portion of Setup.

6. The GUI portion of Setup continues.

7. Setup begins to detect your computer hardware (this can take quite a while, so be patient).

8. You are then asked to set the regional settings for the computer. You need to select the system or user locale as well as the keyboard layout.

9. Enter you name and organization.

10. Enter your CD-KEY.

11. Next, you are asked to enter a computer name. Windows 2000 generates a computer name by using your organization name, adding a dash, and then adding 13 autogenerated characters—for example, xyzcompany-GH38DJE63HQD8. You also need to enter a password for the administrator account.

12. Verify the date and time, and set your time zone information.

13. The network services install starts next. You are asked whether you want to use the typical or custom settings. If you choose custom, you are then asked to add any clients, protocols, or services that are necessary.

14. At this point, you can connect to a domain or workgroup. If you connect with a domain, you must have a computer account in the domain, or you can create one by entering a username and password of a domain account that has permission to create computer accounts.

15. Setup then copies the files that it needs to install the components you have selected.

16. After some final tasks are completed, Setup installs Start Menu items, registers components, saves settings, and removes all temporary files.

17. Setup finishes and reboots the system.

18. Setup then presents a dialog box, asking whether you want all users to enter a login and password, or if you want the system to automatically log on a user.

19. Setup then finishes.

Automatic Installation Options

Deploying a new operating system can become a major chore. The more workstations in your network, the larger the chore becomes. If you only have five computers in your network, you might be better off just going through the install process on each one. If you have 5000 computers, it could take a long time to roll out Windows 2000. Microsoft recognized this problem and worked hard to come up with a number of options to automate the process of setting up Windows 2000 as your desktop operating system of choice.

Automated Installation Scripts

The first way that Microsoft has given us to install Windows 2000 is to create automated scripts to answer all the questions in the Setup program. Although this won't make the Setup program run faster, you can run the script on multiple computers and install the operating system with little or no user intervention.

To create an automated install, you must have an answer file. This file can be either your best friend or your worst enemy. There are hundreds of settings for this file. Listing 2.1 shows an example of a very basic answer file.

Listing 2.1   A simple example of an answer file.

```
[Data]
    AutoPartition=1
    MsDosInitiated="0"
    UnattendedInstall="Yes"

[Unattended]
    UnattendMode=FullUnattended
    OemSkipEula=Yes
    OemPreinstall=No
    TargetPath=\WINNT

[GuiUnattended]
    AdminPassword=password
    OEMSkipRegional=1
    TimeZone=20
    OemSkipWelcome=1

[UserData]
    FullName="User Name"
    OrgName="Organization Name"
    ComputerName=*

[Identification]
    JoinDomain=DOMAIN
    DomainAdmin=administrator
    DomainAdminPassword=password

[Networking]
    InstallDefaultComponents=No

[Display]
    BitsPerPel=24
    Xresolution=1024
    YResolution=768
    Vrefresh=70

[TapiLocation]
    CountryCode=1
    Dialing=Tone
    LongDistanceAccess="9,"

[FavoritesEx]
    Title1="Coriolis.url"
    URL1="http://www.coriolis.com"
    Title2="Microsoft.url"
    URL2="http://www.microsoft.com"
```

```
[Branding]
    BrandIEUsingUnattended=Yes

[URL]
    Home_Page=http://www.yahoo.com

[Proxy]
    Proxy_Enable=0
    Use_Same_Proxy=0

[NetAdapters]
    Adapter1=params.Adapter1

[params.Adapter1]
    INFID=*

[NetClients]
    MS_MSClient=params.MS_MSClient
    MS_NWClient=params.MS_NWClient

[params.MS_NWClient]
    LogonScript=No

[NetServices]
    MS_SERVER=params.MS_SERVER

[NetProtocols]
    MS_TCPIP=params.MS_TCPIP
    MS_NWIPX=params.MS_NWIPX

[params.MS_TCPIP]
    DNS=Yes
    UseDomainNameDevolution=No
    EnableLMHosts=Yes
    AdapterSections=params.MS_TCPIP.Adapter1

[params.MS_TCPIP.Adapter1]
    SpecificTo=Adapter1
    DHCP=Yes
    WINS=No
    NetBIOSOptions=0
    NetworkNumber=00000000
```

You can create this file on your own. You only need a text editor, the guide to
Unattended Setup (you can find this in the Windows 2000 resource kit), and the will
to create the document. This can become a huge task given that the Unattended
Setup guide is about 130 pages in length and contains hundreds of settings.

Setup Manager

Setup Manager is the answer to the dilemma of creating an answer file. The Setup Manager is a GUI-based tool that assists you in creating the answer file. Although the Setup Manager doesn't configure every possible key in the answer file, it does configure the most common options.

You can find the Setup Manager program on the resource kit in the deployment tools. You can also find Setup Manager in the \support\tools folder on the Windows 2000 CD-ROM. When you run the Setup Manager program, it asks whether you want to create a new answer file, create an answer file that duplicates your computer's configuration, or modify an existing answer file (see Figure 2.1). Regardless of the option you choose, the rest of the program is the same. The only difference is if you choose to modify an answer file or duplicate your computer's configuration, some of the options will already be filled in. You can change these answers because they are just defaults.

You need to decide on the kind of answer file you want to create. Three variations of answer files are available: a Windows 2000 unattended installation file, a Sysprep file, or a Remote Installation Service file. The Sysprep and Remote Installation Service files are discussed later in this chapter, in the "Remote Installation Services (RIS)" section. For now, focus on the Windows 2000 unattended install. You must choose whether this file is for Windows 2000 Professional or Windows 2000 Server. The files created are similar and could be used for either install. Some of the sections and settings for the Server product, however, will not work on the Workstation product. You are better served by creating different answer files for Server and Professional installations.

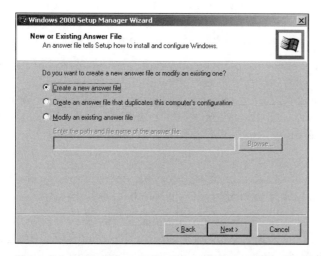

Figure 2.1   Determining whether to create a new answer file or to modify an existing one.

Figure 2.2 These are the available User Interaction Level options.

You then must determine the level of user interaction that you will allow (see Figure 2.2). Five options of supplying answers are available. The first option is Provide Defaults. As you go through the Setup procedure, it allows you to stop at every entry instead of just the blank entries. The entries are then replaced by what you have in your answer file. This is useful for users (who are installing the operating system) who may not know what all the settings are for. This way, the users can change the settings they do know, and the settings they don't know are already provided for their network.

The next option is Fully Automated. The Setup program will not stop as long as all the answers have been provided. This method is useful when you want to install the operating system on many computers. It allows you to start the install process and walk away. When you return, the system should be set up for the user.

The Hide Pages option allows you to create an install for your users, but it limits them to seeing only the pages on which you allow them to make changes. In this way, if you have some settings that should not be changed, the Setup program bypasses those screens and doesn't show them to the user. This method may be an alternative to Provide Defaults because you have more control over which options the user can change.

The Read Only option allows the user to see what has been entered in the Setup program, but does not allow her to change any option that has been set.

The last option is GUI Attended. This option automates only the text portion of the Setup program. If you have users who will perform the install, automating the text portion can be useful because it's often the most difficult portion for users to understand. This also allows you to change the partition you are installing on or load a different mass storage device driver, if needed.

The Setup Manager program then asks the standard questions that you would normally be asked during a regular install. As you follow along with the wizard, you are able to set the options you need for the type of install that you have chosen. Near the end of the wizard, choose to run the automated install from a CD-ROM drive locally or to perform a network install.

If you decide to install over the network, Setup Manager asks where you would like to create the distribution folder and what name you would like to share it as. You are also allowed to add drivers to the setup as well as other files if you need them. Within the distribution folder, Setup Manager creates a folder called oem, where any individual files you have added to the setup are stored. These files usually include additional drivers for Plug and Play devices that do not come with Windows 2000. However, Microsoft does provide a great many drivers with Windows 2000. Although you may not find many instances of hardware that are not recognized in your current system, it doesn't take long for hardware manufacturers to introduce new hardware to the market. Obviously, this new hardware will not have drivers included with Windows 2000. By placing these new drivers in this folder, the Setup program will be able find, and install, the new drivers automatically. Setup Manager then copies the setup files from your CD-ROM or from a location that you specify.

To add these drivers to your automated install, you need to add a folder under the path \$OEM$\$1$. If you name the folder "drivers", you also need to add a line to your unattended installation file. In the section called Unattended, you must add the following line:

```
OEMPnPDriversPath = "drivers"
```

You can create multiple subfolders, just be sure that you add all the directories in the path. If you create subfolders under drivers (like video, audio, scsi, and net), you would add the following line:

```
OEMPnPDriversPath = "drivers"; "drivers\video"; "drivers\audio";
"drivers\scsi"; "drivers\net"
```

If you decide to use the unattended text file with the CD-ROM locally, you are asked where you want to store the file. The disadvantage to this option is that you are not allowed to add any drivers to the Setup. The advantage to this option is that you will be allowed to partition or format your system drive. It also doesn't require you to be connected to a network.

Setup Manager creates a file by default called unattend.txt. The big difference between these two setup methods is this line in the CD-ROM install file:

```
MsDosInitiated = "0"
```

This line informs the Setup loader that the installation is being performed from the CD-ROM. This line usually doesn't exist in a network install. If you decide later that you want to use the file for a network install, you can change the file by setting the value to 1 and the network install will work, or if you started with a network install, you can add this line to the [Data] section.

After you have created unattend.txt with Setup Manager, you may or may not need to make any manual changes to the file. Be sure to follow the guidelines in the unattend.doc file, which you will find in the resource kit. You are now ready to start your unattended install.

UDF (Uniqueness Database File)

The UDF is provided to help you create unique installs without having to create a completely new unattend.txt for every computer in your organization. You can use the UDF to override the answers in the answer file with unique values. The main reason for doing this is to make sure that every computer has a unique computer name. You might also use this file if you are in a multiple domain environment. You can have the UDF file change the parameters based on which domain you would like to belong to.

The UDF file has the same basic structure as the answer file. The difference is that you must specify which ID the section relates to. Listing 2.2 shows a basic UDF file.

Listing 2.2   A simple example of a basic UDF file.

```
[UniqueIds]
    one=UserData
    two=UserData
    three=UserData

[one:UserData]
    ComputerName=ComputerOne

[one:GuiUnattended]
    TimeZone=4

[two:UserData]
    ComputerName=ComputerTwo

[two:GuiUnattended]
    TimeZone=10

[three:UserData]
    ComputerName=ComputerThree

[three:GuiUnattended]
    TimeZone=20
```

In this UDF file, you can see that there are three IDs, and each of the IDs is associated with two different sections. The UserData section assigns a computer name, and the GuiUnattend section assigns different time zones. Regardless of what answers have been placed in the answer file, if you specify an ID that is in the UDF, the UDF overrides it and places its answer in the Setup program.

Putting this file together can be a lengthy procedure. In Windows NT, you would have been forced to create a UDF if for no other reason than to assign unique computer names. Windows 2000 has the added feature of autogenerating computer names. This may mean that you can get away with not having to use a UDF, which makes the procedure much quicker and easier.

Winnt or Winnt32

Now that you have created your answer file and your UDF, you are ready to test it out and roll out your installation of Windows 2000. Two questions to consider at this point are, "How do I specify which answer file I'm going to use?" and "If I have a UDF, how do I let it know which computer ID I want to install?"

To start the Setup program, you have to invoke either the winnt.exe or the winnt32.exe program. The choice is easy; if you are running Setup from DOS or Windows 3.1, you use winnt.exe. If you are running Windows 95, Windows 98, Windows NT 3.51, or Windows NT 4, you use winnt32.exe.

Warning: In Windows NT, if you were running Setup from an operating system other than a Windows NT system, you used winnt.exe. However, in Windows 2000, you have to remember to use the winnt32.exe if you are running Setup from Windows 95.

The options are similar between the two Setup programs. If you are using winnt.exe, the two switches you need are /u and /udf. In these options, you specify your answer file and your UDF. See the following syntax:

```
Winnt.exe /u:answer_file /udf:id,UDF_file
```

You need to replace *answer_file* with the exact path and name of the appropriate answer file. You also need to replace the *id* with whichever ID you specified in the UDF, and replace the *UDF_file* with the exact path and name of that file.

If you are using winnt32.exe, the syntax changes only slightly, as shown in the following line:

```
Winnt32.exe /unattend[num]:answer_file /udf:id,UDF_file
```

The key difference here is that you use /unattend instead of /u. Also, notice the [*num*] after the unattend. This is used to specify the number of seconds between the time that Setup finishes copying the files and when it reboots the system. The [*num*] is effective only if winnt32 is being run from Windows NT or Windows 2000.

If you use the Setup Manager program to create your answer file and UDF, Setup Manager also creates a file called unattend.bat. This is a sample batch file that helps you start your automated install. Although you are certainly not required to use this batch file, it can provide a good starting place. Listing 2.3 shows a batch file that was created with Setup Manager.

Listing 2.3 An example of a sample unattend.bat file.

```
@rem SetupMgrTag
@echo off

rem
rem This is a SAMPLE batch script generated by the Setup Manager Wizard.
rem If this script is moved from the location where it was generated, it
may have to be modified.
rem

set AnswerFile=.\unattend.txt
set UdfFile=.\unattend.udf
set ComputerName=%1
set SetupFiles=D:\i386

if "%ComputerName%" == "" goto USAGE

D:\i386\winnt32 /s:%SetupFiles% /unattend:%AnswerFile% /
udf:%ComputerName%,%UdfFile% /makelocalsource
goto DONE

:USAGE
echo.
echo Usage: unattend ^<computername^>
echo.

:DONE
```

To run this batch file, type "unattend", followed by the ID you used in the UDF.

If you want to run an unattended install from the CD-ROM when it boots, you don't have the option of adding switches to the command. The Setup program is run automatically. In this case, you just need to rename your answer file to winnt.sif. It is vital that this file uses this exact name. If you are going to install from the CD-ROM, you must have the following section in the answer file—if this data section is not present, the install will not work:

```
[Data]
unattendedinstall = yes
msdosinitiated = 0
autopartition = 1
```

Warning: If you view your answer file in Notepad and save the file, Notepad automatically puts a .txt extension on your file. If you have the extensions hidden, which is the default setting, you will not see this extension. Your file looks like winnt.sif in Explorer, but it's true name is actually winnt.sif.txt, which will not work.

Copy the file to a floppy disk and have it in the drive when the Setup program runs. The Setup program automatically checks for this file every time it runs, and if it finds the file, it uses the answers provided in the file to complete the installation. The disadvantage to this is that you are not able to use a UDF for this type of install.

Warning: Make sure that the floppy disk is in the drive when Setup runs. One of the first things the Setup program does is to check for this file. If your CD-ROM drive is the first device in your boot order, put the floppy in the drive as the computer starts.

Disk Imaging

Disk imaging has become popular in the last couple of years. It revolutionized the way many companies roll out their systems. The advantage to using disk imaging is that it allows you to take your time installing the operating system and all of your applications. To use disk imaging, test the installs to make sure that everything is working properly, then use an imaging program that saves an exact replica of the hard drive to a file on your network. You can then take that file and download it to any number of computers on the network, which results in each computer having an exact replica of the original hard drive. Microsoft doesn't have a disk imaging tool, but you can purchase a third-party imaging tool for this purpose.

Although this technology has a great many advantages, it does have some drawbacks. You are required to change the computer name because you must have uniqueness in your network. If you are not using DHCP (Dynamic Host Configuration Protocol), you have to change the IP address. If your computers are not exactly the same, you have to change the drivers for your hardware and in some cases, your operating system will not even come on line. If you are running the Windows NT operating system and each computer's autogenerated SID (Security Identifier) number is not unique on the network, it can cause problems; so you are required to run a program that will regenerate these numbers. As you can see, there can still be quite a few things left to do after the new computer has been imaged, so you may have to create many images depending on how many configurations of computers you have.

Sysprep

Microsoft has remedied many of the problems associated with these drive imaging programs. They have created a tool called Sysprep. The idea behind this tool is to make the imaging process much smoother than with previous operating systems. When you run the Sysprep tool, it removes all of the unique information from the computer, and then has the system regenerate all of this information on the next reboot. Sysprep tells the system to regenerate the SID numbers. This is critical because the system uses these numbers to communicate. Here's an example of a SID: {17CCA71B-ECD7-11D0-B908-00A0C9223196}. As you can see, this is not a number you would want to have to remember. You refer to computers by their names, whereas Windows 2000 refers to computers by their SID numbers. Not only is the computer assigned a SID, but virtually every other component, user, group, and so on is given a SID number.

Sysprep also strips away all the user information from the system. When you reboot the system, the user name and organization will have been deleted. You need to configure a number of settings in the system to make it functional again.

To prepare your computer for imaging, you must install the operating system and your applications. Make sure all the applications are working and settings are configured the way you want them. When you are configuring your applications, it is important that you use the same account to install and configure those applications. Usually you would use the local administrator account to install all applications. No matter which account you use, make sure that it has administrator privileges. Assume that you are using the administrator account. After you have configured everything, you must create a temporary account that has administrator privileges. Log into the system using your new temporary account. You need to copy the administrator profile to the default user profile. You can find more information about user profiles in Chapter 14. You will want all the application settings that you made to be available for all users on the system. If you perform the following steps, all the settings will be available to everyone:

1. In the Control Panel, double click on the System icon.

2. Select the User Profile tab.

3. Highlight the Administrator account (or whichever account you used), and click on the Copy To button.

4. Click on the browse button and navigate to the following path: *x*:\Documents and Settings\Default User (replace the *x* with the drive letter that contains your system files). See Figure 2.3.

5. Click on OK. Every user who logs on will now obtain the proper application settings.

6. Log back in as administrator, and delete the temporary account.

Note: *Do not set up your computer to the domain. Before running Sysprep, you must remove all the networking properties. Only have the computer set as part of a workgroup. After running Sysprep, you will be able to set up the computer on the network.*

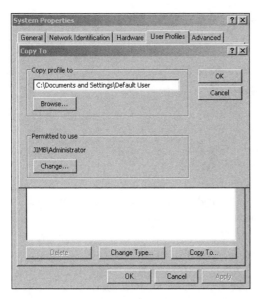

Figure 2.3 The Copy To dialog box, which will allow you to copy the contents of a profile to another location.

After your system is set up, you need to create the folder %*systemdrive*%\sysprep (%*systemdrive*% should be replaced with the drive letter on which you installed the Windows 2000 system files). Copy the sysprep.exe and setupcl.exe files from the \support\tools\deploy.cab into this folder.

Note: A cab file contains compressed versions of other files. Windows Explorer allows you to see the contents of a cab file by double-clicking on the file. If you copy a file from Windows Explorer to another location, the file will be automatically decompressed and usable.

It is important that you put the setupcl.exe file in this folder, or Sysprep will not work. Both of these files can be found in the Windows 2000 resource kit. Now you only need to run Sysprep. You can run Sysprep by itself, but some command line options can be used in conjunction with it. See the following syntax and Table 2.1:

```
Sysprep.exe -sysprep.inf -nosidgen -quiet -pnp -reboot
```

Table 2.1   Command line options for sysprep.exe.

Option	Description
Sysprep.inf	Automates the mini-setup routine after the system reboots.
Nosidgen	Tells the setupcl.exe not to regenerate the SIDs when the system reboots.
Quiet	Bypasses the confirmation dialog boxes.
Pnp	Tells the system to run the Plug and Play detection utility when the system reboots.
Reboot	Tells the system to reboot the system automatically after Sysprep is run instead of shutting down. Reboot adds some time to the reboot process.

Don't worry about the Sysprep folder that you created, because after you run Sysprep, the folder and its contents are deleted. After running Sysprep, the program shuts down the system. At this point, run your disk imaging tool. This part of the procedure varies, depending on the program you purchased to create your images. If you start the computer again, you will have to restart the procedure.

Most likely, you will also want to reduce the size of your image files. There are a few very large files that you can delete, which may help: hyberfil.sys and pagefile.sys. Hyberfil.sys is the hibernation file that is used when the system goes into standby. The other file is a little trickier. Pagefile.sys is a system file that contains your virtual memory. This file is usually 1.3 times the size of memory in your computer. For example, if your system has 128MB of RAM, then your pagefile will start out at 192MB. The default size of the pagefile is 1.5 times the amount of RAM in the system. The only problem with deleting this file is that you cannot delete it while the system is running. If you formatted your hard drive with NTFS, you may not be able to delete this file. If your hard drive is formatted with FAT, you can use a boot disk from DOS, Windows 95, or Windows 98 to access the drive. You can then delete pagefile.sys. Windows 2000 automatically re-creates these files.

Before you decide to download the disk image to another computer, you should keep a few things in mind. Make sure that the HAL (Hardware Abstraction Layer) works on the new computer. Not all HALs will work on all computers. The mass storage controller must also be identical. If it's different on your destination system, the operating system will not be able to load, and you won't be able to change it. You also need to make sure that the destination computer has as much hard drive space as the source computer. Most disk imaging applications allow you to repartition the drive on the fly, so as long as the destination hard drive has enough space for the files from the source computer, the imaging process should work. If the BIOS versions on both computers are different, test the image first because a BIOS may not be compatible and can cause problems. If the devices on the two systems are not identical, there should not be a problem because Windows 2000 is a Plug and Play operating system. The new devices should be found automatically and the drivers loaded. Although this procedure may work most of the time, you will want to test it first to make sure.

Mini-Setup Wizard

After you download the image to the new computer and start it, you need to enter all the unique values for the computer. Now a Mini-Setup Wizard runs, which guides you through the process of entering all the required information.

The Mini-Setup Wizard tool assists in getting your imaged computer ready to function. You will be required to enter information, such as your name and organization, the administrator password, the location, and the network properties. You will also have the opportunity to set up the system on a domain.

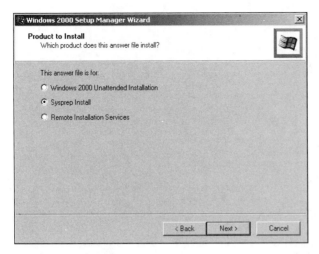

Figure 2.4 The Setup Manager dialog box, with choices for the type of answer file you would like to create.

The Mini-Setup Wizard takes only five or ten minutes to complete. Although it's much faster than performing the install manually, it can still take longer than you may expect. Here again, Microsoft provides a way to automate the answers for the Mini-Setup Wizard by using the Setup Manager program. This time, however, you must choose to create an answer file for Sysprep Install (see Figure 2.4).

You need to create a file called sysprep.inf, which contains the answers to the questions asked in the Mini-Setup Wizard. This file is similar to the unattended answer file that was created earlier. Using Setup Manager allows you to create a basic version of the sysprep.inf file. You can modify this file in the same way that you modified the unattend.txt file; however, some options may not work, so test the file prior to rollout.

Listing 2.4 shows an example of a sysprep.inf file. To use this file, place it in the same folder as the syspref.exe file, usually c:\sysprep.

Listing 2.4 An example of a sysprep.inf file.

```
;SetupMgrTag
[Unattended]
    OemSkipEula=Yes
    InstallFilesPath=C:\sysprep\i386
    OemPnPDriversPath=C:\drivers
    TargetPath=\WINNT

[GuiUnattended]
    AdminPassword=password
    OEMSkipRegional=1
```

```
            TimeZone=20
            OemSkipWelcome=1
            OEMDuplicatorstring="Version 1"

    [UserData]
            FullName="Test User"
            OrgName="Test Org"

    [SetupMgr]
            ComputerName0=computername
            ComputerName1=Computername

    [Identification]
            JoinDomain=DOMAIN
            DomainAdmin=administrator
            DomainAdminPassword=password

    [Networking]
            InstallDefaultComponents=No

    [Display]
            BitsPerPel=16
            Xresolution=800
            YResolution=600

    [TapiLocation]
            AreaCode=414
            LongDistanceAccess="9,"

    [Branding]
            BrandIEUsingUnattended=Yes

    [Proxy]
            Proxy_Enable=0
            Use_Same_Proxy=0

    [NetClients]
            MS_MSClient=params.MS_MSClient
            MS_NWClient=params.MS_NWClient

    [params.MS_NWClient]
            LogonScript=No
```

Distributing your operating system by using images can be one of the best tools you can use to set up a network. If your users aren't storing data on their local hard drives, you can simply re-image a user's computer if there are problems. Problems arise in making sure that your images are up-to-date with the newest versions of software and service packs. It is generally assumed that you need to re-create or update your images every three months. This task can become daunting if you created many images.

Remote Installation Services (RIS)

RIS is really a tool that is more closely related to Windows 2000 Server than to Windows 2000 Professional. Because this tool is used to distribute Windows 2000 Professional, some of the basics of working with RIS are covered in this section.

RIS is Microsoft's answer to the currently available imaging technologies. It isn't quite as easy to use, and it doesn't have all the features of some third-party products, but it does allow you to send images to client computers in a quick and easy fashion. RIS can only be used to distribute Windows 2000 Professional images, so it's limited in its scope. RIS allows you to boot your PC from the network card, connect to a RIS server, and download the proper image to the client computer.

Setting Up a RIS Server

RIS has some very specific requirements that you need to adhere to when you set up a server. RIS has been designed to work with a Windows 2000 network. If you set up your network to work with Active Directory, you should be able to implement a RIS server.

Your network needs to have a DHCP server, Active Directory, and a DNS (Domain Name Service) Server. Active Directory already requires a DNS server, so if you have that set up, you will meet those requirements. Your DNS server must support SRV (service) records, and your DHCP server has to be authorized by Active Directory to distribute TCP/IP addresses.

Your RIS server requires that you have a 2GB or larger partition, which has been formatted as NTFS. This partition cannot contain either your boot or system partition. It is generally considered best practice to dedicate a physical hard drive to store and distribute your RIS images to obtain better performance.

Note: *There has been much confusion about the boot and system partitions because they are exactly the reverse of what you might expect. The system partition is the partition that contains the boot files. It is usually on the c: drive on most systems and contains files like ntldr, boot.ini, bootsect.dos, and ntdetect.com. Your boot partition is the partition that contains your system files. These files are contained in the Winnt and Program Files directories. The boot and system partitions can be the same partition, but it is not required.*

After you have met the requirements for setting up a RIS server, you need to install the service. Go to the Control Panel and open Add/Remove Programs. Select Add/ Remove Windows components, and then choose the Remote Installation Services and install them. When you have the services installed, you need to configure them; you can do so by running the program Risetup. The installation wizard asks for information about how you want to set up RIS. You need to decide on a location for the Remote Installation Folder. This folder cannot be on a Dfs (Distributed File System) shared folder or on an EFS (Encrypting File System) volume. You also need to specify if you want the server to respond to clients that are requesting the service. It's probably a good idea not to allow the RIS server to respond to these requests at this point. You are better off waiting until you have the server configured before allowing it to respond to requests.

RIS also creates a CD-based image. You are required to have at least one CD-ROM-based image on your RIS server. To do this, the RIS Setup Wizard asks for the Windows 2000 Professional source files. After you complete the required information, the wizard creates the RIS folder structure, copies all the supporting files, creates the default CD-based image, and starts the RIS services (see Figure 2.5).

After RIS is installed, you need to authorize the RIS server to distribute its images. The purpose of this authorization is to prevent unauthorized users from setting up a RIS server, which might create problems on your network. You authorize an RIS server in exactly the same way that you authorize a DHCP server in Active Directory. Simply open the DHCP console from Administrative tools, right-click on DHCP, and choose Manage Authorized Servers. Then just add your RIS server to the list. You must be a member of the Enterprise Admins group to authorize a server. The last thing you need to do is make sure that users installing the RIS images are able to create computer accounts in the organizational units in which you want the accounts to go.

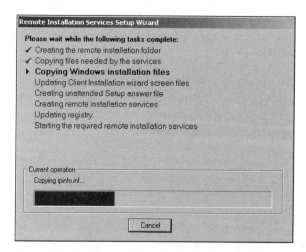

Figure 2.5   The Remote Installation Service will copy a number of files during the install process. This window shows the installation tasks that RIS needs to perform during installation.

2

You can also set up a client-naming format. If you want to autogenerate computer names for your clients, you define a system for doing this. By default, RIS names the computer based on the user name of the person initiating the install. You can use the variables in Table 2.2 to create a custom naming format.

You can set this naming feature by going to the properties of the RIS computer, navigating to the Remote Install tab, and then clicking on the Advanced Settings button (see Figure 2.6).

Creating and Managing RIS Images

Before you deploy Windows 2000 Professional, you need to create some images for RIS to send out. As mentioned previously, when you install RIS, it automatically creates a CD-based image. You must have the CD-based image on the RIS server at all times. This image is a standard Windows 2000 Professional install. This install package contains a file called ristandard.sif, which is the default answer file for this installation.

Table 2.2   Variables used by RIS to autogenerate computer names.

Variable	Description
%MAC	Inserts the MAC address of the network card in the computer
%First	Inserts the first name of the user doing the install
%Last	Inserts the last name of the user doing the install
%Username	Inserts the username of the user doing the install
%#	Inserts an incremental number

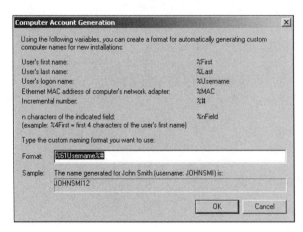

Figure 2.6   Computer Account Generation options.

You may want to create a Riprep image of your Windows 2000 installation. The advantage of creating Riprep images is similar to that of the Sysprep images; they contain applications and user settings. You can set up your operating system, and then install and configure your applications. After that is done, you can create an image of the installation. However, rather than using a third-party application, you can use the Riprep utility to create the image. Creating the Riprep image is easy: Simply go to Start|Run, and type "\\ris_server\reminst\admin\i386\riprep.exe". This command removes all SIDs and unique registry entries, and creates the image on the RIS server. A default answer file that matches your current configuration is also created. Make sure that you follow the same steps for creating the Riprep image as you did for a Sysprep image.

You may want to create or modify the answer file that is associated with your image. To change the associated answer file, go back to the properties of the server and select the Remote Install tab. Click on the Advanced Setting button, and select the Image tab. Then click on the Add button. This starts an Add wizard from which you can choose to associate a new answer file to an existing image. In the wizard, you can select an existing sample image, copy an answer file from another RIS server, or select an alternative location. When the wizard is complete, your answer file will be modified.

If you want to create your own answer file, you can use the Setup Manager program. This time, you need to choose to create a Remote Installation Service answer file. You may notice a couple of new options in this install, For example, when you try to set up the time zone information, you can choose to set the time zone to whatever is set on the server.

When you create this file, notice that quite a few changes occurred in the answer file. One in particular is the [RemoteInstall] section. If this section appears, the repartition=yes value is set, and the install process deletes all the current partitions on the system and formats the drive as one NTFS partition. If this value isn't set, the default parameters in the client answer file are used. If your computer manufacturer has a partition that it uses for power management or system settings, it will not be affected by this setting. Listing 2.5 shows an example of a RIS answer file, which by default is named Ristndrd.sif.

Listing 2.5 An example of an RIS file.

```
;SetupMgrTag
[Data]
    AutoPartition=1
    MsDosInitiated="1"
    UnattendedInstall="Yes"
    floppyless="1"
    OriSrc="\\%SERVERNAME%\RemInst\%INSTALLPATH%"
    OriTyp="4"
    LocalSourceOnCD=1
```

```
[SetupData]
    OsLoadOptions="/noguiboot /fastdetect"
    SetupSourceDevice="\Device\LanmanRedirector\%SERVERNAME%\RemInst\
        %INSTALLPATH%"

[Unattended]
    UnattendMode=ProvideDefault
    OemPreinstall=No
    TargetPath=\WINNT
    FileSystem=LeaveAlone
    NtUpgrade=No
    OverwriteOemFilesOnUpgrade=No

[GuiUnattended]
    AdminPassword=*
    OEMSkipRegional=1
    TimeZone=%TIMEZONE%

[UserData]
    FullName="%USERFULLNAME%"
    OrgName="%ORGNAME%"
    ComputerName=%MACHINENAME%

[Display]
    BitsPerPel=8
    Xresolution=1024
    YResolution=768

[SetupMgr]
    DistFolder=C:\win2000dist
    DistShare=win2000dist

[Identification]
    JoinDomain=%MACHINEDOMAIN%
    DoOldStyleDomainJoin=Yes

[Networking]
    InstallDefaultComponents=No
    ProcessPageSections=Yes

[NetAdapters]
    Adapter1=params.Adapter1

[params.Adapter1]
    INFID=*

[NetClients]
    MS_MSClient=params.MS_MSClient
```

```
[NetServices]
    MS_SERVER=params.MS_SERVER

[NetProtocols]
    MS_TCPIP=params.MS_TCPIP

[params.MS_TCPIP]
    DNS=Yes
    UseDomainNameDevolution=No
    EnableLMHosts=Yes
    AdapterSections=params.MS_TCPIP.Adapter1

[params.MS_TCPIP.Adapter1]
    SpecificTo=Adapter1
    DHCP=Yes
    WINS=No
    NetBIOSOptions=0

[RemoteInstall]
    Repartition=Yes

[OSChooser]
    Description="Windows Professional - Standard Installation"
    Help="This will install Windows Professional in a standard configuration."
    LaunchFile="%INSTALLPATH%\%MACHINETYPE%\templates\startrom.com"
    ImageType=Flat
```

There is no way to restrict access to the list of images for a user who has permission to log on to the RIS server. The only way to restrict the images a user can use is to set the NTFS permissions to not allow a user access to the data files. The only permissions required for a user to employ the images are the Read and Read & Execute permissions. Finally, you need set the RIS server to respond to client requests in the RIS properties.

Deploying Images to Clients

After you set up the RIS server, and create the images and answer files, it's time to distribute these images to your client computers. This is where RIS really shines because connecting the client to the RIS server can be easy and quick.

You have two ways to connect to the RIS server. The first way is to do a Network boot, which actually boots the computer from the network card and connects to a RIS server. Usually you can accomplish this by pressing F12 during the boot process. You need to have a network card that supports the PXE (Pre-boot eXecution Environment) standard. The PXE version on the network card must be version .99c or later for your card to work. The most recent PCs you may have purchased will likely meet this requirement because it is one of the requirements that Microsoft established in their Net PC and PC98 specifications. Check in the Windows 2000 HCL or in the specifications on the network card to make sure your card meets this requirement. If you see a message during boot that prompts you to press F12 for a network boot, your system probably supports this card. After you press F12, the system boots and looks for a DHCP server. You may need to press F12 again, or the system may jump to booting from the hard drive. If your system supports this card and the boot process continues, the RIS startup screen is displayed.

If your system doesn't support PXE .99c (or later), you still may not be out of luck. There is also an option for creating a startup disk that boots the system to the RIS server. There is no guarantee that this will work, but it is certainly worth giving it a shot. To create the startup disk, run this command: "*RIS_server*\reminst\admin\ i386\rbfg.exe". Replace *RIS_server* with the name of your RIS server. Choose your network adapter from the list, and then create the disk. If this does work, you are prompted to press F12 to connect to the RIS server.

Regardless of which way you connect to the RIS server, you need to log in. You then are given a choice of images to load onto the client workstation. After you select an image and it starts copying files to the workstation, make sure that you remove the boot disk (if you used one to boot the computer).

RIS can only distribute Windows 2000 Professional, so it may not be a replacement for your third-party drive imaging tool if you need to distribute other operating systems. If you can use RIS, however, you will find a useful tool.

Upgrading from a Previous OS

Windows 2000 has made a number of advancements in how Windows 2000 upgrades a computer compared to Windows NT 4. With Windows NT 4, you could upgrade from Windows NT 3.51, but generally, you had to perform a clean install of the operating system.

Windows 2000 allows you to upgrade from Windows NT 3.51 and from Windows NT 4. Performing an upgrade from previous Windows NT systems is probably the easiest upgrade. Windows 2000 was originally named Windows NT 5, so the architecture and much of the system is similar to the other Windows NT operating systems, which makes the upgrade to Windows 2000 a fairly smooth process.

Windows 2000 also allows you to upgrade from Windows 95 and Windows 98. The upgrade from Windows 95 seems to be a smoother process than that from Windows 98. Windows 98 and Windows 2000 both use a driver for their hardware call WDM (Win32 Driver module). The idea behind WDM is that the hardware developer can create one driver that works on both Windows 2000 and Windows 98. There have been a number of problems with drivers in Windows 98 that do not comply with WDM when the system is upgraded to Windows 2000.

The process of upgrading your operating system is straightforward. Simply insert the Windows 2000 CD into the system, and the auto-run feature asks if you want to upgrade the system. If you choose to upgrade, the setup almost mirrors a clean install. However, you are asked far fewer questions because the install program obtains setup answers from your current operating system. If you are upgrading from Windows NT Workstation, you shouldn't have to configure any settings after Windows 2000 Professional is installed. If you are upgrading from Windows 95 or Windows 98, you may have to obtain some upgrade packs for your applications. You need to check with the software manufacturer to see if upgrades are needed. Some applications use different .dll files or possibly different Registry settings when the application is installed on Windows 95 or 98 rather than on Windows NT. The upgrade packs are available to make changes in the applications, so they will run properly on Windows 2000. Windows 2000 also does an upgrade check before starting the upgrade and generates a report on potential problems it finds. It may ask you to delete some programs or let you know that some programs will not work. Some programs need to be reinstalled after the upgrade process. This procedure doesn't find every problem, but if it finds an issue, you should take it seriously.

Make sure that your previous operating system is running perfectly before beginning an upgrade. Check to make sure that all the applications are working and that you have no errors in your event log. Many people have tried to fix a problem by upgrading, and this usually just makes the problem worse. If everything is running smoothly, there should be no problems.

My opinion on upgrading: Do it only if you have to. My experience has been that when you upgrade, you seem to have more problems than with a clean install. This seems true of all products, not just Windows 2000. So, although performing a clean install is preferable, I'm not saying that doing an upgrade won't work.

After the Install

When you have Windows 2000 installed, you still may need to do a few things. First, check the Event Viewer to see if there are any problems. Pay particular attention to warning or error messages. You can find the Event Viewer in the Control Panel under Administrative tools. While you are in the Event Viewer, you should also check the services, and make sure that all the services that you need have started or can start. You will also want to check your system properties in the Hardware Manager to make sure that all your hardware was detected correctly and is running properly.

You may also need to install a service pack at some point. After you have installed the operating system, you simply run the update.exe from the service pack. If you are going to perform a network install, you can apply the service pack to the install files. Run the update.exe file with the /slip switch, which copies over the install files and allows you to install the operating system with the service pack intact. If you later have to install other services, you can do so from this network share and will not have to reapply the service pack after you install the new service.

Chapter Summary

Correctly installing your operating system is the core to using your computer effectively. This can become a major challenge when you are trying to install a new operating system on many computers. Depending on the size of your company, an installation project could take anywhere from a couple of days to over a year to complete. The larger the rollout, the more time that you will want to spend planning and testing the installation.

A straight Windows 2000 installation works great when you are installing on one computer or on a small number of computers, and possibly when you have a highly specialized install. With the bootable CD-ROM and the over-the-network installs, the straight Windows 2000 installation can be easy to start. You can also upgrade the operating system, including Windows 95 and Windows 98. Windows 2000 also gives you the option of setting up a dual-boot situation if you need to run two operating systems at the same time. Remember that you should use caution if you use the NTFS file system when you are going to be dual-booting because previous operating systems will not be able to use an NTFS drive—only Windows NT 4 will be able to read information from the drive, as long as it has Service Pack 4 or later installed.

An automated installation may be helpful because you can set up installations of the operating system with minimal user intervention. It may also be useful if you want to create an install with just the default entries for users to use at later time, so they can make minor changes to some of the options. By performing an automated install, you can also create unique installations by adding a UDF.

Sysprep allows you to take full advantage of drive imaging programs. Sysprep removes all user and unique information from an image, so that when the image is reused on multiple computers, each one will be unique. Prior to Sysprep, this kind of installation caused problems on the network because the installs were not truly unique. Sysprep fixes this problem and gives you the Mini-Setup Wizard to make sure that all the required information is added to the system.

RIS is a great new tool that allows you to take advantage of the PXE tools on your network card. Make sure that your network card supports PXE .99c or later. RIS combines the idea of an automated install and a drive imaging program. RIS images auto-install Windows 2000 Professional and load the applications onto the system in one shot.

The Setup Manager program is invaluable for automating your install. Whether you want to automate a straight installation, use the Sysprep Mini-Setup Wizard, or use the RIS install, Setup Manager makes the task much easier by helping you create an answer file. Although Setup Manager will not help you with every possible setting in the answer file, it will create almost all the settings you will need in your setups. After you have the structure of the answer file, you may need to tweak it here and there; more likely, you won't need to do a thing to it.

Microsoft spent a great deal of time and energy working on automating the installation of Windows 2000, and it gives many options. Rather than just selecting what it thought was the best way to perform an install, Microsoft provided a number of ways of getting the operating system on the desktop.

Review Questions

1. You are planning to use RIS to install your operating system, and you would like to fully automate the installation procedure. Which tool do you need to accomplish this?

   a. Setup Manager

   b. Sysprep

   c. Makeboot.exe

   d. RIS

2. You want to install Windows 2000, and you want to automate the install. What do you need to be able to install Windows 2000 with different parameters on different computers? [Check all correct answers]

   a. CD-ROM

   b. UDF

   c. Boot disk

   d. Setup Manager

3. You want to automate the install of your Windows 2000 installation and boot the system from the CD-ROM drive. Which file do you need to place on a floppy disk to have this install automated?

   a. Unattend.txt

   b. Setup.bat

   c. Winnt.sif

   d. Install.bat

2

4. You created an install that you are going to deploy with a third-party imaging tool. You are putting this image on slightly different computers. Which switch would you use with sysprep.exe to make the system automatically detect any new hardware when the system reboots?

   a. Nosidgen

   b. Pnp

   c. Reboot

   d. Detect

5. You created an install that you are going to deploy with a third-party imaging tool. You are preparing to run the Sysprep utility. What file other than sysprep.exe will you need to run this utility?

   a. Setup.exe

   b. Setupcl.exe

   c. Setuppci.exe

   d. Setuppnp.exe

6. You want to deploy a RIS image to a client workstation. You want to boot directly from the network card to the RIS server. What standard must the network card support for this to work?

   a. 802.1p

   b. 802.1q

   c. 802.3

   d. PXE

7. You are deploying a RIS image to a client workstation. You cannot boot to the RIS server from the network card. What utility must you run to create a RIS boot disk?

   a. Makeboot.exe

   b. Risboot.exe

   c. Pxeboot.exe

   d. Rbfd.exe

8. What is the minimum PXE version that you can use to boot to a RIS server from a network card?

   a. 2.0b

   b. 1.0c

   c. 99c

   d. 99a

9. You are going to run the installation of Windows 2000 from Windows 95. What program should you run to start the installation?

   a. Setup.exe

   b. Winnt32.exe

   c. Install.exe

   d. Winnt.exe

10. You are going to automate the install of a RIS image. What file name must you give to the answer file?

    a. Unattend.txt

    b. Winnt.sif

    c. Remboot.sif

    d. Doesn't matter

11. A user wants to run Windows 2000 in a dual-boot situation but is concerned because she is using the FAT32 File System. Which of the following should you tell the user before she starts her upgrade? [Check all correct answers]

    a. Windows 2000 fully supports the FAT32 File System.

    b. She should make sure that she converts all her drives to the NTFS file system during the install.

    c. Windows 2000 supports only the FAT16 File System.

    d. She should make sure that she does *not* convert any drives to the NTFS file system during the install.

12. A user wants to install Windows 2000 Professional but he is concerned about having enough drive space available. What is the minimum space needed for the installation?

    a. 1.2G

    b. 374MB

    c. 650MB

    d. 875MB

13. You would like to automate the installation of Windows 2000; however, your new PCs contain some hardware that was unavailable when Windows 2000 was released. The hardware is compatible, but you would like Windows 2000 to automatically find the hardware. You create a directory in the distribution folder and add the files. What do you need to add to the answer file so that the installation program will look there for the files?

    a. OemPnpDriversPath

    b. OemDrivers

2

    c. DriversPath

    d. OemPnpDrivers

    e. OemPath

14. You are installing Windows 2000, and you have a hard drive that is 1.6GB. If you choose to format this drive FAT, which version of FAT will be used to format the Drive?

    a. FAT8

    b. FAT16

    c. FAT32

    d. FAT64

15. You are setting up a RIS autonaming structure for your clients. You would like all the computer names to be the same as their MAC address. What variable should you use to accomplish this?

    a. #MAC

    b. %MAC

    c. &MAC

    d. @MAC

16. You would like to apply a service pack to the Windows 2000 installation files so, when you install the operating system, the service pack is also installed. What switch would you use to update these files?

    a. /overwrite

    b. /s

    c. /installfiles

    d. /slip

17. A user has created an automated install that runs the installation from a bootable CD-ROM. You want to use this same answer file, but you want to use it for doing an over-the-network install. What do you need to change or add to the answer file to make this possible?

    a. NetworkInstall=Yes

    b. SourceFiles=Network

    c. MSDosInitiated=1

    d. CDRomInstall=NO

18. You want to have Windows 2000 installed on your desktop computer with all the applications already installed and configured. Which of the following installation methods can you use? [Check all correct answers]

    a. Sysprep install, with a third party imaging software

    b. CD-ROM installation

    c. RIS Installation

    d. Automated Install with a UDF File

19. What is the minimum amount of RAM required to install Windows 2000 Professional?

    a. 16MB

    b. 32MB

    c. 64MB

    d. 128MB

Real-World Projects

Sarah is working at her desk one day when her boss comes and tells her that the company wants to roll out Windows 2000 Professional to all the desktops at the company's three locations. Sarah asks what kind of time frame they are looking at. Her boss gives her a two-month span to prepare for the project, and that the company wants the rollout to last two weeks at the most, from beginning to end.

After her boss leaves, Sarah gets nervous about this project and thoughts of getting her resume together start popping into her head. She first sits down and calculates the number of desktops in the three locations. Headquarters has the most desktops, with a little over 800. The second and third remote locations have 75 and 200 desktops, respectively. The next step in the process is to start looking over the inventory. Sarah wants to make sure that the desktops will be able to handle the new operating system. She also wants to make sure that, if any new hardware needs to be ordered, it happens right away so that everything is installed before the upgrade time.

Sarah is happy to note that the third location (with 250 desktops) has all new PCs that were installed less than six months ago and that all the PCs are the same. Headquarters has mostly new PCs that can handle Windows 2000, but there are few nonstandard configurations from two different vendors. Sarah verifies that all the hardware is on the HCL and prepares to replace or upgrade those items that are not compatible.

The second location seems to be the most problematic, even though it is the smallest. This location contains a hodge-podge of many computers by different vendors with many different configurations. Sarah works through the list and orders the upgrades that will be needed for that location.

Sarah then needs to verify that all the company's applications will run on Windows 2000. She checks with the application department to determine the status of the applications. She is assured by the department that everything was tested, and is working well.

Once Sarah is confident that all the PCs and applications will handle the new operating system, she starts contemplating the best way to roll out the new OS. Sarah thinks that the easiest location to roll out will be at the third location. All the PCs are the same and no users are storing data on their local hard drives. Sarah decides to use a third-party imaging tool to roll out the operating system at this location. She contemplates using RIS at this location, but the location does not have servers that can take on this load. There are 250 PCs at this location, so she wants the whole process to be automated. Sarah gets one of these PCs and starts Project 2.1.

Project 2.1

To automate the distribution of a third-party drive image:

1. Install the operating system.

2. Install and test all applications.

3. Create a network boot disk that starts up the system, connects to a network drive, runs the third-party disk imaging tool, and automatically loads the image onto the computer.

4. Use Setup Manger to create a Sysprep automated install script called sysprep.inf that sets the appropriate settings for the environment.

5. Make all appropriate manual modifications to the sysprep.inf file.

6. Create a folder off the root of the C: drive called Sysprep.

7. Copy sysprep.exe, setupcl.exe, and syprep.inf into the Sysprep folder.

8. Run sysprep.exe.

9. Create the image of the computer when the system shuts down.

10. Use the boot disk to download the image back to the computer to make sure that the whole process happens automatically.

11. Make all needed modifications to the system or automated files and repeat Steps 6 through 10 until the systems go through the whole process with no user intervention.

Now that Sarah has a plan to upgrade the third location, she focuses her energies on the second location. This is going to be more difficult because most of the PCs are different. Many users have custom applications on their machines, and they are storing data on their local hard drives. Sarah decides that the only way to make this process go as quickly and easily as possible is to run the Windows 2000 upgrade. Sarah obtains a couple of PCs that have setups that are similar to the setups at the second location.

Project 2.2

To automate the upgrade process to Windows 2000:

1. Go through the upgrade process manually, and document the places that user intervention is required.

2. Create an unattended answer file with the appropriate answers for the setup.

3. Create a network share that contains the Windows 2000 installation files.

4. Create a batch file that runs Winnt32.exe with the /unattend switch that specifies the answer file you created and the /s switch that contains the path to the source files.

5. Run the batch file, and test the process.

At this point, Sarah is feeling pretty good. She has estimated that with 10 people working, she can get both remote locations installed in just a few days time. Now she is starting to plan the rollout at headquarters. This project is going to be big. Again, Sarah wants to make the process as easy as possible. For headquarters, she decides to implement RIS. She verifies that all the network cards are PXE .99c or later and should support booting to a RIS server. Sarah obtains a couple of test machines. She also contacts the server team and has them set up the RIS servers.

Project 2.3

To create an automated RIS installation:

1. Install and configure the operating system and applications.

2. Run Setup Manager and configure a remboot.sif file.

3. Create the RIS image by running the following command:
   "**ris_server**\reminst\admin\i386\riprep.exe"

4. Associate the remboot.sif file with the image.

5. Boot a test system from the network card and connect to the RIS server.

6. Download the image and test it to make sure that it installs without user intervention.

7. If needed, make any modifications necessary to the remboot.sif file.

8. Repeat the process for as many images as needed.

Now that Sarah has a good plan in place to roll out the systems and enough people to help set up the computers, she feels much better about the two-week time limit and is actually now thinking that completing the task is possible. Her actual plan is to have the installations completed in a week's time, which leaves her and her staff another week to troubleshoot and fix any problems that arise with specific PCs.

2

CHAPTER THREE

Microsoft Management Console (MMC)

After completing this chapter, you will be able to:

✓ Start the MMC

✓ Add a snap-in to the MMC

✓ Use predefined consoles

✓ Configure a custom console

✓ Distribute a custom console

✓ Create a taskpad and tasks

Managing your computer can sometimes be a tedious and frustrating process. The Microsoft Management Console (MMC) provides a new way for users to manage their computers and networks.

To manage a computer until Windows 2000, you had to use many different tools, and you often had to physically be at the computer you wanted to manage. The MMC pro-vides you with a common interface for all of your management tools. It also allows you to manage your entire network from a single location.

In this chapter, you'll learn how to configure the MMC as well as how to use some of the configuration options available. Creating a custom console by including the utilities you need helps you to complete your work as quickly as possible. You can also create taskpads, which will give you a customized view of a snap-in. In a task-pad, you can create tasks that run common commands or run an external program or script.

The New Admininstrative Tool

With the release of Windows 2000, Microsoft takes the MMC to the next level. Microsoft first released the MMC with Internet Information Server (IIS) 4. As new back office products have been released, Microsoft has based all of its administrative tools on the MMC (SQL7, SMS 2.0). The current version of the MMC in Windows 2000 is 1.2. If you have an MMC on Windows NT, you are probably running version 1.0. From this point on, all new tools will be based on the MMC. You need an administrative tool to manage your entire network. Microsoft has also asked third-party software vendors to integrate their management tools into the MMC as well.

The MMC brings a completely new world of features and functionality to the network administrator. In Windows NT 4, administrators were always opening up a new application to perform some task or switching back and forth between windows. Some tasks couldn't even be completed unless the administrator was physically at the computer being worked on. With the MMC, all your administrative tasks can be done from a single application, and these tools can be used on your local computer or from a remote computer.

The MMC is really just the framework for other administrative applications. If you run MMC from a command prompt or from the Run dialog box, you will see that the MMC is actually empty (see Figure 3.1). To make the MMC useful, you need to add tools to the console. These tools are called *snap-ins*. A snap-in is the core unit of the MMC. As you work with different administrative tools, you will need to add the appropriate snap-in that contains the required functionality to the MMC. Not only can you add a snap-in to the console, but you can also add folders to organize the snap-ins, and you can add links to Web sites. Besides the advantages that the

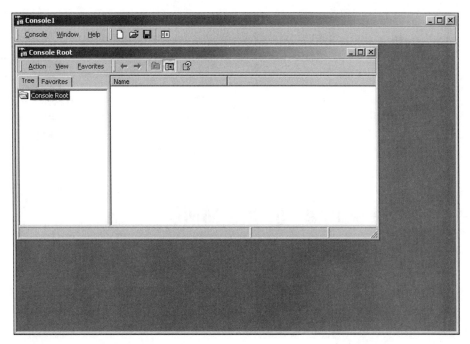

Figure 3.1   The basic MMC window.

MMC offers for managing your network, the MMC also provides a consistent look and feel for all of your administrative processes. In the past, every tool had its own program and many of them were very different from each other. The idea behind the MMC is the same as the idea behind other products, such as Microsoft Office. When you switch between Office programs, such as Word, Excel, and Power Point, you will notice that the look and feel of these applications are similar, even though these products do very different things. By making these programs consistent, the user knows how to use them. The same is true with the MMC. As the MMC gets more popular, its look and feel will remain consistent, so you will always know how to complete an administrative task. You will be able to manage your local system, your network, your database, and your mail system from a single standard interface.

Microsoft's goal for all administrative tools as well as the MMC is for them to be entirely based on Internet technologies. However, at this time, Internet technologies are not mature enough to handle some of the more complex tools that you need to manage your network. It is likely that this situation will be resolved soon with Microsoft and other companies working to develop new Internet tools and applications. The MMC can already display Web pages and can handle anything that your Web browser can handle. Therefore, in the future, you should start to see more snap-ins being ported to the Internet. When this happens, it will allow for many different types of network management.

The MMC makes life easier for administrators because they are able to use the MMC from their client workstations. In the past, many administrative tools simply didn't run on some client computers. The MMC now manages all administrative tasks from the client.

The MMC also allows you to create and save your own configuration settings. This is very useful in an organization where you want to allow certain users to manage different parts of your network. You can now build a custom tool that gives users only the specific objects they need to complete the task, but does not give them unneeded, extraneous tools.

Behind the Scenes of the MMC

The MMC is based on the concept of a multiple document interface. Microsoft is pushing third-party software vendors to develop their applications using the MMC as their management tool. A snap-in will have to run in the MMC; it will not run on its own. This concept is similar to Microsoft Word. With Microsoft Word, you can open multiple documents at the same time, but if Microsoft Word is unavailable, you will not be able to use your documents. The documents are dependent upon Microsoft Word in the same way snap-ins are dependent on the MMC.

Microsoft has given you a way to create your own snap-ins. The Microsoft Platform Software Developer Kit (MSDK) is available for general use. With this kit, you can design your application with the MMC in mind. For more information on this kit, go to the Microsoft Developer Network Web site at **http://msdn.microsoft.com/downloads/sdks/platform/platform.asp**.

The MMC is based on the Windows Management Services. These services are integrated into the operating system, and they provide a sophisticated method for developing a management tool. Windows Management Services provide developers with base functionality and access to the operating system to create a new tool.

The Windows Management Service consists of three layers. The first, or highest, layer is the presentation layer; this is sometimes referred to as the Presentation services. This high-level service is used by developers to tie their application into the operating system. The MMC is part of this layer along with other automation, scripting, and Extensible Markup Language (XML) services.

The second, or middle, layer is the management logic layer. This layer is divided into two areas. The first area is the value-added management solutions. It consists of task-based solutions provided by Microsoft and third-party software developers. The Group Policy snap-in functions at this level. The second area is the standard management tools area. This area controls the functions of storage management, security management, problem tracking, network quality of service, health monitoring, and change and configuration management.

The last layer is the common services layer. This is the lowest layer and provides the base functionality of the Windows Management Services. This layer includes services like COM+, Active Directory, Event Notification, Windows Management Instrumentation (WMI), replication, load balancing, and scheduling.

This section gave a fairly brief overview of the architecture of the MMC. The intention was to explain how the MMC works behind the scenes so you would have a better understanding of the MMC concept. Microsoft continues to provide and improve many tools to make the process as easy as possible for developers to create applications for the MMC.

Configuring the MMC

Before you can make use of the MMC, you must add at least one snap-in to it. The MMC offers a great many tools and functions to the administrator. After you add a snap-in, you can then choose among many options to make the MMC usable by yourself and other administrators.

After you start the MMC, click on the Administrative Tools icon in the Control Panel to find the preconfigured consoles. Microsoft has provided some of the most frequently used snap-ins in the preconfigured consoles. Depending on your needs, these may be sufficient. To open the MMC, run the mmc.exe file, which is located in the System32 directory.

Two startup switches are associated with the MMC. The first switch is /a, which opens the MMC in author mode and allows you to make changes to previously saved consoles. The other switch is /s, which just prevents the splash screen from popping up.

Let's look at the MMC user interface. See Figure 3.2 to associate the parts of the MMC with their descriptions in the following list. The MMC is similar in design and function to the Windows Explorer layout.

➤ *Action toolbar*—This menu bar contains the Action, View, and Favorites menus. To the right of these menus, you will find navigation buttons. Also, notice that as you use different snap-ins, the buttons may be added or removed from this toolbar.

➤ *Console Tree pane*—This is the left window; it contains the console root, snap-in root nodes, containers, and the favorites list.

➤ *Details pane*—This window shows you the contents of a snap-in, a management utility associated with a snap-in, a Web page, or a taskpad view.

➤ *Main toolbar*—This menu bar contains the Console, Window, and Help menus. This menu is available only in Author Mode or User Mode—Full Access.

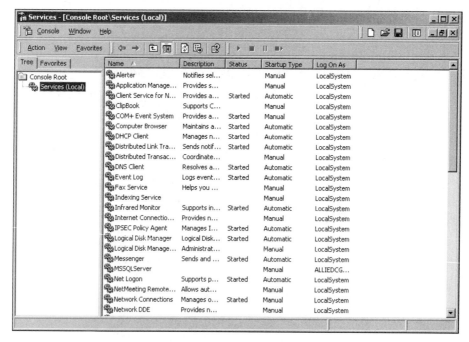

Figure 3.2   An example of the MMC with the Services snap-in loaded.

Adding and Configuring Your Snap-Ins

After opening a blank console, add a snap-in. Select Console | Add/Remove Snap-In. The Add/Remove Snap-In Window is displayed. Click on the Add button to get a list of all the loaded snap-ins that are available on the computer. When you add a snap-in, you are usually asked whether you want the snap-in to be directed to the resources of the local computer or whether you want to enter the name of a remote computer you would like to manage. Some of the snap-ins allow you to right-click on them to connect the snap-in to a different computer, whereas others may need to connect the snap-in to the other computer at the time you add it. Make sure that when you add the snap-in, you select the checkbox that says the following: "Allow The Selected Computer To Be Changed When Launching From The Command Line. This Applies If You Save The Console."

As you add different applications to your system, you may notice that new snap-ins are available for you to add to your console. Two tabs are available from the Add/Remove Window. The first tab is the default, which lists the snap-ins that you have already loaded. You can organize your snap-ins by clicking on the drop-down button located next to Snap-Ins Added To. From here, you can navigate through the list of snap-ins and folders that you have added to the console. You can load a snap-in inside of another snap-in or add a folder and put specific snap-ins in that folder. Because you may wind up with many snap-ins loaded in a console, folders will enable you to organize them. There is no add folder button, so you have to add a folder the same way you add a snap-in. In the list of available snap-ins, you will see one called Folder. When you add a folder, it will be called New Folder. There is no way to change the name at this point. When you return to the main console windows, you can right-click on the folder and choose to rename it.

In addition to the standalone snap-ins that are available, there are also extensions that are associated with them. An extension snap-in is a snap-in that extends the functionality of a standalone snap-in. Some snap-ins can act as standalone snap-ins and extend other snap-ins. By default, when you add a standalone snap-in, all of the extensions to that snap-in are loaded. After you have added the snap-ins, go to the Extensions tab in the Add/Remove Snap-In window and view the extensions that exist or can be loaded. If you want all the extensions loaded, select the Add All Extensions checkbox. You may want to remove some of the extensions that are irrelevant to what you are doing. For example, you may want to remove the Removable Storage Extension setting from Computer Management because you don't have any removable storage to manage (see Figure 3.3). If later on you do obtain some removable storage, you can then re-enable the extension.

At this point, you should be able to add some snap-ins and organize them into folders efficiently. There are many snap-ins available, and the number grows dramatically as you start adding applications. Therefore, you will want to use folders to plan a useful structure for the snap-ins that you use for a basic console (see Figure 3.4).

You may also want to create some favorite locations in your console. Some of the snap-ins have many layers that you will have to navigate through, and it can be

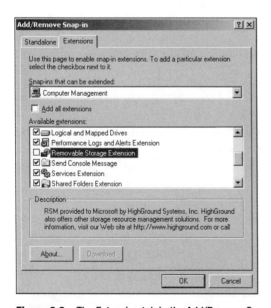

Figure 3.3 The Extension tab in the Add/Remove Snap-in window.

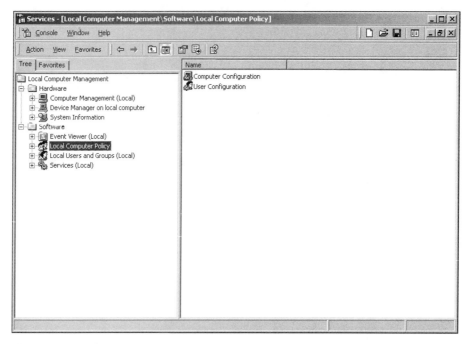

Figure 3.4 A basic console with a few snap-ins loaded and organized into folders.

difficult to remember exactly where some options are located. As you find locations that you want to return to, you can create a favorites list. The favorites list in the MMC is similar to the concept of favorites in Internet Explorer. Once you are at a certain location, simply click on the favorites drop-down menu and select Add Favorites. The location will then be displayed in your favorites list. By clicking on a favorite location in the list, you will automatically be taken to that location.

You also may want to open multiple windows to work with your snap-ins. From the Window drop-down menu, you can create multiple windows that allow you to easily switch back and forth between different snap-ins that you have loaded. You can also open a new window that uses your current location as the root location for any new windows. Select Action | New Window. This may be useful when you are trying to complete tasks that require you to make changes in multiple snap-ins.

Taskpad View

The taskpad view is another page that you can add to your console. It can contain a snap-in view or tasks. With the taskpad view, you can show the contents of a snap-in in a way that makes it easier for you to view them. The tasks allow you to create a shortcut to a task that you created. The task can be a function that you perform often and that requires multiple snap-ins or automates a task for a new user. You may also want to group different tasks into one area. You can create a task that navigates to a particular location in the console, runs a menu command, runs a script, or runs another program. This can be a powerful tool if you use batch files and scripts, which allow you to do just about anything with Windows.

Creating a taskpad view is fairly easy. Navigate to a snap-in, and select Action | New Taskpad View. This option starts a wizard that walks you through the process of creating a taskpad view. Once you have created the taskpad, you can start the new task wizard. See Figure 3.5 for a view of a sample taskpad. The new task wizard allows you to create a task in the taskpad view that you just created. You can create three types of tasks: You can navigate throughout the console tree; however, you can only choose a location from the favorites list; you can create a task that runs one of the commands from the menu; or you can create a task that runs a shell command, which is the most powerful task you can create. The shell command option allows you to run a batch file, a script, or a shell command.

Saving a Custom Console

Now that you have spent all this time creating and configuring your console, you will want to reuse that console. You can also distribute your custom console to other users. However, you may not want your console to be modified, so you can provide the use of the same console to multiple people or a specific group.

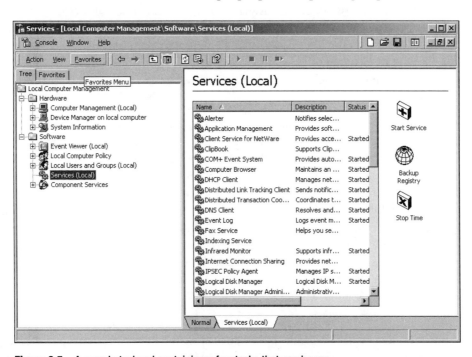

Figure 3.5   A sample taskpad containing a few tasks that can be run.

By default, the console is saved with an .msc extension. This extension is registered with Windows 2000, and it automatically opens the file in the MMC. By default, the MMC saves your custom consoles in the following path: *systemdrive*\Documents and Settings*user*\Start Menu\Programs\Administrative Tools. After you save the files, they are available to you in the Administrative Tools folder in your start menu, but they are only available to you. You may want to consider changing the location if you want other users to access your consoles. If you replace *user* in the previous path with default user and save the file, the console will be available to all users.

You can save a console in one of four modes. The first mode is author mode. Use this mode when creating a custom console. Enter author mode by opening a blank MMC or by opening a saved console with the /a option. This mode is the default setting for all new consoles that you create. Note that if you already have the MMC open, any new console that you open will open in author mode. When you are in author mode and you exit from the console, you will be asked whether you want to save your changes to the console.

You can set your console to one of three other modes. To change the mode for your console, click on the console drop-down menu and choose Options. Then select one of three user modes presented. After you change to any of these user modes, three checkboxes will become available. The first checkbox allows users to see context menus in the console. When they right-click on an item, a menu appears. The second option allows users to save changes to the console. Users will not be prompted to save their changes; the console will automatically save changes when users close the console. The third option allows users to access the custom view dialog box.

The three user modes allow users to access a console and use the functionality of the snap-ins that are loaded. However, users will not be able to add any new snap-ins to the console. The first mode is User Mode—Full Access. In this mode, users have full functionality of the tools that are available as well as the different viewing options. The save command is not available because only changes that do not affect the snap-ins will be saved. The second mode is User Mode—Limited Access, Multiple Window. Users are able to access multiple child windows in this mode, but they are not able to close them. The same restrictions as Full Access apply. Users are also limited in their access to the console tree. The last mode is User Mode—Limited Access, Single Windows. The same restrictions apply in this mode except that users cannot open any child windows.

Although the MMC is a great tool for administrators, you may not want other users to access it at will. The group policy snap-in is the key to restricting this access. Group policies provide two restrictions the MMC. The first restricts a user or group of users from opening the MMC in author mode. The second restricts access to all or individual snap-ins. To find these options, add the group policy snap-in, and then navigate down the following path: User Configuration\Administrative Templates\ Windows Components\Microsoft Management Console.

The Included Snap-Ins

Now that you understand how to configure and manage the MMC, it is time to actually start using the available tools. Some of the concepts involved in managing the MMC will start making more sense after you start using the console to manage your system. A number of snap-ins is included with Windows 2000 Professional. Certainly, these are not all the available snap-ins. You can find many more snap-ins in the Server product as well as other third-party applications. The following is a list of snap-ins included with Windows 2000 Professional, accompanied by a short description of each:

➤ *ActiveX Control*—This tool introduces an ActiveX Control at the specified location in the tree.

➤ *Certificates*—This tool allow you to manage the certificates for a user, service, or computer account.

➤ *Component Services*—This tool allows you to manage COM and COM+ applications as well as distributed transaction applications.

➤ *Computer Management*—This is a collection of the most commonly used snap-ins that you can use for managing your system.

➤ *Device Manager*—This tool is the main tool that you use to manage the hardware on your system. You can use Device Manager to scan for new hardware or uninstall hardware. You can also use this tool to enable or disable hardware.

➤ *Disk Defragmenter*—This tool allows you to analyze and defragment your hard drive. It is actually a copy of Diskeeper Lite from Executive Software.

➤ *Disk Management*—This tool allows you to manage your hard drives. It provides the capability to manage your partitions, drive letters, and dynamic volumes.

➤ *Event Viewer*—This tool allows you to manage and clear the system, security, and application logs.

➤ *Fax Service Management*—This tool allows you to manage the built-in fax tools.

➤ *Folder*—This tool allows you to create folders in the console for organizing your snap-ins.

➤ *Group Policy*—This tool helps you manage and create policies that allow you to designate different system settings, manage software deployment, and assign scripts.

➤ *Indexing Service*—This tool allows you to manage the index service and determine which directories you would like to be a part of the index catalog on the local system.

➤ *Link to Web Address*—This tool allows you to create a Web page link within your console. The Web page will be displayed in the console. This can be useful to link to different vendor support pages that have documentation or drivers that you need to configure your system.

➤ *Local Users and Group*—This tool allows you to manage and maintain users that are authorized to use the local computer and manage the local groups and their membership.

➤ *Performance Logs and Alerts*—This tool allows you to monitor your hardware utilization and configure alerts to notify you when your hardware utilization reaches critical levels.

➤ *Removable Storage Management*—This application allows you to set up your removable storage media, such as tape drives and optical disks.

➤ *Security Configuration and Analysis*—This tool allows you to create a security database. Using a security template, you can compare your system against the template and also have the tool automatically configure the system based on the settings in the template. If you run the analysis, you can view each object and see how it's currently configured, compared to what the template suggests is the best configuration.

➤ *Security Templates*—This tool contains some preconfigured templates and allows you to create new templates that contain different security options. It doesn't allow you to actually set options, but you can use the templates with the Security Configuration and Analysis tool or set the policies in the Group Policy object.

➤ *Services*—This tool enables you to manage the services on your system. You can start, stop, and pause the services from here as well as manage when the service starts and, if needed, as what user account the service should log on to the system.

➤ *Shared Folders*—This snap-in allows you to manage the shares on a computer, the current sessions, and the files a particular user has open. You can disconnect a user from a particular resource. You can create new shares from this tool as well.

➤ *System Information*—This tool gives you detailed information about your system. It reports nearly anything you need to know about the system—for example, which drivers are loaded, the settings of environment variables, what document a user has open in Word, and so on.

Throughout the remaining chapters of this book, you get a better understanding of the full functionality of the snap-ins in the preceding list.

Let's look quickly at the preconfigured consoles that come with Windows 2000 Professional. You will find the following consoles in the Control Panel by clicking on the Administrative Tools icon:

➤ *Component Services*—This console contains the component services, event viewer, and services snap-ins. You can use this tool to make sure your services are functioning properly, and if they are not functioning properly, you can check the event viewer for errors.

➤ *Computer Management*—This console contains just about every snap-in that you will use to manage your system, including the computer management snap-in. It consists of two folders: Storage, and Services and Applications (the latter two contain other snap-ins).

➤ *Event Viewer*—This console simply contains the event viewer snap-in.

➤ *Local Security Settings*—This console contains the group policy snap-in.

➤ *Performance*—This console contains the system monitor and the performance monitor logs and alerts.

➤ *Services*—This console contains only the services snap-in.

Note that in the administrative tools folder there are two other icons. These tools do not work with the MMC. One is the Data Sources tool, which you can use to manage connectivity with ODBC (Open Database Connectivity) data sources. The other is the Telnet Server Administration, which runs the program tlntadmn.exe, which allows you to manage the telnet server functions of Windows 2000.

Chapter Summary

Now that you have a better understanding of how the MMC works, you will find that it is a useful and valuable tool. It's a good idea to become familiar with (and use) it because it's what you will be seeing from Microsoft for the foreseeable future. Obviously, Microsoft will make improvements and changes in the program, but the basic concepts and functionality will probably remain similar to what they are now.

By itself, the MMC really can't do anything; it's there as the interface that the snap-ins will use to access the Windows 2000 operating system. Microsoft has ported virtually every management application into an MMC snap-in. You may still find the occasional application that is not a snap-in, but it seems highly likely that it won't stay that way for long.

The MMC provides a number of configuration options that assist you in making the tool usable for your location. You can restrict user access to the tools with group policies. You can create custom views with the taskpad and launch common routines with tasks in the taskpad. You can use folders to organize your snap-ins, and you can enhance the snap-ins by creating a link to a Web page that contains useful information. You can also restrict users from modifying your custom console by setting the console to user mode.

Review Questions

1. Which command would you use to open the Microsoft Management Console in author mode?

   a. MMC /a

   b. MMC /s

   c. Console /s

   d. Console /a

2. Which of the following types of tasks can you create within the MMC?

   a. Menu commands

   b. Shell command

   c. Script

   d. Navigate to a favorite

3. You would like to create a custom console for your help desk to use. You don't want users to be able to add any new snap-ins to the console. In which mode should you save the console?

   a. User Mode—Full Access

   b. User Mode—Limited Access, Multiple Window

   c. User Mode—Limited Access, Single Window

   d. Author Mode

4. You would like to create a custom console for your help desk to use. You don't want users to be able to add any new snap-ins to the console. However, you would like to allow users to open new windows. What mode should you save the console in?

   a. User Mode—Full Access

   b. User Mode—Limited Access, Multiple Window

   c. User Mode—Limited Access, Single Window

   d. Author Mode

5. You would like to create a custom console for your help desk to use. You would like to give each user an individual copy of the console file. You would also like users to be able to modify the console. In which mode should you save the console?

   a. User Mode—Full access

   b. User Mode—Limited Access, Multiple Window

c. User Mode—Limited Access, Single Window

d. Author Mode

6. You have created a custom console and you would like your help desk to use it. In this console, you have created a number of windows. You don't want users of this console to be able to remove any of these windows. In which mode should you save the console?

    a. User Mode—Full Access

    b. User Mode—Limited Access, Multiple Window

    c. User Mode—Limited Access, Single Window

    d. Author Mode

7. You need to manage the hardware on your local system. You need to look at the drivers that the hardware is using and ensure that all the devices are indeed loaded and functioning properly. Which snap-ins can you load to accomplish this?

    a. Component Services

    b. Device Manager

    c. Computer Management

    d. Event Viewer

8. What is the default extension that the MMC uses when saving a custom console?

    a. .con

    b. .cus

    c. .msc

    d. .mcs

9. You have created a custom console that some of your users employ. You are receiving complaints that every time your users open the console, it is changed. Your users would like to be able to open new windows within the console as well. Which of the following will you need to do to alleviate your users' concerns?

    a. Select Do Not Save Changes To This Console in the Options dialog box.

    b. Set the mode to User Mode—Full Access.

    c. Set the mode to User Mode—Limited Access, Multiple Window.

    d. Select Allow Users To Customize Views.

10. You are creating a custom console and you realize that you do not want your users to have the full functionality of a particular snap-in. They will need to do certain things with the snap-in, but parts of it are not needed. How would you try to remove some of the functionality?

    a. Get a modified DLL from the vendor.

    b. Try to set a group policy.

    c. Check the extensions to see if the functionality can be removed.

    d. Get a third-party blocking program.

11. Which of the following external services can you link to with the MMC?

    a. SMTP

    b. HTTP

    c. ARP

    d. FTP

12. You would like to set up an easier way to navigate through the snap-in structure to certain areas. Which tool would you use?

    a. Tasks

    b. Links

    c. Views

    d. Favorites

13. You would like to be able to run a script file that you generated from the MMC. Which tool would you use to make this possible?

    a. Tasks

    b. Links

    c. Views

    d. Favorites

14. You are looking at a console, and you realize that the console drop-down menu isn't available. What do you need to do to make it available?

    a. Restart the MMC

    b. Reboot the computer

    c. Open the console in author mode

    d. Open the console file from a fresh MMC instance

15. You have to physically be at the computer you are managing when using a snap-in in the MMC. True or false?

    a. True

    b. False

16. You would like to have access to the System log in the event viewer. What snap-ins could you add to a console to accomplish this?

    a. Computer Management

    b. Event Viewer

    c. Services

    d. Disk Management

17. You would like to create a new partition on your hard drive. What snap-ins could you add to a console to accomplish this?

    a. Computer Management

    b. Event Viewer

    c. Services

    d. Disk Management

18. You would like to disable one of your hardware components. What snap-ins could you add to a console to accomplish this?

    a. Computer Management

    b. Device Management

    c. System Information

    d. Disk Management

19. You would like to add a local user to your computer. What snap-ins could you add to a console to accomplish this?

    a. Computer Management

    b. System Information

    c. Local Users and Groups

    d. Services

20. You would like to stop a service on your computer. What snap-ins could you add to a console to accomplish this?

    a. Computer Management

    b Services

    c. System Information

    d. Component Services

3

Real-World Projects

Steve is working with the rollout team as they put together a plan to roll out Windows 2000 Professional. The team is concerned with the level of administrative tools that are available to the standard user. They decide that they want to remove the administrative tools from the users, but want the desktop support staff to be able to access the hardware and system configuration tools for the desktop. They want to make sure that the desktop support staff does not have access to other administrative tools, and that all staff uses the same tools for ease of training and support later on.

Steve is assigned the task of making sure that all the goals of the team are taken care of when the OS is rolled out. Steve starts by taking a look at what the desktop support staff is required to do and determines what tools they are going to need to accomplish these tasks. After Steve has spoken with the staff, he creates a list of snap-ins and a couple of scripts that the team will run. Steve is now ready to create the console by following the steps in Project 3.1.

Project 3.1

Create a custom console in the MMC:

1. Open the MMC by typing "MMC" at the Run command.

2. Add two folders to the MMC by clicking on the Console menu and selecting Add/Remove Snap-in. Then click on the Add Button. Highlight the Folder snap-in and click on Add twice. Click on the Close button, and then click on OK.

3. Rename the root folder to Desktop Support by right-clicking and then clicking on Rename. Rename the two folders you added. Name one "Hardware Support" and the other "Software Support".

4. Add the following snap-ins to the Hardware Support folder: Device Manager, Removable Storage, Performance Logs and Alerts, and Disk Manager.

5. Add the following snap-ins to the Software Support folder: Event Viewer, Component Services, Services, and System Information. The console should now look like the one shown in Figure 3.6.

6. Set up two Favorites, one to the system error log and the other to the environment variable. Navigate to the event viewer, and then click on the system log. Click on the Favorites drop-down list, and click on Add to Favorites. Do the same for the environment variables, which are found in System Information—Software Environment.

7. Click on the services icon. Then click on the Action drop-down menu, and click on New Taskpad View.

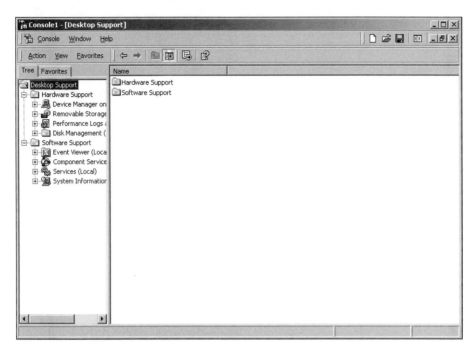

3

Figure 3.6 Your console should look something like this when you have completed Step 5.

8. Click on Next. Leave the defaults as they are, and click on Next again. Again, leave the defaults as they are, and click on Next. Change the name to "Service Management", and click on Next. Make sure that the Start New Task Wizard checkbox is selected, and click on Next.

9. In the New Task Wizard, click on Next, click on Shell Command, and click on Next. Now enter the name of the script that was created for your system in the command window, and click on Next. Name the task "Script", and click on Next. Then choose an icon, and click on Next. Then click on Finish.

10. Click on the console drop-down menu and click on Options. Set the console mode to User Mode—Limited Access, Single Window. Also, select the checkbox Do Not Save Changes To This Console. Then click on OK.

11. Click on the console drop-down menu, and click on Save. Give the console a name, and click on OK.

12. Copy the console file to a secure network location where only your desktop support people will have read access to the file.

Now that Steve has created the custom console, he will need to work with the desktop support team to test it. More modifications may need to be made, but at this point, they have a good start and should have the functionality needed to do their job with the new operating system.

CHAPTER FOUR

Configuring Disks

After completing this chapter, you will be able to:

✓ Describe the disk storage types supported by Windows 2000 Professional

✓ Use the Disk Management Snap-in to perform disk management tasks

✓ Convert from basic to dynamic storage

✓ Explain the differences between the file systems supported by Windows 2000 Professional

✓ Describe the advantages of using NTFS 5

✓ Describe the Encrypting File System and why it is used in Windows 2000 Professional

✓ Describe volume mount points and how to create a volume mount point

✓ Compress a file and folder on an NTFS volume

✓ Describe disk quotas and how to enable them

✓ Describe how the Disk Defragmenter and Disk Cleanup tools are used

Disk Management

An important aspect of disk management is determining the type of disk drive storage that would be best for your system. After you decide on the type of disk storage to use, the drives must be partitioned and initialized.

Disk Storage Types

Windows 2000 Professional provides support for two types of disk storage: basic storage and dynamic storage. You can use either basic or dynamic storage on a disk, but not both at the same time. All volumes on a disk must be either basic or dynamic storage.

Basic Storage

Basic storage is the industry standard. Basic storage divides disks into partitions. A partition is a physical unit of storage. Windows 2000 Professional recognizes disks that are partitioned as a basic disk. A basic disk can contain primary partitions, extended partitions, and logical disks. Basic disk is the default hard disk storage for Windows 2000. Basic disk is supported on all previous versions of Windows and MS-DOS.

Features of Basic Disk

Basic disk supports up to four partitions. One of these partitions can be an extended partition, as with Windows NT. You do not have to confirm changes or restart the computer for changes to become effective when using Disk Management in Windows 2000, as you do in Windows NT. The system will execute the changes without user confirmation as long as the changes don't affect existing files on the disk. Basic disk cannot be used to create multiple volume sets or fault-tolerant volumes.

Dynamic Storage

Dynamic storage is introduced in Windows 2000. In dynamic storage, the entire disk is created as a single partition. A dynamic disk is a disk that has been initialized for dynamic storage. Dynamic disks cannot contain partitions and logical drives. They are not accessible from MS-DOS or previous versions of Windows.

Dynamic disks are divided into volumes. A volume can consist of all or a portion of a disk or multiple physical disks. A dynamic disk can be divided into simple volumes, spanned volumes, or striped volumes. A dynamic disk is created by upgrading a basic disk.

Dynamic disks can be resized without having to restart Windows 2000. Dynamic disks, however, do have some limitations:

➤ They are not supported on portable computers, removable disks, Universal Serial Bus (USB), and IEEE 1394 interfaces.

➤ Windows 2000 cannot be installed on a dynamic volume that is created from unallocated space on a dynamic disk. Windows 2000 Setup will recognize only dynamic volumes that contain partition tables. Partition tables appear in dynamic volumes that were created from basic volumes. A new dynamic volume created on an existing dynamic disk does not contain a partition table.

➤ Windows 2000 can be installed on a dynamic volume that has been upgraded from a basic volume, but the dynamic volume cannot be extended. The boot volume, which contains the Windows 2000 files, cannot be part of a spanned or extended volume.

4

Both basic and dynamic disk support allow you to do the following:

➤ Check disk properties

➤ View volume information and partition properties

➤ Establish drive-letter assignments

➤ Establish disk sharing

➤ Establish security for volumes and partitions

Disk Partitions

Basic disks can be divided into primary and extended partitions. They can be divided into a maximum of four partitions. You can either have four primary partitions or three primary partitions and one extended partition.

Primary Partition

One primary partition is the *active partition*. In the active partition, Windows 2000 looks for the boot files to start the operating system. You can have only one active partition on a single hard disk. You can have multiple primary partitions with Windows 2000, which enables you to dual boot with other operating systems, such as MS-DOS and Windows 95. The primary partition must be formatted as FAT if you want to dual boot Windows 2000 with Windows 95. If you want to dual boot Windows 2000 Professional with Windows 95, OSR2, or Windows 98, the primary partition must be formatted as FAT or FAT32.

Extended Partition

Only one extended partition can be created on a hard disk. The extended partition is created from free space on the disk. Extended partitions are divided into segments called logical disks.

Dynamic Volumes

Basic disks are converted to dynamic storage. Dynamic volumes are created from dynamic storage. Windows 2000 Professional supports three types of dynamic

volumes—simple, spanned, and striped. Windows 2000 Server supports two additional types of dynamic volumes—mirrored and RAID 5 volumes.

Simple Volumes

A simple volume is created from the disk space on a single disk. Simple volumes are
not fault tolerant.

Spanned Volumes

A spanned volume can contain disk space from up to 32 disks. Windows 2000
Professional writes data on the first disk completely before continuing on to the
next disk in the spanned volume. As with simple volumes, spanned volumes are not
fault tolerant.

Striped Volumes

On a striped volume, free space is combined from multiple disks into one logical
volume. A striped volume can combine up to 32 hard disks into one logical volume.

Disk Management Tasks

Users with the proper permissions can manage local and remote hard disks. Disk
management tasks may include adding or upgrading simple, spanned or striped
volumes, viewing and updating disk information, and changing the disk storage
type. Users may also have to diagnose disk problems.

Disk Management

Disk Management is used to configure and manage disk storage. Disk Management
replaces the Disk Administrator tool used in previous versions of Windows NT (see
Figure 4.1).

Disk Management offers several new features. These include:

➤ *Dynamic disks*—Dynamic disks are new to Windows 2000. Users can create,
extend, or mirror partitions without having to restart the computer. Changes
take effect immediately after the change is made.

➤ *Local and network drive management*—Users with administrator privileges can,
in addition to their local computer, remotely manage any computer on the
network.

➤ *Mounted disks*—Local drives can be mounted to an empty folder on an NTFS
formatted volume.

➤ *Simplified user interface*—Tasks are easier to accomplish with the right-click menus
and wizards that guide the user through most tasks.

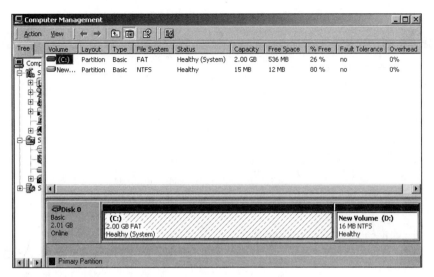

Figure 4.1 Disk Management Snap-in tool.

To Open Disk Management, take these steps:

1. Select Start | Settings | Control Panel.

2. Double-click on Administrative Tools.

3. Double-click on Computer Management.

4. Click on Disk Management.

Disk Management can also be added to the Microsoft Management Console (MMC) as a snap-in tool. To add the Disk Management snap-in tool to the MMC:

1. Open the Microsoft Management Console.

2. Select Console.

3. Click on Add/Remove Snap-in.

4. Click on the Add button.

5. Highlight Disk Management from Available Standalone Snap-ins, and click on the Add button.

6. Select the computer you want to manage with the snap-in, and click on Finish.

7. Click on Close to close the Add Stand-alone Snap-in dialog box.

8. Click on OK.

The Disk Management snap-in is added to the Microsoft Management Console. Information displayed in the Properties dialog box for a disk is presented in Table 4.1.

Table 4.1   The Disk Properties dialog box for a disk.

Category	Description
Disk	The number of the disk in the system
Type	The type of storage (basic, dynamic, removable)
Status	The current status of the disk (online, offline, foreign, unknown)
Capacity	The total capacity of the disk
Unallocated Space	The amount of available space
Device Type	Type of device (IDE, SCSI, EIDE)
Hardware Vendor	The hardware vendor for the disk and the disk type
Adapter Name	The type of controller to which the disk is attached
Volumes Contained On this Disk	The volumes that exist on the disk and their total capacity

Table 4.2   Properties dialog box for a volume.

Tab	Description
General	Lists the volume label, type, file system, and used and free space
Tools	Provides single location to perform error checking, backup, and disk defragmentation
Hardware	Checks properties and troubleshoots the physical disks
Sharing	Sets network-shared volume parameters and permissions
Security	Sets NTFS permissions
Quota	Sets user quotas for NTFS 5 volumes

Information shown in the Properties dialog box for a volume is presented in Table 4.2.

Adding Disks

New hard disks are added as basic storage by default in Windows 2000 Professional.

To add a new disk, take these steps:

1. Insert the hard disk in the computer.

2. Go to the Disk Management snap-in.

3. Click on Rescan Disks on the Action menu.

You should not have to restart the computer for the newly installed hard disk to be recognized. You must use Rescan every time you add or remove a disk from the computer. After the disk is added as a basic disk, it can be upgraded to a dynamic disk.

Note: You may have to restart the computer after adding a disk if it is not detected in Disk Management after you run Rescan Disks.

Converting from One Disk Type to Another

Disks can be upgraded from basic disk to dynamic disk at any time without loss of data. Partitions on basic disks become simple volumes when you upgrade from basic to dynamic storage. Striped volumes that were created in Windows NT 4 become dynamic striped volumes, and spanned volumes created in Windows NT 4 will become dynamic spanned volumes after upgrading from basic to dynamic storage.

There must be at least 1MB of unallocated space on the hard disk for the conversion from basic to dynamic disk to be successful.

4

Converting from Basic to Dynamic Storage

To convert from basic storage to dynamic storage:

1. Go to the Disk Management snap-in.

2. Right-click on the basic disk that you want to upgrade.

3. Click on Upgrade To Dynamic Disk.

4. Follow the instructions provided by the wizard.

You must restart your computer for the process to be completed.

Note: Only Windows 2000 can access information on dynamic disks.

Reverting from Dynamic Storage to Basic Storage

To revert from dynamic storage to basic storage:

1. Open Disk Management.

2. Right-click on the dynamic disks that you want to revert to basic storage.

3. Click on Revert To Basic Disk.

Note: All data will be lost when you revert from dynamic disk to basic disk.

Formatting a Dynamic Volume

You must be logged in as an administrator or a member of the Administrators group to complete the following procedure.

1. Open Disk Management.

2. Right-click on the dynamic volume that you want to format.

3. Click on Format.

4. Select options for the drive, and then click on OK.

Deleting a Dynamic Volume

You must be logged in as an administrator or be a member of the Administrators group to complete the following procedure:

1. Open Disk Management.

2. Right-click on the dynamic volume that you want to delete.

3. Click on Delete Volume.

Configuring File Systems

Windows 2000 Professional supports the FAT, FAT32, and NTFS file systems. NTFS is used when end users want to utilize features of Windows 2000, such as file and folder level security, disk quotas, and encryption. Windows 2000 and Windows NT can access data on NTFS formatted disks. Previous versions of Windows and MS-DOS cannot. FAT and FAT32 provide compatibility with other operating systems.

A combination of file systems (FAT, FAT32, and NTFS) can be used on a single computer, but each file system must be located on a separate volume.

FAT

FAT was created for use on small disks. It is not recommended for volumes larger than 511MB and cannot be used on volumes larger then 4GB. FAT can be used by MS-DOS, Windows 3.x, Windows 95, Windows 98, and Windows 2000. Some Unix operating systems can also use FAT. One advantage of FAT is that if there is a problem with the computer, it can be started with a bootable floppy disk. A second advantage of FAT is that it is an efficient file system for small disks. One of the disadvantages of FAT is that the root folder has a limitation of 512 entries. In addition, FAT is inefficient on large volumes. Additionally, no built-in file security or compression is available. FAT is provided with Windows 2000 Professional for backward compatibility with earlier versions of Windows.

FAT32

FAT32 was introduced with Windows 95 OEM Service Release 2 (OSR2). Windows 2000 Professional supports FAT32. FAT32 has several advantages: It does not have a limit to the number of entries that can be in the root folder; it uses smaller clusters and allocates disk space more efficiently than FAT16; and it provides support for larger hard disks than does FAT16. FAT32 has several disadvantages: The largest FAT32 volume Windows 2000 can format is 32GB, and FAT32 volumes cannot be accessed by operating systems other than Windows 95 OSR2, Windows 98, and Windows 2000. As with FAT, FAT32 has no built-in file security or compression.

NTFS

NTFS is now extended to version 5. NTFS 5 is the recommended version for use with Windows 2000 Professional. Version 5 supports version 4 in previous Windows NT systems, but has several enhancements. NTFS 5 supports striped partitions for high-speed data access. It has data encryption for protection of files. Partitions can be extended without restarting the computer. Disk quotas can be used to monitor and limit disk usage. Distributed Link Tracking can be utilized to preserve shortcuts when files are moved from one location on the hard disk to another. Mount points are supported to allow a volume to be grafted onto an NTFS folder. Faster retrieval of documents is provided through text and property indexing.

NTFS has many advantages, including the following:

➤ NTFS uses transaction logging and recovery techniques. Users seldom need to run disk repair utilities on an NTFS volume. NTFS is a recoverable file system and automatically restores the consistency of the file system.

➤ NTFS supports file compression on files and folders.

➤ There are no restrictions on the number of entries in the root folder.

➤ Volumes can be formatted up to 2 terabytes using NTFS.

➤ NTFS manages disk space more efficiently than do FAT and FAT32.

➤ Permissions can be set on shares, folders, and files.

➤ NTFS supports Encrypting File System (EFS).

➤ NTFS supports disk quotas.

NTFS has the following disadvantages:

➤ NTFS volumes are not accessible from MS-DOS, Windows 95, or Windows 98.

➤ Many of the advanced features of Windows 2000 NTFS are not available in Windows NT NTFS.

➤ The overhead of managing NTFS can cause a performance drop on very small volumes.

File and folder permissions can be set on NTFS volumes. This allows administrators to specify the level of access users and groups have to data. The NTFS version provided with Windows 2000 provides support for inheritable permissions. NTFS file and folder permissions are covered in greater detail in Chapter 13.

EFS

Encrypting File System (EFS) is a new feature introduced with Windows 2000. With EFS, users can encrypt files and folders on NTFS volumes. Once users encrypt the file, they can use it just as they would any other file on an NTFS volume. The encryption is transparent to the user. The user does not have to decrypt the encrypted file to use it. Users can open, copy, move, and rename the file as they would any other file. Any other user who tries to access the encrypted file will receive an access denied message. EFS is supported only on the NTFS version provided on Windows 2000.

There are several important details to remember about EFS:

➤ Compressed files cannot be encrypted using EFS.

➤ Only files and folders on NTFS volumes can be encrypted using EFS.

➤ The encrypted file can be opened only by the user who encrypted it.

➤ Encrypted files cannot be shared.

➤ If you move or copy encrypted files to a volume that is not an NTFS volume, the file will become decrypted.

➤ System files cannot be encrypted.

➤ Files and folders can be encrypted on remote computers as long as the user has the correct access permission to the remote computer's NTFS volume.

The Cipher Command

EFS is implemented from Windows Explorer or from the command line using the Cipher command. To encrypt a file or folder using Windows Explorer, take these steps:

1. Open Windows Explorer.

2. Right-click on the file or folder you want to encrypt.

3. Click on Properties.

4. Click on Advanced on the General tab.

5. Select the Encrypt Contents To Secure Data checkbox, and click on OK.

6. Click on Apply, and then click on OK.

7. If you have selected a file to encrypt that isn't in an encrypted folder, you will be asked if you want to encrypt the file and parent folder or only the file itself. Select your answer, and click on OK.

8. Click on OK to exit the file or folder Properties dialog box.

Files and folders can also be encrypted from the command line using the Cipher command. To learn more about the Cipher command, type "cipher /?" at the command prompt. EFS is discussed in further detail in Chapter 13.

Volume Mount Points

The Disk Management tool can be used to mount local drives to an empty folder on an NTFS folder. When a local drive is mounted to a folder, it is assigned a drive path rather than a drive letter. Mounted drives are not limited to the 26-drive limitation imposed by drive letters. A mounted drive can be formatted by any file system supported by Windows 2000. Drive paths retain their association with drives, so storage devices can be rearranged without the drive path failing.

4

Mounting a Drive

You must be logged in as an administrator or be a member of the Administrators group to complete the following procedure.

To create a mounted drive:

1. Open Disk Management.

2. Right-click on the partition or volume you want to mount.

3. Click on Change Driver Letter And Path.

4. To mount the volume, click on Add.

5. Click on Mount In This NTFS folder.

6. Type the path to an empty folder on an NTFS volume.

Drive paths are available only on empty NTFS volumes. These volumes can be basic or dynamic. You cannot modify a drive path directly. You must remove it and re-create it. If you are administering a remote computer, you cannot browse the NTFS folder. You must type the path to an existing NTFS folder. The Mountvol tool allows administrators to identify and manage volume mount points.

Sparse Files

Windows 2000 Professional supports the use of sparse files. A sparse file is a file that has an attribute that causes only meaningful (nonzero) data to be allocated on the disk. Meaningless data (zeros) is not allocated to the disk. This provides more efficient file system storage and retrieval.

Change Journal

The Change Journal is another new feature of Windows 2000 Professional. Change Journal tracks changes made to files on an NTFS volume. A record is added to the Change Journal any time a file is created, modified, or deleted. The Change Journal is used in Windows 2000 components, such as the Indexing Service.

Distributed Link Tracking

Distributed Link Tracking is used to maintain shortcut references. It allows objects to be moved transparently on a local computer or within a Windows 2000 domain. Distributed Link Tracking uses a unique object identifier (ID) to track objects and their source files. Distributed Link Tracking works if the following is true:

➤ The link source file has been renamed.

➤ The name of the target file has changed.

➤ The target file has moved within the same volume, between volumes on the same computer, or between computers in the same Windows 2000 Server-based domain.

➤ The name of the network share containing the source file has been changed.

➤ The computer containing Windows 2000 Professional has been changed.

NTFS Compression

File, folder, and NTFS volume compression is supported in Windows 2000 Professional. Files that are compressed can be read by any Windows-based application. Files are automatically decompressed when they are read and then compressed again when they are saved or closed. Compressed files and folders are identified in Windows Explorer with a C attribute.

Files, folders, and volumes on an NTFS volume are either compressed or decompressed. Not all files in a compressed folder have to be compressed. Files within a compressed folder can be selectively decompressed.

Files and folders can be compressed using Windows Explorer or by using the command-line utility Compact. To compress a file or folder, follow these steps:

1. Open Windows Explorer.
2. Right-click on the file you want to compress.
3. Select Properties.
4. Click on the Advance button.
5. Select the Compress Contents To Save Disk Space checkbox under Compress and Encrypt Attributes.
6. Click on OK to exit the Advanced attributes dialog box.
7. Click on Apply, and then click on OK.

Files and folders that are compressed can be displayed in alternate colors in Windows Explorer. To display a compressed file or folder in an alternate color, perform the following steps:

1. Open Windows Explorer.

2. Click on the drive where the file is located.

3. Select Tools | Folder Options.

4. Click on the View tab.

5. Select the Display Compress Files And Folders With Alternate Color checkbox in the Advanced settings list.

6. Click on Apply, and then click on OK to save the changes.

Compressed files and folders are displayed in blue in Windows Explorer. Files and folders can also be compressed from the command line using the Compact command. To learn more about the Compact command, type "compact /?" at the command prompt.

Copying Compressed Files and Folders
When a file is copied, it takes on the attributes of the target folder. If the folder is compressed, the file will be compressed. If the folder is not compressed, the file will not be compressed.

Moving Compressed Files and Folders
When you move a compressed file to a folder that is not compressed, it will remain in its compressed state.

Copying and Moving Files and Folders between NTFS and FAT Volumes
FAT partitions do not support compression. Any compressed files or folders moved or copied from an NTFS volume to a FAT volume will automatically be decompressed.

Copying and Moving Files and Folders to Floppy Disks
Compressed files and folders that are copied or moved to a floppy disk are automatically decompressed.

Converting from One File System to Another

Windows NT 4 volumes are automatically converted to NTFS 5 when they are mounted in Windows 2000 Professional. FAT16 and FAT32 volumes can be converted to the new NTFS 5 by using the Convert tool. The Convert tool converts the volume without loss of data. To learn more about the Convert command, type "convert /?" at the command prompt.

Disks Quotas

Administrators can control how much disk space is allocated to users on NTFS volumes by using Disk Quotas (see Figure 4.2). Quotas can be allocated on a per-user or per-volume basis. Quotas cannot be administered for network shares or folders. When quotas are enabled, administrators can set disk quota limits and the disk quota warning level. Events can be logged when users exceed a specified disk space limit or when they exceed a specified disk space warning level. Disk Quotas are transparent to the user. Users are charged only for the files they own. If users exceed their allocated amount of disk space, they will receive an error indicating that the disk is full. If users receive a message indicating that they are out of disk space, they can do one of the following:

➤ Delete some of their files.

➤ Have someone else take ownership of some of his or her files.

➤ Have the administrator increase their quota allowance.

The following rules apply to quotas:

➤ Disk quotas apply only to the volume they are enabled on.

➤ Disk quotas cannot be set on individual files and folders.

➤ Disk quotas are based on decompressed file sizes, not compressed.

➤ If the computer is to dual boot to Windows NT 4, users can exceed their quota limitations. The limits will be applied when they resume running Windows 2000.

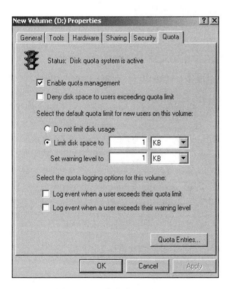

Figure 4.2 Disk quota properties tab.

➤ The volume must be formatted with NTFS to support quotas.

➤ You must be a member of the Administrators group to administer quotas.

To enable disk quotas, take these steps:

1. Open My Computer.

2. Right-click on the NTFS volume on which you want to enable disk quotas and select Properties.

3. Select the Quota tab.

4. Select Enable quota management.

5. Select any additional options for the quota.

6. Click on OK.

When quotas are applied to a volume, the volume usage is automatically tracked for new users. Existing users must be added to the Quota Entries window to be tracked. To enable disk quotas on existing users, take these steps:

1. Open My Computer.

2. Right-click on the NTFS volume that disk quotas have been enabled on.

3. Select Properties in the Quota tab.

4. Select Quota Entries.

5. Click on Quota, and select New Quota Entry.

6. Highlight the user you want to apply quotas to.

7. Click on Add, and then click on OK.

8. Select the quota limits, and click on OK.

9. Select Quota, and click on Close to exit the Quota Entries dialog box.

10. Click on OK.

There are three quota states: quota disabled, quota tracked, and quota enforced:

➤ *Quota disabled*—Quota changes are not tracked, but the limits are not removed.

➤ *Quota tracked*—Quota usage is tracked, but quota limits are not enforced.

➤ *Quota enforced*—Quota usage is tracked and enforced.

Disk quotas can be administered on local and remote computers. The volume on the remote computer must be formatted with the Windows 2000 version of NTFS and shared from the root folder of the volume.

Note: When administering disk quotas on a local computer, systems files are included in the sum of volume usage by the person who installed Windows 2000 Professional.

Disk Defragmenter

Windows NT did not have a disk defragmenter tool. If you wanted to consolidate fragmented files and folders on your hard drive in previous versions of Windows, you had to purchase a third-party utility. Windows 2000 includes a Disk Defragmenter tool that rearranges unused space on your hard drive (see Figure 4.3).

Performance of the computer is increased as fragmented files are stored in contiguous space on the disk. Disk Defragmenter can defrag FAT16, FAT32, and NTFS 5 volumes. To start Disk Defragmenter, select Start | Programs | Accessories | System Tools, and then click on Disk Defragmenter. You must have Administrator privileges to run Disk Defragmenter.

Disk Cleanup

Disk Cleanup is used to clear space on your hard drive (see Figure 4.4). Disk Cleanup searches the hard drive for Internet cache files, temporary files, and files that can be safely deleted. The Disk Cleanup wizard calculates the amount of free space that can be freed up by deleting the following files:

➤ Downloaded program files

➤ Temporary Internet files

➤ Files in the Recycle Bin

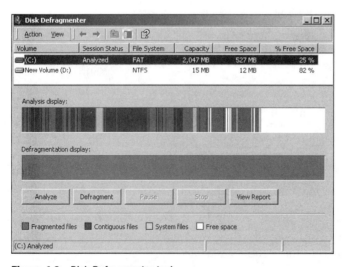

Figure 4.3   Disk Defragmenter tool.

Figure 4.4   Disk Cleanup tool.

➤ Temporary files

➤ Temporary offline files

➤ Offline files

To start Disk Cleanup:

1. Select Start | Programs | Accessories | System Tools.

2. Click on Disk Cleanup.

3. Select the drive you want to run Disk Cleanup on, and click on OK.

Disk Cleanup analyzes the drive and shows how much disk space it can free up.

File System Tools

Several file system tools are provided with Windows 2000 Professional. All of the tools are executed from a command-line prompt. To learn more about each command, go to the command prompt and type the name of the command, followed by "/?". The following tools are available on the Windows 2000 Resource Kit CD-ROM and/or the Windows 2000 operating system CD-ROM:

➤ *Calcs*—Displays and modifies NTFS Access Control Lists.

➤ *Cipher*—Displays or alters encryption of files and folders.

➤ *Compact*—Compresses and decompresses NTFS files and folders.

➤ *Compress*—Compresses files and folders.

➤ *Convert*—Converts a volume from FAT to NTFS.

➤ *Diruse*—Scans a folder and reports on disk space usage.

➤ *Efsinfo*—Displays information on encrypted files and folders.

➤ *Expand*—Expands compressed files.

➤ *Mountvol*—Displays, creates, and deletes volume mount points.

Managing Disks on Remote Computers

You must be a member of the Administrators group or the Server Operators group to manage disks on computers running Windows 2000. The computer must be a member of a domain or trusted domain running Windows 2000.

To manage disks on remote computers with Windows 2000 Professional, you must have the same account with the same password on the local and remote computers. If the passwords do not match, the service will fail.

The best way to manage disks on a remote computer is to create a custom console through the MMC. You can create a custom console by performing the following steps:

1. Select Start|Run.

2. Type "mmc", and click on OK

3. Click on Add/Remove Snap-In.

4. Click on Add.

5. Click on Disk Management, and then click on Add.

6. Click on Another Computer in the Choose Computer dialog box (see Figure 4.5).

7. Type the name of the computer where you want to remotely manage the hard disk.

8. Click on Finish.

Chapter Summary

Windows 2000 Professional supports two types of disk storage: basic and dynamic. Basic storage is the industry standard for disk storage. Basic disks can contain partitions and logical disks. Dynamic storage is new to Windows 2000 and supports

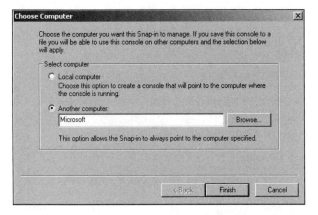

Figure 4.5 Creating a custom console for managing hard disks on remote computers.

dynamic disks. Dynamic disks can be resized without having to restart the computer. Dynamic disks are created by upgrading basic disks.

Disk Management is the Windows 2000 Professional tool used to manage and configure disk storage. Disk Management replaces the Disk Administration tool found in Windows NT. Disk Management is used to install, configure, and manage basic and dynamic disks.

Windows 2000 Professional supports the FAT, FAT32, and NTFS file systems. NTFS 5 is new to Windows 2000 and is the recommended version for use with Windows 2000 Professional. NTFS supports disk compression, disk quotas, Distributed Link Tracking, and Mount Points. Encrypting File System (EFS) is a new feature of Windows 2000. Users can encrypt files using EFS. Only the user who creates the file can open the encrypted file. Both FAT and FAT32 volumes can be converted to NTFS 5 volumes. The Convert command is used to convert the volumes.

Volume Mount Points allow users to mount local drives to empty folders on NTFS volumes. When a drive is mounted to an empty folder, it is assigned a drive path rather than a drive letter. File, folder, and NTFS volume compression is supported in Windows 2000 Professional. Compressed files are automatically decompressed when opened and recompressed when saved or closed. Disk Quotas are supported on NTFS volumes in Windows 2000 Professional. Using disk quotas, administrators can allocate disk space on NTFS volumes on a per-user and per-volume basis.

Several disk utilities are available. You'll find Disk Defragmenter in Windows 2000. In some previous versions of Windows, users had to use a third-party tool to defrag their hard disks. Disk Defragmenter can defrag FAT16, FAT32, and NTFS volumes. Disk Cleanup is used to clear unnecessary files off your hard disks.

Several command-line tools are provided with Windows 2000 Professional. These include Calcs, Cipher, Compact, Compress, Convert, Diruse, Efsinfo, Expand, and Mountvol.

Finally, you have remote computer management. Members of the Administrators and Server Operators groups can manage disks on remote computers by creating a custom console through the MMC.

Review Questions

1. Volume points are used to do which of the following?

    a. Mount local drives to a folder on a FAT volume.

    b. Mount local drives to an empty folder on an NTFS volume.

    c. Mount local drives to a subfolder on an NTFS volume.

    d. Connect to remote volumes.

2. EFS stands for which of the following phrases?

    a. Enhancement File System

    b. Encrypting File System

    c. Encrypted File System

    d. Encrypted File Setup

3. Dynamic Disks are not supported on which of the following hardware?

    a. Portable computers

    b. File Servers

    c. Removable disks

    d. USB interfaces

4. What is the purpose of the Change Journal?

    a. It provides a log of changes to a FAT volume.

    b. It monitors changes to hard drive space.

    c. It logs system error messages.

    d. It provides a log of changes to an NTFS volume.

5. What system tool is used to convert a FAT partition to an NTFS partition?

    a. Calcs

    b. Expand

    c. Mountvol

    d. Convert

6. For which of the following procedures would you use Disk Management?

    a. To prevent system files from being deleted or altered by users

    b. To configure and manage network storage space

    c. To set up users and groups

    d. To assign disk quotas to individual users

7. Disk Quotas can be administered on network shares. True or false?

    a. True

    b. False

8. To manage disks on remote computers, users must be a member of which of the following groups?

    a. Administrators

    b. Power Users

    c. Guests

    d. Server Operators

9. Which utility allows users to compress and decompress files on an NTFS volume from a command-line prompt?

    a. Cipher

    b. Convert

    c. Compact

    d. Expand

10. Disk Cleanup is used to perform which of the following actions?

    a. Identifying unnecessary files that can be deleted from the hard disk

    b. Rearranging files and folders on the hard disk

    c. Converting a FAT to an NTFS volume

    d. Backing up files on the hard disk

11. What do users type at the command line to learn more about the Cipher command?

    a. Cipher /help

    b. Cipher

    c. Cipher /?

    d. Cipher use help

12. What happens to a compressed file when it is copied from an NTFS volume to a FAT volume?

    a. The file retains its compressed attribute.

    b. The file is decompressed.

    c. The file is first decompressed and then recompressed on the FAT volume.

    d. The file is compressed and encrypted.

13. Which file systems can be used on Windows 2000 Professional? [Check all correct answers]

    a. FAT16

    b. NTFS

    c. FAT32

    d. Unix

14. Which of the following choices describes Dynamic disks?

    a. Dynamic disks are physical disks that contain only dynamic volumes.

    b. Dynamic disks are the same as basic disks.

    c. Dynamic disks can be used on non–NTFS partitions.

    d. Dynamic disks can be on the same volume as a basic disk.

15. What happens if a user reverts from a dynamic disk to a basic disk?

    a. All information on the volume is left intact.

    b. All data on the disk is lost.

    c. The disk is automatically converted to NTFS.

    d. The disk is not usable.

16. A basic disk can have which of the following?

    a. Three primary partitions and one extended partition

    b. Five primary partitions

    c. Two primary partitions and two extended partitions

    d. Three primary partitions and two extended partitions

17. Disk Quotas can be allocated on a per-user basis. True or false?

    a. True

    b. False

18. A compressed file can be encrypted? True or false?

    a. True

    b. False

19. Which of the following files will Disk Cleanup search for on the hard drive? [Check all correct answers]

    a. Temporary Internet files

    b. Offline files

    c. Files in the Recycle Bin

    d. System files

20. Dynamic disks can be resized without having to restart Windows 2000 Professional. True or false?

    a. True

    b. False

Real-World Projects

For the following projects, you need a computer running Windows 2000 Professional and a hard disk with at least one NTFS partition.

Project 4.1

Create a folder on an NTFS partition, create a file using Notepad, and then encrypt that file:

1. Open My Computer.

2. Open your NTFS volume.

3. Select File | New | Folder.

4. Name the new folder "Encrypted Folder".

5. Double-click on the folder you just created to open it.

6. Right-click inside the new folder and select New and Text Document.

7. Name the text document "Encrypted File".

8. Right-click on Encrypted File, and select Properties.

9. Click on Advanced.

10. Select the Encrypt Contents To Secure Data checkbox, and click on OK.

11. Click on Apply.

12. You will get an Encryption Warning message asking you if you want to encrypt the parent folder that the file is in. At this time, encrypt only the file. Select Encrypt The File Only and click on OK.

13. Click on OK to exit the properties dialog box.

14. Check the attributes of the file in Windows Explorer. The file is encrypted.

Project 4.2

Create a new user and access the encrypted file from Project 4.1 with the new user account:

1. Create a new user named "Test1 User". Select Start | Settings | Control Panel.

2. Double-click on Administrative Tools.

3. Double-click on Computer Management.

4. Under Local Users and Groups, right-click on Users.

5. Select New User. Enter "Test1 User" in the User name box, and click on Create.

6. Click on Close.

7. Log in as Test1 User.

8. Open Windows Explorer.

9. Double-click on the NTFS volume.

10. Double-click on the encrypted file. What happens?

11. The Test1 User will get an access denied dialog box. The user is unable to open the encrypted file.

Project 4.3

Create a new user, enable Disk Quotas, and assign a disk quota to the user you just created:

1. Create a new user named "Test User". Select Start | Settings | Control Panel.

2. Double-click on Administrative Tools.

3. Double-click on Computer Management.

4. Under Local Users and Groups, right-click on Users.

5. Select New User. Enter "Test2 User" in the User name box, and click on Create.

6. Click on Close.

7. Exit Computer Management.

8. Double-click on My Computer.

9. Right-click on the NTFS volume and select Properties.

10. Select the Quota tab.

11. Select the Enable Quota Management checkbox and click on Apply.

12. Click on OK to enable the quota system.

13. Click on Quota Entries.

14. Select Quota and New Quota Entry.

15. Select the computer in the Look In box.

16. Highlight Test2 User, and click on Add.

17. Click on OK.

18. Set the disk space limit and warning level for Test2 User, and click on OK.

19. Select Quota, and click on Close to exit the Quota Entries Dialog box.

Project 4.4

Create a file on the NTFS volume, compress the file, and display compressed files in an alternate color in Windows Explorer:

1. Open My Computer.

2. Open your NTFS volume.

3. Select File|New Folder.

4. Name the new folder "Compressed Folder".

5. Double-click on the folder you just created to open it.

6. Right-click inside the new folder and select New and Text Document.

7. Name the text document "Compressed File".

8. Right-click on Compressed File and select Properties.

9. Select the Compress Contents To Save Disk Space checkbox.

10. Click on OK, and then click on Apply.

11. Click on OK to close the Properties dialog box.

12. Open Windows Explorer.

13. Select Tools|Folder Options.

14. Click on the View tab.

15. Select the Display Compressed Files And Folders With Alternate Color checkbox in the Advanced Settings list.

16. Click on OK.

Compressed files and folders are now displayed in blue (provided that you used the Windows Standard scheme) within Windows Explorer.

CHAPTER FIVE

Customizing Windows 2000 Professional

After completing this chapter, you will be able to:

✓ Work with the Accessibility tools

✓ Customize a system to a user's needs with the Accessiblity Options

✓ Customize menus

✓ Use the Control Panel utilities

✓ Work with the MultiLanguage version of Windows 2000

✓ Manage an Active Desktop

Microsoft has taken many of the customizable portions of its previous operating systems and included them with Windows 2000. Microsoft has also added to these utilities and improved them where needed.

If you are comfortable customizing Windows 95, Windows 98, and Windows NT, you will likely find that customizing Windows 2000 is fairly similar. Microsoft has made a number of improvements in some of its tools and in some cases has combined features that worked well in Windows 98 with features that worked well in Windows NT. Hopefully, you will find improvements that make the system easier to use and customize. You may also find some changes that make the system harder to use for power users; however, these "features" can be removed.

Window 2000 remains in the same user interface mode that was introduced with Windows 95, most likely because the user interface is fairly stable and people are familiar with it. In Windows 2000, Microsoft has fine tuned the user interface as well as many of the tools and utilities that are available. Although this chapter deals with Windows 2000 specifically, you may find that many of the options and tools are also available in Windows 95, Windows 98, or Windows NT.

Customizing Your Desktop

Because your desktop is so heavily used, how you set up your desktop and Start menu can effect how efficiently you use your system. If you take the time to organize your system, you will find that it is easier and faster to access your programs and utilities.

Working with the Start Menu

The Start menu is probably one of the most used tools since its advent in Windows 95. Virtually every program that you install puts its startup icon into the Start menu. As a result, the Start menu can become a gigantic mess in a hurry. Managing the Start menu is not necessarily at the top of most people's list of activities, but having a well-organized Start menu certainly makes life much easier when you need to find a program that you don't use often.

On the Start menu, there are a number of ways to modify the contents, but a few items cannot be removed. Run, Help, Search, Settings, Documents, and Programs are permanent selections. The Run command is used to execute a command. Help brings up the Windows 2000 Help program, and Search allows you to find files, people, or Web sites on the Internet.

You can configure the Start menu in a number of different ways. Basically, the Start menu is a graphical representation of a folder with shortcuts. There are two locations that are combined to produce the Start menu. The first location, *Systemdrive*:\Documents and Settings\All Users\Start Menu (*Systemdrive* represents the drive letter that contains your system files), contains the standard items. The other location, *Systemdrive*:\Documents and Settings*profile*\Start Menu (*profile* represents your profile name), contains your personal items. The advantage of this two-pronged approach to the Start menu is that users are able to make changes to their own icons, and as an administrator, you can set icons that every user on the system will see and not be able to change. Most, if not all, normal users do not have the appropriate permissions to change items in the All Users folder.

There are a few ways to access and manage the Start menu. The first way to access the Start menu is to simply use Windows Explorer and navigate to the proper folder, creating your subfolders or shortcuts from that folder. You can also right-click on the Start button. If you click on the option Explore, Windows Explorer opens directly to your individual profile options. You will see another option named Explore All Users, which opens Windows Explorer and navigates to the All Users Start menu. Two other options, Open and Open All Users, open the Start menu into a window that contains either your personal profile or the All Users Start menu.

Another way to manage the Start menu is to right-click on the taskbar, select Properties, and navigate to the Advanced tab, where you will see four buttons in the Customize Taskbar section (see Figure 5.1). The first button allows you to add a new icon to the Start menu. When you click on the Add button, a wizard starts that allows you to select what you want the icon to point to and where in the Start menu you want to place it. When you click on the remove button, you are allowed to navigate throughout your Start menu and choose which icons you want to remove. The Advanced button opens Explorer and displays the current profile's Start menu. The Re-sort button goes through your Start menu and sorts it alphabetically. As

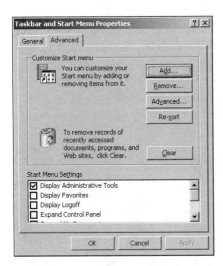

Figure 5.1   The Advanced tab of the Taskbar and Start Menu Properties dialog box.

you install applications, they will simply be added to the bottom of the Programs menu. You can click and drag the icons or menus to rearrange their order, but if you want them to be alphabetical, the Re-sort button provides the easiest way to arrange them. If you want an icon to appear at the top of the Start menu, simply drag the icon to the top of the Start menu.

You can also modify how the Start menu displays some of the items that are available. In the Taskbar Properties on the Advanced menu, the options at the bottom allow some modifications to the Start menu (refer to Figure 5.1). The first option allows you to display the Administrative Tools, which is selected by default only for the Administrator account. The next option displays your Favorites from Internet Explorer. The Display Logoff option will appear on the Start menu instead of your having to hold down Ctrl+Alt+Del to get this option. The remaining options, Expand Control Panel, Expand My Documents, Expand Network And Dial-Up Connections, and Expand Printer will react like any other menu in the Start menu and will expand to show you what is available. The last option, Scroll The Programs Menu, is only useful if you wind up having a large number of icons in the Programs menu. It allows you to scroll up and down the Programs menu instead of having a second level of the menu appear, which can make it unwieldy.

Regardless of how you decide to work with the Start menu, it is probably a good idea to at least think about its structure and organization. If you have many programs installed on your system, the Programs menu can become very messy, so organizing this menu will make it more functional and efficient.

Personalized Menus

Although it has always been possible to manage the Start menu in each version of Windows that contained a Start menu, not many people have taken advantage of this option. At one time or another, you have probably sat down at a computer and selected Start | Programs, resulting in the entire screen being filled with program items. Many users simply don't uninstall programs that are no longer used and therefore, all of their programs continue to appear on the menu. Users actually use only about ten programs on a regular basis, but they hesitate to remove those that are not used.

Microsoft has introduced a new way to manage the Start menu, and the best part is that it works automatically. This feature is called Personalized Menus, and its technology was actually introduced in Office 2000. This feature is based on the idea that more often than not, a user only uses only a small subset of all the icons on the Start menu on a regular basis. Many of the icons are actually special use icons and are very rarely used.

Personalized Menus tracks the icons you use and the ones you don't. Once the system has a good feel for how often you use a particular program or icon, it starts

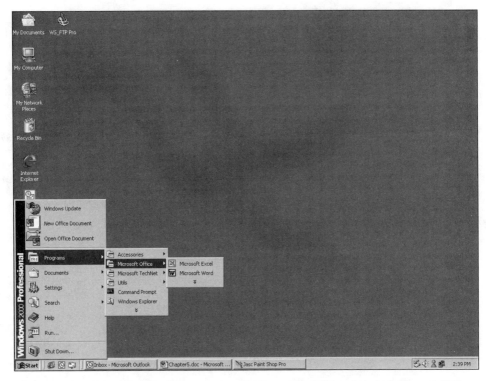

Figure 5.2   The Microsoft Office Program menu after Personalized Menus has started to work. Notice that only Word and Excel appear.

making the display determination. If you haven't used a particular icon for some time, it becomes hidden (see Figure 5.2). After this feature is invoked, you will see a downward-pointing chevron at the bottom of the Programs menu. The chevron lets you know that Personalized Menus has been invoked and if you want to access an infrequently used icon, you must click on the chevron or if you hold the mouse still for four or five seconds, the menu will expand. The strange part, for the end user, about this feature is that it doesn't start working for a few days after you install the operating system and start working with it. You may want to make sure that all the users on the system know about this feature or you will be flooded with support calls.

Once you click on the chevron, all the icons appear, although the hidden icons are now depressed, so you can tell which ones were hidden (see Figure 5.3). After an icon is hidden, it doesn't always stay that way. If you start using a particular icon more frequently, it will show up again on the regular menu.

Many power users are reluctant to use this new technology and many just want to know how to shut if off. However, I suggest that you give it some time to grow on you. At first, it can be frustrating, but after using it for a while, you won't want to

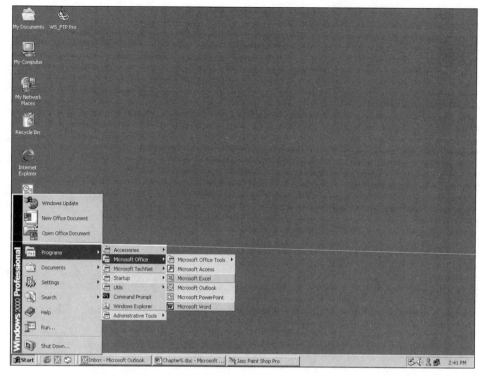

Figure 5.3 The Microsoft Office Programs menu, after clicking on the chevron. Notice that the icons other than Word and Excel are depressed.

give it up. If you do want to turn off the Personalized Menus feature, simply go to the Taskbar Properties and clear the Use Personalized Menus checkbox at the bottom of the list.

Active Desktop

The Active Desktop feature is certainly not new in Windows 2000; it's been available since Internet Explorer 4 and was available with every version of Windows from Windows 95 on. Windows 2000 and Internet Explorer 5 have improved versions of the Active Desktop. Prior to these improvements, loading the Active Desktop could have a serious impact on the performance of the system.

The new version of Active Desktop is actually just a different wallpaper for your system. The wallpaper can be an HTML document or an active Web page on the Internet. The Active Desktop uses the Internet Explorer engine to display the Web page, so it can handle HTML content, ActiveX controls, or just about anything that you can display in Internet Explorer 5.

To configure the Active Desktop, simply right-click on a blank part of the desktop and highlight Active Desktop. You can then add a new desktop icon or customize your desktop. If you choose to customize the desktop, you can add new Web content to the list of choices that are available. Microsoft also has a gallery of different items that you may want to place on your desktop. When you add an item, the wizard that appears has a button called Visit Gallery, which takes you to the Web site that contains a variety of applets. The Web page is found at **http://www.microsoft.com/ windows/ie/ie40/gallery/**. You don't necessarily have to use these applets, instead you can substitute any valid Web page address (see Figure 5.4). Active Desktop, by default, downloads the Web page for offline viewing. The content is basically static at this point and you will need to update the content. You can set a schedule to update the content periodically, or after you have the content set up, you can tell Active Desktop to manually synchronize the content.

You can also lock the Active Desktop once it is set up. Right-click on the desktop, choose Active Desktop, and click on Lock Desktop Items. If you are planning to add Active Desktop items, please note that it could have an effect on your system resources. Some of the items that you place on the desktop can take up a considerable amount of memory.

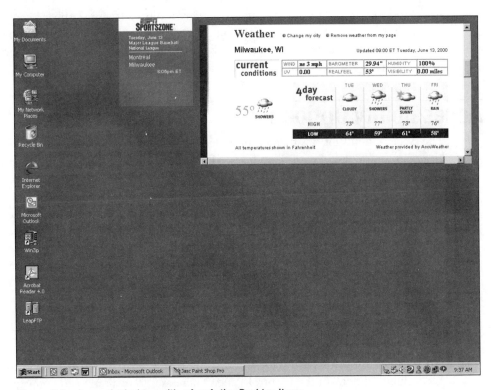

Figure 5.4 A sample desktop with a few Active Desktop items.

Working with the Taskbar and Toolbars

The taskbar at first glance looks similar to other versions of Windows. The Start button is still present as well as the status area containing the clock. By default, you will also find the Quick Launch toolbar next to the Start button.

You can also add other toolbars. Simply right-click on the taskbar to see an option for Toolbars. In this menu, you will see four different preconfigured toolbars. The Quick Launch bar is already selected. To add an item to the Quick Launch bar, simply drag any shortcut, program, file, folder, or Internet shortcut onto the toolbar. To remove an item, just click and drag the item off the toolbar to another location. The address toolbar adds an address box to the taskbar. The links toolbar adds some predefined links to the taskbar. You can drag other links on and off the links toolbar as well. The last predefined toolbar adds all the desktop icons to the taskbar.

You can also create your own toolbar from a folder that you create in the system. If you choose to add your own toolbar, the system will ask for the folder you would like to use. It then places its contents onto the taskbar.

It's all too easy to create or try to use too many toolbars. If your taskbar becomes overly cluttered with toolbars, you may find that instead of helping your productivity, these toolbars will hinder your efficiency because the programs that you were hoping to find quickly are now hidden by too many choices.

Accessibility Options

The Accessibility Options that are provided with Windows 2000 help to make life a bit easier for any users with disabilities. Microsoft has included a number of utilities to assist users who have impaired vision, hearing loss, or difficulty typing or using a mouse. The current version of the Accessibility Options hasn't changed much from earlier versions, so there shouldn't be a lot of retraining needed for users already familiar with these options. Although these options work well for many users that have a disability, you may need to purchase some third-party programs if these features do not satisfy the needs of the user.

The Accessibility Options are located in the Control Panel. You can modify the different options that are available.

Keyboard Options

The Keyboard Options is usually the first tab that appears when you open the Accessibility options in the Control Panel. There are a few alterations you can make to change the way the keyboard reacts to the user.

Sticky Keys

The first option displayed is the Sticky Keys option. With Sticky Keys, a user doesn't have to press two keys at the same time to get an effect. For example, if a user wants a capital letter, he would have to press Shift at the same time as a letter key, or if he wanted to get to the Windows Security dialog box, the user would have to press Ctrl+Alt+Del at the same time. This can be a difficult task for some users. Sticky Keys allows users to first press Shift, and then press the letter that they need to make a capital letter, or press the Ctrl key, and then the Alt key, and finally the Delete key in sequence to get to the Windows Security dialog box.

You may not want the Sticky Keys option on all the time, as it may affect how the average user uses the system. In the Sticky Keys settings, you can turn on the shortcut for Sticky Keys. This is turned on by default and if a user wants to use this feature, she simply has to press the Shift key five times. By default, the system will then make a noise and bring up a dialog box that informs her that Sticky Keys has been activated.

Other options that are available allow the user to press a modifier key (Shift, Alt, Ctrl, or Windows) twice to lock its status on. By pressing Shift, for instance, the result is similar to pressing the Caps Lock key, except that even the numbers will react as if the Shift key is pressed. You can also set the system so that if two keys are pressed at the same time, the Sticky Keys function is disabled until someone presses Shift five times. The system can be instructed to make a sound every time a modifier key is pressed, and to display an icon. This icon appears next to the clock, which shows that Sticky Keys is enabled on the system.

Filter Keys

The Filter Keys option changes how Windows reacts when a user either presses a key multiple times in a row or holds down a key. The Filter Keys option can be turned on by a shortcut. You simply need to hold down the right Shift key for eight seconds, and the feature will be activated.

This option has two settings that you may need to manage for users, depending on their needs. The first option is to ignore repeated keystrokes. With this option turned on, the system ignores a keystroke if it is repeated within the time frame you select. The time frame can be as brief as a half second and as long as 2 seconds. If your user wants to press the same key twice, she will have to wait the specified time before the system will accept the keystroke. Also, if you hold down a key, it will react as though you have only pressed the key once.

The next option listed ignores any quick keystrokes and slows down the repeat rate if a key is held down. This option tells the keyboard not to repeat the keystroke no matter how long the key is pressed. The only way to get multiple keystrokes is to press the key as many times as needed. If you don't want to disable this feature entirely, you can just slow down the repeat rate. You can manage how long a key is depressed before it starts to repeat the keystroke, and you can manage the rate at which the repeated key is sent to the system.

The Slow Keys option requires the user to press the key for the specified period before the system will accept the keystroke. The default setting is one second, so if the user holds down the key for only half-second, the system ignores the keystroke.

You can also have the system beep every time a key is accepted by the system, as well as display the Filter Keys icon next to the clock.

Toggle Keys

Toggle Keys allows a user to be notified by a tone when the Caps Lock, Num Lock, or Scroll Lock keys are depressed. The shortcut for this function is to press the Num Lock key for five seconds.

Note: If you would like to use the Toggle Keys shortcut, make sure that the system has a Num Lock key. Many laptops do not have them.

The last keyboard option shows additional keyboard help available within an application. Usually, it is a good idea to leave the Keyboard options available at all times. If a user doesn't need them, they will not affect how that user uses the system. If a user happens to need them, he just needs to activate the option with the shortcut that is available.

Sound Options

The Sound Options are available to make the system display a message when a sound is generated by the system. Users that are hard of hearing may need to have a display informing them that a sound has been activated.

The Sound Sentry monitors your system and reacts when a sound is generated. The system flashes an active caption bar, flashes the active window, or flashes the desktop. This alerts the user that a sound has been generated, and the user can then investigate to see if it was important. Many times the system will generate sounds that are not relevant to the user.

You can also use the Show Sounds option, which tells the programs that you are working with to provide a caption for any sound or speech that it is using. This will only work with programs that have been programmed to handle this functionality.

Display Options

Many times the standard colors that are used by the system are not viewable by some users. To make it easier for users to switch to a display that they can use, there is a shortcut available. If the user presses the left Alt key, the left Shift key, and the

Print Screen key simultaneously, the system automatically shifts to a high contrast display. You can set up the system to automatically jump to a high contrast display with white lettering on a black background or black lettering on a white background, or to choose a custom display that you have created.

It is easy to activate the custom display with the shortcut, but switching back is a little trickier. To switch back to the original display, go to the Display Properties, and on the Appearance tab, choose the Scheme that you want.

Mouse Options

The mouse can be a very tricky item for some people to use. The Mouse Options allow the keyboard instead of the mouse to control the pointer on screen. To activate the mouse keys, a user needs to hold down the left Alt key, the left Shift key, and the Num Lock key simultaneously.

After this feature is activated, the user can use the numeric keypad to control the movement of the mouse. You have a few options to control how these mouse functions will react. You can control the speed of the mouse and the acceleration speed of the mouse. One nice feature is that each user can easily speed up and slow down the mouse on an individual basis. If users hold down Ctrl, they can speed the mouse up, and if they hold down Shift, they can slow it down.

You can use the Num Lock key to control whether or not the mouse keys are activated. You can decide whether they should be active if the Num Lock key has been activated or deactivated. You can also have an icon appear when the mouse keys have been activated.

General Accessibility Options

On the General tab there a few options that don't really fit into any of the other categories. There is an automatic reset of the options. You can specify a time limit when the Accessibility Options will be turned off if they haven't been used. This may be useful for a general purpose computer, where many users use the system. However, this could be annoying to a user who uses these features on a regular basis.

You can set the system to notify you when Accessibility Options are activated. You can have the system automatically notify you by either presenting a dialog box that tells you which option has been activated, and you can have the system make a sound when the options are activated. This can be very useful for all users. The users that need the options will be assured that they are activated and the users who don't need the options will know that they just pressed the wrong keys.

Windows 2000 also has the capability to allow you to replace the keyboard and mouse with an alternative Serial Key device. A number of devices are on the market that assist people in using a system, and you can configure where the hardware is plugged into the system. You may also need to load drivers or configure other settings, so be sure to check the documentation that accompanies the hardware you purchase.

There are also a few administrative options that you can set. You can apply all the Accessibility Options to the logon desktop. You can also have the system automatically apply the settings as defaults for all new users to the system.

It is probably a good idea to always leave the Accessibility Options with its shortcuts available on the system. It requires no overhead on the system to have these options available, and you never know when they will be needed.

Accessibility Options Available on the Start Menu

There are some other options available from the Start menu. Select Start | Accessories to find a variety of other options that you can use.

The Magnifier tool uses part of the screen as a display window to magnify where the mouse is pointing. See Figure 5.5. This can be very useful to someone who has trouble reading the text and needs magnification.

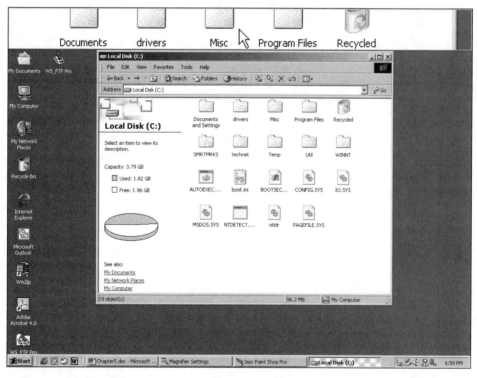

Figure 5.5 The Magnifier tool.

The Narrator tool reads the contents of the windows on the screen out loud through the sound card and speakers on the system. The Narrator also pronounces letters as you type them. The only problem with this tool is that you have to type fairly slowly for the system to keep up with you. Again, this tool can be useful for users who have trouble reading the text on the system.

The On Screen Keyboard tool allows you to display an onscreen keyboard in the foreground. You can use this keyboard to type on the system. This tool is useful for someone who has trouble using regular keyboards. With this tool, you can use either the keyboard or the mouse to type characters into the system.

There is also an Accessibility Wizard, which walks you through the available options, so you can set up the system according to your needs.

The Utility Manager allows you to set the Accessibility Options to automatically start. You can have the options start when Windows starts and when Utility Manager starts. You can also use this tool to stop and start an option manually.

Control Panel Utilities

Since the beginning of the Windows line of operating systems, the Control Panel has always been at the heart of configuring the system. In Windows 2000, some of the functionality of the Control Panel has been moved to Microsoft Management Console (MMC) snap-ins, but you still use the Control Panel for most system configuration.

Many of the options and settings in the Control Panel can be accessed by other means throughout the system, but they are all collected in the Control Panel to make them easy to find. Depending on your system's configuration, some options in the Control Panel may or may not be present. Don't be surprised if the contents of the Control Panel change from system to system. Also, you may need to have Administrator permissions to make many of the available changes.

Accessibility Tool Options

The Accessibility tool allows you to set the options for the accessibility features. Refer to the "Accessibility Options" section in the first part of this chapter for more details concerning these features.

Add/Remove Hardware

The Add/Remove Hardware tool allows you to manage any physical device attached to the computer. Generally, your hardware is preconfigured by the system when you install Windows 2000. This tool allows you to add or change the current configuration.

Note: You must be logged in as the Administrator or have Administrator privileges on the system to make changes to the hardware configuration.

There are a few common tasks that can be accomplished with this tool. You can install or uninstall hardware devices. If your hardware device is Plug and Play compatible, it should be autodetected by the system and installed without having to use this tool. However, sometimes a device isn't detected or if it isn't Plug and Play compatible, this tool checks the system in a more thorough fashion by querying all the possible hardware settings; it should find your new hardware and set it up.

You can use this tool to update your device drivers. You can find out the current version of the driver you are using and if needed, update the driver to a newer version. This is a common task in troubleshooting a device. Usually, if a piece of hardware isn't functioning properly, you should first check to see if a newer driver can fix the problem. Most hardware vendors will not help you troubleshoot the system unless you are using the latest driver. You may also want to update the driver to access any new functionality added to the driver for the hardware component.

You can use this tool to troubleshoot a device that is not functioning properly. If you are having trouble with a device, point this tool at the particular piece of hardware, and it will check the system and try to tell you why it is not functioning. If the device is broken, this tool will not help. If the device is simply not configured properly, the Add/Remove Hardware tool attempts to give you some assistance in diagnosing where the problem seems to be and how to resolve it.

It also assists you in unplugging or ejecting a device from the system. Not all hardware can be unplugged from the system while it is running, but if it can, this utility is advantageous. It's most commonly used for this purpose in portable or laptop computers. You can use this tool to unplug a laptop from a docking station or eject a PCMCIA (Personal Computer Memory Card International Association) device, such as a modem or network card.

Add/Remove Programs

The Add/Remove Programs tool helps you manage the programs that you have installed on your system. When you open this utility, you see a list of programs that have been installed on your system. You can highlight a program and then either remove the program entirely or modify the installation by removing or adding different features of the program.

This utility has been upgraded from previous versions, and you can use it to obtain different information about a program as well. Windows tracks the number of times that you use a particular program over a 30-day period and lets you know how often it has been used. Windows has three different classifications of use: rarely, occasionally, and frequently, which is the only information you receive about usage, but it might help determine whether a program should remain or be removed. You will also see the date that shows the last time the program was used. Windows also estimates the size of an application. This measurement can be inaccurate, but you can get a decent idea of how much hard drive space is taken by an application. Some programs may also include support information.

You can use the Add New Programs section to have Windows 2000 assist you in adding a program from a CD-ROM or a floppy disk. From this section, you can launch Windows Update, which connects you to the Microsoft Web site and lets you know if any programs are available that may add functionality to the system or fix a known problem. If you happen to be working on a network, you may also see a list of programs that are available on the network to install. Additionally, you can use this tool to add or remove Windows components from the system.

Administrative Tools

In the Administrative Tools window, you can find many tools that are available to administer the system. Most of the tools available in this window are custom consoles for the MMC. There are a couple of tools that are not MMC consoles, like the Data sources tool, which allows you to manage your ODBC sources, and the Telnet Server Administration tool, which assists you in configuring the system to allow telnet connections.

Client Services for NetWare (CSNW)

CSNW isn't found in the Control Panel unless you have configured your system to connect to a NetWare server. This tool allows you set the options you need to connect to a NetWare environment. You are also able to set some print options and select an option to run NetWare login scripts.

Date/Time

The Date/Time utility allows you to set the system time and date. The system uses this setting to assign a date and time to created or modified files. You also should set the time zone property for your location. This utility can be important if you are using a scheduling program. For example, if you schedule an online meeting and want to invite people from other time zones, the scheduling program may change the time for users outside your time zone, so that everyone will be at the meeting at the same time. You also want to make sure that you set your system to adjust the time when daylight savings comes around if you change times in your local area.

Display

The Display program allows you to manage how your desktop looks and how the monitor displays information. Many people like to personalize their desktop, and this tool allows many configuration options.

You can set your wallpaper on the Background tab of the display options. This background image sits on the desktop behind the icons. You can choose to use an HTML document or just about any picture document. Windows 2000 comes with a number of pictures that you can use as well as many patterns that you can tile across the screen. If you have a specific picture that you like, you can stretch the picture to fill the screen although sometimes this may distort the picture.

You can set a screen saver in this utility. Windows 2000 comes with a number of preconfigured screen savers. You can determine which one you like and when it will start. The system times your inactivity with the computer, and when it reaches the time set in this utility, the screen saver starts. Depending on the screen saver you choose, you may also be able to configure some settings to display how it will look on screen.

The Appearance tab allows you to change the colors of the system. There are a number of predefined schemes that have different colors set. You can also create a custom scheme and set the colors to the way you want them. You can change the color of a certain type of object or change the colors of many options.

The Web tab allows you to set some of your Active Desktop options. Refer to the "Active Desktop" section earlier in this chapter for more information.

The Effects tab allows you to change the feel of the system. You can change the icon used for some system tools, like My Computer, Recycle Bin, My Documents, and My Network Places. You can set whether you want the transition effects for menus and tool tips to have a fade effect or a scroll effect. You can set the system to not use all available colors for the icons. Effects can be useful if you want the system to be able to refresh the screen quicker. You can also have the system use large icons to make them easier to view.

The Settings tab allows you to work with the resolution, video card, and monitor options. You can tell the system to use a specific resolution as well as how many colors to display. Windows 2000 bases the options it makes available on what it knows about the video card and monitor you are using. It does this to prevent you from setting the system to an unusable setting. You can also set the monitor you are using as well as the video card. The Color Management utility allows you to choose how you want to see the colors on your system. You can use an .icm or .icc document, which have definitions for how the colors should be displayed on the system. Using these documents assures that when you print a document, the colors that are on the screen are the same as the color that are printed.

Windows 2000 also has the capability to work with multiple monitors at the same time. You may need to use this feature if you are doing certain types of work that requires you to be able to see many things at the same time. You can be actively working on a document in one screen and referring to figures on another.

Fax

The Fax setting allows you to set some options for sending and receiving faxes. You need to have a Fax Modem on your system to use this setting. Once you have set up the fax modem, this tool allows you to specify your personal settings as well as the cover pages you would like to use. The status monitor allows you to set options for how you want the system to inform you of your faxing status. The Advanced options help you to set up the fax service as a printer object and to take you to the fax service management console.

Folder Options

The Folder Options tool does more than just manage the Folder Options. There are many different settings you can configure with this tool.

The General tab allows you to determine how similar you would like Windows 2000 to act to your Web browser. You can set whether or not you would like Web content on the desktop. You can set your folders to allow for Web content in them or whether they should act the same as previous versions of Windows. When you browse folders, you can decide to open all folders in a new window or stay in the same window you are currently working in. You can also change the default behavior of double-clicking on an item to use it to single-clicking the item as you would in a Web browser.

The View tab gives you many options on how you would like your folders displayed. By default, Windows 2000 hides many file extensions, system files, and protected operating system files. If you would like to see these files or file extensions, you can change the setting on the View tab. You can also set how the system displays compressed files and whether the full path to files is shown in the title bar.

The File Types tab shows which file extensions are associated with which program. This information can be very important, because sometimes programs fight over using a particular file extension. For example, you double-click on a file with a certain extension and expect program A to run and instead program B runs. You can use this utility to change the associated program. You can also set up an extension from scratch if it has not been used to automatically open a program.

The Offline File tab is useful to you only if you are working on a network that has offline files activated. If you are in this situation, you can determine how often the files should be synchronized and how much hard drive space should be used for the offline files.

Fonts

The Fonts Program lists all the fonts that you have available in the system. To add a new font, simply click on the File menu, and choose Install New Fonts. Point to the font file and the new font will be added. You can then use these fonts in any program that allows you to choose a font.

Game Controllers

The Game Controllers utility allows you to add the proper drivers for your joystick. You can also add rudder and pedal devices.

Infrared and Wireless Link

The Infrared and Wireless Link allows you to manage your infrared device. If you have an infrared device attached to your system, it should be autodetected by the system. If it is, then this link will be available in the Control Panel.

This utility assists you in making a connection to another system through the infrared port. You can transfer files to other systems, print to a printer with an infrared port, or make a connection to another device that has infrared capabilities. This tool is often used to synchronize data between a laptop or personal computer and a handheld device.

Internet Options

The Internet Options in the Control Panel are the same Internet Options that you see in Internet Explorer 5. In this utility, you are able to set many parameters for your Internet connection. The nice thing about this utility is that many other programs can share this information and use these settings, so you only have to set these parameters once.

Keyboard

The Keyboard utility allows you to adjust your keyboard. You can adjust the repeat delay and repeat rate when you hold down a key. You can also adjust how fast the cursor blinks.

The Locales tab allows you to change the keyboard, so that it functions as a keyboard in another language. You can also set up a series of keystrokes that allows you to switch between locales as you use the system.

Mouse

The Mouse utility allows you to customize how the mouse acts according to your personal preference. You may want to change the order of the buttons if you are right- or left-handed. You can turn on a feature that allows you to single-click on items to open them instead of double-clicking. You can also adjust the double-click speed if it is too fast or too slow.

You can adjust the look of the pointer. You can create your own pointer icons or choose from a number of pointer schemes included with Windows 2000. Mouse speed and acceleration rate can also be adjusted. Additionally, you can have the mouse jump to the default dialog box when a new window opens, although this can be disconcerting to some users until they get used to it.

Network and Dial-Up Connections

Network and Dial-up Connections allow you to configure your network settings. You can set the system up to work on a local network with all the protocol and client options that are necessary. You can also set up dial-up networking through this tool. These options are covered in more detail in Chapter 10.

Phone and Modem Options

With the Phone and Modem Options utility, you can configure your dialing options. You are able to specify the type of modem that you are using and any properties to make the modem dial properly. You are also able to set up dialing rules for your locations. If you work from different locations, you can set different configurations for where you are going to be. You may be in places that require you to dial a number or sequence before you can dial the number you are calling. You can also set the system to use a calling card instead of dialing a long-distance number.

Power Options

The Power Options allow you to specify how you would like your system to manage the power features of your computer. These options may be more critical on a laptop computer when you are using a battery, but they can just as easily be used on your desktop computer to reduce your power consumption.

The power schemes help you to manage the length of time your devices stay active. You can have the monitor power down as well as the hard drives. There are many schemes available with different times available for when and if you would like these devices to power down. If you decide to have the monitor power down, when you return to your system, you will have to wait for the monitor to warm up, but the system will come back to full functionality very quickly. If you decide to power down the hard drives, you will have to wait a little longer for the hard drives to spin back up before you can use the system. Either way it shouldn't take more than a few seconds for the system to be functional again.

The Advanced options allow you to display a power management icon on the taskbar. This can be especially useful on a laptop because it tells you whether you are plugged into the wall or if you are running on the battery. Some laptops have a problem with the power cord coming loose, so this feature will help you make sure that you are not using the battery when you don't need to.

The Hibernate feature takes everything that is currently in memory and saves it on the hard drive. When you initiate the hibernation feature, the memory information is written to the hard drive and the system is powered off. When you want to use the system again, you don't have to reboot the system, so it will come back online again very quickly by comparison. The programs that were being used at the time of hibernation will be available again automatically. This is another feature that laptop users employ extensively. This feature is only available if your system board tells the operating system that it can handle this feature.

If your system reports that it can handle hibernation, you can enable the Advanced Power Management options. If you enable this feature, you will see some new options. You will be able to set the power options, which not only allows you to manage the monitor and hard drive power down, it also sends the system into standby mode. You will be able to set the option differently, depending on whether you are running the system plugged in or off the battery. You may want to be more aggressive with the time setting when the battery is being used. You can also set warnings to alert you when you reach a low battery state. When the battery gets low, you can specify what you would like the system to do. The system can jump to standby or power off automatically. You can also configure a program of your choice to run when the power gets low. If your system goes into standby mode, you can set the system to require a password to get back into the system.

An uninterruptible power supply (UPS) can also be configured for your system. You can configure where the UPS is connected to the system and what should happen if the UPS detects a power failure. Usually the UPS keeps the system on for a while to see if the power comes back. Most often, power failures are very short, so the UPS keeps the system up without a hitch. If there is a long power outage, the UPS is usually configured to shut down the system to ensure that nothing is lost and that the system gets a clean shut down. When the power comes back online, the system can be restarted.

Printers

The Printers folder allows you to add a new printer or manage any printer that you currently have on the system.

Regional Options

The Regional Options allows you to determine what locale you are in and to make necessary changes. The locale determines how options, such as the date and currency are displayed. Usually, you set the locale to where you are currently, so if you travel you may need to change this depending on the country or locale that you are in.

You may want to simply change how the currency is displayed on your system or how your system displays numbers. You can also decide how you would like dates displayed on your system and how the system should deal with a two-digit year.

Scanners and Cameras

Scanners and Cameras shows you the scanners or cameras that have been added to the system and allows you to add others.

Scheduled Tasks

Scheduled Tasks allows you to create a task and have the system run that task on a scheduled basis.

Sounds and Multimedia

The Sounds and Multimedia utility allows you to manage the sounds that are associated with system events. Windows 2000 has been set up to play different sounds when different events occur, like minimizing or maximizing a window, receiving an email, or clicking on a link in Internet Explorer. A couple of preconfigured schemes are available that you can set, and other schemes can be added to the system. You also can modify any sound on the system and change it to your favorite sound.

You can modify the hardware that is available for your sounds on the system. If you have multiple sound devices, you can choose which ones are preferred for sound playback and recording.

System

The System tool allows you get some basic information about the system. The Network Identification tab allows you to manage your computer name and join a domain.

Note: *The Join Domain Wizard is now located in the System Properties of the Control Panel. This has changed from Windows NT 4, where this information was located in Network Properties.*

This tool helps you to manage the hardware on your system. Mostly, it has links to other utilities to manage your drivers and add new hardware. You can configure multiple hardware profiles with this utility. Setting up multiple hardware profiles is very common on a laptop or a desktop with removable devices. Occasionally, if a device is not attached to the system, it can prevent the system from booting or may generate many errors. To resolve this problem, you can set up a separate hardware profile, and then configure the two profiles with separate hardware information. When you boot the system, you are given a choice of which profile to use, and you can choose the one that matches the hardware you currently have attached to the system. You can also set a default profile, which will be activated if you don't make a choice during the boot process.

On the Advanced tab, you are allowed to set different environment variables that may be needed for your applications. You can also set some performance options, which optimize the system based on whether you want the system priority to be given to background services or to the applications you are running. Usually, you will want to choose applications unless you are using your system to share data with other users, which is more important. You can also set the initial and maximum size that you want to use for your pagefile. If you have multiple hard drives, you can move the pagefile to a different disk.

The Startup and Recovery options allow you to set the startup defaults as well as what happens when there is a problem with the system. When you boot the system, a Startup menu is displayed, where you can choose to change the default operating system or the amount of time you are given to choose which system you would like to boot. The Startup Option makes the necessary changes in the boot.ini file that controls this menu. The Recovery options determine what should happen when the system suffers a stop screen. You can have the system write an event to the Event Viewer, send an administrative alert, or automatically reboot the system. You can also have the system do a memory dump at the time of the error. The contents of memory can be dumped to a file on the local hard drive. This file may be very large because it will be as big as the amount of physical memory in the system. However, you may need this information if the stop screen that you received is a recurring problem.

Managing User Profiles

You can set some options for your user profiles in the system utility. The User Profile tab shows you what profiles are currently being stored on your system. Your user profile defines different individual settings for a user. Your display settings, network connections, icons, and other items are stored in the profile, so that they are always available and unique to the individual that logs on to the system.

Your profiles are stored on the boot partition under a folder named Documents and Settings. After you install the system, you will find three default profiles in this folder. The first is the Default User Profile. This is usually a hidden folder, so unless you have chosen to see hidden folders, you will not see it. This profile, in essence, is a template for all new profiles that are generated. If you want something to show up in all future profiles, you can place it in this default profile. When a profile is created, the contents of this default profile are copied to the new profile. If a user wants to remove a custom item you have added, he or she can do so.

The All Users Profile applies to every user on the system. Users are not able to remove any items in this profile. All items will always show up when a user logs in. If you want to add a custom item and don't want users to be able to remove or change it, you should add the item in this profile. You will also see the Administrator Profile, which is simply a user profile for the Administrator account.

The user profiles that are created on the system contain all of your user settings. There are a number of folders in the profile that contain different types of data. See Table 5.1 for the folders and what they contain.

Your user profile doesn't have to be stored in the default location or on the local system. You can highlight the profile you would like to use and click on copy, which

Table 5.1   A list of folders in a user profile and their contents.

Folder	Contents
Application Data	Customization files to save your applications with the options that you like
Cookies	Internet Explorer cookies
Desktop	Your custom desktop shortcuts
Favorites	Your individual favorites from Internet Explorer
Local Settings	Temporary Internet files and Application data and history files
My Documents	A default location for storing your documents
NetHood	A listing of network places that you have visited
PrintHood	A listing of network printers that you have used
Recent	A listing of documents that you have used recently
Send To	You can send different files or objects to different locations, such as to a floppy disk or email recipient, that are listed
Start Menu	This is where the shortcuts are stored that are available on the Start menu
Templates	Some programs may use this location to store template files

will make a copy of the profile in the new location. You can then use this profile instead of the old one.

Users and Passwords

The Users and Passwords tool assists you in creating users for the local system. You have more options if you use the MMC snap-in for local users and groups, but this tool makes it easy to handle some basic configuration of the users on your local system. Windows 2000 Professional does give you the option of disabling the secure login and will automatically log on to the system in this utility. This option is only useful if security is not an issue and only one user is using the system

Multilanguage Support

Although you may work with Windows in an English-speaking environment, you may not be aware of some of the trials and problems associated with users who would like to use a different language. In the past, Microsoft had created different localized versions of their products. For example, you could purchase a Japanese or French version of other Windows products. There were and are many localized versions of the operating system available.

The problem with a localized version is that only a user who speaks that language is able to use the system. Also many different versions of an operating system may need to be rolled out in a worldwide organization. This means creating different installation scripts and testing applications on each version of the operating system that is being used.

Windows 2000 again has followed this standard and allows you to purchase a localized version of the operating system. Microsoft has also created a MultiLanguage edition of Windows 2000 known as the MUI edition. Microsoft wanted Windows 2000 to have a worldwide presence, and to accomplish this, the MUI edition was developed and introduced. The main advantage of the MUI edition is that one person can be using the system in one language and another can use it in a different language. All that is required to change languages for these users is to log on to the system. The following list contains the supported languages in the MUI version:

➤ Arabic

➤ Brazilian

➤ Chinese (Simplified)

➤ Chinese (Traditional)

➤ Czech

➤ Danish

➤ Dutch

➤ English

➤ Finnish

➤ French

➤ German

➤ Greek

➤ Hebrew

➤ Hungarian

➤ Italian

➤ Japanese

➤ Korean

➤ Norwegian

➤ Polish

➤ Portuguese

➤ Russian

➤ Spanish

➤ Swedish

➤ Turkish

You wouldn't think that the problems associated with multiple languages on an operating system would be that extensive, but in reality it is quite a big problem. A number of areas are affected by the language. First, displaying the text of the language, including being able to enter that language from the keyboard, is a problem. Second, there is the issue of ensuring that all operations of the system act the same way, such as saving files and sharing folders. Third, all of the dialog boxes, menu items, icons, help features, and basic tools of the operating system are affected.

The localized versions of the operating systems seem to be able to take care of these issues fairly well. The operating system is built from the ground level with that specific language in mind, so all features are built with the language. There are also some issues with the localized versions, however. The user will always have to use that language, and there may be problems trying to connect and get resources from a different localized version. The MultiLanguage version has some limitations in this regard.

With the MultiLanguage version, you may have some problems sharing resources with users with another language version installed. The downside of the MUI version is that many of the pieces of this version are still in English: Bitmaps and Registry keys are in English, any 16-bit OS pieces are still in English, and all files that make up Windows 2000 are in English, which affects the Start menu and desktop items because they are displayed in English. You also need more hard drive space because every language that is being used needs to be loaded on the system.

The MUI version of Windows 2000 is most advantageous for a user who wants to work in multiple languages or for a system that is going to have users who speak different languages. Although much of the background of the system is in English, users are still able to use their applications and enter information in the language of their choice. As a user switches between languages, the keyboard defaults to the keyboard type that is the default for that language. Many users who employ multiple languages will want to keep the keyboard the same regardless of the language they are using. If the languages or characters used are similar, this shouldn't be a problem. For example, if a user is working in English and she switches to French, then she would be able to use the same keyboard layout. If the user is switching from the English to Chinese, however, it is unlikely that the English keyboard would be of any use.

The problem with using the MUI version for your worldwide organization is that the administrators of the system need to know English. Because much of the backend of Windows 2000 MUI is in English, they need to be able to administer the system in that language. The localized versions do make all the backend processes in the language of choice, so the administrators don't need to work in English. Depending on how your network is administered and based on the capabilities of the administrators, this may affect how the systems are rolled out. If you do have to roll out a localized version, you will need to re-create any automated scripts and retest all your applications on the localized system. You can eliminate this redundancy by working with the MultiLanguage version.

The Application Programming Interfaces (APIs)

There are two APIs that handle languages within Windows 2000: the NLSAPI (National Language Support API) and the MLAPI (Multilingual API).

The NLSAPI provides the system or applications with the user's locale, input locale, character mapping, and sorting information. The MLAPI contains the functions to process the input from a user and display it in the proper format on the screen. This is important, as many languages may display certain items right to left, some may use a left to right format, and others may display items vertically.

Windows 2000 supports the Unicode standard. Unicode supports all the characters of the main languages in the world, so that all will be able to be displayed. If the application is designed to handle Unicode and uses the MLAPI and the NLSAPI, it should be fully functional regardless of what language the user is working in. This is a tremendous boon for independent software vendors for creating and distributing their software in other languages. In the past, it has been a long and sometimes painstaking process to port an application to another language and consequently, many applications were only written in a single language. The one limitation you may find is that Windows 2000 is only able to run one language application at a time and may require you to change system locales to run some applications.

However, the main advantage is that if the program is developed properly, you will be able to run a single application in multiple languages across your worldwide network with very little user modification.

Chapter Summary

Many users will want to make their system their own by modifying how the system looks and feels. They may want to change the background of the desktop, change the color scheme, or change other features.

The Control Panel is really the key element to get inside the guts of Windows 2000 Professional to customize your system. Although you can access many of the tools in other ways, the Control Panel is the central location for a collection of tools that allows users to make just about any necessary modification to the system.

Although the Control Panel utilities are among the most powerful tools you can use, please note that these tools can also get you into trouble if you make a mistake.

Make sure that you document the exact procedures needed to make adjustments to the system to prevent your users from creating problems on the system.

If you are part of an organization that must support many languages, take a long look at the options available in the MultiLanguage version. This may not be the best option for your particular needs, but it does have many nice features, which may make it useful in your environment.

Review Questions

5

1. You want to add a Windows 2000 Professional computer to a domain. Which tool in the Control Panel do you use to accomplish this?

   a. Network and Dial-Up Connections

   b. Add/Remove Programs

   c. System

   d. Regional Options

2. You want to remove a piece of hardware from your system. Which tools in the Control Panel will enable you to do this?

   a. System

   b. Add/Remove Programs

   c. Add/Remove Hardware

   d. Display

3. You want to configure a screen saver to come on after five minutes of inactivity. Which tool in the Control Panel do you use to set this?

   a. System

   b. Display

   c. Power Options

   d. Regional Settings

4. You would like to configure the screen to power off after five minutes of inactivity. Which tool in the Control Panel would you use to set this?

   a. System

   b. Display

   c. Power Options

   d. Regional Settings

5. You would like to enable the advanced power management features of your computer. Which tool in the Control Panel would you use to enable this?

   a. Add/Remove Hardware

   b. Add/Remove Software

   c. Folder Options

   d. Power Options

6. A user mentions that he is having a hard time reading the text on the screen. He can see most things just fine, but some of the text is too small for him to read. Which utility would you suggest he use to make the system better for him?

   a. Sticky Keys

   b. HighContrast

   c. Magnifier

   d. Narrator

7. A user is having difficulty pressing two keys at the same time on the keyboard. What utility allows him to have full functionality of the keyboard without ever having to press more than one key at a time?

   a. Sticky Keys

   b. Toggle Keys

   c. Magnifier

   d. Filter Keys

8. A user would like to change the keyboard layout for his system. Which tool would he use to accomplish this?

   a. System

   b. Keyboard

   c. Power Options

   d. Regional Settings

9. A user calls and says that some of her icons that were on her Start menu are no longer there. What feature has hidden these icons?

   a. Active Desktop

   b. Accessibility Options

   c. Personalized Menus

   d. Plug and Play

10. You would like to find out how much disk space is required to put your system into hibernation. Which tool would have this information?

    a. System

    b. Display

    c. Folder Options

    d. Power Options

11. A user wants to have the Date on his system displayed in a different format. Which tool would you tell him to use to set this?

    a. Date/Time

    b. Keyboard

    c. System

    d. Regional Options

12. A user is having a problem with the system doubling entered keystrokes. You would like to limit the time before the system reenters a keystroke. Which utility would you use?

    a. Sticky Keys

    b. Toggle Keys

    c. Filter Keys

    d. On-Screen Keyboard

13. A user wants to shorten the time that the system waits for her to choose an operating system when the system boots up. Where you would direct her to make this change?

    a. System

    b. Display

    c. Power Options

    d. Regional Settings

14. You would like to add a Hardware Profile to the system. Where would you find the utility that would make this possible?

    a. Add/Remove Hardware

    b. Display

    c. Network and Dial-Up Connections

    d. System

5

15. You need to change the time zone that you are located in. Which tool would you use to accomplish this?

    a. Regional Options

    b. System

    c. Date/Time

    d. Folder Options

16. A user calls and tells you that he would like to change the colors of the menus on the system. Where you would direct him to make this change?

    a. Regional Options

    b. System

    c. Display

    d. Add/Remove Programs

17. You have just purchased a new modem and you want to make sure it is installed and working. Which utility would use to set this up?

    a. Phone and Modem Options

    b. Network and Dial Up Connections

    c. System

    d. Fax

18. In your organization, you have some users who speak English and others who speak Japanese. You also have some users who speak both languages. Which of the following will you need to install to support these users?

    a. English Localized version

    b. Japanese Localized version

    c. MultiLanguage version

19. You have some users who are currently using the Chinese Localized version of Windows 2000. These users are having trouble connecting to shares on your English Windows 2000 Server. What can you do to allow these users to connect to your server.

    a. Reinstall your file server with the Chinese Localized version of Windows 2000 Server.

    b. Create your Shares on the file server with the Chinese language.

    c. Install the English version of Windows 2000 on the Chinese users' computers.

    d. Install the MultiLanguage version of Windows 2000 on the Chinese users' computers.

Real-World Projects

Linda is a member of the Help Desk at her organization. She has been noticing that since her company installed Windows 2000, she and her coworkers have been answering many of the same questions repeatedly.

At the Help Desk's weekly planning meeting, Linda brings up her concerns and it is decided that the Help Desk staff will put together a list of the most commonly asked questions. The Help Desk tracks the types of calls they receive, so the data should be fairly easy to collect. Linda is assigned the task of documenting how to resolve these calls and then posting this information on the company's intranet.

To start this project the staff decides to post the most commonly asked questions, and then continue to expand the list as time goes on. Linda goes through the Help Desk software and identifies the top few items that people are calling about.

Project 5.1

To change the background on the desktop:

1. Select Start|Settings, and click on the Control Panel.

2. Double-click on the Display icon.

3. Click on the Background tab.

4. Select one of the predefined backgrounds or browse to a file of your choice.

5. If needed, adjust the pattern to your liking.

6. Click on OK when you are finished, and close the Control Panel.

Project 5.2

To remove the click sound on a link in Internet Explorer 5:

1. Select Start|Settings, and click on the Control Panel.

2. Click on the Sounds And Multimedia icon.

3. Click on the drop-down arrow in the Sound Events box and scroll down until you find the Section for Windows Explorer.

4. Highlight the Start Navigation item.

5. The name box should contain the file named start.wav. Click on the down arrow, and click on the item None.

6. Click on OK when you are finished, and close the Control Panel.

Project 5.3

To change the colors of menus and dialog boxes:

1. Select Start|Settings, and click on the Control Panel.

2. Click on the Display icon.

3. Click on the Appearance tab.

4. Choose a predefined Scheme or find the item you would like to change and choose a color from the Color Picker.

5. Click on OK when you are finished, and close the Control Panel.

Project 5.4

To configure the system to shut down when the battery reaches critical state (this assumes that Advanced Power Features have been activated):

1. Select Start|Settings, and click on the Control Panel.

2. Click on the Power Options icon.

3. Click on the Alarms tab.

4. In the Critical Battery Alarm section, make sure the option Activate Critical Battery Alarm When Power Level Reaches has been selected.

5. Adjust the percentage of battery you would like left before the critical alarm goes off. The default is 3%.

6. Click on Alarm Action.

7. Under the Power Level section select the When The Alarm Goes Off The Computer Will checkbox (see Figure 5.6).

Figure 5.6 Critical battery alarm actions.

8. You can choose whether you would like the system to shut down or go to standby mode when this happens.

9. Click on OK twice when you are finished, and close the Control Panel.

5

CHAPTER SIX

Files and Folders

After completing this chapter, you will be able to:

✓ Describe the new features in Windows 2000 Professional that make file access easier

✓ Describe the purpose of the My Documents, My Pictures, and My Network Places folders

✓ Describe the uses of AutoComplete

✓ Customize folders in Windows 2000 Professional

✓ Identify the types of NTFS permissions used in Windows 2000 Professional

✓ Compress files and folders to save disk space

✓ Describe what happens when you move and copy files and folders between NTFS volumes

✓ Describe what happens when you move and copy files and folders between NTFS and FAT volumes

✓ Explain the uses of Offline Files

✓ Describe how users can share folders

✓ Understand permissions that apply to shared folders

✓ Know what caching is and how it is used for offline file use

✓ Understand the Distributed Files System and its use

✓ Explain the search options available with Windows 2000 Professional

Windows 2000 Professional makes working with files and folders easier than in previous versions of Windows.

Working with Files and Folders

Several new features give users easier access to files. These include:

➤ My Network Places keeps track of a user's favorite files and folders on the local network.

➤ By default, all files are saved in the My Documents folder.

➤ Windows 2000 Professional has a new common dialog box for opening and saving files from any program.

➤ Folders provide users in Windows 2000 Professional with a way to organize their files.

➤ AutoComplete saves previous entries and suggests possible matches when users type information.

➤ Windows 2000 Professional keeps track of the user's most recently used files and folders in the History folder.

My Documents Folder

The My Documents folder is the default location for the storage of a file, as well as the default location for Open and Save As commands. The contents of the My Documents folder are saved on a per-user basis. An icon is created on the desktop for easy access to the My Documents folder.

The My Documents folder is a system folder that cannot be deleted. However, it can be renamed and redirected by using Group Policies. The My Documents folder is stored with other user profile settings in the Documents and Settings folder.

Windows Explorer opens to the My Documents folder by default. The My Documents folder shortcut appears immediately below the Desktop icon. The actual folder is located in the user's profile under the Documents and Settings*username*\\ My Documents. This location can be changed by right-clicking on the My Documents shortcut and selecting Properties from the pop-up menu (see Figure 6.1).

The My Documents folder also can be accessed from the Documents submenu of the Start menu. By selecting the Expand My Documents checkbox, users can open the My Documents folder with a Documents submenu that displays all files and folders located in the folder. The Expand My Documents checkbox is located on the Advanced tab of the Taskbar and Start Menu Properties dialog box.

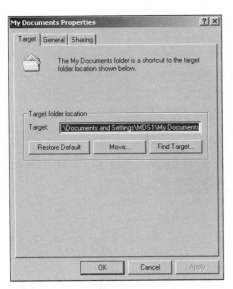

Figure 6.1   The Properties page, used to change the location of the My Documents folder.

My Pictures Folder

The My Pictures folder is a subfolder under the My Documents folder. The My Pictures folder provides a centralized place to store images. The folder is the default storage location for images from scanners, digital cameras, and other digital devices. Images can be previewed through Windows Explorer as thumbnails or in full-screen mode. Users can pan left, right, up, and down and zoom in and out without opening the images in a viewer. As with the My Documents folder, the contents of the My Pictures folder is stored on a per user basis (see Figure 6.2).

My Network Places

My Network Places replaces Network Neighborhood from previous versions of Windows. My Network Places provides a comprehensive group of network resources to which a computer connects. Unlike Network Neighborhood, not all of the network resources are displayed. Instead, the following three icons are displayed (see Figure 6.3):

➤ *Add Network Place*—Used to add a shortcut to a network resource.

➤ *Entire Network*—Allows users to browse other domains and workgroups on their network.

➤ *Computers Near Me*—Presents the user with a list of network resources in the user's domain or workgroup. This icon is used when Windows 2000 Professional is used in combination with Active Directory.

Figure 6.2   The My Pictures folder.

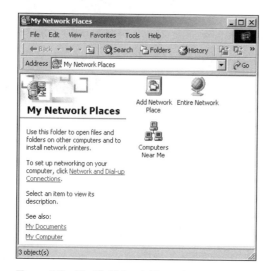

Figure 6.3   The My Network Places folder.

Note: Mapped drives do not appear in My Network Places.

History Folder

The History folder tracks all documents you have opened. The History folder is selected by clicking on the History button on the Windows Explorer toolbar. Users can select to view documents sorted By Date, By Site, By Most Visited, or By Order Visited Today (see Figure 6.4).

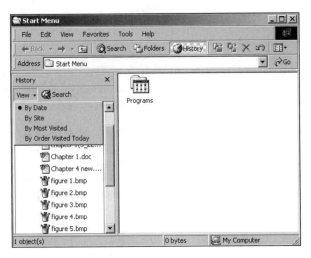

Figure 6.4   The History folder.

AutoComplete

AutoComplete in Windows 2000 Professional caches typed information and displays entries similar to those previously entered by a user. AutoComplete works with other applications in Windows 2000 Professional, including Windows Explorer and Internet Explorer. For example, AutoComplete helps users type URLs previously input in Internet Explorer, improving the accuracy of what the user types (see Figure 6.5). AutoComplete can be turned on and off through the AutoComplete settings properties dialog box. This box is accessed by clicking on the AutoComplete button on the Content tab of the Internet Properties dialog box.

Customizing Folders

Windows 2000 Professional provides two ways for users to customize their folders. Folders can be customized by using the Folder Options under the Tools menu in Windows Explorer or by using the Customize This Folder Wizard.

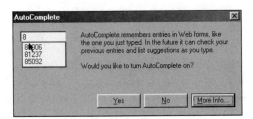

Figure 6.5   Turning on AutoComplete.

Folder Options

The Folder Options selection has four tabs:

➤ *General*—Used to enable Active Desktop and Web View. On this tab, users can select to open folders in the same window or a separate window. They also can select to open a folder by single-clicking or double-clicking on the folder.

➤ *View*—Used to set folder options. The Advanced Settings section has an extensive list of options that can be set for viewing files and folders (see Figure 6.6).

➤ *File Types*—Used to display a list of registered file types and the programs that are associated with them. It can also be used to add and delete file types.

➤ *Offline Files*—Used to set up the computer to make files stored on a network available when working offline (see Figure 6.7).

Customize This Folder Wizard

The Customize This Folder Wizard is accessed from Windows Explorer or My Computer. The wizard allows the user to choose or edit an HTML template for the folder, modify background picture and file name appearance, and add a comment to the folder (see Figure 6.8).

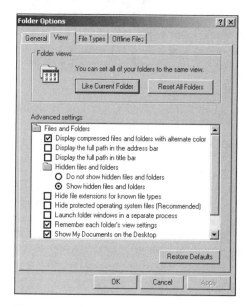

Figure 6.6   The View tab of the Folder Options dialog box.

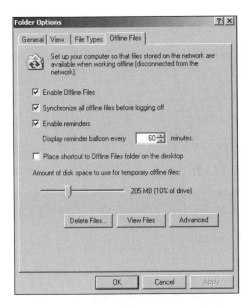

Figure 6.7   The Offline Files tab of the Folder Options dialog box.

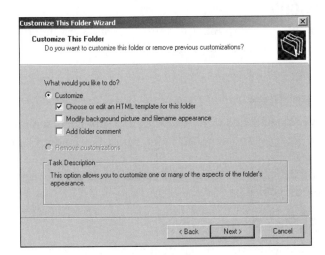

Figure 6.8   The Customize This Folder Wizard.

NTFS Permissions

NTFS permissions allow users to specify who has access to their files and folders. NTFS permissions are available only on NTFS volumes. There are two types of NTFS permissions: file and folder.

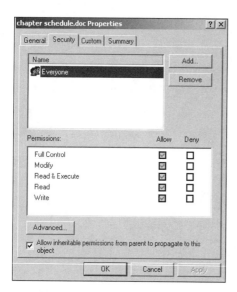

Figure 6.9   NTFS permissions on the Security tab of the Properties dialog box.

NTFS File Permissions

NTFS file permissions can be applied to files to control user access to the files. Figure 6.9 shows the standard NTFS permissions on the Security tab of the Properties dialog box.

NTFS Folder Permissions

NTFS folder permissions can be applied to folders, files, and subfolders within the folder. The standard NTFS folder permissions are Read, Write, List Folder Contents, Read & Execute, Modify, and Full Control. NTFS file permissions take precedence over folder permissions. By default, permissions of a parent folder are inherited by subfolders and files within the folder.

Special File and Folder Permissions

In situations in which file and folder permissions do not provide the access control that users want, they can apply NTFS special access permissions to the files and folders. There are 14 special access permissions (see Figure 6.10). The two special permissions that are the most useful for controlling access to resources are Change Permissions and Take Ownership. Change Permissions allows users to change permissions of files or folders without them having Full Control permission over the file or folder. Take Ownership permission allows users to transfer ownership of files and folders from one user or group to another. Two rules apply to the Take Ownership permission:

➤ Any user with Full Control or the owner of the file or folder can assign the Take Ownership special access permission to another group.

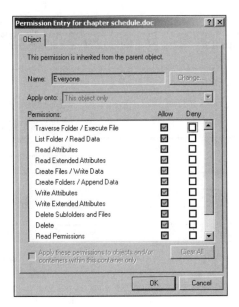

Figure 6.10   Special NTFS permissions as shown on the Permissions Entry dialog box.

➤ An administrator can take ownership of a file or folder, regardless of any other permissions applied to the file or folder.

To apply special permissions to a file or folder, take the following steps:

1. Right-click on the file or folder.

2. Select Properties.

3. Click on the Security tab.

4. Click on the Advanced button.

5. Click on View/Edit.

6. Select the Allow checkbox or the Deny checkbox for each permission you want to apply to the file or folder.

7. Click on OK.

8. Click on both Apply and OK twice.

Table 6.1 lists each file permission and specifies which special permissions are associated with that permission. Table 6.2 lists each folder permission and specifies which special permissions are associated with that permission.

Share permissions can also be set on NTFS volumes. Share permissions operate on shared files and folders in combination with file and folder permissions. Figure 6.11 shows the standard NTFS share permissions as listed on the Sharing tab of the Properties dialog box.

Table 6.1 Special permissions associated with file permissions.

Special Permissions	Full Control	Modify	Read & Execute	Read	Write
Traverse Folder/Execute File	X	X	X		
List Folder/Read Data	X	X	X	X	
Read Attributes	X	X	X	X	
Read Extended Attributes	X	X	X	X	
Create Files/Write Data	X	X			X
Create Folders/Append Data	X	X			X
Write Attributes	X	X			X
Write Extended Attributes	X	X			X
Delete Subfolders and Files	X				
Delete	X	X			
Read Permissions	X	X	X	X	X
Change Permissions	X				
Take Ownership	X				
Synchronize	X	X	X	X	X

Table 6.2 Special permissions associated with folder permissions.

Special Permissions	Full Control	Modify	Read & Execute	List Folder Contents	Read	Write
Traverse Folder/Execute File	X	X	X	X		
List Folder/Read Data	X	X	X	X	X	
Read Attributes	X	X	X	X	X	
Read Extended Attributes	X	X	X	X	X	
Create Files/Write Data	X	X				X
Create Folders/Append Data	X	X				X
Write Attributes	X	X				X
Write Extended Attributes	X	X				X
Delete Subfolders and Files	X					
Delete	X	X				
Read Permissions	X	X	X	X	X	X
Change Permissions	X					
Take Ownership	X					
Synchronize	X	X	X	X	X	X

Access Control Lists (ACLs)

NTFS uses ACLs to determine who has access to files and folders. The ACL is a list of user accounts and groups that have been given access to files and folders, and it specifies the type of access users and groups have to those files and folders. If a user requests access to a file or folder, his or her account must have an access control entry (ACE) in the ACL for the resource. The ACE must match the type of access being requested before the user is allowed access to the resource.

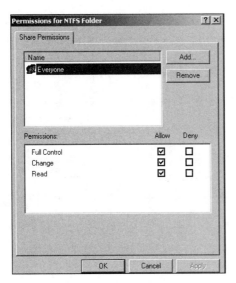

Figure 6.11   The Share Permissions tab of the Properties dialog box.

Multiple NTFS permissions can be assigned to user accounts. Permissions can be assigned to the individual user account and to the group accounts that the user belongs to. Several rules apply for assigning multiple NTFS permissions:

➤ NTFS permissions are cumulative. A user's effective permissions are the sum of the permissions for the user's individual account and all group accounts to which the user belongs.

➤ NTFS file permissions have priority over NTFS folder permissions.

➤ Deny permission overrides all other permissions.

Inherited File Permissions

NTFS file permissions of a parent folder are inherited by subfolders and files by default. Permissions assigned to the parent folder are automatically assigned to subfolders and files contained within that folder. Users can prevent permissions from being inherited to files and folders within a folder. Inherited file permissions are set on the Security tab of the Properties dialog box of the file or folder. Refer to Figure 6.9 earlier in the chapter for more information.

Compression

Windows 2000 Professional uses file and folder compression to store more data on disk partitions. All files and folders on an NTFS partition have one of two states: compressed or uncompressed.

Compressed files are read and written by any Microsoft Windows–based application or MS-DOS application without first being uncompressed by another program. When a program, such as Microsoft Word, opens a file that has been compressed, the file is automatically uncompressed. It is compressed again when it is saved.

NTFS disk space is allocated based on the uncompressed size of files. If a user tries to copy a compressed file to an NTFS partition that does not have enough disk space for the file in an uncompressed state, the file will not be copied. There must be enough space on the disk for the uncompressed file.

Files and folders are compressed using Windows Explorer. The user must have Write permission to change the compressed state of a file or folder. To compress a file or folder:

1. Open Windows Explorer.

2. Right-click on the file you want to compress.

3. Select Properties.

4. Click on the Advanced button.

5. Click on the Compress Contents To Save Disk Space checkbox under Compress Or Encrypt Attributes.

6. Click on OK to exit the Advanced attributes dialog box.

7. Click on Apply, and then click on OK.

Compressed files and folder can be displayed in Windows Explorer in an alternate color. To display a compressed file or folder in an alternate color, perform the following steps:

1. Open Windows Explorer.

2. Click on the drive where the file is located.

3. Select Tools | Folder Options.

4. Click on the View tab.

5. Select the Display Compressed Files And Folders With Alternate Color checkbox in the Advanced Settings list.

6. Click on Apply, and then click on OK to save the changes.

Note: Compressed files and folders will be displayed in blue in Windows Explorer.

Files and folders can also be compressed from the command line using the **compact** command. To learn more about the **compact** command, type "compact /?" at the command prompt.

A compressed folder can contain uncompressed files and subfolders. Alternately, an uncompressed folder can contain compressed files and subfolders. Encrypted files cannot be compressed, and compressed files cannot be encrypted.

Copying and Moving Compressed Files and Folders

Several rules apply that determine the compressed state of files and folders when they are copied and moved between NTFS and FAT volumes. The following list details these rules:

➤ *Copying a file within an NTFS volume*—A file that is copied from one location to another on the same NTFS volume inherits the compression state of the target folder.

➤ *Moving a file within an NTFS volume*—A file that is moved from one location to another on the same NTFS volume retains its original compression state.

➤ *Copying a file between different NTFS volumes*—A file that is copied from one NTFS volume to another NTFS volume inherits the compression state of the target folder.

➤ *Moving a file between different NTFS volumes*—A file that is moved from one NTFS volume to another NTFS volume inherits the compression state of the target folder. This is because Windows 2000 treats a move as a copy, and then a delete.

➤ *Copying or moving a file or folder from an NTFS volume to a FAT volume*—A compressed file or folder that is moved or copied from an NTFS volume to a FAT volume loses its compression state. FAT does not support compression.

➤ *Copying or moving a file or folder from an NTFS volume to a floppy disk*—A compressed file or folder that is moved or copied from an NTFS volume to a floppy disk loses its compression state.

Offline Files and Folders

Windows 2000 Professional allows users to work with network files and programs when they are not connected to the network. Offline Files makes this possible. Using Windows Explorer, users can select network-based files and folders that they want to use offline. The network files are then cached on the local hard disk. Users can continue to use the files and folders as if they were still connected to the network. When the user reconnects to the network, the files and folders are automatically synchronized with those stored on the network.

When the status of the network connection changes, Offline Files notifies the user with an Offline Files icon in the status area. An informational balloon appears to notify the user that the network connection has changed. Users can continue to work with their files and folders as they normally would.

If the user is working offline, she can still browse shared folders and network drives in My Computer and My Network Places. However, she will be able to see only those files and folders that have been configured for offline use. Permissions to the files and folders remain the same as they were when the user was connected to the network.

Any computer that supports Server Message Block (SMB)–based file and print sharing has the capability for offline files and folders. This includes Windows 95/98 and Windows NT 4 systems. Offline files are not supported in Novell NetWare or Windows 2000 running Terminal Services.

A database in the hidden system folder (%systemroot%/CSC) stores information on offline files. The %systemroot%/CSC directory contains all offline files and folders requested for use on the computer. The database in this directory emulates the original network resource. Permissions are retained from the original files. A user must be a member of the Administrators group to view and open files in the CSC directory.

Files are cached to the computer that requests them using either automatic caching or manual caching. Automatic caching does not guarantee that the files will be available offline. They are marked as Temporarily Available Offline and are deleted from the cache if the cache fills up. Files are manually cached when specified by the user to be made available offline. This is done by selecting Make Available Offline on the File menu. Manually cached files and folders are marked as Always Available Offline. Manual caching is the default cache setting in Windows 2000 Professional.

Three conditions must be met for the network share to be available when the network resource comes back online:

➤ No offline files on the network share can be open on the user's computer.

➤ No offline files can have changes that need to be synchronized.

➤ The network connection cannot be a slow link.

Synchronizing Files

Once the user is reconnected to the network, the Synchronization Manager updates network files with any changes that were made while the user was working offline. Synchronization can occur manually or automatically. Several options are available to synchronize files when the network resource becomes available. Files can be synchronized in the following ways:

➤ Automatically at log on

➤ Automatically at log off

➤ Manually at any time

➤ When the computer is idle for a specific amount of time

➤ Automatically at a specific time

Offline Files and Folders on Mobile Computers

Offline files and folders are especially beneficial for use on mobile computers. For information on using offline files on mobile computers, see Chapter 12.

Offline Web Pages

Web pages can be cached for offline use. Windows 2000 Professional includes the Offline Web Page Wizard, which makes it easier to make Web content available offline. To make a Web page available offline, it must be on an Internet shortcut, such as a Web entry in Links or Favorites. This feature is an update of the subscriptions feature in Internet Explorer 4. When choosing to make a Web page available offline, you have two decisions to make. The first decision is whether or not to download linked pages. Many Web pages have multiple linked pages that could affect the amount of time required to update the page. The second decision is to specify a time when the offline Web page will be updated. The default is to update the page when Synchronization is run. Users can also define a specific time to schedule the Web page update.

Shared Folders

Windows 2000 Professional users can share their folders with others on the network. Users can decide who has access to the folders by applying permissions to the folders. Shared folder permissions have several characteristics:

➤ Permissions on shared folders are applied to the folders only, not files or sub-folders within the shared folder.

➤ Shared folders do not restrict access to users who have access to the local computer on which the folder is stored.

➤ Shared folders are the only way to secure network resources on a FAT volume.

➤ By default, the shared folder permission is Full Control to the Everyone group.

Table 6.3 lists the shared folder permissions and what they allow the user to do with the folder.

Table 6.3 Shared folder permissions.

Shared Folder Permission	Permits User To
Full Control	Change permissions, take ownership of files, perform tasks permitted by the Change permission
Change	Create folders, add files to folders, change data in folders, change file attributes, delete files and folders, and perform tasks permitted by the Read permission
Read	Display folder names, file names, file data, and file attributes; change folders within the shared folder

Creating Shared Folders

To share folders in Windows 2000 Professional, users must be a member of the Administrators group or the Power Users group.

Note: If the shared folder resides on an NTFS volume, users must also have Read permission for the folder in order to share it.

To share a folder, take these steps:

1. Log on as a member of the Administrators or Power Users group.

2. Right-click on the folder you want to share, and click on Properties.

3. Enter a share name for the folder in the Share Name box.

4. Enter a description for the share in the Comment box.

5. Select the number of users who can concurrently access the shared folder under User Limit.

6. Assign the appropriate access permissions. By default, the Everyone group has Full Control permission to the shared folder.

7. Select the Cache settings for offline access to the shared folder.

Note: Windows 2000 Professional is limited to 10 concurrent connections.

Combining Shared Folder Permissions and NTFS Permissions

If you share folders on a FAT volume, users are limited to shared folder permissions. If the shared folder is on an NTFS volume, NTFS permissions can be assigned to individuals and groups to control access to the files and subfolders within the shared folders. When combining shared folder permissions and NTFS permissions, the most restrictive permission is the overriding permission.

Several rules apply when using shared folders on an NTFS partition:

➤ NTFS permissions can be applied to files and subfolders within the shared folder. Different NTFS permissions can be applied to each individual file and subfolder within the shared folder.

➤ Users must have NTFS permissions to the files and subfolders within the shared folder. This is in addition to the shared folder permissions.

➤ When combining shared folder permissions and NTFS permissions, the most restrictive permission is the overriding permission.

Administering Shared Folders on Remote Computers

Computer Management is a desktop tool that provides easy access to Windows 2000 administrative tools. It consolidates them into a single console tree that uses a two-pane view, much like Windows Explorer (see Figure 6.12). Computer Management can be used to manage local and remote computers, create and manage shares, and view a list of users connected to a local or remote computer. Shared Folders is accessed through Computer Management. Other administrative tasks are available through the System Tools, Storage, and Services and Applications nodes of the console tree.

Only members of the Administrators group can take full advantage of Computer Management. You must be a member of this group to perform administrative tasks.

The properties of shared folders can be managed through Shared Folders. To open Shared Folders, select Start | Settings | Control Panel. Double-click on Administrative Tools, double-click on Computer Management, and then double-click on Shared Folders. Shared resources are administered through the Shares, Sessions, and Open Files folders.

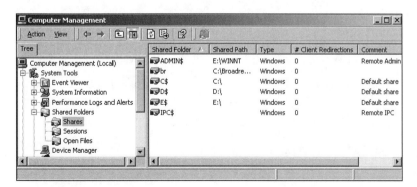

Figure 6.12   Computer Management console.

Shares

The Shares folder is used to create new shares, manage the properties of a shared resource, and change the sharing permissions for a shared resource. The information for Shares is provided in columns. The Shared Folder column lists the available shared folders. The Shared Path column displays the path to the shared folders. The Type column displays the type of network connection (i.e., Windows, NetWare, or Macintosh). The # Sessions column displays the number of users connected to shared folders. The Comment column is used to describe the share.

To create a new share, do the following:

1. Open Shared Folders, and click on Shares in the console tree.

2. Click on Action|New File Share.

3. Enter the name of the folder to share in the Folder To Share box, or click on the Browse button to browse for a folder to share.

4. Enter a share name for the folder in the Share Name box, and click on Next.

5. Select the share permissions for the folder, and click on Finish.

To manage properties of a shared folder, take these steps:

1. Open Shared Folders, and click on Shares in the console tree.

2. Right-click on the shared folder you want to manage properties for, and click on Properties.

3. Make the changes you want on the General or Security tab, and click on OK.

To change permissions for a shared resource:

1. Open Shared Folders, and click on Shares in the console tree.

2. Right-click on the shared folder you want to change permissions for, and click on Properties.

3. On the Security tab, click on the name of the user or group you want to change.

4. In Permissions, click on Allow or Deny for each permission, and then click on OK.

To limit the number of users of a shared folder:

1. Open Shared Folders, and click on Shares in the console tree.

2. Right-click on the shared folder you want to set a user limit for, and click on Properties.

3. Click on the Allow radio button under User Limit.

4. Enter the maximum number of users to be able to connect to the shared folder, and click on OK.

Note: The maximum number of users that can connect to a shared folder in Windows 2000 Professional is 10.

Sessions

Sessions is used to view which users are connected to a shared folder (see Figure 6.13). It is also used to disconnect users from a shared folder. The information for Sessions is provided in columns. The User column lists users who are connected to the shared folders. The Computer column displays the computer name of the user. The Type column displays the type of network connection (Windows, NetWare, or Macintosh). The Open Files column displays the number of files or resources open on this computer by this user. The Connected Time column displays the amount of time in hours and minutes that have elapsed since the start of the session. The Idle Time column displays the amount of time that has elapsed since the last action was initiated by the user. The Guest column displays whether the user is connected as a Guest.

To disconnect a user from a shared folder:

1. Open Shared Folders, and click on Sessions in the console tree.

2. Right-click on the user's name, and then click on Close Session to disconnect the user.

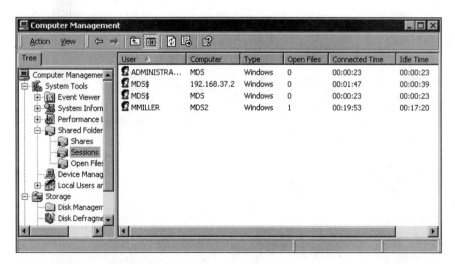

Figure 6.13   Shared Folders Sessions.

To disconnect all users from a shared folder:

1. Open Shared Folders, and click on Sessions in the console tree.

2. Click on Action, and then click on Disconnect All Sessions.

Note: Loss of data may occur when disconnecting users. It's good policy to warn users before disconnecting them.

Open Files

Open Files is used to see which files and resources are open on a share (see Figure 6.14). It is also used to close files that are open. The information for Open Files is provided in columns. The Open File column lists the names of all open files. An open file can be a file, a named pipe, a print job in a print spooler, or a resource of an unrecognized type. The Accessed By column displays the name of the user who opened the file. The Type column displays the type of network connection (i.e., Windows, NetWare, or Macintosh). The # Locks column displays the number of locks on the particular resource. The Open Mode column displays the permission granted when the resource was opened.

Monitoring Access to Shared Folders

Windows 2000 provides several resources to monitor access to shared folders. The Shares folder in the Shared Folders snap-in can be used to view a list of all shared folders on a computer. It also can be used to view how many users are connected to each shared folder. This information is provided in several columns (see Figure 6.15). The Shared Folder column shows all shared folders on the computer. The Shared Path column shows the path to the folder. The Type column tells what type of operating system must be running on the computer that is trying to access the

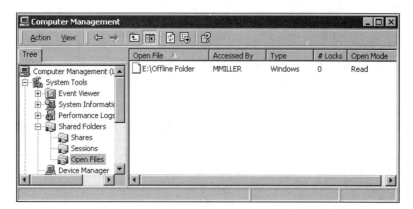

Figure 6.14 Shared Folders Open Files.

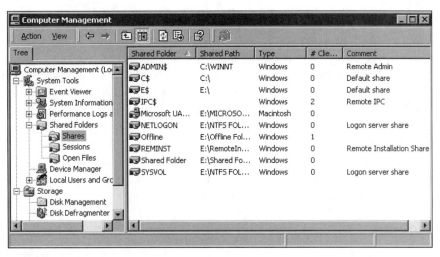

Figure 6.15 The Shared Folder snap-in.

shared folder. The # Client Redirections column lists the number of clients who have made a remote connection to the shared folder. The Comment column is used to provide descriptive text about the shared folder.

Note: The information in the shared folder list is not updated automatically. You must click on Action and Refresh to update the list.

The Shared Folders snap-in can also be used to manage and monitor any Windows 2000 and Windows NT 4 system.

Shared Folders allows you to view summary information of connection and resource use for local and remote computers. With the Shared Folders snap-in, you can create, view, and set permissions for shares as well as view a list of files opened by remote users. You can also view a list of users connected to the shared folders over a network and disconnect one or all of them. The shared folder information is provided in columns. The Shares column provides information about the shared resource on the computer. The Sessions column provides information about every network user currently connected to the computer. The Open Files column provides information about all open files on the computer. Shared Folders replaces the resource-related components in the Server Manager Control Panel tool in Windows NT 4.

Note: Only members of the Administrators and Power Users groups can use Shared Folders on Windows 2000 Professional. Members of the Administrators, Power Users, and Server Operators group can use Shared Folders on Windows 2000 Server.

Using the Shared Folder Snap-In

Windows 2000 provides several resources to monitor access to shared folders. The Shares folder in the Shared Folder snap-in can be used to view a list of all shared folders on a computer. It also can be used to view how many users are connected to each shared folder. This information is provided in several columns (refer to Figure 6.15). The Shared Folder column shows all shared folders on the computer. The Shared Path column shows the path to the folder. The Type column tells what type of operating system must be running on the computer that is trying to access the shared folder. The # Client Redirections column lists the number of clients who have made a remote connection to the shared folder. The Comment column is used to provide descriptive text about the shared folder.

Caching

A new feature that has been introduced in Windows 2000 Professional is the caching of network documents for offline use. This is similar to the Briefcase in Windows 95/98 and Windows NT 4. Caching documents allows users of laptop computers to create a copy of network documents from shared folders onto their local hard drive. Laptop users can modify the documents while not connected, and then these users can resynchronize them when they are reconnected to the network. Three caching schemes are available: manual document caching, automatic document caching, and automatic program caching. Manual document caching requires that users specify the particular files they want to have cached offline for their use. Automatic document caching caches all files that are accessible over the network. Automatic program caching allows users who run applications off a network share to continue using the program even after they have been disconnected from the network. This reduces network traffic because the local cached copy is used even if the user is connected to the network.

To set caching options for a shared folder:

1. Open Shared Folders, and click on Shares in the console tree.

2. Right-click on the shared folder you want to set caching options for, and click on Properties.

3. Click on Caching.

4. Select the Allow Caching Of Files In This Shared Folder checkbox.

5. Select the caching option you want from the Setting drop-down list, and click on OK (see Figure 6.16).

6. Click on OK again to close the shared folder Properties box.

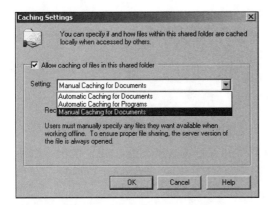

Figure 6.16   The Caching Settings dialog box.

Special Shares

Special shares are shares created by the system. These are in addition to any shared resources created by users and the administrator. Depending on the configuration of the computer being administered, some or all of the following special shares may appear:

➤ *[drive]$*—This share allows administrators to connect to the root directory of a remote computer's storage device (i.e., C$, D$, or E$).

➤ *ADMIN$*—This share is used during remote administration of a computer and is the path to the Windows 2000 system root (i.e., C:\Winnt).

➤ *IPC$*—This share is essential for communication between programs and is used during remote administration and viewing of shared resources.

➤ *PRINT$*—This share is used during remote administration of printers.

➤ *NETLOGON*—This is a resource used by the Net Logon service of Windows 2000 to processes login requests. This resource is only provided for Windows 2000 Server.

Dfs

The Distributed File System (Dfs) can also be used to manage and monitor shared folders. With Dfs, an administrator can create a directory tree consisting of shares located anywhere on the network. Users can transparently access files anywhere on this directory tree and automatically connect to the appropriate server. Dfs eliminates the problems inherent in drive mapping. In drive mapping, each drive being mapped is assigned a specific letter of the alphabet. This limits the number of connections a user can have. Also, users must know which server the drive is on and must create a separate connection to that server. With Dfs, users are not limited in the number of

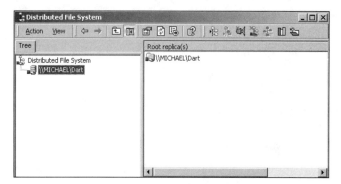

Figure 6.17 Distributed File System dialog box.

connections they can have, and they don't have to track which server the shared resource is located on. Users are able to map a single network drive and connect to all shared resources that the administrator has configured in the Dfs tree.

Dfs is administered through the Distributed File System utility in the Administrative Tools group (see Figure 6.17). Dfs uses a tree structure, which contains root and child nodes. The administrator first creates the root, which can have multiple child nodes beneath it. Each child node points to a shared folder. There are two types of Dfs: standalone Dfs and fault-tolerant Dfs. Standalone Dfs stores the Dfs topology on a single computer. It provides no fault tolerance if the computer that holds the shared folder fails. Fault-tolerant Dfs stores the Dfs topology in Active Directory. In this topology, the child nodes point to multiple identical shared folders. A duplicate copy of the information in the original shared folder is replicated to another shared folder. This replication can be done manually or automatically.

Note: Dfs consists of both a server and a client-based component. Only computers with the Dfs client software can gain access to Dfs resources. Both Windows NT 4 and Windows 98 have a Dfs client. A Windows 95 client is available, but it must be downloaded.

Searching

Windows 2000 Professional provides several ways for users to search for files and folders. Searching can be executed from the Start menu, Windows Explorer, My Computer, My Network Places, or My Documents. No matter where the search is executed, users are provided with access to the Search Assistant, History folder, and Indexing Service (see Figure 6.18).

Searching for Files and Folders

The Search Assistant provides a universal way for users to perform searches. The Search Assistant is integrated into Windows Explorer. Files and folders can be

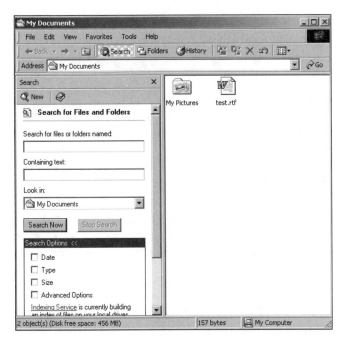

Figure 6.18   The Search pane.

searched by name, by location, by date, by type, by size, and other advanced options. Users can search for files and folders in any of the following ways:

➤ Select Start | Search | For Files Or Folders.

➤ From Windows Explorer, click on the Search button on the toolbar. Enter the files or folders to search for in the Search For Files Or Folders Named text box.

➤ Double-click on My Computer, My Documents, or My Network Places. Click on the Search button on the toolbar. Repeat the search entry process.

Searching for Network Resources

If the Windows 2000 Professional computer is a member of an Active Directory domain, users can search for computers, shared files and folders, and printers. Users can also search the Internet for Web pages.

Indexing Service

Indexing Service creates a database of keywords found in each file on the computer. When a user searches the computer for keywords, the operating system displays any matches it finds. Indexing Service can be used on Windows 2000 Professional, but it is not activated by default. To enable content indexing, users can click on the Indexing Service link under Search Options. The Indexing Service can also work with Active Directory to provide system-wide searching, including Web pages.

Once an index is created, users can query the database for keywords, phrases, or properties. Indexing Services indexes HTML, text, and Microsoft Office 95 or later documents. It can also index Internet mail and news.

Chapter Summary

Windows 2000 Professional provides several methods to make accessing user files and folders easier. The My Documents folder is the default storage location for files. Windows Explorer opens to the My Documents folder by default. An icon is created on the desktop for the My Documents folder to make accessing the folder easier. My Documents is also the default location for Open and Save As commands. The My Pictures folder is the default storage location for images. The My Pictures folder is a subfolder under the My Documents folder and is used as a centralized storage folder for images from digital devices and scanners. Images in the My Pictures folder can be viewed from Windows Explorer without having to open the file.

My Network Places replaces Network Neighborhood from previous versions of Windows. Three icons are displayed in My Network Places: Add Network Place, Entire Network, and Computers Near Me. Unlike previous versions of Windows NT, network resources aren't shown by default in My Network Places. The Add Network Place Wizard is used to create a shortcut to network resources. Users must double-click on Entire Network to see all available network resources. Computers in the user's workgroup or domain can be accessed with the Computers Near Me icon.

The History folder tracks documents that users have previously opened. Items in the History folder can be viewed by Date, by Site, by Most Visited, or by Order Visited Today.

AutoComplete caches previously typed information and displays entries similar to those typed by a user. AutoComplete can be used to complete forms and URLs.

Windows 2000 Professional provides two ways to customize folders. Users can select Tools under the Folders Options menu selection, or they can use the Customize This Folder Wizard. Users can view their folders as Web pages or enable Active Desktop for integration with IE 5. Folders can be customized to open in the same or separate windows. An extensive list of options is available to allow the users to determine how they want to view their files and folders.

Windows 2000 Professional supports NTFS file and folder permissions. In situations where file and folder permissions don't provide the level of access control that users want, users can apply NTFS special access permissions. There are 14 special access permissions. The two most used are Change Permissions and Take Ownership.

NTFS uses Access Control Lists to determine who has access to files and folders. An ACL is stored with every file and folder on an NTFS partition. The ACL contains a list of all user and group accounts and what resources they have access to.

Permissions of parent folders are inherited by default by subfolders and files within the folder. This includes all new files or folders created under the folder. Permissions can be prevented from being inherited from parent folders.

Windows 2000 Professional supports file and folder compression. Files are compressed with Windows Explorer or with the command-line utility, compact. Compressed files can be read by any Microsoft Windows-based application without being uncompressed first. When a compressed file is opened, NTFS uncompresses the file for use. It recompresses when the file is closed. Identifying compressed files can be made easier in Windows Explorer by displaying them in an alternate color.

6

Offline files allow users to work on network-based files when they are not connected to the network. Files are synchronized when the user reconnects to the network. Users can still browse shared folders and network drivers in My Computer and My Network Places. Permissions for offline files and folders are the same for offline use as they are on the network. Web pages can be cached for offline use. All images associated with the Web paged are also cached for viewing.

Windows 2000 Professional users can share their folders with others on the network. Permissions are applied to the folders only, not files and subfolders. Shared folders do not restrict access to only those users who have access to the computer the folders are located on. Shared folders are the only way to secure network resources on a FAT volume. The Shared Folders snap-in is used to monitor shared folders. Shared Folders is accessed through Computer Management.

Several special shares are created by the operating system. The {drive}$ share is used by administrators to connect to the root of the computers hard drive. The Admin$ share is used to remotely administer a computer. The Print$ share is used for remote administration of printers. The Netlogon share is used by the Net Logon service of the operating system to process logon requests.

Distributed File System can be used to monitor and manage shared folders. Using Dfs, administrators can create a directory tree of shares located anywhere on the network.

The Search Assistant is used to search for files and folders in Windows 2000 Professional. If the computer is a member of an Active Directory domain, users can also search for people, computers, shared files, and printers.

Indexing Service creates a database of keywords that users can search the computer for. The Indexing Service can be used by Windows 2000 Professional, but it isn't enabled by default.

Review Questions

1. In which folder are Documents stored by default?

   a. My Documents

   b. My Pictures

   c. My Network Neighborhood

   d. My Network Places

2. Shared folders can be located on what types of partitions?

   a. FAT

   b. NTFS

   c. Both FAT and NTFS

   d. Neither FAT nor NTFS

3. Which folder is the default location where images are stored?

   a. My Documents

   b. My Pictures

   c. History

   d. My Computer

4. What is Indexing Service used to do?

   a. Return a list of all documents that meet specific search criteria

   b. Search for files on the Internet

   c. Apply permissions to files and folder

   d. Keep track of users' favorite files and folders

5. What does ACL stands for?

   a. Access Control List

   b. Active Control List

   c. Advanced Control List

   d. Administrator Control List

6. What does Dfs stands for?

   a. Distributed File System

   b. Domain File System

   c. Dynamic File Servers

   d. Dynamic File Security

7. Shared folder permissions are sufficient to gain access to files and folders on an NTFS volume. True or false?

    a. True

    b. False

8. What happens to a compressed file when it is copied from an NTFS volume to a FAT volume?

    a. The file loses its compressed state.

    b. The file keeps its compressed state.

    c. The file is encrypted.

    d. The file is encrypted and compressed.

9. What happens to a compressed file when it is moved from an NTFS volume to another NTFS volume?

    a. The file loses its compressed state.

    b. The file keeps its compressed state.

    c. The file is encrypted.

    d. The file is encrypted and compressed.

10. Files can be both compressed and encrypted. True or false?

    a. True

    b. False

11. Which groups can administer shared folders? [Check all correct answers]

    a. Administrators

    b. Server Operators

    c. Power Users

    d. Guest

12. For which of the following is caching used?

    a. Making network documents available for offline viewing

    b. Storing most recently used documents

    c. Creating a database of keywords to search

    d. Synchronizing files and folders

13. The Shared Folders snap-in can be used to do which of the following? [Check all correct answers]

    a. View a list of all shared folders

    b. View how many users are connected to each shared folder

    c. Apply permissions to shared folders

    d. Allow users to take ownership of shared folders

14. The History folder tracks all documents that the user opens. True or false?

    a. True

    b. False

15. How can files be synchronized? [Check all correct answers]

    a. Automatically at log in

    b. Automatically at log off

    c. Manually at any time

    d. When the computer is idle

Real-World Projects

For these projects, you need a computer running Windows 2000 Professional and a hard disk with at least one NTFS partition.

Project 6.1

To create a folder on an NTFS partition and assign it NTFS permissions:

1. Log on as Administrator.

2. Open My Computer.

3. Open your NTFS volume.

4. Select File | New | Folder.

5. Name the new folder "NTFS Folder".

6. Right-click on the folder.

7. Click on Properties.

8. Select the Security tab on the Properties dialog box.

9. Click on Add, and select the users or groups that you want to have access to the folder. Click on Add.

10. Repeat Steps 6 through 9 for each user or group you want to add.

11. Click on OK.

12. Select the user or group under Name.

13. Select the Allow checkbox or the Deny checkbox next to the appropriate permissions.

14. Click on Apply, and then click on OK.

Project 6.2

To log on as a different user and take ownership of a file:

1. Log on as Administrator.

2. Open My Computer.

3. Open your NTFS volume.

4. Right-click on a file in the NTFS volume, and select Properties.

5. Click on the Security tab.

6. Under Name, click on the user that you want to give ownership to.

7. Click on the Advanced button.

8. Select the user under Permissions Entries, and click on View/Edit.

9. Select the Allow checkbox next to Take Ownership, and click on OK.

10. Click on Apply, and then click on OK.

11. Click on OK again to close the Properties dialog box for the file.

12. Log off as Administrator and log on as the user.

13. Open My Computer.

14. Open your NTFS volume.

15. Right-click on a file in the NTFS volume, and select Properties.

16. Click on the Security tab.

17. Click on the Advanced button.

18. Click on the Owner tab.

19. Highlight the user in the Change Owner To box, and click on Apply.

20. Click on OK.

21. Click on OK again to close the Properties dialog box.

Project 6.3

To create a shared folder on a FAT partition and limit the number of users that can access the folder to three:

1. Log on as Administrator.

2. Open My Computer.

3. Open your FAT volume.

4. Right-click on a folder on the FAT volume, and select Properties.

5. Click on Sharing.

6. Click on the Share This Folder button.

7. Type a name for the shared folder in the Share name box.

8. Click on the Allow button under User Limit.

9. Type "3" in the Users box.

10. Click on Apply, and then click on OK.

Project 6.4

To create a shared folder on an NTFS partition and set caching options for offline viewing of the folder:

1. Log on as Administrator.

2. Open My Computer.

3. Open your NTFS volume.

4. Right-click on a folder on the NTFS volume, and select Properties.

5. Click on the Sharing tab.

6. Click on the Share This Folder button.

7. Type a name for the shared folder in the Share name box.

8. Click on the Caching button.

9. Select the Allow Caching Of Files In This Shared Folder checkbox.

10. Select Automatic or manual caching from the Setting box.

11. Click on OK.

12. Click on Apply, and then click on OK.

CHAPTER SEVEN

Printing

After completing this chapter, you will be able to:

✓ Understand the Windows 2000 printing process

✓ Install and configure Windows 2000 printers

✓ Monitor and manage print jobs

✓ Enforce printer access through permissions

✓ Understand and install advanced printing configurations

✓ Troubleshoot common printing issues

Printing, in addition to file sharing, is the most commonly used network application. For years, people have been exhorting the coming of the paper-less office, however, many of us realize that it is merely a myth. Thanks to low-cost laser printers, printing and overall paper use is higher than ever. Windows 2000 supplies an easily implemented printing solution that supports a variety of clients, including Windows NT 4/3.51, Windows 95/98, Windows for Workgroups, MS-DOS, Macintosh, Unix, and Novell NetWare.

Printing Overview

Windows 2000 is an excellent printing platform, both locally and across the net-work. By combining a variety of software and hardware components, Windows 2000 provides a robust and versatile printing environment. It also provides support for almost all printers on the market. Although it may appear to be overly complex, in reality, printing in Windows 2000 is extremely easy to install and configure.

Let's first go over some of the terms you will see mentioned throughout this chapter:

➤ *Local Printer*—A printer that is attached to the local computer.

➤ *Network Printer*—A printer that is directly attached to the network.

➤ *Print Device*—The physical hardware device used for printing.

➤ *Print Driver*—A software component that enables applications to communicate properly with the associated print device.

➤ *Print Jobs*—The file that is created by the application to be sent to the print device. The print job contains the information (i.e., printer commands and data) for the print device to create a finished printed sheet.

➤ *Print Queue*—The list of print jobs waiting to be sent to a print device. As print jobs are sent to a print device, the print server queues the jobs. After a job is completed, the next job in the queue is sent to the print device.

➤ *Print Server*—The computer that hosts one or more print devices. The print server holds the spool files for the printer and manages the print queue.

➤ *Print Spooler*—The software component that receives, stores, and distributes print jobs. The Print Spooler places print jobs in the print queue. When the print device is available, the Print Spooler sends the next print job to the print device. In the Windows 2000 Printing Process, there are actually two spoolers: The Client-side Spooler and the Server-Side spooler. These two components interact to make network printing possible.

➤ *Printer*—The most commonly mistaken term in the Windows 2000 printing process. A printer represents the software interface between the print device and the clients, not the actual physical printer (the print device).

The Windows 2000 Printing Process

To the unfamiliar eye, the printing process may appear as black magic. The Windows 2000 printing process, however, (see Figure 7.1) is a powerful and flexible operation. The following section reviews the general architecture of the process and defines

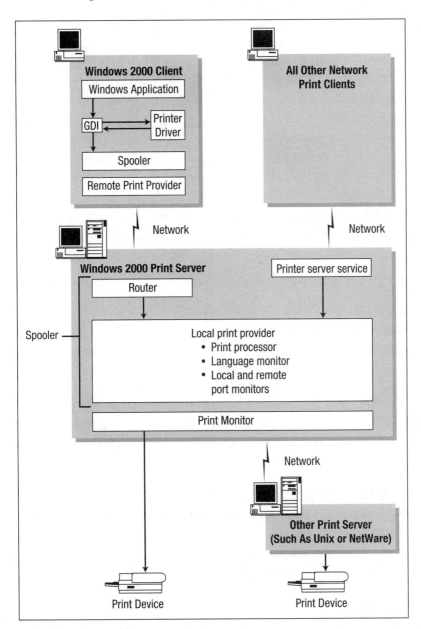

Figure 7.1   The Windows 2000 printing process.

the various components involved. Although a user does not need to know this much detail about the process, an administrator familiar with it will be better prepared to troubleshoot printing issues.

The printing process begins when the user chooses to print a document at a client workstation. The application on the client calls the graphical device interface (GDI), which in turn calls the print driver for the selected print device. After obtaining device dependent information from the print driver, the GDI renders the print job using the print device's supported printer language. Once complete, the application calls either the *client-side spooler* (WINSPOOL.DRV) if the printer is local or the *server-side spooler* (SPOOLSV.EXE) if the printer is a network printer.

For local printers, the client-side spooler contacts the server-side spooler (SPOOLSV.EXE) via remote procedure calls (RPC). The server-side spooler makes an application programming interface (API) call to the *print router* (SPOOLSS.DLL). The print router then sends the print job to the *local print provider* (LOCALSPL.DLL).

For network printers, the print router examines the *remote print providers* to see if they are available. The remote print provider (WIN32SPL.DLL) creates an RPC connection to the server-side spooler located on the print server. The print server's server-side spooler then sends the print job to the local print provider.

The local print provider contacts two of its subcomponents, the print processor and the separator page processor. The print processor alters the print job according to the document's data type. If needed, the separator page processor adds separator pages. A separator page is more commonly known as a banner page, which includes information about who printed the job and when. Separator pages can also be used to have the print provider switch languages between jobs (such as from PCL to PostScript). The local print provider then writes the job to a spool file and keeps track of the job.

The local print provider sends the print job to the *port monitor*. The port monitor's job is to communicate with the print device. When the print device is available, the port monitor sends the print job.

Graphics Device Interface (GDI)

The GDI controls how objects are graphically represented. This includes the video display as well as printing. In printing, the GDI contacts the print driver of the selected printer to determine the fully qualified path name of the printer and the appropriate printer language to use.

Print Drivers

The print driver is a software component that acts as a translator between the GDI and the print device. The print driver understands the language of the print device, allowing computer commands to be translated into printer-specific commands.

Because it is a translator, multiple drivers need to be installed if multiple print devices or operating systems are used. Windows 2000 does ship with three generic drivers that provide basic functionality for most print devices:

➤ *HPGL/2 Plotter Driver*—This print driver is used for plotters that support the HPGL/2 plotter language.

➤ *PostScript Printer Driver*—This print driver supports Adobe v4.3 PostScript printer description (PPD) files.

➤ *Universal Printer Driver (Unidriver)*—This print driver supports most printers.

Print Spooler

The print spooler is actually a group of components that work together to provide spooling services. There is a client-side spooler (WINSPOOL.DRV) if the printer is local or a server-side spooler (SPOOLSV.EXE) if the printer is a network printer.

Print Router

The print router takes the print job from the GDI and locates an available print provider that can handle the print job. Once the print provider is located, the print router sends the job to the local print provider (for local printing) or to a remote print provider (for network printing).

Remote Print Providers

It's important to remember that the remote print provider is located on the client-side spooler. This is called the remote print provider because its function is to relay the print job to the local print provider on the remote print server.

Local Print Providers

The local print provider does most of the work in the spooler. It receives the print job, writes it to a spool file, and keeps track of the file. The local print provider also contains two subcomponents, the print processor and the separator page processor.

Port Monitors

Windows 2000 includes a number of port monitors to enable printing in various network environments:

➤ *AppleTalk Port Monitor*—This port monitor allows you to view and manage queues on AppleTalk (i.e., Macintosh) networks.

➤ *Local Port Monitor*—This is the preferred local port monitor in Windows 2000. This port monitor is used when the print device is attached to the LPT or COM port.

➤ *NetWare Port Monitor*—This port monitor enables you to view and manage NetWare queues.

➤ *Standard TCP/IP Port Monitor (SPM)*—This is the preferred network port monitor in Windows 2000. It uses the Simple Network Management Protocol (SNMP) to configure and monitor printer ports.

Print Job Formats

Print jobs can be created in a variety of formats, depending on the environment being used:

➤ *Enhanced Metafile (EMF)*—The default print job format in Windows 2000. This print job format is generated by the GDI. Once the print job is sent to the spooler, control of the application is returned to the user.

➤ *PSCRIPT1*—The print job format used by Macintosh printers using Level 1 monochrome PostScript printing. The print job is translated into a bitmap by the spooler, allowing the print job to be printed on non-PostScript print devices.

➤ *RAW*—For non-Windows 2000 clients, such as Windows NT 4 and Windows 95, RAW is the default print job format. The RAW format is created by the print driver.

➤ *RAW (FF Appended)*—The same format as RAW, with the exception that a form feed (FF) has been appended to the job. This may be necessary with a print device that doesn't print the last page of the print job.

➤ *RAW (FF Auto)*—The same format as RAW, but the spooler checks the print job for a form feed. If no form feed is present, the spooler automatically adds it.

➤ *Text*—This print job only contains ASCII text. The print job is printed using the print device's default font.

The Printers Folder

The Printers Folder is where all activities relating to printing in Windows 2000 can be found. In this folder, a user can add a printer via the Add Printer Wizard or modify the properties of printers already installed. To call the Printers Folder a "folder" is really a misnomer. Actually, it should be called the Printers Control Panel. Besides adding and modifying printers, the Printers Folder also controls the print server properties for the computer.

As with almost anything else in Windows 2000, you can open the Printers Folder in a variety of ways. To find the Printers Folder, select Start | Settings | Printers, or follow these steps:

1. Double-click on the My Computer icon on the Desktop.

2. Double-click on the Control Panel icon.

3. In the Control Panel, find the Printers applet, and double-click on it.

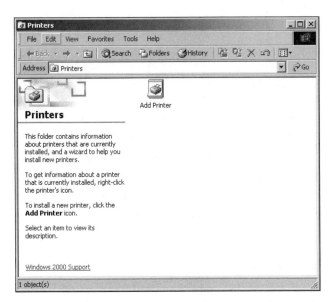

Figure 7.2   The Printers Folder.

After the initial install of Windows 2000 Professional, the Printers Folder contains only the Add Printer applet (see Figure 7.2), which starts the Add Printer Wizard. The Add Printer Wizard is used to install local printers or attach to existing network printers. The printer can then be managed or shared at that point.

Installing Printers

There are several ways to install printers in Windows 2000 Professional. Depending on the situation, one of the following methods may be used.

Plug and Play

One of the easiest and most convenient methods of installing a printer in Windows 2000 is by using Plug and Play.

The Plug and Play specification allows a computer to automatically detect and configure components that have been added. This specification also includes printers, where Plug and Play automatically adds the printer and installs the appropriate printer drivers. It's important to remember that Plug and Play works only for printers directly attached to the computer (i.e., a local printer). It will not work for network printers.

Plug and Play is extremely easy to use. Simply plug the printer into the computer. Plug and Play begins to initialize the printer and to install the printer drivers. It also allocates any needed resources. Amazingly, no reboot is necessary! All Plug and Play compatible printers use Institute of Electrical and Electronic Engineers (IEEE) 1394 cables, Universal Serial Bus (USB) cables, or Infrared Data Association (IrDA).

Although Plug and Play works 99 percent of the time, in a few situations it will not work. Usually this occurs because the printer itself is older and doesn't support the Plug and Play specification.

If the printer isn't automatically installed after being connected, Plug and Play can be started manually by forcing Windows 2000 to look for new hardware using the Add Hardware Wizard or by restarting Windows 2000 (the operating system looks for new hardware at boot up). Another possibility is to use the Add Printer Wizard. If any of these methods detects the printer, Plug and Play finishes the installation.

Another possible installation problem may be the lack of a printer driver. Although Windows 2000 ships with drivers for many popular printers, the print driver for the printer being installed may not be included. In this case, the user needs to supply the print driver when prompted.

Using the Add Printer Wizard

In all situations, the Add Printer Wizard can be employed to install local printers, even after Plug and Play has failed to install the printer. When a local printer is installed via the Add Printer Wizard, a logical printer is created that connects to the physical print device.

To start the Add Printer Wizard, simply double-click on the Add Printer icon in the Printers Folder. You are then prompted for configuration information relating to the printer, such as the following:

➤ Select the port that the printer is attached to.

➤ Select the manufacturer and model of the printer.

➤ Enter a name for the printer.

➤ Whether the printer should be the default printer for the workstation.

➤ Whether or not the printer should be shared.

➤ Supply the share name.

➤ Optionally supply location and description information for the printer (which may help users identify the printer).

➤ Print a test page to verify proper installation of the printer.

Once complete, the new logical printer will have an icon in the Printers Folder (see Figure 7.3). Applications will now be able to utilize the printer, unless of course the application itself has special needs.

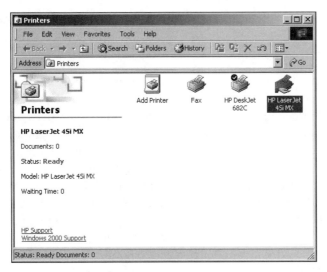

Figure 7.3   A new printer in the Printers Folder.

Using Windows Update

Windows 2000 comes with a dandy new feature that takes a lot of the headache out of searching for new drivers. This new feature is called Windows Update. Windows Update is an online extension of Windows 2000 (see Figure 7.4). Windows Update

Figure 7.4   Windows Update.

contains a list of fixes, enhancements, and updates to the Windows 2000 operating system. If you need a printer driver that wasn't shipped with Windows 2000, you can try Windows Update to see if the driver has been added.

Because Windows Update is an online extension, Internet connectivity via analog modem, cable modem, or Digital Subscriber Line (DSL) is required. Additionally, as always, you must be either an administrator or a user with administrative permissions to update system files and drivers. Windows Update can be started by selecting Start | Windows Update. When connected, Windows Update scans your computer to determine which components have been installed and then presents a list of components that were updated or can be added. There are different categories of components: Critical Updates, Picks of the Month, Recommended Updates, Additional Windows Features, and Device Drivers. In the case of printers, view the Device Drivers category and see if your printer has been added. If listed, select the printer driver. You can then decide on which other components to install. Windows Update then downloads the selected components and automatically installs them.

Note: Windows Update does not send any scanned information back to Microsoft. It is only used to determine what is necessary to keep your computer up-to-date.

Installing Network Printers

The real power in networking is the capability to share network resources with other users. A printer is one such commonly shared resource. Installing network printers in Windows 2000 can be accomplished in a number of ways. Some of these are familiar and are the same as those in Windows NT and Windows 95/98. Some features are new to Windows 2000.

Using the Add Printer Wizard

You can use the Add Printer Wizard in the same way as you added a local printer. The only difference is when asked whether to install a local printer or a network printer, select network printer. You will then be given three choices to locate a network printer:

➤ Find a printer using Active Directory.

➤ Enter the printer's Universal Naming Convention (UNC) name, or click on Next to browse.

➤ Enter the printer's Uniform Resource Locator (URL) to connect to a printer via the Internet or an intranet.

Using Point and Print

Point and Print is a great feature that can be used on network printers. It significantly simplifies the network printer installation for users, much as Plug and Play does for local printers. This in turn reduces the administrative overhead required in configuring and maintaining printers.

Point and Print allows users to install a printer from across a network. Users simply "point" to a print server and select the printer they would like to install. The print server sends important configuration information to the workstation, including

➤ The print drivers

➤ The location of the print drivers (i.e., the server where they are stored)

➤ The printer model

To install a printer using Point and Print, follow these steps:

1. Find the print server where the printer is located using Find, My Network Places, entering its UNC in the Run dialog box or the Add Printer Wizard.

2. Double-click on the server, then double-click on the server's Printers Folder.

3. Right-click on the desired printer, then click on Connect.

Internet Printers

Another exciting feature found in Windows 2000 is the ability to print to a URL over an intranet or the Internet. This is possible via the use of the Internet Printing Protocol (IPP), defined in a set of RFCs (2565, 2566, 2567, 2568, and 2569).

IPP may someday replace the fax machine and email when its ease of use is considered. Rather than sending a fax via long distance or sending an email with an attachment, a user can simply use a Web browser to view the print server to which the recipient's printer is attached. From the list of printers displayed, the user selects the appropriate printer and prints the document. The user doesn't need to worry about long distance costs or whether the recipient received and opened the email.

On the print server, IPP requires either Peer Web Services for Windows 2000 Professional or Internet Information Server (IIS) for Windows 2000 Server to be installed. Jobs are submitted using IPP 1.0 as the protocol, which controls job configuration information (job name, paper tray, duplexing, notification, and so on). The Hypertext Transfer Protocol (HTTP) transmits the print job from the client to the print server.

With IPP, the user's Web browser provides the necessary interface (via Active Server Pages) to view printer status, perform installation and configuration, print job status, and print job submission (see Figure 7.5).

Installing an Internet printer is much like installing a local printer, except that the port that the printer is attached to is an IP address or URL. To applications, the Internet printer appears the same as a local printer (see Figure 7.6).

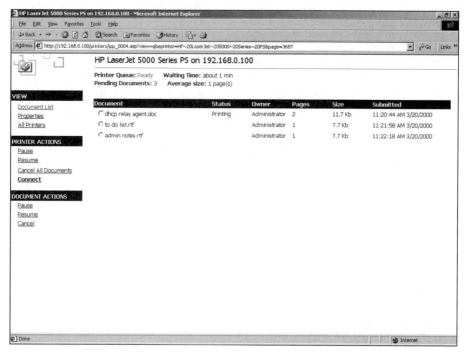

Figure 7.5 The status screen of an Internet printer.

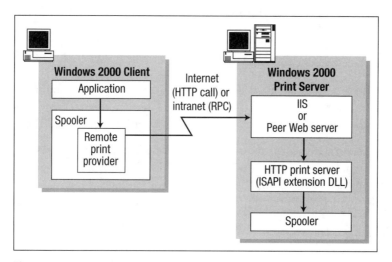

Figure 7.6 Internet printing process.

To install an Internet printer, follow these steps:

1. Open Internet Explorer.

2. In the Address box, type the print server's URL or IP address, and press Enter.

3. Select the printer you want to print to and click on Connect (see Figure 7.7).

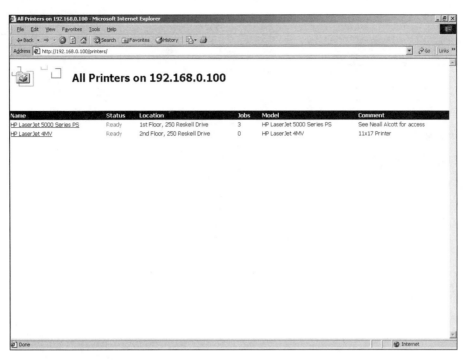

Figure 7.7   Connecting to an Internet printer.

After the Internet printer is installed, it will appear in the Printers Folder like any other installed printer.

Configuring Printers

Once a printer has been installed, an icon representing the logical printer appears in the Printers Folder. Further configuration of printer settings (ports settings, device settings, and so on) can be accomplished via the printer's Properties dialog box. Several methods are available to access the Properties dialog box, but the most common method is to open the Printers Folder, right-click on the printer, and select Properties.

The General Tab

The General tab is shown in Figure 7.8. This tab displays basic information about the installed printer, such as the printer model and what features it supports. It also allows you to do the following:

➤ Specify the name of the printer.

➤ Specify the location of the printer (e.g., 1st Floor, Bldg. 110).

➤ Add any additional comments (e.g., Call Neall Alcott @ x5555 for assistance).

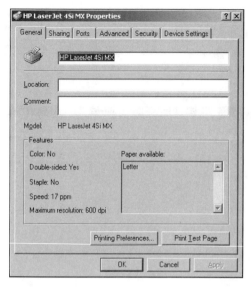

Figure 7.8 The General tab.

➤ Set any Printing Preferences.

➤ Print a test page.

Printing Preferences

Printing Preferences allows a user to specify print settings that will be maintained across different documents. This determines the default print job settings, although they can be overridden by using the Print dialog box.

The Printing Preferences dialog box is activated by clicking on the Printing Preferences button on the General tab or by right-clicking on the printer in the Printers Folder and selecting Printing Preferences. This dialog box consists of two tabs, Layout and Paper/Quality. An Advanced button may also be available, if the printer supports advanced features as described here:

➤ The Layout page allows you to specify the orientation (portrait or landscape) of the page as well as the ordering of pages when printed (front to back/back to front).

➤ Pages per Sheet allows you to print multiple pages of a document to a single piece of paper.

➤ The Paper/Quality page can be used to specify information, such as the default paper tray, print quality (Draft/Normal/Best), and whether to print in color or black and white.

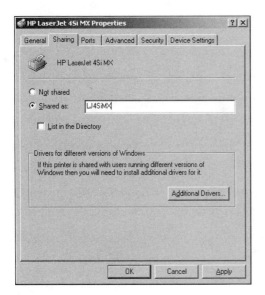

Figure 7.9   The Sharing tab.

The Sharing Tab

The Sharing tab is used to designate whether the printer will be shared with other users on the network (see Figure 7.9).

By default, a printer is not shared. To share a printer, select the Shared As radio button and enter the printer's share name. The share name is limited to 80 characters, so a very descriptive name can be entered. In practice however, the name should be kept to a smaller standard, especially if older clients such as Windows 3.x and MS-DOS are in the environment. These clients cannot see names longer than eight characters with a three-character extension (for example, printer.pcl); you'll need to make sure that the old MS-DOS 8.3 naming convention is used.

Additional print drivers can be added for other operating systems, such as Windows NT 3.51/4 and Windows 95/98.

The Ports Tab

The Ports tab, shown in Figure 7.10, is used to configure printer ports on the local machine. On this tab, you can:

➤ Select the port or ports the printer will print to

➤ Add, delete, and configure local ports

➤ Enable bi-directional support

➤ Enable print pooling

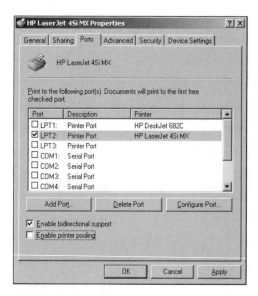

Figure 7.10 The Ports tab.

Printer pooling is an advanced concept and will be discussed in "Printer Pooling" later in this chapter.

The Advanced Tab

Under the Advanced tab (see Figure 7.11), features such as scheduling, priorities, and spooler settings can be found.

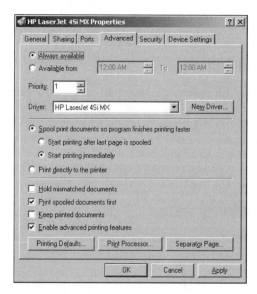

Figure 7.11 The Advanced tab.

Scheduling

Scheduling allows an administrator to specify when a printer is available for use. This feature may be useful if an organization wants to limit printer use to standard business hours or if the printer is maintained during certain hours. If any print jobs are sent to the printer when the printer is unavailable, the jobs will sit in the spooler until the printer becomes available again.

This feature is also beneficial when used to manage large print jobs. In this case, an administrator can create two logical printers both pointing to the same print device. The first logical printer is used for regular print jobs and is always available. The second logical printer is used for large print jobs and is available only after business hours. Users are instructed to send all large print jobs to the second logical printer. This way, large print jobs won't overburden the print device during normal work hours when other users are printing regular print jobs.

The administrator can specify that the printer is always available or that the printer is only available within a specified time frame.

7

Priorities

Priorities can be defined per logical printer. If multiple logical printers point to the same physical print device, priorities can determine which logical printer will print first. Priorities can range in descending order from 99 through 1, with 99 having the highest priority.

As an example, a printer may be used by two groups of employees: supervisors and workers. The supervisors may want their print jobs to print sooner, so they have the administrator set the priority for their logical printers to 99. Because the default priority is 1, the worker's logical printers don't need to be modified. When one of the supervisors prints, her print job will be processed first because supervisors have a higher print priority. The workers' print jobs remain in the spooler until the print device is finished printing the supervisor's job.

Spooler Settings

Spooler settings determine if and how the spooler should be employed. Using the spooler allows a document to be printed in the background. This is accomplished by first storing the print job on the hard drive after which it is sent to the print device.

Select Spool Print Documents So Program Finishes Printing Faster to enable spooling. When this option is selected, you can have the spooler wait until after the last page is spooled before printing or have printing begin immediately.

Select Print Directly To The Printer to disable spooling and have the print job sent immediately to the print device.

When spooling is enabled, a number of additional options are available, such as:

➤ If a user sends a print job that needs a different type of paper than the one loaded into the print device, the print device stops printing all jobs until the requested paper is installed. To make printing more efficient, the print processor can check the print job's destination print device to see if its settings match the settings needed by the print job. If there is a mismatch, the spooler holds mismatched documents until all other documents have been printed.

➤ By selecting Print Spooled Documents First, the spooler prints jobs that have completed spooling. Incomplete jobs, even those with a higher priority, will be printed after the complete jobs.

➤ The user can specify that the spooler not delete print jobs from the queue after they are printed. This allows the job to be printed again via the queue and not from the application.

The Security Tab

The Security tab controls the access control list (ACL) for the printer (see Figure 7.12). This tab provides access to the list of users or groups permitted to use the printer as well as the type of access they have been granted.

There are three different rights that can be granted to a user:

➤ *Manage Documents*—The user can change the properties of a job, manipulate jobs in the queue, and change printing defaults.

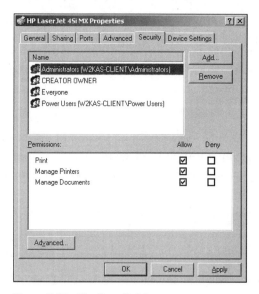

Figure 7.12 The Security tab.

➤ *Manage Printers*—The user can administer the printer including printing defaults, creating a printer share, modifying printer properties, and deleting a printer.

➤ *Print*—The user can submit print jobs to the printer and view the list of print jobs in the queue.

Advanced Security

By clicking on the Advanced button, more security options can be viewed or modified, such as special permissions, auditing, and ownership.

The Permissions tab gives a more granular view of the ACL, displaying the type of access granted, the user to whom it is granted, the right granted, and where the permissions are applied (see Figure 7.13).

To view which permissions are granted for the Print, Manage Printers, and Manage Documents rights, select a user with that right and click on View/Edit (see Figure 7.14). You can also add or remove users from the ACL from this dialog box.

The Auditing tab controls which events are audited for a specific printer object. Auditing is useful in tracking the printer's usage. This dialog box allows you to specify which types of access should be audited for which groups (see Figure 7.15). Auditing can be set to take place if the object is successfully or unsuccessfully accessed.

Events that have been audited can be viewed with the Event Viewer.

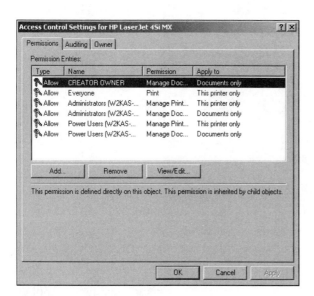

Figure 7.13 The Permissions tab.

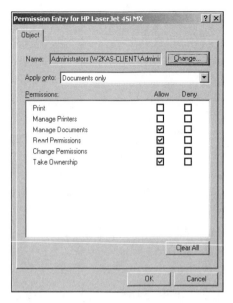

Figure 7.14 Viewing a user's permissions entry.

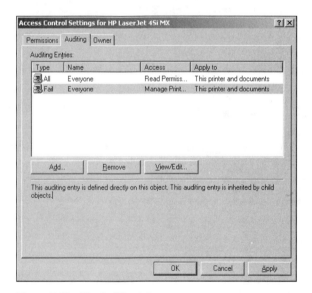

Figure 7.15 The Auditing tab.

The Owner tab displays which user is the current owner of the printer object (see Figure 7.16). If you have Take Ownership permission, you can take ownership of the object by selecting your user or group account and clicking on Apply or OK. A common situation in which ownership needs to be taken is where the previous owner's account has been deleted and the current administrator does not have the proper rights to this object. Because an administrator has the Take Ownership right, the administrator can take ownership of the object and grant himself access.

Figure 7.16   Viewing and modifying ownership.

The Device Settings Tab

The Device Settings tab, displayed in Figure 7.17, allows you to specify and configure device-specific settings for the print device. This includes items such as paper
tray selection, printer resolution, font cartridges, and so on.

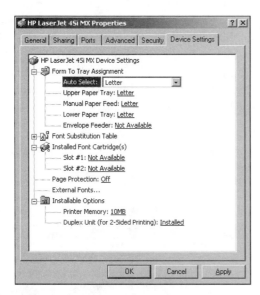

Figure 7.17   The Device Settings tab.

Monitoring and Managing Print Jobs

After the printer has been installed and configured, you will need to monitor and manage print jobs that have been sent to the queue. The following sections explain the features that help you to do so.

The Print Queue Window

The Print Queue window displays a list of print jobs that are waiting to be printed (see Figure 7.18). Each print job in the list will include information such as:

➤ *Document Name*—The name of the document.

➤ *Owner*—The user who sent the document to the printer.

➤ *Pages*—The number of printed pages and the total number of pages in the document.

➤ *Port*—The printer port being used.

➤ *Size*—Document size in kilobytes.

➤ *Status*—The current status (Spooling, Paused, or Printing) of the document.

➤ *Submitted*—The time and date that the document was sent to the printer.

Besides simply providing a list of print jobs, the Print Queue window allows a user or administrator to manage the print jobs in the queue. A regular user, by default, is given only the Print right. This allows the user to submit his or her print jobs and modify the printing preferences for those jobs only. Administrators, on the other hand, are granted the Manage Printer and Manage Documents rights. These rights give administrators full control of the print queue. They can submit, modify, and delete any print job in the queue. They can also modify or delete the printer itself. Table 7.1 lists the different printer permissions and their capabilities.

Managing print jobs can be accomplished by selecting the desired print job and selecting one of the following commands from the Document pull-down menu:

➤ *Cancel*—Stops the printing of a print job and deletes it from the queue.

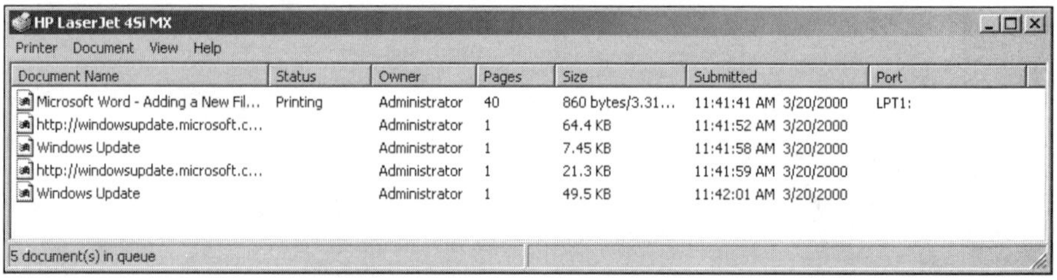

Figure 7.18 The Print Queue window.

Table 7.1   Printer permissions.

Capabilities	Print	Manage Documents	Manage Printers
Print Documents	X	X	X
Pause, resume, restart, and cancel the user's own print jobs	X	X	X
Connect to a printer	X	X	X
Control print job settings for all jobs		X	X
Pause, restart, and delete all print jobs		X	X
Share a printer			X
Modify printer properties			X
Delete printers			X
Modify printer permissions			X

➤ *Pause*—Suspends the printing of an already printing print job or pauses the print job in the queue.

➤ *Restart*—Starts a print job from the beginning, allowing the entire print job to be reprinted in the event of a print device error.

➤ *Resume*—Allows a paused print job to be released.

Managing the entire print queue is attained by using the following commands from the Printer pull-down menu:

➤ *Cancel All Documents*—Stops and deletes all print jobs from the queue.

➤ *Pause Printing*—Suspends the printing of all print jobs in the queue. Any print jobs submitted after the queue is paused will still be accepted, but not printed. To release the pause, simply reselect Pause Printing from the Printer pull-down menu.

➤ *Set as Default Printer*—Designates this printer as the default printer for the workstation. All print jobs sent without specifying a print device are sent to this printer. After setting the printer as the default printer, a checkmark will be displayed next to the command on the Printer pull-down menu. To change the default printer, select another printer as default.

Note: *Pausing or canceling print jobs will not instantly stop all printing at the print device. If the print device has a significant amount of RAM, printing may continue until all print jobs are removed from its memory. Simply turning off the print device and clearing any paper jams will remove any jobs from memory.*

Managing the Print Server

In addition to managing print jobs and printers, you can manage the overall operation of the print server. All changes made to the print server affect all attached logical printers. Management of the print server is provided via the Printers Folder's File pull-down menu. From this menu, select Server Properties.

The Forms Tab

When the Server Properties dialog box is displayed, the first tab shown is the Forms tab (see Figure 7.19). This is where forms for the print server are defined. A form defines the dimensions of the paper (letter, legal, A4, and so on) and the margins for right, left, top, and bottom of the paper. From the Forms tab, you can:

➤ Define a new form by specifying the form name, the paper size, and the margins.

➤ Delete forms from the print server.

The Ports Tab

The Ports tab is used to configure printer ports on the local machine. On this tab, you can:

➤ Select the port or ports the printer will print to.

➤ Add, delete, and configure local ports.

The following ports can be added to a Windows 2000 Professional workstation:

➤ *Local Port*—This gives you the ability to connect to a network printer via its UNC name (such as *servername**sharename*).

➤ *Standard TCP/IP Port*—Sometimes referred to as an Line Printer Remote (LPR) port, the Standard TCP/IP Port gives you the ability to print directly to TCP/IP

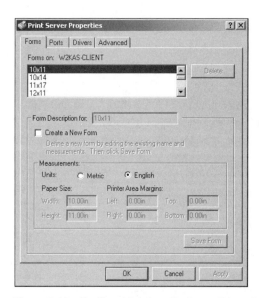

Figure 7.19 The Forms tab from the Server Properties dialog box.

enabled devices. To configure this port, you must specify the IP address or host name of the printer, along with an optional device name.

The Drivers Tab

The Drivers tab, shown in Figure 7.20, provides a centralized area where you can view, add, remove, and update any print drivers installed. It lists the printer model and the operating system that the installed print driver supports.

The Advanced Tab

The Advanced tab, shown in Figure 7.21, is used to manage advanced properties of the print server. On the Advanced tab you can:

➤ Specify the spool folder location where print jobs are kept before being sent to the print device. The default location is %systemroot%\System32\spool\ PRINTERS.

➤ Enable logging of spooler events (Errors, Warnings, Informational) in the event log.

➤ Enable the computer to beep when it encounters an error with a remote document.

➤ Send a notification to the user when a remote document is printed.

➤ Send a notification to the computer when a remote document is printed.

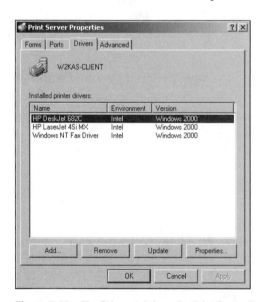

Figure 7.20   The Drivers tab from the Print Server Properties dialog box.

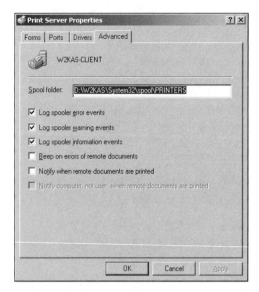

Figure 7.21 The Advanced tab from the Print Server Properties dialog box.

Printer Pooling

Printer pooling is an advanced printing technique that allows two or more identical print devices to be associated with a single logical printer (see Figure 7.22). This technique helps alleviate printing bottlenecks in situations where many print jobs are being sent to one printer. By attaching multiple identical print devices, the logical printer can send one print job to one print device and send the next print job to another available print device.

The print devices need to be identical because the print jobs are formatted for a particular device's features. If different print devices are in the same printer pool, print output may not be the same.

To create a printer pool:

1. Add a printer using the Add Printer Wizard.

2. After the printer is created, right-click on the Printer, and select Properties.

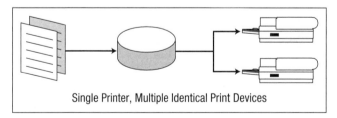

Single Printer, Multiple Identical Print Devices

Figure 7.22 Printer pooling.

3. Select the Ports tab, and select the Enable Printer Pooling checkbox.

4. Select the ports that the print devices are attached to.

5. Click on OK.

Troubleshooting

Troubleshooting printers can really be an art, considering the many different components, both software and hardware, that come together to produce the final product. As such, the key to troubleshooting printer problems is to be patient and methodical. Test a component and observe how it behaves. The following list contains some common details to check when troubleshooting:

➤ *Is one user having the problem, or is the same problem affecting all jobs going to the printer?* This is *the* first question to ask. Observe the environment. If a single user is complaining that the printer is down, but other users are sending and printing their jobs, the problem is with the user. It may be an issue with the user's configuration, a permissions issue, or a training issue.

➤ *Is the printer plugged in, both power and communications cables?* Always start with the simple solutions first, no matter how simple they may seem. It's obvious if the printer has lost power, but a loose cable (network or printer) can cause the printer to stop communicating. By verifying and reseating the cables, you can eliminate bad connections from the equation.

➤ *Is there a printer jam or other physical problem causing the printer to not print?* This is another simple problem, but one that can cause users to complain that the printer is down. Verify that there are no physical problems with the printer.

➤ *Does the printer have network connectivity?* With network printers, it's important to verify that they have network connectivity. Try pinging the printer's IP address. If you get no response, verify that the printer's network configuration is correct.

➤ *Are print jobs getting to the queue?* Using the printer's Print Queue window, verify that print jobs are actually reaching the queue. You can also see if the print queue is paused or if jobs are just sitting there waiting to be serviced.

➤ *Are the print jobs stalled in the queue?* If the print jobs are stalled in the queue, try restarting the Print Spooler service on the print server.

➤ *Is there enough free disk space on the print server or workstation to spool the print jobs?* Verify that there is plenty of disk space available for printing operations. If there isn't enough disk space, move the spool folder location, which is found under the Server Properties Advanced tab.

7

Chapter Summary

Printing is one of the most important components in a networking environment. Everyone, from the people in the mail room to the president of the company, uses this service. Windows 2000 provides a robust printing architecture that supports multiple operating systems, such as Windows NT 4/3.51, Windows 95/98, Windows for Workgroups, MS-DOS, Macintosh, Unix, and Novell NetWare.

The Windows 2000 printing process is comprised of many parts, mostly software (with the exception of the print device). The combination of these components creates a logical printer, from which users print.

The Printers Folder is the centralized hub of all printing activity in Windows 2000. In this folder, printers can be added and removed, printer configurations can be modified, and print server properties can be adjusted.

Installing a printer in Windows 2000 is a simple process that can be accomplished in several ways. Using the Add Printer Wizard, a user is walked through the steps required to install the printer. Using Point and Print, the user simply browses to the printer via My Network Places and connects to the printer. Windows 2000 automatically installs the print driver. Finally, Plug and Play can install local printers upon detection.

Through the Print Queue window, print jobs can be paused, canceled, and resumed. The queue itself can also be paused or resumed, affecting all print jobs in the queue.

Printer pooling is an advanced printing feature that helps alleviate printing bottlenecks in networking environments.

Review Questions

1. Which print process component provides device specific information to the GDI?

   a. Local Print Provider

   b. Client-side spooler (WINSPOOL.DRV)

   c. Port Monitor

   d. Print Driver

2. For printer pooling, what do the print devices need to be?

   a. Identical

   b. Use parallel cables

   c. HP printers

   d. PostScript

3. At what two places can additional print drivers be installed for other operating systems?

    a. The Sharing tab from Printer Properties

    b. Advanced Properties tab

    c. Control Panel

    d. The Drivers tab from Server Properties

4. Which one of the following statements is correct?

    a. Internet Printing can be used with the IPX protocol.

    b. Internet Printing is not standardized.

    c. Internet Printing requires IIS on the print server.

    d. Internet Printing requires SQL Server.

5. Where is the default spooling location?

    a. %systemroot%\spooler\FILES

    b. %systemroot%\System32\spool\PRINTERS

    c. %systemroot%\System\spool\PRINTERS

    d. %systemroot%\System32\spool\JOBS

6. Windows 2000 does not support which of the following print job formats?

    a. PSCRIPT1

    b. RAW (AF)

    c. EMF

    d. RAW

7. If print jobs are stalled in the print queue, what can be done to get them printed?

    a. Restart the print spooler service.

    b. Redirect the print jobs to another print device.

    c. Delete the printer and re-create it.

    d. Use another print driver.

8. Which port monitor is the preferred port monitor for network printing in Windows 2000?

    a. NLSP

    b. SPM

    c. SNMP

    d. TCP/IP

7

9. Which statement best describes the difference between a logical printer and a physical printer?

    a. A logical printer represents all software components belonging to the Windows 2000 printing process. The physical printer, known as a print device, is the actual hardware.

    b. A physical printer represents all software components belonging to the Windows 2000 printing process. The logical printer, known as a print device, is the actual hardware.

    c. Both printer types are exactly the same.

    d. A logical printer represents the components on the client side of the printing process. The physical printer represents the components on the server side of the printing process.

10. When using Windows 3.x or DOS clients, how many characters should the print share name use?

    a. 255

    b. 31

    c. 11

    d. 5

11. A print jam occurs in the middle of a very long document. After fixing the print jam, what command do you use to continue printing the document?

    a. Restart from the Document menu.

    b. Restart from the Printer menu.

    c. Resume from the Printer menu.

    d. Resume from the Document menu.

12. To print to an Internet printer, TCP/IP must be installed. True or false?

    a. True

    b. False

13. What can you do if the print server has run out of disk space?

    a. Move the spool folder to another drive with free space.

    b. Pause some print jobs to allow others to print.

    c. Restrict the number of users using the printer.

    d. Send the print jobs to another printer port.

14. The Pause Printing command:

   a. Stops the print device from printing immediately.

   b. Stops the print queue from sending data to the print device.

   c. Stops new jobs from entering the print queue.

   d. Allows jobs in the queue to print, but pauses any new jobs.

15. You have a network with 100 Windows NT 3.51 clients. You install three Windows 2000 computers to the network to be used as print servers. What must you do to enable the clients to print to these servers?

   a. Install the Windows NT 3.51 print drivers on each of the print servers.

   b. Map a network drive from each client computer to the new printer servers.

   c. On each client computer, create a share name for each of the printers.

   d. On each print server, create a client account for each client with the appropriate printer permissions.

16. Your supervisor demands that his print jobs be printed before anyone else's. What must you do?

   a. On his computer, configure his logical printer's priority to 1.

   b. On all computers except his, configure the logical printers' priority to 99.

   c. On his computer, configure his logical printer's priority to 99.

   d. On all computers except his, configure the logical printers' priority to 1.

17. Where can forms be added to a print server?

   a. The Advanced Properties tab from the Printer Properties.

   b. Forms cannot be added.

   c. The Forms tab from the Server Properties.

   d. The Device Settings tab from the Server Properties.

18. To manage their own print documents, what right do users need?

   a. Manage Documents

   b. Print

   c. Manage Printers

   d. Full Control

19. All Windows 2000 printing requires the TCP/IP protocol. Is this statement true or false?

   a. True

   b. False

20. Which dialog box controls auditing?

    a. Security

    b. General

    c. Advanced Properties

    d. Ports

21. If a print job is paused, what happens to other print jobs in the queue?

    a. They continue to print.

    b. They wait for the paused print job to be resumed.

    c. They are hidden in the queue.

    d. Their priority is raised.

22. The print spooler service can be stopped and started using which utility?

    a. The Printers Folder

    b. The Services applet

    c. Add/Remove Hardware applet

    d. Windows NT Explorer

23. What happens if the printer's port is set to FILE?

    a. The print job is sent to the spooler as a file.

    b. The print job is saved to the %systemroot% directory.

    c. The user is prompted for a file name.

    d. The user must cut and paste the file into the spooler.

24. Which components are part of the local print provider?

    a. Print router

    b. Print processor

    c. Separator page processor

    d. GDI

Real-World Projects

Your boss has just notified you that you will be receiving the company's first Windows 2000 Professional workstation. He wants you to test the printing capabilities of the new operating system.

After receiving the workstation, you attach an HP LaserJet 5000 laser printer to the computer and begin the installation process. The workstation's computer name is W2K.

Project 7.1

To install a locally attached printer:

1. Open the Printers Folder by clicking Start | Settings | Printers.

2. In the Printers Folder, double-click on the Add Printer icon to start the Add Printer Wizard.

3. The Welcome screen is displayed. Click on Next.

4. This screen asks if the printer to be installed is a local or network printer. Select Local printer and clear the Automatically Detect And Install My Plug And Play Printer checkbox. Click on Next.

5. Select LPT1 as your printer port, and click on Next.

6. Select the correct print driver for the print device. Select HP as the manufacturer and HP LaserJet 5000 Series PS as the model. Click on Next.

7. Name the printer and click on Yes to make the printer the default printer for the workstation.

8. On the Sharing screen, select Do Not Share This Printer. Click on Next.

9. Click on Yes to send a test page to the print device. Click on Next.

10. Click on Finish to complete the installation.

After installing the printer, you need to share the printer so other employees in the department can access it. There is a mixed environment of Intel-based Windows 98 and Windows NT 4 workstations. Presently your department uses a workgroup security structure.

Project 7.2

To share a local printer:

1. Open the Printers Folder by selecting Start | Settings | Printers.

2. Right-click on the icon for the printer, then click on Sharing. The Sharing tab is displayed.

3. Select the Shared As radio button, and enter LJ5000 as the share name.

4. Click on Additional Drivers. The Additional Drivers dialog box is displayed.

5. Select both the Intel Windows 95 or 98 and the Intel Windows NT 4 drivers and click on OK. If prompted, insert the Windows 2000 CD-ROM.

6. Click on OK to complete the operation.

You must now connect the department's workstations to the printer share you just created.

Project 7.3

To connect to a printer share:

1. Open the Printers Folder by selecting Start | Settings | Printers.

2. In the Printers Folder, double-click on the Add Printer icon to start the Add Printer Wizard.

3. The Welcome screen is displayed. Click on Next.

4. This screen asks if the printer to be installed is a local or network printer. Select Network printer. Click on Next.

5. Locate a network printer. Select Type The Printer Name, or click on Next to browse for a printer. Enter "\\W2K\LJ5000", and click on Next.

6. Select the correct print driver for the print device. Select HP as the manufacturer and HP LaserJet 5000 Series PS as the model. Click on Next.

7. Click on Yes to make the printer the default printer for the workstation. Click on Next.

8. Click on Finish to complete the installation.

Users in your department can now start sending print jobs to the printer.

CHAPTER EIGHT

Plug and Play

After completing this chapter, you will be able to:

✓ Define the function of Plug and Play

✓ Identify the architecture of the Plug and Play system

✓ Determine the functions of the drivers

The idea of Plug and Play is that the operating system has control over the system's resources. Before Plug and Play, it was a major undertaking to add a hardware device to the system. You had to check the IRQ (Interrupt ReQuest), DMA (Direct Memory Access), and IO (Input/Output) for all the hardware on your system. You then had to make them all function at the same time. This could be a long and involved process, especially if the only way to change these settings was to move jumpers around on the hardware.

With the advent of Plug and Play, much of this hassle has been eliminated. The operating system receives word from the system board that a new piece of hardware has been added to the system, and the operating system then tells the hardware how it should be configured. For the most part, it is now a seamless and simple procedure to add new hardware. In addition, with the vast amount of drivers already included with Windows 2000, the driver is usually loaded automatically, and you don't have to do a thing except start using your new device.

Windows 2000 is the first operating system in the NT line that supports Plug and Play. In the last few years, new technologies like Universal Serial Bus (USB) and infrared ports have really taken off, allowing users to hot-plug devices into their system. Plug and Play allows these types of devices to be identified and configured on the spot. Before Plug and Play, you had to tell the system that the new device was there. Windows 2000 often configures these devices in the background, allowing you to simply start using the new device. Occasionally, you may run into devices whose drivers Windows 2000 does not have. In this case, Windows 2000 prompts you for the location of the drivers.

Plug and Play's Evolution

Plug and Play was first introduced to Microsoft operating systems with the release of Windows 95. At the time, many people called it "plug and pray" because it was a new technology and many different devices didn't support it fully. Many times with these devices, you were better off just turning the Plug and Play support off and configuring the device manually. Since then, however, Plug and Play has been drastically improved, and it is unlikely that you will find any systems today that are not Plug and Play compliant.

The OnNow initiative has helped to bring about Plug and Play's evolution. This initiative defines a system-wide method for controlling system configuration, device configuration, and power management. The idea is to standardize how the hardware and the operating system can work together so that everything functions properly.

When Windows 95 introduced Plug and Play, it relied on a Plug and Play BIOS and Advanced Power Management (APM) to function. These two BIOS implementations were designed for Windows 95; they are superseded by Advanced Configuration and Power Interface (ACPI) version 1, which is a product of the OnNow initiative. ACPI defines a system board and a BIOS that includes power management under the operating system's control. With ACPI in place, you can manage how the system handles power-down options without having to enter the BIOS to configure them.

Windows 2000 extends the existing I/O infrastructure to support the new power management and Plug and Play features, and it has been optimized to work with computers that have ACPI system boards. Microsoft has also made sure to provide support for existing hardware standards. The BIOS and APM implementations are still supported, but only for backward-compatibility purposes.

Additionally, Microsoft has defined a common device driver that works with both Windows 98 and Windows 2000. The Win32 Driver Model (WDM) is Microsoft's new set of classes for the driver developers. If a driver is created with the WDM, it should function on both Windows 98 and Windows 2000, reducing the development time. This model also allows the operating system to have full control over the particular hardware for which it was developed.

8

Support for Plug and Play

Windows 2000 supports Plug and Play in a number of ways. One of the most important to the end user is that the proper drivers are loaded. The Plug and Play manager attempts to determine what driver will work with a particular device. Windows 2000 also has new functionality to communicate with the system board to receive Plug and Play information.

Windows 2000 automatically detects hardware in two ways. It detects hardware in the initial boot process to determine if there has been a change since the last boot. It also detects hardware when a runtime event occurs. A runtime event could be docking or undocking a laptop or inserting a USB or PCMCIA device.

The system must allocate resources for the hardware. The Plug and Play manager is in charge of assigning resources to a device. The driver has no control over this. When the Plug and Play manager finds a new device, it asks the device what kind of resources it needs. The device responds with what it needs from the system. The Plug and Play manager then assigns free resources to the device. If needed, the Plug and Play manager reallocates resources to other devices if it finds that it needs to shift things around to get all the devices to work properly.

Plug and Play also works together with power management to handle dynamic events. Besides adding and removing devices, these two processes work together to put devices to sleep and to awaken them again when needed.

Windows 2000 Plug and Play Architecture

Plug and Play works in both kernel and user mode. This section covers the different components and how they interact with the rest of the Windows 2000 architecture. Figure 8.1 shows the architecture of the Plug and Play system and how it fits into the rest of the Windows 2000 architecture.

Kernel Mode

Kernel mode in Windows 2000 is where the operating system functions close to the hardware. It is separated from the hardware by the HAL (Hardware Abstraction Layer). This is where the low-level operating system functionality happens. The Plug and Play Manger, Power and Policy Manager, and IO Manger all function on this level.

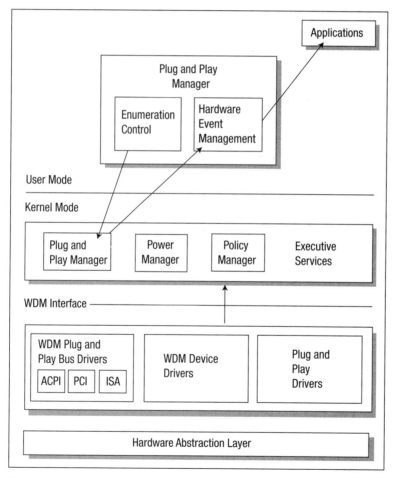

Figure 8.1 Plug and Play architecture for Windows 2000.

Plug and Play Manager

The kernel-mode Plug and Play manager is the heart of the Plug and Play system. It is responsible for coordinating all the activities required of the system. It makes requests of the hardware, directs device drivers to load or unload, or determines whether a device can safely be paused or stopped.

Power Manager and Policy Manager

The power manager works with the policy manager to handle power management tasks. These kernel-mode components work together to coordinate power events. The power manager handles the power requests and determines if they can be filled or if other events need to occur before the requests can be fulfilled. The policy manager develops a power management policy based on how you use your system. This policy keeps track of driver, application, and system status. The policy manager may on occasion attempt to change device power states.

I/O Manager

The I/O manager is the primary interface for the device drivers. This kernel-mode component translates user-mode read or write requests into I/O Request Packets (IRPs). The I/O manager in Windows 2000 works exactly as it did in Windows NT 4, so in theory, if you installed a Plug and Play driver in Windows NT, it will work as a Windows 2000 Plug and Play driver.

User-Mode Plug and Play Components

The user-mode application programming interfaces (APIs) are available to applications. These APIs allow the applications to use hardware events and to create new ones based on the application's needs. These routines provide a standard method of access to the kernel-level drivers.

Drivers

Drivers are what allows Windows 2000 to use different pieces of hardware and manufacturers the capability to add new things to the operating system. A Plug and Play driver will allow the operating system to manage how that piece of hardware will use available system resources.

Device and Driver Support

To obtain full Plug and Play support, both the device and the driver must support Plug and Play. If one or the other does not fully support Plug and Play, you may have some difficulties with the device. In other words, you may have issues with one or more legacy ISA cards taking up potentially needed resources. The following list details these difficulties:

➤ If the device and driver support Plug and Play, you should have full support. For optimal support, the hardware should comply with the OnNow initiative, including the ACPI standard.

➤ If the device has full Plug and Play support but the driver does not, no Plug and Play support is available. Regardless of the support that's available in the hardware, the driver must support Plug and Play in order to take advantage of Plug and Play's features.

➤ If the device isn't Plug and Play but the driver supports it, you have some support. Although the system cannot automatically detect the hardware or load the drivers, Plug and Play may be able to handle some of the resource allocations for the hardware. In addition, having a Plug and Play driver registers the driver in the device manager.

➤ If neither the device nor the driver supports Plug and Play, you get no Plug and Play support. The device should continue to function but the operating system cannot manage it.

Types of Drivers

There are three types of drivers in Plug and Play mode: the *bus driver*, the *function driver*, and the *filter driver*. The bus driver is a required driver that has responsibility over the bus controller or a device that has child devices. You usually use the driver that Microsoft provides, although hardware vendors may create their own bus drivers. If a hardware vendor makes a custom bus driver, you should use that driver. Each bus type on the system requires its own bus driver.

The function driver provides the operational interface to a device. The main driver is usually required, although the device can be used in raw mode. When a device is used in raw mode, the I/O is done with only the bus driver and the bus filter drivers. This implementation isn't used very often. The function driver usually has two parts: a class driver and a minidriver, which creates the function driver. The class driver is usually created by Microsoft; it defines the basic parameters that all devices of that type will use. The minidriver is usually created by the device manufacturer; it provides the unique functionality of the device. One function driver is loaded for each device.

The filter driver sorts the I/O requests that are sent to the device, bus, or class of devices. The filter driver is not required, but if it is used, you can load any amount of these drivers. A low-level filter modifies how a device behaves. A low-level filter on the keyboard may determine how long a key needs to be held down before it starts repeating. An upper-level filter provides some additional functionality to a device. An upper-level filter on a keyboard may allow you to add a security feature to your system.

Device Objects

A device object is created by the driver; it represents the device to the driver. There are three types of device objects:

➤ *Physical Device Object (PDO)*—Represents a device on a bus

➤ *Functional Device Object (FDO)*—Represents the functionality of the device

➤ *Filter Device Object*—Represents the filter driver

WDM Bus Drivers

Both Plug and Play and power management are controlled by WDM bus drivers, which expose the bus functionality. A bus driver responds to Plug and Play and power management IRPs. The bus driver can also be extended with filter drivers.

The bus driver has a number of responsibilities. It enumerates the devices, handles the general administration, reports any dynamic events to the operating system, responds to IRPs, and may handle multiplexing access to certain buses.

Microsoft provides built-in support for the most common buses like PCI, Plug and Play ISA, SCSI, and USB. Hardware vendors may implement their own bus drivers.

WDM Device Drivers

Device drivers support the operational interface for the device as well as help with power management. Device drivers supply information about the capabilities of a system and the current state of the devices.

Additional Windows Interfaces

Windows 2000 is not limited to using WDM interfaces. Windows 2000 allows drivers to make calls as they did in Windows NT. Although Windows 2000 does support the Windows NT drivers and the calls that they make, you will not have full functionality of the Plug and Play system if you use these other interfaces.

The Windows 2000 Implementation

A few things have changed in Windows 2000 from Windows NT 4. Developers who created device drivers for Windows NT 4 need to keep the following in mind:

➤ The bus drivers have now been separated from the Hardware Abstraction Layer (HAL).

➤ Many of the user-mode components have new capabilities and extensions.

➤ The Plug and Play APIs that read and write information to the Registry have been updated to support the changes and extensions that have been made to the Registry structure.

Windows 2000 supports older drivers but those older drivers cannot take advantage of the new Plug and Play support or the new power management features.

Chapter Summary

Although Plug and Play seems like a complicated system to work out, the end user will not be aware of all the complexity below the surface. Users can easily use the devices that they add to the system. When everything is working properly, it is a very smooth experience. When things go wrong, however, it can be very frustrating. Knowing the architecture of the Plug and Play system allows you to narrow down problems. You may need to determine if the problem is from a third-party driver or if it is native to the operating system.

Review Questions

1. Which of the following operating systems support Plug and Play? [Check all correct answers]

   a. Windows 3.1

   b. Windows 95

   c. Windows 98

   d. Windows NT 4

   e. Windows 2000

2. Which of the following operating systems was the first operating system to support Plug and Play?

   a. Windows 3.1

   b. Windows 95

   c. Windows 98

   d. Windows NT 4

   e. Windows 2000

3. Windows 2000 supports drivers from other operating systems if they meet the Windows 2000 criteria. From which of the following operating systems does Windows 2000 try to use drivers?

   a. Windows 3.1

   b. Windows 95

   c. Windows 98

   d. Windows NT 4

4. A Plug and Play device is attached to the computer. The driver for this device is not Plug and Play compliant. The device receives full Plug and Play support.

   a. True

   b. False

5. A non-Plug and Play device is attached to a computer. The driver for this device is Plug and Play compliant. The device receives full Plug and Play support.

   a. True

   b. False

6. A Plug and Play device is attached to a computer. The driver for this device is Plug and Play compliant. The device receives full Plug and Play support.

   a. True

   b. False

7. A non-Plug and Play device is attached to a computer. The driver for this device is not Plug and Play compliant. The device receives full Plug and Play support.

   a. True

   b. False

8. A developer creates a WDM device driver. With which of the following operating systems will the driver function? [Check all correct answers]

   a. Windows 3.1

   b. Windows 95

   c. Windows 98

   d. Windows NT 4

   e. Windows 2000

9. You are purchasing a new computer. The systems that you are looking at have different power management systems available. Which of the following should you choose to receive the best support from Windows 2000?

   a. APM

   b. ACPI

   c. No power management support

8

10. When a driver is implemented in raw mode, which of the following driver types are used? [Check all correct answers]

    a. Bus driver

    b. Function driver

    c. Filter driver

    d. IRP

11. Which part of the computer has control over a Plug and Play device?

    a. System board

    b. Processor

    c. BIOS

    d. Operating system

12. When a Plug and Play device is attached to a system, which of the following does the user need to do to gain functionality of the device?

    a. Install a driver

    b. Have the system check for the new device

    c. Run the Plug and Play detection utility

    d. Do nothing

13. Windows 2000 detects a device that has been added to the system. Windows 2000 does not have a driver for the device. What does the operating system do?

    a. It does not install any driver.

    b. It asks you where the drivers are or asks where it should search for the driver.

    c. It informs you that you must remove the device and install the driver before adding the device.

    d. It chooses a similar driver and sees if it works.

14. Which of the following has the responsibility for allocating resources to the hardware device?

    a. BIOS

    b. Bus

    c. Plug and Play manager

    d. Power manager

15. Which two of the following handle power management tasks?

    a. Plug and Play manager

    b. Policy manager

    c. Power manager

    d. Bus driver

CHAPTER NINE

Hardware Devices and Support

After completing this chapter, you will be able to:

✓ Describe the hardware supported in Windows 2000 Professional

✓ Describe power management and how it is used in Windows 2000 Professional

✓ Describe how to use a USB device in Windows 2000 Professional

✓ Describe how Windows 2000 Professional supports the use of infrared devices

✓ Describe how Windows 2000 Professional provides DirectX 7.0 support

✓ Explain what ICM is and how it is used

✓ Explain what ACP is and how it is used

✓ Describe multiple monitor support in Windows 2000 Professional

✓ Describe DVD support in Windows 2000 Professional

✓ Explain removable media and how it is supported in Windows 2000 Professional

✓ Upgrade a uniprocessor to a multiprocessor in Windows 2000 Professional

✓ Describe the function of Device Manager

✓ Explain device driver signing

✓ Create hardware profiles

✓ Describe troubleshooting tools available in Windows 2000 Professional

Windows 2000 Professional supports over 11,000 hardware devices, including new categories of hardware devices such as smart cards and digital video disc (DVD). It also supports existing legacy hardware used with previous versions of Windows.

New Hardware Support

This section covers what's new in Windows 2000 Professional, including how much of this new technology interrelates both with other new features and with features carried over from Windows 95/98 and NT 4. In this section, you learn about the new hardware devices that are supported in Windows 2000 Professional. You also learn about hardware support that has been included from previous versions of Windows and how it relates to Windows 2000.

Plug and Play

Plug and Play support is included in Windows 2000 Professional. Plug and Play was originally introduced in Windows 95 and improved upon in Windows 98. Windows NT 4 did not include Plug and Play. Plug and Play support for Windows 2000 has been optimized to include support for Advanced Configuration and Power Interface (ACPI) system boards and the Win32 Driver Model (WDM). The following benefits are realized with the introduction of Plug and Play in Windows 2000 Professional:

➤ Dynamic loading, initialization, and unloading of drivers

➤ Automatic allocation of resources

➤ Notification to other drivers and applications when a device is available for use

➤ Consistent driver and bus interface for all devices

➤ Support for a wide range of device types

Plug and Play is discussed in greater detail in Chapter 8.

WDM

WDM allows hardware vendors to develop device drivers that are compatible with both Windows 98 and Windows 2000. Device drivers developed under the WDM architecture can participate in Plug and Play and the advanced power management functions of Windows 2000 Professional. WDM has four distinct features:

➤ It provides compatibility between Windows 98 and Windows 2000, which allows developers to develop a single device driver for both operating systems.

➤ It supports Plug and Play in Windows 2000 Professional.

➤ It provides power management functions that comply with the OnNow initiative.

➤ It expands on the minidriver model used with small computer system interface SCSI and Network Driver Interface Specification (NDIS) drivers.

More information on WDM is also provided in Chapter 8.

IEEE 1394

IEEE 1394 is a serial bus interface that compliments the Universal Serial Bus (USB). IEEE 1394 ports support transfer rates of 100, 200, and 400 Mbps. Devices with different transfer rates can be interconnected, and the maximum rate supported is the highest rate supported by the slowest device.

Many high-end computers currently have IEEE 1394 ports built into their motherboards. IEEE 1394 can provide the transfer rates needed for streaming video and applications that require fast throughput rates. Up to 63 devices can be attached to a single IEEE 1394 bus. Up to 1,023 buses can be connected to form a network with over 64,000 devices. IEEE 1364 supports isochronous and asynchronous transfer modes.

Digital Audio

Windows 2000 Professional can support digital audio through USB and IEEE 1394. Both USB and IEEE 1393 provide the bandwidth necessary for digital audio and the isochronous and asynchronous services that distributed audio systems need. Multiple streams of audio can be handled simultaneously under the WDM architecture. Previous versions of Windows did a poor job of mixing sound from multiple hardware and software sources. Users could only hear sound from one application at a time. In Windows 2000 Professional, two applications can simultaneously output sound because WDM can handle multiple streams of audio. Audio can be redirected to any available output, including external USB and IEEE 1394 devices. This provides higher fidelity because there is no radio frequency noise interference as with internal audio devices.

Still Images

Window 2000 professional is the first version of Windows to support still images. The still-image architecture is comprised of the following components:

➤ The Scanners and Camera icon in the Control Panel, which allows users to add, remove, and configure still images devices.

➤ The still-image event monitor, which monitors events, such as the pushing of a button on a scanner to launch the scanning application.

➤ Technology without an interesting name (TWAIN), an Application Programming Interface (API) that facilitates seamless communications between imaging devices and software.

➤ The still-image device driver interface (DDI), which provides support for SCSI, serial, infrared, parallel, and USB devices.

➤ WDM still-image drivers, which use the WDM to enable delivery to USB or SCSI buses.

Users can install non-Plug and Play still image devices though the Scanner and Camera icon in the Control Panel.

OnNow

OnNow is a design initiative specification that enables a computer to provide the same instant-on capability as other devices, such as televisions and VCRs. In legacy computers, the BIOS controls power states of system devices. There was a delay before the user could resume using the computer when it was in a low power state. With OnNow, the operating system can coordinate power management at all levels. The computer is immediately available after waking from a low power state.

Note: OnNow is only an initiative. It is not a technology. There is not an OnNow feature in Windows 98 or Windows 2000. It does, however, have an influence on specifications for such features as ACPI.

Advanced Power Management (APM)

APM, the precursor to ACPI, was introduced in Windows 95 and has limited support in Windows 2000 Professional. Windows 2000 Professional recognizes three categories of APM support:

➤ *AutoEnable APM*—APM is automatically installed and enabled during Windows 2000 Professional installation.

➤ *Disable APM*—If it is determined that APM will not work properly on the system, APM is not installed.

➤ *Neutral System*—The functionality of APM cannot be determined and APM is installed, but not enabled.

APM support in Windows 2000 is only for legacy notebook computers. It isn't designed to run on desktop computers. If your computer supports APM, it must be enabled by selecting the Enable Advanced Power Management Support checkbox. This checkbox is located on the APM tab of the Power Options icon in the Control Panel (see Figure 9.1).

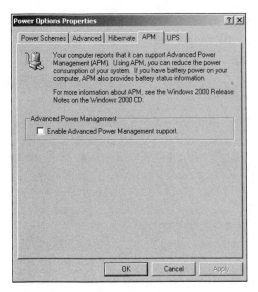

Figure 9.1   The APM tab on the Power Options Properties dialog box.

ACPI

ACPI (Advanced Configuration and Power Interface) is an open industry standard, which is the foundation for the OnNow initiative. Employing ACPI, the operating system can manage power requirements for the computer's hardware and software. ACPI allows the operating system to control power management. Individual devices, such as hard disks, network adapters, and printers, can be put in a low power state when they are not needed. With ACPI, the operating system has direct control over how the computer's power is consumed.

To use ACPI and the OnNow initiative, the BIOS of the computer must support ACPI. The Windows 2000 Professional Setup program checks to see if a computer has ACPI support before it tries to implement ACPI. You can also use the Microsoft System Information (MSInfo) utility to determine if the computer's BIOS has ACPI support.

The ACPI specification has two parts: configuration and power management. Power management features in Windows 2000 Professional include the following:

➤ *System Power Management*—Mechanisms for determining and controlling the computer's sleep and wake states defined by ACPI.

➤ *Device Power Management*—A device can be put in a low power state depending on its level of usage.

➤ *Processor Power Management*—The processor's power state can be controlled to meet certain goals.

➤ *System Events*—A mechanism can be defined as to how ACPI handles system events, thermal events, docking, and device insertion/removal.

In Windows 2000 Professional, power management allows the computer to turn on instantly, respond to wake up events, adjust software to changing power states, and incorporate new devices into power management.

Power schemes can be configured to manage the behavior of the power management system. Power schemes are created by using the Power Options icon in the Control Panel. Windows 2000 Professional has six predefined power scheme configurations: Home/Office Desk, Portable/Laptop, Presentation, Always On, Minimum Power Management, and Max Battery (see Figure 9.2).

Troubleshooting Power Management

In older legacy systems, if the system stopped responding when it was in standby mode, it was probably a hardware problem. With ACPI-compliant systems, the cause of system lockup is probably due to incompatible device drivers. To handle this problem, try to obtain an updated driver if it is available. If that does not work, try to disable power management.

HIDs

Windows 2000 Professional provides support for Human Interface Devices (HIDs). HIDs include keyboards, mice, and joysticks for use with vehicle simulation and virtual reality programs. Plug and Play support and power management for these devices is supported without the need for additional device drivers. Windows 2000 also supports HIDs connected to legacy ports.

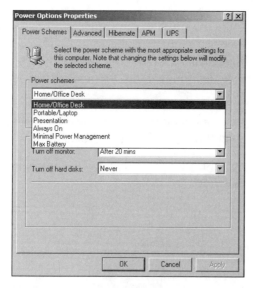

Figure 9.2 The Power Schemes tab.

I/O Devices

In this section, you learn the advantages of using USB ports. You learn how to use infrared devices (to send and receive files between devices) and to connect to a network.

USB

The use of the USB was introduced in Windows 98. USB provides users with a hot-pluggable Plug and Play serial interface. It provides an industry-standard port for the installation of external hardware devices. The majority of new computers today have two USB ports. Most new portable computers have one USB port. USB has several advantages:

➤ USB devices have the same I/O connector.

➤ USB supports hot-pluggable Plug and Play.

➤ Multiple USB devices can be plugged into a single port. Up to 127 devices can be tiered to a single USB port.

USB devices planned or already produced include the following categories:

➤ *Input*—Keyboards, pointing devices, and joysticks

➤ *Storage*—Hard disks, CD-ROM drives, and removable media

➤ *Communications devices*—Modems, ISDN adapters, and network adapters

➤ *Output devices*—Monitors, printers, and audio devices

➤ *Imaging*—Scanners and cameras

Two transfer rates are supported by USB. The transfer rate supported depends on the bandwidth requirement of the device. The transfer rate is determined by the host devices, such as mice and keyboards, don't require a lot of bandwidth and operate at speeds up to 1.5 Mbps. Devices that require more bandwidth, such as modems, operate at 12 Mbps. The actual transfer rate determined by the host depends on the transfer mode of the device.

IrDA

Windows 2000 Professional supports infrared devices in accordance with the Infrared Data Association (IrDA) standards and protocols. Most new notebook computers have IrDA ports that support transmission speeds of either 115,000 bits per second (bps) or 4 Mbps. Both of these transmission speeds are supported in Windows 2000. IrDA-SIR is the most common implementation of infrared. It is a half-duplex system that has a maximum transfer rate of 115,000 bps. It provides short-range, infrared asynchronous serial transmission. IrDA-FIR provides transmission rates of up to 4 Mbps. Most new notebook computers have IrDA-FIR transceivers. IrDA-FIR devices can communicate with IrDA-SIR devices without additional hardware.

Windows 2000 Professional is installed with the Wireless Link file transfer program, infrared printing support (IrLPT), and infrared image transfer capability (IrTran-P). The Wireless Link program can be used to send files and folders to computers running Windows 2000 or Windows 98. To send files, an infrared link must first be established. An icon appears on the taskbar when the infrared device is in range. A data connection can be made only when the infrared transceiver is in range. Infrared printing ports are seen as local ports on the Add Printer dialog box. IrTran-P image exchange is used to transfer digital images from cameras and other devices that support the IrTran-P protocol.

All infrared transmissions occur from the primary (commanding) device to the secondary (receiving) device. The computer that initiates the connection usually assumes the primary role. Some devices can only assume a secondary role.

Several programs can work simultaneously over a single IrDA link. A single IrDA device cannot link simultaneously with more than one IrDA device. You can install multiple IrDA devices in a computer to provide simultaneous links to multiple IrDA devices. You can view properties for infrared devices by opening the Wireless Link icon in the Control Panel. You configure infrared devices by using the Device Manager.

Infrared network connections are supported, which allow a direct connection to another computer without the use of network hardware. Users can create a connection to another computer using an infrared port with the Network and Dial-Up Connections Wizard. The Point-to-Point Protocol (PPP) is the default protocol used for infrared network connections in Windows 2000. When setting up a network connection, the computer that has the information that you want to access is the host, and the computer that is accessing the information is the guest.

Note: *Before accessing a computer using Infrared network connections, the user must be a member of a group on the host computer.*

Multimedia

This section shows how Windows 2000 Professional improves on the multimedia capabilities introduced in Windows 98. Here, you learn about support for DirectX 7 and the new OpenGL 1.2 specification. You also learn how multiple monitor support is provided for both PCI and AGP video adapters, and how to use ICM to ensure consistent color output across different devices and platforms.

DirectX

Windows 2000 Professional supports DirectX 7. DirectX 7 provides enhanced multimedia capabilities, such as full-color graphics, theater surround sound, immersive audio, video, and 3-D animation. DirectX consists of two APIs. The APIs are grouped into two classes: the DirectX Foundation layer and the DirectX Media layer. By using these two APIs, programs are able to directly access many of the computer's hardware devices.

The DirectX Foundation layer provides improved access to advanced hardware, such as 3-D graphics acceleration chips and sound cards. Several components make up the DirectX Foundation layer. These include the following:

➤ *Microsoft DirectDraw*—Provides support for fast and direct access to the accelerated hardware capabilities of the computer's video adapter.

➤ *Microsoft Direct3D Immediate Mode*—Provides developers with features to interface to the 3-D rendering functions of new video cards. These features include

  ➤ Switchable depth buffering

  ➤ Flat and Gourard shading

  ➤ Multiple lights and light types

  ➤ Full material and texture support

  ➤ Transformation and clipping

  ➤ Hardware independence

  ➤ Full hardware acceleration on Windows 2000

  ➤ Built-in support for MX, Pentium III architectures, and the 3D!Now architecture

➤ *Microsoft DirectSound*—Provides a link between programs and an audio adapter's sound mixing and playback capabilities.

➤ *Microsoft Direct Music*—Provides developers with the capability to create dynamic soundtracks that respond to user input.

➤ *Microsoft DirectInput*—Provides advanced input for games with joysticks, mice, keyboards, and other game controllers.

The DirectX Media layer works with the DirectX Foundation layer to provide high-level animation, media streaming, and interactivity. The DirectX Media layer is comprised of the following components:

➤ *Microsoft Direct3D Retained Mode*—Provides support for realtime 3D graphics.

➤ *Microsoft DirectAnimation*—Provides support for the animation of 2D and 3D images, 3D objects, sounds, movies, and text.

9

➤ *Microsoft DirectPlay*—Provides support for game connections. These connections can be over a modem, a LAN, or the Internet.

➤ *Microsoft DirectShow*—Captures multimedia streams from video cards and plays video and audio content in various formats, such as MPEG and WAV.

➤ *Microsoft DirectX Transform*—Provides developers with the ability to create, edit, and animate digital images.

Troubleshooting DirectX

Two tools are provided to aid with troubleshooting DirectX: the DirectX Diagnostic Tool and the Multimedia and Games Troubleshooter. The DirectX Diagnostic Tool (Dxdiag.exe) is installed directly from DirectX. It is used to diagnose problems, to test the functionality of DirectX, and to optimize DirectX performance. The Multimedia and Games Troubleshooter is used to diagnose and repair DirectX driver and game problems (see Figure 9.3).

ICM

Image Color Management (ICM) 2.0 is supported in Windows 2000 Professional. ICM is an API that provides the user with the ability to produce consistent colors across output devices. This ensures that the color on a display is the same color that is reproduced on a printer. ICM ensures that color is portable across applications. Windows 2000 Professional includes ICM support for monitors, printers, and scanners.

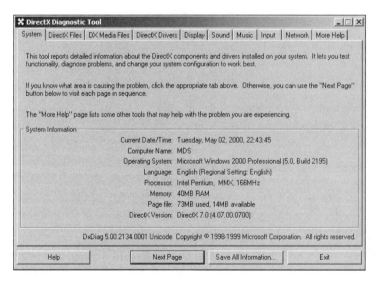

Figure 9.3   The DirectX Diagnostic Tool.

ICM uses color profiles to communicate color characteristics, so that accurate colors are produced on each output device. An example of an application that uses ICM is Adobe Photoshop. Adobe Photoshop uses the color profiles to ensure color accuracy on each device.

Windows 2000 Professional includes several color profiles:

➤ Diamond Compatible 9300K G2.2

➤ Hitachi Compatible 9300 K

➤ NEC Compatible 9300K G2.2

➤ SRGB Color Space Profile

➤ Trinitron Compatible 9300K G2.2

ICM is based on color profiles. Color profiles ensure color consistency between different devices and platforms. Color profiles are installed by right-clicking on the profile file and choosing Install Profile from the pop-up menu. After the profile is installed, users associate devices with the profile by selecting Associate from the profile's pop-up menu. Multiple devices can be associated with each color profile.

Accelerated Graphics Port (AGP)

Intel introduced AGP, which is an expansion slot designed specifically for video adapters. To utilize AGP, the computer must have an AGP graphics controller. It also must have an AGP compatible chipset, such as the Pentium II LX chipset. AGP has several improvements over PCI video adapters. These include:

➤ Peak bandwidth, which can be four times higher than with PCI adapters.

➤ A dedicated bus, which reduces contention by other devices.

➤ The CPU, which is able to write directly to shared memory instead of local memory. This makes processing of information faster.

➤ Information, which can be read from shared memory while other data is being written to local memory. This improves 3-D resolution.

➤ Graphics data, which can be executed directly from system memory. This eliminates having to first move it into video memory before it can be displayed.

Scanners

Windows 2000 Professional supports scanners and digital still and video cameras. Scanners are installed automatically through Plug and Play. If the operating system does not detect the devices, users can add the scanner or camera by using the

Scanners and Cameras icon in the Control Panel. By clicking on Add, users start the Scanner and Cameras Installation Wizard, which walks them through installing the device.

Documents can be associated with programs, so that when the document is scanned, it automatically opens using the associated program.

Multiple Monitor Support

Windows 2000 Professional supports the connection of up to 10 individual monitors. A single document can be displayed across multiple monitors, or each monitor can be used to display a different document or application. Multiple monitor support is provided for both PCI and AGP video adapters.

The monitor that is defined as the Primary Monitor in the Display Properties dialog box is the default monitor used for prompts and pop-up messages. It's also the only monitor that will be able to run DirectX applications in full-screen mode.

For a monitor to be used as a secondary monitor, it must be either a PCI or AGP device, and it must have the appropriate Windows 2000 drivers. Multiple monitors are configured using the Display icon in the Control Panel.

Note: Each additional monitor added to the system increases the use of system resources and compromises system performance.

To add a second monitor to your computer, take these steps:

1. Install the video adapter for the second monitor.

2. Start your computer and confirm that the video adapter has been detected.

3. Click on Search when prompted for a driver, and then click on Next.

4. Select the appropriate driver from the Windows 2000 CD, and click on Finish twice.

5. Open the Control Panel.

6. Double-click on the Display icon.

7. Click on the Settings tab in the Display Properties dialog box. Both monitors should be displayed.

8. Click on the icon for the new monitor and make any necessary adjustments.

9. Select Extend My Windows Desktop To This Monitor, and click on Restart.

10. Double-click on the Display icon.

Troubleshooting Multiple Monitors

Several ways are available to troubleshoot problems with multiple monitors, which are listed here:

➤ Make sure the video adapters are on the Hardware Compatibility List (HCL).

➤ If the system doesn't detect the second video adapter, make sure you have the correct drivers for the monitors.

➤ Make sure VGA is disabled on the secondary display.

OpenGL 1.2

Windows 2000 Professional includes support for Open Graphics Library (OpenGL) 1.2. OpenGL is a new standard for 3-D graphics, which provides improved functionality for programming in computer aided design and scientific visualization applications.

DVD

Windows 2000 Professional supports DVD, which employs optical disk storage technologies. DVD is a natural progression from CD-ROMs and laser discs and supports multimedia applications as well as the storage of full-length movies. DVD is supported with multiple device drivers in Windows 2000 Professional. DVD is currently supported for movie playback and storage as well as writeable devices in the near future. A single digital video disc can store up to 4.7GB of data or two hours of high-quality audio and video.

The DVD file system is based on the Universal Disk Format (UDF), which is the successor to CDFS (CD-ROM File System). Windows 2000 professional doesn't currently support writing to DVD, but it will in the near future.

Windows 2000 Professional supports DVD in the following formats:

➤ *DVD-Video*—A DVD disk that contains full-length motion pictures. The pictures can be played on a computer's DVD-ROM drive or on a home DVD-video player.

➤ *DVD-ROM*—A DVD disk that contains data that can be read by a DVD-ROM drive. A DVD-ROM can have up to 17GB of data storage space.

➤ *DVD-WO*—A DVD disk that is similar to compact disc recordable discs in that it supports one-time recording of data to the disk. A DVD-WO requires third-party software to operate with Windows 2000 Professional.

➤ *DVD-RAM*—A DVD disk that supports multiple recording capabilities, such as those with magneto-optical (MO) disks. DVD-RAM also requires third-party software to operate with Windows 2000 Professional.

9

To use DVD-Video, there are specific hardware and software requirements. On the hardware side, the computer needs a DVD drive and decoder. The decoder can be a hardware decoder card, a software decoder card, or a combination of both. Currently there are several decoder cards that are directly supported in Windows 2000. These include:

➤ Toshiba Tecra 760, 780, 8000, Toshiba Infinia

➤ Quadrant 1.2 and 3.0 and Dell EXP series

Several software components are supported in Windows 2000 Professional: MPEG-2, Dolby Digital (AG-3), Subpicture, DVD-ROM Class Driver, UDF File System, DirectShow, and DirectDraw.

Troubleshooting DVD

Troubleshooting DVD is relatively straightforward. There are several ways to troubleshoot DVD problems:

➤ Check the Device Manager to make sure that the DVD drive is displayed.

➤ Use Windows Explorer to make sure that Windows 2000 Professional can read the DVD data on the DVD device.

➤ Use the Device Manager to ensure that the hardware decoder is working properly.

➤ Verify that the hardware decoder is on the HCL.

➤ Use the Device Manager to ensure that the software decoder is working properly.

Removable Media

Windows 2000 Professional supports removable media, such as disks, tapes, and optical media. The Removable Storage snap-in makes managing removable storage media easier. Removable Storage uses media pools to organize and control access to media. A media pool is a collection of media with the same management properties. Media can be 8mm tapes, magnetic disks, optical disks, or CD-ROMs. Removable Storage manages two classes of physical locations: libraries and offline media physical locations. A library is comprised of the data storage media and the device used to read and write to the media. There are two major types of libraries: robotic libraries and stand-alone drive libraries. Robotic libraries are automatic units that hold multiple tapes or drives. Stand-alone drive libraries are nonautomated and hold a single tape or CD-ROM drive. Offline media physical locations list media that is not in a library. Removable storage provides a comprehensive way to manage all media in your library. Removable storage works in conjunction with data management programs, such as the Windows Backup utility, to manage the actual data on the media.

Mobile Computer Support

Windows 2000 Professional is the ideal operating system for mobile computer users. Support for mobile computers is discussed in detail in Chapter 12.

Multiple Processing Units

Windows 2000 Professional supports symmetric multiprocessing (SMP). Symmetric multiprocessing allows multiple processors to share the workload of the operating system. Up to two processors can be installed in a computer running Windows 2000 Professional. In Windows NT 4, to upgrade a uniprocessor system to a multiprocessor system, users had to reinstall the operating system or use a utility called *uptomp* from the Resource Kit. Users in Windows 2000 Professional can upgrade from a uniprocessor system to a multiprocessor system by using the Device Manager.

To upgrade from a uniprocessor to a multiprocessor using the Device Manager, take these steps:

1. Go to the Control Panel.

2. Click on the System icon, and select the Hardware tab.

3. Click on Device Manager.

4. Select the computer node, and expand it.

5. Double-click on the object listed, and choose the Driver tab.

6. Click on Update Driver.

7. Click on Next on the Upgrade Device Driver Wizard.

8. Select Display A Known List Of Drivers For This Device So That I Can Choose A Specific Driver, and click on Next.

9. Select Show All Hardware Of This Device Class on the Select Device Driver page.

10. Select the HAL that matches your computer configuration, and click on Next.

11. Make sure the wizard is showing the configuration you want, and then click on Next.

Device Manager

The Device Manager provides the user with a graphical representation of the hardware in the computer (see Figure 9.4). This is known as the device tree. The device tree is created in RAM when the computer is started or when there is a dynamic change to the system configuration. The Device Manager can be used to do the following:

➤ Determine whether hardware is working properly

➤ Change configuration settings

➤ Identify the device drivers loaded for each hardware device

➤ Install device drivers

➤ Enable, disable, and uninstall devices

➤ Identify device conflicts

➤ Print a summary of device information

Note: You must be logged on as a member of the Administrator group to complete procedures with the Device Manager.

The device tree has branches that define a device node. Each node has the following items.

➤ A unique identification code or device ID

➤ A list of resources, including interrupts and memory range

Figure 9.4 Device Manager.

➤ A list of allocated resources

➤ An indication if the node is a bus

To view devices on your computer, follow these steps:

1. Open the Device Manager.

2. Select one of the following on the View menu:

   ➤ *Devices By Connection*—To see devices by connection type, for example, COM2.

   ➤ *Resources By Type*—To see the status of allocated resources, DMA channels, I/O ports, IRQs, and memory addresses by the type of device using the resource.

   ➤ *Resources By Connection*—To see the status of allocated resources, DMA channels, I/O ports, IRQs, and memory addresses by the connection type.

Note: To see hidden devices in the Device Manager, click on Show Hidden Devices on the View menu. Non-Plug and Play devices and devices that have been removed but have not had their drivers uninstalled are hidden by default in the Device Manager.

Driver Signing

Windows 2000 introduces device driver signing, which ensures that the highest quality device drivers are being used. Windows 2000 Professional ships only with device drivers that have been digitally signed by Microsoft. Driver signing uses digital cryptographic technology. Authenticating information is stored in a catalog (.cat or CAT) file. The information in the catalog file verifies that the device driver has been tested by the Windows Hardware Qualify Lab (WHQL). A CAT file is created for each device driver and is stored in the systemroot\System32\CatRoot folder. Users can verify that a device driver is digitally signed through Device Manager.

Windows 2000 Professional provides the capability to warn or block users from installing unsigned drivers. Windows 2000 Professional can be configured to ignore device drivers that are not digitally signed, display a warning when it detects a device driver that is not digitally signed, or prevent the user from installing device drivers that have not been digitally signed (see Figure 9.5).

To configure how the operating system responds to unsigned files:

1. Open the Control Panel.

2. Double-click on the System icon.

3. Click on the Hardware tab, and then click on Driver Signing.

4. Select the type of verification you want, and click on OK.

9

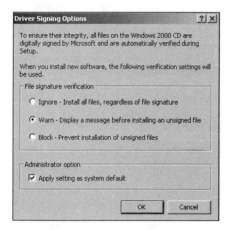

Figure 9.5   Driver Signing Options dialog box.

Troubleshooting Driver Signing

The Device Manager can be used to monitor the digital signatures of files. Two command line utilities, System File Checker (SFC) and File Signature Verification, can also be used to check the digital signature of files.

Hardware Profiles

Hardware profiles are not new to Windows. Hardware profiles tell the computer what devices to start when the user starts the computer and what settings to use for those devices. A default hardware profile called Profile 1 is created when Windows 2000 Professional is first installed. If you install Windows 2000 Professional on a portable computer, the default hardware profile is called Docked Profile or Undocked Profile. Support for docking stations has been built into Windows 2000 Professional. Hardware profiles allow portable computer users to select particular devices when the computer is docked and a different set of devices when it is undocked. Hardware profiles are managed from the System icon in the Control Panel (see Figure 9.6).

After a profile is created, devices within the profile can be enabled and disabled though the Device Manager. If a device is disabled through the Device Manager, the device drivers for the device are not loaded then the computer is started.

To copy a hardware profile, take the following steps:

1. Double-click on the System icon in the Control Panel.

2. Click on Hardware Profiles on the Hardware tab.

3. Click on the existing profile you want to copy in the Available Hardware Profiles box.

4. Click on Copy to open the Copy Profile dialog box.

5. Enter the name for the copy.

Figure 9.6   Hardware Profiles dialog box.

Note: You must be a member of the Administrator group to create, copy, delete or rename hardware profiles.

Troubleshooting

This section covers the tools and methods to resolve problems with Windows 2000 Professional. Here, you learn how to use the troubleshooter wizards to aid in identifying and resolving problems. You learn how the Device Manager can be used to ensure that hardware devices are configured and working properly. You'll also look at some of the diagnostic utilities provided with Window 2000 Professional to aid in resolving hardware problems.

Troubleshooters

Windows 2000 Professional contains Troubleshooters to aid users in resolving their computer problems. The following Troubleshooters are available in Windows 2000 Professional:

➤ Client Service for NetWare

➤ Displays

➤ Hardware

➤ Internet Connections

➤ Modems

➤ MS-DOS programs

➤ Multimedia and games

➤ Networking and TCP/IP

➤ Printing

➤ Remote access to networks

➤ Sound

➤ System setup

➤ Windows 3.0 and Windows 3.1 programs

Additional Troubleshooters are provided in Windows 2000 Server. To start online Troubleshooter help:

1. Go to the Help menu.

2. Choose Troubleshooting and Maintenance.

3. Select Use The Interactive Troubleshooters (see Figure 9.7).

Troubleshooting Hardware Problems

The most common cause of hardware problems in Windows 2000 is hardware that is not on the HCL. To avoid problems, make sure that devices you are using are on the HCL.

Troubleshooting Tools

Additional troubleshooting tools are provided to aid in diagnosing problems with your computer hardware. They are discussed in the following sections.

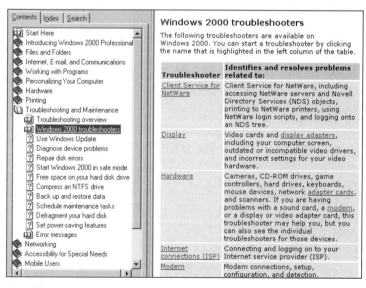

Figure 9.7   Windows 2000 Troubleshooter Wizard.

Device Manager

The Device Manager can be used to troubleshoot many devices in Windows 2000 Professional. Through the Device Manager, users can see if devices are configured correctly and are working properly.

To troubleshoot a device using Device Manager:

1. Right-click on My Computer.

2. Click on Manage.

3. Select Device Manager under System Tools.

4. Double-click on the device type in the Details pane.

5. Double-click on the device you want to troubleshoot.

6. Click on Troubleshooter.

7. Continue with the Troubleshooter Wizard for the selected device.

System Information Utility

Windows 2000 Professional includes the System Information Utility, which can aid in diagnosing and correcting problems. This utility can be used to gather information about hardware resources. It can also provide device driver status and a snapshot of the current software environment (see Figure 9.8). To access the System Information Utility tool, type "MISINFO32" from the Run command.

The System Information Utility can also be used as a snap-in. By adding the System Information Utility to a custom console, users can troubleshoot local and remote computers.

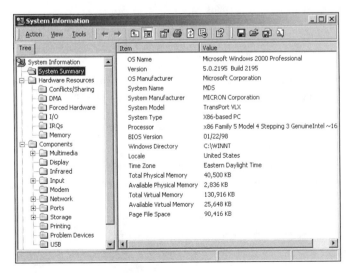

Figure 9.8   System Information.

To add the System Information Utility as a snap-in to a console:

1. Select Start|Run.

2. Type "MMC", and click on OK.

3. Select Console and Add/Remove Snap-in.

4. Click on Add.

5. Select System Information, and click on Add.

6. Select whether you will manage a local or remote computer, and click on Finish.

7. Click on Close to close the Add Standalone Snap-in dialog box.

8. Click on OK. The System Information Utility is added to your console.

The System Information Utility also provides access to the following tools:

➤ *Disk Cleanup*—Disk Cleanup searches the hard drive and displays files that can be safely deleted.

➤ *Dr. Watson*—Dr. Watson is a program error debugger, which can be used to diagnose program errors on computers running Windows 2000.

➤ *DirectX Diagnostic Tool*—DirectX Diagnostic is a Windows-based tool for troubleshooting Direct X problems.

➤ *Hardware Wizard*—Hardware Wizard is useful for installing devices not recognized by Plug and Play.

➤ *Network Connections*—Network Connections can be used to open, create, and access settings for network connections on your computer.

➤ *Backup*—Backup is used to prevent accidental loss of data in the event of a hardware failure.

➤ *File Signature Verification Utility*—File Signature Verification Utility is used to ensure that file integrity is maintained in Windows 2000 Professional.

➤ *Update Wizard Uninstall*—Update Wizard Uninstall is used to remove a patch or driver that was installed and then restore the previous version.

➤ *Windows Report Tool*—Windows Report Tool collects information about your computer that can be used to aid in diagnosing and troubleshooting problems.

DiskProbe

The DiskProbe tool is used to examine and change information on individual disk sections. DiskProbe cannot be used on dynamic disks.

DiskMap

DiskMap is a tool used to display the layout of partitions and logical volumes on a disk.

AVBoot

AVBoot is a virus scanner that scans the master boot record and boot sectors on physical disks for viruses. If a virus is found, AVBoot can remove it.

Chkdsk

Chkdsk is a command-line tool that scans and repairs volumes on hard disks. Chkdsk can scan FAT16, FAT32, and NTFS volumes. Chkdsk cannot be run on CD-ROM and DVD-ROM disks.

Diagnostic Boot Options

If Windows 2000 Professional does not boot properly, users have several boot options to aid them in troubleshooting. These are:

➤ *Safe Mode*—Windows 2000 Professional is started with the minimum amount of files and drivers.

➤ *Safe Mode with Networking*—This is the same as Safe Mode, but includes networking support.

➤ *Safe Mode with Command Prompt*—Starts Windows 2000 Professional with the minimal files and drivers, and it boots to a command prompt.

➤ *Enable Boot Logging*—Windows 2000 professional is started normally, but all drivers and services are logged in systemroot\ntbtlog.txt

➤ *Enable VGA Mode*—Windows 2000 Professional is started with the basic VGA driver.

➤ *Last Known Good Configuration*—Starts Windows 2000 Professional with the last known good configuration, which the operating system saved before its most recent shut down. Registry settings are restored to the state the operating system was at before its last shut down.

➤ *Directory Services Restore Mode*—This applies to Windows 2000 Server, not Windows 2000 Professional.

➤ *Debugging Mode*—This also does not apply to Windows 2000 Professional.

To start Windows 2000 Professional in safe mode, press F8 when prompted for the operating system.

9

Chapter Summary

Windows 2000 Professional provides support for both legacy and new hardware devices, such as DVDs and smart cards. Plug and Play support has been added to Windows 2000 Professional. Plug and Play has been optimized to include support for WDM. WDM allows developers to develop device drivers that are compatible with both Windows 98 and Windows 2000.

Windows 2000 Professional now supports many new areas, such as IEEE 1394 ports, which are high-speed serial interfaces that complement USB. They are designed for applications requiring fast throughput, such as streaming video and desktop teleconferencing. Up to 63 devices can be attached to one IEEE 1394 port. Digital audio is also supported in Windows 2000 Professional through USB and IEEE 1394. Multiple streams of audio can be handled simultaneously, affording users the capability to listen to audio from two sources at the same time.

IrDA device support in Windows 2000 Professional is enhanced with transmission speeds of 115,000 bps and 4 Mbps. Users can send and receive files with the Wireless Link file transfer program. No additional hardware is required for communicating between infrared devices. Both infrared printing and infrared network connections are supported. PPP is the default protocol for infrared network connections in Windows 2000.

Windows 2000 is the first version of Windows to support still images. The Scanners and Camera icon in the Control Panel is provided to allow users to install and configure devices such as digital still cameras.

Windows 2000 Professional has limited APM support. Support is provided for notebook computers only. APM is the precursor to ACPI. ACPI, which is the foundation for the OnNow initiative, manages power requirements for computer hardware and software. ACPI allows the operating system to manage power requirements for all system components. Several power schemes are provided with Windows 2000 Professional to allow the user to manage power consumption. Users can also create their own power schemes if one of the predefined schemes does not meet their needs.

Windows 2000 Professional supports DirectX Version 7.0. DirectX provides enhanced multimedia capability, including enhanced 3-D animation and theater surround sound. ICM provides consistent color across multiple output devices. ICM uses color profiles to communicate color characteristics. Several default color profiles are installed with Windows 2000 Professional.

AGP is an expansion slot designed specifically for video adapters. The computer must have an AGP graphics controller to utilize the AGP expansion slot. AGP video adapters provide several improvements over PCI video adapters.

The use of multiple monitors is supported in Windows 2000 Professional. A single image can be displayed across multiple monitors, or each monitor can display a different application or document. Multiple monitor support is provided for both PCI and AGP video adapters.

DVD support is provided for DVD-Video, DVD-ROM, DVD-WO, and DVD-RAM. DVD is based on the Universal Disk Format (UDF), which is the successor to CDFS, or the CD-ROM file system.

The Device Manager is a tool that gives a graphical representation of hardware in the computer. The Device Manager can be used to troubleshoot hardware and device driver problems.

Driver Signing allows users to verify that their device drives have been digitally signed by Microsoft for use in Windows 2000. Driver Signing ensures the integrity of device drivers used in Windows 2000 and verifies that they have been tested by the WHQL. Troubleshooter wizards are provided to aid users in solving hardware problems. Additional troubleshooting tools, such as the System Information Utility, also aid users in resolving problems with their computer.

Review Questions

9

1. ICM is which of the following?

   a. An API

   b. A device driver

   c. A port emulator

   d. Windows system driver

2. Why would there be no APM tab in the Power Options menu in the Control Panel?

   a. The tab is hidden behind another tab.

   b. The computer does not support APM.

   c. The APM tab is located in the Scanners and Cameras menu in the Control Panel.

   d. The computer does not support APCI.

3. AGP stands for which of the following phrases?

   a. Accessible Graphics Peripheral

   b. Accelerated Graphics Port

   c. Accelerated Graphics Peripheral

   d. Advanced Graphics Port

4. Windows 2000 Professional supports connecting up to _____ monitors.

    a. 2

    b. 15

    c. 10

    d. 5

5. CAT files are stored in the _____ folder.

    a. systemroot\System32\Color

    b. systemroot\System32\CatRoot

    c. systemroot\temp

    d. systemroot\System32\drivers

6. For which of the following does DVD stand?

    a. Divided Video Disks

    b. Digital Version Disks

    c. Digital Video Disc

    d. Domain Video System

7. APCI is the same as APM. True or false?

    a. True

    b. False

8. Windows 2000 Professional currently supports writing to DVD devices. True or false?

    a. True

    b. False

9. Up to how many processors does Windows 2000 Professional support?

    a. 1

    b. 4

    c. 2

    d. 32

10. Windows 2000 Professional has a Troubleshooter for DHCP. True or false?

    a. True

    b. False

11. Which of the following can be USB devices?

    a. Keyboards

    b. Modems

    c. Printers

    d. Scanners

12. IrDA supports transmission rates of up to_____.

    a. 115,000 bps

    b. 350,000 bps

    c. 4 Mbps

    d. 16 Mbps

13. Which version of DirectX does Windows 2000 Professional support?

    a. Version 5.0

    b. Version 7.0

    c. Version 6.5a

    d. Version 1

14. Only members of the Administrator group can create hardware profiles. True or false?

    a. True

    b. False

15. Up to how many devices can be tiered to a single USB port?

    a. 2

    b. 100

    c. 127

    d. 250

16. Which of the following actions does driver signing perform?

    a. Trigger security negotiations for communications based on source

    b. Ensure that the highest quality device drivers are being used

    c. Allow a client to find a shared resource on a network

    d. List all drives currently running on a computer

17. AVBoot is used to examine and change information on disk sections. True or False?

    a. True

    b. False

9

18. Windows 2000 Professional supports Plug and Play. True or false?

    a. True

    b. False

19. Which boot option starts Windows 2000 Professional while logging drivers and services to a text file?

    a. Safe Mode

    d. Enable Boot Logging

    b. Safe Mode with Networking

    d. Enable VGA Mode

Real-World Projects

For the following projects, you need a computer running Windows 2000 Professional and a hard disk with at least one NTFS partition.

John has recently started his job as a network administrator for a local company. He notices that several of the computers that individuals are using seem to go into standby mode almost immediately after they are turned on. Users are complaining that they are constantly having to hit the Enter key or move the mouse to keep their desktop up. John believes that an improper power scheme has been selected for each computer, and he decides to configure the computers to use the Home/Office Desk power scheme.

Project 9.1

To select a power scheme for your desktop computer:

1. Open the Control Panel.

2. Double-click on the Power Options icon.

3. Select the Power Schemes tab.

4. Select a power scheme from the Power schemes drop-down box.

5. Click on Apply, and then click on OK.

Jennifer mentions to John that she cannot access the network. John finds out that Billy recently installed a second network adapter in Jennifer's computer. John tells Jennifer to print out a report of system settings on her computer to make sure that they are no IRQ conflicts with the second network adapter card Billy installed.

Project 9.2

To print out a report with all your system settings:

1. Open the Control Panel.

2. Double-click on the System icon.

3. Click on the Hardware tab.

4. Click on Device Manager.

5. Click on Print.

6. Select the type of report to print, and click on Print.

Mark has a notebook computer that he uses at home and at the office. Mark is tired of getting a network logon error when he is trying to use his computer at home. He asks John for help. John tells Mark that he can set up his notebook with two hardware profiles—one for the office and one for home. The profile for at-home use will not prompt for a network logon.

Project 9.3

To create a hardware profile:

1. Open the Control Panel.

2. Double-click on the System icon.

3. Click on the Hardware tab.

4. Click on the Hardware Profiles button.

5. Select the name of the hardware profile that you want to use as the base for the new hardware profile, and click on Copy.

6. Enter a name of the hardware profile you are creating, and click on OK.

7. Open Device Manager

8. Double-click on the item you want to configure for this profile, and click on Properties.

9. Make the changes to the item, and close Device Manager.

10. Click on OK to exit Systems Properties.

Martha is always going on the Internet and downloading files to her desktop computer. On several occasions, she has overwritten important device drivers. John is frustrated with having to constantly reinstall critical system files on her computer. He decides to set driver signing on her computer to ensure that only digitally signed drivers are copied on to her computer.

Project 9.4
To select the level of driver signing for your computer:

1. Open the Control Panel.

2. Double-click on the System icon.

3. Click on the Hardware tab.

4. Click on Driver Signing.

5. Select a level of driver signing under the File Signature Verification box.

6. Click on OK twice.

CHAPTER TEN

Networking

After completing this chapter, you will be able to:

✓ Define the basic components of a network

✓ Configure local area connections

✓ Configure remote connections

✓ Configure Virtual Private Network connections

✓ Configure Internet Connection Sharing

S ince the beginning of time, the human race has been driven to communicate. Cavemen drew on the walls of caves in prehistoric times. Around 5000 B.C., the Egyptians developed hieroglyphics. The first books started to appear around 70 A.D. In 1452, Gutenberg conceived of movable type and a mass-production paper-making technique, setting the stage for the printing press. The first computer was invented in the mid-1800s. A little over a century later, the Internet was born.

Networking Overview

Today, networking is so pervasive that it's hard to believe that merely ten years ago, many people didn't even know what the Internet was, let alone have access to it. Today the Internet is used for nearly everything: communication, research, commerce, weather, and so on. All this is possible through the advent of computer networking.

Networking Defined

A *network* is a group of computers connected via an electronic medium and associated hardware devices. The computers may share a common operating system, such as Windows 2000, but more important, they must be running a common network protocol.

Network protocols process requests from computers and handle the delivery of data from one computer to another. Network protocols have many functions. Some connection oriented network protocols, such as TCP or SPX, will retransmit any data that is corrupted or lost. Other network protocols are known as unreliable or non-connection oriented. These protocols, such as IP or IPX, are only concerned with the transmission of data, not whether it gets to the destination. The network protocol can also send notification messages when a data connection fails or a computer cannot be found.

Networking Hardware

There are various types of hardware that make networking possible. Working together, these hardware components create a synergistic entity that brings the network to life. Although they may not all be required in some network designs, they all play an important role in a network.

Network Media

The *network medium* provides the physical path on which communication occurs. There are two different classes of network media: bound and unbound.

Bound network media essentially consists of wired-based media. This includes un-shielded twisted pair (UTP), shielded twisted pair (STP), coaxial, and fiber optics.

➤ UTP cabling is by far the most common network medium. Originally used for telephone wiring, it has long held its place in the world of networking. UTP cabling consists of two or more insulated copper wires that are twisted together and wrapped in insulation. It is not shielded against interference, such as electro-magnetic interference (EMI) or radio frequency interference (RFI). By twisting the wires together, susceptibility to EMI is reduced. UTP is classified using a five-level category. The categories designate the number of twists per foot and the grade of insulation. Cat 1 is the lowest grade of UTP cabling. It works well for voice use only. Cat 3 is voice grade, but can be used for data. Cat 5 is recommended for data use. Cat 5 provides data capacity to 100 Mbps. UTP is extremely cost-effective in local area network (LAN) environments.

➤ STP provides better protection for data lines because it is shielded. The shielding is added under the outer jacket of the cabling with a drain wire that connects the shielding to an electrical ground. The shielding traps any EMI or RFI, which is then dissipated into the ground. STP typically forms the foundation of Token Ring networks. STP provides data capacity to 155 Mbps. Because of the additional shielding, STP is a more expensive alternative than UTP.

➤ Coaxial cabling provides higher bandwidth than UTP or STP, although it is not as flexible when designing the physical layout of the network. Coaxial cabling consists of two conductors. The first conductor is typically a solid copper wire that runs in the center of the cable. This conductor is surrounded by insulation. The outer conductor, which is a wire mesh, surrounds the insulation. Coaxial resists EMI and RFI better than UTP or STP. Although coaxial is typically used for television and cable transmissions, in LAN environments, it is used in a bus configuration.

➤ Fiber optic cabling doesn't experience any of the problems faced by the other bound media. Fiber optic uses light pulses instead of electrons to transmit data. It is not affected by EMI or RFI, it has much higher bandwidth, and it can be used in distances measured in kilometers, not meters. The downside of fiber optics is its high cost. It is typically used as a high-speed network backbone.

Unbound network media consists of wireless media. This area of technology is constantly expanding, but it includes radio, microwave, and infrared. Unbound network media allows a network to span larger geographic distances.

➤ When used as a networking media, radio tends to be used in the unregulated radio bands: 902 through 928MHz, 2.4GHz, and 5.72 through 5.85GHz. These bands are used because there are few restrictions and no licensing fees placed on them. Systems based on radio can operate at 1 Mbps through 10 Mbps. These speeds are increasing with the latest advancements in technology.

➤ Microwave operates at frequencies that are even higher than those used in radio. The frequency ranges are 6GHz through 11GHz and 21GHz through 23GHz for ground-based microwave; and 11GHz through 14GHz for satellite microwave.

➤ Infrared communication is essentially unbound fiber optic technology. Similar to fiber optics, Infrared relies on light to send data back and forth. Infrared cannot pass through walls or solid objects; it is usually used in line-of-sight applications. There are two different types of Infrared communications: Point-to-Point and Broadcast:

> ➤ Point-to-Point Infrared is the most typical infrared application. It can be used between two systems, such as a laptop and a laser printer. By lining up the infrared ports between the two systems, the laptop can create a connection with the printer and send print jobs to it.

> ➤ Broadcast Infrared is used when an access point is installed in a room, typically the ceiling, and communicates with multiple infrared receiving devices. Because the light is highly diluted throughout the room, bandwidth is very low.

Hubs

A *hub* is a network device that provides a central point of connectivity to a physical network. Each individual computer connects to the hub with its own network cable. Network traffic that enters the hub is then replicated and sent back out every port in the hub.

Bridges

A *bridge* is a network device that connects two or more physical networks. The bridge maintains a table consisting of hardware addresses. When the bridge receives a *frame* from one physical segment, it checks the destination hardware address for the frame against the table. A frame is a segment of data that includes source and destination hardware addresses. Picture a frame as though it's a postal envelope, in which you place your letter (the data). You then address the envelope (the frame) with the recipient's mailing address (the destination hardware address) and your return address (the source hardware address). If the hardware address is located on the other side of the bridge, it allows the frame to cross. If it isn't, the frame is not permitted to cross.

Switches

A *switch* is a network device that combines the features of bridges and hubs. Like a hub, a switch contains ports that interconnect multiple computers or physical networks. Like a bridge, the switch analyzes the destination hardware address in a frame and sends the frame out the appropriate port. Because the frame is not replicated on all ports (like a hub), using a switch results in greater bandwidth for the individual workstations.

Routers

A *router* is a network device that connects two or more logical networks. The router maintains a routing table that tells the router which logical networks it knows the routes *to*. When the router receives a packet, it analyzes the packet's logical destination address to determine where it should route the packet. If the router is aware of a route to the destination, it forwards the packet to the next hop according to the routing table. If the router is not aware of a suitable route, the router discards the packet and sends a notification to the sender that the destination was not reachable.

Types of Networks

Networks are organized according to their desired function. Consider, for example, the administrative model and geographic locations.

Workgroup Networks

The workgroup, also known as a *peer-to-peer network*, is the simplest type of network. Workgroup networks are ideal for file and print sharing among a small number of users and computers. Typically, workgroup networks are used in homes and small offices, where a centralized administrative model is not required. A workgroup is a group of computers associated by name only. All computers in a workgroup maintain their own security database. As a result, user administration is more complex because a user needs to have valid user accounts on each computer. Most peer-to-peer networks are based on Windows 95 or 98 as well as Windows NT Workstation or Windows 2000 Professional.

Domain-Based Networks

Domain-based networks are much more common in larger businesses. Domain-based networks are used for many network applications, such as file and print sharing, and also messaging, database, and intranet applications. Domain-based networks benefit from a centralized administration, which results in a stronger security model and efficient user administration. A user requires a single user account to access network resources. Domain-based networks are usually built using NetWare, Unix, Windows NT, and Windows 2000, or a combination of these operating systems.

Windows 2000 Component Architecture

Windows 2000 supports a modular component architecture to support networking. These components are all software based. Figure 10.1 shows the components from bottom to top.

Network Driver Interface Specification (NDIS) Layer

The NDIS layer provides a way for a network transport (TCP/IP, NWLink, or NetBEUI) to communicate with a network adapter. This layer contains the drivers that communicate directly with the network adapters.

Network Protocol Layer

The Network Protocol layer provides services that allow data to be sent across the network. These protocols include IP, NWLink, NetBEUI, AppleTalk, Infrared Data

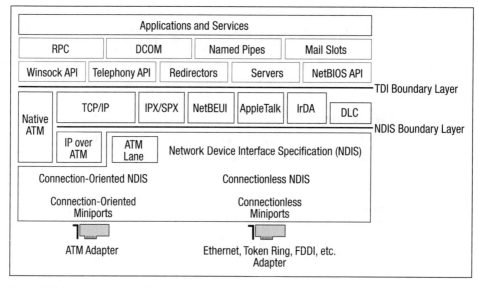

Figure 10.1   Windows 2000 Component Architecture.

Association (IrDA), Asynchronous Transfer Mode (ATM), and Data Link Control (DLC).

Transport Driver Interface Layer

The Transport Driver Interface (TDI) layer provides an interface between the Network Protocol layer and the Network Application Programming Interface layer. This allows an application programming interface (API) to operate independently of any particular network protocol.

Network Application Programming Interface Layer

The Network Application Programming Interface layer is a set of APIs that applications can use to access network services. These APIs provide a set of standard routines that the applications can use to perform low-level network activities. By employing APIs, the application doesn't need to contain its own code to perform network functions. APIs include Winsock, NetBIOS, Telephony, Messaging, and WNet.

Interprocess Communications Layer

The Interprocess Communications (IPC) layer supports applications that rely on communications for client/server and distributed processing technology. Some of these services include remote procedure calls (RPC), Named Pipes, Mailslots, the Distributed Component Object Model (DCOM), and the Common Internet File System (CIFS).

Basic Network Services Layer

Basic Network Services support user applications by providing networking services. These services include simple I/O requests, such as reading and writing to a file across the network. Services at this layer include the Server service, Workstation service, and Network Resource Access.

Creating and Managing Connections

In today's networking environments, a workstation may be required to connect to a number of different types of networks. Windows 2000 allows a number of connections to be created. These include local area connections or LAN-based connections, remote connections, Virtual Private Network (VPN) connections, and direct connections. All connections are created in the Network and Dial-up Connections folder (see Figure 10.2).

Local Area Connections

Local area connections are LAN-based connections and are the fastest connection type. These connections use one of the following communication methods: Ethernet, Token Ring, Cable Modem, Digital Subscriber Line (DSL), Fiber Distributed Data Interface (FDDI), IP over ATM, Wireless, IrDA, T1, and Frame Relay.

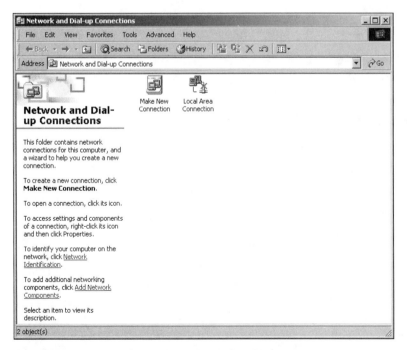

Figure 10.2   The Network and Dial-up Connections folder.

A local area connection is created by default for each network adapter installed in the system. For example, if a Windows 2000-based computer contains two network adapters, two local area connection icons will be displayed in the folder. To modify an existing local area connection, you need to right-click on the connection and select Properties. The Local Area Connection Properties dialog box is displayed (see Figure 10.3).

The Local Area Connection Properties dialog box shows which network adapter is being used by the connection. It also displays the components that are in use with this connection. The components are divided into three categories: Clients, Services, and Protocols.

Clients

A Client is a software component that provides access to computers and files on the local area network. The following clients are shipped with Windows 2000:

➤ *Client for Microsoft Networks*—This client provides access to all Microsoft-based file and print services, such as Windows 95/98 or Windows NT. The client sends requests to the servers using the Server Message Block (SMB) protocol.

➤ *Gateway (and Client) Services for NetWare*—This client provides access to all NetWare file and print servers. This client sends requests to the servers using the NetWare Core Protocol (NCP).

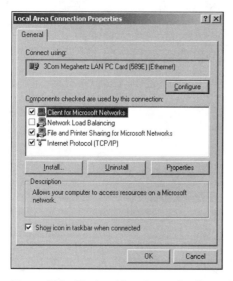

Figure 10.3   The Local Area Connection Properties dialog box.

Services

A Service is a software component that provides additional features to the operating system, such as file and print sharing. The following services are shipped with Windows 2000:

➤ *File and Printer Sharing for Microsoft Networks*—Essentially, this Server service allows a Windows 2000-based system to share its files and printers across the network.

➤ *QoS Packet Scheduler*—Quality of Service (QoS) allows an administrator to control bandwidth on the network. For example, if a user needs to use a network intensive application, such as Voice over IP (VoIP), QoS can be implemented to prioritize VoIP traffic over regular network traffic.

➤ *SAP Agent*—The Service Advertisement Protocol (SAP) Agent collects and distributes SAP information and responds to client SAP requests. Used on a NetWare IPX-based network, SAP creates a list of services available on the network and their corresponding IPX internetwork addresses.

Protocols

A Protocol is a software component that allows the computer to communicate with other computers on the network. A protocol is a common language that the computer uses for the communication. The following protocols are shipped with Windows 2000:

10

➤ *AppleTalk*—The AppleTalk protocol allows a Windows 2000-based computer to communicate on Apple Macintosh networks. It is a routable protocol.

➤ *DLC*—The DLC protocol allows a Windows 2000-based computer to connect to an IBM host, such as the AS400. DLC is also used with HP JetDirects for network printers without using TCP/IP. It is a nonroutable protocol.

➤ *NetBEUI*—The NetBEUI protocol is a simple, nonroutable protocol. It works well on small networks with less than 10 computers.

➤ *NWLink (IPX/SPX)*—NWLink, more commonly known as IPX/SPX, allows a Windows 2000-based computer to communicate with Novell NetWare networks. A routable protocol can be used in small, medium, or large networks.

➤ *TCP/IP*—By far the most commonly used protocol in the world, TCP/IP allows a Windows 2000-based computer to communicate via the Internet or across a LAN. It is a routable protocol.

Remote Connections

Remote connections provide a network connection for mobile users who need to dial in to their corporate LAN. Most corporations have a dial-in infrastructure that supports remote access with modem and integrated services digital network (ISDN) lines. Remote connections can also be employed to establish a connection to the Internet via an Internet Service Provider (ISP).

When creating a remote connection with Windows 2000, you have two choices: connect to a private network or connect to the Internet. In most operating systems, there is no difference between the two. In Windows 2000, however, File and Print Sharing for Microsoft Networks is automatically disabled if a connection to the Internet is created. This protects your computer from unauthorized access via the Internet.

To create a remote connection to a private network, follow these steps:

1. Open the Network and Dial-up Connection folder by selecting Start | Settings | Network and Dial-up Connections.

2. Double-click on the Make New Connection icon. The Network Connection Wizard starts.

3. On the Network Connection Type screen, select Dial-Up To A Private Network, and click on Next.

4. On the Select A Device screen, the devices currently installed in the computer and that are capable of establishing remote connections are displayed (see Figure 10.4). Select the device you want to use, and click on Next.

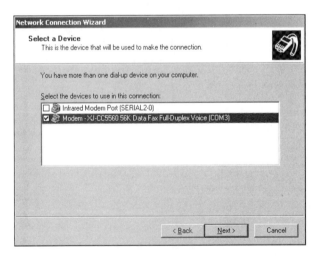

Figure 10.4 Selecting a remote connection device.

5. On this screen, you enter the phone number of the dial-up connection to the private network. Specify the phone number and area code in the appropriate box. Click on Next.

6. The Connection Availability screen is displayed. This screen allows you to specify if the remote connection being created can be used by other users. Select For All Users, and click on Next.

7. The Internet Connection Sharing (ICS) screen is displayed. ICS is discussed later, in "Internet Connection Sharing" in this chapter. Click on Next.

8. Finally, name the remote connection. Type "Dial-up to Corporate Network" and click on Next.

To create a remote connection to the Internet, follow these steps:

1. Open the Network and Dial-up Connection folder by selecting Start | Settings | Network and Dial-up Connections.

2. Double-click on the Make New Connection icon. The Network Connection Wizard starts.

3. On the Network Connection Type screen, select Dial-Up To The Internet, and click on Next.

4. The Internet Connection Wizard starts. This wizard gives you three options:

   ➤ I Want To Sign Up For A New Internet Account. (My Telephone Line Is Connected To My Modem.)

   ➤ I Want To Transfer My Existing Internet Account To This Computer. (My Telephone Line Is Connected To My Modem.)

   ➤ I Want To Set Up My Internet Connection Manually, Or I Want To Connect Through A Local Area Network (LAN).

   If you select either of the first two options, Windows 2000 connects you to the Microsoft Referral Service, which presents you with phone numbers for ISPs.

   If you select the last option, you are expected to supply (if required by the ISP) an IP address and a DNS server address.

Virtual Private Network (VPN) Connections

A VPN is a private network that uses a public network infrastructure, such as the Internet (see Figure 10.5). Because using a public network infrastructure creates a security risk, a VPN relies on a tunneling protocol to maintain privacy and security. With a VPN, a user can connect to the corporate LAN and access resources and data as though they were directly connected. The connection is secure because the tunneling protocol encrypts and encapsulates the data at one end of the connection, and then decrypts the data on the far side connection.

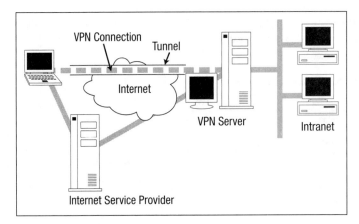

Figure 10.5   A Virtual Private Network.

Windows 2000 supports two tunneling protocols to create a VPN environment: Point-to-Point Tunneling Protocol (PPTP) and Layer 2 Tunneling Protocol (L2TP).

PPTP

PPTP is a simple, yet secure, way of creating a VPN for clients. PPTP is a TCP/IP protocol that can encapsulate TCP/IP, IPX/SPX, or NetBEUI protocols. Using the authentication, encryption, and compression capabilities of the Point-to-Point Protocol (PPP), Windows 2000 clients with a PPP connection to an ISP can take advantage of the security found in PPTP to connect to their corporate LANs.

L2TP

L2TP combines the features of PPTP and Layer 2 Forwarding, developed by Cisco Systems, is another tunneling protocol. L2TP is similar to PPTP, but uses User Datagram Protocol (UDP), which is a connectionless transport protocol. Although L2TP was designed to run over a number of different networks, such as Frame Relay, ATM, and X.25, in Windows 2000, L2TP supports only IP networks.

Because L2TP itself doesn't provide data encryption, L2TP relies on Internet Protocol Security (IPSec). IPSec is a group of open standards that define methods of using public key cryptography for secure IP connections. IPSec is discussed in the "Data Encryption" section later in this chapter.

When a connection is created between two computers using L2TP and IPSec, it goes through a couple of stages.

1. Both computers, the VPN client and the VPN host, are authenticated. This is known as *mutual authentication*. At this stage, the two computers exchange computer certificates to establish an IPSec Encapsulating Security Payload (ESP) security association (SA). In order for the exchange to occur, a computer certificate must be installed on both computers. Certificates can be created

by using the Certificates snap-in. Both computers then agree on an encryption algorithm, a hash algorithm, and encryption keys.

2. The user is authenticated via the user authentication protocols found in PPP: Extensible Authentication Protocol (EAP), Microsoft Challenge Handshake Authentication Protocol (MSCHAP), Challenge Handshake Authentication Protocol (CHAP), Shiva Password Authentication Protocol (SPAP), and Password Authentication Protocol (PAP). These protocols are discussed in the "Authentication Protocols" section later in this chapter.

To create a VPN Connection, follow these steps:

1. Open the Network and Dial-up Connection folder by selecting Start|Settings| Network and Dial-up Connections.

2. Double-click on the Make New Connection icon. The Network Connection Wizard starts. Click on Next.

3. On the Network Connection Type screen, select Connect To A Private Network Through The Internet, and click on Next.

4. On the Destination Address screen, enter the name or IP address of the computer that will be hosting the VPN connection. Click on Next.

5. On the Connection Availability screen, determine whether this VPN connection should be stored in your profile only or be available to all users. Click on Next.

6. The Internet Connection Sharing screen is displayed. ICS is discussed in "Internet Connection Sharing" later in this chapter. Click on Next.

7. Name the VPN connection. Type "VPN to Corporate Network", and click on Next.

By default, the VPN Connection is set to Automatic, where L2TP is attempted first, then PPTP. If you are sure of the type of VPN connection to use, configure the setting to L2TP or PPTP by following these steps:

1. Open the Network and Dial-up Connection folder by selecting Start|Settings| Network and Dial-up Connections.

2. Right-click on the desired VPN connection, and select Properties.

3. The Virtual Private Connection Properties dialog box is displayed. Select the Networking tab to display the Networking page (see Figure 10.6).

4. From the Type Of VPN Server I Am Calling drop-down list, select PPTP or L2TP.

5. Click on OK to save your selections.

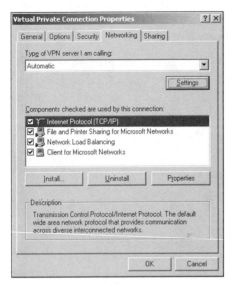

Figure 10.6 Setting the tunneling protocol.

Direct Connections

Another type of remote connection supported by Windows 2000 is direct connections. Direct connections are typically used to synchronize information between a Personal Digital Assistant (PDA), such as a Palm Pilot or Windows CE device, and a desktop computer. Windows 2000 supports three different direct connection types: Serial, Infrared, and Parallel.

Security for Remote Connections

Now that we have reviewed the several methods of creating a remote connection using Windows 2000, you need to consider an issue that is becoming more and more important in today's networking environments: security.

Because the very nature of remote connections means that users from outside the corporate LAN can establish a connection and access the network's resources, it is important that measures are in place to verify that the user is permitted access. It is also important to ensure the integrity of the data being transmitted.

Authentication

Authentication is the process in which the system validates the user's logon credentials. In other words, the user's user name and password are compared to an authoritative database, such as the Security Accounts Manager (SAM). If the credentials match those in the database, access is granted. If they do not match access is denied.

Interactive Authentication

Interactive authentication occurs when the user logs in at the keyboard of a Windows 2000 computer. The Winlogon process passes the user's credentials to the Local Security Authority (LSA), which then attempts to verify them. If the credentials match, Winlogon creates an interactive session on the computer and provides access. If they do not match, access is denied.

If the account is issued on the local computer where the logon is occurring, the LSA itself verifies the credentials. If the account is issued from another security entity, such as a domain, the LSA contacts the issuing authority for verification.

Network Authentication

Network authentication occurs when the user attempts to access any network resource or service. This type of authentication can be provided by Kerberos, Secure Socket Layer/Transport Layer Security (SSL/TLS), and Windows NT LAN Manager (NTLM), which is used by Windows NT 4.

If users access a local account (one that was issued by the LSA) when logging on, they will be prompted for a user name and password whenever they attempt to access network resources. Users who log in with a domain account do not receive such challenges if the resource being accessed trusts the domain.

Authentication Protocols

10

Authentication Protocols are responsible for the transmission and reception of user names and passwords.

PAP

PAP is the least sophisticated authentication protocol. It transmits the password in plaintext, that is, unencrypted. PAP tends to be the least common denominator in authentication protocols, and it is used when two computers cannot negotiate a more secure means of authentication.

SPAP

SPAP is a proprietary authentication protocol used to connect Windows 2000 dial-in clients to a Shiva dial-in server.

CHAP

Designed to address some of the concerns of transmitting passwords via plaintext, CHAP uses an encrypted authentication based on a hashing method known as Message Digest 5 (MD5). CHAP operates by having the server send a challenge to the client computer. The client computer, using MD5, hashes both the challenge and the password and sends it to the server. The server, knowing the challenge and the user's password from its security database, creates its own hash. The server then compares the two hashes. If the hashes match, the requested access is permitted.

Because CHAP operates in this way, the password itself is never actually transmitted across the network.

MSCHAP

MSCHAP uses the same challenge-response type of authentication found in CHAP. Instead of MD5, MSCHAP uses MD4 for its hashing method.

MSCHAP v2

MSCHAP v2 provides more advanced features than CHAP or MSCHAP. These features include mutual authentication, stronger initial data encryption keys, and different encryption keys for sending and receiving data.

The MSCHAP v2 authentication process operates as follows:

1. The server sends a challenge to the client that includes a unique session identifier and an arbitrary challenge string.

2. The client sends a response with a user name, an arbitrary peer challenge string, a hashed copy of the challenge string, the peer challenge string, and the user's password.

3. The server receives and checks the response from the client. It then sends a response to the client containing an indication of whether the authentication was successful.

4. The client verifies the authentication response from the server. If authentication is successful, the client begins to use the connection. If authentication fails, the client terminates the connection.

MSCHAP v2 also allows users to change their passwords when the passwords expire.

EAP

EAP is an extension to PPP that works with dial-in, PPTP, and L2TP clients. EAP allows additional authentication methods with PPP. These methods include smart cards, such as Secure ID, public key authentication, and certificates. EAP is generally used in VPN networks that require stronger authentication methods.

To configure the Authentication Protocol used by the remote connection, follow these steps:

1. Open the Network and Dial-up Connection folder by selecting Start | Settings | Network and Dial-up Connections.

2. Right-click on the desired remote connection, and select Properties.

3. The Dial-up Connection Properties dialog box is displayed. Select the Security tab to display the Security page.

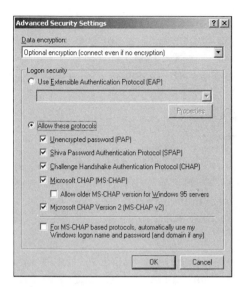

Figure 10.7   The Advanced Security Settings dialog box.

4. Select Advanced, and then click on the Settings button. The Advanced Security Settings dialog box is displayed (see Figure 10.7).

5. Select EAP or one of the other authentication methods.

6. Click on OK to save your selections.

Data Encryption

Data encryption is a way to secure the actual transmission of the data across a network. Data is encrypted using a key algorithm, which can only be decrypted by a computer with the appropriate key. Windows 2000 supports two types of data encryption: Microsoft Point-to-Point Encryption (MPPE) and IPSec.

MPPE

MPPE uses Rivest-Shamir-Adlemen (RSA) RC4 encryption. MPPE can be used only if EAP-TLS, MSCHAP, or MSCHAP v2 is used for authentication.

MPPE can use 40-bit, 56-bit, or 128-bit encryption keys. The client and the server negotiate the encryption key, and the highest key supported by both is used. If the server requires a key higher than the client can support, the connection is terminated.

IPSec

IPSec is a group of services and protocols that use cryptography to protect data. Typically used for L2TP-based VPNs, IPSec provides machine-level authentication and data encryption.

Because IPSec is implemented at the Internet Layer of the OSI model, IPSec encapsulates data provided from upper layer applications and becomes transparent to the user. In this way, IPSec packets are encrypted at the transmitting end of a connection and decrypted at the receiving end. The encapsulated data is then presented to the upper layer applications.

Internet Connection Sharing

ICS is a new feature found in Windows 2000 that allows a single computer to host an Internet connection for a network. For example, if you have a small office with 10 computers, only one of the computers (running Windows 2000 and ICS) would require a physical dial-up connection. The other nine computers would be ICS clients and would access the Internet via the ICS computer.

ICS provides IP address allocation, network address translation (NAT), and name resolution services for all ICS clients. Clients can use Internet applications (e.g., Internet Explorer and Outlook) as though the computers themselves were connected. If the ICS connection to the Internet isn't active when one of the clients attempts access, ICS automatically dials the ISP and creates the connection. The client is then able to access the requested resource.

Configuring ICS

The computer running ICS needs two connections: one for the internal network (i.e., the connection for computers in the office) and one for the connection to the Internet.

To enable ICS, follow these steps:

1. Create a remote connection to the Internet as described earlier in this chapter.

2. Open the Network and Dial-up Connection folder by selecting Start | Settings | Network and Dial-up Connections.

3. Right-click on the desired remote connection, and select Properties.

4. The Dial-up Connection Properties dialog box is displayed. Select the Sharing tab to display the Sharing page (see Figure 10.8).

5. Select the Enable Internet Connection Sharing For This Connection checkbox.

By enabling ICS, the computer automatically becomes a Dynamic Host Configuration Protocol (DHCP) server for the office network. DHCP automatically assigns IP addresses to the hosts on the office network along with TCP/IP configuration information, such as DNS servers. Table 10.1 displays the settings that are configured when ICS is enabled.

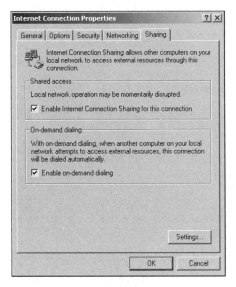

Figure 10.8 Enabling ICS.

Note that these default settings cannot be modified, nor can any particular service, such as DHCP or DNS Proxy, be disabled.

Configuring ICS Clients

Configuring ICS clients is simple. Verify that the ICS client is configured as follows:

➤ The local area connection is using Client for Microsoft Networks, Internet Protocol (TCP/IP), and File and Printer Sharing.

➤ TCP/IP is configured to obtain an IP address and DNS server addresses automatically from a DHCP server.

Table 10.1   ICS settings.

Item	Configuration	Description
IP address	192.168.0.1	IP address for the office network adapter.
Subnet mask	255.255.255.0	Subnet mask for the office network adapter.
Autodial	Enabled	If Internet connection is not present, ICS autodials the modem to create the connection.
Static default route	Created when the dial-up connection is established	Provides a default route from the office network to the Internet.
Internet Connection Sharing Service		Starts automatically.
DHCP Allocator	Enabled	Allocates IP addresses from 192.168.0.2 through 192.168.0.254, with a subnet mask of 255.255.255.0.
DNS Proxy	Enabled	ICS receives DNS queries from clients and forwards them to a DNS server.

10

After verifying that the previous settings are correct, configure the ICS client as follows:

1. Start Internet Explorer.

2. From the Tools drop-down menu, select Internet Options.

3. In the Dial-up Settings, select Never Dial A Connection. Next, click on LAN Settings.

4. In Automatic Configuration, select Automatically Detect Settings. Clear the Use Automatic Configuration Script checkbox.

5. In Proxy Server, clear the Use A Proxy Server checkbox. Click on OK to close the LAN Settings dialog box. Click on OK to close the Internet Options dialog box.

At this point, the ICS client can access and browse the Internet using the ICS host. Note that the previous steps configure only Internet Explorer. If other applications, such as Outlook, need to be configured, refer to the instructions for the application.

Chapter Summary

In this chapter, you learned that Windows 2000 is a robust networking platform. Microsoft provides the means to connect a Windows 2000 Professional computer to practically every networking environment.

A number of devices are combined to form a functional network. The network media facilitates the network communication. The network media may be bound or cabling, or it may be unbound, such as radio, microwave, or infrared. A hub is a network device that provides a central point of connectivity for several work-stations. A bridge connects two or more physical network segments and divides traffic according to the physical addresses of the hosts on each segment. A switch operates much like a hub except that it also operates like a bridge, where it divides traffic according to the destination physical address. This results in greater bandwidth for individual workstations. A router connects two or more logical networks and divides the traffic according to the logical network address.

There are two different network administrative models supported by Windows 2000. The first is the workgroup, which is a collection of network computers by name only. A workgroup has a noncentralized administration, where each computer maintains its own database of user accounts. The second is a domain-based network. A domain-based network is a group of network computers that share a common database of user accounts. This results in a centralized administrative model.

Windows 2000 is based on a software component architecture to provide network connectivity. There are a number of different levels to this architecture, starting with the NDIS layer. This layer consists of the network adapter drivers. The next layer is the Network Protocol layer, which provides services for network communication. Windows 2000 supports TCP/IP, NWLink, NetBEUI, AppleTalk, IrDA, ATM, and DLC. The TDI layer provides an interface between the Network Protocol layer and the Network Application Interface layer. TDI allows upper layer applications to operate independently of any particular protocol. The Network Application Programming Interface layer is a set of APIs that contain common routines, which applications can employ to use the network. The IPC layer supports applications that rely on bidirectional communication, typically client/server based applications. The Basic Network Services layer supports applications by providing basic networking services, such as drive mapping and file I/O requests across the networks.

Windows 2000 supports a number of network connections, both local and remote. This gives Windows 2000 the capability to connect to a number of varied networking environments. Windows 2000 supports local area connections over Ethernet, Token Ring, FDDI, ATM, IrDA, T1, and Frame Relay.

Remote Connections can be dial-up or VPN connections. For dial-up connections, Windows 2000 provides the capability to connect either to private networks or to the Internet via an ISP. If the connection is to the Internet, Windows 2000 automatically disables File and Printer Sharing to protect the workstation from unauthorized access. Windows 2000 is capable of creating VPN connections via the use of tunneling protocols, such as PPTP and L2TP. A VPN provides a secure, private network connection via a public infrastructure, such as the Internet.

10

To provide security for remote connections, Windows 2000 supports a number of authentication protocols: PAP, SPAP, CHAP, MSCHAP, MSCHAP v2, and EAP. Data encryption is supplied by using either MPPE or IPSec.

Windows 2000 provides a new service known as ICS. This feature allows a single computer to host an Internet connection that other computers on the network can share and utilize. When ICS is enabled, the ICS host becomes a DHCP server that provides IP addresses to the internal network. It also provides a DNS Proxy that accepts name resolution requests from the network and directs them to a DNS server.

Review Questions

1. Which authentication protocol provides unencrypted transmission of passwords?

   a. L2TP

   b. ISDN

   c. PAP

   d. CHAP

2. Which network device provides a central point of network connectivity and replicates any signals received to all ports?

   a. Switch

   b. Hub

   c. Router

   d. Gateway

3. Which network model is based on separate account databases being maintained by each computer?

   a. Domain

   b. Client/Server

   c. Distributed

   d. Workgroup

4. Which network service allows an administrator to control the bandwidth usage on the network?

   a. SAP Agent

   b. Throttle Service

   c. File and Printer Sharing for Microsoft Networks

   d. QoS Packet Scheduler

5. Which network clients are included with Windows 2000?

   a. Client for Linux Networks

   b. Client Services for NetWare

   c. Client for Microsoft Networks

   d. AppleTalk Client Services

6. Which tunneling protocol relies on IPSec to provide data encryption?

   a. L2TP

   b. IPSec

   c. PPTP

   d. PPP

7. With CHAP, when is the password transmitted across the network?

   a. During the challenge

   b. During the response

   c. Never

8. What is the function of the NDIS layer of the Windows 2000 Component Architecture?

   a. Provides a design structure for network adapters

   b. Provides a connectivity between network protocols and APIs

   c. Provides services between network adapters and network protocols

   d. Provides communications from APIs to network adapters.

9. Which authentication protocol is used with smart cards?

   a. PPTP

   b. EAP

   c. VPN

   d. MSCHAPv2

10. Which network device connects two or more physical networks?

   a. Bridge

   b. Hub

   c. Gateway

   d. Router

11. A Windows 2000 computer hosting ICS can be configured with a DHCP address. True or false?

   a. True

   b. False

10

12. You have some clients that need to connect to your corporate network using third-party communication software. The server they are dialing into supports MSCHAP v2. What other authentication protocol should you configure the server to use?

   a. MS-CHAP v2 only

   b. CHAP

   c. MSCHAP

   d. PAP

13. Which network protocols provide connectivity between Windows 2000 Professional and Novell NetWare 5?

   a. NWLink

   b. TCP/IP

   c. NetBEUI

   d. DLC

14. The Windows 2000 Component Architecture is comprised of what type of components?

    a. Software

    b. Hardware

    c. Network

    d. Both software and hardware

15. Which network device connects two or more logical networks?

    a. Bridge

    b. Hub

    c. Gateway

    d. Router

16. Windows 2000 supports only local area and remote connections. True or false?

    a. True

    b. False

17. What connection media cannot be used for a local area connection?

    a. ATM

    b. Ethernet

    c. X.25

    d. Token Ring

18. Which network device provides a centralized point of network connectivity and routes signals received to the proper destination port only?

    a. Router

    b. Gateway

    c. Switch

    d. Bridge

19. Which network protocol provides connectivity between Windows 2000 Professional and Novell NetWare 3.12?

    a. NWLink

    b. TCP/IP

    c. NetBEUI

    d. DLC

20. Which protocol is not shipped with Windows 2000?

    a. AppleTalk

    b. NetBEUI

    c. Localtalk

    d. TCP/IP

21. Which network model is based on a centralized account database being shared by all member computers?

    a. Domain

    b. Client/server

    c. Centralized

    d. Workgroup

22. What is the function of the Network Protocol layer of the Windows 2000 Component Architecture?

    a. Provides services that facilitates the transmission of data across the network

    b. Provides services between transport protocols and network adapters

    c. Provides communication paths between APIs and network adapters

    d. Provides services that facilitates the communication of data via network adapters

10

Real-World Projects

You have just been assigned to a team to redesign your corporation's remote access capabilities. You have been assigned the task of determining and configuring the dial-in clients.

Project 10.1

To create a remote dial-up connection:

1. Open the Network and Dial-up Connection folder by selecting Start | Settings | Network and Dial-up Connections.

2. Double-click on the Make New Connection icon. The Network Connection Wizard starts.

3. On the Network Connection Type screen, select Dial-Up To A Private Network, and click on Next.

4. On the Select a Device screen, the devices currently installed in the computer that are capable of establishing remote connections are displayed (refer to Figure 10.4). Select the device you want to use, and click on Next.

5. This screen is for entering the phone number of the dial-up connection to the private network. Specify the phone number and area code in the appropriate box. Click on Next.

6. The Connection Availability screen is displayed. This screen allows you to specify if the remote connection being created can be used by other users. Select For All Users, and click on Next.

7. The Internet Connection Sharing screen is displayed. Click on Next.

8. Name the remote connection. Type "Dial-up to Corporate Network", and click on Next.

After consulting with the security engineer on the team, you decide that you want to use VPN connections for the remote clients. The security engineer configures the dial-in architecture to use L2TP for the tunneling protocol. The IP address for the server hosting the VPN connection is 10.123.1.1.

Project 10.2

To create a remote VPN connection:

1. Open the Network and Dial-up Connection folder by selecting Start | Settings | Network and Dial-up Connections.

2. Double-click on the Make New Connection icon. The Network Connection Wizard starts.

3. On the Network Connection Type screen, select Connect To A Private Network Through The Internet, and click on Next.

4. On the Destination Address screen, type "10.123.1.1". Click on Next.

5. On the Connection Availability screen, decide whether this VPN connection will be available to all users. Click on Next.

6. The Internet Connection Sharing screen is displayed. Click on Next.

7. Type "VPN to Corporate Network", and click on Next.

Next, you need to configure the VPN connection to use L2TP as the tunneling protocol.

Project 10.3

To select L2TP for the remote VPN connection:

1. Right-click on the VPN connection, and select Properties.

2. The Virtual Private Connection Properties dialog box is displayed. Select the Networking tab to display the Networking page.

3. From the Type Of VPN Server I Am Calling drop-down list, select L2TP.

4. Click on OK to save your selections.

After the project is complete, you are assigned a small project. This project consists of establishing Internet connectivity for a small office. Because the clients computers use Windows 2000 Professional workstations, you decide to use Internet Connection Sharing. You order a DSL line from a local provider.

Project 10.4

To install ICS:

1. Open the Network and Dial-up Connection folder by selecting Start|Settings| Network and Dial-up Connections.

2. Rename the local area connection on the Windows 2000 Professional machine to Office Network. Power down the computer.

3. The DSL line requires the use of a second network adapter. Install the second network adapter. Power up the computer, and install the network adapter's device driver if Plug and Play does not detect it.

4. Open the Network and Dial-up Connection folder by selecting Start|Settings| Network and Dial-up Connections.

5. Rename the new local area connection to Internet Connection.

6. Right-click on Internet Connection, and select Properties.

7. Select the Sharing tab to display the Sharing page.

8. Select the Enable Internet Connection Sharing For This Connection checkbox.

Next, you need to configure the clients on the office network.

Project 10.5

To configure ICS clients:

1. Right-click on My Network Places, and select Properties.

2. Select Internet Protocol, and click on the Properties button.

10

3. Verify that the system is set to obtain an IP address automatically from a DHCP server. Also, verify that it will obtain DNS server addresses automatically.

4. Start Internet Explorer.

5. From the Tools drop-down menu, select Internet Options.

6. In the Dial-up Settings, select Never Dial A Connection. Next, click on LAN Settings.

7. In Automatic Configuration, select Automatically Detect Settings. Clear the Use Automatic Configuration Script checkbox.

8. In Proxy Server, clear the Use A Proxy Server checkbox. Click on OK to close the LAN Settings dialog box. Click on OK to close the Internet Options dialog box.

CHAPTER ELEVEN

A TCP/IP Primer

After completing this chapter, you will be able to:

✓ Define an IP address

✓ Determine a basic subnet mask

✓ Identify the network ID and broadcast ID

✓ Identify the class of an IP address

Windows 2000 networking is based on Transmission Control Protocol/Internet Protocol (TCP/IP). Although this is not a book on TCP/IP, understanding it is essential to knowing Windows 2000. TCP/IP is a vendor-neutral protocol. It was deveoped and has since been improved upon by many different people and organizations. It is an open protocol; anyone can suggest a change or an improvement.

TCP/IP is made up of request for comments (RFC) documents, each of which provides the details of different portions of the protocol. Most of these documents are very clear as to what they are trying to accomplish and how TCP/IP works. These source documents will become useful to you as you continue to work with TCP/IP. You can find the RFCs in many locations on the Internet by searching for "RFC" on any of the major search engines. We like to use **http://sunsite.cnlab-switch.ch/cgi-bin/search/standard/nph-findstd?show_about=yes** because it has a good search engine for looking up RFC documents. You may also want to check **www.rfc-editor.org**, which has the RFCs and information about how to publish an RFC. You'll also find some of the more interesting and important RFCs on this book's companion CD-ROM.

As you look through the RFCs, you will see many different names and companies—names such as Microsoft, Cisco, Novell, Sun Microsystems, and others—that have created the TCP/IP protocol. The advantages to this are that no one vendor can control what happens with the protocol, and all can take advantage of the protocol's strengths and weaknesses.

This chapter provides a basic overview of some of the protocol's major aspects. If you are familiar with TCP/IP, this chapter may not bring forth much new information. If, however, you are new to TCP/IP, it should give you a beginning. A great deal of information is available on TCP/IP; this chapter is by no means meant to be a complete reference on the subject. There simply isn't enough space here to cover it in depth. We recommend that you study this topic more; many TCP/IP-specific books are currently available.

IP Addresses

The IP address is the basis for how the TCP/IP protocol functions on your network. Every computer and peripheral device that wants to communicate on the network must contain a unique IP address. An *IP address* is a logical address, meaning that it is not fixed with a piece of hardware. One system can be using an address; if that system removes itself from the network, another system could start using that address and the device communicates without any problems.

An IP address is made up of four octets. Each octet contains a number between 0 and 255. The range of possible addresses is therefore 0.0.0.0 through 255.255.255.255. No number in an octet can be larger than 255 because the IP address is actually a binary number. The IP address we know of is just a representation of the binary to make our life easier, but the computer always looks at the address in the binary representation. To fully understand IP addressing, you must figure out how to convert an address from decimal to binary and back.

In a binary number, each number can be either a 0 or a 1 only. If you start at the right of the binary number, the first place has a value of 1, the second has a value of 2, then 4, then 8, then 16, and so on. Each place to the left is double the amount of the place before it. In an IP address, there are only eight places total. If the value is a 1 in the binary address, you add the number to the total. If the value is 0, you do not. So, if all eight places have a value of 1, the total is 255: 128+64+32+16+8+ 4+2+1=255.

The easy way to convert a number to its binary format is to use the Windows Calculator. To start Calculator, go to the View menu and click on Scientific. Type a number and then click on the Bin radio button. This shows the representation of the number you typed in, in binary. You also can type a binary value into the Calculator and then click on the Dec radio button to get the decimal value of the number.

Note: If you are using the Calculator to convert decimal numbers to binary, be aware that it shows only the numbers that are relevant. Therefore, when you work with the binary values, you must place the leading 0 in there so that you have eight places in every IP address. For example, if you use Calculator to convert the number 61 to binary, the result is 111101. This result has only six places. To make this a valid IP octet, you need to add the two leading zeros to make an 8-place total, with a result of 00111101.

11

Therefore, if you see an IP address of 210.164.87.218, you can convert it into the binary address of 11010010.10100100.01010111.11011010. Although the average user never needs to know how to do this, it becomes important later, when you start calculating routes for packets.

Subnet Masks

The *subnet mask* is what allows different groups of IP addresses to be divided into networks. After you have divided IP address ranges into networks, you can route among them. All IP addresses require a subnet mask.

Every IP address has two parts to it: the network portion and the host portion. The subnet mask defines which part of the IP address is network and which is host. The subnet mask is defined by starting at the far left of and 4 IP octets and placing a value of 1 in each binary placeholder. As an example, if the subnet mask is 255.255.0.0, then the binary equivalent of the number is 11111111.11111111.00000000.00000000. If the subnet mask is 255.255.240.0, then the binary equivalent is 11111111.11111111.11110000.00000000.

The subnet mask should match the IP address, and wherever there is a 1 in the subnet mask, it means that that value in the IP address is part of the network ID. Where there is a 0 value in the subnet mask, that portion of the IP address is part of the host portion. So, if the subnet mask is 255.0.0.0, then anytime the IP address has the same number in the first octet, all those addresses are considered to be on the same network. Then, for example, the network consists of the IP address range w.0.0.0 through w.255.255.255. If the subnet mask is 255.255.0.0, then when the first two octets contain the same number, the IP addresses are on the same network. Then, the network consists of the IP address range w.x.0.0 through w.x.255.255.

Note: Throughout this chapter, when w.x.y.z is used in an IP address, it is used as a generic placeholder and will represent any valid IP number.

When you start getting into partial octet subnetting, or values in the subnet mask other than 255, things can get a little more complicated. This topic is a little too advanced for the space available here, so look at RFCs 950, 1878, and 1219 for more information on this topic.

Network IDs and Broadcast IDs

After you calculate the range of values for your network, there are two addresses that you cannot use. The first and last addresses in every network range are reserved. The first address in every network is the *network ID*. This number is used to refer to a whole range of addresses. You often see this in routers and other similar devices. If your subnet mask is 255.255.255.0, the network ID is *w.x.y.*0.

The last address in every network is the *broadcast ID* for the network. If a packet needs to reach all computers on a network, then the destination address for the packet is the last address in the network. If your subnet mask is 255.255.255.0, the broadcast ID of the network is *w.x.y.*255.

Classes of Addresses

If you are going to use your IP address on the Internet, you need to have a unique IP address. If your company is going to go on the Internet, you may need multiple IP addresses, and this is where the classes of addresses come in. Three classes of addresses are available for use on the Internet and within your private company. The classes are simply there as a way of distributing multiple IP addresses to a particular company or organization. Table 11.1 lists the network IDs that are available,

Table 11.1 Classes of addresses.

Class	IP Network ID Range	Subnet Mask	Networks Available	Hosts Available
A	1.0.0.0 through 126.0.0.0	255.0.0.0	126	16,777,214
B	128.0.0.0 through 191.255.0.0	255.255.0.0	16,382	65,534
C	192.0.0.0 through 223.255.255.0	255.255.255.0	2,097,052	254

the number of networks available for each class of address, and the number of hosts available in each network. The Class A network 127.0.0.0 is reserved for local loopback and interprocess communications on the local computer.

Address Resolution Protocol

The IP address is a logical address, which means that it can be used on any system. It is not tied to a particular piece of hardware. The problem with this is that at some point when you send a packet from one system to another, the packet needs to know what piece of hardware to send the packet to. Address Resolution Protocol (ARP) maps an IP address to the media access control (MAC) address. The MAC address is hard coded into the network card. Every network card has a unique MAC address when it comes from the manufacturer. The local computer sends out an ARP request broadcast packet. The packet basically asks who is using the destination IP address. When the device using the IP address receives the packet, it returns a packet with its MAC address and then the two systems can begin to communicate. For more information on ARP, refer to RFC 826.

Dynamic Host Configuration Protocol (DHCP)

Once you have determined what IP addresses you are going to use on your network, you must decide how you are going to assign the addresses to your clients. You may have only a few devices or you might have hundreds to assign. You can manually assign the IP addresses to your clients. If you decide to take this course, you must keep track of the IP addresses that you assign. If you don't keep track of where you are assigning your addresses, it can be difficult to track down duplicate addresses. It can also be difficult if you ever change your addressing scheme because you must visit every device on the network.

Dynamic Host Configuration Protocol (DHCP) allows you to automatically distribute IP addresses to your clients. On the DHCP server, you must define a *scope* of addresses. The scope contains a range of IP addresses available to be distributed along with the subnet mask. Each scope also has a *lease time*, which is the time that the client may use a distributed address; after that time, the client must get a new address. You may also define other scope options to be distributed with the address. You may distribute things like a default gateway, a Windows Internet Name Server (WINS) server address, and a domain name system (DNS) server address.

After a client computer receives an address from a DHCP server, it keeps this address for the time of the lease. When half the time of the lease has expired, the client attempts to renew the lease on the address it has been given. As long as everything is the same, the address should be renewed. If the address cannot be renewed for whatever reason, the client waits until seven-eighths of the time has expired and then tries to renew the address again. If this is still unsuccessful, then when the time has expired, the client releases its address and requests a new one from a DHCP server. The client will also try to renew its address whenever the system is booted.

If you want to check to see that you did get an address and what options were set, you can run **ipconfig** from the command prompt. Doing so gives you your current IP address, subnet mask, and default gateway. To get a more complete picture of what your TCP/IP settings are, run **ipconfig /all**. Entering this lists all the relevant IP settings that have been made on your system. You should note that if you have two or more network cards or a network card and a modem, each of these can have different settings and each is listed under the devices title. This can also present a decent amount of data, and it may scroll off the screen. You should make sure you can scroll in your command prompt.

You can get rid of an IP address and request a new one manually if you would like to. This is a useful troubleshooting tool because sometimes the address is not distributed properly, and just requesting a new one fixes the problem many times. To get rid of your IP address, just run the **ipconfig /release** command. If you run **ipconfig** at this point, you will see that your current address is 0.0.0.0, which means you won't be able to connect to anything on the network until you get a new address. If you run **ipconfig /renew**, your system requests a new IP address from the DHCP server. For more information on DHCP, refer to RFC 2132.

Routing

Routing is another one of these topics that can become very large and very complex. This section deals with how the client interacts with the router. The basic idea behind a routed network is that you want to reduce the amount of broadcast traffic. A router does not forward broadcast packets, so those packets are confined to the subnet where they started. The problem with this is that the client still needs to be able to find and communicate with devices that are on different subnets.

Based on the IP address of the destination device, the local computer can determine whether the destination is on the local subnet or a remote subnet. The local computer uses a process called *Anding*. To And the IP addresses, you need to first convert both the local and destination addresses as well as the subnet mask to binary. In the first step, the computer lines up the local address with the subnet mask. Anytime both bits have a 1 value, a 1 value is put in the result; if there is any other combination, a 0 is placed in the result. The first part of the process is to And the local IP address against the Subnet Mask, as follows:

```
11000000.10101000.11010100.10000011   Local IP Address
11111111.11111111.00000000.00000000   Subnet Mask
11000000.10101000.00000000.00000000   Result
```

Now the system needs to get a result set with the destination address and the local subnet, as shown here:

```
11000000.10101001.11010100.10000011   Destination Address
11111111.11111111.00000000.00000000   Subnet Mask
11000000.10101001.00000000.00000000   Result
```

Now that the system has the two result sets, it compares them. If they are the same, the system knows that the destination address is on the local subnet. If the result sets are different, the system knows that the destination address is on a remote subnet.

If the local system determines that the destination address is on a remote subnet, it forwards the packet to the default gateway. The default gateway, which is a router, then transfers the packet to the network where it belongs. The local computer's only responsibilities here are to determine whether the destination is local or remote and, if the destination is remote, to let the default gateway find out how to get the packet to its destination. After the router receives the packet, it may have to do a great deal to get the packet to its destination. The routers on your network may communicate with one another to determine the best way for the packet to get to its destination.

Routing is a huge topic, and dozens of RFCs define different aspects of routing. Take a look at RFCs 1518 and 1519.

Name Resolution

TCP/IP addresses are not very friendly to most users. Certainly, the Internet probably wouldn't have taken off as it has if everyone had to remember an IP address. Imagine the commercial for some company saying "Just go to 10.187.42.16" instead of "Just go to company.com."

11

Being able to use a name instead of an IP address makes it dramatically easier for a user to be able to use the network. Microsoft currently uses two different types of name resolution. Windows 2000 supports NetBIOS name resolution and host name resolution. Both of these simply resolve a name to an IP address for the system, so it is redundant to have both. Microsoft has decided to phase out NetBIOS name resolution and use host name resolution instead. NetBIOS name resolution is still in Windows 2000; although you cannot use this form of name resolution, it's still there for backward compatibility.

NetBIOS Name Resolution

A number of possible steps are involved when you are resolving a NetBIOS name to an IP address. Each Windows computer uses the computer name as its NetBIOS name. To resolve a name, the system goes through the following steps by default:

1. Checks the NetBIOS name cache.

2. Querys the WINS server.

3. Sends out a local broadcast.

4. Checks the LMHOSTS file (described in the "LMHOSTS File" section later in this chapter).

5. Checks the Hosts file (described in the "Hosts File" section later in this chapter).

6. Queries DNS.

You can change the order of the steps, though they seem to work best for most systems in this order.

Name Cache

The NetBIOS name cache on the local system stores the names you have recently resolved. The idea here is that after you resolve a name, you are likely to use that name again in the near future. The NetBIOS name cache stores the names you have resolved for 10 minutes by default.

The NBTSTAT.exe utility allows you to work with the name cache. Table 11.2 lists the options of this utility.

Note: These switches are case-sensitive and can give very different results if the case is not followed. Replace the placeholder information (which is in italics) with the actual remote name and IP address.

WINS

WINS is a NetBIOS name server that stores NetBIOS names and their IP addresses. If a client is configured with a WINS server address, that client registers its name and IP address with the server when the system boots. When the system shuts down, it tells the WINS server that it is doing so, and the server removes the name from its list.

Table 11.2   The switches and their purpose for the NBTSTAT utility.

Parameter	Definition
-a *remotename*	Lists the remote computer's name table
-A *IP Address*	Lists the remote computer's name table
-c	Lists the current contents of the name cache, giving the IP address and name for each system you have resolved
-n	Lists local NetBIOS names
-R	Purges the local cache and then reloads the LMHOSTS file
-r	Lists statistics for the number of names resolved by the local system
-S	Lists client and server sessions, displaying remote computers by IP address
-s	Lists client and server sessions, displaying remote computers by name if it can resolve them

After the client registers itself with the WINS server, it can then resolve names from the server. Although the WINS server gladly resolves a name to an IP address, it can also handle requests for services. When a client comes online, it tells the WINS server about all the services it can handle. This way, when a client needs to find a domain controller to authenticate it to the network, it can simply ask the WINS server for a domain controller in the network to which it would like to authenticate. If you look at the WINS database of information, you may notice that a particular computer name is listed multiple times. The difference between ComputerName[20h] and ComputerName[1Bh] is the 16 characters of the name, which has a value of 00–FF in hexadecimal form (this always indicates a resource type). Table 11.3 defines the different sixteenth characters that are available and when they are used. These services are registered only if the particular service is active on your network.

The advantage of working with a WINS server is that it dynamically builds its table of names and addresses. The client also needs to be configured with the address of the WINS server so that clients on multiple networks can use the same WINS server. The clients can also resolve the names of computers on remote networks.

Local Broadcasts

A local broadcast is made to find a computer that responds to the NetBIOS name request. The issuing computer sends a message to every computer. The receiving

Table 11.3   The different types of services that can be registered in a WINS server.

Format	Description
Computer_name[00h]	This is the name registered by the workstation service. This is the name usually referred to as the NetBIOS name.
Computer_name[03h]	This name is registered by the messenger service.
Computer_name[06h]	This name is registered by the Routing and Remote Access Service.
Domain_name[1Bh]	This is registered by a Windows NT 4 domain controller.
Computer_name[1Fh]	This is registered the Network Dynamic Data Exchange (NetDDE) Service.
Computer_name[20h]	This is registered by the Server service.
Computer_name[21h]	This is registered by Remote Access Services (RAS) clients.
Computer_name[BEh]	This is registered by the Network Monitoring Agent Service.
Computer_name[BFh]	This is registered by the Network Monitoring Utility.
Username[03h]	This is the user name of currently logged-on users.
Domain_name[00h]	This is registered by the workstation service to receive browser broadcasts.
Domain_name[1Ch]	This is registered for use by the domain controllers.
Domain_name[1Dh]	This is registered for use by the Master Browser.
Group_name[1Eh]	This is a normal group.
Group_name[20h]	This is an Internet group used for administrative purposes.
MSBROWSE [01h]	This is registered by the Master Browser for each subnet.

11

computers check to see if they have the matching name in the request, and if they do, they send back a response with the IP address.

The problem with a local broadcast is that your routers are probably not configured to forward these broadcast packets, so if the computer you are looking for is on the other side of a router, then you receive no response. This is why you should implement a WINS server on a routed network.

LMHOSTS File

The LMHOSTS file is a static file that is located on the local system. A sample named lmhosts.sam is located in the c:\winnt\system32\drivers\etc directory. This is also where you must place an LMHOSTS file if you are going to use one. For the LMHOSTS file to work, it must be named "LMHOSTS" with no extension.

The LMHOSTS file is just a text file that has some NetBIOS names and their IP addresses. For the most part, you simply enter an IP address followed by a NetBIOS name. You can include a number of options with the LMHOSTS file. If you follow a NetBIOS name with "#PRE", that particular entry is preloaded into the NetBIOS name cache when the system boots. You may want to add this kind of entry for computers you will be accessing regularly. You can also follow a NetBIOS name with "#DOM:<*domain*>", replacing "*domain*" with the domain name for a domain controller. You may want to do this in a situation where you would like a domain controller to be the preferred option for login authentication.

If you have multiple entries for a particular system, only the first entry is used. When the computer goes through the LMHOSTS file, it starts at the top and then stops as soon as it finds the entry that it's looking for.

The problem with using LMHOSTS is that it is a static file, so you shouldn't place any entries in this file for systems that are getting their addresses from a DHCP server. The other issue is that each computer on your network has its own LMHOSTS file, so if you want to make a change, you must either change every computer or direct your LMHOSTS file to include information from a network LMHOSTS file.

Host Name Resolution

Host name resolution is actually a huge topic in and of itself. You can find books dedicated just to this topic. This section focuses on the client's perspective in name resolution. The advantage of using host name resolution is that just about all systems that support TCP/IP use host name resolution. The Internet uses host name resolution and the idea of domains and sub-domains. A *domain name* is something like "company.com," and the host name is whatever comes before the domain. So, if you see an address like "www.company.com", then the domain name is "company.com" and the host name is "www".

To resolve a host name, the system goes through the following steps by default:

1. Checks the Hosts file.

2. Queries DNS.

3. Checks the NetBIOS name cache.

4. Queries the WINS server.

5. Sends out a local broadcast.

6. Checks the LMHOSTS file.

These settings can be changed, but they seem to work best for most environments.

Hosts File

The Hosts file is very similar to the LMHOSTS file. As with the LMHOSTS file, the entries in the Hosts file consist of an IP address followed by a host name. That's it for the Hosts file. As with the LMHOSTS file, only the first entry for a host name is used if you have multiple entries for a host.

For the system to use the Hosts file, it must be named "Hosts", with no extension, and placed in the c:\winnt\system32\drivers\etc folder. The file is a simple text file that you can open and edit with Notepad or any other available plain text editor.

DNS

Working with and managing a DNS server can be a very complicated task. This section covers using DNS from the client perspective and assumes that the DNS servers have been configured appropriately. For the most part, as long as the client computer has been configured with the appropriate IP address of the DNS server, the clients system can then resolve a hostname to an IP address. The client needs only to be configured with the address of one DNS server; if the DNS server does not have the address for which the client is looking, the DNS server checks with other DNS servers to resolve the name.

If the DNS server that you are using supports dynamic registration, Windows 2000 can register its host name when the client boots up. If for some reason you want to change your host name when it has been registered dynamically, run the **ipconfig /registerdns** command.

For more information on DNS, see RFCs 1034, 1035, and 2181. You can also reference the documentation for the DNS server that you are using.

11

Chapter Summary

TCP/IP is a large topic. Most people don't think it's as complex as it is because, after all, it is just a protocol. Well, it is more than that. Although TCP/IP allows you to have two or more devices connect and transfer data, it also routes your information around a large network and transfers data in different ways.

This chapter does not go into a great amount of detail on some of the topics; it is meant as an overview. We hope that after reading this, you will be motivated to study TCP/IP more. Microsoft has determined that TCP/IP is going to be the basis of Windows 2000. In fact, you cannot have an Active Directory network without TCP/IP. TCP/IP is certainly the most-used protocol in the world at the current time, so you must understand it well. You may want to start with RFC 1180, which is a tutorial on TCP/IP.

Review Questions

1. Convert the following IP address to binary: 37.162.47.96.
   a. 00100101.10100010.00101111.01100001
   b. 00100101.10100010.00101111.01100000
   c. 00100101.10101010.00101111.01100001
   d. 00100101.10100010.00101111.01100011

2. Convert the following IP address to binary: 218.47.236.118.
   a. 11011011.00101111.11101100.01110110
   b. 11011010.00101111.11101101.01110110
   c. 11011010.00101111.11101100.01110111
   d. 11011010.00101111.11101100.01110110

3. Convert the following IP address to binary: 18.247.136.128.
   a. 00010011.11110111.10001001.10000000
   b. 00010010.11110111.10001000.10000001
   c. 00010010.11110111.10001000.10000000
   d. 00010010.11110111.10001010.10000001

4. Convert the following binary address to decimal:
11011001.11111101.00100110.11101110.

   a. 217.253.38.238

   b. 216.253.68.236

   c. 217.253.36.64

   d. 216.253.64.230

5. Convert the following binary address to decimal:
10011001.11111100.00100111.01101110.

   a. 151.234.92.111

   b. 212.92.66.84

   c. 118.215.183.99

   d. 153.252.39.110

6. Convert the following binary address to decimal:
10011101.11001100.00111111.11011110.

   a. 157.204.63.222

   b. 137.202.73.222

   c. 157.204.63.232

   d. 117.202.73.222

7. Your address is 192.168.2.37 and your subnet mask is 255.255.255.0. The destination address is 192.168.1.64. Is this address local or remote?

   a. Local

   b. Remote

8. Your address is 192.168.2.37 and your subnet mask is 255.255.0.0. The destination address is 192.168.1.64. Is this address local or remote?

   a. Local

   b. Remote

9. Your address is 11000000.10101000.00000010.00100101 and your subnet mask is 11111111.11111111.11111111.00000000. The destination address is 11000000.10101000.00000001.01000000. Is this address local or remote?

   a. Local

   b. Remote

11

10. Your address is 11000000.10101000.00000010.00100101 and your subnet mask is 11111111.11111111.00000000.00000000. The destination address is 11000000.10101000.00000001.01000000. Is this address local or remote?

    a. Local

    b. Remote

11. You are trying to resolve a NetBIOS name. The computer you are trying to reach has entries in both the WINS server and the LMHOSTS file, but the entries are different. Which entry is used?

    a. WINS.

    b. LMHOSTS.

    c. Neither is used.

    d. Both are used.

12. You are trying to resolve a host's name. The computer you are trying to reach has entries in both the DNS server and the Hosts file, but the entries are different. Which entry is used?

    a. DNS.

    b. Hosts.

    c. Neither is used.

    d. Both are used.

13. You are having trouble communicating and you realize that you do not have an IP address. You are on a network that is using DHCP. What command requests a new IP address?

    a. **ipconfig /registerdns**

    b. **ipconfig /release**

    c. **ipconfig /renew**

    d. **ipconfig /flushdns**

14. You have changed the host name of your local computer and you would like to add this new host name to a DNS server that supports dynamic updates. What command should you use to update this entry without rebooting the system?

    a. **ipconfig /registerdns**

    b. **ipconfig /release**

    c. **ipconfig /renew**

    d. **ipconfig /flushdns**

15. You want to check which DNS and WINS server has been distributed to the local computer via DHCP. What command allows you to see this information?

    a. **ipconfig /registerdns**

    b. **ipconfig /displaydns**

    c. **ipconfig /showclassid**

    d. **ipconfig /all**

16. You have received an IP address from a DHCP server. When does the local system try to renew this address? [Check all correct answers]

    a. When half the lease time has expired.

    b. When seven–eighths of the lease time has expired.

    c. When the lease time expires.

    d. You must renew the address manually.

    e. When the system reboots.

17. You have recently accessed a system using a NetBIOS name, and then you changed the IP address of the remote system. Now you cannot access the system and you notice that the wrong name is being resolved. What can you do from the local computer to resolve the name properly?

    a. Run the command **NBTSTAT -r**.

    b. Run the command **NBTSTAT -R**.

    c. Add an entry to the LMHOSTS file.

    d. Add an entry to the Hosts file.

18. You are trying to resolve a host name and you have multiple entries for the host name. Which of the following provides the name resolution for the local system if all options have entries for the host?

    a. DNS

    b. WINS

    c. Local broadcast

    d. Hosts file

19. IP addresses are logical addresses that need to be mapped to a physical piece of hardware. Which of the following allows that to happen?

    a. DHCP

    b. DNS

    c. WINS

    d. ARP

11

20. Where should your Hosts file and LMHOSTS file be placed for the system to use them?

    a. c:\winnt\system32\drivers

    b. c:\winnt\system32

    c. c:\winnt\system32\drivers\etc

    d. c:\winnt\system32\wins

Real-World Project

Nora's company has decided to implement TCP/IP as its protocol. Nora has been assigned the responsibility of making sure that the workstations on the network can communicate. Other people are responsible for making sure the routers communicate and for setting up the server components. Nora will decide how to distribute the IP addresses to the clients and what settings should be in place.

Nora decides that the company will be better served by using DHCP instead of manually assigning the addresses. A few of the workstations will require a static IP address, so those will be configured separately. To handle the name resolution, Nora must decide a few things. First, Nora decides to look at NetBIOS name resolution. The network is divided into three subnets, so relying on broadcast traffic will not work. She realizes that if she decides to implement LMHOSTS for the network, there may be problems with this because she has decided to use DHCP to distribute the addresses, and LMHOSTS is a static file. Nora checks with the server group and finds that it can install a WINS server, so she gets the IP address of the server and uses that for NetBIOS name resolution.

As far as hostname resolution is concerned, Nora realizes that implementing the Hosts file will cause the same problems as implementing LMHOSTS. Therefore, the only alternative is to implement DNS. She checks with the server group again and finds out the current domain name it is using and the address of the DNS server. She also finds out that the DNS server being used does support dynamic updates and convinces the server group to enable this feature.

Nora then consults with the router group and gets the IP addresses for the routers and the ranges of addresses that she is allowed to use for the clients.

Now that Nora has the addresses and the name resolution addresses, she puts this together to determine the scope for DHCP. Nora lists the options that are needed for each scope and has the server team enter them into the DHCP servers. Nora decides to have a short lease time on the DHCP servers so that if changes need to be made, they can go into effect quickly.

Once the servers have been configured, she starts setting up the client workstations to obtain their IP addresses automatically through DHCP.

Project 11.1

Configuring Windows 2000 Professional to obtain a DHCP address:

1. Select Start | Settings | Control Panel.

2. Double-click on Network and Dial-Up Connections.

3. Right click on Local Area Connection and choose Properties.

4. Highlight Internet Protocol (TCP/IP) and then click on Properties.

5. Select Obtain an IP Address Automatically.

6. Select Obtain DNS Server Address Automatically.

7. Click on OK twice.

A few clients are running a special piece of software that requires that they have a static IP address. Nora configures these systems by following the steps in Project 11.2.

Project 11.2

Configuring Windows 2000 Professional with a static IP address:

1. Select Start | Settings | Control Panel.

2. Double-click on Network and Dial-Up Connections

3. Right click on Local Area Connection and choose Properties.

4. Highlight Internet Protocol (TCP/IP) and then click on Properties.

5. Select Use The Following IP Address.

6. Enter the workstation's IP address, subnet mask, and default gateway.

7. Select Use The Following DNS Server Address.

8. Enter the IP address of the DNS server.

9. Click on OK two times.

Now that Nora has the systems up and running, she is finding that some of the computers have authentication to the wrong domain controller. She decides to implement a LMHOSTS file on these computers to point them to the proper domain controller.

Project 11.3

Create an LMHOSTS file that specifies a domain controller and preloads the entry:

1. Open Notepad.

2. Type the following line into Notepad:

```
IP Address      domain controller       #PRE #DOM:domainname
```

Replace *IP Address* with the IP address of the domain controller, *domain controller* with the name of the domain controller, and *domainname* with the name of the domain.

3. Save the file as lmhosts.

4. Copy the file to c:\winnt\system32\drivers\etc.

Mobile Users

After completing this chapter, you will be able to:

✓ Describe the different types of network connections supported in Windows 2000 Professional

✓ Describe how security is implemented for network connections

✓ Describe the authentication protocols supported for network connections

✓ Configure portable computers for Offline Files And Folders

✓ Describe dynamic hardware support

✓ Describe the various methods of power management used for portable computers in Windows 2000 Professional

✓ Configure power schemes on portable computers

✓ Describe what hardware profiles are and how they are used

✓ Describe what smart cards are used for in Windows 2000 Professional

Windows 2000 Professional is the perfect operating system for mobile users. It has improved on many features introduced in Windows 98 to support notebook computers. Connecting to remote computers has been made easier with the Network And Dial-Up Connections Wizard. You can dock and undock notebook computers without having to reconfigure the system. In addition, enhanced power-management tools provide users with longer battery life and better management of the computer's resources.

Network Connections

Users gain access to network resources from local or remote locations by using Network And Dial-Up Connections. Connections are created using the Network And Dial-Up Connections Wizard. Configuration information is stored in the Network And Dial-Up Connections folder.

Network Connection Wizard

The Network Connection Wizard is accessed through the Network And Dial-Up Connections icon in the Control Panel. Double-click on Make New Connection to start the Network Connection Wizard. Figure 12.1 shows the Network and Dial-Up Connections screen.

You can choose the type of network connection you want to make from among the five types of network and dial-up connections (see Figure 12.2). They are:

➤ *Dial-Up To Private Network*—This uses dial-up connections to access a corporate network. Access can be provided through a modem, integrated services digital network (ISDN), or X.25. File and Print Sharing is automatically enabled.

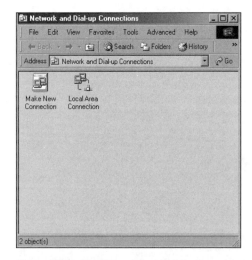

Figure 12.1 The Network And Dial-Up Connections screen.

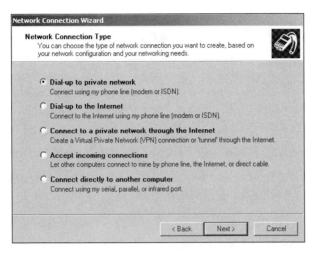

Figure 12.2 Choosing the type of network connection with the Network Connection Wizard.

➤ *Dial-Up To The Internet*—This uses dial-up connections to access the Internet. Access can be provided through a modem, ISDN, or X.25. The Internet Connection Wizard is automatically launched when you select this option. File and Print Sharing is disabled. If users select this option, the Internet Connection Wizard connects them to the Microsoft Referral Service to aid them in selecting an Internet Service Provider (ISP).

➤ *Connect To A Private Network Through The Internet*—This creates a Virtual Private Network (VPN) connection or "tunnel" to the Internet. Access is provided through Point-to-Point Tunneling Protocol (PPTP) or Layer 2 Tunneling Protocol (L2TP).

➤ *Accept Incoming Connections*—This allows other computers to connect to yours through dial-up connections, VPN, or a direct cable.

➤ *Connect Directly To Another Computer*—This allows users to connect to another computer through a serial cable, DirectParallel cable, or infrared link. A DirectParallel cable is a special parallel cable that connects two computers through standard ports and enhanced ones—Extended Capabilities Ports (ECPs).

Dial-Up Connection

A dial-up connection allows users to connect to a LAN or the Internet with a device that uses the telephone network. Windows 2000 Professional supports dial-up con-nections that use a modem, an ISDN line, or an X.25 network. Those who use Windows 2000 Professional on a notebook computer have the same dial-up connection sup-port as local area network (LAN) users, except for slower connection speeds. Dial-up connections are created using the Network And Dial-Up Connection Wizard.

12

Virtual Private Connection

VPNs provide secure transmission across public and private networks. VPNs can be created in two ways: by dialing an ISP or by connecting directly to the Internet. When users dial an ISP, a connection is first made to the ISP. Then, another connection is made to the remote access server (RAS). The second call establishes the PPTP or L2TP tunnel. Users can use the remote server after they are authenticated.

If users are directly connected to the Internet through a cable modem, asynchronous digital subscriber line (ADSL) service, or LAN, the VPN connection is used to dial the RAS.

VPNs support PPTP and L2TP. Both of these protocols are automatically installed on your computer when you install Windows 2000 Professional.

Using VPNs over other dialing options has several advantages:

➤ *Savings*—Users save money because they use the Internet as a connection instead of a long-distance number. The ISP is responsible for all communications hardware.

➤ *Simplicity*—Users do not have to worry about maintaining telephony equipment. Users make a local call to the telephone company or ISP, and then they are connected to a RAS running Windows 2000 or to their corporate network. The telephone company or ISP manages the modems and telephone lines.

➤ *Security*—VPN connections are encrypted and secure. Authentication is enforced by the remote server, and data is hidden from all Internet users except for the intended parties.

➤ *Compatibility*—VPNs support the most common protocols, such as Transmission Control Protocol/Internet Protocol (TCP/IP) and Internet Protocol Exchange (IPX).

➤ *Protection*—Internal IP addressing schemes are protected. The Internet sees only the external IP address specified.

Incoming Connections

As with previous versions of NT, Windows 2000 Professional can be set up as a RAS. Incoming connections can be set to support the following dial-up connection types:

➤ Dial-up (modem)

➤ VPN (PPTP and L2TP)

➤ Direct connect (discussed in the next section)

A computer that is running Windows 2000 Professional can accept up to three incoming connections simultaneously: one dial-up, one VPN, and one direct connection.

Any user that connects to your computer must have a local user account on the computer. User accounts that can make incoming connections to the computer are added on the Users tab of the Incoming Connections Properties dialog box, shown in Figure 12.3.

Note: You must be a member of the Administrator group to create incoming connections.

You can combine multiple modems, ISDN, or X.25 lines into a logical bundle. The Network And Dial-Up Connections feature uses Point-to-Point Protocol (PPP) Multilink dialing over multiple physical links. The resulting link increases connection bandwidth. To use Multilink, both the remote and server computers must have Multilink enabled.

Direct Connect

Direct connections involve creating a physical connection between computers. The physical connection can be made through a serial cable, modem, infrared port, or DirectParallel cable.

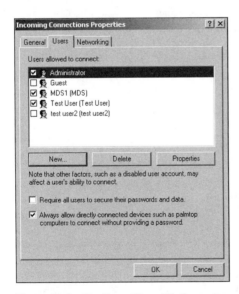

Figure 12.3   The Users Allowed To Connect screen of the Users tab.

12

Security

Security for Windows 2000 Professional for Network And Dial-Up Connections is provided through authentication, data encryption, and callback features. Security settings are configured on the Advanced Security Settings dialog box, shown in Figure 12.4.

To access this dialog box, click on the Settings button on the Security tab of the Dial-Up Connections dialog box.

Authentication

Once users are connected to a network or computer, resources are allocated depending on whether their credentials are authenticated. You can configure dial-up, VPN, and direct connections to require various levels of authentication.

Authentication in Windows 2000 Professional is implemented using two processes: the interactive logon process and network authorization.

The interactive logon process involves confirming the user's identification to a domain or local account. If it is a domain account, the user logs on to the network using a password or smart card. Kerberos 5 is used for both passwords and smart cards. If users have a local account, they log on using credentials stored in the Security Account Manager (SAM) database.

Network authorization involves confirming the identification of the users and the network resources they have access to. Network authorization is provided using

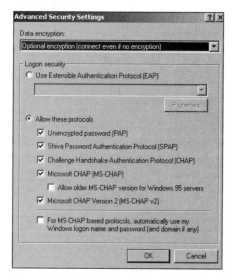

Figure 12.4 The Advanced Security Settings dialog box.

Kerberos 5, Secure Sockets Layer/Transport Layer Security (SSL/TLS), and Windows NT LAN Manager (NTLM) for compatibility to Windows NT 4.

Network And Dial-Up Connections supports the following authentication protocols:

➤ *Password Authentication Protocol (PAP)*—This uses unencrypted text for the passwords. It is the least secure of the authentication protocols. You can use it to authenticate to non-Windows-based servers.

➤ *Shiva Password Authentication Protocol (SPAP)*—This allows Shiva clients to dial in to Windows 2000 servers.

➤ *Challenge Handshake Authentication Protocol (CHAP)*—This is a secure form of encrypted authentication. It uses the Message Digest 5 (MD5) hashing scheme to transfer data into a unique form that cannot be recreated to its original form.

➤ *Microsoft Challenge Handshake Authentication Protocol (MS-CHAP)*—This is an extension of CHAP. MS-CHAP uses a challenge–response mechanism with one-way encryption on the response. This is also used with CHAP. MS-CHAP was specifically designed for computers running Windows 95, 98, NT, or 2000.

➤ *MS-CHAP 2*—This is the latest version of MS-CHAP. Different encryption keys are used for sending and receiving. It also provides mutual authentication. Both VPN and dial-up connections can use MS-CHAP 2 in Windows 2000. Only VPN connections can use MS-CHAP 2 in Windows 98 and NT.

➤ *Extensible Authentication Protocol (EAP)*—This is an extension to PPP. EAP was created to provide remote users with authentication that used third-party security devices. When you use EAP, you have access to additional authentication methods. These include token cards, public-key authentication using smart cards, and one-time passwords. EAP provides stronger security methods than the older password-based authentication methods and is a critical component for secure VPN connections.

Data Encryption

Data encryption involves locking data with a key algorithm. The data is unreadable if you don't know the key. Data encryption can be initiated by the remote computer or the server. Network And Dial-Up Connections supports two types of data encryption: Microsoft Point-to-Point Encryption (MMPE) and IP Security (IPSec).

MPPE

MPPE uses the Rivest-Shamir-Adlemen (RSA) RC4 stream cipher. To use MPPE for dial-up or VPN connections, you must use the MS-CHAP, MS-CHAP 2, or EAP authentication methods. These methods generate keys that are used in the encryption process. MPPE supports 128-bit key, 56-bit key, and 40-bit key encryption schemes.

12

IPSec

IPSec is actually a suite of cryptography-based protection services and security protocols. IPSec can use all standard PPP-based authentication protocols to authenticate users after an IPSec connection is established. IPSec is used if the remote computer is using a VPN connection to an L2TP server. IPSec supports the Data Encryption Standard (DES) with a 56-bit key and Triple DES (3DES), which uses three 56-bit keys. 3DES is designed for high-security environments.

Callback

The Callback feature in Windows 2000 Professional is similar to Callback in previous versions of Windows NT. Callback instructs the server that the remote computer is calling to disconnect the call and to immediately call back a predetermined number. This reduces phone charges. Callback increases security by ensuring that only users from specific locations have access to the server and its resources. Three options are available when you are configuring your computer for Callback:

➤ Do Not Allow Callback

➤ Allow The Caller To Set The Callback Number

➤ Always Use the Following Callback Number

Callback is not supported on VPN connections.

Offline Files and Folders

Users may find that they need to work on network-based files when they are not connected to the network. Windows 2000 Professional has a new feature, Offline Files and Folders, which allows users to make any files and folders available offline for use when they are not connected to their network. Files are synchronized to the original when the users reconnect to the network. Offline Files and Folders is similar to Briefcase in previous versions of Windows. Unlike Briefcase, however, users can make shared files and folders available offline.

With Offline Files and Folders, networked files are cached to the local hard drive. Files are available for use when users are not connected to the network. When they reconnect to the network, the files are synchronized with the original files.

Configuring a Computer for Offline Files in Shared Folders

Before you can use files offline, you must configure them for caching to the local hard drive on the portable computer. Two options are available for determining how nonexecutable files from a shared network folder are cached on the portable computer. Files can be stored using automatic caching or manual caching.

Automatic caching stores a local copy of the file on the portable computer when the file is opened. Automatic caching is good when users are connecting to a network with an unreliable network connection.

Manual caching makes a file available offline when it is manually marked (or pinned) on the user's computer. Manual caching is good for users who need access to files all the time. When a file is pinned for offline use, a copy is put in the local cache of the portable computer. All users have permission to pin files and folders by default in Windows 2000 Professional. When a folder that contains subfolders is manually pinned, users are prompted if they want to also make the subfolders available offline.

To cache executable (program) files for offline use, select Automatic Caching For Programs. This setting stores a copy of the network program on the portable computer, allowing users to run the application when they are offline. Files that have been configured for automatic caching can be manually pinned to the local cache. This forces the file to be stored.

Configuring Options for Offline Files

Several options are available for configuring offline files. Offline Files allows users to determine how much disk space is used on the portable computer to store the offline files and folders. This option applies only to files that have been made available through automatic caching. By default, the amount of space is limited to 10 percent of the disk size. The disk size for manually cached files and folders is limited only to the amount of available disk space.

Offline Files also allows users to determine what happens when network connections are lost. Two options are available: Notify Me And Begin Working Offline or Never Allow My Computer To Go Offline. The first of these is the default setting and gives users access to offline files and folders when the network connection is lost. With the second option, users don't have access to the offline files or folders whether they have a network connection or not.

If users lose their network connection, they can still browse shared folders and network drives in My Network Places or My Computer. A red X appears over the network drive indicating that the connection is currently not available. Users can still use any offline files or folders that were made available before the network connection was lost.

If the status of your network connection changes, an Offline Files icon appears in the status area of the taskbar. An informational balloon indicating that a change in your network connection has occurred is displayed. Click on the Offline Files icon to receive more information about the status of your connection.

Offline files are stored in the Offline Files folder. This folder is machine specific, not user specific. This means that there is only one Offline Files folder on a portable

12

computer, regardless of how many people use the computer. This folder is protected by administrative-level permissions by default.

Portable computer users may find that they need to delete files stored in the Offline Files folder on their local hard drive. They have two options for deleting files from the cache without affecting the network files or folders. One way is to open the Offline Files folder and delete the files that are no longer needed.

To delete files from the Offline Files folder:

1. Open Windows Explorer on a shared network folder.

2. Select Tools | Folder Options.

3. Click on the Offline Files tab.

4. Click on View Files.

5. Click on the files you want to delete.

6. Select File and click on Delete.

Note: If you delete a file from a folder that is pinned, the file is copied to the cache the next time offline files are synchronized.

The second way is to delete files from a network share. Using this method, you can delete batches of files from the shared folder that contains them. When you use this method, the files in manually pinned folders are no longer pinned. To make them available for offline access, you must pin them again.

To delete files from a network share:

1. Open Windows Explorer on a shared network folder.

2. Select Tools | Folder Options.

3. Click on the Offline Files tab in the Folder Options dialog box.

4. Click on Delete Files.

5. In the Confirm File Delete dialog box, select the shared folders that contain the offline files you want to delete.

6. Click on the Delete Only The Temporary Offline Versions checkbox if you want to delete only files that were automatically stored. Click on the Delete Both The Temporary Offline Versions And The Versions That Are Always Available Offline checkbox if you want to delete both automatically and manually stored files.

To permanently remove offline files from the portable computer, reinitialize the Offline Files cache. Doing so deletes all offline files from the Offline Files folder and resets the Offline Files database.

To reinitialize the Offline Files cache:

1. Open Windows Explorer on a shared network folder.

2. Select Tools | Folder Options.

3. Click on the Offline Files tab in the Folders Options dialog box.

4. Press Ctrl+Shift and click on Delete Files.

Note: All files are permanently deleted from the cache when it is reinitialized. This process cannot be undone.

You can change the size of the Offline Files cache by doing the following:

1. Open Windows Explorer on a shared network folder.

2. Select Tools | Folder Options.

3. Click on the Offline Files tab in the Folders Options dialog box.

4. Move the slider until the file size (or a percentage of the hard drive) shows the desired size.

Synchronization Manager

The Synchronization Manager is used to control how offline files and folders are synchronized with the original files on the network. Users can initialize either a full or a quick synchronization. The network resources must be available for synchronization to work.

The Synchronization Manager can synchronize individual files, folders, and offline Web pages. Items can be synchronized when users log on or off the computer, or both. These elements can be synchronized at specified intervals during idle periods or at predetermined times.

Users can choose to synchronize files and folders:

➤ Automatically at logon

➤ Automatically at logoff

➤ Manual at any time

➤ When the computer is idle for a specific period

➤ Automatically at predetermined times

Users can define and schedule specific times for synchronization. Synchronization can be scheduled to occur at a specific time and on a specific date. In addition, users can schedule it to automatically run every day, on weekdays, or every x number of

12

Chapter 12

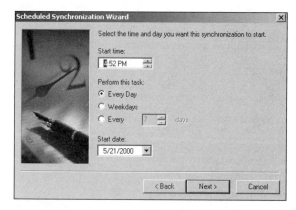

Figure 12.5 The Scheduled Synchronization Wizard.

days. The Scheduled Synchronization Wizard, shown in Figure 12.5, steps users through setting up a synchronization schedule.

You can configure the computer to connect to the network when synchronization is scheduled to occur. This is not recommended for portable computers, however. Windows 2000 does not try to connect if there is not a network connection at the time of a scheduled synchronization.

By default, synchronization does not occur when a portable computer is in an idle state when running on battery power. Although it is not recommended to synchronize files when you are running the portable computer on battery power, it can be done.

To change synchronization so that it occurs during an idle state when the computer is running on a battery:

1. Click on Start | Programs.

2. Select Accessories and click on Synchronize.

3. Click on Setup in the Items To Synchronize dialog box.

4. Click on the On Idle tab in the Synchronization Settings dialog box.

5. Click on Advanced.

6. Click on the Prevent Synchronization When My Computer Is Running On Battery Power checkbox in the Idle Settings dialog box.

Windows 2000 Professional supports synchronization over slow links, usually defined as connections that operate at 64Kbps or slower. However, slow links affect synchronization in two ways:

1. They can prevent automatic transmission of shared network folders to an online state.

2. They can prevent newly added files from being copied from the network share to the portable computer's local cache.

When a network shared resource is brought back online, it is not available to users until three conditions are met:

1. No offline files from the network share can be open on the computer.

2. None of the offline files from the network share can have changes that need to be synchronized.

3. The network connection cannot be a slow link.

After the three conditions are met, users are working from the network share. All changes made to the file or folder are saved both on the network share and on the local Offline Files folder.

If any of the three conditions are not met, users are still working offline although the network share is available. Changes are saved to only the offline version of the file.

Users who connect to a network share through a slow link are working offline although the network folders are available. To work online, the files must be synchronized.

Dynamic Hardware Support

Windows 2000 Professional provides dynamic hardware support for PC cards and Integrated Drive Electronics (IDE) devices. *Dynamic hardware support* means that you don't have to restart the computer after the device is installed or removed. Dynamic hardware support is possible only if the computer is Plug and Play compliant and enabled with Advanced Configuration and Power Interface (ACPI). (ACPI is discussed in greater detail later in this chapter.) If the computer is Plug and Play compliant but not ACPI enabled, users must reboot before the computer recognizes the change.

12

PC Cards

Windows 2000 Professional supports PC cards and CardBus devices through card information structure (CIS). If CIS is present on the card, Windows 2000 creates a unique ID for the device. This ID contains information about the device. The operating system uses this information to dynamically configure the device and load the appropriate device drivers. The device is then enabled without users having to restart the computer. If the computer is not ACPI enabled, it must be restarted before the configuration is complete.

A *surprise removal* occurs when a PC card or CardBus device is removed from the computer and Windows 2000 is not notified before the device is removed. In such

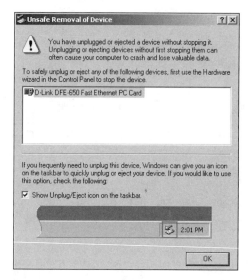

Figure 12.6 The Unsafe Removal Of Device dialog box.

a case, an Unsafe Removal Of Device dialog box, shown in Figure 12.6, appears. It indicates that the device should be stopped first before it is removed.

ACPI-enabled computers usually can recover from a surprise removal. It is recommended that you stop the device first and then remove it using the Unplug/Eject icon on the taskbar or the Hardware Wizard in the Control Panel.

Note: *Although Windows 2000 Professional can automatically configure PC cards and CardBus devices, it is good practice to notify the operating system before removing them.*

IDE Devices

Windows 2000 Professional supports hot swapping of IDE devices. The IDE devices can be floppy drives, CD-ROM drives, and hard disks. As with PC cards, dynamic configuration of IDE devices requires that the computer be ACPI-enabled. If it is not, the computer must be restarted after the device is removed or installed.

Power Management

Portable computer users have more special power requirements than desktop computer users. Windows 2000 Professional provides portable computer users with many options for managing power consumption on their computers. By using Power Options in the Control Panel, users can reduce the consumption of battery power on their computers and still keep them available for immediate use. Predefined power schemes are available for users to help them manage the computers' power consumption. Users can also create their own power schemes to meet their particular needs.

Advanced Power Management (APM)

APM is a legacy power-management scheme that was first supported in Windows 95. Windows 2000 Professional supports the APM 1.2 specification. APM is supported in Windows 2000 Professional only for legacy APM computers. It is not designed for desktop system support.

APM was designed to support battery status, suspend, resume, and auto-off for hibernate mode (discussed shortly). It was not designed to support timer wakeup, wake on LAN, and wake on ring states.

APM systems have the following three classes under Windows 2000:

➤ *AutoEnable APM*—This indicates that the system has passed testing at Microsoft and has been placed on the AutoEnable APM List. The Windows 2000 operating system checks this list during installation and enables APM support automatically on these systems.

➤ *Disable APM*—This indicates that APM does not work properly on these systems. Windows 2000 will not install or enable APM on such systems.

➤ *Neutral System*—This indicates that Microsoft doesn't know whether or not these systems will work with APM. Users can manually enable APM support on such systems.

APM is not enabled by default. Rather, it is enabled through the APM tab in the Power Options Properties dialog box. The APM tab is present only if APM is detected on the computer system.

Note: *The computer system has to be rebooted when APM support is turned on. It does not have to be rebooted when APM support is turned off.*

APM should not be used on computer systems that are on the Windows 2000 Disable APM List. Windows 2000 Professional provides a support tool, ampstat.exe, to determine if your computer BIOS is APM compatible. This tool is located in the Support\Tools folder on the Windows 2000 Professional CD and is run from a command line. It has only one option, the **–v** command line switch. This runs ampstat.exe in verbose mode.

Note: *APM support is available only for Windows 2000 Professional. It is not available for Windows 2000 Server, Windows 2000 Advanced Server, or Windows 2000 Datacenter.*

ACPI

In Windows 2000 Professional, APM has been superseded by ACPI. An open-industry specification enables the operating systems to directly manage power on a computer system. ACPI allows the operating system to manage power for all its subsystems and peripherals.

12

ACPI is based on the OnNow design initiative for power management. With the OnNow design initiative, computers are always available for immediate use. The PC may be perceived as off when not in use, but it must be capable of responding to wake-up events. The operating system and applications must work together to effectively deliver power management.

ACPI specifications have two parts: configuration (Plug and Play) and power management. Windows 2000 and the device drivers have full control over power management. The BIOS allows the operating system to determine when to turn devices on or off.

ACPI allows the operating system to control not only standard devices (such as CD-ROMs and network adapters) but also consumer devices connected to the computer (such as a VCR).

Computer systems that are ACPI compliant have the following features:

➤ Low-power processor, system, and device states

➤ Battery management

➤ Hibernation

➤ Hot and warm docking and undocking (discussed later in this chapter)

➤ Hot swapping of IDE devices, floppy devices, PC cards, and CardBus cards

Hibernate Mode

When a computer is put in hibernate mode, the current system state is saved to the hard drive and the computer is turned off. When a computer is restarted after being in hibernate mode, all settings, including network connections, are returned to their original state.

Hibernate mode is disabled by default in Windows 2000 Professional. You can enable it by checking the Enable Hibernate Support checkbox on the Hibernate tab in the Power Options Properties dialog box.

The contents of the computer's memory is written to disk when it enters hibernate mode. To go into hibernate mode, you must have at least as much disk space as you have RAM for the computer.

Computers that are not enabled with ACPI or APM cannot automatically be put into Hibernate mode. Instead, users must manually put the computer in hibernate mode. In addition, they must enter a username and password when resuming use from a hibernate state.

Standby Mode

When a computer goes into standby mode, it enters a low-power state. The monitor and hard disk are turned off and power consumption is reduced. When the computer comes out of standby mode, the desktop is returned to its original state. A loss of power while in standby mode could result in loss of data because the data is not saved to the hard disk as it is when the computer enters hibernate mode.

The computer prompts users for a username and password after it resumes from standby mode. This is the default setting and can be turned off by deselecting the Prompt For Password When Computer Goes Off Standby checkbox.

Standby mode is enabled by default on ACPI- and APM-enabled computers. It is not available on computers not based on ACPI or APM.

Power Schemes

Windows 2000 Professional has six default power schemes that allow users to configure power consumption:

➤ *Home/Office Desk*—This is the default power scheme for Windows 2000 Professional. It was designed for desktop computers.

➤ *Portable/Laptop*—This power scheme is optimized for portable computer use. It includes settings for battery operation.

➤ *Presentation*—This power scheme is intended for use when you are giving presentations. It prevents the computer from going into standby mode.

➤ *Always On*—This is the default power scheme for servers. The standby time is disabled.

➤ *Minimum Power Management*—Several power-management options, such as time hibernation, are disabled with this power scheme.

➤ *Max Battery*—This power scheme is for conserving battery power. The computer is put into a power-saving state after a short period of inactivity.

If the computer is enabled with ACPI or APM, you can set separate power schemes for standby and hibernate modes. In addition, you can configure separate settings for when the computer is powered by an alternating current or a battery. By default, the Home/Office Desk scheme is selected. This isn't the best setting for portable computer users, however. At a minimum, portable users should select the Portable/Laptop power scheme. The Presentation scheme is also a good selection because it keeps the computer from going into hibernate and standby modes.

12

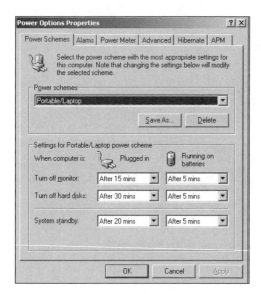

Figure 12.7 The Power Schemes tab of the Power Options Properties dialog box.

Figure 12.7 shows the settings for the Portable/Laptop power scheme, which allows users to configure separate settings for the computer when it is running on an alternating current or batteries.

Portable computer users can create their own power scheme if the predefined schemes do not meet their needs. To create your own power scheme, take these steps:

1. Select Start | Settings | Control Panel | Power Options.

2. Select the time setting you want in the Turn off monitor and Turn off hard disks lists.

3. Click on Save As and enter a name for the new power scheme.

4. Click on OK.

Alarms

Windows 2000 Professional has an option that allows users to set alarms when battery power is low. You can set this option through the Alarms tab of the Power Options Properties dialog box, as shown in Figure 12.8.

Alarms can be set for a low-battery alarm and a critical-battery alarm. Computer users can be notified through an audible alarm and with a displayed message.

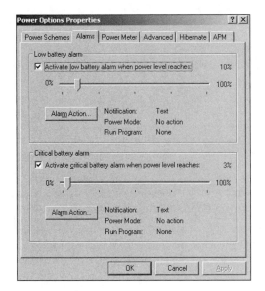

Figure 12.8   The Alarms tab of the Power Options Properties dialog box.

Hardware Profiles

Hardware profiles tell the operating system what devices to start when you turn your computer on. A default profile called Profile 1 holds the settings for all devices that were installed when you initially installed Windows 2000 Professional.

Computers that are Plug and Play compliant automatically create separate hardware profiles for when the computer is docked and/or undocked. These profiles are called Docked Profile and Undocked Profile. Users do not have to designate which profile to use; the operating system automatically detects whether to use a docked or undocked profile. If your computer is not fully Plug and Play compliant, you may have to create a hardware profile.

Docking/Undocking

Three methods are available for docking and undocking portable computers. The first method is a *cold dock*. In a cold dock, the computer is shut down before it is docked or undocked from its docking station. Cold docking should be used if the computer is not enabled with ACPI or APM. The second method is a *warm dock*. In a warm dock, the operating system unloads device drivers and puts the computer in standby mode before it is docked or undocked. The computer must be ACPI enabled to perform a warm dock. The third method is a *hot dock*. In a hot dock, the computer is running while being docked or undocked from its docking station. You can do a hot dock by using the Eject PC command or by physically removing the computer from the docking station.

Note: Undocking a computer from its docking station is not recommended when it is in hibernate mode.

Smart Cards

Windows 2000 Professional introduces support for smart cards and smart card readers. A *smart card* is a device the size of a credit card that contains integrated circuit cards (ICCs). Smart cards store public and private keys, passwords, and other forms of personal information. They are used to perform operations such as authentication and digital signing. Smart cards provide tamper-resistant storage for protecting public keys and personal information. They isolate security-critical computations from those parts of the operating system that don't need this information. They enable portability of private information and credentials among work, home, and remote computers.

Smart card technology is an important component of Windows 2000 Professional's public-key infrastructure security feature. Users can be authenticated using private- and public-key information stored on the card.

A Personal Identification Number (PIN) is used instead of passwords with smart cards. Only the smart card owner knows this PIN, and it is required before the smart card can be used. The card locks if an incorrect PIN is entered after a predetermined number of times.

A smart card reader is required to use smart cards. Windows 2000 Professional supports industry standard Personal Computer/Smart Card (PC/SC)-compliant Plug and Play smart cards and smart card readers. These devices must meet Microsoft's implementation of the PC/SC Workgroup 1.0 specification and Windows platform requirements for Plug and Play. They must conform to the physical and electrical requirements defined in the International Organization for Standardization (ISO) 7816-1, 7816-2, and 7816-3 standards. Smart card readers can be attached to standard peripheral interfaces such as Universal Serial Bus (USB), RS-232, PC, and PS/2 ports.

Microsoft has implemented a Windows-compatible logo program for smart card readers. You can download a smart card reader test kit from the Windows Hardware Quality Lab (WHQL) Web site (www.microsoft.com/HWTEST/TestKits/default.asp) to determine whether a reader is compatible with the Windows 2000 operating system.

Windows 2000 Professional automatically detects Plug and Play-compliant smart card readers and installs them through the Hardware Wizard.

Note: Non-Plug and Play smart card readers are not recommended for use with Windows 2000 Professional. If you do use one, you must use the installation instructions provided by the device's manufacturer. Microsoft does not support non-Plug and Play smart card readers.

Chapter Summary

Windows 2000 Professional was designed for mobile computer users. Features such as ACPI provide users with the ability to work on their notebook computers longer. Several features introduced in Windows 98 have been improved on in Windows 2000.

Network And Dial-Up Connections is used to access network resources. The Network Connection Wizard steps users through setting up network and dial-up connections. Users can connect to a private network and the Internet using a modem, ISDN, or X.25. When connecting to the Internet, the Internet Connection Wizard allows users to make a connection with an existing Internet account. If they do not have an existing account, the wizard will walk them step by step through setting up a new account. VPN connectivity is provided through PPTP and L2TP. By employing VPNs, users can establish secure connections through an untrusted network. A connection to the user's ISP must be established before he can connect to the VPN.

Direct connections can be between computers using serial cables, a modem, an infrared port, and DirectParallel cables. Direct connections are a good way to transfer files between computers.

Windows 2000 Professional can support incoming connections through dial-up, VPN, and direct connections. Users must have a local account on the computer they are dialing into. Up to three incoming connections can be made to a computer running Windows 2000 Professional, but they cannot all be of the same connection type.

Security for Network And Dial-Up Connections is provided through authentication, data encryption, and callback. Network And Dial-Up Connections supports the PAP, SPAP, CHAP, MS-CHAP, MS-CHAP 2, and EAP authentication protocols.

Two types of data encryption are supported in Network And Dial-Up Connections: MMPE and IPSec. MMPE is specifically used for a VPN connection that is configured to connect to a PPTP server. IPSec is used for a VPN connection to a L2TP server.

12

The Callback feature in Windows 2000 Professional is similar to Callback in previous versions of Windows NT. Users can configure the Callback feature to call a specific number, to always call the same number, or to not allow Callback at all. Callback is not supported on VPN connections.

Offline Files And Folders allows users to work on network-based files when they are not connected to the network. Files are synchronized when users reconnect to the network.

Windows 2000 Professional provides dynamic hardware support for PC cards, CardBus devices, and IDE devices. Devices can be removed or installed from computers without rebooting.

Windows 2000 Professional provides APM to support legacy-based notebook computers. ACPI, an industry standard for power management on a computer system, supersedes APM. When a system is put into hibernate mode, all data is saved to the hard disk. Portable computers that are not enabled with ACPI or APM cannot be put into hibernate mode. A computer goes into an idle state when it goes into standby mode. You can set alarms to indicate a low battery on a notebook computer.

Windows 2000 Professional comes with six predefined power schemes. The Portable/Laptop and Presentations power schemes are the best to use with portable computers. If none of the predefined schemes suits the users' specific needs, they can create her own.

Separate hardware profiles are created in Windows 2000 Professional for when a computer is docked and undocked. Hardware profiles provide users with the ability to control which device drivers are loaded when their notebook computers are started.

Smart cards provide a secure method for authenticating portable computer users. A smart card uses a PIN instead of a password to authenticate users. You must have a smart card reader installed on the computer to use a smart card.

Review Questions

1. What happens when a notebook computer is put into hibernate mode?

   a. The current state of the computer is saved to disk.

   b. The current state of the computer is saved to RAM.

   c. The current state of the computer is saved to a CD in the CD-ROM drive.

   d. All data is lost.

2. What is the difference between warm and hot docking?

   a. A warm dock is performed when the computer is running, and a hot dock is performed when the computer is in standby mode.

   b. A hot dock is performed when the computer is running, and a warm dock is performed when the computer is in standby mode.

   c. A hot dock means the computer is completely shut down before docking, and a warm dock means it is turned on before docking

   d. There is no difference between warm and hot docking.

3. Of which of the following does Windows 2000 Professional support hot swapping?

   a. IDE devices

   b. CD-ROMs

   c. Memory cards

   d. Offline files

4. What does it mean to pin a file or folder?

   a. The file or folder is copied to the network share.

   b. The file or folder is copied to the local cache on the portable computer.

   c. The file or folder is copied to the local cache on the server.

   d. The file or folder is redirected to another location.

5. Windows 2000 Professional does not synchronize files over a slow link. True or false?

   a. True

   b. False

6. How do you change the size of the Offline Files cache?

   a. You cannot change the size of the Offline Files cache.

   b. By moving the slider under Amount Of Disk Space To Use For Temporary Offline Files.

   c. By editing the Registry.

   d. By reinitializing the cache.

7. Where do you enable APM on a portable computer?

   a. On the APM tab in the Power Options Properties dialog box

   b. On the Power Meter tab in the Power Options Properties dialog box

   c. On the Hibernate tab in the Power Options Properties dialog box

   d. By clicking on the Alarm Action button

12

8. What is the purpose of running ampstat.exe?

   a. To check for APM BIOS compatibility

   b. To compress a disk

   c. To check for ACPI BIOS compatibility

   d. To synchronize offline files

9. APM is enabled by default on portable computers. True or false?

   a. True

   b. False

10. Windows 2000 Professional has six default power schemes. True or false?

    a. True

    b. False

11. Standby mode is enabled by default on ACPI- and APM-enabled computers. True or false?

    a. True

    b. False

12. What is a surprise removal?

    a. Removing a CD-ROM from the CD-ROM drive

    b. Removing a PC card before Windows 2000 is notified to stop the device

    c. Removing a PC card after Windows 2000 has been notified to stop the device

    d. Removing RAM from your portable computer

13. Which two options are the best power schemes to use with portable computers?

    a. Always On

    b. Portable/Laptop

    c. Max Battery

    d. Presentation

14. Which dial-up connection types does Incoming Connections support? [Check all correct answers]

    a. VPN

    b. Direct connect

    c. Modem

    d. T1

15. Which of the following authentication protocols are supported by Network And Dial-Up Connections? [Check all correct answers]

    a. SPAP

    b. MS-CHAP

    c. EAP

    d. CHAP

16. What is the purpose of the Callback feature?

    a. To allow a user to make toll-free calls using a portable computer

    b. To have a remote server call a user back at a preset number

    c. To have a portable computer call a server at a preset number

    d. To enable video-conferencing on a portable computer

Real-World Projects

For all of the following projects, you need a portable computer running Windows 2000 Professional. You need to have a hard disk with at least one NT File System (NTFS) partition.

Project 12.1

To create a new power scheme for your portable computer:

1. Open the Control Panel.

2. Double-click on the Power Options icon.

3. Select the Power Schemes tab.

4. Select Options For The New Power Scheme.

5. Click on Save As.

6. Enter the name for the new power scheme in the Save This Power Scheme As box and click on OK.

7. Click on OK to close the Power Options Properties dialog box.

Project 12.2

To configure your portable computer to synchronize at a predetermined time:

1. Click on Start | Programs.

2. From the Programs menu, select Accessories | Synchronize.

3. Select the item you want to synchronize.

12

4. Click on the Setup button.

5. Click on the Scheduled tab.

6. Click on Add button to add a synchronization task. The Scheduled Synchronization Wizard starts.

7. Click on Next.

8. Select a network connection for the synchronization task and click on Next.

9. In the Start Time box, select the time when you want the synchronization task to start.

10. In the Perform This Task box, select when you want the synchronization task to run.

11. Select the start date for the synchronization task to begin and click on Next.

12. Enter a name for the task in the Type A Name For This Scheduled Synchronization box and click on Next.

13. Click on the Finish button to add the synchronization task to the Windows schedule.

Project 12.3

To configure your notebook computer to automatically make a network connection for synchronization and to configure it to synchronize when the computer is idle and running on battery power:

1. Click on Start | Programs.

2. From the Programs menu, select Accessories | Synchronize.

3. Select the item you want to synchronize.

4. Click on the Setup button.

5. Select the On Idle tab.

6. Select a network connection for the synchronization task and click on Next.

7. In the Synchronize The Following Checked Items selection box, add a checkmark beside each item to synchronize.

8. Click on the Synchronize The Selected Item While My Computer Is Idle checkbox.

9. Click on the Advanced button.

10. Deselect the Prevent Synchronization When My Computer Is Running On Battery Power checkbox and click on OK.

11. Click on the Schedule tab. The Scheduled Synchronization Wizard starts.

12. Click on Next.

13. Click on the If My Computer Is Not Connected When This Scheduled Synchronization Begins, Automatically Connect For Me checkbox and click on Next.

14. Select a network connection for the synchronization task and click on Next.

15. Select the items to synchronize.

16. In the Start Time box, select the time when you want the synchronization task to start.

17. In the Perform This Task box, select when you want the synchronization task to run.

18. Select the start date for the synchronization task to begin and click on Next.

19. Enter a name for the task in the Type A Name For This Scheduled Synchronization box and click on Next.

20. Click on the Finish button to add the synchronization task to the Windows schedule.

Project 12.4

To create alarms to indicate low-battery and critical-battery levels:

1. Select Start | Settings | Control Panel.

2. Double-click on the Power Options icon.

3. Select the Alarms tab.

4. Check the Activate Low Battery Alarm When Power Level Reaches checkbox.

5. Move the slider to the battery level at which a low battery is activated.

6. Click on the Alarm Action button and select the type of Notification to receive.

7. Click on OK.

8. Check the Activate Critical Battery Alarm When Power Level Reaches checkbox.

9. Move the slider to the battery level at which you want the low battery alarm to activate.

10. Click on the Alarm Action button and select the type of Notification to receive.

11. Click on OK.

12. Click on OK again to exit the Power Options Properties dialog box.

12

CHAPTER THIRTEEN

Working Securely

After completing this chapter, you will be able to:

✓ Describe the security groups available in Windows 2000 Professional

✓ Describe group policies and how they are implemented

✓ Describe security policies and identify the security policy settings available in Windows 2000 Professional

✓ Explain the difference between user rights and permissions

✓ Explain how to audit events in Windows 2000 Professional

✓ Describe public key security and how it is used in Windows 2000 Professional

✓ Describe a certificate's uses

✓ Describe the two types of user authentication in Windows 2000 Professional

✓ Describe RAS authentication protocols that are available in Windows 2000 Professional

✓ Explain VPN

✓ Explain IPSec

✓ Explain how EFS is used in Windows 2000 Professional

Protecting your data is important whether the computer you use is a standalone desktop or notebook computer. Although security is an important aspect of any computer operation, networked computers bring additional security risks. Users must have a way of verifying individuals or groups that are trying to access their resources. Windows 2000 Professional provides users with several ways to keep their computers secure.

Security Groups

Several security groups are built into Windows 2000 Professional. These predefined groups give users the rights and permissions they may need to access the computer. Users who need access to a particular resource can be added to the appropriate security group. The predefined security groups are described in the next few sections.

The Administrators Group

Administrators have full access to all resources on the computer. This includes the Registry and file system objects. The Administrators group is the first group created when Windows 2000 is installed. Individuals or groups who are members of the Administrator group can:

➤ Install the operating system and any additional components

➤ Install Service Packs

➤ Upgrade and repair the operating system

➤ Configure system parameters such as audit policy, password policy, and access control

➤ Take ownership of files and folders that may have become inaccessible

➤ Monitor and maintain system and auditing logs

➤ Back up and restore the system

The Users Group

As members of the User group, individuals can run programs installed by members of the Administrators group. They have full control over their own data files but cannot remove programs installed by other users. Nor can they modify system-wide settings, or system or program files. They have read-only permission for most of the operating system. Members of the User security group have read/write permission over their own profile folders. They can shut down workstations but not servers. They can create local groups but can manage only the groups they create.

The Guest Group

The Guest security account is for users who need one-time access to the system. This group allows users to log on to a workstations's built-in Group account. The Guest Group account is disabled by default, as it is in Windows NT. Members of this group have very limited capabilities but they can shut down the workstation.

The Power Users Group

The Power Users group in Windows 2000 Professional has the same permissions as the Power Users group in Windows NT. Members of the Power Users group have more permissions than those in the User group but not as many permissions as those in the Administrators group. The Power Users group can perform any operating system tasks except those specifically reserved for the Administrators group. Power Users cannot add themselves to the Administrators group and do not have access to other users' data on an NT File System (NTFS) volume unless they have been granted permission to access the data. Power Users can:

➤ Install programs that do not modify operating system files

➤ Install programs that do not install system services

➤ Create and manage local user accounts and groups

➤ Customize system-wide groups such as Printers and items in the Control Panel

➤ Start and stop services that are not configured to start by default

The Backup Operators Group

Backup Operators are given permission to back up and restore files on the computer. The files can be backed up regardless of the permissions protecting the files. Backup Operators cannot change security settings on a computer, but they can log on and shut the system down.

13

Special Security Groups

In addition to the predefined groups, Windows 2000 Professional has several other groups that are created by default during installation:

➤ *Interactive*—The Interactive group contains the user who is currently logged on to the computer.

➤ *Network*—The Network group contains users that are currently accessing the system over the network.

➤ *Terminal Server Users*—The Terminal Server User group contains any user who is currently logged on to the system via Terminal Server.

Group Policies

Administrators can use group policies in Windows 2000 Professional to set security policies for domain-based environments and locally for individual workstations. Group policies are a collection of settings that the operating system enforces. The user cannot modify them. The Group Policy snap-in, shown in Figure 13.1, is used to manage group policies on local computers. (Despite the title of the snap-in in Figure 13.1, this is the Group Policy snap-in.) You must have administrative rights to manage group policies. Group Policy settings are not enabled by default.

The Group Policy snap-in supercedes System Policy Editor in previous versions of Windows. In Windows NT 4, 72 policy settings could be applied to NT Workstation, Windows 95, and Windows 98 computers. In Windows 2000, administrators can set group policies for more than 100 security-related settings and over 450 registry-based settings. Group Policy objects are located in \%SystemRoot%System32\ GroupPolicy on the local computer.

Administrators can set the following group policy settings on the local computer:

➤ Security settings for the local computer

➤ Administrative templates to allow for 450 operating system behaviors

➤ Scripts for automating procedures at computer startup or shutdown and when users log on and off

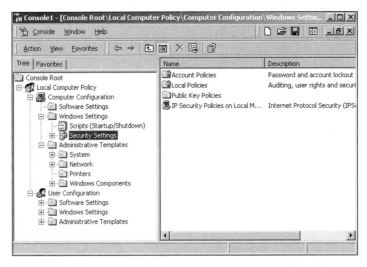

Figure 13.1   The Group Policy snap-in tool.

Note: Group Policy settings take precedence over user settings. Local Group Policy settings can be applied to the computer configuration or the user configuration. Computer-related Group Policy settings take affect when the system is initialized. User-related Group Policy settings take affect when the user logs on to the computer.

The Windows 2000 Professional Resource Kit contains a utility that can be used to view both local and domain Group Policy settings. GPResult.exe is located on the Windows 2000 Professional Resource Kit companion CD and provides the following information:

➤ *Operating System*—Including type (Professional, Server, Domain Controller), build number, and Service Packs

➤ *User Information*—Username, location in Active Directory (if applicable), domain name and type, security group membership, and security privileges

➤ *Computer Information*—Including computer name and location in Active Directory (if applicable), domain name, and type and site name

Security Policies

Security policies are a subset of group policies. As with group policies, security policies can be managed on a domain-based network and on local workstations. Nine groups of security policy settings are defined in Windows 2000 Professional. They are:

➤ *Password Policy*—Passwords can be modified to meet your organization's needs. Complex passwords, in addition to minimum or maximum password lengths, can be required.

➤ *Account Lockout Policy*—User accounts can be locked out after a predefined number of failed logon attempts. The account can be locked out for a specified amount of time.

➤ *Kerberos Authentication Policy*—This policy can be modified on domain settings. Its settings are not available for a local security policy.

➤ *Audit Policy*—As in Windows NT, Window 2000 Professional can record security events such as user logon and logoff. Successful and unsuccessful attempts of a particular action can be recorded and logged.

➤ *User Rights Assignment*—Rights can be assigned to users and security groups for a variety of tasks on local computers.

➤ *Security Options*—Options can be set for a variety of security options on the local computer.

13

➤ *Encrypted Data Recovery Agent*—Rights can be assigned for the encrypted data recovery agent.

➤ *Internet Protocol (IP) Security Policies*—Policies can be set for how requests for IP Security (IPSec) communications are handled. IPSec is discussed in more detail later in this chapter.

Security Options

Security on local computers can be increased by using security options available under the Security Options node of the Local Policy. Approximately 40 security options are available to increase security on the local machine. The following discusses several of these options.

Ctrl+Alt+Delete

Unlike in Windows NT, users in Windows 2000 Professional do not have to press the Ctrl+Alt+Delete combination to log on. This feature can be activated if increased security is needed. In addition, Ctrl+Alt+Delete can be used to lock and disable the workstation, as in Windows NT 4.

To require that Ctrl+Alt+Delete be pressed before users can log on:

1. Select Start | Settings | Control Panel and click on Users And Passwords.

2. Click on the Advanced tab.

3. In Secure Boot Settings, click on the Require Users To Press Ctrl-Alt-Delete Before Logging On option.

Clear Virtual Memory Pagefile When System Shuts Down

Windows 2000 Professional does not clear the virtual memory pagefile when the computer is shut down. This can be a security risk in that sensitive data in the pagefile could be accessible to users who are not authorized to view it. To force the operating system to clear the pagefile when the system is shut down:

1. Open the Group Policy snap-in.

2. Expand Local Computer Policy.

3. Expand Computer Configuration.

4. Expand Windows Settings.

5. Expand Security Settings.

6. Expand Local Policies and select Security Options.

7. Right-click Clear Virtual Memory Pagefile When System Shuts Down and click Security.

8. Click the Enabled button and click OK.

Do Not Display Last User Name in Logon Screen

By default, the name of the last user who logged onto a Windows 2000 Professional computer is displayed in the Log On To Windows dialog box. For security reasons, administrators may want to disable this so that unauthorized users do not see valid user accounts displayed on the screen. To prevent the last username from appearing in the Log On To Windows dialog box, perform the following steps:

1. Open the Group Policy snap-in.

2. Expand Local Computer Policy.

3. Expand Computer Configuration.

4. Expand Windows Settings.

5. Expand Security Settings.

6. Expand Local Policies and select Security Options.

7. Right-click Do Not Display Last Username In Logon Screen and click Security.

8. Click the Enabled button and click OK.

Security Templates

A security template is a file that contains security settings that can be applied to local and domain-based computers. Windows 2000 Professional provides a set of security templates (see Figure 13.2) that can be used to apply consistent security settings for a large number of computers. These security settings can also be imported into a group policy object and applied to specific classes of computers.

Security templates are not active until they are imported into a group policy object or the Security Configuration and Analysis snap-in. The Security Configuration

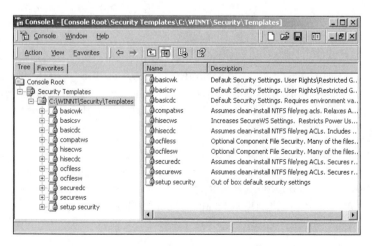

Figure 13.2   Security templates.

and Analysis snap-in is used to view and modify security templates. You can also use it to compare security settings of a template to those on a local computer. Before you can use security templates, you must define the level of user access using the built-in Windows 2000 groups such as Administrator and Power User.

After you have defined the level of user access, you can use the following security templates:

➤ Basic

➤ Optional Component File Security

➤ Compatible

➤ Secure

➤ High Secure

User Rights

User rights allow administrators to assign specific rights to users and groups. These rights define what actions the users or groups can perform. User rights are applied to user accounts; they differ from permissions, which are applied to objects. User rights can be applied to individual users, but it is better to apply the rights to groups and then put the individual users into the groups. If users are members of multiple groups, their user rights are cumulative.

Windows 2000 Professional has two types of rights: privilege rights and logon rights. A *privilege right* allows a user to perform specific tasks on the network or local computer. A *logon right* specifies how a user can log onto a system.

Permissions

File and folder permissions can be set in Windows 2000 Professional only on NTFS volumes. This is the same as with Windows NT except that the NTFS version supplied in Windows 2000 provides for inheritable permissions. With inheritable permissions, the files or folders inherit the permissions from their parent folder. Inheritable permissions are enabled by default. To prevent a file or folder from inheriting the permissions from its parent folder, clear the Allow Inheritable Permissions From Parent To Propagate To This Object checkbox on the Security tab of the Properties dialog box.

Permissions can be applied to files and folders for local computer and network resources. Members of the Administrators and Power Users security groups can assign permissions to shared folders. Rights cannot be assigned to files and folders. File permissions in Windows 2000 Professional include Full Control, Modify, Read And Execute, Read, and Write. Users with Full Control permission can change permissions, take ownership of files and folders, delete files and subfolders, and perform all actions permitted by the other NTFS permissions. Users with the Modify permission can delete files and perform actions permitted by the Read and Execute permission. Read and Execute permissions allow users to run applications and perform actions permitted by the Read permission. Users with the Write permission can overwrite files, change file attributes, and view file ownership and permissions. The Read permission permits users to read the file and view its attributes, ownership, and permissions.

Folder permissions are the same as file permissions except for the addition of the List Folder Contents permission. The List Folder Content permission allows the user to see the names of files and subfolders in the folder.

Special Permissions

Users can customize permissions on files and folders by using special permissions. The special permissions that can be set on NTFS volumes are described in the following sections.

Traverse Folder/Execute File

Traverse Folder allows or denies moving through folders to reach other files or folders, even if users have no permissions for the traversed folders (this permission applies to folders only). Execute File allows or denies running program files (this permission applies to files only).

List Folder/Read Data

List Folder allows or denies viewing file names and subfolder names within the folder (this permission applies to folders only). Read Data allows or denies viewing data in files (this permission applies to files only).

Read Attributes

Read Attributes allows or denies viewing the attributes, such as read-only and hidden, of a file or folder. NTFS defines the attributes.

Read Extended Attributes

Read Extended Attributes allows or denies viewing the extended attributes of a file or folder. Extended attributes are defined by programs and may vary by program.

Create Files/Write Data

Create Files allows or denies creating files within the folder (this permission applies to folders only). Write Data allows or denies making changes to the file and overwriting existing content (this permission applies to files only).

13

Create Folders/Append Data

Create Folders allows or denies creating folders within the folder (this permission applies to folders only). Append Data allows or denies making changes to the end of the file but not changing, deleting, or overwriting existing data (this permission applies to files only).

Write Attributes

Write Attributes allows or denies changing the attributes, such as read-only or hidden, of a file or folder. NTFS defines the attributes.

Write Extended Attributes

Write Extended Attributes allows or denies changing the extended attributes of a file or folder. Extended attributes are defined by programs and may vary by program.

Delete Subfolders and Files

Delete Subfolders and Files allows or denies deleting subfolders and files, even if the Delete permission has not been granted on the subfolders or files.

Delete

Delete allows or denies deleting the file or folder. If you don't have the Delete permission on a file or folder, you can still delete it if you have been granted Delete Subfolders and Files on the parent folder.

Read Permissions

Read Permissions allows or denies reading permissions, such as Full Control, Read, and Write, of the file or folder.

Change Permissions

Change Permissions allows or denies changing permissions, such as Full Control, Read, and Write, of the file or folder.

Take Ownership

Take Ownership allows or denies taking ownership of the file or folder. The owner of a file or folder can always change permissions on it, regardless of any existing permissions that protect the file or folder.

Synchronize

Synchronize allows or denies different threads to wait on the handle for the file or folder and synchronize with another thread that may signal it. This permission applies only to multithreaded, multiprocess programs.

Table 13.1 lists the special permissions associated with each of the file permissions. Table 13.2 lists the special permissions associated with each of the folder permissions.

Table 13.1   Special permissions associated with file permissions.

Special Permissions	Full Control	Modify	Read And Execute	Read	Write
Traverse Folder/Execute File	X	X	X		
List Folder/Read Data	X	X	X	X	
Read Attributes	X	X	X	X	
Read Extended Attributes	X	X	X	X	
Create Files/Write Data	X	X			X
Create Folders/Append Data	X	X			X
Write Attributes	X	X			X
Write Extended Attributes	X	X			X
Delete Subfolders And Files	X				
Delete	X	X			
Read Permissions	X	X	X	X	X
Change Permissions	X				
Take Ownership	X				
Synchronize	X	X	X	X	X

Table 13.2   Special permissions associated with folder permissions.

Special Permissions	Full Control	Modify	Read And Execute	List Folder Contents	Read	Write
Traverse Folder/Execute File	X	X	X	X		
List Folder/Read Data	X	X	X	X	X	
Read Attributes	X	X	X	X	X	
Read Extended Attributes	X	X	X	X	X	
Create Files/Write Data	X	X				X
Create Folders/Append Data	X	X				X
Write Attributes	X	X				X
Write Extended Attributes	X	X				X
Delete Subfolders And Files	X					
Delete	X	X				
Read Permissions	X	X	X	X	X	X
Change Permissions	X					
Take Ownership	X					
Synchronize	X	X	X	X	X	X

13

Shared Permissions

Shared permissions are applied to folders only, not files or subfolders within the shared resource. Shared permissions do not restrict users who access the computer locally (on which the shared resource is stored). Shared permissions are enforced by the operating system, not the file system, and are applied equally to NTFS and file allocation table (FAT) volumes. Shared permissions are set in the same way as file and folder permissions are set on NTFS volumes.

The security levels of network access for shared folders and resources are as follows:

➤ *Full Control*—Allows users to take ownership of files and folders and to change file access rights. It is assigned to the Everyone group by default.

➤ *Change*—Allows users to create and add files, modify files, change the attributes of files, and delete files. Users are granted all the permissions of the Read level of security.

➤ *Read*—Allows users to display and open files, display the attributes of files, and execute program files.

➤ *No Access*—Prevents users from displaying, accessing, or modifying files.

Auditing

Windows 2000 Professional allows you to track user and group access to files, folders, and other objects by enabling auditing. You can also use it to track operating system activity. Audited activities or events are written to the security log. An audit entry that is written to the security log contains the following information:

➤ The action that was performed

➤ The user who performed the action

➤ Whether the event was a success or failure when it occurred

Before you can audit objects, you must specify in an audit policy the type of auditing you want to implement. Events recorded in the security log are defined by the audit policy. Administrators can audit file, folder, and printer access, user logon and logoff, computer startup and shutdown, and changes made to user and group accounts.

To administer auditing on a Windows 2000 computer, you must have the Manage Auditing And Security Log user right for the computer. This right is granted to the Administrator group by default. Files and folders being audited must be on NTFS volumes. Auditing is not supported on FAT volumes.

Windows 2000 allows auditing of the following events:

➤ Account logon events

➤ Account management

➤ Directory service access

➤ Logon events

➤ Object access

➤ Policy change

➤ Privilege use

➤ Process tracking

➤ Systems events

The Event Viewer is used to view events that Windows 2000 Professional has recorded in the security log on the computer in which the event occurred. You can view the security log for other computers if you have administrative privileges for that computer. You do this by creating a custom console in the MMC that points to the Event Viewer for the remote computer.

Public Key Security

Public key security is a key component of Windows 2000 security. To understand security in Windows 2000 Professional, you must understand the difference between the two types of encryption used in public key security. The first is *private key encryption*, also known as *symmetric encryption*. With private key encryption, one secret key is used to encrypt and decrypt data; the same private key to encrypt to data is used to decrypt it. An example of private key encryption is Data Encryption Standard (DES).

The second type of encryption is *public key encryption*, also known as *asymmetric encryption*. Unlike with private key encryption, public key encryption uses two keys—one public and one private. The two keys are mathematically related to each other. One key encrypts the data whereas the other decrypts it.

Both parties share the same key in symmetric encryption. In asymmetric key encryption, the private key is used to encrypt the data and the public key is used to decrypt it. The user who originally encrypted the data using the private key publishes the public key to whomever he or she wants to have access to the data. (In some systems of encryption, however, the situation may be reversed; the public key is used to encrypt, while the private key is used to decrypt the encrypted data. Make sure that you are aware of the system being used before sending a key.)

The following Windows 2000 security systems use public key technology:

➤ Network logon authentication.

➤ Routing and Remote Access Service (RAS), including Remote Authentication Dial-In User Service (RADIUS), user authentication based on Extensible

13

Authentication Protocol (EAP) and Transport Layer Security (TLS), communication over the Internet using Point-to-Point Tunneling Protocol (PPTP) and Layer 2 Tunneling Protocol (L2TP), and remote network access and logging. EAP and RADIUS are discussed in more detail later in this chapter. TLS, PPTP and L2TP are discussed in more detail in Chapter 12.

➤ Microsoft Internet Information Services.

➤ IPSec, described later in this chapter.

➤ Encrypting File System (EFS), described later in this chapter.

The following components comprise public key security in Windows 2000:

➤ Windows 2000 Certificate Services

➤ Microsoft CryptoAPI and cryptographic service providers (CSPs)

➤ Certificate stores

➤ Certificate consoles

➤ Certification authority trust model

➤ Certificate enrollment and renewal methods

➤ Public key group policy

➤ Certificate revocation lists

➤ Preinstalled trusted root certificates

➤ Smart card support

Note: For further information on the public key security components in Windows 2000 Professional, see the Microsoft Windows 2000 Professional Resource Kit.

Certificates

The public key is published with a certificate, which is used to ensure the public key's integrity. It holds specific information about the public key such as its name, purpose, owner, and the actual key itself. The certificate is digitally signed by a certificate authority such as VeriSign. Certificates are very important in Windows 2000 Professional and are used to:

➤ Allow data to be encrypted

➤ Allow data to be signed

➤ Allow a recovery agent to recover encrypted data

➤ Allow secured communications over the Internet

➤ Ensure that email came from the correct sender

➤ Ensure that only the intended recipient can view the content of email messages

➤ Guarantee the identity of remote computers

➤ Protect device drivers and system components from tampering

The Certificate Manager, shown in Figure 13.3, manages certificates in Windows 2000 Professional.

With Certificate Manager, users can:

➤ Remove certificates

➤ Import and export certificates

➤ Request new certificates from certificate authorities

Normally, Windows 2000 Professional does not have to manage certificates using Certificate Manager. It is most commonly used to export certificates to a backup file.

User Authentication

Authentication validates users' credentials against their local or domain database. They are allowed access to resources depending on the rights and privileges assigned to them. The security system in Windows 2000 Professional provides two types of authentication: interactive logon and network authentication.

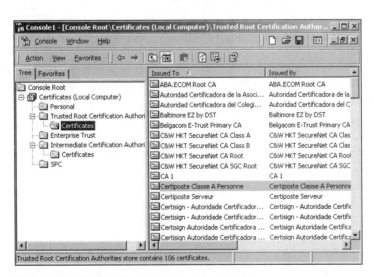

Figure 13.3   The Certificate Manager snap-in tool.

13

Interactive Logon

With interactive logon, users are confirmed depending on whether they are connecting to a local computer or a domain account. On a local computer, a user's identification is confirmed based on credentials stored in the Security Account Manager (SAM). The SAM is the local security account database. On a networked computer, a user logs on to the network using Single Sign-On (SSO) credentials stored in Active Directory. Kerberos 5 is used for authentication.

Network Authentication

Network authentication provides confirmation of a user's identification and the resources he or she is permitted to access. Users who log on to a local computer account must provide some type of credential such as a username and password before they are granted access to network resources. Domain-based users do not see network authorization when logging on to the network. Windows 2000 provides network authentication through several methods, including smart cards, Kerberos 5, or NTLM.

Smart Cards

One of the new features of Windows 2000 is the support of smart cards and smart card readers. A smart card looks like a credit card but acts like a computer. Smart cards allow users to authenticate credentials among computers at home, work, or on the road in a portable manner.

Smart cards can be used to verify users' identities to enable them to log on to the network. The holders of the smart cards are authenticated via a Personal Identification Number (PIN). Users must have the correct PIN to be authenticated. Smart cards produce a digital certificate that authenticates the users' credentials and authorizes their access to resources. Smart cards offer very high levels of security.

To use smart cards, users must install a smart card reader on the computer. It is recommended that you use only those smart card readers that the Windows Hardware Quality Lab (WHQL) has tested.

Kerberos

Kerberos is an industry-standard network authentication protocol. Kerberos, or SSO, allows users to access multiple network resources after a single logon authentication. Kerberos 5 is the default protocol used for authentication in domains for Windows 2000. The protocol uses a dual verification known as *mutual authentication*. Mutual authentication verifies the identity of users and the network services they have access to.

Three elements are essential to Kerberos authentication in Windows 2000: the client, the server, and the Key Distribution Center (KDC). The KDC is the network service that issues a ticket-granting ticket (TGT) that contains encrypted data about the user. The TGT gets a service ticket (ST) that provides the access to the network services.

The process for Kerberos authentication is as follows:

1. A client requests authentication from an authentication server.

2. The server creates two session keys. These keys are sent to the client in an encrypted message. The encrypted message contains the client's private key and the server's encrypted private key.

3. Copies of the session key are sent to the server from the client. The server uses its private key to open the encrypted key.

4. The client is verified and can now communicate with the server and access the appropriate resources.

Account information about network users and resources in stored in the Key Database (KDB). The KDC uses the KDB to verify Kerberos clients.

NTLM

NTLM is the default authentication protocol for Windows NT 4 networks. NTLM is used in Windows 2000 for backward compatibility to earlier versions of Windows. Windows 3.x, 9x, and NT computers use the NTLM protocol to authenticate to Windows 2000 domains. Windows 2000 computers use NTLM when authenticating to a Windows NT computer to access its resources.

NTLM is based on challenge/response authentication. Three methods of challenge/response are supported in Windows 2000 Professional:

➤ *LAN Manager (LM)*—LM is the least secure form of challenge response authentication. It allows Windows 2000 computers to attach to file shares on computers running Windows 3.x, 95, and 98.

➤ *NTLM version 1*—This is more secure than LM and allows Windows 2000 computers to connect to servers in Windows NT 4 domains.

➤ *NTLM version 2*—This is the most secure of the three challenge/response authentication methods. It allows Windows 2000 computers to connect to Windows NT 4 domain servers that are running Service Pack 4 or later. It also connects Windows 2000 computers to Windows NT servers that are operating in a Windows 2000 domain.

Note: The three challenge/response authentication methods used in NTLM are enabled by default in Windows 2000 Professional.

13

RAS Authentication Protocols

Windows 2000 Professional supports several authentication protocols. Protocols vary in how they handle authentication and security. Authentication protocols are configured using the Network And Dial-Up Connections folder.

Password Authentication Protocol (PAP)

PAP is the least secure of the authentication protocols available in Windows 2000 Professional. It uses plain-text passwords and can be used to connect to non-Windows-based servers. PAP does not support encrypted passwords. This is not a recommended authentication protocol because anyone using a protocol analyzer can easily read the unencrypted password.

Shiva Password Authentication Protocol (SPAP)

SPAP allows Shiva clients to dial into Windows 2000 servers. In addition, Windows 2000 clients can use it to dial into Shiva clients. SPAP is more secure than PAP but not as secure as Challenge Handshake Authentication Protocol (CHAP). SPAP always uses the reversible encrypting method when sending passwords. This makes it susceptible to playback attacks, where an intruder can record the data exchange and play it back to gain fraudulent access.

CHAP

CHAP uses Message Digest 5 (MD5) to negotiate authentication. MD5 is an industry hashing scheme that is unique and cannot be reversed back to its original format.

CHAP uses a three-way handshake method to provide encrypted authentication. A challenge string is sent to the client from the authenticator. The client returns a one-way encrypted value of the challenge string. The authenticator verifies the value of the string and acknowledges the authentication. The challenge string is changed every time it is sent.

Microsoft Challenge Handshake Authentication Protocol (MS-CHAP)

MSCHAP is Microsoft's extension of CHAP. It supports password changes during authentication and one-way authentication. MSCHAP supports LM authentication by default.

MSCHAP 2

MS-CHAP 2 is the latest version of MS-CHAP. It uses different encryption keys for sending and receiving, and provides mutual authentication. Windows 2000 attempts to use MS-CHAP 2 first on Virtual Private Network (VPN) connections, discussed shortly. MSCHAP 2 supports stronger encryption than MSCHAP and does not support LM authentications.

Note: If you configure your computer to use only MSCHAP 2 and the computer you are dialing doesn't support it, the connection will fail.

EAP

EAP is a critical component for secure VPN connections. It is an extension to Point-to-Point Protocol (PPP) and supports token cards, one-time passwords, public key authentication, and smart cards. Like MSCHAP 2, EAP is a mutual authentication protocol.

RADIUS

RADIUS is an authentication protocol that supports third-party accounting and auditing packages. A Windows 2000 computer can act as a RADIUS client, RADIUS server, or both. Internet Service Providers (ISPs) commonly use RADIUS. Windows 2000 Internet Authentication Protocol performs authentication for RADIUS clients.

VPN

Users of Windows 2000 Professional can securely access resources on their company network by using a VPN. A VPN uses PPTP or L2TP (with IPSec) to create a secure connection through either a public or a private network. A VPN connection is made by dialing an ISP or through a direct connection to the Internet.

Authentication for VPNs can be made through the standard PPP user-level protocols, including PAP, SPAP, CHAP, MS-CHAP, and EAP.

If the VPN is using a L2TP connection, IPSec and EAP can provide remote users with increased security.

VPNs provide several advantages over long-distance dial-up connections, including lower cost, easier administration, better security, and support for existing protocols such as Transmission Control Protocol/Internet Protocol (TCP/IP) and Internet Protocol Exchange/Sequence Packet Exchange (IPX/SPX).

PPTP

PPTP provides a secure way to transmit data from a remote computer to a private server over TCP/IP networks. PPTP is supported by Windows 95, 98, NT, and 2000. Data is encrypted in PPTP VPN connections by Microsoft Point-to-Point Encryption (MPPE). PPTP was developed as an extension to PPP.

13

L2TP

L2TP creates a tunnel similar to PPTP, but the data isn't encrypted. Security for L2TP is provided through IPSec. L2TP is supported in Windows 2000 Professional for client-to-server and server-to-server tunneling only. L2TP also supports dynamic IP address assignment. As with PPTP, transmitting data via L2TP over a VPN connection is as secure as transmitting data over a corporate network.

The implementation of L2TP in Windows 2000 Professional does not support tunneling over X.25, Asynchronous Transfer Mode (ATM), or Frame Relay networks.

Both PPTP and L2TP are automatically installed in Windows 2000 Professional.

IPSec

IPSec allows for the transmission of encrypted data over the Internet. Employees can access the company network by enabling an IPSec policy and connecting through their local ISP. IPSec is implemented through policies. The policies decide the type of hashing used and the encryption standard used to encrypt the data.

IPSec provides machine-level authentication for VPN connections that use the L2TP protocol. IPSec ensures that a secure communication channel is established before data is exchanged. Microsoft uses two authentication methods to ensure the integrity and authentication of IP packets. The first method used is MD5, which uses a 128-bit hash value that is tacked to the end of the data packet. Once the packet is received at the destination, the hash value is compared to the original hash value. If they don't match, the packet is discarded.

The second method used is Secure Hash Algorithm (SHA). SHA is like MD5 but uses a 160-bit hash value instead of a 128-bit one. SHA is more secure than MD5.

Microsoft uses DES to encrypt IP packets for transmission. DES is a widely used method of encryption. It applies a 56-bit private key to every 64-block of data. Both the sender and receiver of the data must know and use the same private key. Triple DES is a variant of DES in which the algorithm is applied three times on the data to be encrypted before it is sent.

IPSec is actually two separate protocols: Authentication Header (AH) and Encapsulated Security Payload (ESP). AH provides authentication, integrity, and anti-replay. The data is not encrypted with AH. It is readable but cannot be modified. AH is used when a secure connection is needed but data being transmitted is not sensitive.

ESP provides authentication, integrity, anti-replay, and data encryption. It is used when you want to protect sensitive data.

You can configure IPSec through the IP Security Policy Management snap-in. IPSec policies can be used to:

➤ Specify the level of authentication used among IPSec clients

➤ Specify the lowest level of communication allowed between IPSec clients

➤ Allow or prevent communications between IPSec clients

➤ Specify whether to use encrypted or plain-text communication

IPSec policies can be stored in Active Directory or locally in the Registry of stand-alone computers.

Windows 2000 Professional provides several predefined IPSec policies:

➤ *Client (Respond Only)*—Used by computers that should not secure communications most of the time

➤ *Server (Request Security)*—Used by computers that should secure communications most of the time

➤ *Secure Server (Require Security)*—Used by computers that require secure communications all the time

EFS

EFS is the core technology of Windows 2000 Professional file encryption on NTFS volumes. Once users encrypt a file or folder, they can work with it as they do with any other files or folders. EFS is transparent to users. They do not have to decrypt the file to use it; they can open and close the file as they normally would. If individuals who did not encrypt the file try to access it, they receive an access denied message.

If a folder is encrypted, all files and subfolders under the folder are encrypted. Files and folders are encrypted using the Properties dialog box for the file. You can also encrypt them from a command line using the cipher.exe utility. The syntax for this utility is Cipher [/e] [/d] [/s:*folder*] [/a] [/i] [/f] [/q] [/h] [/k] [*pathname* [...]]. Table 13.3 lists the command-line options for encrypting files and folders for using cipher.exe.

13

Some limitations apply:

➤ EFS does not apply to FAT volumes. Files and folders on FAT volumes cannot be encrypted. Only files and folders on NTFS 5 volumes can be encrypted.

➤ Compressed files and folders cannot be encrypted. If you want to encrypt a file that is compressed, you must first uncompress it. The only individual who can open an encrypted file can also encrypt it.

Table 13.3   Command-line options for cipher.exe.

Command	Description
/e	Encrypts the specified folders
/d	Decrypts the specified folders
/s:*folder*	Performs the specified operation on folders in the specified folder and all subfolders
/i	Continues encrypting even if cipher.exe finds errors
/a	Specifies the operation for files as well as for folders
/f	Forces encryption of all specified directories even if they have already been encrypted
/q	Causes cipher.exe to report only essential information
/h	Displays files with hidden or system attributes
pathname	Specifies a file or folder
/?	Displays user help

➤ Encrypted files cannot be shared. If an encrypted file or folder is moved to a non-NTFS volume, encryption is lost. System files (files in the \%SystemRoot\% folder) cannot be encrypted.

➤ Users should not use drag and drop to move encrypted files. The encrypted file must be moved with the cut and paste technique or it will not keep its encrypted state.

➤ Files and folders can be encrypted on remote computers provided an administrator enables encryption on the remote computer.

You can use a recovery policy to recover encrypted files. Recovery policies are part of the Group Policy snap-in. EFS doesn't work if the recovery policy does not exist. Windows 2000 Professional creates a default recovery policy for all standalone computers. EFS is disabled if the Encrypted Data Recovery Agents folder is emptied. To recover encrypted files, users must be logged on as the recovery agent.

Chapter Summary

Windows 2000 Professional provides several methods for users to keep their computers secure:

➤ *Security groups*—These are built into Windows 2000 Professional. These predefined groups give users the rights and permissions they need to access resources on local and networked computers.

➤ *Group policies*—These are used to set security policies for domain-based and standalone computers. Group policies are managed with the Group Policy snap-in.

➤ *Security policies*—These are a subset of group policies. Windows 2000 Professional has nine predefined security policies.

➤ *Security templates*—These can be used to applied security settings to multiple computers. Security templates are not active until they are imported into a group policy object or the Security Configuration And Analysis snap-in.

➤ *User rights*—These define what actions users can perform on their computer or a network. User rights are applied to user or group accounts, and permissions are applied to objects. The two types of user rights are privilege right and logon right.

➤ *File and folder permissions*—These can be set in Windows 2000 Professional as they were in Windows NT. Members of the Administrator and Power Users groups can assign permissions. Users can customize permissions on files and folders by using special permissions. Shared permissions can be applied to folders only, not files or subfolders. The Everyone group has Full Control to shared folders by default.

➤ *Auditing*—This can be enabled in Windows 2000 to track user and group access to resources. Audit entries are written to the security log.

Public key security is the core technology of Windows 2000 Professional security. Public key security is also known as asymmetric key encryption. In asymmetric key encryption, two keys—one private, one public—are used. The private key is used to encrypt the data, and the public key is used to decrypt the data. Public keys are published in certificates. Certificates are managed in Windows 2000 Professional with the Certificate Manager snap-in tool. (Remember our previous comment about how on occasion, the key use is the reverse of this. Always verify key usage before sending a key.)

Two types of user authentication are supported in Windows 2000 Professional: interactive logon and network authentication. On a local computer, users are authenticated against their credentials stored in the SAM. On a networked computer, users are authenticated by Kerberos or SSO. Kerberos 5 is the default authentication protocol for Windows 2000 networks. Kerberos allows users to have access to multiple network resources with a single logon authentication. NTLM is the default authentication protocol for Windows NT 4 networks. NTLM is based on challenge response for authentication. You can also use smart cards to authenticate users.

Windows 2000 Professional supports the PAP, SPAP, CHAP, MS-CHAP, EAP, and RADIUS RAS authentication protocols. Of these protocols, PAP is the least secure. SPAP is used to authenticate Shiva clients and is more secure than PAP, but not as secure as CHAP. CHAP or Challenge Handshake Authentication Protocol, provides encrypted authentication with challenge/response. MS-CHAP is Microsoft's extension of CHAP and was originally created to authenticate remote Windows workstations.

13

VPNs can be used to transmit data securely over a public or private network. VPNs are created by using tunneling protocols such as PPTP and L2TP. PPTP provides a way to transmit data over TCP/IP networks. PPTP is an extension of the Point-to-Point Protocol. L2TP creates a tunnel for transmitting data such as PPTP but uses IPSec for encryption of the data. IPSec is implemented in Windows 2000 Professional through policies. IPSec is configured and managed through the IP Security Policy Management snap-in.

EFS is the core technology of Windows 2000 Professional encryption on NTFS volumes. EFS cannot be implemented on FAT volumes. Encrypted files cannot be shared. Encryption through EFS is transparent to the end user. Only the creator of the file can access it. They can open, edit, and save files are they normally would. EFS automatically decrypts the file for usage and re-encrypts it when it is saved or closed. Files that are compressed cannot be encrypted.

Review Questions

1. What does SSO stand for?
    a. Single Sign-Online
    b. Single Sign-On
    c. Single System On
    d. Systems Solutions Online

2. Which of the following are included in the Windows 2000 Professional security groups? [Check all correct answers]
    a. Users
    b. Backup Operators
    c. Administrators
    d. Group

3. The Guest security group can install Service Packs. True or false?
    a. True
    b. False

4. Members of the Power Users group can do which of the following? [Check all correct answers]
    a. Take ownership of files
    b. Install Service Packs
    c. Create and manage local user accounts
    d. Install programs that do not alter system files

5. What are the types of rights in Windows 2000 Professional?

    a. Privilege and logon

    b. Permissions and privileges

    c. Logon and permissions

    d. Interactive and special

6. Users in Windows 2000 Professional must use the Ctrl+Alt+Delete combination to log onto their workstation. True or false?

    a. True

    b. False

7. The owner of a file can always change permissions on it, regardless of any existing permissions applied to the file. True or false?

    a. True

    b. False

8. Which of the following special permissions allow users to change the attributes of a file?

    a. List Folder

    b. Create Files

    c. Write Attributes

    d. Delete Subfolders

9. Which of the following events can be audited? [Check all correct answers]

    a. Account management

    b. Object access

    c. Policy change

    d. System events

10. Certificates are managed with which snap-in?

    a. Disk Defragmenter

    b. Certificate Manager

    c. Group Policy

    d. Security templates

11. The two types of user authentication in Windows 2000 Professional are interactive logon and network authentication. True or false?

    a. True

    b. False

13

12. Kerberos is the default authentication protocol for Windows NT 4 networks. True or false?

   a. True

   b. False

13. Which of the following RAS authentication protocols are supported in Windows 2000 Professional? [Check all correct answers]

   a. PAP

   b. CHAP

   c. MS-SLAP

   d. WAP

14. IPSec is the default authentication protocol used for L2TP VPN connections. True or false?

   a. True

   b. False

15. The cipher.exe utility is used to do which of the following?

   a. Defragment an NTFS volume

   b. Encrypt a file from the command line

   c. Specify the level of authentication for RAS clients

   d Update certificates for a local computer

Real-World Projects

For all of these projects, you need a computer that is running Windows 2000 Professional. You also need to have a hard disk with at least one NTFS partition. Your supervisor has requested that you perform an audit. To do so, you'll need to activate Audit Policy on the computer in question. Then you'll need to set up the audit file. Finally, you've been requested to set up a Windows 2000 Professional workstation to accept an incoming connection.

Project 13.1

To enable auditing for selected events:

1. Log on as Administrator.

2. Click on Start | Programs.

3. Select Administrative Tools.

4. Click on Local Security Policy.

5. Double-click on Local Policies in the Local Security Settings window.

6. Click on Audit Policy.

7. Right-click on the event you want to audit and select either the Success checkbox or the Failure checkbox for the Audit These Attempts settings.

8. Close the Local Security Settings window.

9. Restart the computer for the settings to take effect.

Project 13.2

To create a file and then set up auditing of the file:

1. Log on as Administrator.

2. Click on Start|Programs|Accessories|Windows Explorer.

3. Create a text file on your NTFS partition and save it as auditfle.txt.

4. Right-click on the auditfle.txt file and click on Properties.

5. Select the Security tab and click on the Advanced button. Click on the Auditing tab.

6. Click on Add.

7. Double-click on Everyone in the Select User, Computer, Or Group dialog box.

8. Select the Successful checkbox in the Audit Entry For Audit dialog box for Change Permissions and Delete.

9. Click on OK twice.

Project 13.3

To configure your Windows 2000 Professional workstation to accept an incoming connection:

1. Log on as Administrator.

2. Choose Start|Settings|Network And Dial-Up Connections.

3. Double-click on Make New Connection. The Network Connection Wizard appears.

4. Click on Next.

5. Select Accept Incoming Connections and click on Next.

6. Select the modem device option for the workstation in the Connection Devices list and click on Next.

13

7. Select Allow Virtual Private Connections and click on Next.

8. Select Administrator and click on Next.

9. Click on Internet Protocol (TCP/IP) and click on Properties.

10. Select Specify TCP/IP addresses and enter a range of IP addresses.

11. Click on OK.

12. Click on Next.

13. Enter a name for the incoming connection and click on Finish.

CHAPTER FOURTEEN

Managing and Maintaining Windows 2000 Professional

After completing this chapter, you will be able to:

✓ Create a task

✓ Schedule a task to complete at a certain time

✓ View the performance of your system in real time

✓ Create a log file of your system performance

✓ Analyze the data from a log file

✓ Create an alert that will notify you of an event on your system

✓ Create and manage hardware profiles

Managing your Windows 2000 computer can be a frustrating task. There are often different events that you would like to happen on your computer at regular intervals. Also, finding out why your system isn't performing up to your expectations can be a complicated task.

There are many ways to make the job of maintaining a Windows 2000 Professional computer easier. Having some common tasks run on a scheduled interval certainly reduces the time you spend on each computer. Ensuring that your computers are running well and are not bogged down by the software that is being run is also important. Maintaining a schedule for monitoring your system's performance will help in planning for new hardware and anticipating problems with computers that might run out of resources.

This chapter discusses three popular tools you can use to manage and maintain Windows 2000 Professional: Task Scheduler, Performance Monitor, and Hardware Profiles. It is by no means meant to cover everything you might need to manage a computer. This chapter is meant to provide you with some of the common tools that you can use to make your life managing the system a little easier.

Task Scheduler

The Task Scheduler is provided in Windows 2000 to allow you to run a task at a certain time. The Windows operating systems have incorporated a Task Scheduler since the introduction of Windows 95. Many other applications also contain different task-scheduler programs. Backup software, utility programs, and many others contain scheduling programs. Unfortunately, if you have a number of these programs on your system, problems can occur when more than one of these schedulers run at the same time, consuming valuable system resources. Windows 2000 includes an enhanced Task Scheduler, which has also been made easier for developers to use. Microsoft provided these enhancements in hopes that independent software vendors employ the Windows 2000 Task Scheduler, so that users have a standard interface and won't have to deal with a variety of other schedulers.

The Windows 2000 Task Scheduler has been implemented as a service, which makes it a little easier to start and stop, especially if you want to use it remotely. By default, the service has been set up to start automatically when the system starts.

The Task Scheduler provides a full set of programmable interfaces for the developer. It is based on COM (Component Object Model) objects. One nice thing about the Task Scheduler is that the developer can program the task and have it run with both the Windows 2000 and Windows NT Task Scheduler.

The Application Programming Interfaces (APIs) that are available for the Task Scheduler provide the full functionality of the scheduler to the developer. They are intended to help developers in programming some applications, so developers won't have to duplicate work that has already been done. The scheduler already exists and is complete; developers just need to take advantage of it.

For more information about the development process and the tools available, check out these two Web sites: **www.microsoft.com/workshop/prog/inetsdk/** and **www.microsoft.com/msdn/sdk**.

Creating a Scheduled Task

Prior to creating a scheduled task, you first need to decide what task you want to schedule. After you determine what you want to accomplish, you need to determine how to make it happen. You can create tasks that run programs, scripts, batch files, or just about any code that runs under Windows 2000. However, the task must be self-sufficient, meaning that the task needs to be able to run and have full functionality with no user interaction. Although you can create a task that requires user interaction, most likely it is not what you want to do this because it will defeat the idea of having the task scheduled—you would have to be present to complete it.

When you know what it is you want to schedule, you can create the task. You can find the Task Scheduler in the Control Panel. You may notice that a task already exists. The Windows Critical Update Notification task may have been installed on your system. This task checks the Microsoft Update Web site throughout the day and lets you know if Microsoft has released a fix for Windows 2000.

To get to the Task Scheduler, open the Control Panel, and then double-click on the icon labeled Scheduled Tasks. A window appears that lists all the currently scheduled tasks. Also on this window is an icon to access the Add Scheduled Task Wizard. The wizard is probably the easiest way to create a task, although you may be required to add options that are more advanced.

If you run the wizard, you are first asked for the program you want the task to use. You are given a list of all the currently registered programs on the system; however, you can also browse to an application that is not listed. After you choose the application, the wizard queries you for a task name as well as how often you want the task to be completed (see Figure 14.1). Depending on the type of schedule you choose, you are then asked for more specifics about the schedule—for example, what time or which day of the week the task should run.

The task must run under the context of a specific user. Some users may not have the proper permissions to run a particular program, so each task runs according to the permissions of the user you specify. You must supply the user login name and the appropriate password. After completing the task wizard options, you are asked if you want to open the advanced properties of the task, which can also be accessed by right-clicking on a task and choosing Properties.

When you open Properties, the first tab displayed is the Task tab. This tab allows you to specify the command that you want to run. Make sure that this command is

14

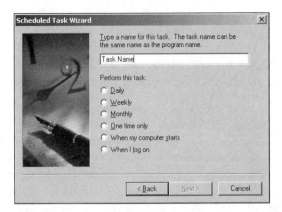

Figure 14.1 Schedule Task Wizard showing the different scheduling options that are available.

a self-sufficient command and can run with no user intervention. For example, the following command automatically backs up the hard drive with no user intervention:

```
C:\WINNT\system32\ntbackup.exe backup "@C:\Documents and
Settings\userfiles\Local Settings\Application Data\Microsoft\Windows
NT\NTBackup\data\System Backup.bks" /n "Media created 5/21/2000 at 4:03 PM"
/d "Set created 5/21/2000 at 4:04 PM" /v:no /r:no /rs:no /hc:off /m normal
/j "System Backup" /l:n /f "c:\temp\Backup.bkf"
```

The Task tab also allows you to specify in which folder you want the command to start, which may be required for some programs. You can also set comments and change the user context that the task runs under. Make sure that the user context you choose has permission to run the program. An Enabled checkbox is also displayed. If you clear this checkbox, the task stays on the system but doesn't run. This option can be useful to retain a task on the system that you don't want to run right away.

The Schedule tab allows you to set the schedule for the task. You can create multiple schedules for a particular task. If you want to set multiple schedules, select the Show Multiple Schedules checkbox. You can then create a new schedule and delete existing schedules.

The Settings tab allows you to specify how the task interacts with the operating system (see Figure 14.2). The first section on the tab allows you to set the task so that it is automatically deleted if it isn't scheduled to run again. You can also set the task to automatically stop if, for some reason, the task doesn't complete. The default time is set at 72 hours, and depending on the task you are running, you may want to increase or decrease that time.

The Idle Time section requires that the task be run only when nothing else on the system is running. If this option is selected, the task only runs when the system is idle for the specified time frame. If the system is not idle, the task is retried for the

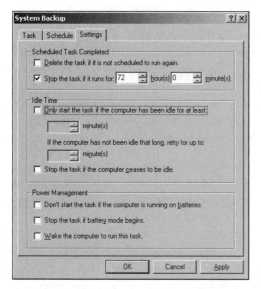

Figure 14.2   The Settings tab in the Properties of a system backup task.

following 60 minutes by default. You can also have the task stop if the system ceases to be idle.

Additionally, a few power management options are also available for the system. You may not want a particular task to run if the system is currently running on batteries. If you have a number of tasks that consume a large amount of power from the battery, these tasks can be disabled to retain the life of the battery. You may also want the task to stop if the system goes to battery power while the task is running. If your computer is set to go into sleep mode, you can instruct the task to wake the computer to run the task. If you do not select this particular option and the computer is in sleep mode, the task will not run.

Managing Scheduled Tasks

After you create the task, you can make any needed modifications to it. Most of the modifications you need to make can be made in the Properties of the task, which were described in the preceding section.

The Task Scheduler also provides more enhanced options. The Advanced drop-down menu in the Task Scheduler allows you to stop, start, and pause the Task Scheduler service. Moreover, you can have the system automatically notify you of tasks that fail to run. If you do not set this option, you will need to check the log file to make sure that your tasks are completing. You can check the log by selecting Advanced|View Log.

The last option on the menu is for the AT service account. In Windows NT, the task scheduling was completed by using the **AT** command at the command prompt.

14

When you upgrade your system to Windows 2000, any tasks that you had scheduled with the **AT** command are automatically added to the list of tasks in the Task Scheduler. These tasks continue to be a part of the AT infrastructure. The tasks are listed when you type "AT" at the command prompt. The tasks are also displayed in the Task Scheduler window. The task is usually given the name "AT*xxxx*", where four randomly generated numbers replace the *x* characters. You can make changes to these tasks as you would any task that was created in Windows 2000. Once you modify one of these tasks, it will be upgraded and will no longer be listed as an AT task.

All AT tasks under Windows 2000 run under the same user context. Select Advanced|AT Service Account. There are two types of accounts that can be used for the AT service. You can choose a local system account or a user account. If you choose a local system account, all the tasks will run with full permissions, but only tasks that work on the local computer will function. If you have tasks that need to make connections to other computers, you need to choose a user account that has the appropriate permissions on all the computers that need to be connected.

Each task that you create becomes a file with a .job extension. These files are not displayed on the local hard drive, but you can drag any file from the Task Scheduler to any location on your hard drive. You can move a file to any Windows 2000 computer, drag it into the Task Scheduler, and use the task. Some tasks may take time to set up. You can also copy a task to other computers and use the same task throughout your network.

Performance Monitor

The Windows 2000 Performance Monitor allows you to track the system's usage of resources. It allows you to manage and maintain the use of resources on a particular system, identify bottlenecks, and determine where an upgrade would be useful.

Managing a system's performance can be a tricky undertaking because it is sometimes difficult to determine where a problem or slow down occurs. Often, a problem can be caused by another problem in a different area. It's important to establish a baseline of system performance. The baseline is simply a collection of data from the system, which you can refer to later to see what has changed. A baseline helps to reduce the amount of time you spend looking at the data because when you compare the current results against the baseline, the problem usually jumps out at you.

You will tend to look at four key areas for hardware bottlenecks: memory, disk, processor, and network—the four major areas of a computer. Although these areas may not seem like a great deal to monitor, there are many functions that you may need to check in each of these areas.

Performance Monitor consists of objects and counters. Objects are containers for the counters. There are numerous counters, and by placing them in objects, it's easier to find a counter that relates to what you are trying to monitor. Table 14.1 lists the objects that are available by default on Windows 2000 Professional. As you add programs and services to your computer, you may notice that objects are added and removed, so don't be alarmed if you have some different objects available on your system.

Table 14.1   Windows 2000 Professional Performance Monitor objects available by default.

Object Name	Description
ACS/RSVP Service	Monitors QoS (Quality of Service) operations, which prioritize network resources.
Browser	Monitors the Browser service and the different types of network traffic generated by the service. The Browser service is available for backward compatibility with Windows 3.x, Windows 95, Windows 98, and Windows NT.
Cache	Reports on the usage of the system cache.
Distributed Transaction Coordinator	Reports on Distributed Transactions. This used to be part of Transaction Server and is used to coordinate two-phase transactions.
HTTP Indexing Service	Reports on the Indexing service and how it is handling the queries of the indexed catalogs.
IAS Accounting Clients	Reports on how the IAS (Internet Authentication Service) is managing the usage of remote clients.
IAS Accounting Server	Reports on how the IAS is managing the usage of remote servers. If this service is not installed, all counters report zeros.
IAS Authentication Clients	Reports on how the IAS is managing remote client authentication.
IAS Authentication Servers	Reports on how the IAS is managing remote client authentication. If this service is not installed, all counters report zeros.
ICMP	Reports on the ICMP (Internet Control Messaging Protocol), which provides packet information and error correction.
Indexing Service	Reports on creating and merging indexes.
Indexing Service Filter	Reports on the filtering of indexes.
IP	Reports on the IP layer of TCP/IP.
Job Object	Reports on the usage of the processor and accounting of named job objects.
Job Object Details	Reports detailed information about named job objects.
Logical Disk	Reports on the usage of the logical disk partitions. To activate these counters, type "diskperf –y" at the command prompt, and reboot the system; to deactivate these counters, type "diskperf –n" at the command prompt.
Memory	Reports on the usage of RAM (Random Access Memory).
NBT Connection	Reports on statistics of data that is sent using the NetBT protocol, which is used to provide NetBIOS support for TCP/IP.
Network Interface	Reports on the statistics of how much your network adapter is being used. You may notice several instances of network adapters for each type of connectivity device (modem, network interface card, WAN interface, etc.). You can obtain statistics about each device individually.
Objects	Reports about system events and software objects.

14

(continued)

Table 14.1 **Windows 2000 Professional Performance Monitor objects available by default** *(continued)*.

Object Name	Description
Paging File	Reports on the usage of the paging file.
Physical Disk	Reports on the usage of physical hard disks. It is different from the Logical Disk object, which reports on an individual partition. This counter returns statistics based on all the partitions that reside on a physical hard drive. To activate these counters, type "diskperf –y" at the command prompt, and reboot the system; to deactivate these counters, type "diskperf –n" at the command prompt.
Print Queue	Reports on the statistics of a queue on a print server. This object is new to Windows 2000.
Process	Reports on a process and its activity.
Processor	Reports on the CPU and its activity.
Redirector	Reports on the activity of the redirector, which forwards requests to a network server.
Server	Reports on the activity of the Server service, which responds to incoming requests for information and system resources.
Server Work Queues	Reports on the objects and length of the queue for requests that are made of the Server service.
System	Statistics for systemwide counters.
TCP	Reports on the TCP packets that are sent and received.
Telephony	Reports on the usage of telephony devices.
Thread	Reports on the activity of a thread.
UDP	Reports on the UDP packets that are sent and received.

Within each of the objects are numerous counters. These counters return values based on the use of the system. Generally, counters fall into one of two categories: instantaneous or averaging. Instantaneous counters provide you with the most current measurement. These counters are useful for watching what is currently happening on a system or for observing the peak values for a counter. Averaging counters usually display a value based on a percentage or the number of times an event happens within a specified time frame. These types of counters may create a slight delay in their reporting because they must be calculated. These counters are most useful when you want to find the number of times an event occurs or the average usage.

Counters and objects assist you in determining where you might have a bottleneck on your system. To work with counters, you need to work with the Performance Monitor tools.

Performance Monitor Tools

The Performance Monitor gives you a number of tools to view system performance. You can watch the counters in realtime, or you can send the data to a log file and analyze it later on.

System Monitor

You can use the System Monitor tool to view and analyze the data you collect. You can view realtime data in this tool or view the data you have collected in a log file. If you have worked with the Performance Monitor in Windows NT, this tool will be familiar. There have been, however, a number of improvements made to this tool.

The System Monitor graph display is more flexible, and it's easier to change colors, borders, and other attributes. The graphs that you create can be saved in HTML documents, and you can print them. The reports can be saved as tab-separated files and used with Microsoft Excel. The System Monitor is now part of the MMC, which means that you can create charts and graphs and move them to other computers. Additionally, charts and graphs are provided by an ActiveX control, which means that this control can be added to applications or Web pages.

You can start System Monitor by double-clicking on Performance in the Administrative tools folder, or you can type "perfmon.msc" at the Run prompt or the command prompt. When you open Performance Monitor, you see a standard MMC console with two snap-ins: System Monitor and Performance Logs and Alerts. System Monitor opens to a blank graph, and as you add counters to it, you start to see the real-time data of your system. See Figure 14.3.

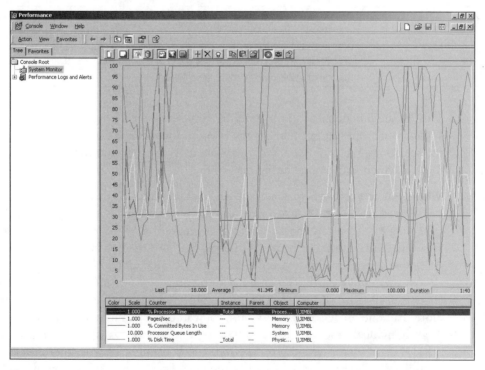

Figure 14.3 An example of the System Monitor using a few counters to monitor real-time data.

Table 14.2   The System Monitor toolbar icons and their functions.

Icon	Description
New Counter Set	This icon clears all the current counters from the display and starts over from scratch.
Clear Display	This icon simply clears the display of the activity it is showing, but does not remove any of the counters.
View Current Activity	This icon allows you to add counters and view the results in real time. All the activity displayed is current and no log of the information is kept.
View Log File Data	This icon allows you to display data from a log file that you have created. When you press this button, you are asked to select a log file that you would like to use.
View Chart	This icon displays the result of the counters in a line chart.
View Histogram	This icon displays the result of the counters in a column chart.
View Report	This icon displays the result of the counters in report format.
Add	This icon allows you to add counters to your display. The counters that you add can be for your computer or another computer.
Delete	This icon deletes the selected counter from the display.
Highlight	This icon highlights the selected counter in the display.
Copy Properties	This icon copies the properties to the clipboard.
Paste Counter List	This icon pastes the information from the clipboard into the counter list.
Properties	This icon allows you to change the appearance of the System Monitor. You can change the font or the colors. You can change the scale of information and give titles to the axes of the chart.
Freeze Display	This icon can be used to stop the System Monitor from collecting data and leave the current results on the screen.
Update Data	This icon is used in conjunction with Freeze Display. Once you have frozen the display, you can click this to manually update the data displayed on the screen.
Help	This icon displays Help for the System Monitor.

Most of the functionality of the System Monitor can be accessed from the toolbar. If you point your mouse at any of the icons in the toolbar, a message tells you what the icon does. Table 14.2 lists each button and its function starting on the left of the toolbar, which you can see in Figure 14.3.

When you add counters to the graph, the Add Counters dialog box appears, which can be seen in Figure 14.4. You need to choose from which computer you will be collecting data. You can choose the local computer or any other computer as long as you have the computer name and permission. You then need to select an object. After you select an object, you can monitor all the counters from an object or choose them individually. Depending on the object and counter, you may need to choose an instance of the device you are monitoring. As an example, if you have more than one processor in the system, you can choose to monitor all the processors or an individual processor. Many different counters are available, and many of the titles of the counters are not as descriptive as you might like, so Microsoft has included the Explain button, which gives a brief description of each counter. When you have chosen the counters you want to add to the chart, simply click on the

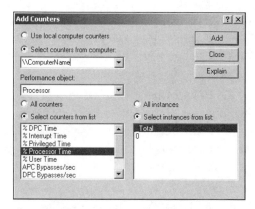

Figure 14.4   The Performance Monitor's Add Counters dialog box.

Add button. The dialog box remains open until you click on the Close button, so you can add more items.

You can print the contents of the System Monitor in a couple of ways. You can copy the contents to the clipboard by pressing Alt+PrtScn, and then paste the information into a paint program and print from the program. You can also right-click on the chart and save it as an HTML document. You can then open the document with Internet Explorer or some other Web browser and print it.

The System Monitor can be a powerful tool that shows you how your system is running. The following section covers how to create a log file that can be displayed in the System Monitor

Creating Log Files

Although looking at your system in real time can be useful for getting a quick picture of the usage on your system, you may want to see how the system is doing over an extended period. Log files allow you to save the usage information over a specified period. You may want to see how your system is doing during periods of high activity, so the log files allow you to schedule when you want to monitor your system's performance.

You can create two types of logs. When Performance Monitor is open, you see Performance Monitors Logs and Alerts. When you expand this folder, you see two types of logs: *counter logs* and *trace logs*.

A counter log is just a file that contains the results of the counters you have chosen to track. A counter log samples the counters you have chosen at a predefined interval and returns the values to the log file.

A trace log does not sample the data; rather, when an event occurs, the event is tracked from start to finish instead of just sampled. There must be a data provider that supports the tracing of a particular type of data. Windows 2000 has a built-in

14

kernel trace program that traces system events, such as thread activity, process creation, or page faults. Other programs may include other providers that you may use as well to monitor other events. You also need to have a parsing tool to interpret the log file. Unfortunately, Windows 2000 does not come with a parsing tool.

After you decide to create a log, you must select the flavor of log that you want to create. Create the new log settings by selecting Action | New Log Settings, or right-click in the MMC and choose New Log Settings. You are first asked to name the new log. The only restriction is that the name must be unique among all log files. After this is complete, the Properties for the log file opens, and you can set the different parameters.

The first tab you see is the General tab. On this tab, add the counters that you want the system to monitor. When working with a log file, make sure that you monitor all the counters that you think might be relevant. If you have forgotten a counter, you will have to redo the log file. Then choose the interval in which you want the counters to be sampled. The shorter the interval, the larger the log file you create. You can have the system sample as often as every second. However, this creates a very large log file. Also, you need to consider that when the system samples the counters, it will have an impact on the system resources. The more often you sample the data, the more of an impact it will have.

The Log File tab allows you to set different properties for the file you are creating. Check the file name and location that you want the system to use. You can have your file name end with a sequential number or a date. An example window on this tab shows you what the file name will look like. You also have to choose the format of the file you are creating. You can create either a text file or a binary file. Choose a text file if you want the file to be opened by another application, such as Microsoft Excel. If you choose a binary file, there are two options. The first option is a standard binary file, which can grow as large as you need. You can also set a size limit, so when the file reaches a particular size, it closes out and a new file is created. The second option is a circular binary file. With a circular file, the system collects data until the file reaches the specified limit, and then it starts over at the beginning of the file. This option can be useful in a system with limited disk space.

You also may want to schedule the log to be run. You can either set a date and time when the system should start the log, or set the log to only be started manually. A time and date can be set for when the log should stop, or you can have the log run for a specified time frame, such as for one day or 2 weeks. You can also set the log file to only stop when you manually stop it or when the file reaches, for example, 1,000KB. Depending on how you choose to stop the file, you may have the system automatically create a new file. You can also have a command run when the log file stops. Additionally, you may have a batch file that copies the log file to a network location.

After you create the log file, you can save it as an HTML document. If you save the log settings as an HTML file, you can transport that file to any other Windows 2000 computer. To create a new log based on the file, simply select Action | New Log Setting From. This allows you to browse to the HTML file that you saved. You can open the file in Internet Explorer, which opens the log file like it is being opened in System Monitor, and you can work with it just as if you were in System Monitor.

Alerts

You can create alerts on your system that let you know when part of your system is not functioning as you want or is being used too much. You can have the system watch a particular counter and if it rises or falls to a specified level, the system alerts you or runs a program.

To create an alert, right-click on Alerts, choose New Alert Settings, and give the Alert a name. The name must be unique among all the logs and alerts. Three tabs that configure the properties of the alert are then displayed. Working with the Schedule tab is almost identical to working with the log schedule. You must set a time to start and stop the alert, or you can set it to be manually run.

The General tab lets you set the counter you want to monitor. You can choose to monitor any number of counters and have the alert fire when the value of the counter either rises above the value you've set or falls below that level. You also need to set the interval in which these values are checked. In Figure 14.5, the alert fires whenever the value of the % Processor Time rises above 80%. The counter is checked every 5 seconds for the % Processor Time being used.

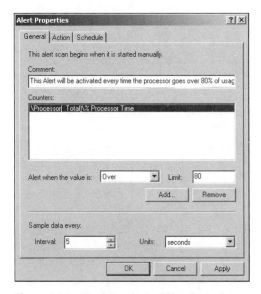

Figure 14.5 The General tab of Alert Properties.

The Action tab allows you to specify a response to the alert being fired. You can have the alert write a message into the event viewer in the application log. You need to check this log to see when the alert was fired. A network message can be sent to a computer to inform the user that the alert was fired. This should be used as a backup method of notification because if the computer is off, the message will never arrive. You can also have one of the performance logs start running. At times, this may be useful because you can have this log start one of your logs, so you can see what is happening with the system immediately after the alert is fired. Additionally, you can run a program, batch file, or script when the alert fires.

Auditing

Auditing is the ability to track events on your computer. There are a number of events that can be audited and that you can check later to learn when a particular event occurred and, possibly, who triggered the event. For Windows 2000 Professional, you may not need to audit every computer. Auditing is often used on Professional to find out why a system fails or to track a user's actions to determine why a problem is occurring.

When you start auditing, your system keeps all the records of the audit in the event viewer in the security log. Make sure that you either clear out this log or set the size large enough so that it does not fill up. You can also set the event viewer to overwrite old events. If the log fills up and cannot overwrite the entries, all auditing on the system stops, which results in some missed events that you wanted to track.

To start auditing the system, select Start | Settings | Control Panel | Administrative Tools and click on Local Policies. When you open the Local Security Policy, navigate to Local Policies | Audit Policy. Under Audit Policy, you will find a number of polices that you can set to track different kinds of events (see Figure 14.6). For all of the events listed, you can track whether the action that has been taken has been successful or whether the action failed. After you turn on the auditing for these events, you will see that a lot of activity is logged to the event log. You may not be concerned when users log on successfully, but you'll want to know when they fail to log on. The log can show you that someone is having trouble remembering passwords or that someone is trying to hack into the system. The following is a list of the types of events that can be audited in Windows 2000 Professional:

➤ Account logon events

➤ Account management

➤ Directory service access

➤ Logon events

➤ Object access

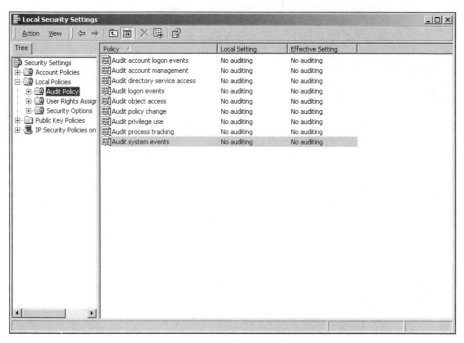

Figure 14.6   The Local Policies snap-in opened to the Audit Policy.

➤ Policy change

➤ Privilege use

➤ Process tracking

➤ System events

Auditing object access is the only option that doesn't immediately provide results. When you choose to audit object access, you must determine which objects you want to monitor. For example, to audit files, you need to go to the properties of the file or folder that you want to audit, navigate to the Security tab, and then click on the Advanced button. The Auditing tab appears. You need to add a user or group to be tracked. You can then determine what type of access you want to audit. You may only want to track a user's successful deletion of an item, or you may want to track a user who failed to change permissions on the object.

When you start auditing the system, you need to check the event viewer in the security log to find out what has been tracked. The following list contains the many different types of entries that you might receive in the event viewer:

➤ System restart

➤ System shutdown

➤ Authentication package loading

14

➤ Registered logon process

➤ Audit log cleared

➤ Number of audits discarded

➤ Logon successful

➤ Unknown user name or password

➤ Time restricted logon failure

➤ Account disabled

➤ Account expired

➤ Invalid workstation

➤ Logon type restricted

➤ Password expired

➤ Failed logon

➤ Logoff

➤ Open object

➤ Close handle

➤ Assign special privilege

➤ Privileged service

➤ Privileged object access

➤ Process created

➤ Process exit

➤ Duplicate handle

➤ Indirect reference

➤ Privilege assigned

➤ Audit policy change

➤ Domain changed

➤ User changed

➤ User created

➤ User deleted

➤ Global group member removed

➤ Global group member added

➤ Domain local group changed

➤ Domain local group created

➤ Domain local group member removed

➤ Domain local group member added

➤ Domain local group member deleted

Within the preceding kinds of entries in the event viewer, you will see more specific information regarding the event that occurred.

Auditing is a powerful function that allows you to track virtually every activity on the computer. This can potentially create a huge amount of data, which you will probably not want to sort through. Make sure that you determine the exact nature of what you are trying to identify through auditing and audit only that activity to find the information you need. This makes the process of examining the security log much easier and quicker.

Hardware Profiles

The idea behind hardware profiles is to eliminate the errors that happen when the hardware on your system changes. The hardware profile can also specify that different services can be loaded with the different profiles. This is usually the case with notebook computers, but the profile can affect desktop computers also. A notebook computer, for example, might be used at the office in a docking station to connect to the network and may be used at home as well. You may receive error messages when the system is not in the docking station because the operating system is trying to initialize hardware that is not currently attached to the system.

A hardware profile allows you to have different hardware configurations for the computer. Usually, Windows 2000 does not need different hardware profiles because of its Plug and Play functionality. The system is often able to detect whether the hardware is present and if it is not, it doesn't load the driver. You may notice that some laptop systems automatically create a docked and undocked profile and automatically know whether or not the system is docked.

However, there is a chance you may run into hardware that either is not Plug and Play or still wants to load the drivers if the hardware is not attached to the system. Sometimes, only annoying error messages occur, but other times the system may fail to boot. In either case, you can usually correct the problem by creating hardware profiles and booting under the correct profile depending on the hardware attached to the system.

14

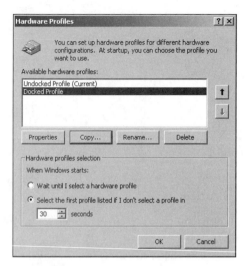

Figure 14.7 The Hardware Profiles utility.

To create a hardware profile, you usually start out with your current profile, and then make modifications to it. To get to the Hardware Profile tab, open the System Properties in the Control Panel. Click on the Hardware tab, and then click on the Hardware Profiles button. This opens the utility that allows you to manage the hardware profiles (see Figure 14.7).

You may see more than one profile in the list; if you do, then the one you are currently using is listed as the current profile. Highlight one of the profiles and copy it. After copying the profile, you must rename the profile. It is best to give it a descriptive name. You can rename any of the profiles at any time in this utility. Go to the Properties of the profile and select the Always Include This Profile As An Option When Windows Starts checkbox. When this checkbox is selected, you will be asked with which profile you want to boot during the boot process. You can have Windows wait indefinitely for you to select a profile, or you can have the first profile listed as the default and set a time to wait for a choice. When you have multiple hardware profiles, you can move them up and down in the list by clicking on the arrows on the right of the screen so that the profile you use most often will be listed first and be the default profile.

Chapter Summary

If you are using new hardware and the hardware is Plug and Play compliant, it's unlikely that you will ever have to use hardware profiles. The system may use them automatically for you, but you won't have to make a choice because the system automatically detects the profile to use. If you do need to set up different hardware profiles, Windows 2000 makes the process relatively easy.

Review Questions

1. You have a task that continually fails to complete. When you log in and run the command that is supposed to be scheduled, it completes, but when you run the scheduled task, it fails. Which of the following could be the problem?

    a. The task is disabled.

    b. The task is running with the context of a user who doesn't have permission to run the task.

    c. The task scheduler service hasn't started.

    d. The task requires user intervention.

2. You would like to schedule a task to run on the system, but you do not want the task to run if the computer is busy performing other tasks. Which option should you set to make sure this happens? [Check all correct answers]

    a. Don't start the task if the computer is running on batteries.

    b. Stop the task if battery mode begins.

    c. Only start the task if the computer has been idle.

    d. Stop the task if the computer ceases to be idle.

3. If you copy a task to another location on the hard drive, the task has which of the following extensions?

    a. .tsk

    b. .job

    c. .sch

    d. .scd

4. If you copy a task to another Windows 2000 Professional computer, what do you need to do to the task to make it function on the new system?

    a. Reset the Schedule.

    b. Enable the task.

    c. Rename the task.

    d. No configuration is necessary.

5. What is the difference between Performance Monitor objects and counters? [Check all correct answers]

    a. Counters are categories of objects.

    b. Objects are categories of counters.

    c. Counters contain objects.

    d. Objects contain counters.

14

6. You would like to view Performance Monitor data in real time. Which of the following tools should you use to accomplish this?

   a. System Monitor

   b. Counter Log

   c. Trace Log

   d. Alerts

7. You would like to store Performance Monitor data to view later. Which of the following tools should you use to accomplish this? [Check all correct answers]

   a. System Monitor

   b. Counter Log

   c. Trace Log

   d. Alerts

8. You have some stored performance log data and you want to view it. Which of the following tools should you use to accomplish this?

   a. System Monitor

   b. Counter Log

   c. Trace Log

   d. Alerts

9. You would like to be notified when your system performance reaches certain levels. Which of the following tools should you use to accomplish this?

   a. System Monitor

   b. Counter Log

   c. Trace Log

   d. Alerts

10. You would like to save your counter log file settings so that you can use them on another computer. What file type can you use to save these settings?

    a. Web page

    b. Tab delimited, .tsv file

    c. Excel file

    d. Log file

11. You are viewing some of the data from a log file in System Monitor. You want to export the data to be used in another program. What file type can you use to save this data? [Check all correct answers]

   a. Web page

   b. Tab delimited, .tsv file

   c. Excel file

   d. Log file

12. You want to view data in System Monitor. In which of the following ways can the data be presented? [Check all correct answers]

   a. Chart

   b. Log

   c. Histogram

   d. Report

   e. Pie

   f. Bar

13. You have turned on audit object access, yet you are getting no results. Which of the following do you need to do to complete the process of auditing object access on the system?

   a. Start the auditing service.

   b. Turn on the auditing on each object you want to track.

   c. Do nothing; it should be working.

   d. Reboot the computer.

14. You want to track when users are authenticated to the system. Which of the following audit policies must you enable?

   a. Audit logon events

   b. Audit object access

   c. Audit system events

   d. Audit policy change

15. You want to track which users delete files on the system. Which of the following audit policies must you enable?

   a. Audit logon events

   b. Audit object access

   c. Audit system events

   d. Audit policy change

14

16. You want to track when someone changes how you are tracking activities on your system. Which of the following audit policies must you enable?

    a. Audit logon events

    b. Audit object access

    c. Audit system events

    d. Audit policy change

17. You want to view the data that has been collected from the auditing process. Which log in the event viewer should you use to view that data?

    a. Application

    b. Security

    c. System

    d. Audit

18. Which of the following conditions will determine that you need to create hardware profiles for your system? [Check all correct answers]

    a. You have specific hardware that is not connected to the system all the time.

    b. When certain hardware is not connected, you receive error messages.

    c. When certain hardware is not connected, the system doesn't boot.

    d. When some of your hardware isn't Plug and Play compliant.

Real-World Projects

Jeff works on the desktop support team. His team has determined that, to reduce some of its support issues, it will automate certain tasks and track which users are logging on to systems that are not theirs. The team would also like to track the performance of its systems so that it can determine when the systems need to be upgraded. Jeff has been given the task of implementing this strategy.

One of the developers has created a program that imports the log files from Performance Monitor and generates an analysis of the systems. The desktop support team just needs to create the logs and save them to a network location.

Jeff first decides to create the two automated tasks that need to be implemented. The first task is to back up the system state and user profiles on each system and have the backup stored in a networked location.

Project 14.1

To create a task to backup the system nightly:

1. Select Start | Settings | Control Panel | Scheduled Tasks.

2. Click on Add Scheduled task, and then click on Next. The Scheduled Task Wizard appears on screen.

3. Choose the backup program, and click on Next.

4. Name the task, choose to perform this task daily, and click on Next.

5. Choose a start time of 11:30 P.M., Perform This Task only on Weekdays, and click on Next.

6. Enter the user name "administrator" and the password for the administrator account, and click on Next.

7. Select the Open Advanced Properties For This Task When I Click Finish checkbox, and then click on Finish.

8. Change the **run** command to the following:

   C:\WINNT\system32\ntbackup.exe backup "@C:\Documents and Settings\ userfiles\Local Settings\Application Data\Microsoft\Windows NT\NTBackup\ data\System Backup.bks" /n "Media created 5/21/2000 at 4:03 PM" /d "Set created 5/21/2000 at 4:04 PM" /v:no /r:no /rs:no /hc:off /m normal /j "System Backup" /l:n /f "\\server\backup\computername.bkf"

9. Click on the Settings tab, select the Wake The Computer To Run This Task checkbox, and then click on OK.

10. Copy the job from the scheduled task to a network location. Then copy it to the scheduled task on each of the other workstations.

Jeff then creates the second task, which runs the chkdsk program nightly to make sure that the files and directories on the hard disk have no errors.

Project 14.2

To create a task to run chkdsk nightly:

1. Select Start | Settings | Control Panel | Scheduled Tasks.

2. Click on Add Scheduled task, and click on Next.

3. Click on Browse, browse to the file c:\winnt\system32\chkdsk.exe, and then click on OK.

4. Name the task, choose to perform this task daily, and click on Next.

5. Choose a start time of 10:00 P.M., Perform This Task only on Weekdays, and click on Next.

6. Enter the user name "administrator" and the password for the administrator account, and click on Next.

14

7. Select the Open Advanced Properties For This Task When I Click Finish checkbox, and click on Finish.

8. Change the **run** command to this: "C:\WINNT\system32\chkdsk.exe c:".

9. Click on the Settings tab, select the Wake The Computer To Run This Task checkbox, and then click on OK.

10. Copy the job from the scheduled task to a network location. Then copy it to the scheduled task on each of the other workstations.

Jeff then decides to create the Performance Monitor log for the developer's program. Jeff has been given a list of counters to log and a network location to store the logs.

Project 14.3

To create a Performance Monitor log file for a custom analysis application:

1. Open Performance Monitor by typing "perfmon" at the Run prompt.

2. Expand Performance Logs And Alerts, and click on Counter Logs.

3. Right-click on counter logs and choose New Log Settings.

4. Name the log file "Analysis".

5. Click on the Add button, and choose the counters that were supplied by the developer.

6. Click on the Log Files tab, and enter the network location and file name for the log files that the developer has provided.

7. Click on the Schedule tab, have the log file start at 8:00 A.M. and end at 5:00 P.M., and then click on OK.

8. Right-click on the Analysis log, and click on Save Settings As.

9. Save the setting as analysis.htm.

10. On each of the other systems in your network, right-click on Counter Logs, choose New Log Settings From, and point to the analysis.htm file.

Now that certain functions have been automated, some of the administrative tasks should be reduced. More tasks may need to be automated in the future, and the results from the log file analysis will need to be evaluated. At this point, the process is in place and as more tasks are able to be automated, the support process will become easier.

CHAPTER FIFTEEN

System Recovery

After completing this chapter, you will be able to:

✓ Prevent and troubleshoot system problems

✓ Plan backup strategies

✓ Perform backups using Windows 2000 Backup

✓ Perform restores using Windows 2000 Backup

✓ Use Safe Mode options to boot a troublesome system

✓ Access and use the Recovery Console

✓ Use the ERD and the emergency repair process

U sually, a Windows 2000-based system runs pretty much flawlessly; however, there are times when a system doesn't work, and you, as the administrator, need to take certain actions to restore services. You may be aware of what caused the problem, such as faulty hardware or a misbehaving application, or you may not. If you are not aware of the cause, you'll need to troubleshoot the situation to determine what is at fault.

Prevention of System Problems

There are basically three types of system problems to be aware of:

➤ Device driver problems

➤ System file problems

➤ Hardware related problems

Device Driver Problems

By far the most common system problems are device driver problems, which can result when a new device and its associated device driver are installed in a Windows 2000 machine. A device driver is a small application that allows Windows 2000 to communicate with the hardware device. The device driver may be incompatible with Windows 2000. It may also conflict with other device drivers by overwriting their memory address spaces.

To prevent problems with device drivers, the administrator should

➤ Read the documentation for configuration and compatibility information that shipped with the device. Also, always read any addenda or readme files for changes and notifications that have occurred since the shipped documents were published.

➤ Check the Hardware Compatibility List (HCL) to verify that Microsoft has certified the device. The HCL can be obtained from the Windows 2000 CD-ROM or from Microsoft's Web site (**www.microsoft.com/hcl**).

➤ Obtain the latest device driver from the manufacturer. Check the manufacturer's Web site for the device driver as well as any notices or alerts about potential problems with the device driver.

To correct problems with device drivers, the administrator should

➤ Check the Event Viewer if the system boots. By checking the Event Viewer, the administrator may be able to determine what is causing the device driver to fail; for example, it may be an interrupt conflict or a missing system file. Once the cause is determined, the administrator can take steps to resolve the situation.

➤ Restart the computer using the Last Known Good Configuration. The Last Known Good Configuration restores Registry settings that Windows 2000 saved during the last successful boot up. If the administrator recently changed the configuration, this setting may restore the old configuration, allowing the computer to boot.

➤ Restart the computer in Safe Mode. In Safe Mode, Windows 2000 will load using basic system files and device drivers only. Drivers and system files for base video, mouse, keyboard, and storage media will be loaded. No system files or drivers will be loaded for networking services. Booting in Safe Mode allows the administrator to double-check configuration settings and reinstall the device driver if necessary.

➤ Obtain the latest device driver from the manufacturer. The administrator can check the manufacturer's Web site for the latest device driver and install the new device driver.

System File Problems

If device driver problems are the most common problems, then system file problems are by far the most annoying and difficult to troubleshoot. If system files become corrupt or damaged, the computer may not run properly. It is also possible that system files may become mismatched—that is, a version of a system file may conflict with other system files. System files include the following:

➤ The Registry

➤ DLL files

➤ Operating system files

➤ Device drivers

➤ Boot files

To prevent problems with system files, the administrator should

➤ Perform regular backups that include the System State information. The System State information includes the boot files, the Registry, performance counter configuration information, and the Component Services Class registration database.

➤ Use an uninterruptible power supply (UPS) to protect the computer from power surges and outages. System files can be corrupted if power failures occur during file write operations.

To correct problems with system files, the administrator should

➤ Check the Event Viewer.

15

➤ Restart the computer using the Last Known Good Configuration.

➤ Restart the computer in Safe Mode.

➤ Restore the System State from a recent backup.

Hardware-Related Problems

Hardware related problems can occur with the hard drive, a network card, memory, the CPU, or other hardware devices.

To prevent hardware related problems, the administrator should

➤ Check the Event Viewer. By checking the Event Viewer, the administrator will be able to observe problems as they develop.

➤ Perform regular backups that include the System State information. The System State information includes the boot files, the Registry, performance counter configuration information, and the Component Services Class registration database.

➤ Use a UPS to protect the computer from power surges and outages. System files can be corrupted if power failures occur during file write operations.

➤ Implement fault tolerance. The administrator can implement fault tolerance on some hardware devices, such as hard disks.

Backup Strategies

One of the most important aspects to recovering a Windows 2000 configuration is to perform regular backups. A regular backup helps prevent data loss caused by faulty hardware, user error, power outages, virus infections, and so on. These days, computer data is an integral part of a business, and as such, a company's backup strategy needs to be carefully planned and executed.

Windows 2000 supports the following backup types:

➤ *Copy*—Backs up all selected files and does not mark the files as backed up.

➤ *Daily*—Only backs up files that have changed that day, and does not mark the files as backed up.

➤ *Differential*—Only backs up files that have changed since the last normal backup, and does not mark the files as backed up.

➤ *Incremental*—Only backs up files that changed since the last normal or incremental backup, and marks the files as backed up by setting the files' archive bit.

➤ *Normal*—Backs up all selected files and marks each file as backed up by setting the files' archive bit.

One of the first details to consider is what needs to be backed up and how important the data is. Any data that changes frequently and is critical to the business should be backed up on a daily schedule using the Normal backup type. This data would include network file servers, information stores, databases, and so on. Any data that is lost or corrupted can be restored to the state of previous backups. One problem with performing Normal backups with a large amount of data everyday is the amount of time and backup capacity needed. In spite of this, most organizations opt for the daily backup schedule if their equipment and backup capacity allows for it.

Any data that is static or changes infrequently does not need to be backed up as vigorously. An example of this would be a user's workstation. If the user stores data files on a network share, that data is backed up daily from the file server. Because data is not stored on the workstation, a Normal backup can be performed once a month with Incremental backups performed nightly. This gives the user or administrator the ability to restore the system and most files.

Using Windows 2000 Backup

Windows 2000 ships with Microsoft Windows Backup 5 (see Figure 15.1). This full-featured graphical utility allows an administrator to perform backup and restore operations to a variety of backup media. Backup also includes the Windows 2000 Job Scheduler for automating the execution of backup jobs.

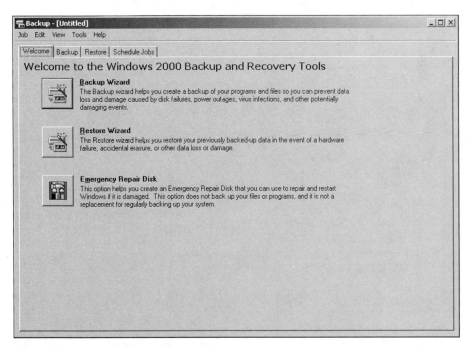

Figure 15.1   Microsoft Windows Backup 5.

All file systems that are supported by Windows 2000 are also supported by Backup. When Backup backs up data, all attributes and security permissions are also preserved.

Removable Storage

The management of backup tapes and disks are performed using the Removable Storage Console (see Figure 15.2). Backup media is allocated according to media pools. When a user configures Backup for a backup job, the user must specify which media pool Backup should allocate media to. This is a significant change from previous versions of Backup found in Windows NT.

For example, in earlier versions of Backup, the user would specify any available tape cartridge when configuring backup jobs. If the user wanted to perform backups every night, the user would create a single job.

In the new Backup, tapes are managed by Removable Storage. A user must select a media pool to back up the data to. Once the media pool is selected, Removable Storage determines which tape is available to be written to.

Backup

Creating a backup job is fairly simple. The user has two choices: use the Backup wizard found on the Welcome page or choose to back up manually from the Backup page. From the Backup page (see Figure 15.3), take these steps:

1. Select the drivers, directories, files, and/or System State to be backed up.

2. Select the Backup destination. The Backup Destination designates which media pool will be used. Remember that the media pools are managed by Removable

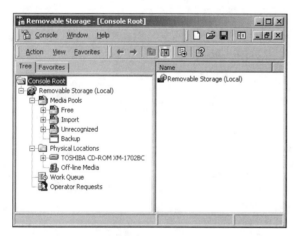

Figure 15.2 The Removable Storage Console.

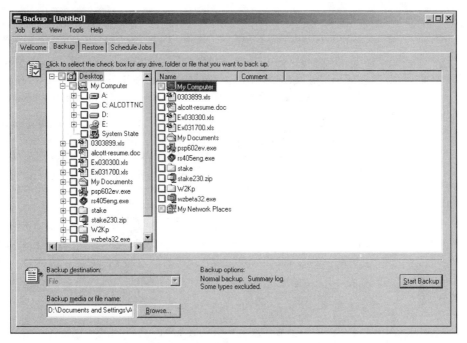

Figure 15.3   Manually configuring a backup job.

Storage Service. If the media pool selected is File, the user can enter the file name and destination.

3. Click on the Start Backup button. The Backup Job Information dialog box is displayed (see Figure 15.4). The following information can be supplied:

➤ *Backup Description*—Allows the user to enter a useful description for the backup job—for example, "Full Backup/March 13, 2000."

➤ *Append This Backup To The Media*—Allows the backup job to be appended or added to an existing backup media.

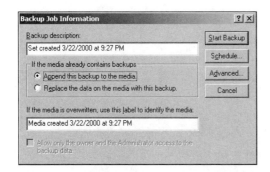

Figure 15.4   The Backup Job Information dialog box.

➤ *Replace The Data On The Media With This Backup*—Causes Backup to erase any existing backup data on the backup media before writing the new data.

➤ *If The Media Is Overwritten, Use This Label To Identify The Media*—Allows a user to label the backup media. Labeling the backup media causes the tape to be erased, so it cannot be used when the backup job is being appended.

➤ *Allow Only The Owner And The Administrators Access To The Backup Data*—Allows the tape to be secured. Only members of the Administrators group or the Creator/Owner of the tape will be able to restore the data. If the backup job is being appended, this option cannot be used because the security for the tape has already been created.

➤ *Schedule*—Allows the user to schedule the backup job.

➤ *Advanced*—Allows the user to specify advanced settings, such as the backup type, compression, verification, and so on.

To set the default Backup type, select Tools | Options | Backup Type. From the Backup Type page, the user can select the desired Backup Type.

To back up data, the user must be a member of the Administrators or Backup Operators group.

Backing Up and Restoring System State Information

In previous versions of Windows NT, Backup could back up and restore the Registry and system files. In Windows 2000, Backup backs up these items in what is known as the System State. The System State includes the following items:

➤ Boot files

➤ System files

➤ Windows File Protection (WFP) protected files

➤ Performance counter configuration information

➤ Component Services Class registration database

➤ The Registry

When System State is selected for backup, all of these items are backed up. Backup will not allow individual items to be selected. To back up the System State, follow these steps:

1. Click Start | Programs | Accessories | System Tools, and select Backup.

2. Go to the Backup page. Select the System State checkbox.

When the System State checkbox is selected, the System State is backed up along with any other files selected in the backup job.

If a user wants to restore the System State, the user must be a member of the Administrators group. During a restore, the Registry and system files can be restored to an alternate location. The Component Services Class registration database can only be restored to its original location.

Restore

Restoring data is as simple as backing it up. Again, as with a backup, the user has two choices: using the Restore wizard found on the Welcome page or choosing to do so manually from the Restore page.

From the Restore page, a list of media pools is displayed (see Figure 15.5). To restore data, the user selects the media pool that contains the appropriate backup set. Once the media pool is displayed, the user can select the backup set and the desired files. To restore data, the user must be a member of the Administrators or Backup Operators group.

Warning: When backing up encrypted files (EFS), it is important that user keys and certificates are also backed up. When encrypted files are restored, they remain encrypted; only the user with the correct key can decrypt the file. The Certificate console furnishes ways to export keys to removable media, such as floppy disks.

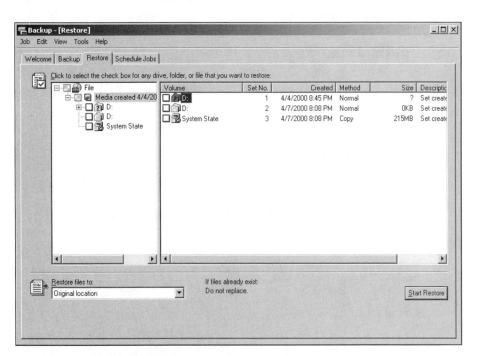

Figure 15.5   Manually configuring a Restore Job.

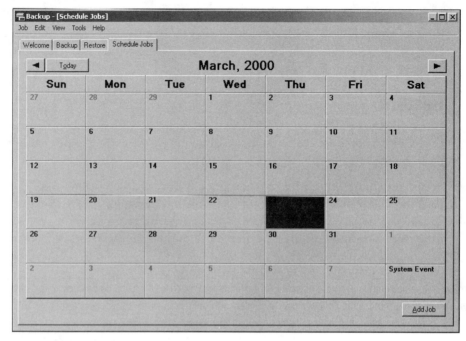

Figure 15.6 The Schedule Jobs page.

Schedule Jobs

To schedule backup jobs, users have a variety of options to customize job schedules to suit their needs. The Schedule Jobs page displays a monthly calendar (see Figure 15.6).

To schedule a backup job, take these steps:

1. From Backup, select the Schedule Jobs page.

2. Select the day that the backup job should start running. Click on Add Job.

3. The Backup Wizard will start. Click on Next.

4. Specify what should be backed up:

   ➤ Backup everything on my computer

   ➤ Backup selected files, drives, or network data

   ➤ Only backup the System State data

5. Click on Next.

6. Select the backup media type and the backup media.

7. Select the type of backup to be performed (Normal, Copy, Incremental, Differential, or Daily) from the drop-down list.

8. Click on Next.

9. Specify verification and compression options. Click on Next.

10. Select whether the backup job should be appended to or overwrite the media. Click on Next.

11. Enter backup and media labels if desired. Click on Next.

12. Select Later to specify a time for the backup job to start. Click on Set Schedule.

13. From the Schedule Job dialog box, select the Schedule Task from the drop-down list:

   ➤ Daily

   ➤ Weekly

   ➤ Monthly

   ➤ Once

   ➤ At System Startup

   ➤ At Logon

   ➤ When Idle

14. Click on OK. Click on Next.

15. A summary of the scheduled backup job will be displayed. Click on Finish to schedule the job.

Using Safe Mode Options

Safe Mode is a tool that allows a user to control how Windows 2000 starts. Although this tool was first introduced in Windows 95, it was never added to Windows NT 4. With Windows NT, a user had a limited number of options to diagnose and trouble-shoot system problems that may have been related to device drivers and system files. Problems with these types of files may prevent the computer from booting properly, so Safe Mode allows the user to boot a computer with the minimum required drivers and system files.

To access the Safe Mode boot menu, press F8 when the message "For troubleshooting and advanced startup options for Windows 2000, press F8" is displayed. You can

15

then select the Safe Mode option you would like to use or press ESC to return to the boot menu. After pressing F8, the following menu will be displayed:

```
Windows 2000 Advanced Options Menu
Please select an option:
    Safe Mode
    Safe Mode with Networking
    Safe Mode With Command Prompt
    Enable Boot Logging
    Enable VGA Mode
    Last Known Good Configuration
    Directory Services Restore Mode (Windows 2000 domain controllers only)
    Debugging Mode
    Boot Normally
Use - and ‾ to move the highlight to your choice.
Press Enter to choose.
```

To enter an option, use the arrow keys to highlight the option and press Enter. You then can select from the following modes:

➤ *Safe Mode*—This mode loads Windows 2000 with a minimum number of basic device drivers and system services to load the operating system. No other services or applications are started.

➤ *Safe Mode with Networking*—This mode loads the same devices and services as Safe Mode, but also loads drivers and services associated with networking. This option allows the administrator to access resources on the network. No other services or applications are started.

➤ *Safe Mode with Command Prompt*—This mode loads the same devices and services as Safe Mode, but loads cmd.exe instead of explorer.exe as the user shell.

➤ *Enable Boot Logging*—This mode boots the system under normal conditions (i.e., all device drivers and services designated to start automatically will be loaded). It creates a log file called ntbtlog.txt that logs the name and status of device drivers in memory. The log file is stored in the %systemroot% folder.

➤ *Enable VGA Mode*—This mode starts the system using the basic VGA mode. This option is useful when you are experiencing video driver problems.

➤ *Last Known Good Configuration*—This mode starts the system using the last successfully started system configuration.

➤ *Directory Services Restore Mode (Windows 2000 Domain Controllers Only)*—As indicated in the option name, this mode is used only on Windows 2000 domain controllers. It doesn't apply to Windows 2000 Professional.

➤ *Debugging Mode*—This mode starts Windows 2000 in kernel debug mode. This mode is useful in troubleshooting, where another system (the debugger) can break into the Windows 2000 kernel for precise analysis.

The Recovery Console

Another exciting feature that is new in Windows 2000 is the Recovery Console. The Recovery Console is a command-line interface that an administrator can use to access the hard disk of a Windows 2000 system. Windows 2000 does not need to be operating when using the Recovery Console, so it is very useful in troubleshooting and recovery situations.

The Recovery Console provides access to the file systems on the hard disk, whether it is FAT, FAT32, or NTFS. With this level of access, an administrator can access files and directories. More importantly, the administrator has the capability to start and stop services and therefore repair the system.

Starting the Recovery Console

The Recover Console can be accessed from the Windows 2000 installation CD-ROM or from the Windows 2000 Setup floppy disks. It can also be installed to the local hard disk by typing the following command from a command prompt:

```
D:\I386\WINNT32.EXE /cmdcons
```

In this prompt, D: represents the CD-ROM drive where the Windows 2000 installation CD-ROM is located.

Note: *The Recovery Console cannot be installed on a mirrored disk. To install the Recovery Console on the system, break the mirror, install the Recovery Console, and re-create the mirror.*

To start the Recovery Console using the installation media, take these steps:

1. Boot the computer from the Windows 2000 installation CD-ROM or from the Windows 2000 Setup floppy disks. At the Setup Notification screen, press Enter.

2. On the Welcome to Setup screen, press R to repair a Windows 2000 installation.

3. Press C to start the Recovery Console.

4. Select the Windows 2000 installation you want to repair, and press Enter.

5. Enter the password for the local administrator account.

15

To start the Recovery Console that was installed to the local hard disk:

1. Boot the computer. At the Operating System selection screen, select Windows 2000 Recovery Console.

2. Select the Windows 2000 installation you want to repair and press Enter.

3. Enter the password for the local administrator account.

Using the Recovery Console

The Recovery Console is a command-line interface. Most of the commands are derived from MS-DOS commands, so if you are familiar with MS-DOS, you can figure out what the command does. If you are not sure what a command does, help can be obtained by typing the command followed by /?. Table 15.1 lists the commands supported by the Recovery Console.

Table 15.1   Recovery Console commands.

Command	Description
Attrib	Changes attributes on one file or directory.
Batch	Executes commands specified in a text file.
Cd/chdir	Displays the name of the current directory or switches to a new directory.
Chkdsk	Checks a disk and displays a status report.
Cls	Clears the screen.
Copy	Copies a single file to another location.
Del/delete	Deletes one file.
Dir	Displays a list of files and subdirectories in a directory.
Disable	Disables a Windows system service or driver.
Diskpart	Manages the partitions on your hard disk volumes.
Enable	Enables a Windows system service or driver.
Expand	Expands a compressed file.
Fixboot	Writes a new boot sector onto the system partition.
Fixmbr	Repairs the master boot code of the boot partition.
Help	Displays information about commands supported by the Recovery Console.
Listsvc	Lists all available services and drivers on the computer.
Logon	Lists the detected installations of Windows 2000 and requests the local administrator password for those installations.
Map	Lists the drive letter to physical device mappings that are currently active.
Md/mkdir	Creates a directory.
More/type	Displays a text file to the screen.
Rd/rmdir	Removes (deletes) a directory.
Ren/rename	Renames a single file.
Set	Displays and sets Recovery Console environment variables.
Systemroot	Sets the current directory to %systemroot%.

By default, the Recovery Console only permits access to the following directories:

➤ %systemroot%

➤ The root directory of local disks

➤ \cmdcons and any subdirectories

➤ Directories on floppy disks and CD-ROMs

Access can be gained to other directories by changing the local Group Policy settings:

1. Select Start|Run, and enter "MMC".

2. Click on the Console drop-down menu, and select Add/Remove Snap-in.

3. Click on Add.

4. From the list of Snap-ins, select Group Policy, and click on Add.

5. The Select Group Policy Object dialog box will be displayed. Verify that Local Computer is listed, and click on Finish.

6. Click on Close on the Add Stand-alone Snap-in dialog box.

7. Click on OK to close the Add/Remove Snap-in dialog box.

8. Double-click on Local Computer Policy.

9. Double-click on Computer Configuration.

10. Double-click on Windows Settings.

11. Double-click on Security Settings.

12. Double-click on Local Policies.

13. Select Security Options.

14. Double-click on Recovery Console: Allow floppy copy and access to all volumes and folders.

15. The Local Security Policy Setting dialog box will be displayed. Select Enabled, and click on OK.

The set command is disabled by default. Once this access has been granted via Group Policy, the set command is enabled. The following set command can provide several functions:

```
Set [variable = value]
```

Here, *variable* can be the following

➤ *AllowWildCards*—This variable enables wild-card support for some commands, such as copy.

➤ *AllowAllPaths*—This variable provides access to all files and folders on the system.

➤ *AllRemovableMedia*—This variable allows files to be copied to removable media, such as floppies.

➤ *NoCopyPrompt*—This variable causes the confirmation prompt during over-writes to be disabled.

Replacing the Registry by Using the Recovery Console
Problems with the Registry can be remedied by using the Recovery Console. Registry files can be replaced by using the copy command. Backup copies of the Registry files are kept in either the %systemroot%\repair folder or the %systemroot%\repair\regback folder.

To replace the Registry using the Recovery Console, follow these steps:

1. Start the Recovery Console, and enter the local administrator password.

2. You will start in the %systemroot% directory (e.g., C:\WINNT). Enter the following commands:

```
cd repair\regback
copy filename C:\WINNT\SYSTEM32\CONFIG
```

Here, *filename* is the name of the Registry file to be copied. We recommend that you rename the current Registry files before replacing them. In case a problem occurs, this gives you the opportunity to return to the system's original condition.

Warning: Files located in %systemroot%\repair\regback represent the Registry state the last time that the System State was backed up. Any changes made to the Registry files since then will be lost.

Disabling a Device Driver or Service by Using the Recovery Console
Problems with the device drivers and services can be remedied by using the Recovery Console as well. By using the enable and disable commands, troublesome device drivers and services can be disabled. To disable a device driver using the Recovery Console, take the following steps:

1. Start the Recovery Console, and enter the local administrator password.

2. You will start in the %systemroot% directory (e.g., C:\WINNT). Type "listsvc" to obtain a list of currently installed device drivers and services. Locate the name of the troublesome device driver.

3. Enter the following command:

```
disable servicename
```

Here, *servicename* is the name of the device driver and service. For example, if you needed to disable the device driver for a 3Com Network Adapter, you would enter:

```
disable EL90BC
```

The following output will be displayed:

```
The registry entry for the EL90BC service was found.
The service currently has a start_type SERVICE_DEMAND_START.
Please record this value.

The new start_type for the service has been set to SERVICE_DISABLED.
The computer must now be restarted for the changes to take effect.
Type EXIT if you want to restart the computer now.
```

4. The disable command will display the current start type. Write this down so you know what it should be set back to when it is enabled.

5. Type "exit" to restart the computer.

To enable a device driver using the Recovery Console:

1. Start the Recovery Console, and enter the local administrator password.

2. You will start in the %systemroot% directory (e.g., C:\WINNT).

3. Enter the following command:

```
enable EL90BC SERVICE_DEMAND_START
```

The following output will be displayed:

```
The registry entry for the EL90BC service was found.
The service currently has a start_type SERVICE_DISABLED.
Please record this value.

The new start_type for the service has been set to SERVICE_DEMAND_START.
The computer must now be restarted for the changes to take effect.
Type EXIT if you want to restart the computer now.
```

4. Type "exit" to restart the computer.

15

ERD and the Emergency Repair Process

The Emergency Repair Disk (ERD) is a floppy disk that is created with Backup. The ERD contains the following files from the %systemroot%\repair directory:

➤ *Autoexec.nt*—This file is used to initialize the MS-DOS subsystem.

➤ *Config.nt*—This file is used to initialize the MS-DOS subsystem.

➤ *Setup.log*—This file contains a list of files installed during Setup. It also contains cyclic redundancy check (CRC) numbers. The list and the CRC numbers will be used by the Emergency Repair Process to diagnose whether any of the files are missing or corrupt.

It is important to note what is missing. In earlier versions of Windows NT, the ERD also contained copies of the Registry. In Windows 2000, the Registry is no longer copied to the ERD. To back up the Registry, you must use Backup. To create an ERD, follow these steps:

1. Select Start|Programs|Accessories|System Tools, and select Backup.

2. On the Welcome screen, click on Emergency Repair Disk.

3. When prompted, insert a formatted, high-density 3.5" floppy disk into the disk drive (see Figure 15.7).

   If desired, select the checkbox to have the Registry files backed up to the %systemroot%\repair directory. The Registry files located in this directory are the original Registry files created during initial setup.

4. Once complete, label the disk "Emergency Repair Disk" and store it in a safe place.

The Emergency Repair Process can repair corrupt or missing system files and make it possible for the system to boot again. It performs the following operations:

➤ Restores the system partition boot sector (on the first hard disk only)

➤ Restores the Registry

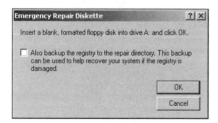

Figure 15.7 Creating the ERD.

➤ Checks and replaces any missing or corrupt system files

➤ Inspects and repairs the startup environment

During a Registry repair, the Emergency Repair Process restores Registry files contained in %systemroot%\repair. These Registry files are the original Registry files created during initial setup. For this reason, it is recommended that Backup or the Recovery Console be used to restore the Registry. When the System State is backed up, a backup copy of the Registry is stored in %systemroot%\repair\regback. These are the latest copies of the Registry files.

To repair a system using the Emergency Repair Process, take these steps:

1. Boot the computer from the Windows 2000 installation CD-ROM or from the Windows 2000 Setup floppy disks. At the Setup Notification screen, press Enter.

2. On the Welcome to Setup screen, press R to repair a Windows 2000 installation.

3. Press R when prompted for the repair option.

4. Choose the type of repair to be used:

   ➤ Press M for Manual Repair.

   ➤ Press F for Fast Repair.

5. When prompted, insert the ERD.

Manual Repair allows you to select from three options:

➤ *Inspect Startup Environment*—This option verifies that the system startup files (NTLDR, ntdetect.com, boot.ini, ntbootdd.sys, and hal.dll) are correct. If any of the files need to be replaced, the Emergency Repair Process restores them from the Windows 2000 installation CD-ROM.

➤ *Verify Windows 2000 System Files*—This option verifies that the system files are not missing or corrupt. It uses the setup.log file stored on the ERD to perform this check.

➤ *Inspect Boot Sector*—This option verifies that the boot sector on the system points to NTLDR. If it does not, it replaces the boot sector. The Emergency Repair Process can replace the boot sector on the first hard disk and only on the first hard disk only.

Fast Repair runs all three of these options automatically, including the replacement of the Registry files.

15

Chapter Summary

Recovering a Windows 2000 installation can be a real lifesaver. Luckily, Windows 2000 comes with a number of utilities to help an administrator diagnose, trouble-shoot, restore, and recover a Windows 2000 system.

Before attempting to recover a system, the administrator needs to diagnose the problem. The types of problems encountered in Windows 2000 generally fall into three categories: device driver problems, system files problems, or hardware problems. Each category has its own method of diagnosing and remedying the problem.

Windows 2000 includes a full-featured backup utility, simply called Backup. The Backup utility allows data to be backed up to any removable media. Once the data is backed up, individual files or even the full system can be restored. This can include the System State, which includes the Registry, boot files, system files, Windows File Protection (WFP) protected files, performance counter configuration, and the Component Services Class registration database.

Windows 2000 now includes Safe Mode options upon boot up. These options allow an administrator to start a Windows 2000 system with the minimum required device drivers and services. These options are useful when diagnosing and repairing a troublesome workstation.

Another new feature in Windows 2000 is the Recovery Console. The Recovery Console is a command-line interface that provides an administrator with access to the file system, whether the file system is FAT, FAT32, or NTFS. An administrator can also start and stop device drivers and services with the Recovery Console. It is a powerful tool that may repair a system that previously would have required a full restore.

Finally, this chapter covered the Emergency Repair Process and the ERD. The Emergency Repair Process allows an administrator to repair the boot files, system files, the boot sector, or replace the Registry. The ERD contains three files that the Emergency Repair Process utilizes: autoexec.nt, config.nt, and setup.log.

Review Questions

1. The ERD is a bootable floppy disk. True or false?

   a. True

   b. False

2. What is the easiest way to recover boot files that are missing or corrupt?

    a. Reinstall the operating system.

    b. Copy the files from a Windows NT workstation.

    c. Use the ERD.

    d. Run the SYS command in the Recovery Console.

3. How can you back up the Windows 2000 Registry?

    a. Use the ERD.

    b. Boot using Safe Mode with Registry Backup.

    c. Export the Registry to tab delimited text files.

    d. Perform a backup using the Backup utility, and select the System State.

4. Which service or device driver is not loaded when booting in Safe Mode?

    a. Mouse device driver

    b. Logical Disk Manager services

    c. Network Adapter device driver

    d. Basic VGA device driver

5. What is one method of starting the Recovery Console?

    a. Boot the system with the ERD.

    b. Boot the system with the Windows 2000 installation CD.

    c. Press F8 when starting.

    d. Boot with an MS-DOS disk.

6. Which Windows 2000 repair option allows an administrator to disable a device driver?

    a. Safe Mode

    b. The Emergency Repair Process

    c. The Recovery Console

    d. Safe Mode with Command Prompt

7. Backup found in Windows 2000 does not support which of the following media?

    a. QIC Tape

    b. DLT Tape

    c. Floppy

    d. CD-ROM

15

8. Using Recovery Console, what directories can be accessed? [Check all correct answers]

    a. %systemroot%

    b. Directories on floppy disks and CD-ROMs

    c. The root directory of local disks

    d. \cmdcons and any subdirectories

9. If the Safe Mode startup option Enable Boot Logging is selected, where is the log file stored?

    a. %systemroot%

    b. C:\ntbtlog.txt

    c. %systemroot%\repair

    d. The Event Viewer

10. You are having difficulties with an application in Windows 2000. It has corrupted some application specific device drivers that are causing the system to crash. You need to install a service pack for the application that will fix the problem, but it only resides on a network share. How can you utilize the system to get to and install the service pack?

    a. Boot with Safe Mode

    b. Boot with Safe Mode with Command Prompt

    c. Use the Recovery Console

    d. Boot with Safe Mode with Networking

11. The ERD contains a compressed copy of the Windows 2000 Registry. True or false?

    a. True

    b. False

12. How do you access Safe Mode options in Windows 2000?

    a. Press F8 on the OS selection menu.

    b. Boot with the ERD.

    c. Select the Restart in Safe Mode option upon shutdown.

    d. Hold down Ctrl+Alt+Esc.

13. When restoring the Registry using the Emergency Repair Process, from where is the Registry restored?

    a. ERD

    b. Backup Tape

    c. %systemroot%\repair\regback

    d. %systemroot%\repair\

14. When restoring the System State to a Windows 2000 Professional system, individual Registry files can be selected. True or false?

   a. True

   b. False

15. You need to check your system's startup files only. Using the Emergency Repair Process, what options should you select?

   a. Manual Repair, Inspect Startup Environment

   b. Fast Repair, Inspect Startup Environment

   c. Fast Repair, Check Startup Files

   d. Manual Repair, Inspect Boot Sector

16. Which Recovery Console command can be used to set the start_type of a service or device driver?

   a. Enable

   b. Set start_type

   c. Start_type

   d. Re-enable

17. Which Safe Mode startup option provides you with a list of loaded device drivers and services?

   a. Safe Mode

   b. Enable Boot Logging

   c. Safe Mode with Networking

   d. Debugging Mode

18. How do you create a new ERD?

   a. Rerun Setup.

   b. From a command prompt, use the ERD command.

   c. In Control Panel, select the System applet.

   d. Use the Backup utility.

19. Which Recovery Console command creates a new boot sector on the system partition?

   a. Fixmbr

   b. Fixboot

   c. Fixbootsector

   d. Fixsys

15

20. You need to restore the Registry on your Windows 2000 Professional system. You boot the system using the Windows 2000 installation CD and access the Recovery Console. You change to the %systemroot%\repair directory and notice that there is no regback subdirectory. Why is this so?

    a. The Recovery Console does not provide access to the regback directory.

    b. An ERD has not been created.

    c. The System State has never been backed up.

    d. The Set command must be run first.

21. The Recovery Console does not allow full access to which file system?

    a. FAT

    b. FAT32

    c. NTFS

    d. CDFS

22. How do you install the Recovery Console as a startup option?

    a. From a command prompt, type "D:\I386\WINNT32 /cmdcons".

    b. From the Control Panel, select Recovery Console from Windows Setup.

    c. It cannot be installed as a startup option.

    d. Reinstall Windows 2000, and select Recovery Console from Advanced Options.

Real-World Projects

You have just been given a new Windows 2000 Professional-based workstation. Although your workstation is connected to the network, you prefer to save your data to the local hard disk. The workstation includes an internal DLT tape drive.

You want to create a backup schedule where a Normal backup occurs every Friday night with Differential backups taking place Monday through Thursday. No backups will be performed on the weekend. You want to back up everything on your workstation, including the System State.

Project 15.1

To create a scheduled Normal Backup:

1. Select Start|Programs|Accessories|System Tools|Backup to open the Backup utility.

2. From the Welcome Screen, click on the Backup tab to open the Backup page.

3. On the left pane, select the local disk to be backed up (C:). Also, select the System State to back up the Registry and related system files.

4. Select DLT from the Backup destination drop-down list.

5. Click on Start Backup.

6. The Backup Job Information dialog box will be displayed. Enter "Full Normal Friday Backup" in the Backup description box.

7. Select Replace The Data On The Media With This Backup. This will overwrite any data on the DLT tape.

8. Click on Schedule. A dialog warning displays to notify you that you must save the backup selection before proceeding. Click on Yes to save the selection. The Save Selections dialog box will be displayed. Enter "Friday-Normal" as the file name. Click on OK.

9. The Set Account Information dialog box will be displayed. Enter the user account that the backup job will use as a security context when run. Remember that the user account must be in the Administrators group because the System State is also being backed up. By default, the local Administrator account is selected. Enter the Administrator password and verify the password. Click on OK.

10. The Schedule Job Options dialog box will be displayed. Enter "Friday-Normal Backup" in the Job name box. Click on Properties to schedule the job.

11. The Schedule Job dialog box will be displayed. From the Schedule Task drop-down list, select Weekly. Clear the default selection Monday checkbox, and select the Friday checkbox. In the Start Time box, enter "10:00 P.M". Click on OK to save the scheduled job. Click on OK to close the Schedule Job Options dialog box.

Next, you need to create the Daily Differential backup job.

Project 15.2

To create a scheduled Differential Backup:

1. Select Start|Programs|Accessories|System Tools|Backup to open the Backup utility.

2. From the Welcome Screen, click on the Backup tab to open the Backup page.

3. From the Job drop-down menu, select Load Selections. Select FridayNormal.bks because it contains the desired job selection set (Local C: and the System State).

4. Select DLT from the Backup destination drop-down list.

5. From the Tools drop-down menu, select Options. From the Default Backup Type drop-down list, select Differential. Click on OK to close the Options dialog box.

15

6. Click on Start Backup.

7. The Backup Job Information dialog box will be displayed. Enter "Daily Differential Backup" in the Backup description box.

8. Select Append This Backup To The Media. This will append the backup job to any data on the DLT tape.

9. Click on Schedule.

10. The Schedule Job Options dialog box will be displayed. Enter "Daily Differential Backup" in the Job name box. Click on Properties to schedule the job.

11. The Schedule Job dialog box will be displayed. From the Schedule Task drop-down list, select Weekly. Keep the default selection of Monday and also select the Tuesday, Wednesday, and Thursday checkboxes. In the Start Time box, enter "10:00 P.M.". Click on OK to save the scheduled job. Click on OK to close the Schedule Job Options dialog box.

You have a Windows 2000 Professional workstation that will be used for testing new applications and hardware. You want to use the Recovery Console to help troubleshoot any problems resulting from the testing.

Project 15.3

To install the Recovery Console:

1. Open a Command Prompt by selecting Start|Run. Type "cmd" in the Run dialog box. Click on OK.

2. Insert the Windows 2000 Installation CD in the CD-ROM drive. At the command prompt, type "D:\I386\WINNT32.EXE /cmdcons" (where D: is the letter of the CD-ROM drive), and press Enter.

3. A dialog box will be displayed, asking if you want to install the Recovery Console on the hard disk. Click on Yes.

4. The Windows 2000 Setup Wizard will start to install the necessary files. Click on OK when the wizard is finished.

After installing a new Adaptec SCSI adapter in your system along with its associated device drivers, strange application faults start occurring. After rebooting your system, Windows 2000 will not boot normally. Because the SCSI adapter's device driver was the last change made to the workstation, you decide that you want to disable it using the Recovery Console.

Project 15.4

To disable a device driver using the Recovery Console:

1. Boot the computer. At the Operating System selection screen, select Windows 2000 Recovery Console.

2. Type the number for the Windows 2000 Professional installation, and press Enter.

3. Type the password for the local administrator account installation, and press Enter.

4. At the Recovery Console command prompt, type "listsvc" to display a list of all device drivers and services installed. From the list, identify the troublesome device driver, aic78xx.

5. At the command prompt, type the command "disable aic78xx". The following text is displayed:

```
The registry entry for the aic78xx service was found.
The service currently has a start_type SERVICE_DEMAND_START.
Please record this value.

The new start_type for the service has been set to SERVICE_DISABLED.
The computer must now be restarted for the changes to take effect.
Type EXIT if you want to restart the computer now.
```

6. Type "exit" at the command prompt to restart the workstation.

After restarting, the workstation boots normally. You check the Adaptec Web site and find a technical article describing the problem with the device driver. You download the updated device driver and install it on the workstation. You will not see the previously encountered problems resurface.

15

CHAPTER SIXTEEN

The Windows Network Environment

After completing this chapter, you will be able to:

✓ Identify the different types of networks found in Windows 2000 Professional

✓ Identify and access network resources

✓ Join a workgroup or domain

✓ Implement Group Policies on the local computer

✓ Configure network protocols in a Windows network

Many organizations and individuals benefit from networks by cost-effectively using resources, such as disk space and printers. A company with 20 computers in a non-networked environment would need to use more costly measures to access resources. For example, they would need to purchase 20 individual printers for the computers or resort to printer sharing using an unreliable patchwork of switchboxes and cables. To share files, they would have to resort to "sneakernet," where individual users copy files to floppy disks and walk them to other computers. Using sneakernet is very inefficient because the computers end up with multiple copies of the same files. Another problem with sneakernet is that file size is limited to whatever can fit on a floppy. Other more advanced features found in networks, such as email and databases, are not even possible in non-networked environments.

Networking and Communications

Most Microsoft operating systems include built-in networking support. Windows 95/98, Windows NT 3.51/4, and Windows 2000 provide networking capabilities that many organizations use for network services. Because Microsoft operating systems are widely used, chances are that the network you will be attaching Windows 2000 Professional to will be a Microsoft Windows network.

Although Windows 2000 Professional is a great standalone platform, its power is truly found when it is attached to a network. In a network environment, it can take advantage of a myriad of network resources including file and print servers, databases, messaging, application servers, intranets, and perhaps most important, the Internet. Windows 2000 Professional provides file and print sharing, peer Web services, and many other network features.

Accessing Network Resources

Windows 2000 Professional can access many network resources straight out of the box.

Microsoft wisely included support for the most popular network protocols, such as TCP/IP, NWLink (IPX/SPX), NetBEUI, and AppleTalk. By supporting these protocols, Windows 2000 Professional can speak the same language as the servers supplying network resources, such as databases and messaging. For example, a client/server-based database may use TCP/IP via a particular port to facilitate communication between the client and the server. Messaging applications typically use Simple Mail Transport Protocol (SMTP), a member of the TCP/IP protocol suite, to send email across the network.

Although a network protocol allows Windows 2000 to speak the same language as other network resources, a network client provides the functionality and access to

Table 16.1 Windows 2000 supported network clients.

Client	Network Protocols	Description	Other Information
Client for Microsoft Networks	TCP/IP, NWLink, NetBEUI	Used for accessing file and print services for Microsoft Networks.	Included with Windows 2000 (installed by default)
Client Services for NetWare	NWLink	Used for accessing file and print services on Novell NetWare services.	Included with Windows 2000
Microsoft Windows Services for Unix 2	TCP/IP	Used to provide functionality between Unix hosts and Windows 2000 computers.	Included as an add-on pack
Windows 2000 Services for Macintosh	TCP/IP, AppleTalk	Allows Windows 2000 clients and Macintosh clients to share files over TCP/IP or AppleTalk	Found in Windows 2000 Server and Windows 2000 Advanced Server

these network resources. Microsoft included network clients that allow Windows 2000 Professional to access file and printing resources on Novell NetWare networks, Apple Macintosh networks, Unix networks, and of course, Microsoft Networks. A client/server database would include its own client software. Messaging resources can be accessed from a number of clients that support SMTP, such as Netscape Communicator and Microsoft Outlook. Table 16.1 lists the network clients supported by Windows 2000.

This chapter focuses on the default client found in Windows 2000: Client for Microsoft Networks. We will focus on Client Services for NetWare in Chapter 17 and Microsoft Windows Services for Unix 2 in Chapter 18.

Microsoft Networks

More often than not, Windows 2000 Professional computers will be connected to a Microsoft Network. The network may be built around any of the Microsoft operating systems: Microsoft LAN Manager, Windows 3.x, Windows for Workgroups, Windows 95, Windows 98, Windows NT 4, or Windows 2000.

Microsoft Networks use the Common Internet File System (CIFS) protocol. CIFS is a file and printer sharing protocol that allows a computer to access files and folders on remote computers. Computers using CIFS communicate using four basic command types: session control, file, printer, and message. CIFS is identical to the Server Message Block (SMB) protocol found in Windows NT.

Networks are organized according to their desired function. Details to consider when organizing a network are the administrative model and geographic locations involved.

16

Types of Network Environments

There are two types of network environments found in Microsoft Networks: workgroup-based and domain-based networks. These environment types are based on the security structure of the network.

Workgroup-Based Networks

A workgroup-based network is a single subnet peer-to-peer network. A workgroup is simply a logical grouping of computers that allows a small number of users to share network resources, such as disk space and printers. Security is decentralized, and each computer in the network maintains its own security database. In order to access resources on a computer, a user needs a valid user account and password on that computer.

Workgroup-based networks are ideal for a small office or home, where users want to share resources and security is not the greatest concern. Workgroups typically consist of no more than 10 computers.

Joining a Workgroup

By default, a Windows 2000 Professional computer becomes a member of the workgroup named WORKGROUP. Only a user account that is a member of the Administrators group can change workgroup membership.

A Windows 2000 Professional computer can change workgroup membership via two methods: by using the Network Identification Wizard or by manually joining a workgroup.

The Network Identification Wizard provides a simple interface that allows a Windows 2000 Professional computer to join a workgroup. The Network Identification Wizard is illustrated in Figure 16.1.

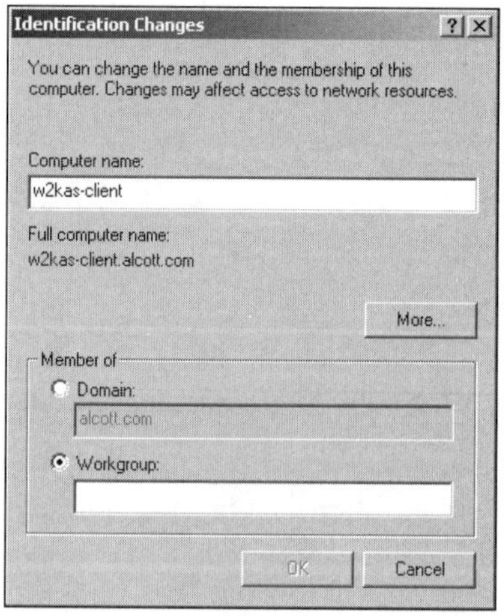

Figure 16.1 The Network Identification Wizard.

To start the Network Identification Wizard, follow these steps:

1. Right-click on My Computer, and then select Properties.

2. Select the Network Identification tab.

3. Click on Network ID, and then click on Next.

4. Select This Computer Is Part Of A Business Network, And I Use It To Connect To Other Computers At Work. Click on Next.

5. To join a workgroup, select My Company Uses A Network Without A Domain. Click on Next.

6. Enter the name of the workgroup. Click on Next.

7. Click on Finish, and restart the computer.

To manually join a workgroup, follow these steps.

1. Right-click on My Computer, and then select Properties.

2. Select the Network Identification tab. Select Properties.

3. The Identification Changes dialog box is displayed. In the Member Of section, select Workgroup.

4. Enter the name of the workgroup. Click on OK.

5. Click on OK to close the Identification Changes dialog box.

6. Click on OK to close the System Properties dialog box.

7. Click on Yes to restart the computer.

Domain-Based Networks

A domain-based network is also a logical grouping of computers with the notable exception that they all share a common security database. This allows a user to have a single user account that, when granted the proper access, can utilize any resources in the domain.

The security database for the domain is housed on domain controllers. These are servers that manage all interactions, such as authentication, account creation and deletion, auditing, and the granting or revoking of rights.

If a domain contains more than one domain controller, the security database is replicated between them. This provides fault tolerance and scalability. If a domain controller fails, the other domain controllers can continue to authenticate users. It provides scalability by distributing the authentication load across the multiple domain controllers.

16

There are two models of domain-based networks. The older model, found in Windows NT 4, is known as a Windows NT 4 Domain, or simply a Domain. The new model is found in Windows 2000 and is called Active Directory.

Windows NT 4 Domains

Windows NT 4 Domains are created with the installation of a Windows NT 4 Server designated as a primary domain controller (PDC). On the PDC resides a read/write copy of the Security Accounts Manager (SAM). The SAM is the security database for the domain. When a user account is created or modified, the result is saved to the SAM located on the PDC.

To create fault tolerance and scalability in a Windows NT 4 Domain, another type of domain controller can be added. This domain controller is known as a backup domain controller (BDC). A BDC houses a read-only copy of the SAM. If the PDC goes down, the BDCs will continue to authenticate users, although changes or additions cannot occur. A BDC can also be promoted to function as the PDC.

Active Directory

Active Directory is the domain-based security model found in Windows 2000. Active Directory is known as a directory service. A directory service provides a place to store information about the network, such as user accounts, computer accounts, files, printers, and applications.

Unlike a Windows NT 4 Domain, which contains a single read/write copy of the SAM, Active Directory is known as a multiple master database. The domain controllers in Active Directory all have read/write access to the directory service.

Active Directory is also more organized than a Windows NT 4 Domain. Active Directory can contain separate trees, domains, and organizational units (OUs) that may mimic the organization or geographic structure of the company.

Joining a Domain

Whether joining a Windows NT 4 Domain or an Active Directory, the method is the same. Only a user account that is a member of the Administrators group can add or remove a computer from a domain. As with workgroup-based networks, a Windows 2000 Professional computer can be added or removed from the domain via two methods: by using the Network Identification Wizard or by manually joining a domain.

The Network Identification Wizard provides a simple interface that allows a Windows 2000 Professional computer to join a domain. To start the Network Identification Wizard, follow these steps:

1. Right-click on My Computer, and then select Properties.

2. Click on the Network Identification tab.

3. Click on Network ID, and then click on Next.

4. Select This Computer Is Part Of A Business Network, And I Use It To Connect To Other Computers At Work. Click on Next.

5. To join a domain, select My Company Uses A Network With A Domain. Click on Next.

6. Enter the name of the domain and a valid user account and password. Click on Next.

7. Click on Finish, and restart the computer.

To manually join a domain, follow these steps:

1. Right-click on My Computer, and then select Properties.

2. Click on the Network Identification tab. Select Properties.

3. The Identification Changes dialog box is displayed. In the Member Of section, select Domain.

4. Enter the name of the domain and a valid user account and password. Click on OK.

5. Click on OK to close the Identification Changes dialog box.

6. Click on OK to close the System Properties dialog box.

7. Click on Yes to restart the computer.

Account Authentication

Whether joining a workgroup or domain, a computer needs to be protected from unauthorized access. Microsoft Networks use account authentication to secure the computer and the resources it contains. Account authentication is the process of verifying a user's identification supplied by the user against the information found in the security database. Once verified, the user is allowed to access resources according to the permissions granted. If authentication fails, the user is denied access.

Authentication in workgroup-based networks occurs at the local account database on each computer. Authentication in domain-based networks occurs at the domain controllers.

In Windows 2000, Kerberos v5 authentication protocol is the default authentication method. Kerberos is a standard security protocol supported by many vendors and operating systems.

Windows 2000 Professional also supports Windows NT Lan Manager (NTLM) security for authentication to Windows NT 4 Domains. When logging into a Windows NT domain, Windows 2000 Professional will first attempt to use Kerberos. If it fails to find the Kerberos Key Distribution Center on the domain controller, it will attempt to use NTLM and the SAM.

16

Logon Names

Windows 2000 requires every user who attempts to access resources to have a valid and unique logon name. A logon name identifies the user to the operating system. In Windows 2000, a user can have two types of logons: a SAM Account Name and a User Principal Name (UPN).

Recall from the first part of this chapter that user accounts in Windows NT are stored in the SAM. The SAM is a security accounts database containing user accounts, group accounts, passwords, and so on. A SAM Account Name is used to provide compatibility with older Windows NT 4 domains and workgroups. In Windows NT 4, each logon name in the SAM must be unique. In other words, if there are two users, one named Mike Witherspoon and another named Mike Walters, only one of them can have the logon name MIKEW. The other user would need to have a logon name that incorporates a middle initial or some other variation to make it unique.

The UPN is a new feature found in Windows 2000 and is used in addition to the SAM Account Name. The UPN looks exactly like an Internet email account. The UPN consists of the user name followed by the @ sign followed by the UPN suffix. The suffix is typically the Active Directory domain in which the logon name is found. For example, if Mike Witherspoon had a logon name in the Active Directory domain helpandlearn.com, his UPN would be mikew@helpandlearn.com.

The UPN is a shortened version of the Distinguished Name and the Relative Distinguished Name. The Distinguished Name uniquely identifies an object in Active Directory by including the full path to its location. The Distinguished Name includes the common name of the object as well as the names of all organizational and domain units that contain the object. For example, the Distinguished Name of Mike Witherspoon, a member of the Engineering department at helpandlearn.com, is cn=MikeWitherspoon, ou=engineering, dc=helpandlearn, dc=com (cn designates the common name, ou designates the organizational unit, and dc designates the domain component).

The Relative Distinguished Name is an attribute of the object that the object itself is naming. For example, given the Distinguished Name of cn=MikeWitherspoon, ou=engineering, dc=helpandlearn dc=com, the Relative Distinguished Name is MikeWitherspoon. The maximum length of the Relative Distinguished Name is 255 characters.

As you can see, the Distinguished Name must be unique in Active Directory because it points to a single object. The Relative Distinguished Name need only be unique at its current organizational level. In other words, there can be only one MikeWitherspoon object in the engineering organizational unit, but there can be another MikeWitherspoon object in other organizational units, such as marketing.helpandlearn.com.

Group and System Policies

Starting with Windows NT 4, Microsoft introduced the System Policy editor. The System Policy Editor allowed an administrator to specify user and computer configuration settings in the Registry. Administrators could then enforce and control the user's work environment. This in turn helped reduce the administrative costs caused by a user changing or misconfiguring (breaking is more like it!) the system.

Windows 2000 includes a new utility called the Group Policy Snap-in. It provides the same basic functionality as the System Policy Editor, but is expanded to include a broad range of user environment options. To access the Group Policy Snap-in, follow these steps:

1. Select Start|Run. In the Run dialog box, type "MMC", and click on OK.

2. From the Console pull-down menu, select Add/Remove Snap-In.

3. From the Add/Remove Snap-In dialog box, click on Add.

4. From the Add Standalone Snap-In dialog box, select Group Policy from the list of snap-ins. Click on Add.

5. When prompted to store the Group Policy in Active Directory or on the local computer, select Local Computer. Click on Finish.

6. Click on Close to close the Add Standalone Snap-In dialog box.

7. Click on OK to close the Add/Remove Snap-In dialog box.

Remember to save the MMC you've just created! When finished, the Group Policy MMC should look like Figure 16.2.

A Group Policy is an object that gets associated with a particular domain or organizational unit in Active Directory or in a local computer. In Windows 2000 Professional, we will focus on the Local Computer Policy.

The local Group Policy allows an administrator to make the following changes to the local computer:

➤ Define security settings.

➤ Modify more than 450 operating system components.

➤ Specify scripts for computer startup and shutdown and user logon and logoff.

Windows 2000 Professional stores Group Policy objects in the %systemroot%\ System32\GroupPolicy directory.

Let's walk through some Group Policy examples.

Pretend you are the administrator for a corporate LAN. The CFO of the company is concerned about the loss of production output for a particular department. The

16

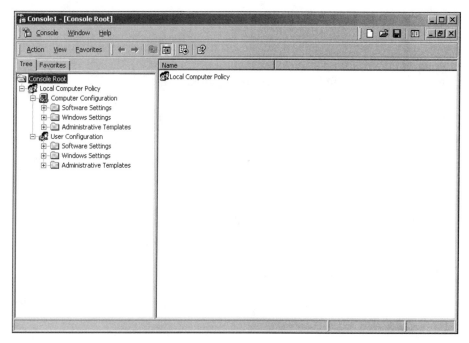

Figure 16.2   The Group Policy Snap-in dialog box.

CFO discovers that a number of employees in the department have been changing the configurations on the workstations. These changes are breaking some of the applications, which in turn results in downtime. The CFO wants you to take measures that will limit the number of changes that can be made.

You decide that you will implement a Group Policy that will eliminate access to the Control Panel, the Run dialog box, My Network Places, Registry tools, and the command prompt.

To accomplish this, follow these steps:

1. Start the Group Policy MMC you created earlier in the chapter.

2. In the left pane, select User Configuration. Expand Administrative Templates, and select Desktop.

3. In the right pane, double-click on the Hide My Network Places icon on the desktop. Select Enable. This hides the My Network Places icon, which prevents users from browsing the network. Click on OK.

4. In the left-hand pane, select Start Menu and Taskbar. Select Remove Run menu from Start menu. Select Enable. This removes the Run menu from the Start menu and the New Task (Run) option from Task Manager. Click on OK.

5. In the left pane, select Control Panel. Double-click on Disable Control Panel. Select Enable. This hides the Control Panel from users. If you want to limit

access to only a few applets on the Control Panel, you could choose Hide Specified Control Panel Applets instead. Click on OK.

6. In the left-hand pane, select System. Double-click on Disable Registry Editing Tools. Select Enable. This disables access to regedit.exe and regedt32.exe. Click on OK.

7. Again under System, double-click on Disable The Command Prompt. Click on Enable. This eliminates access to the command prompt, where a user could enter other commands, such as Net, in an attempt to circumvent your Group Policy. Click on OK.

Test the Group Policy by logging on as a regular user. Notice that the Control Panel, the Run dialog box, and My Network Places are all hidden. Next, try opening the command prompt. You should get a message that it has been disabled by the administrator. Finally, try running regedit.exe. It too displays a message that regedit has been disabled by the administrator.

Group Policy is a powerful tool for locking down Windows 2000 Professional configurations. Although it is more commonly used in domain-based networks, it can also be used in workgroup or standalone environments. Group Policy can save an administrator a lot of time when trying to troubleshoot items broken by a renegade user. It also allows users to do what they are paid to do: work.

Logon Scripts

Logon scripts are typically batch files or scripts (Windows Scripting Host, VBScript, or JavaScript) that are used to configure a user's work environment. Items, such as mapped network drives and printers, are set up automatically. This saves users valuable time and also standardizes their configurations.

Typically, logon scripts are used in domain environments, where the logon script resides on a domain controller. As a user logs on, the logon script executes and configures the user's environment. Logon scripts are executed after the Group Policy has been applied.

Getting Connected

Well, if you want to start using network resources, you need to connect to the network. There are number of ways to accomplish this, depending on your situation.

16

Local Area Connection

If you need to connect to a LAN, you need to create a Local Area Connection. A Local Area Connection is created automatically when a network adapter is installed in the Windows 2000-based computer. For example, if you have one network adapter installed, there is one Local Area Connection found in the Network And Dial-Up

Connections folder. If two network adapters are installed, there are two Local Area Connections.

To open the Network And Dial-Up Connections folder, select Start | Settings | Network And Dial-Up Connections. By default, Windows 2000 configures the Local Area Connection with the following items:

➤ TCP/IP

➤ Client for Microsoft Networks

➤ File and Printer Sharing for Microsoft Networks

Depending on your situation, this may be all the network components you need. However, your situation may require the use of another network protocol, network client, or service. So let's explore the Local Area Connection interface and define what some of the items found there do. Figure 16.3 displays the Local Area Connection Properties dialog box.

Configuring Network Protocols

A network protocol facilitates communication between computers on a network. Before you can start accessing network resources, you need to configure your network protocol. Windows 2000 includes support for a number of network protocols. The three we are covering here—TCP/IP, NWLink (IPX/SPX), and NetBEUI—are the most common network protocols found in LAN environments.

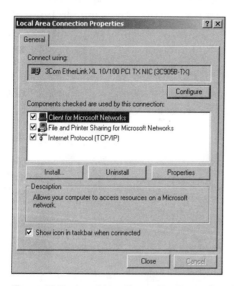

Figure 16.3 Local Area Connection Properties dialog box.

TCP/IP

Transport Control Protocol/Internet Protocol (TCP/IP) is a protocol suite that forms the foundation of many of today's corporate internetworks and, most importantly, the Internet. See Chapter 11 for a thorough and detailed explanation of the TCP/IP protocol suite.

To install TCP/IP in Windows 2000, follow these steps:

1. Open the Network And Dial-Up Connection folder by selecting Start | Settings | Network And Dial-Up Connections.

2. Right-click on the desired Local Area Connection, and select Properties.

3. Click on Install on the Local Area Connection Properties dialog box.

4. Select Protocol from the Select Network Component dialog box. Click on Add.

5. In the Select Network Protocol dialog box, select Internet Protocol (TCP/IP). Click on OK.

6. Reboot.

Dynamic Host Configuration Protocol (DHCP) is a protocol that was designed to make the configuration of TCP/IP hosts much simpler. DHCP is a client/server protocol, where the DHCP client (a TCP/IP host) requests TCP/IP configuration information from a DHCP Server. The DHCP Server is configured by an administrator with scopes (which are a range of available IP addresses) along with other TCP/IP configuration items.

There are different items that can be configured via DHCP:

➤ IP Address

➤ Subnet Mask

➤ Default Gateway

➤ DNS Server IP Addresses

➤ WINS Server IP Addresses

If a DHCP Server is available on your network, you probably will use it to configure TCP/IP. Windows 2000 Professional defaults to obtaining an IP address automatically via DHCP (see Figure 16.4).

If you want to use a static IP address configuration, you must specify the configuration information manually. From the Internet Protocols (TCP/IP) Properties dialog box, select Use The Following IP Address and specify a valid IP address, subnet mask, and if in a routed environment, the default gateway IP address.

16

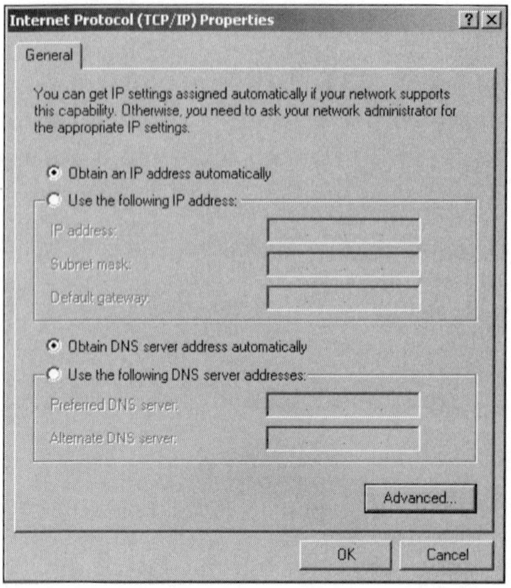

Figure 16.4 Internet Protocol (TCP/IP) Properties dialog box.

By selecting the Advanced button on the Internet Protocols (TCP/IP) Properties dialog box, you can configure more advanced TCP/IP settings.

Figure 16.5 displays the first tab displayed on the Advanced TCP/IP Settings. The IP Settings page is used to configure IP addresses, subnet masks, and default gateways.

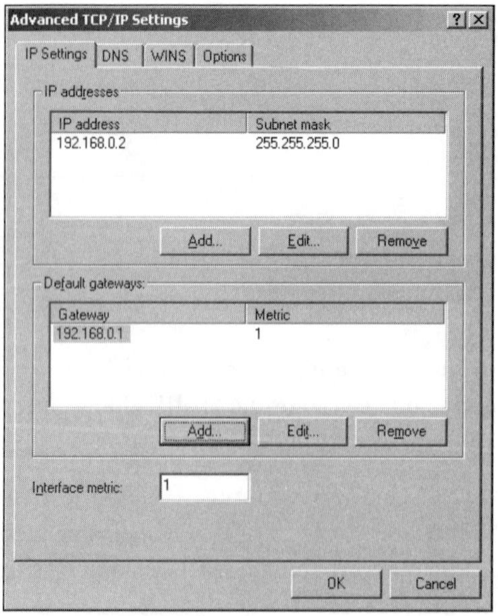

Figure 16.5 IP settings from the Advanced TCP/IP Settings dialog box.

To add an IP address and subnet mask for this network connection, click on the Add button and enter the IP address and the appropriate subnet mask. You can add more than one IP address in Windows 2000. A typical application for this would be a Web server using virtual Web sites. Each Web site would be bound to a separate IP address.

Finally, enter the default gateway address. Windows 2000 also allows you to specify a Metric for this interface. A Metric, sometimes referred to as a "hop," indicates the cost of using the routes associated with this interface. The Metric is placed in the Windows 2000 routing table. If there are multiple routes to a destination, the interface with the lowest Metric is chosen for the route. The default value for the Metric is 1.

The next tab that is displayed is the DNS page (see Figure 16.6). This page is used for configuring host name resolution.

The upper portion of the page is for specifying the IP addresses for DNS servers. These DNS servers resolve host names to IP addresses. For example, when you enter **www.microsoft.com** into your Web browser, your system queries a DNS server to resolve this address into an IP address. The DNS server may know the address, or it can query another DNS server to resolve the name. When the DNS server receives the response, it forwards the resolution to your system.

There are two types of DNS names: fully qualified and unqualified. A fully qualified domain name (FQDN) is the unique name of the host. It starts with the host name,

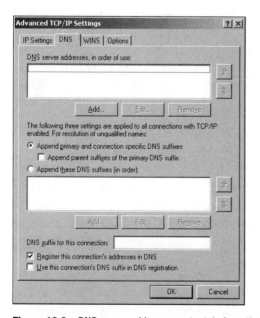

16

Figure 16.6   DNS server addresses entry tab, from the Advanced TCP/IP Settings dialog box.

includes all the domains, and finally ends at the root domain. For example, if your computer's host name is lab1 and it is located in the mycompany.com domain, the FQDN would be lab1.mycompany.com. The unqualified name is simply the host name without the domain names. So in the previous FQDN example, the unqualified name is simply lab1.

The other settings on the DNS page tell the system how to respond to unqualified name resolution requests and Dynamic DNS.

The first setting, Append Primary And Connection Specific DNS Suffixes, specifies that resolution of unqualified domain names be limited to the domain suffixes of the primary and connection specific suffixes. For example, your system's FQDN is lab1.mycompany.com. If you attempt to connect to lab5.mycomputer.com, you can simply specify lab5. Your system automatically appends your primary DNS suffix, mycomputer.com, to the request.

The next setting, Append These DNS Suffixes (in this order), specifies that resolution of unqualified domain names be limited to the specific DNS suffixes listed. The primary and connection specific suffixes are ignored. For example, if you add bldg1.mycompany.com and bldg2.mycompany.com to the list and type "ping lab3" at a command prompt, Windows 2000 queries for lab3.bldg1.mycompany.com and lab3.bldg2.mycompany.com.

You can specify a connection specific DNS suffix on this page as well by entering the DNS suffix in the DNS Suffix For This Connection text box.

The final two settings on this page refer to Dynamic DNS. Dynamic DNS allows a system to register its own host name in the DNS tables. Before Dynamic DNS, the host names had to be entered manually into the DNS tables by LAN administrators. To enable Dynamic DNS registration, select Register This Connection's Addresses In DNS. If you also specified a connection specific DNS suffix, select Use This Connection's DNS Suffix In DNS Registration to register that suffix as well.

The next tab is the WINS page (see Figure 16.7). This page is used for configuring NetBIOS name resolution.

The first portion of the WINS page is for specifying the IP addresses for WINS servers. A WINS server resolves NetBIOS names to IP addresses. For example, when you map a drive to a network share on another Windows 2000 machine, Windows 2000 queries the WINS server to resolve this address into an IP address.

If you are using an LMHOSTS file for NetBIOS resolution as well, enable LMHOSTS lookup.

The final option specifies whether NetBIOS resolution over TCP/IP will be used on this computer. This option is included because Windows 2000 relies on DNS for name resolution, not NetBIOS. If you are operating in a pure Windows 2000

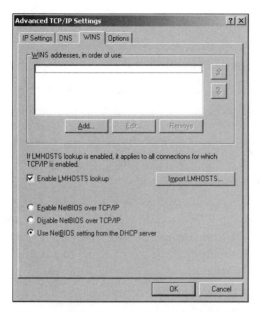

Figure 16.7   WINS server addresses from the Advanced TCP/IP Settings dialog box.

environment, you can disable NetBIOS resolution. However, it is important to realize that you may have applications that rely on NetBIOS. If you disable it, these applications will be broken. Refer to the applications documentation to determine if NetBIOS is required.

The final tab on Advanced TCP/IP Settings dialog box is for configuring optional components, such as IPSec and TCP/IP Filtering.

IP Security (IPSec) is a group of services and protocols that use cryptography to protect data. Typically used for L2TP-based VPNs, IPSec provides machine-level authentication and data encryption.

TCP/IP Filtering allows you to enable or disable specific TCP and UDP ports. This setting is used to secure TCP/IP traffic entering the computer by allowing or disallowing the processing of traffic on those ports.

NWLink (IPX/SPX)

NWLink is Microsoft's fully compatible version of the IPX/SPX protocol. IPX/SPX is a proprietary protocol designed for use in Novell NetWare-based networks. NetWare 4.x and earlier networks relied on IPX/SPX for communications. The latest version of NetWare, NetWare 5, is the first version that operates using TCP/IP as its primary network protocol.

NWLink is a routable network protocol that is suitable for any size network. The only caveat with NWLink is that it cannot be used for Internet connectivity.

16

To install NWLink, follow these steps:

1. Open the Network And Dial-Up Connection folder by selecting Start | Settings | Network And Dial-Up Connections.

2. Right-click on the desired Local Area Connection, and select Properties.

3. Click on Install on the Local Area Connection Properties dialog box.

4. Select Protocol from the Select Network Component dialog box. Click on Add.

5. In the Select Network Protocol dialog box, select NWLink. Click on OK.

6. Reboot.

Compared to TCP/IP, NWLink is a snap to implement and configure. There are only three configurable components in NWLink: internal network number, frametype, and external network number. NWLink uses these components to communicate with computers on the same logical network.

The internal network number is used for internal routing purposes—that is, among the network-related processes within the computer. It is only used if you are running an application, such as File and Print Services for NetWare. By default, Windows 2000 sets the internal network number to 00000000.

A frame is a logical contiguous group of bits. Frames form the data that is being transmitted on the network. The frametype specifies the structure of the frames. There are different frametypes depending on the networking media being used. Windows 2000 supports the following frametypes: Ethernet II, Ethernet 802.3, Ethernet 802.2, Ethernet 802.2 SNAP, 802.5, and 802.5 SNAP. Table 16.2 lists the network topologies and their supported frametypes.

In Windows 2000, the default setting for frametype is autodetect. When Windows 2000 is set to autodetect the frametype, it selects the first one detected and sets it to that frametype. Usually, this is sufficient for most networking implementations. However, some environments may have legacy equipment that require specific frametypes to be implemented. In this case, you must specify each frametype to be used. For example, if you are installing a Windows 2000 Professional workstation in an environment that uses both Ethernet 802.3 and Ethernet 802.2, you would need to specify both frametypes.

Table 16.2   Supported network topologies and frametypes.

Network Topology	Supported Frametypes
Ethernet	Ethernet II, Ethernet 802.3, Ethernet 802.2, Ethernet 802.2 SNAP
Token Ring	802.5 and 802.5 SNAP
FDDI	Ethernet 802.3, Ethernet 802.2, Ethernet 802.2 SNAP

The external network number is used for addressing and routing purposes. The external network number is associated with physical network adapters and networks. All computers on the same network that use a given frame type must have the same external network number to communicate with each other. The external network number must be unique to the IPX internetwork.

NetBEUI

NetBIOS Extended User Interface (NetBEUI) is one of the earliest network protocols available. NetBEUI is a simple protocol meant to be used in small networks with less than 200 computers, although in all actuality it is usually used in small workgroup environments with less than 10 computers. Because NetBEUI does not have any layer 3 components, it is non-routable. It is included with Windows 2000 for compatibility with legacy systems, such as LAN Manager and Windows for Workgroups. NetBEUI is also supported by the Windows 9x and Windows NT families of operating systems.

To install NetBEUI, follow these steps:

1. Open the Network And Dial-Up Connection folder by selecting Start | Settings | Network And Dial-Up Connections.

2. Right-click on the desired Local Area Connection, and select Properties.

3. Click on Install on the Local Area Connection Properties dialog box.

4. Select Protocol from the Select Network Component dialog box. Click on Add.

5. In the Select Network Protocol dialog box, select NetBEUI. Click on OK.

6. Reboot.

There isn't anything to configure with NetBEUI. It doesn't get any simpler than that!

Chapter Summary

This chapter covered many of the aspects of working with Windows 2000 Professional in a Windows network environment.

The chapter began with a discussion of the methods used to access network resources with Windows 2000 Professional. Windows 2000 can access and exploit many types of network resources including file and print servers, databases, messaging, application servers, intranets, and the Internet.

16

Windows 2000 includes many of the components that make network connectivity possible. These components include various networking protocols, such as TCP/IP, NWLink (IPX/SPX), DLC, AppleTalk, and NetBEUI. Networking protocols allow computers to communicate in exactly the same way as people use language to communicate. If two people speak English, they can communicate. If two computers speak TCP/IP, they can communicate.

Another essential networking component is the network client. A network client allows a computer to access network resources, such as file and print services. Windows 2000 ships with support for a number of different networks, including Client for Microsoft Networks and Client Services for NetWare Networks. Windows 2000 also supports, through add on packages, Unix (via Microsoft Windows Services for Unix 2) and Macintosh (via Windows 2000 Services for Macintosh).

A Microsoft Network uses the CIFS protocol to provide network access to file and printer shares. This protocol allows a client computer to open, read, write, and close a file on a file server.

Microsoft Networks support two types of network environments: Workgroups and Domains. Workgroups are peer-to-peer networks grouped logically, without a centralized security database. To access resources on the computers in a workgroup, you need a valid logon with each computer. A domain is a logical grouping of computers with a centralized security database. Windows 2000 Professional can be a member of a workgroup or a domain.

The process where a user, using a logon name and password, is validated by the security database is known as authentication. Windows 2000 supports two methods of authentication: NTLM for older Windows NT 4 domains and Kerberos for Windows 2000. Windows 2000 includes support for System Policies and Group Policies. System and Group Policies allow an administrator to specify use and computer configuration settings in the Registry. These settings help an administrator enforce and control a user's work environment. System Policies were first introduced in Windows NT 4. In Windows 2000, Group Policies have been expanded and have replaced the functionality of System Policies.

The chapter concluded with an overview of the three most popular network protocols used in Windows 2000: TCP/IP, NWLink, and NetBEUI.

Review Questions

1. Which of the following TCP/IP components cannot be configured via DHCP?

   a. IP Address

   b. Subnet Mask

   c. Default Gateway

   d. MAC Address

2. David Murphy has a user account in the domain mycompany.com. His user name is dmurphy. What is his UPN?

    a. dmurphy@mycompany.com

    b. .dmurphy.mycompany.com

    c. cn=dmurphy, dc=mycompany, dc=com

    d. dmurphy/mycompany.com

3. What is the default authentication method for Windows 2000?

    a. NTLM

    b. Kerberos v5

    c. Kerberos v4

    d. NTLM2000

4. In a domain-based network, a user needs only a single logon to access domain resources. True or false?

    a. True

    b. False

5. You are connecting a Windows 2000 Professional workstation to a Token Ring network that uses NWLink. What frametype should be specified?

    a. 802.5

    b. Ethernet 802.2

    c. Ethernet 802.5

    d. Ethernet 802.3

6. A WINS Server is used for what type of name resolution?

    a. IP address to NetBIOS name

    b. host name to IP address

    c. IP address to host name

    d. NetBIOS name to IP address

7. When configuring TCP/IP on a Windows 2000 Professional in a non-routed environment, what items need to be specified? [Check all correct answers]

    a. IP Address

    b. Subnet Mask

    c. Default Gateway

    d. DNS Server Address

16

8. To access resources on a NetWare network, what two components need to be installed? [Check all correct answers]

   a. NWLink

   b. Client Services for NetWare

   c. NetWare for Windows Networks

   d. TCP/IP

9. Which object uniquely identifies a user object in Active Directory?

   a. Relative Distinguished Name

   b. The UPN

   c. Distinguished Name

   d. SAM Account Name

10. To receive an IP address via DHCP, you select which of the following?

    a. Use DHCP For IP Addresses on the Control Panel

    b. Obtain An IP Address Automatically from Internet (TCP/IP) Protocol properties

    c. IPCONFIG /RELEASE from a command prompt

    d. Obtain An IP Address Automatically from the Network Control Panel

11. If a Windows 2000 Professional workstation is attempting to authenticate with a Windows NT 4 domain, what authentication method will it use?

    a. Kerberos

    b. Public Key Cryptology

    c. NTLM

    d. Domain

12. A DNS Server is used for what type of name resolution?

    a. IP address to NetBIOS name

    b. NetBIOS name to IP address

    c. host name to IP address

    d. computer name to IP address

13. Windows 2000 uses what protocol to open and close files on a Microsoft Network?

    a. TCP/IP

    b. NetBEUI

    c. NWLink

    d. CIFS

14. Windows 2000 Professional stores Group Policy objects in which location?

    a. Active Directory

    b. C:\WINNT

    c. %systemroot%\GroupPolicy

    d. % systemroot%\System32\GroupPolicy

15. Which groups can add a Windows 2000 Professional computer to a domain?

    a. Administrators

    b. Users

    c. Power Users

    d. Server Operators

16. Which network client is not supported by Windows 2000?

    a. Client for Microsoft Networks

    b. Client Services for NetWare

    c. Microsoft Windows Services for Unix 2

    d. Client Services for AS400

17. You are attempting to connect a Windows 2000 Professional computer to a network that uses NWLink as its networking protocol. Because of legacy applications, the network uses two frametypes, Ethernet 802.2 and Ethernet 802.3. Which frametypes need to be specified on the workstation?

    a. Ethernet 802.2

    b. AutoDetect

    c. Ethernet 802.3

    d. Ethernet 802.2 and Ethernet 802.3

18. A workgroup is a logical grouping of computers sharing a centralized security database. True or false?

    a. True

    b. False

19. What are the two types of logons found in Windows 2000? [Check all correct answers]

    a. SAM Account Name

    b. Relative Distinguished Name

    c. Distinguished Name

    d. UPN

16

20. Given the Distinguished Name of cn=MichaelGrift, ou=Lab5, ou=Research, dc=NewYork, dc=Pharmaco, dc=com, what is the Relative Distinguished Name?

   a. MichaelGrift@Pharmaco.com

   b. MichaelGrift

   c. Lab5

   d. MichaelGrift.Lab5.Research.NewYork@Pharmaco.Com

Real-World Projects

You have just received your first Windows 2000 Professional computer. After unpacking the computer, you need to attach and configure it to your company's Windows network.

The corporate network uses TCP/IP. After talking with the network administrator, you find out that at this time, the corporation has not implemented DHCP. The network administrator gives you the following information:

```
IP address              10.0.26.5
Subnet Mask             255.0.0.0
Default Gateway         10.0.0.1
Preferred DNS Server    10.0.0.10
Alternate DNS Server    10.0.0.11
Primary WINS Server     10.0.0.20
Secondary WINS Server   10.0.0.21
```

Project 16.1

To configure TCP/IP in Windows 2000 Professional:

1. Select Run|Settings|Control Panel, and click on Network And Dial-Up Connections.

2. Right-click on Local Area Connection and select Properties.

3. Select Internet Protocol (TCP/IP), and then select Properties. The Internet Protocol (TCP/IP) Properties dialog box is displayed.

4. Select Use The Following IP Address. For IP address, enter "10.0.26.5". Enter "255.0.0.0" as the subnet mask and "10.0.0.1" as the default gateway.

5. Select Use The Following DNS Server Addresses. For the Preferred DNS Server, enter "10.0.0.10", and for the Alternate DNS Server, enter "10.0.0.11".

6. Click on the Advanced button to open the Advanced TCP/IP Properties dialog box.

7. Select the WINS tab to display the WINS properties page.

8. Click on Add to enter a WINS Server IP address. Enter "10.0.0.20", and click on Add. Click on Add again to enter the other WINS Server IP address. Enter "10.0.0.21", and click on Add.

9. On the same tab, select Enable NetBIOS Over TCP/IP.

10. Click on OK to close the Advanced TCP/IP Properties dialog box.

11. Click on OK to close the Internet Protocol (TCP/IP) Properties dialog box.

12. Click on OK to close the Local Area Connection Properties dialog box.

After you configure TCP/IP, it's time to have your computer join the corporation's domain. To join a domain, the account you are using must be a member of the Domain Admins group or have been granted the Add A Machine To The Domain user right.

You call the network administrator to let him know that you need to add the computer to the domain. He tells you that the domain name is CorpDomain. There is a special user account called AddMachine with the password AddMore. The account has the Add A Machine To The Domain user right.

Project 16.2
To join a domain with Windows 2000 Professional:

1. Right-click on My Computer, and then select Properties.

2. Click on the Network Identification tab. Select Properties.

3. The Identification Changes dialog box is displayed. In the Member Of section, select Domain.

4. Enter "CorpDomain" as the name of the domain.

5. When prompted, enter "AddMachine" as the user account and "AddMore" as the password. Click on OK.

6. You should get a message welcoming you to the domain. Click on OK.

7. Click on OK to close the Identification Changes dialog box.

8. Click on OK to close the System Properties dialog box.

9. Click on Yes to restart the computer.

16

After you have joined CorpDomain, you want to map some network drives to shares on servers named CorpServer1 and CorpServer2. The following list contains the shares and their corresponding drive mappings:

```
H:      \\CorpServer1\Data
K:      \\CorpServer1\Finance
Y:      \\CorpServer2\Marketing
```

Project 16.3

To map network drives with Windows 2000 Professional:

1. Right-click on My Network Places, and then select Map Network Drives.

2. Select H: from the Drive Letter drop-down list. Type "\\CorpServer1\Data" in the folder. If needed, you can also browse the network.

3. Click on Finish.

4. Repeat the process for the remaining network drives.

CHAPTER SEVENTEEN

The Novell NetWare Environment

After completing this chapter, you will be able to:

✓ Identify the different members of the NetWare family

✓ Configure IPX

✓ Configure the client for NetWare networks

✓ Access NetWare resources

✓ Troubleshoot NetWare connectivity problems

Novell NetWare, once a powerhouse in the world of local area networks (LANs), is a family of robust network operating systems. Novell was one of the first companies to realize that organizations could benefit greatly by pooling their resources. Connecting a group of PCs together on a LAN, users were able to share data and printers quickly and easily.

An Overview of Novell NetWare

NetWare has always been based on a dedicated PC-based server. The first version of NetWare, released in 1984, ran on an IBM PC XT using the Intel 8086 processor. It was a multitasking operating system, so it was perfect for LANs, where it could handle multiple connections and requests simultaneously. NetWare, a centralized server-based network operating system (NOS), cannot be used as a workstation operating system.

By creating a NOS that provided file and print services in a secure fashion, Novell quickly cornered the networking market. Throughout the years, Novell continued to enhance NetWare, further pushing the envelope. Many of the newer NOSs, including Windows NT and Windows 2000, owe their very existence to the path forged by Novell NetWare.

Novell NetWare 3.12

In 1993, Novell introduced NetWare 3.12, which was a powerful, standalone server NOS that provided file, print, and application services. NetWare 3.12 used a concept known as the *Bindery*. This contained all of the user and group accounts, as well as users' passwords and trustee assignments. *Trustee assignments* are comparable to access control lists (ACLs) in Windows 2000. They provide the access list to server objects such as files, directories, print queues, and so on. Internet Protocol Exchange/ Sequenced Packet Exchange (IPX/SPX) was the default network protocol for NetWare 3. 12. IPX/SPX is a proprietary network protocol, designed by Novell.

All NetWare 3.12 servers, because they were standalone, contained their own Bindery. In other words, if a user wanted to access files on two separate NetWare 3.12 servers, he or she would need a user account on each server. This is analogous to the *Workgroup* network type in Windows 2000, where each computer manages its own local security database. As networks grew, the Bindery approach to network security became increasingly unwieldy. Thus, Novell went back to the drawing board.

Novell NetWare 4.x

With NetWare 4.x, Novell unveiled a new concept in networking: the directory service. NetWare Directory Service (NDS) created a global directory of network objects. These network objects included users, groups, servers, volumes, Organizational Units (OUs), and so on. NDS allowed a user to have a single user account, through which he could access any network resources.

NDS organizes these objects using a tree-style architecture. An NDS tree is divided into two object types: containers and leaf objects. *Container objects* are used to organize resources. An NDS tree is usually divided into OUs (container objects that can hold other OUs or leaf objects) that represent a group of resources or geographic locations. For example, an NDS tree may have OUs that represent major cities such as New York, Chicago, Philadelphia, and Los Angeles. Any resources, such as servers, volumes, and printers, located in those cities would be placed in the OU. These resources are known as *Leaf objects.* Items such as user accounts, servers, volumes, printers, and so on are considered Leaf objects.

In NDS, a user logs in to the NDS tree, not in to an individual server. When logging in, the user needs to specify a *default context*, which points to the location in the NDS tree (the container object) where the user's user object is. For example, if a user account called Joe is located in an OU called Users and Users is located in the Philadelphia OU, Joe's default context is USERS.PHILADELPHIA.

All the NDS objects are stored in a database, which is then replicated to all servers within the tree. By replicating the database, NDS increases both the performance of user login authentication and fault tolerance. The database is replicated to all servers, so if any server goes down, users can still log in to the tree. Therefore, the tree won't go down.

Although NDS greatly improved the NetWare operating system, NetWare still suffered from a major drawback: it was dependent on IPX/SPX. With the growing popularity of the Internet and open standards such as Transmission Control Protocol/Internet Protocol (TCP/IP), NetWare's dependence on a proprietary protocol such as IPX/SPX quickly became a liability. Microsoft, realizing the importance of the Internet, steered its NOSs, such as Windows 95 and Windows NT, toward adopting TCP/IP. This gave Microsoft a toehold against the supremacy of NetWare in the NOS market.

So again, Novell went back to the drawing board.

Novell NetWare 5.x

In 1999, Novell introduced the latest addition to the NetWare family; NetWare 5.x. NetWare 5.x continued the formidable advancement that Novell had achieved with NDS. In NetWare 5.x, NDS was improved with the capability to hold over a billion objects! For an organization with a large, enterprise network, this new version of NDS provided plenty of capacity for growth and change.

17

More important, NetWare 5.x was completely redesigned to use TCP/IP as its core network protocol. This allows NetWare 5.x servers to be used as Web and FTP servers on the Internet. It also allowed many corporate networks to run more efficiently with only one network protocol, TCP/IP.

Although NetWare may have lost its market dominance to Windows NT, it is still widely used in many businesses and organizations. The jury is still out on NetWare 5.x. It is being deployed, although not at a blistering pace. NetWare 4.x is the most popular version of NetWare, and, even though NetWare 3.12 is older, many organizations still use it. This is why we cover Windows 2000 Professional in a NetWare environment. Odds are, you will need to connect a Windows 2000 Professional computer to a NetWare network at some point in your career.

The IPX/SPX Protocol Suite

Before delving into the client components, let's spend some time detailing the protocol suite that NetWare depends upon for communication. The IPX/SPX protocol suite is a descendant of another protocol, Xerox Network Systems (XNS). This protocol was developed by the Xerox Corporation as a client/server protocol. IPX/SPX supports a number of different network media such as Ethernet/Institute of Electrical and Electronics Engineers (IEEE) 802.3, Token Ring, and Fiber Distributed Data Interface (FDDI).

The protocol suite itself is comprised of a number of protocols that together form the functionality required by the NetWare operating system. When you install NWLink (described later in this chapter) on Windows 2000 Professional, only some of these protocols (IPX and SPX) are implemented. The others are needed only for server and routing functions.

IPX

IPX is a network protocol that operates on Layer 3 of the Open System Interconnection (OSI) Model. This protocol makes it possible for packets to be routed across an internetwork. It is a connectionless protocol, meaning that it does not require the use of a virtual circuit for connectivity. It does not provide any error correction or flow control. IPX is analogous to the IP protocol found in the TCP/IP protocol suite.

Network addressing with IPX is represented in a hexadecimal format and, like IP, consists of two parts: the IPX network number and the node number. The IPX *network number* is 32 bits long and is assigned by the network administrator. The *node number* is 48 bits long and is derived from the network adapter's media access control (MAC) address. As a result of using the MAC address for the node number, IPX does not need to use any type of address translation. IP, on the other hand, requires the use of another protocol, Address Resolution Protocol (ARP).

SPX

SPX is a connection-oriented protocol located on Layer 4 of the OSI Model. SPX is considered a reliable protocol because it requests that missing datagrams be retransmitted. SPX is typically used for applications that require a continuous connection between the client and server.

SAP

Service Advertising Protocol (SAP) is used by network devices to advertise the services they provide. Devices such as file servers and print services use this protocol. These devices send out SAP advertisements every 60 seconds. The services being advertised are represented by a SAP identifier, a hexadecimal number. For example, a file server has a SAP identifier of 4, while a print server has a SAP identifier of 7.

RIP

Routing Information Protocol (RIP) is used for route and router discovery with IPX. RIP is used in internetworks. Without RIP, an administrator would need to configure static routes for each logical network. With RIP, a router will send its routing table to its neighbors every 30 seconds. This allows a router or server to build a route table to determine where to forward IPX packets.

Operating Windows 2000 and NetWare Together

When using Windows 2000 Professional on a NetWare network, you have two choices for connectivity. First, you can use Client Service for NetWare, a network component that is installed on each workstation. Once it is installed, the Windows 2000 Professional computer can access NetWare resources on the network. This option gives you the best performance and speed when accessing NetWare resources.

Another alternative is to install Gateway (and Client) Service for NetWare. This network component is installed on a Windows 2000 server. It's a gateway to NetWare servers through which Windows 2000 clients can access NetWare resources. This can be a useful alternative. If you don't want to install Client Service for NetWare on every Windows 2000 machine, you need only install Gateway (and Client) Service for NetWare on one Windows 2000 server. The downside of this approach is that performance takes a hit. It creates a funnel effect because the Windows 2000 server running the gateway must host all connections to NetWare resources.

NWLink (IPX/SPX)

Regardless of which client you decide to use, you need to use NWLink as the network protocol. Although Microsoft did their best to confuse everyone by referring to IPX/SPX as NWLink, make no mistake; they are one in the same. NWLink is

17

simply Microsoft's implementation of IPX/SPX. Let's spend a few moments discussing the different parameters in NWLink that you need to configure.

Internal Network Numbers

The *internal network number* is used for internal routing purposes (among the network-related processes within the computer). This is used only if you are running an application such as File And Print Services for NetWare. By default, Windows 2000 sets the internal network number to 00000000. Normally, the internal network number does not need to be changed.

Frametypes

A *frame* is a logical contiguous group of bits. These form the data that is being transmitted on the network. The *frametype* specifies the structure of the frames. There are different frametypes depending on the networking medium being used. Windows 2000 supports the following frametypes: Ethernet II, Ethernet 802.3, Ethernet 802.2, Ethernet 802.2 SNAP, 802.5, and 802.5 SNAP. Table 17.1 lists the network topologies and their supported frametypes.

On Ethernet, NetWare uses a couple of different frametypes, depending on the version of NetWare. NetWare 3.11 and earlier (that's not a typo; Novell changed the default frametype at NetWare 3.12!) use Ethernet 802.3. In NetWare 3.12 and later, Novell decided to use Ethernet 802.2. Also, remember—of course—that NetWare 5.x uses TCP/IP as the default network protocol, so this discussion does not apply unless it is running IPX/SPX.

In Windows 2000, the default setting for Frametype is Autodetect. When Windows 2000 is set to autodetect the frametype, it selects the first one detected and sets it to that frametype. Usually, this is sufficient for most networking implementations. However, some environments may have legacy equipment that requires specific frametypes to be implemented. In this case, you must specify each frametype to be used. For example, if you are installing a Windows 2000 Professional workstation in an environment that uses both Ethernet 802.3 and Ethernet 802.2, you must specify both frametypes.

External Network Numbers

The *external network number* is used for addressing and routing purposes. It is associated with physical network adapters and networks. All computers on the same

Table 17.1   Supported network topologies and frametypes.

Network Topology	Supported Frametypes
Ethernet	Ethernet II, Ethernet 802.3, Ethernet 802.2, and Ethernet 802.2 SNAP
Token Ring	802.5 and 802.5 SNAP
FDDI	Ethernet 802.3, Ethernet 802.2, and Ethernet 802.2 SNAP

network that use a given frametype must have the same external network number to communicate with each other. The external network number must be unique to the IPX internetwork. This is analogous to the network portion of an IP address.

Client Service for NetWare

Client Service for NetWare is the client component installed on a Windows 2000 Professional computer that allows it to access NetWare resources. Client Service for NetWare accomplishes this by allowing the Windows 2000 Professional computer to communicate directly with the NetWare server using the NetWare Core Protocol (NCP). NCP facilitates the opening, closing, writing, and so on of files between the client and server, as shown in Figure 17.1.

When you are installing Client Service for NetWare, you must configure a number of items, discussed in the next few sections.

Preferred Server or Default Tree and Context

In order to access NetWare resources, the user needs to be authenticated. The first component, Preferred Server or Default Tree and Context, is used for authentication to the NetWare server (in bindery-mode) or the NDS tree.

Preferred Server is used when you are authenticating to a NetWare server running in bindery-mode. NetWare 3.12 and earlier rely on the Bindery for user authentication. Later versions of NetWare, including NetWare 5.x, can also run in bind-

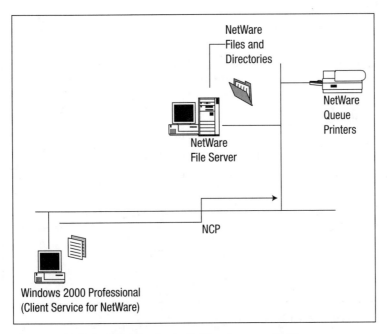

Figure 17.1 Using Client Service for NetWare to access NetWare resources.

17

ery-mode. Regardless of the version of NetWare, if it's running in bindery-mode, you need to specify a Preferred Server.

Default Tree and Context is used when you are authenticating to an NDS tree. NetWare 4.x and later support NDS for user authentication. The Default Tree is simply the name of the NDS tree to which you want to be authenticated. The Context is the location in the NDS tree where your user account is located. Figure 17.2 helps illustrate the concept of the Default Tree and Context.

NDS is always described as an upside-down tree. At the top is the root object of the tree. This is the NDS tree's name. In Figure 17.2, the tree's name is SOMECO. This would be entered as the Default Tree. Spreading out below the root object are various OUs. We need to determine the Context for the user account JEFFT. In Figure 17.2, JEFFT is located in ou=design.ou=newyork.ou=east.o=someco. Specifying the Context like this is known as specifying the *typefull name format*. The o= type in the typefull name signifies the NDS tree name. A much simpler form is the *typeless name format*, which would be .design.newyork.east.someco.

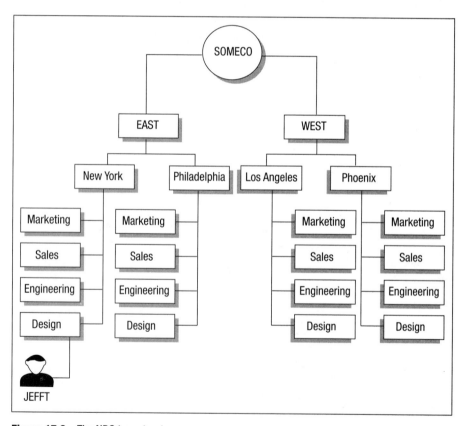

Figure 17.2 The NDS tree structure.

Run Login Script

A NetWare login script, much like a Windows 2000 logon script, is a series of commands that are used to configure a user's environment. The login script is executed
each time the user logs in. A login script is used to set up network and search-drive
mappings, printers, and environment variables. It can also be used to distribute
software updates, such as the latest virus definitions for antivirus software.

If you want the NetWare login script to execute on a Windows 2000 Professional
computer with Client Service for NetWare installed, simply check the radio button
for Run Login Script.

Installing Client Service for NetWare

To install Client Service for NetWare, follow these steps:

1. Open the Network And Dial-Up Connections folder (Start | Settings | Network
   And Dial-Up Connections).

2. Right-click on Local Area Connection. Select Properties.

3. Click on Install.

4. The Select Network Component Type dialog box is displayed. Select Client
   and click on Add.

5. The Select Network Client dialog box is displayed. Select Client Service For
   NetWare. Click on OK.

6. Windows 2000 Professional now installs Client Service for NetWare. NWLink
   is also installed (if it wasn't previously).

7. The Select NetWare Logon dialog box is displayed.

   If you are connecting to a NetWare server that is running in bindery-mode,
   select Preferred Server. From the drop-down list, select the NetWare server
   where your user account is located. Windows 2000 Professional generates this
   list by compiling what is known as a SAP list. NetWare servers use SAP broadcasts via IPX to advertise their file and print services.

   If you are connecting to a NetWare server that is running NDS, select Default
   Tree And Context. Enter the name of the Tree and the Context where your
   user account is located.

   Finally, if you wish to execute the NetWare login script, select Run Login Script.

8. Click on OK to save your settings.

17

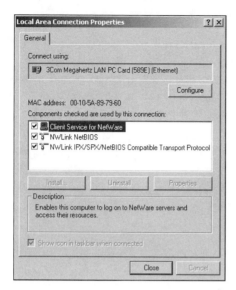

Figure 17.3   Client Service for NetWare.

Figure 17.3 shows that the following components were added after these eight steps were completed:

➤ Client Service for NetWare

➤ NWLink NetBIOS

➤ NWLink IPX/SPX/NetBIOS Compatible Transport Protocol

Gateway (and Client) Service for NetWare

Gateway (and Client) Service for NetWare allows a Windows 2000 server to act as a gateway to NetWare resources on the network. This allows Windows 2000 Professional computers to access NetWare resources without having Client Services for NetWare installed. Figure 17.4 illustrates how Gateway (and Client) Service for NetWare operates on a network.

The gateway translates Common Internet File System (CIFS) requests sent by Windows 2000 computers into NCP requests that the NetWare servers understand. The NetWare servers then respond with NCP requests to the Windows 2000 server that hosts the gateway. The gateway translates the NCP requests back into CIFS requests and sends them to the Windows 2000 Professional computers, as shown in Figure 17.5.

Using the gateway alleviates many of the concerns about supporting multiple clients on workstations. The technical staff needs to be trained to support Client for Microsoft Networks as well as Client Service for NetWare. With the gateway, most of the staff needs to support only Client for Microsoft Networks. Another more

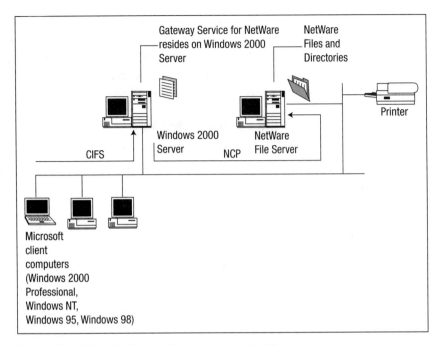

Figure 17.4   Using the Gateway Service to access NetWare resources.

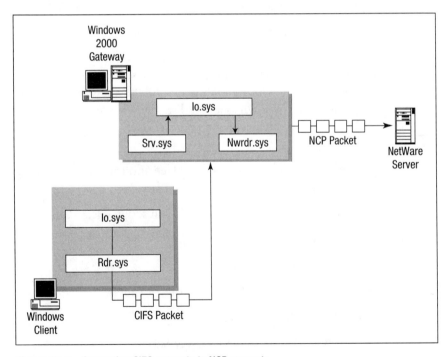

Figure 17.5   Converting CIFS requests to NCP requests.

17

critical concern is supporting multiple network protocols on the network infrastructure. Windows 2000 Professional computers that are running both clients need TCP/IP to connect to Microsoft Network resources and NWLink to connect to NetWare resources. Using both of these may cause the network to take a performance hit if the network infrastructure has limited bandwidth.

Installing Gateway (and Client) Service for NetWare

To install Gateway and Client Service for NetWare, follow these steps:

1. Open the Network And Dial-Up Connections folder (select Start | Settings | Network And Dial-Up Connections).

2. Right-click on Local Area Connection. Select Properties.

3. Click on Install.

4. The Select Network Component Type dialog box is displayed. Select Client and click on Add.

5. The Select Network Client dialog box is displayed. Select Gateway (And Client) Service For NetWare. Click on OK.

6. The Windows 2000 server now installs Gateway (and Client) Service for NetWare. NWLink is also installed (if it wasn't previously installed).

7. The Select NetWare Logon dialog box is displayed.

   If you are connecting to a NetWare server that is running in bindery-mode, select Preferred Server. From the drop-down list, select the NetWare server where your user account is located. Windows 2000 Professional generates this list by compiling what is known as a SAP list. NetWare servers use SAP broadcasts via IPX to advertise their file and print services.

   If you are connecting to a NetWare server that is running NDS, select Default Tree And Context. Enter the name of the Tree and the Context where your user account is located.

   Finally, if you want to execute the NetWare login script, select Run Login Script.

8. Click on OK to save your settings.

9. Reboot your computer if prompted.

10. Open the Control Panel (Start | Settings | Control Panel).

11. Double-click on the GSNW applet.

12. Click on Gateway to configure the Gateway Service.

13. Click on Enable Gateway to start the Gateway Service.

14. In Gateway Account, enter the NetWare user account you created. Also, enter and confirm the password for the user account.

15. Click on Add to begin mapping network drives to NetWare volumes.

16. The New Share dialog box is displayed. Enter the Share Name. This is the name that Windows 2000 Professional computers see when browsing the Windows 2000 server that hosts the gateway.

17. Enter the Network Path to the NetWare resource. The path needs to be entered in Uniform Naming Convention (UNC) format. For example, if you want to access the volume DATA on a NetWare 3.12 server named NW312, the UNC path is \\NW312\DATA.

18. From the drop-down list, select the local drive letter that you want to map the drive to. Click on OK to save the settings.

19. Click on OK to close the Configure Gateway dialog box.

20. Click on OK to close the Gateway Service For NetWare dialog box.

Configuring Gateway (and Client) Service for NetWare

Before actually configuring Gateway (and Client) Service for NetWare on the Windows 2000 server, you need to prepare the NetWare server or NDS tree.

First, create a unique NetWare user account using either NetWare Administrator (NetWare 4.x or later) or SYSCON (NetWare 3.12 or earlier). The gateway uses this account to authenticate to the NetWare network. The password for this account must match the password used to configure the gateway.

Next, create a unique NetWare group called NTGATEWAY. Assign the appropriate trustee assignments for the NTGATEWAY group to any NetWare resources to which the gateway will provide access. Make the NetWare user account created in the preceding paragraph a member of the NTGATEWAY group.

The initial configuration of the Gateway (and Client) Service for NetWare is exactly like that of the Client Service for NetWare (you need to configure the client with Preferred Server or Default Tree and Context). Using this and the NetWare user account authenticates the gateway with NetWare resources.

Once the gateway is authenticated, you can configure the gateway to host connections to NetWare resources. Configuring the gateway is relatively simple. The Windows 2000 server that is running the gateway maps one of its drives to a NetWare volume. The mapped drive is then shared on the Microsoft Network. Windows 2000 Professional computers see the share as a resource on the Windows 2000 server, although it is actually a volume located on a NetWare server.

17

Accessing NetWare Resources

After you have installed Client Service for NetWare, accessing NetWare resources is a lot like accessing resources on Microsoft networks. Many of the NetWare utilities have functional equivalents in Windows 2000. Table 17.2 lists some of the NetWare utilities and their Windows 2000 counterparts.

As you can see, most of the functionality for NetWare networks can be accomplished by using the **net** command in Windows 2000. You can also use My Network Places or the Add Printer Wizard to browse and connect to NetWare file and print servers.

Accessing NetWare Resources

To access NetWare files, folders, printers, and volumes, simply map a network drive to the resource. You can accomplish this either via My Network Places or by using the **net use** command at a command prompt.

To connect to a volume via My Network Places, follow these steps:

1. Double-click on My Network Places.

2. Double-click on Entire Network, and then double-click on NetWare or Compatible Network.

3. Browse through the NetWare network to locate the volume to which you want to map a drive. When you have located it, right-click on the volume and select Map Network Drive. Select an available drive letter from the drop-down list and click on OK.

To connect to a volume via the **net use** command, follow these steps:

1. Open a command prompt (click on Start|Run, type "cmd", and then press Enter).

2. Type "net use [*drive_letter*]: *Servername**Resourcename*".

Here is a description of the above syntax:

Table 17.2   NetWare utilities and their Windows 2000 counterparts.

Task	NetWare Utility	Windows 2000 Counterpart
View NetWare resources on the network	SLIST	**net view /network:nw**
Log in and log off the NetWare network	ATTACH, LOGIN, or LOGOUT	**net use**
Map network drives to NetWare volumes	MAP	**net use**
Map a local printer port to a NetWare printer	CAPTURE	**net use**
View current logon and configuration	WHOAMI	**net config workstation** or **net config server**

➤ *[drive_letter]*—The letter of the local drive to be mapped to the volume

➤ *Servername*—The name of the NetWare server that contains the volume

➤ *Resourcename*—The name of the volume or print queue

For example, if you want to map drive Z: to the volume MYDATA on the NetWare server PRODUCT, you can enter "net use Z: \\PRODUCT\ **MYDATA**".

Accessing NetWare Print Queues

To access NetWare printers, you can use the Add Printer Wizard or the **net use** command.

Using the Add Printer Wizard, take these steps:

1. Open the Printer folder (Start|Settings|Printers).

2. Double-click on Add Printer to start the Add Printer Wizard. Click on Next.

3. Click on Network Printer. Click on Next.

4. Type the UNC path to the network printer, or click on Next to browse the network.

5. Click on Next to finish the Add Printer Wizard.

Using the **net use** command, follow these steps:

1. Open a command prompt (click on Start|Run, type "cmd", and then press Enter).

2. Type "net use *[lpt_port]*: *Servername**Printer*".

Here is a description of the above syntax:

➤ *[lpt_port]*—The lpt port (e.g., LPT1, LPT2) to be mapped to the printer

➤ *Servername*—The name of the NetWare print server

➤ *Printer*—The name of the printer

Troubleshooting NetWare Problems

Connecting Windows 2000 Professional computers to Novell NetWare servers is a relatively simple task. However, something inevitably goes wrong, and as an administrator, you must diagnose and fix whatever problems pop up. This section reviews some of the areas where connectivity problems tend to arise.

17

Are Client Service for NetWare and NWLink Installed?

Always remember to start with the simplest solution when troubleshooting. If a user cannot access NetWare resources, verify that Client Service for NetWare and NWLink are installed. To do so, first, open the Local Area Connection Properties dialog box and visually inspect that these two components are installed. If they are not installed, go through the installation procedure described in the previous "Installing Client Service for NetWare" section in this chapter.

Next, check that the Client Service for NetWare service is started by following these steps:

1. Open the Services applet (Start | Programs | Administrative Tools | Services).

2. Find Client Service For NetWare and verify that it says Started Under The Status Column.

3. If it isn't started, right-click on the service and select Start.

Is NWLink Configured Correctly?

Remember that in order for two computers to communicate via NWLink, they must both be using the same frametype and external network number. Novell NetWare 3.11 and earlier use Ethernet 802.3 as their default frametype. NetWare 3.12 and later use Ethernet 802.2. If you are connecting to either of these versions of NetWare, you can leave the Frame Type field as Autodetect. However, if you need to connect to servers that are using both frametypes, you must manually add both Ethernet 802.2 and Ethernet 802.3.

You must also verify that the external network number matches the external network number configured on the NetWare servers.

Is the Preferred Server or Default Tree and Context Correct?

In order to authenticate to the NetWare network, you must configure Client Service for NetWare for the Preferred Server or Default Tree and Context. If you are connecting to a NetWare server that supports bindery-mode, select the Preferred Server whose Bindery contains your NetWare user account.

If you are connecting to a NetWare 4.x or later server running NDS, enter the name of the Default Tree and specify the Context where your NetWare user account is located.

Chapter Summary

This chapter covered many aspects of working with Windows 2000 Professional in a Novell NetWare environment. Novell NetWare, once the undisputed market leader in LAN technology, is a powerful and versatile NOS. NetWare comes in three flavors that all operate in a centralized server architecture.

NetWare 3.12 is deployed as a standalone server NOS that provides fast and efficient file, print, and application services. This version of NetWare uses what is known as the Bindery, which contains all user and group accounts as well as passwords and trustee assignments.

With NetWare 4.x, Novell introduced a new concept in local area networking: the directory service. NDS created a global directory of network objects, which is then replicated and distributed among all NetWare 4.x servers. This type of architecture improved authentication speed and fault tolerance.

The architecture of NDS is known as a tree. Objects in an NDS tree can be one of two types: container or leaf. There are two container-type objects: an organization (O) object that represents the top-level of the NDS tree and an OU. Container objects can contain other OUs or leaf objects. Leaf objects represent actual resources, such as users, groups, servers, or printers, on the network.

NetWare 5.x is the first version of NetWare to not rely on IPX/SPX as its network protocol. It relies on the network protocol that built the Internet: TCP/IP. NetWare 5.x also introduced an improved version of NDS that could support a billion objects in the tree.

IPX/SPX was the default network protocol for NetWare 3.12 and NetWare 4.x. It is a proprietary network protocol whose predecessor, XNS, was developed by Xerox. IPX/SPX is a routable network protocol, meaning that you can develop and deploy large internetworks. NWLink is Microsoft's implementation of IPX/SPX.

When needing to interconnect NetWare networks with Windows 2000, a network designer has two choices: use Client Service for NetWare or Gateway (and Client) Service for NetWare.

Client Service for NetWare is installed on a Windows 2000 Professional computer. The client, along with NWLink, gives the workstation access to NetWare resources on the network. This configuration gives the workstation its best network performance.

Gateway (and Client) Service for NetWare takes a different approach, installing the gateway on a Windows 2000 server. Windows 2000 clients can then access NetWare resources. The gateway accomplishes this by converting CIFS requests sent by Windows 2000 clients into NCP requests that the NetWare servers understand. The NetWare servers respond by using NCP, which the gateway converts back into

17

CIFS. The gateway then sends the requested data to the Windows 2000 clients. This solution eliminates the need to install two clients and two network protocols on the Windows 2000 workstations. The downside of this solution is that it does not perform as well as Client Service for NetWare because all workstations are sharing the single gateway connection.

Review Questions

1. When you are configuring Gateway (and Client) Service for NetWare, what item is required?

   a. A valid NetWare user account that is a member of the NTGATEWAY group on NetWare

   b. A valid NetWare user account that is a member of the NTGATEWAY group on Windows 2000

   c. A valid Windows 2000 user account that is a member of the NTGATEWAY group on Windows 2000

   d. A valid Windows 2000 user account that is a member of the NTGATEWAY group on NetWare

2. NetWare 3.12 is fault tolerant because the Bindery is replicated and distributed to all NetWare 3.12 servers on the network.

   a. True

   b. False

3. What represents the location of a user account in NDS?

   a. Login

   b. Common Context

   c. Default Tree

   d. Context

4. When you are connecting to a NetWare 3.12 server, what two network components need to be installed on a Windows 2000 Professional workstation? [Check all correct answers]

   a. Client Service for NetWare

   b. Client for Microsoft Networks

   c. TCP/IP

   d. NWLink

5. You need to connect to the NetWare 5.x server, DATASRV. This server is using a Bindery context for user authentication. How does Client Service for NetWare need to be configured?

   a. Preferred Server

   b. Default Tree

   c. Context

   d. NetWare 5 Context

6. You are installing Gateway (and Client) Service for NetWare. The gateway needs to be configured to access resources on NetWare 3.11, NetWare 3.12, and NetWare 4.x servers. How does the frametype for NWLink need to be configured? [Check all correct answers]

   a. Autodetect

   b. Ethernet 802.2

   c. Ethernet 802.3

   d. Autoswitch

7. What is the name of the NetWare group that Gateway (and Client) Service for NetWare uses?

   a. NTGATEWAY

   b. NWGATEWAY

   c. NSGATEWAY

   d. NMGATEWAY

8. You use a DOS application that prints to the LPT1 printer port. Unfortunately, you cannot upgrade this application because the company that produced it went out of business. You need print jobs from this application to go to a NetWare printer named PRT1 on NetWare server PRINTSRV. What command do you use?

   a. **capture LPT1: \\PRINTSRV\PRT1**

   b. **map LPT1: \\PRINTSRV\PRT1**

   c. **net use LPT1: \\PRINTSRV\PRT1**

   d. **LPT1:=\\PRINTSRV\PRT1**

9. When you are installing Gateway (and Client) Service for NetWare, all Windows 2000 Professional workstations need to install NWLink as well. True or False?

   a. True

   b. False

17

10. The internal network number normally does not need to be changed. True or False?

    a. True

    b. False

11. In Windows 2000, what command allows you to map the network drive Y: to the volume DATASTORE on NetWare 3.12 server NW312?

    a. **net use \\nw312\datastore Y:**

    b. **net use Y: nw312\\datastore**

    c. **net use Y: \\nw312\datastore**

    d. **map root Y: nw312:datastore**

12. You need to install a Windows 2000 Professional workstation on IPX subnet B4, which contains no NetWare servers. The NetWare servers are located on IPX subnet B1. What do you need to set the external network number to for NWLink?

    a. B4

    b. B1

    c. B★

    d. Autodetect

13. When you are connecting to a NetWare 3.12 server, what needs to be configured on Client Service for NetWare?

    a. Default Tree and Context

    b. Default Context

    c. Preferred Server

    d. Default Tree

14. What did Novell first introduce with the NetWare 4.x operating system?

    a. TCP/IP

    b. NDS

    c. Bindery

    d. NetBIOS support

15. What is the name of the object that stores all user and group accounts, passwords, and trustee assignments in Novell NetWare 3.12?

    a. XNS

    b. NDS

    c. Bindery

    d. Ethernet 802.2

16. Your user account is DAVIDS. Your account is located in an OU named ENGINEERING, which itself is located in another OU named PARIS. The NDS tree is named SOMECO. What is your typefull Context?

    a. ou=ENGINEERING.ou=PARIS.o=SOMECO

    b. cn=DAVIDS.ou=ENGINEERING.ou=PARIS.o=SOMECO

    c. .ENGINEERING.PARIS.SOMECO

    d. DAVIDS.ENGINEERING.PARIS.SOMECO

17. You are the network administrator for a large corporation. Your company has recently acquired a smaller company whose network uses NetWare 4.x servers. The management of your company wants employees to access the data on the NetWare servers; however, it does not want another network client deployed. What should you do?

    a. Install only Client Service for NetWare on workstations that require access.

    b. Install a Windows 2000 Professional computer with Gateway (and Client) Service for NetWare.

    c. Install a Windows 2000 server with Gateway (and Client) Service for NetWare.

    d. Migrate all NetWare data to Windows 2000 servers.

18. How does Gateway (and Client) for NetWare operate?

    a. It translates SMB to NCP.

    b. It translates CIFS to NCP.

    c. It translates TCP to NCP.

    d. It translates SPX to NCP.

19. When you are configuring Gateway (and Client) Service for NetWare, how do Windows 2000 clients locate NetWare resources?

    a. By connecting to shares on the Windows 2000 server

    b. By connecting to volumes on the NetWare server

    c. By mapping a network drive to the NetWare volume

    d. By mapping a network drive to the NetWare server

20. What command can be used to view NetWare resources on the network via a command prompt?

    a. **net use /network:nw**

    b. **net /network:nw**

    c. **net view /network:nw**

    d. **net view /network:netware**

17

21. You are installing Client Service for NetWare on your Windows 2000 Professional workstation. You need to access NetWare 3.11 servers. Which frametype do you use?

    a. Ethernet 802.2

    b. Ethernet 802.5

    c. Ethernet 802.3

    d. Ethernet 802.4

22. When you are connecting to a NetWare 5.x server, what needs to be configured on Client Service for NetWare? [Check all correct answers]

    a. Default Tree

    b. Preferred Server

    c. Common Name

    d. Context

23. Which version of NetWare was the first NetWare operating system with the capability to be used as a Web server on the Internet?

    a. NetWare 2.2

    b. NetWare 3.12

    c. NetWare 4.x

    d. NetWare 5.x

24. Objects in an NDS tree can be of which two types?

    a. Container

    b. User

    c. Leaf

    d. Common

25. Which version of the Novell NetWare operating system relies on the Bindery for storing user and group account information?

    a. NetWare 5.x

    b. NetWare 4.1

    c. NetWare 4.11

    d. NetWare 3.12

Real-World Projects

You work for a large corporation whose network includes Windows 2000, Windows NT 4, and Novell NetWare 4.x servers. The NDS tree is called SOMECO. Your NetWare user account is located in the .SALES.MIAMI container. You have been given a Windows 2000 Professional workstation to use to access the corporate network. It has already been configured to access the corporate Windows domain. You need to install and configure Client Service for NetWare.

Project 17.1

To install and configure Client Service for NetWare:

1. Open the Network And Dial-Up Connections folder (Start | Settings | Network And Dial-Up Connections).

2. Right-click on Local Area Connection. Select Properties.

3. Click on Install.

4. The Select Network Component Type dialog box is displayed. Select Client and click on Add.

5. The Select Network Client dialog box is displayed. Select Client Service For NetWare. Click on OK.

6. Windows 2000 Professional now installs Client Service for NetWare. NWLink is also installed (if it wasn't previously).

7. The Select NetWare Logon dialog box is displayed.

   The corporate network is using NetWare 4.x, so you need to specify Default Tree and Context.

   Enter the name of the tree: SOMECO.

   Enter the Context: .SALES.MIAMI.

   You are concerned about conflicts, so you do not want to execute the NetWare login script. Verify that Run Login Script is not selected.

8. Click on OK to save your settings.

9. Reboot if prompted.

Next, you want to map to some volumes on the NetWare network. The volumes are listed below:

Y: \\MIAMISRV\DATA

K: \\NYSRV\DATA

Q: \\LASRV\DATA

17

Project 17.2

To map drives to NetWare resources:

1. Open a command prompt (click on Start | Run, type "cmd", and then press Enter).

2. Type "net use Y: \\MIAMISRV\DATA".

3. Type "net use K: \\NYSRV\DATA".

4. Type "net use Q: \\LASRV\DATA".

One of the applications you use is a DOS application. This DOS application is set up to print to LPT2 only. You want to send some print jobs from this application to a printer located in Philadelphia. The printer's name is LASER1, and it is located on the PHILLYSRV print server.

Project 17.3

To map printer ports to NetWare printers:

1. Open a command prompt (click on Start | Run, type "cmd", and then press Enter).

2. Type "net use LPT2: \\PHILLYSRV\LASER1".

The Unix Networking Environment

After completing this chapter, you will be able to:

✓ Identify the origins of the Unix operating system

✓ Identify the different Unix variants

✓ Install and configure Services for Unix

✓ Access files and directories on Network File System (NFS) servers

✓ Host files and directories on an NFS network

The Unix operating system is a powerful and versatile operating system that can handle many of the roles needed in today's enterprise network environment. Unix achieves this power from its utilities and scripting tools as well as from its support for powerful hardware systems. It also supports a large number of programming languages, which allows programmers and administrators to customize and automate many tasks.

Most importantly, Unix is arguably the operating system of the Internet. Most large commercial Web sites use Unix because of its powerful features and scalability. Consequently, it was imperative that Microsoft provide a means to integrate Windows 2000 into an existing Unix network infrastructure.

History of Unix

The history of Unix begins in the early 1960s as a project headed by AT&T. The goal of this project was to develop an operating system that could be deployed throughout the United States. In other words, AT&T wanted to accomplish with computer services what it had achieved with its national telecommunications network. During this early development, Unix was unwieldy and difficult to use and maintain.

In the early 1970s, the C programming language was introduced. With the power of C, the architects of Unix rebuilt the entire operating system. By using C, Unix became much more flexible and easily modifiable. This allowed administrators and programmers to develop solutions to many of the problems encountered in a networking environment.

Because licenses for Unix were either very inexpensive or free, many universities adopted the operating system. As more and more students who were exposed to it started moving into the business industry, Unix began infiltrating corporate networks.

Unix Variants

Unix combines open standards, such as C and TCP/IP, along with a common command set. Because Unix was developed using open standards, eventually there were many different flavors of Unix available on the market. These Unix variants have all been developed for a special need in the Unix market. Because of the expense in upgrading and implementing new hardware, the different flavors of Unix allow different hardware platforms to be used.

Linux

Linux is by far the most widely used Unix variant for Intel-based hardware platforms and is a freely distributed Unix operating system. Linux is also available on other platforms, such as the Motorola Power PC, Digital Alpha, Sun Sparc, and MIPS. Because it is free and runs on the Intel platform, many people simply download Linux from the Internet and install it on their home PC.

Solaris

Solaris is a version of Unix developed by Sun Microsystems. It is primarily run on Sun workstations and hardware; however, it has also been ported to the Intel platform as well.

HP-UX

HP-UX is another version of Unix, which was developed by Hewlett Packard (HP) for its workstations and servers.

Introducing Services for Unix 2

As Windows NT and Windows 2000 were adopted and implemented into more and more networking environments, Microsoft introduced Services for Unix 2 as a way for these operating systems to connect with Unix servers and workstations. Services for Unix 2 is a robust add-on package that provides many components that allow Windows NT and Windows 2000 computers to be integrated into a Unix-based networking environment.

Table 18.1 lists the components found in Services for Unix 2, as well as with which operating systems the component is compatible. The following components are included with Services for Unix 2 and provide connectivity services:

➤ *Client for NFS*—This component allows Windows-based computers to access files on NFS servers.

Table 18.1 Windows operating systems compatibility chart in relation to Services for Unix 2.

Component	NT 4 Workstation	NT 4 Server	2000 Professional	2000 Server
Client for NFS	X	X	X	X
Server for NFS	X	X	X	X
Gateway for NFS		X		X
Telnet Client	X	X	X	X
Telnet Server	X	X	X	X
Server for NIS				X
Server for PCNFS	X	X	X	X
User Name Mapping	X	X	X	X
Password Synchronization		X		X
Server for NFS Authentication		X		X
Remote Shell Service	X	X	X	X
CRON Service	X	X	X	X
ActivePerl	X	X	X	X
Unix Shell and Utilities	X	X	X	X

18

➤ *Server for NFS*—This component allows a Windows NT Server or a Windows 2000 Server to act as an NFS server, exporting Windows directories as NFS file systems.

➤ *Gateway for NFS*—This component acts as a bridge between Unix-based NFS servers and Windows clients. The Gateway for NFS server presents NFS file systems as shared directories. Windows clients can then access NFS data without requiring Client for NFS to be installed.

➤ *Telnet Client*—This component allows a Windows NT or Windows 2000 computer to make a Telnet connection to a remote computer.

➤ *Telnet Server*—This component provides a Windows NT or Windows 2000 computer with the capability to host a Telnet session from a Telnet client.

The remaining components included with Services for Unix 2 provide administrative functions:

➤ *Server for PCNFS*—This component supports an authentication method originally found in Services for Unix 1. Services for Unix 2 provides another authentication method, User Name Mapping.

➤ *Server for NIS*—This component enables a Windows NT Server or a Windows 2000 Server to act as an NIS server. This allows a domain controller to act as a master NIS server, thus integrating Active Directory domains and NIS domains.

➤ *Password Synchronization*—This component allows users to maintain a single password for both Windows domains and Unix systems.

➤ *User Name Mapping*—This component creates a map that associates Windows and Unix user accounts, which allows users to log on to Unix resources without needing a separate Unix user account.

➤ *Remote Shell Service*—This component allows a user to execute commands on a remote computer.

➤ *CRON Service*—This component is a scheduling utility that allows commands to be executed at specified times and dates.

➤ *ActiveState ActivePerl*—This component allows Perl scripts to be executed on a server.

➤ *Unix Shell and Utilities*—This component provides the Korn shell that allows Unix scripting and Perl scripting.

System Requirements

To install Services for Unix 2, your computer requires the following:

➤ Windows NT or Windows 2000 operating system

➤ 60MB free disk space

➤ 16MB RAM (in addition to the operating system's minimum recommendations)

➤ CD-ROM drive

➤ Network adapter

Installing Services for Unix 2

Services for Unix 2 is available as an add-on pack for Windows NT 4 and Windows 2000. It does not support the clustering feature found in Windows NT 4 Enterprise or Windows 2000 Advanced Server. Also, it does not run on Windows 95 or Windows 98. To install Services for Unix 2, take these steps:

1. Start the Services for Unix 2 installation routine. The Services for Unix Setup Wizard starts. Click on Next.

2. On the Customer Information screen, enter your user name and company name. You also need to enter the 25 character product key. You can find this key on the back of the Services for Unix 2 CD case. Click on Next.

3. The License and Support screen appears. This screen displays the End User License Agreement (EULA). If you enjoy this type of reading material, take the time to read the entire EULA. Click on I Accept The Agreement, and then click on Next. (Of course, if you don't agree with the EULA, click on I Don't Accept The Agreement. If you select this option, the wizard exits the installation without installing the software.)

4. The Installation Options screen is then displayed. You can select either a standard installation or a customized installation.

   The Standard Installation option installs certain components depending on the operating system the computer is running.

   If your computer is running Windows NT Workstation 4 or Windows 2000 Professional, the following components are installed during a standard installation:

   ➤ Telnet Client

   ➤ Telnet Server

   ➤ Unix Shell and Utilities

   ➤ Client for NFS

   If your computer is running Windows NT Server 4 or Windows 2000 Server, the following components are installed during a standard installation:

   ➤ Telnet Client

   ➤ Telnet Server

18

➤ Unix Shell and Utilities

➤ Server for NFS

If your computer is also a domain controller, Server for NFS Authentication is also installed.

A customized installation allows you to specify which components you want to install. Select Standard Installation, and click on Next.

5. The User Name Mapping screen appears. This screen is used to specify the name of a User Name Mapping server. If you know the name of the server, enter it. If you are not sure of the server's name, leave it blank. You can configure this item later. Click on Next.

At this point, the wizard begins installing the components selected.

You can administer the different components in Services for Unix 2 from the Services for Unix Administration console. The Services for Unix Administration console is an MMC-based utility that provides an interface to manage the different components found in Services for Unix 2. To start the console, select Start | Programs | Services for Unix | Services for Unix Administration. See Figure 18.1 for a display of the Services for Unix Administration console.

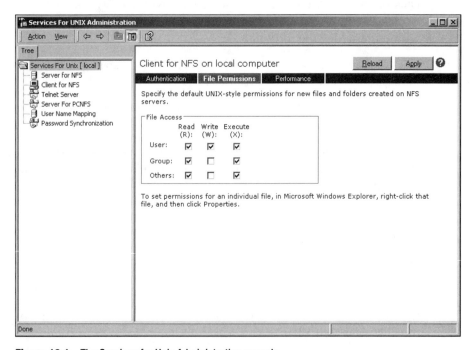

Figure 18.1 The Services for Unix Administration console.

Accessing Files Using NFS

NFS is a standard client/server protocol used to access files across a Unix-based network. NFS is defined in Request for Comments (RFCs) 1094 and 1813.

NFS is analogous to the native network file sharing protocol found in Windows 2000: Common Internet File System (CIFS), formerly known as Server Message Block (SMB). It provides a common language that allows both Unix and Windows computers to open, close, read, and write files across the network.

Client for NFS

Client for NFS allows a Windows 2000 computer to access files on an NFS server (see Figure 18.2). Much like accessing files on a Microsoft-based network, Client for NFS allows a user to connect to and disconnect from NFS shares. These connections can be created by either using the command prompt, that is, **\\servername\share**, or by browsing My Network Places. Client for NFS provides a new selection in My Network Places called NFS Network.

To configure Client for NFS, follow these steps:

1. Open the Windows Services for Unix Administration console (Start | Programs | Services for Unix).

2. Click on Client for NFS.

3. Click on the Authentication tab.

4. Type the name of the mapping server you want to use for authentication, and then click on Apply.

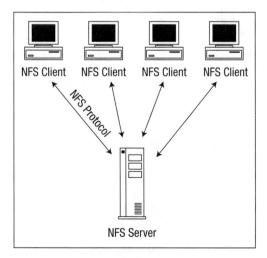

Figure 18.2   Accessing NFS files using Client for NFS.

18

Chapter 18

To map a network drive to an NFS share, follow these steps:

1. Open Windows Explorer (Start | Programs | Accessories).

2. On the Tools menu, click on Map Network Drive.

3. In the Drive list, click on the drive letter to use.

4. To locate the NFS share, you can either click on Browse to browse to the NFS share, or, in Folder, type the path to the share. Specify the path as:

   serverName:/*path* (for example: nfsserv:/data/export)

   or as:

   *serverName**path* (for example: \\nfsserv\data\export)

5. To connect using a different NFS user name or password, click on Connect using a different user name, and type the NFS user name and password. Click on OK.

Server for NFS

Server for NFS allows NFS clients to access files on a Windows 2000 computer (see Figure 18.3). These NFS clients can be either Unix-based workstations or Windows 2000 computers running Client for NFS.

To configure Server for NFS, follow these steps:

1. Open the Windows Services for Unix Administration console (Start | Programs | Services for Unix).

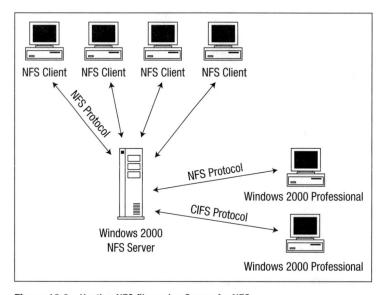

Figure 18.3 Hosting NFS files using Server for NFS.

2. Click on Server for NFS.

3. Click on the Authentication tab.

4. Type the name of the mapping server you want to use for authentication, and then click on Apply.

To create an NFS share, take the following steps:

1. Start Windows Explorer.

2. Locate the directory you want to share. In the details pane, right-click on the directory.

3. Click on Sharing.

4. Click on NFS Sharing.

5. Click on Share this folder and, in the Share name text box, type a share name.

To set up NFS permissions on an NFS share, follow these steps:

1. Start Windows Explorer.

2. Locate the directory you want to share. Right-click on the directory for which you want to set permissions.

3. Click on Sharing.

4. Click on NFS Sharing. If the folder is not already being shared, click on Share this folder.

5. Click on Permissions. Select the user or group for which you want to set permissions.

6. In the Type of Access list, select the permissions you want to set, and then click on OK twice to exit the dialog box.

Gateway for NFS

Gateway for NFS allows Windows-based computers without Client for NFS installed to access NFS files located on NFS servers (see Figure 18.4).

Comparable to Gateway Services for NetWare, Gateway for NFS is loaded on a Windows 2000 Server. The Gateway creates connections to NFS servers and in turn hosts these connections as shares. When Windows-based clients want to access NFS servers, they make a connection to the appropriate share found on the Gateway server using the CIFS protocol.

To configure Gateway for NFS, follow these steps:

1. Open the Windows Services for Unix Administration console (Start | Programs | Services for Unix).

18

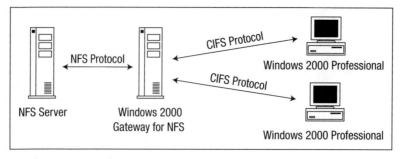

Figure 18.4   Using Gateway for NFS to access NFS files.

2. Click on Gateway for NFS.

3. Click on the Authentication tab.

4. Type the name of the mapping server you want to use for authentication, and then click on Apply.

To set up an NFS share on the Windows network, follow these steps:

1. Start Gateway for NFS Configuration.

2. To connect to an NFS share, you can do one of the following:

   ➤ Double-click Default LAN in the Network Resources list. Next, double-click on the server that contains the directory, and then click on the desired directory name.

   ➤ Enter the name of the NFS server and the exported directory into the Network Resource box.

3. In the Share Name box, enter the name of the drive you are going to share. Note that this is the share name by which the Windows clients will gain access to the resource.

4. In the Drive list, click on the drive letter you want to assign to the NFS share.

5. Use the Comment box to enter a brief description of the network share.

6. If you want to limit the number of users that can connect to the share, click on Allow, and in the Users box, type the number of users to allow. If it doesn't matter, click on Maximum Allowed.

7. Click on Permissions.

8. In Gateway for NFS Share Permissions, select the user or group that you want to set permissions for.

9. In the Type of Access list, select the permissions you want to assign.

Authentication Using Services for Unix 2

User authentication can quickly become a problem in a network where multiple security authorities are present. For example, if a user needs to access data on both Unix and Windows 2000 servers, the user would need user accounts in both Active Directory and Network Information Service (NIS). NIS is a security database used in Unix environments.

Resembling Active Directory, NIS is structured in an NIS Domain, where NIS clients perform lookup services on NIS servers. The NIS servers hold the NIS lookup database. The database itself is replicated among the NIS servers.

Server for NIS

Server for NIS is another component found in Services for Unix 2. It integrates Active Directory and NIS by allowing an Active Directory domain controller to act as a master NIS server. This permits an Active Directory administrator to create, modify, and delete user accounts in both security domains.

Server for PCNFS

Server for PCNFS allows a user to supply his or her Unix user name and password to be authenticated. Once verified, the Windows 2000 server running Server for PCNFS returns the user identifier (UID) and group identifier (GID). The user's computer then connects to the Unix server.

Server for PCNFS was first included in Services for Unix 1. It relied on Unix servers to run the PCNFS daemon. It is included in Services for Unix 2 to provide support for earlier Services for Unix clients.

Password Synchronization

Another task that users in a multiple network infrastructure find difficult is maintaining multiple passwords. If users change their Unix password, they need to either change their Windows password to match or remember both passwords.

One way to simplify this task is through password synchronization. Password synchronization provides a means of keeping these passwords the same. When users change their password in Active Directory, their Unix password is also changed automatically. Password synchronization can also be configured to work in the opposite direction: When users change their Unix password, their Windows password is updated as well.

User Name Mapping Server

User Name Mapping provides a way to create maps between Windows and Unix user and group accounts. For example, a Windows user account is mapped to a Unix account. When a user (running either Client for NFS, Server for NFS, or Gateway

18

for NFS) attempts to access data on a Unix server, the client contacts a User Name Mapping Server, which in turn matches the Windows account to the appropriate Unix account.

Remote Administration Using Services for Unix 2

One of the great features found in many of the Unix variants, but unfortunately not found in many of the Windows operating systems, is the ability to remotely administer and run applications. Unix includes a utility called Telnet that allows a user or administrator to run applications on a remote computer. Telnet is a command-line-based interface. Services for Unix 2 includes an improved Telnet Client and adds a Telnet Server to the Windows NT and Windows 2000 operating system.

Telnet Client

The Telnet Client allows a user to connect via the Telnet protocol (port 23) to a remote computer over a TCP/IP-based network. The remote computer needs to be running a Telnet server that hosts the Telnet connection. The Telnet Client can also be used to access other server-based applications, such as SMTP and POP3. To do this, simply specify the IP address for the server and the port address for the application. For example, SMTP uses port 25 and POP3 uses port 110.

There are two different modes that the Telnet Client operates in when connecting to a remote computer: command mode and session mode.

Command mode allows a user to open or close a connection, set Telnet options, or change the display properties. In session mode, the Telnet Client opens a connection to the remote computer, allowing the user to execute any character-based applications on the remote computer. The following list describes the Telnet commands.

➤ **Open**—The **Open** command is used to establish a Telnet connection to a host. Syntax: **Open** *hostname*, where *hostname* is the name of the Telnet server.

➤ **Close**—The **Close** command is used to close or end an existing Telnet connection.

➤ **Display**—This command is used to view the current operating parameters for the Telnet Client. The following operating parameters are available: WILL AUTH (NTLM Authentication), WONT AUTH, WILL TERM TYPE, WONT TERM TYPE, LOCALECHO off, and LOCALECHO on.

➤ **Quit**—The **Quit** command is used to exit Telnet.

➤ **Set**—The **Set** command is used to set the terminal type for the connection, set authentication to NTLM, set the escape character, turn on local echo, and set up logging.

➤ **SET NTLM**—Turns on NTLM. While you are using NTLM Authentication, your user name and password are automatically verified. Therefore, you are not prompted for a logon name and password.

➤ **SET LOCALECHO**—Turns on local echoing.

➤ **SET TERM {*ANSI | VT100 | VT52 | VTNT*}**—Sets the terminal type to the appropriate terminal type.

➤ **ESCAPE Character**—Sets the key sequence to use for switching from session to command mode. For example, type "set escape", press CTRL+X, and then press Enter. This will set CTRL+X as your escape character.

➤ **LOGFILE FileName**—Sets the file to be used for logging Telnet activity. The log file is a text file that is saved to your local computer. Logging automatically begins when this option is set.

➤ **LOGGING**—Turns on logging.

➤ **Unset**—The **Unset** command can be used to turn off local echo or to set authentication to logon/password prompt.

➤ **UNSET NTLM**—Turns off NTLM.

➤ **UNSET LOCALECHO**—Turns off local echoing.

➤ **Status**—The **Status** command is used to determine whether the Telnet Client is currently connected.

➤ **CTRL+]**—The **CTRL+]** command is used to go to the Telnet command prompt from a connected session.

➤ **Enter**—The **Enter** command is used from the command prompt to go to the connected session.

➤ **?/help**—Prints Help information.

Telnet Server

The Telnet server hosts connections from remote Telnet Clients. The Telnet Clients can run applications on the Telnet server. Please note that applications that interact with the desktop cannot be executed via Telnet.

There are some licensing issues to consider when using the Telnet Server in Services for Unix 2. With each Windows 2000 installation, there is one license for Telnet Server. However, this means that several Telnet Clients can be connected to the Telnet server. Table 18.2 lists the maximum number of Telnet Client connections available for each Telnet Server.

18

Table 18.2   Maximum number of Telnet Client connections.

Operating System	Maximum Number of Connections
Windows 2000 Server	Number of client access licenses installed
Windows 2000 Professional	10
Windows NT Server 4	Number of client access licenses installed
Windows NT Workstation 4	10

Chapter Summary

In this chapter, the history and origins of the Unix operating system (as it was developed in the early 1960s at AT&T) were discussed. Also discussed were some of the Unix variants from the different Unix vendors, such as HP and Sun.

Next, Services for Unix 2 was introduced as Microsoft's solution to facilitate the integration of Windows NT and Windows 2000 into an existing Unix environment. This was followed by a brief description of the different components found in Services for Unix 2.

The subsequent section described the different methods of accessing and hosting NFS data on a network. Client for NFS allows a Windows NT or Windows 2000 computer to access NFS data on the network. Server for NFS allows a Windows NT or Windows 2000 computer to host NFS data on the network, just like a Unix-based NFS server. And, the Gateway for NFS component allows a Windows NT or Windows 2000 server to act as a gateway for other Windows clients to connect to NFS data.

The different methods of integrating authentication services between Active Directory and Unix were described. Server for NIS allows a Windows 2000 domain controller to participate in an NIS domain, thereby synchronizing Active Directory and NIS user accounts automatically. User Name Mapping Server creates a user map between Windows and Unix accounts.

The Telnet Client and Telnet Server were discussed. These components allow a user or administrator to execute applications on a remote computer.

Review Questions

1. Which Intel-based Unix variant is distributed freely via the Internet?

   a. Linux

   b. HP-UX

   c. AIX

   d. SunOS

2. Which component allows Windows NT and Windows 2000 computers to directly access files on an NFS network?

   a. Server for NFS

   b. Client for NFS

   c. Gateway for NFS

   d. NFS Direct for Windows

3. Services for Unix is included with Windows 2000. True or false?

   a. True

   b. False

4. How much free disk space is required to install Services for Unix 2?

   a. 100MB

   b. 40MB

   c. 80MB

   d. 60MB

5. What is the standard file sharing protocol found on Unix-based networks?

   a. SMB

   b. NCP

   c. CIFS

   d. NFS

6. Which Services for Unix component integrates Active Directory domains and NIS domains?

   a. Server for PCNFS

   b. Server for NIS

   c. Password Synchronization

   d. User Name Mapping Server

7. Which component creates user maps between Windows user accounts and Unix user accounts?

   a. User Name Mapping Server

   b. Server for NFS

   c. Server for PCNFS

   d. Server for NIS

18

8. What is the maximum number of connections the Telnet Server can host on a Windows 2000 Professional workstation?

    a. The total number of client access licenses installed.

    b. 1.

    c. 10.

    d. None. It cannot be installed on Windows 2000 Professional.

9. If you are installing Services for Unix 2 on a Windows 2000 Professional workstation and select Standard Installation, which component is not installed?

    a. Client for NFS

    b. Telnet Client

    c. Telnet Server

    d. Server for NFS

10. Which utility allows a user to connect and execute applications on a remote computer?

    a. Server for NIS

    b. Remote Server

    c. Telnet Server

    d. Telnet Client

11. Which Services for Unix component allows a Windows NT or Windows 2000 Server to export Windows directories as NFS file systems?

    a. Server for NFS

    b. Client for NFS

    c. Gateway for NFS

    d. Windows for NFS

12. Which company spearheaded development of the Unix operating system in the early 1960s?

    a. Microsoft

    b. Sun

    c. AT&T

    d. HP

13. Which Telnet Client command creates a connection between the client and the Telnet Server?

    a. Connect computername

    b. Open hostname

    c. Open connection

    d. Connect hostname

14. Which utility provides a command-line interface that allows a user to execute character-based applications on a remote computer?

    a. Telnet Server

    b. Telnet Client

    c. Shell

    d. Explorer

15. Which component is included with Services for Unix 2 to provide support for earlier Services for Unix 1 clients?

    a. Server for PCNFS

    b. Server for NIS

    c. Password Synchronization

    d. User Name Mapping Server

16. Windows users attempting to access files on NFS shares do not need another user account. True or false?

    a. True

    b. False

17. If you are performing a standard install of Services for Unix on a Windows 2000 domain controller, which component is also installed?

    a. Telnet Server

    b. Server for NFS Authentication

    c. Server for NFS

    d. Unix Shell and Utilities

18. Gateway for NFS can be installed on a Windows 2000 Professional computer. True or false?

    a. True

    b. False

18

19. What programming language is closely related to the Unix operating system?

  a. Java

  b. Visual Basic

  c. C

  d. Cobol

20. Which Services for Unix component allows Windows computers to access NFS using the CIFS protocol?

  a. Client for NFS

  b. Server for NFS

  c. Gateway for NFS

  d. Telnet Server

Real-World Projects

You work for a large corporation whose network includes Windows 2000, Windows NT 4, and Unix-based servers.

You are given a Windows 2000 Professional workstation to use to access the corporate network. It has been configured to access the corporate Windows domain. Your boss notifies you that you will also need to access data on the Unix servers. Consequently, you need to install and configure Services for Unix 2.

Project 18.1

To install and configure Services for Unix 2:

1. Start the Services for Unix 2 installation routine. The Services for Unix Setup Wizard starts. Click on Next.

2. On the Customer Information screen, enter your user name and company name. You also need to enter the 25 character product key. You can find this key on the back of the Services for Unix 2 CD case. Click on Next.

3. The License and Support screen appears. This screen displays the End User License Agreement (EULA). If you enjoy this type of reading material, take the time to read the entire EULA. Click on I Accept The Agreement, and then click on Next. (Of course, if you don't agree with the EULA, click on I Don't Accept The Agreement. If you select this option, the wizard exits the installation without installing the software.)

4. The Installation Options screen appears. You can select either a standard installation or a customized installation. Selecting Standard Installation installs the following components.

➤ Telnet Client

➤ Telnet Server

➤ Unix Shell and Utilities

➤ Client for NFS

5. The User Name Mapping screen appears. This screen is used to specify the name of a User Name Mapping server. If you know the name of the server, enter it. If you are not sure of the server's name, leave it blank. You can configure this item later. Click on Next.

After Services for Unix is installed, you need to configure Client for NFS so you can access the data stored on NFS shares. You first need to configure where your user account should be authenticated. After discussing this with the LAN administrator, you learn that there is a User Name Mapping Server called usermap.ourco.com.

Project 18.2
To configure authentication in Client for NFS:

1. Open the Windows Services for Unix Administration console (Start | Programs | Services for Unix).

2. Click on Client for NFS.

3. Click on the Authentication tab.

4. Type the name of the mapping server you want to use for authentication: "usermap.ourco.com". Click on Apply.

Once your authentication settings have been configured, you need to map a network drive to the NFS data. Your boss tells you that the data is located on the server corpdata.ourco.com in export data/export. You want to map this export to the drive letter F:.

Project 18.3
To map a network drive using Client for NFS:

1. Open Windows Explorer (Start | Programs | Accessories).

2. On the Tools menu, click on Map Network Drive.

3. In the Drive list, select drive F:.

4. To locate the NFS share, you can either click on Browse to browse to the NFS share, or, in Folder, type the path to the share. Specify the path as: "corpdata.ourco.com/data/export".

5. Click on OK.

18

CHAPTER NINETEEN

Sample Test

Question 1

You work for a video controller manufacturer. You are assigned the task of designing the driver that will be used in the Windows family of operating systems. You decide to use WDM (Windows Driver Model). Which of the Windows Operating Systems support this model? [Check all correct answers]

❑ a. Windows 95

❑ b. Windows 98

❑ c. Windows NT 4

❑ d. Windows 2000

Question 2

Convert the IP address, 168.17.24.210 to binary.

○ a. 10101000.00010001.00011000.11010010

○ b. 10110000.00010101.00110000.11101000

○ c. 10100011.10010001.10110000.10101000

○ d. 10110000.10010111.10100111.11010011

Question 3

What is the minimum amount of free disk space required to install Windows 2000 Professional?

○ a. 650MB

○ b. 2.2GB

○ c. 1.2GB

○ d. 128MB

Question 4

Mike is reviewing data that was created from a log file in System Monitor. Mike would like to export this data to another program so he can present the data to people throughout his organization. What file types can be used to export this data? [Check all correct answers]

❑ a. .doc (Word)

❑ b. .html (Web Page)

❑ c. .xls (Excel)

❑ d. .tsv (Tab Delimited)

Question 5

Your workstation has stopped printing for no apparent reason. The print jobs are just sitting in the spooler. You decide that you want to stop and start the spooler service. What snap-ins can you add to a console to accomplish this? [Check all correct answers]

❑ a. Services

❑ b. System Information

❑ c. Printers

❑ d. Computer Management

Question 6

Your Windows 2000 Professional computer is configured with the IP address 143.210.8.12 and the subnet mask 255.255.248.0. On what subnet is your computer located?

○ a. 143.0.0.0

○ b. 143.210.0.0

○ c. 143.210.4.0

○ d. 143.210.8.0

Question 7

In which tool do you configure and administer disk storage space in Windows 2000 Professional?

○ a. In the Computer Management Console, Disk Management

○ b. In the Computer Management Console, Disk Administrator

○ c. In the Control Panel, Disk Management

○ d. In the Control Panel, Disk Administrator

Question 8

Which of the following types of files cannot be encrypted using EFS (Encrypting File System)?

○ a. Text Files

○ b. Bitmaps

○ c. Compressed Files

○ d. HTML Files

Question 9

You would like to install Windows 2000 Professional on 100 workstations. You would also like to automate the install on all the computers. What do you need to use to give each workstation a unique computer name?

○ a. UDF

○ b. PXE

○ c. ANSWER.TXT

○ d. RIS

Question 10

Your company has sent you from New York to Los Angeles on a business trip. Your laptop holds your appointment schedule in Microsoft Outlook. You want to make sure you do not miss any appointments because of the time zone change. Where would you change your laptop's time zone setting from EST to PST? [Check all correct answers]

❑ a. Control Panel, Date/Time applet

❑ b. Control Panel, Regional Settings applet

❑ c. Double-click on the time

❑ d. Right-click on the Desktop

Question 11

Members of the Power Users group in Windows 2000 Professional can do which of the following tasks? [Check all correct answers]

❑ a. Create and manage local user accounts

❑ b. Create and manage domain user accounts

❑ c. Install program files that do not alter system files

❑ d. Install device drivers

Question 12

19

When using the CHAP authentication protocol, when is the user's password transmitted across the network?

○ a. During the challenge

○ b. During the response

○ c. During both challenge and response

○ d. Never

Question 13

You are attempting to access resources on a TCP/IP-based network. You are not able to connect to any other computers. To rule out DHCP as the problem, you want to obtain a new IP address from the DHCP server. What commands allow you to receive a new IP address? [Check all correct answers]

❑ a. ipconfig /registerdns

❑ b. winipcfg /renew

❑ c. ipconfig

❑ d. ipconfig /renew

Question 14

What protocol is used to access files on a Windows 2000 Server from across the network?

○ a. NCP

○ b. CIFS

○ c. IPX

○ d. IP

Question 15

From the following list, select the protocols that are used for authentication. Next, arrange the list on the right from most secure to least secure authentication protocol.

    a. PAP

    b. IPSec

    c. MS-CHAP

    d. SPAP

    e. L2TP

    f. MS-CHAPv2

    g. EAP

    h. PPTP

    i. CHAP

Question 16

Rob, the head of network security for your company, suspects that unauthorized people may be attempting to hack into the network. He requests that you enable auditing for unsuccessful logon attempts. After enabling it, where can Rob view the results?

○ a. Event Viewer, System Log

○ b. Event Viewer, Security Log

○ c. System Monitor, Audit Log

○ d. System Monitor, System Log

Question 17

Up to how many processors can be supported by Windows 2000 Professional?

○ a. 2

○ b. 4

○ c. 1

○ d. 8

Question 18

You need to connect to the NetWare 4.11 server, NWSRV_DATA. This server is using NDS for user authentication. How does Client Service for NetWare need to be configured? [Check all correct answers]

❑ a. Default Tree

❑ b. Context

❑ c. Preferred Server

❑ d. NDS Name

Question 19

The Windows 2000 Professional workstation you are using receives its IP configuration via a DHCP server. You are having difficulty accessing resources on the network. You suspect that your system's IP configuration may be wrong. How can you view your current IP configuration?

○ a. winipcfg /view

○ b. ipconfig /all

○ c. show ip config

○ d. ipconfig /view

Question 20

Lisa is the network administrator for a large corporation. Her company has recently acquired a smaller company whose network uses both Windows NT 4 and Novell NetWare 4.x servers. Although the management of the company wants employees to access the data on the NetWare servers, they do not want another network client deployed. What should Lisa do?

○ a. Install Client Services for NetWare on all computers.

○ b. Install a Windows 2000 Professional computer with Gateway (and Client) Service for NetWare.

○ c. Install a Windows 2000 Server with Gateway (and Client) Service for NetWare.

○ d. Migrate all NetWare data to Windows 2000 Servers.

Question 21

From the following list, identify the network protocols supported by Windows 2000. Next, place each characteristic in one of three groups with its corresponding network protocol.

   a. TCP/IP

   b. The Internet

   c. NWLink

   d. Novell NetWare

   e. Small Networks

   f. Non-routable

   g. MAC Address used for host address

   h. No error correction

   i. Highly configurable

   j. DNS

   k. NetBEUI

   l. SAP

Question 22

Which command displays the NetBIOS name cache?

   ○ a. nbtstat -r

   ○ b. nbtstat -R

   ○ c. nbtstat -c

   ○ d. nbtstat

Question 23

19

You are the network administrator for a large company. You were just notified that another network administrator was fired. Before leaving, the fired administrator changed the permissions on many sensitive documents, revoking all access to the files. He also took ownership of the files. What can you do to gain access to the files?

○ a. Take ownership and grant access.

○ b. Grant access.

○ c. Restore from backup.

○ d. Format the volume containing the files. Restore from backup.

Question 24

What does the tunneling protocol L2TP rely on for data encryption?

○ a. PAP

○ b. EAP

○ c. IPSec

○ d. MS-CHAP v2

Question 25

You need to access data on a Windows 2000 Server with the IP address of 192.168.1.210. Your Windows 2000 Professional computer is configured with the IP address 192.168.5.64 and the subnet mask 255.255.255.0. Is the Windows 2000 Server located on your local subnet or a remote subnet?

○ a. Local

○ b. Remote

Question 26

Mark is attempting to connect to a couple of NetWare servers on the network. One NetWare server, NWSRV1, is a NetWare 3.11 file server. The other NetWare server, NWSRV2, is a NetWare 4.11 file server. What does Mark need to install and configure to access these file servers? [Check all correct answers]

❏ a. Client Services for NetWare

❏ b. NWLink

❏ c. Manually add Frametype 802.2

❏ d. Manually add Frametype 802.3

Question 27

Sam wants to automate the install of his Windows 2000 Professional workstation. He wants to accomplish this by using a boot disk and the CD-ROM drive. What file does Sam need to copy to the boot disk?

○ a. Answer.txt

○ b. UDF

○ c. Autoinstall.bat

○ d. Winnt.sif

Question 28

Mary just purchased a new internal DSL modem from her local computer store. The documentation that comes with the modem states that it is Plug and Play. Following the directions in the manual, Mary proceeds to physically install the modem into her Windows 2000 Professional computer. What else does Mary need to do to start using the modem?

○ a. Install the driver

○ b. Run the Plug and Play Administrator

○ c. Have the computer detect the new hardware

○ d. Nothing

Question 29

You need to manage network shares on a group of remote computers. Of which groups do you need to be a member? [Check all correct answers]

❑ a. Power Users

❑ b. Server Operators

❑ c. Computer Operators

❑ d. Administrators

Question 30

From the following list, select the steps that are used in NetBIOS name resolution. Next, arrange the steps in the order in which they occur. The computer where name resolution is occurring is configured as an h-node. Also, it is configured to use DNS and LMHOSTS for NetBIOS name resolution.

a. Query WINS Servers

b. Check local HOSTS file

c. Query DNS Servers

d. Check the NetBIOS Name Cache

e. Send a Remote Broadcast

f. Send a Local Broadcast

g. Clear NetBIOS Name Cache

h. Check local LMHOSTS file

Question 31

You are a consultant to a company that wants to deploy Windows 2000 Professional to all its desktops. One requirement for the project is to remotely install Windows 2000. You decide to have desktops boot directly from the network card and perform the install from the RIS server. To use this solution, what must the network card support?

○ a. PXE

○ b. Ethernet

○ c. TCP/IP

○ d. PCI

Question 32

Congratulations! This is the first day at your new job. You have been assigned a Windows 2000 Professional laptop. In the office, you connect to the network that has Windows 2000 and Novell NetWare 4.11 servers. You are told that most of the data you need is located on the Windows 2000 servers. The NetWare servers are being migrated to Windows 2000. When connecting remotely, you only require access to a Windows 2000 Server running Exchange Server for email. From the following list, select the network connection with the network protocols to be bound on that interface. Next, arrange the network protocols in the correct binding order to achieve maximum performance.

 a. NWLink

 b. NetBEUI

 c. CIFS

 d. Remote Connection

 e. Modem Connection

 f. TCP/IP

 g. Local Area Connection

 h. AppleTalk

Question 33

Michelle needs to add another volume to her Windows 2000 Professional workstation. Unfortunately, Michelle's network environment requires the use of many mapped drives. Therefore, her workstation has no drive letters available. How can Michelle still add this volume to her workstation?

○ a. By adding a Volume Mount Point to her NTFS drive.

○ b. By removing a mapped drive.

○ c. By adding a Volume Mount Point to her FAT32 drive.

○ d. By adding a Volume Mount Point to her FAT drive.

Question 34

As shown in Exhibit 34, an organization's network consists of four subnets: A, B, C, and D. Place the workstations letters with the appropriate subnet according to its IP configuration.

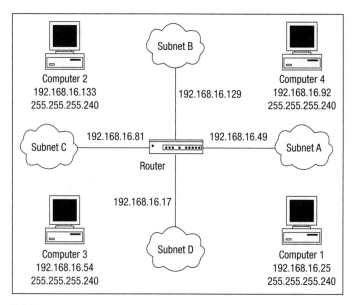

Exhibit 34

- ○ a. Computer 1
- ○ b. Computer 2
- ○ c. Computer 3
- ○ d. Computer 4

Question 35

You suspect that the boot sector on your system partition is damaged. Using the Recovery Console, what command allows you to create a new boot sector?

- ○ a. fixmbr
- ○ b. fixbootsector
- ○ c. fixboot
- ○ d. sys

Question 36

The administrator for your network has sent you, via email, a HOSTS file and an LMHOSTS file. She wants you to use these files until she resolves some DNS and WINS issues. Where do these files need to be placed for your workstation to use them?

○ a. %systemroot%\system32

○ b. %systemroot%\system32\tcpip

○ c. %systemroot%\system32\drivers\etc

○ d. %systemroot%\

Question 37

You need to perform a backup of your Windows 2000 Professional workstation. You also want to back up the Registry files. What do you need to do?

○ a. Boot using the Emergency Repair Disk (ERD), and then copy the Registry files to the ERD.

○ b. Perform a backup using the Backup utility and select the System State.

○ c. Export the Registry files to a comma-delimited text file, and then copy the Registry files to a floppy disk.

○ d. Boot the system in Safe Mode, and then use the Backup Registry option.

Question 38

What is the minimum amount of RAM required to install Windows 2000 Professional?

○ a. 32MB

○ b. 64MB

○ c. 128MB

○ d. 256MB

Question 39

You need to manage disk storage on a group of remote computers. Of the following, which groups do you need to be a member? [Check all correct answers]

❑ a. Power Users

❑ b. Server Operators

❑ c. Computer Operators

❑ d. Administrators

Question 40

Exhibit 40 displays the Advanced tab from the System applet. You want to configure the paging file on your Windows 2000 Professional workstation. Which button provides access to the paging file settings?

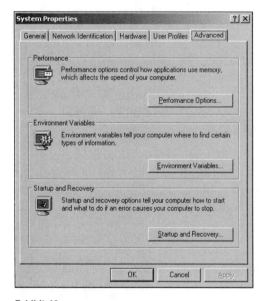

Exhibit 40

○ a. Performance Options

○ b. Environment Variables

○ c. Startup and Recovery

Note: Case studies are a new testing technique Microsoft uses in some of its tests. Although

Note: You probably won't encounter case studies in the Core Four exams, a case study is included in this practice test because it is a valuable way to reinforce the material you've learned.

Case Study 1

Existing Situation

Dynatech Industries is a large corporation specializing in the design, manufacture, and sales of high-tech demolition products. Dynatech's primary customers are demolition firms throughout the United States and Canada. These firms are employed by municipalities and building owners that need large structures imploded without causing damage to other structures.

Most of Dynatech's manufacturing occurs at their headquarters located outside of Chicago. They also have field sales offices in 35 cities throughout the United States and Canada.

Current Situation

To support the headquarters and the field offices, the IT department at Dynatech built a Windows NT 4-based network. Headquarters maintains all the infrastructure services, such as Dynamic Host Configuration Protocol (DHCP), Domain Name Service (DNS), and Windows Internet Naming Service (WINS). HQ also houses the PDC and three BDCs for the corporate domain, DYNATECH, as well as a handful of file and application servers. Each field office contains a BDC and a file server.

On the client side of Dynatech's infrastructure, users are running a mix of Windows 95 and Windows NT Workstation 4. Most of these systems are desktops, although there are a number of sales reps operating out of the field offices with portable computers running Windows 95. Although the company settled on a common hardware platform for the portable computers, there is no common hardware platform for the desktops.

Because of the current IT skills shortage, the IT department is understaffed. The different hardware platforms that need to be supported have added an even heavier burden to the staff. Because of this, Dynatech has hired our firm to provide a common Windows 2000 Professional image for all desktops and portables.

Proposed Goal

Design and implement a common operating system environment for all desktop and portable computers throughout Dynatech's corporate environment. A common operating-system environment will enable standardization, improve problem resolution response time, improve administration, and reduce Total Cost of Ownership (TCO).

Proposal

19

Now, the management team at Dynatech doesn't want to upgrade the current server infrastructure. They feel that more savings can be gained by upgrading and standardizing the clients. They are also hoping that better hardware and standard image will result in better employee satisfaction.

Phase One of this project will focus on the specification and purchase of company-standard computers, both desktops and portables. By purchasing common hardware platforms, Dynatech benefits from the standardization of device drivers and system files. This allows the Dynatech IT department to provide better support for the corporate user community. Because Dynatech already has an existing relationship with IBM, its machines will provide the hardware for the desktops and portables. For the desktop hardware architecture, we have decided on using the IBM 300PL. The 300PL comes with a Pentium III 600MHz processor, 64MB RAM, 10.1GB Hard Drive, 10/100 Ethernet Adapter, and 24x CD-ROM. For the portable architecture, we decided on using the IBM 600X Thinkpad. The 600X comes with a Pentium III 650MHz processor, 64MB RAM, 12GB Hard Drive, DVD/CD-ROM Drive, and 3COM Etherlink III PCCard.

Phase Two of this project will focus on information gathering. We need to know which applications are being used by the current user community as well as how those applications are being used. After a list of applications has been compiled, our team can validate the applications compatibility with Windows 2000 Professional. All applications that are not compatible will need to be upgraded or replaced.

Phase Three of this project will focus on the development and deployment of a standard operating system image using Windows 2000 Professional. This image will be deployed to 5000 desktops and 1500 portables.

Question 1.1

Windows 2000 supplies a new service known as Remote Installation Service (RIS). We want the desktops to automatically boot to the network and start the install using RIS. What version of PXE must the network adapter in the desktops and portables support?

○ a. 2.0a

○ b. a

○ c. .99c

○ d. 1.0

Question 1.2

Using RIS, we want the computer name for the desktops to use the hardware address of the network adapter. What variable allows this?

○ a. %MAC

○ b. %NIC%

○ c. %NIC

○ d. %MAC%

Question 1.3

Given the above information, can RIS be employed?

○ a. Yes

○ b. No

Question 1.4

What are the minimum requirements for RIS? [Check all correct answers]

❑ a. DHCP

❑ b. WINS

❑ c. DNS

❑ d. Active Directory

Question 1.5

Each desktop and portable computer will require its own computer name. What type of file can provide this information?

○ a. .ini

○ b. .oem

○ c. .txt

○ d. .udf

19

Question 1.6

How many unattended answer files need to be created for this project?

○ a. 1

○ b. 2

○ c. 6500

○ d. None

Question 1.7

Some members of the team are investigating the use of disk imaging technology to deploy the image. If disk-imaging technology is used, which Windows 2000 utility allows the Security Identifier (SID) to be regenerated?

○ a. syspart

○ b. RIS

○ c. sysprep

○ d. UDF

Question 1.8

When using sysprep, you need to create a folder called sysprep on the system. Which files need to be copied to this folder? [Check all correct answers]

❏ a. sysprep.ini

❏ b. sysprep.inf

❏ c. setupcl.exe

❏ d. sysprep.exe

Question 1.9

When installing applications on an image that will be distributed via sysprep, we used a user account called APPINSTALLER. We need to make sure that all application settings are available to all users. What needs to be done?

○ a. Have users log on as APPINSTALLER

○ b. Use APPINSTALLER as a template when creating user accounts

○ c. Reinstall all applications once a user logs on

○ d. Copy APPINSTALLER's user profile to the Default User user profile

Question 1.10

Given the above information, which automated installation method should be used?

○ a. syspart

○ b. sysprep

○ c. bootable CD-ROM

○ d. RIS

CHAPTER TWENTY

Answer Key

1. b, d

2. a

3. a

4. b, d

5. a, d

6. d

7. a

8. c

9. a

10. a, c

11. a, c

12. d

13. a, d

14. b

15. g, f, c, i, d, a

16. b

17. a

18. a, b

19. b

20. c

21. a, b, i, j
    c, d, g, l
    k, e, f, h

22. c

23. a

24. c

25. b

26. a, b, c, d

27. d

28. d

29. a, d

30. d, a, f, h, b, c

31. a

32. g, f, a
    d, f

33. a

34. c, b, d, a

35. c

36. c

37. b

38. a

39. b, d

40. a

1.1. c

1.2. a

1.3. b

1.4. a, c, d

1.5. d

1.6. b

1.7. c

1.8. b, c, d

1.9. d

1.10. b

Question 1

Answers b and d are correct. WDM was created after Windows 95 and Windows NT 4.0 were released. Therefore, only Windows 98 and Windows 2000 support WDM. (Chapter 8)

Question 2

Answer a is correct. The IP address 168.17.24.210 displayed in binary is 10101000.00010001.00011000.11010010. (Chapter 11)

Question 3

Answer a is correct. Windows 2000 Professional requires 650MB of free disk space, although it is recommended that you have 1.2GB of free disk space. (Chapter 2)

Question 4

Answers b and d are correct. System Monitor can export files as either html or tsv. Html files can be viewed via a web browser such as Internet Explorer. Tsv files can be imported into Microsoft Excel. (Chapter 14)

Question 5

Answers a and d are correct. The Services snap-in gives you direct access to all services. The Computer Management snap-in also contains the Services snap-in. (Chapter 3)

Question 6

Answer d is correct. By examining the subnet mask, you can see that the first three octets are part of the network ID. Since the computer's IP address is 143.210.8.12, its subnet must be 143.210.8.0. (Chapter 11)

Question 7

Answer a is correct. Disk Management is the utility that allows you to configure and manage disk storage. It is found in the Computer Management Console. (Chapter 4)

Question 8

Answer c is correct. Compressed files cannot be encrypted. To encrypt compressed files, uncompress the file and then encrypt it. (Chapter 4)

Question 9

Answer a is correct. You need to use a UDF (Uniqueness Database File) file. The UDF file will override the answer file with unique answers for each workstation. (Chapter 2)

Question 10

Answers a and c are correct. You can change the time zone two ways. First, go to the Control Panel and open the Date/Time applet. Then select the time zone tab. Also, you can simply double-click on the time found in the System Tray (the lower right corner of the desktop). Then, you can select the time zone tab. (Chapter 5)

Question 11

Answers a and c are correct. Members of the Power Users group can create and manage user accounts for the local computer only. They can also install programs that do not alter system files. (Chapter 13)

Question 12

Answer d is correct. CHAP operates by having the server send a challenge to the client computer. The client computer, using MD5, hashes both the challenge and the password and sends it to the server. The server, knowing the challenge and the user's password from its security database, creates its own hash. The server then compares the two hashes. If the hashes match, the requested access is permitted. As you can see, the password itself is never transmitted across the network. (Chapter 10)

Question 13

Answers a and d are correct. There are two commands that allow you to obtain a new IP address. Ipconfig /renew is the more commonly known command. Ipconfig /registerdns is meant to be used to register the workstation with DNS, but it will also renew the IP address with the DHCP server. (Chapter 11)

Question 14

Answer b is correct. CIFS (Common Internet File System) is the protocol used to open, close, read, and write to files on Windows 2000 computers across the network. CIFS is also known as SMB (Server Message Block) protocol, which is found in earlier Windows operating systems. (Chapter 16)

Question 15

The following order is correct:

g, f, c, i, d, a

EAP (Extensible Authentication Protocol) is the most secure authentication protocol because it provides a way for vendors to incorporate additional authentication methods such as Smart Cards or Secure ID. PAP is the least secure authentication protocol because it provides no encryption for data or passwords. (Chapter 10)

Question 16

Answer b is correct. Rob needs to use the Event Viewer and select the Security Log to view audited events. (Chapter 14)

Question 17

Answer a is correct. Windows 2000 Professional supports two processors. Windows 2000 Server supports four processors and Advanced Server supports eight. Datacenter Server, meant for large enterprise applications, can support 32 processors. (Chapter 9)

Question 18

Answers a and b are correct. When connecting to a NetWare server using NDS, Client Services for NetWare must be configured with the Default Tree (i.e., the name of the NDS tree) and the Context (the location in the tree where the user's account information is located). (Chapter 17)

Question 19

Answer b is correct. ipconfig /all will display all the IP configuration settings on the workstation. (Chapter 11)

Question 20

Answer c is correct. Since management did not want another network client installed, Lisa's only choice was to use the Gateway (and Client) Services for NetWare. The gateway can only be installed on a Windows 2000 Server. (Chapter 17)

Question 21

The items should be placed in the following groups and orders:

a, b, i, j

c, d, g, l

k, e, f, h

From a design standpoint, it is important to know the different network protocols and their characteristics. Although the world is quickly becoming IP only because of the Internet, you will undoubtedly come across other network protocols from time to time.

Question 22

Answer c is correct. nbtstat -c will display the NetBIOS name cache. nbtstat -r will list all names resolved by WINS or broadcasts. nbtstat -R will purge the cache and reload the remote cache name table (NetBIOS names marked #PRE in the LMHOSTS file). (Chapter 11)

Question 23

Answer a is correct. Take ownership of the files and grant access. If you are the Creator/Owner of a file, you can still change permissions even if your access was revoked. By taking ownership, you become the Creator/Owner. (Chapter 13)

Question 24

Answer c is correct. L2TP (Layer 2 Tunneling Protocol) does not have any inherent way of encrypting data. To get data encryption, L2TP always relies on IPSec. (Chapter 10)

Question 25

Answer b is correct. Remote. The first three octets are part of the Network ID. The third octet in the IP addresses of the Windows 2000 Server and your workstation have different values. Therefore, they are located on different subnets. (Chapter 5)

Question 26

Answers a, b, c, and d are correct. All items need to be installed and configured. NetWare servers use NWLink (IPX/SPX) as their network protocol. Windows 2000 computers wanting access to the NetWare servers need to use Client Services for NetWare. By default, the frametype is set to autodetect. However, because the two NetWare servers are using two different frametypes (802.2 for NetWare 4.11 and 802.3 for NetWare 3.11), Mark must manually configure the frametypes. (Chapter 17)

Question 27

Answer d is correct. WINNT.SIF needs to be copied to the boot disk. (Chapter 2)

Question 28

Answer d is correct. Mary does not need to do anything. When the system boots up, it will detect the Plug and Play compatible device and automatically install associated device drivers. There is no such thing as the Plug and Play Administrator. (Chapter 8)

Question 29

Answers a and d are correct. To remotely manage disk storage, you need to be a member of the Administrators or Power Users groups. (Chapter 6)

Question 30

The items should be placed in the following order:

d, a, f, h, b, c

There are many factors to consider when a Windows 2000 Professional workstation is performing NetBIOS name resolution. Items such as node type and configuration settings can greatly affect how resolution occurs. For example, in the question, if the workstation was configured to be a b–node and was not configured to query DNS, it would have sent a local broadcast and checked the LMHOSTS file. It would not query WINS or DNS. (Chapter 11)

Question 31

Answer a is correct. PXE (Preboot eXecution Environment) is an industry standard that allows a system to boot from the network card. (Chapter 2)

Question 32

The items should be placed in the following groups and orders:

g, f, a

d, f

When configuring multiple connections, it is important to bind only the network protocols that are required on the connection. In the question, you need TCP/IP only to access the Exchange Server. For the local network, you need both TCP/IP and NWLink to access the Windows 2000 and Novell NetWare servers. Because the NetWare servers will be gone shortly, it is important to move TCP/IP to the beginning of the binding order. This will give maximum TCP/IP performance for the local connection. (Chapter 17)

Question 33

Answer a is correct. Volume Mount Points allow you to add a volume to a system without using a separate drive letter for the new volume. The Volume Mount Point must be placed in an empty folder on the hosting system's NTFS volume. (Chapter 4)

Question 34

The following items should be matched:

Subnet A, c

Subnet B, b

Subnet C, d

Subnet D, a

Determining which subnet an IP address is on can be one of the most difficult things to learn, especially when the network address is a Class C address that is being divided even further. The way to solve this question is to determine the address ranges of each subnet. First, take the subnet mask 255.255.255.240. We need to be concerned with the last subnet, 240. Converting 240 to binary, we get 1111000. The last bit on from the left (before the zeroes) determines the increment of the address ranges. Here, it is the fourth bit from the left, or 16. Therefore, the address range for each subnet contains 16 host addresses: 192.168.16.16, 192.168.16.32, 192.168.16.48, and so on. Now remember that you can't use the first or last address in a subnet (all zeroes and all ones). So, what are the address ranges for the four subnets? Well, by looking at the router interface for each subnet, you can determine which address range a subnet is using. For example, the router interface for Subnet A is 192.168.16.49. Therefore, the address range for Subnet A is 192.168.16.48 through 192.168.16.63. Therefore, Computer 3 (192.168.16.54) belongs on Subnet A. (Chapter 11)

Question 35

Answer c is correct. The Recovery Console command fixboot will create a new boot sector for the system partition. (Chapter 15)

Question 36

Answer c is correct. The HOSTS and LMHOSTS files need to be placed in %systemroot%\system32\drivers\etc. %systemroot% is a system variable that represents the directory Windows 2000 was installed in (i.e., C:\WINNT). (Chapter 11)

Question 37

Answer b is correct. To back up the registry, use the Backup utility and select the System State. The System State includes a number of items related to the system configuration, including the registry files. (Chapter 15).

Question 38

Answer a is correct. 32MB of RAM is the official minimum requirement from Microsoft, although we highly recommend that you have at least 64MB of RAM for better performance. (Chapter 2)

Question 39

Answers b and d are correct. To remotely manage disk storage, you need to be a member of the Administrators or Server Operators groups. (Chapter 15)

Question 40

Answer a is correct. The Performance Options button provides access to the paging file settings, also known as virtual memory. (Chapter 5)

Question 1.1

Answer c is correct. The network adapter must be running PXE .99c to be used with RIS. (Chapter 2)

Question 1.2

Answer a is correct. The variable %MAC supplies the network adapter's hardware address. (Chapter 2)

Question 1.3

Answer b is correct. No, RIS cannot be used in this situation. Although Dynatech's network infrastructure includes DHCP and DNS, it does not include Active Directory. All three of these items are required to utilize RIS. (Chapter 2)

Question 1.4

Answers a, c, and d are correct. DHCP, DNS, and Active Directory are requirements for RIS. (Chapter 2)

Question 1.5

Answer d is correct. UDF, or Uniqueness Database File, is used along with the unattend.txt file. The UDF file overrides the answers in unattend.txt with unique answers, such as user, computer, and domain names. (Chapter 2)

Question 1.6

Answer b is correct. Since there are two distinct hardware platforms being deployed (desktop and portable), two separate answer files are needed. (Chapter 2)

Question 1.7

Answer c is correct. SYSPREP is a disk imaging utility that will automatically regenerate the computer's SID. (Chapter 2)

Question 1.8

Answers b, c, and d are correct. These files, sysprep.inf, sysprep.exe, setupcl.exe, are used to complete the sysprep process. Once complete, this folder is deleted automatically. (Chapter 2)

Question 1.9

Answer d is correct. For all application configuration settings to be available, the user profile of the account that installed the applications needs to be copied to the Default User user profile. (Chapter 2)

Question 1.10

Answer b is correct. Reviewing the information in the case study, we have already determined that RIS cannot be used because Active Directory is not present. Syspart is meant to be used on systems with differing hardware. A bootable CD-ROM could be used, however the cost of duplicating many CDs (possibly 6500) is too high. This leaves us with SYSPREP. If we made to separate images, one for desktops, one for portables, SYSPREP can be utilized from across the network. (Chapter 2)

Appendix A
Answers to Review Questions

Chapter 1 Solutions

1. **b.** AutoComplete completes words as the user types.

2. **c.** Accelerated Graphics Port.

3. **b.** Image Color Management.

4. **a.** Internet Connection Sharing allows all computers on a local intranet to share the same external connection to the Internet.

5. **a, b, c, d.** DHML, XML, PICS and HTML+Time are all developer tools supported by Windows 2000 Professional.

6. **a.** Windows File Protection prevents system files from being deleted or altered by users.

7. **b.** False. Disk Quotas cannot be administered on network shares.

8. **a, b, c, d.** Disk Defragmenter can defrag NTFS, FAT, and FAT32 volumes.

9. **a.** Encrypting File System is support by NTFS 5.

10. **b.** My Network Places replaces Network Neighborhood in previous versions of Windows.

11. **b.** Files are stored by default in the My Documents folder.

12. **b.** Directory Services is a troubleshooter provided in Windows 2000 Server.

13. **a, b.** IPSec and EFS are examples of security in Windows 2000 Professional.

14. **a.** Dynamic disks are physical disks that contain only dynamic volumes.

15. **a.** Advanced Configuration and Power Interface.

16. **a, b, c, d.** DVD, Plug and Play, USB, and HID are all supported by Windows 2000 Professional.

17. **a.** True. Windows 2000 Professional has support for multiple display devices.

18. **a, b, c.** EAP, MS–CHAP, and SPAP are authentication protocols supported by Windows 2000 Professional.

19. **a.** The Windows Update utility provides a central location to find system files, product enhancements, and service packs.

20. **c.** Logical Disk Manager.

Chapter 2 Solutions

1. **a.** Setup Manager will assist you in creating an answer file.

2. **b.** The Uniqueness Database File will override the answer file with unique answers for a computer.

3. **c.** Winnt.sif is the file that the Windows 2000 professional install is looking for. The file must have this exact name to be used, and all other files will be ignored.

4. **b.** Only the pnp switch causes the system to do a full check for new hardware.

5. **b.** You are required to place both sysprep.exe and setupcl.exe in the Sysprep folder.

6. **d.** The PXE (Preboot eXecution Environment) is the standard used to boot from a network card.

7. **d.** The utility to create a RIS boot disk is rbfd.exe, and it is found on the RIS server.

8. **c.** PXE .99c is the minimum version required to boot from a network card to a RIS server.

9. **b.** With Windows 2000, you use Winnt32.exe to run the installation if you start the installation from Windows 95, 98, or NT. You use Winnt.exe only if the installation is started from DOS or Windows 3.1.

10. **d.** It doesn't matter what you name the answer file for a RIS install. When you associate the answer file with the image, you just need the name. Remboot.sif is the default name created by Setup Manager for a RIS install, but using this name is not a requirement.

11. **a, d.** Windows 2000 fully supports FAT32. You user should not convert any drives to NTFS because Windows 98 doesn't support this file system.

12. **c.** Windows 2000 requires a minimum of 650MB of free space.

13. **a.** OemPnpDriversPath must be added to the answer file for the installation to search there for a compatible driver.

14. **b.** If the partition is smaller that 2GB, Windows 2000 will choose FAT16 for a format done during the install process. If the partion is larger than 2GB, it will be formatted as FAT32.

15. **b.** %MAC is the variable that RIS will use to specify the computers MAC address as the computer name.

16. **d.** /slip is the switch that you would use. Microsoft calls this slipstreaming.

17. **c.** MsDosInitiated=1 informs setup that the files will come from the network install. MsDosInitiated=0 informs setup that the files are on the CD-ROM.

18. **a, c.** RIS and sysprep install allow you to preconfigure and install all your applications.

19. **b.** 32MB of RAM is required to install Windows 2000 Professional. This is the minimum, although you will probably want to install more memory.

Chapter 3 Solutions

1. **a.** MMC.exe is the executable, and if you want to make sure you are in author mode, you must use the /a switch.

2. **a, b, c, d.** You can create all of these tasks.

3. **a.** Full access is probably the best answer because it meets the restrictions and gives the users the most functionality. However, b and c are also correct.

4. **a, b**. Either of these modes will restrict the adding of new snap-ins, but allow new windows to be used.

5. **d.** Only Author Mode will allow users full access to customize the console.

6. **b.** This mode will allow users to use multiple windows, but not remove these windows from the console.

7. **b, c.** Device manager allows you to manage the hardware on your system. The computer management snap-in also contains the device manager.

8. **c.** The MMC saves its consoles with an .msc extension.

9. **a.** By selecting the option Do Not Save Changes To This Console, users will see the same console every time they start the console.

10. **c.** You can check the extensions that are loaded with a particular snap-in. Sometimes, you may be able to remove some of the functionality by unloading an extension.

11. **b, d.** When you load the snap-in Link to a Web Address, you can connect through http or ftp.

12. **d.** Favorites will assist you in navigating to often-used areas of your console tree.

13. **a.** Tasks will allow yo to run a script file from within the MMC.

14. **c.** If the console drop-down menu is not available, you are probably in one of the user modes. You must open the MMC in author mode to make these options available.

15. **b.** False. You can use the MMC to connect to other computers and have full functionality from wherever you are located.

16. **a, b.** You would use the event viewer snap-in. The computer management snap-in also contains the event viewer.

17. **a, d.** You would use the disk management snap-in to modify your partitions. The computer management snap-in also contains the disk management snap-in.

18. **a, b.** You would use the device management snap-in to disable a device. The computer management snap-in also contains the device management snap-in.

19. **a, c.** You would use the local users and groups snap-in. The computer management snap-in also contains the local users and groups snap-in.

20. **a, b.** The Services snap-in will accomplish this goal. The computer management snap-in also contains the services snap-in.

Chapter 4 Solutions

1. **b.** Volume Points are used to mount local drives to an empty folder on an NTFS volume.

2. **b.** Encrypting File System.

3. **a, c, d.** Dynamic Disks are not supported on portable computers, removable disks, and USB interfaces.

4. **d.** Change Journal provides a log of changes to an NTFS volume.

5. **d.** The Convert system tool is used to convert a FAT partition to an NTFS partition.

6. **b.** Disk Management is used to configure and manage network storage space.

7. **b.** False. Disk Quotas cannot be administered on network shares.

8. **a, d.** To manage a hard disk on a remote computer, users must be a member of the Administrator group or the Server Operators group.

9. **c.** The Compact system tool is used to compress and decompress files on an NTFS partition.

10. **a.** Disk Cleanup is used to identify unnecessary files that can be deleted from the hard disk.

11. **c.** cipher /?

12. **b.** When a compressed file is copied from an NTFS volume to a FAT volume, the file is decompressed.

13. **a, b, c.** FAT16, FAT32, and NTFS can be used on Windows 2000 Professional.

14. **a.** Dynamic disks are physical disks that contain only dynamic volumes.

15. **b.** If a user reverts from a dynamic disk to a basic disk, all data is lost.

16. **a.** A basic disk can have three primary partitions and one extended partition.

17. **a.** True. Disk quotas can be allocated on a per-user basis.

18. **b.** False. A compressed file cannot be encrypted.

19. **a, b, c.** Disk Cleanup will search for temporary Internet files, offline files, and files in the Recycle Bin.

20. **a.** True. Dynamic disks can be resized without having to start Windows 2000 Professional.

Chapter 5 Solutions

1. **c.** The System utility has this functionality under the Network Identification tab.

2. **a, c.** The System utility has this functionality under the Hardware tab. You can start the Hardware Wizard from there. You can also go to Add/Remove Hardware.

3. **b.** The Display utility has this functionality under the Screen Saver tab.

4. **c.** The Power Options utility has this functionality under the Power Schemes tab.

5. **d.** The Power Options utility has this functionality under the APM tab.

6. **c.** The Magnifier is probably the best choice for this user, so he can magnify only those items that he is having trouble with.

7. **a.** Sticky Keys allows the user to press only one key at a time on the keyboard and retain full functionality.

8. **b.** The Keyboard utility has this functionality.

9. **c.** The Personalized Menus hide a user's least-often accessed icons from the Start menu.

10. **d.** The Power Options utility gives you this information under the Hibernate tab.

11. **d.** The Regional Options settings allows him to change the format of how the date is displayed. The Date/Time utility only allows you to change the current date.

12. **b.** Toggle Keys allows you to change the settings on whether a key held down will repeat the keystroke and how often it will repeat.

13. **a.** The System utility has this functionality under the Advanced tab in the System and Startup Section.

14. **d.** The System utility has this functionality under the Hardware tab in the Hardware Profiles Section.

15. **c.** The Date/Time utility allows you to change your current time zone.

16. **c.** The Display utility allows you to change the colors under the Appearance tab.

17. **a.** Phone and Modem Options is probably the best choice here, although you could use the System tool and go into the Hardware Wizard. The Phone and Modem Options gives you only modem information.

18. **c.** The MultiLanguage edition would work in this situation. Although you could use the two localized versions, they would require more administration.

19. **d.** Installing the MultiLanguage edition would allow the Chinese users to work in their native language and connect to the English servers.

Chapter 6 Solutions

1. **a.** Documents are stored in the My Documents folder by default.

2. **c.** Shared folders can be located on both FAT and NTFS folders.

3. **b.** The My Pictures folder is the default location for images.

4. **a.** Indexing Service returns a list of all documents that meet a certain search criteria.

5. **a.** ACL stands for Access Control List.

6. **a.** Dfs stands for Distributed File System.

7. **b.** False. Shared folder permissions may not be sufficient to provide access to files and folders on an NTFS volume.

8. **a.** The compressed file or folder loses its compressed state.

9. **b.** The file keeps its compressed state.

10. **b.** False. Files cannot be both compressed and encrypted at the same time.

11. **a, c.** The Administrators and Power Users groups can administer shared folders.

12. **a.** Caching is used to make network documents available for offline viewing.

13. **a, b.** The Shared Folders snap-in can be used to view a list of all shared folders and view how many users are connected to each shared folder.

14. **a.** True. The History folder tracks all documents that a user opens.

15. **a, b, c, d.** Files can be synchronized automatically at logon or logoff, manually at any time, and when the computer is idle.

Chapter 7 Solutions

1. **d.** The Print driver supplies device specific information to the GDI. The GDI in turn uses this information to create the print job that is sent to the spooler.

2. **a.** Because print jobs are sent to any available printer that is a member of the printer pool, the printers need to be identical. If the printers differ, the print job may call for a specific printer function, such as duplexing, that is not supported by one of the printers in the printer pool. Choice b is incorrect because printers in a printing pool can use serial or parallel cables.

3. **a, d.** Windows 2000 supports Point and Print. Point and Print allows a user to simply select the printer and Windows 2000 will automatically install the printer driver. Windows 2000 can install printer drivers for Windows 2000, Windows NT 4 and 3.51, and Windows 95 and 98. Additional printer drivers can be installed in two places—the Sharing tab in Printer Properties and the Drivers tab in Server Properties.

4. **c.** Internet Printing requires the use of Internet Information Server (IIS) on the print server. IIS, through the function of Active Server Pages, supplies the Web-based interface that users can use to connect, install, and manage print jobs. Answer a is incorrect because Internet Printing is based (and relies) on the TCP/IP protocol suite. IPX is not compatible with TCP/IP. Answer b is incorrect because Internet Printing is a standard that is documented in a number of RFCs. Answer d is incorrect because Internet Printing does not require SQL Server.

5. **b.** The default spooler location for Windows 2000 printers is %systemroot%\ System32\spool\PRINTERS. This location can be changed if the boot partition (i.e., where %systemroot% is located) is running out of disk space.

6. **b.** Windows 2000 supports the following print job formats: Enhanced Metafile (EMF), RAW, RAW (FF Appended), RAW (FF Auto), Text, and PSCRIPT1.

7. **a.** The print spooler service controls the print router, remote print provider, local print provider, and port monitors. By restarting the print spooler service, all of these components will restart. They will then restart any jobs located in the spool directory. The print spooler service can be restarted by selecting Control Panel | Administrative Tools | Services or by entering NET STOP SPOOLER followed by NET START SPOOLER at a command prompt.

8. **b.** Standard TCP/IP Port Monitor (SPM) is the preferred port monitor for Windows 2000. It uses Simple Network Management Protocol (SNMP) to configure and monitor ports. Answer a is incorrect. NetWare Link State Protocol (NLSP) is a routing protocol used with IPX. Answer c is incorrect. Although SPM uses SNMP to monitor the ports, Windows 2000 relies on SPM to provide the functionality. Answer d is incorrect. TCP/IP is a protocol suite that consists of many protocols.

9. **a.** The logical printer represents the software-based printing process in Windows 2000. The physical printer represents the actual hardware printing device.

10. **c.** Clients using Windows 3.x or DOS can only see network printers that conform to the 8.3 filename standard. Use eight characters for the file name plus three for the extension for a total of 11 characters.

11. **d.** Using Resume from the Document menu will allow the print job to continue printing. Answer a, Restart from the Document menu, will start the print job from the beginning. Answers b and c are not possible.

12. **a.** True. Because Internet Printing relies on TCP/IP, TCP/IP must be installed on the workstation.

13. **a.** The default spooler location for Windows 2000 printers is %systemroot%\System32\spool\PRINTERS. This location can be changed if the boot partition (i.e., where %systemroot% is located) is running out of disk space. This setting can be changed from Server Properties.

14. **b.** The Pause Printing command stops the print queue from sending data to the print device. The print device will continue to print any data that it has in memory. Once the data in memory is printed, the print device will stop printing.

15. **a.** To enable Windows NT 3.51 clients to use the printers, the Windows NT 3.51 print drivers need to be installed on the print servers. Once installed, the clients can use Point and Print services to install and use the printers.

16. **c.** Remember that priorities go from 99 (highest) to 1 (lowest). By configuring his logical printer to 99 and leaving the remaining logical printers at the default setting of 1, the supervisor's print jobs will print first.

17. **c.** Forms can be added using the Forms tab from Server Properties. On this page, a form can be defined by specifying the margins and paper size.

18. **a.** By default, CREATOR/OWNER is granted the Manage Documents right. With this right, users can manage their own print jobs, but not the print jobs of other users. The Print right, granted to the Everyone group by default, allows users to submit jobs, but they cannot manage the print jobs. The Manage Printers right allows the user to pause or stop the printer. This right is granted to Administrators and Power Users by default.

19. **b.** False. Windows 2000 supports printing in a wide variety of network environments including TCP/IP, IPX/SPX, and NetBEUI.

20. **a.** Auditing can be accessed via the Printer Properties' Security tab. Click on the Advanced button, then the Auditing tab to configure auditing.

21. **a.** When an individual print job is paused, the remaining print jobs in the print queue continue to print as they normally would.

22. **b.** The print spooler service can be restarted by selecting Control Panel | Administrative Tools | Services. Another way of restarting the print spooler is by entering NET STOP SPOOLER followed by NET START SPOOLER at a command prompt.

23. **c.** When FILE is selected as the print port, Windows 2000 prompts the user for a file name. The print job is then written to disk using the supplied file name.

24. **b, c.** The local print provider contains two subcomponents, the print processor and the separator page processor. The print router and the GDI are two separate components.

Chapter 8 Solutions

1. **b, c, e.** Windows 95, Windows 98, and Windows 2000 support the Plug and Play standard.

2. **b.** Windows 95 was the first Microsoft operating system to support Plug and Play.

3. **c, d.** Windows 2000 supports drivers from Windows 98, and it supports Windows NT drivers if the drivers support the WDM model.

4. **b.** False. The driver must be Plug and Play compliant to take advantage of the Plug and Play system.

5. **a.** True. If the driver is Plug and Play, the device can take advantage of the Plug and Play system.

6. **a.** True. This is the optimal situation, where everything is Plug and Play compliant.

7. **b.** False. Nothing here is Plug and Play compliant, so the device does not use the Plug and Play system.

8. **c, e.** Windows 98 and Windows 2000 support the WDM standard.

9. **b.** ACPI is the newest standard, and Windows 2000 can take full advantage of it.

10. **a, c.** A bus driver and filter driver are used in raw mode.

11. **d.** The operating system will be able to control the hardware and use of system resources.

12. **d.** Usually, the user is not required to do anything. The system will automatically make the device available.

13. **b.** Windows 2000 asks you for the device driver, but it also may search for the driver that you need.

14. **c.** The Plug and Play manager is responsible for allocating resources to the hardware.

15. **b, c.** The policy manager and power manager are in charge of the power management tasks.

Chapter 9 Solutions

1. **a.** ICM is an API.

2. **b.** There would be no APM tab if the computer did not support APM.

3. **b.** Accelerated Graphics Port.

4. **c.** Windows 2000 Professional supports up to 10 monitors.

5. **b.** CAT files are stored in the systemroot\System32\CatRoot folder.

6. **c.** Digital Video Disc.

7. **b.** False. ACPI is not the same as APM.

8. **b.** False. Windows 2000 Professional does not currently support writing to DVD devices.

9. **c.** Windows 2000 Professional supports up to two processors.

10. **b.** False. Windows 2000 Professional does not have a troubleshooter for DHCP.

11. **a, b, c, d.** All listed devices can be USB devices.

12. **a, c.** IrDA supports transmission rates of 115,000 bps and 4 Mbps.

13. **b.** Windows 2000 Professional supports version 7.0 of DirectX.

14. **a.** True. Only members of the Administrator group can create hardware profiles.

15. **c.** 127 devices can be tiered to a single port.

16. **b.** Driver signing is used to ensure that the highest quality device drivers are being used.

17. **b.** False. AVBoot is not used to change information on disk sectors.

18. **a.** True. Windows 2000 Professional supports Plug and Play.

19. **b.** Enable Boot Logging starts Windows 2000 Professional while logging devices and services to a text file.

Chapter 10 Solutions

1. **c.** The Password Authentication Protocol (PAP) is the authentication protocol that transmits the password in an unencrypted or plaintext form.

2. **b.** A hub is a network device that provides a central point of connectivity to a physical network. Each individual computer connects to the hub via its own network cable. Network traffic that enters the hub is then replicated and sent back out every port in the hub.

3. **d.** A workgroup is a group of computer resources in name only. All members of a workgroup maintain their own user account databases. In this situation, users need a username and password for each network resource they desire access to.

4. **d.** QoS (Quality of Service) Packet Scheduler allows an administrator to control bandwidth on the network. For example, if a user needs to use a network-intensive application, such as Voice over IP (VoIP), QoS can be implemented to prioritize VoIP traffic over regular network traffic.

5. **b, c.** Windows 2000 ships with support for the two most popular local area networks: Client for Microsoft Networks and Client Services for NetWare.

6. **a.** Windows 2000 provides support for two tunneling protocols: PPTP and L2TP. L2TP relies on IPSec to provide data encryption at a machine level.

7. **c.** With the Challenge Handshake Authentication Protocol (CHAP), the password is never transmitted across the network. CHAP uses the hashing method known as MD5. CHAP operates by having the server send a challenge to the client computer. The client computer, using MD5, hashes both the challenge and the password and sends it to the server. The server, knowing the challenge and the user's password from its security database, creates its own hash. The server then compares the two hashes. If the hashes match, the re-quested access is permitted. The password itself is never actually transmitted across the network.

8. **c.** Network Driver Interface Specification (NDIS) layer provides a way for a network transport (such as TCP/IP, NWLink, and NetBEUI) to communicate with a network adapter. This layer contains the drivers that communicate directly with the network adapters.

9. **b.** The Extensible Authentication Protocol (EAP) is an extension to PPP that works with dial-in, PPTP, and L2TP clients. EAP allows additional authentication methods with PPP. These methods include smart cards, such as Secure ID, public key authentication, and certificates. EAP is generally used in VPN networks that require stronger authentication methods.

10. **a.** A bridge is a network device that connects two or more physical networks. The bridge maintains a table consisting of hardware addresses. When the bridge receives a frame from one physical segment, it checks the destination hardware address for the frame against the table. If the hardware address is located on the other side of the bridge, it allows the frame to cross. If it isn't, the frame is not permitted to cross.

11. **b.** False. When ICS is enabled on a Windows 2000, it configures the Windows 2000 computer with a static IP address of 192.168.0.1.

12. **d.** When third-party software is being used to connect to a network and you are not sure which authentication protocol it uses, the simplest authentication protocol, PAP, should be used. Most software packages support PAP. Another authentication protocol can be used on the server after figuring out what other authentication protocols are supported by the third-party software.

13. **a, b.** NetWare 5.0 is the first version of NetWare to provide support for both IPX/SPX and TCP/IP. Previous versions of NetWare supplied limited TCP/IP support.

14. **a.** The Windows 2000 Component Architecture is comprised of software components, such as network adapter drivers, protocols, and APIs.

15. **d.** A router is a network device that connects two or more logical networks. The router maintains a routing table that tells the router which logical networks it knows the routes to. When the router receives a packet, it analyzes the packet's logical destination address to determine where it should route the packet. If the router is aware of a route to the destination, it forwards the packet out the port closest to the destination. If the router is not aware of a suitable route, the router discards the packet and sends a notification to the sender that the destination was not reachable.

16. **b.** False. Windows 2000 supports local area, remote, VPN, and direct connections.

17. **c.** Windows 2000 supports a number of network media including Ethernet, Token Ring, ATM, Cable Modem, and DSL. X.25 is used for remote dial-up connections.

18. **c.** A switch is a network device that combines the features of bridges and hubs. Like a hub, a switch contains ports that interconnect multiple computers or physical networks. Like a bridge, the switch analyzes the destination hardware address in a frame and sends the frame out the appropriate port. Because the frame is not replicated on all ports like a hub, using a switch results in greater bandwidth for individual workstations.

19. **a.** NWLink, more commonly known as IPX/SPX, is a proprietary network protocol designed to be used by Novell NetWare networks.

20. **c.** Windows 2000 does not ship with support for Localtalk. Localtalk is a simple protocol used with the Apple Macintosh.

21. **a.** A domain-based network model provides a centralized user account database. Any members of the domain use the domain user account database to verify network access. A user needs only one user account to access any resources in the domain.

22. **a.** The Network Protocol layer provides services that allow data to be sent across the network. These protocols include TCP/IP, NWLink, NetBEUI, AppleTalk, IrDA, ATM, and DLC.

Chapter 11 Solutions

1. **b.** 00100101.10100010.00101111.1100000 is the proper conversion.

2. **d.** 11011010.00101111.11101100.01110110 is the proper conversion.

3. **c.** 00010010.11110111.10001000.100000000 is the proper conversion.

4. **a.** 217.253.38.238 is the proper conversion.

5. **d.** 153.252.39.110 is the proper conversion.

6. **a.** 157.204.63.222 is the proper conversion.

7. **b.** This is a remote network because the third octet is part of the network ID and it has a different value than your source IP address.

8. **a.** This is a local network because only the first two octets are part of the network ID and they have the same value.

9. **b.** This is a remote network because the third octet is part of the network ID and it has a different value than your source IP address.

10. **a.** This is a local network because only the first two octets are part of the network ID and they have the same value.

11. **a.** The WINS entry is the one used here because WINS is checked before the LMHOSTS file.

12. **b.** The Hosts entry is the one used here because the Hosts file is checked before the DNS entry.

13. **c. ipconfig /renew** requests a new address from the DHCP server, though **ipconfig /registerdns** refreshes the DHCP lease as well. It also registers the computer again with the DNS server and, if only a DHCP address is needed, then this option will create more bandwidth.

14. **a. ipconfig /registerdns** refreshes the DHCP lease and registers the system with the DNS server.

15. **d. ipconfig /all** displays all of the settings for your TCP/IP configuration.

16. **a, b, c, e.** The client first attempts to renew the address at half the lease time; if unsuccessful, it tries at seven-eighths the time. The client will also renew the address whenever the system reboots.

17. **b.** Running **NBTSTAT −R** purges the local NetBIOS name cache and allows the new IP address to be resolved.

18. **d.** The Hosts file is the first item checked to resolve a host name.

19. **d.** ARP maps an IP address to a MAC address.

20. **c.** c:\winnt\system32\drivers\etc is the path where these files need to be for the system to find and use them.

Chapter 12 Solutions

1. **a.** The current state of the computer is saved to disk when it goes into hibernate mode.

2. **b.** A hot dock is performed when the computer is running, and a warm dock is performed when the computer is in standby mode.

3. **a.** Windows 2000 Professional supports hot swapping of IDE devices.

4. **b.** When a file is pinned, it is copied to the local cache on the portable computer.

5. **b.** False. Windows 2000 Professional does synchronize over slow links.

6. **b.** The Offline File cache is changed by moving the slider under Amount Of Disk Space To Use For Temporary Offline Files.

7. **a.** APM is enabled on the APM tab in the Power Options Properties dialog box.

8. **a.** The ampstat.exe utility is used to check for APM BIOS capability.

9. **b.** False. APM is not enabled by default on portable computers.

10. **a.** True. Windows 2000 Professional has six predefined power schemes.

11. **a.** True. Standby mode is enabled by default on ACPI- and APM-enabled computers.

12. **b.** A surprise removal is when a PC card is removed before Windows 2000 has stopped the device.

13. **b, d.** The two best power schemes for use with portable computers are Portable/Laptop and Presentation.

14. **a, b, c.** Incoming Connections supports VPN, direct connect, and modem connections.

15. **a, b, c, d.** Network And Dial-Up Connections supports all these choices.

16. **b.** Callback allows a remote server to call a user back at a preset number.

17. **b.** The Security log shows you all the data collected from the auditing.

Chapter 13 Solutions

1. **b.** SSO stands for Single Sign-On.

2. **a, b, c, d.** All of the groups listed are included in the Windows 2000 Professional security groups.

3. **b.** False. The Guest group cannot install Service Packs.

4. **c, d.** Members of the Power Users group can create and manage local user accounts and install programs that do not alter system files.

5. **a.** The types of rights in Windows 2000 Professional are privilege and logon rights.

6. **b.** False. Windows 2000 Professional can be set up to not require the Ctrl+Alt+Delete key combination when users are logging on.

7. **a.** True. The owner of a file can change the permissions on the file regardless of any other permissions applied to the file.

8. **c.** The Write Attributes special permission is used to allow users to change the attributes of a file.

9. **a, b, c, d.** All of the listed events can be audited.

10. **b.** Certificates are managed using the Certificate Manager snap-in.

11. **a.** True. Interactive logon and network authentication are the two types of user authentication used in Windows 2000 Professional.

12. **b.** False. Kerberos is the default authentication protocol for Windows 2000.

13. **a, b.** PAP and CHAP are RAS authentication protocols supported in Windows 2000 Professional.

14. **a.** True. IPSec is the default authentication protocol used for L2TP VPN connections.

15. **b.** The cipher.exe utility is used to encrypt files from the command line.

Chapter 14 Solutions

1. **b.** This is the most likely solution because the task runs well when you are logged in. If the task were disabled or the task scheduler service was not started, the task wouldn't start at all.

2. **c, d.** The idle options make sure that the computer does not have other active processes running when your task is running.

3. **b.** Tasks by default have a .job extension.

4. **d.** Nothing should be required of the task on the new system. When you copy a task, all the parameters for the task are included.

5. **b, d.** Counters are individual objects that are grouped together in objects.

6. **a.** System Monitor allows you to view the data in real time.

7. **b, c.** The counter log is the tool used most often for storing data; however, the trace log stores data as well.

8. **a.** The System Monitor allows you to view the data from a counter log file.

9. **d.** An Alert informs you when your hardware reaches certain performance levels.

10. **a.** You can save the counter log settings to a Web page and use that Web page to create counter logs on other computers.

11. **a, b.** You can save the data from System Monitor to a Web page or to a tab delimited file.

12. **a, c, d.** System Monitor allows you to view the data in a chart, histogram, or report format.

13. **b.** You need to enable auditing on each object that you want to track.

14. **a.** Audit logon events allows you to monitor who logs into the system.

15. **b.** Auditing object access allows you to track who is deleting files, but you must enable auditing for each file or directory that you want to track.

16. **d.** Auditing is a policy and enabling this policy allows you to track any changes to the system policy.

17. **b.** The Security log shows you all the data collected from the auditing process.

18. **b, c.** Windows 2000 is Plug and Play and can usually function just fine with the addition and removal of hardware, but if the system produces error messages or cannot boot, you may need a hardware profile.

Chapter 15 Solutions

1. **b.** The ERD is not bootable. To use the ERD, you must boot the system with either the Windows 2000 installation CD or the Windows 2000 Setup floppy disks. Once booted, select R for the Repair option.

2. **c.** Use the ERD to recover missing or corrupt boot files. To use the ERD, you must boot the system with either the Windows 2000 installation CD or the Windows 2000 Setup floppy disks. Once booted, select R for the Repair option. Select the Inspect Startup Environment option.

3. **d.** Perform a backup using the Backup utility, and select the System State. By selecting the System State, Backup backs up the Registry files. It also places a copy of the files in %systemroot%\repair\regback.

4. **c.** When booting in Safe Mode, only essential drivers and services are loaded. These include the mouse, keyboard, basic VGA, the Event Log, Remote Procedure Call (RPC), and the Logical Disk Manager services.

5. **b.** The Recovery Console can be started by booting the system either with the Windows 2000 installation CD or with the Windows 2000 Setup floppy disks. Once booted, select C to start the Recovery Console.

6. **c.** Device drivers can be disabled by using the disable *servicename* command found in the Recovery Console, where *servicename* is the name of the device driver or service to be disabled.

7. **d.** Backup in Windows 2000 supports the following media types: QIC tape, DLT tape, 8mm tape, digital audio tape, floppy disks, hard disks, optical disks, CDR, and CDRW.

8. **a, b, c, d**. By default, the Recovery Console only permits access to %systemroot%, the root directory of local disks; \cmdcons and any subdirectories; and directories on floppy disks and CD-ROMs. Access can be gained to other directories by changing the local Group Policy setting named Allow Floppy Copy And Access To All Volumes And Folders.

9. **a.** The log file is stored in the %systemroot% folder and is called ntbtlog.txt.

10. **d.** The Safe Mode with Networking option loads the minimum required device drivers including device drivers required for network connectivity.

11. **b.** The ERD in Windows 2000 does not contain any copy of the Registry. In previous versions of Windows NT, the ERD did contain compressed copies of the Registry. In Windows 2000, the only files on the ERD are autoexec.nt, config.nt, and setup.log.

12. **a.** The Safe Mode options can be accessed by pressing the F8 key when the OS selection menu is displayed.

13. **d.** The Emergency Repair Process restores the Registry files from the %systemroot%\repair directory. The Registry files stored in this directory are the Registry files created after the initial install of Windows 2000.

14. **b.** False. Individual components in the System State cannot be selected. The System State is restored as a whole because there are dependencies that occur between the different components.

15. **a.** When using the Emergency Repair Process, two options are presented: Fast Repair and Manual Repair. Fast Repair executes all options including restoring the initial Registry created during setup. Manual Repair provides the opportunity to run three separate options: Inspect Startup Environment, Verify Windows 2000 System Files, and Inspect Boot Sector. The Inspect Startup Environment option checks the startup files and replaces any that are missing or corrupt.

16. **a.** The Enable command can be used to set the start type for a device driver or service. The syntax of the Enable command is as follows:

```
enable servicename start_type
```

17. **b.** Enable Boot Logging boots the system under normal conditions (i.e., all device drivers and services designated to start automatically will be loaded). It creates a log file called ntbtlog.txt that logs the name and status of device drivers in memory. The log file is stored in the %systemroot% folder.

18. **d.** The ERD in Windows 2000 is created using the Backup utility.

19. **b.** The Recovery Console command Fixboot creates a new boot sector on the system partition.

20. **c.** The regback directory is created when the System State is backed up. The regback directory is used to store backup copies of the Registry at the time that the System State was backed up.

21. **d.** CDFS is the file system for CD-ROMs. As such, read-only access is only possible, not full access.

22. **a.** The Recovery Console can be installed as a startup option. To install, insert the Windows 2000 installation CD into your CD-ROM drive. At the command prompt, type "D:\I386\WINNT32 /cmdcons", where D: is the drive letter of the CD-ROM drive.

Chapter 16 Solutions

1. **d.** DHCP can provide an IP address, a subnet mask, a default gateway, DNS server addresses, and WINS server addresses. MAC addresses are configured in the network adapter at the factory.

2. **a.** The user principal name looks exactly like an Internet email account. The UPN consists of the user name followed by the @ sign followed by the user principal name suffix.

3. **b.** Kerberos v5 authentication protocol is the default authentication method. Kerberos is a standard security protocol supported by many vendors and operating systems.

4. **a.** True. A domain-based network is a logical grouping of computers that all share a common security database. This allows a user to have a single user account that can employ, when granted the proper access, any resources in the domain.

5. **a.** IPX/SPX or NWLink uses the 802.5 frametype when operating on a Token Ring network.

6. **d.** WINS is used to resolve NetBIOS names to IP addresses.

7. **a, b.** The key word here is non-routed. The default gateway is the IP address of a router. When the workstation needs to send data on another subnet, it sends the data to the default gateway.

8. **a, b.** Connectivity between Windows 2000 Professional and NetWare requires the networking protocol NWLink, also known as IPX/SPX, and Client Services for NetWare, which provides access to NetWare file and print services.

9. **c.** The Distinguished Name uniquely identifies an object in Active Directory by including the full path to its Active Directory location. For example, the Distinguished Name of Samuel Watson, a member of the Marketing department at mycompany.com, is of cn=SamuelWatson, ou=Marketing, dc=mycompany, dc=com (cn designates the common name, ou designates the organizational unit, dc designates the domain component).

10. **b.** Because an IP address is a property of TCP/IP, Obtain An IP Address Automatically from Internet (TCP/IP) Protocol properties will configure TCP/IP in Windows 2000 to use DHCP.

11. **c.** Windows 2000 Professional first attempts to use Kerberos. Because the Windows NT 4 domain does not contain the Kerberos Key Distribution Center on the domain controller, it then attempts to use NTLM and the SAM.

12. **c.** DNS is used to resolve host names to IP addresses.

13. **d.** Microsoft Networks uses the Common Internet File Service (CIFS) protocol to access file and print resources on a Microsoft Network. CIFS is identical to the Server Message Block (SMB) protocol that is used in earlier Microsoft network operating systems such as Windows NT. The other protocols listed are network protocols that facilitate communication between computers on a network.

14. **d.** Windows 2000 Professional stores Group Policy objects in the %systemroot%\System32\GroupPolicy directory.

15. **a.** Only a member of the Administrators group can change workgroup or domain membership.

16. **d.** Windows 2000 does not include a client for the AS400.

17. **d.** When accessing a network with multiple frametypes, you must specify each frametype. AutoDetect sets the frametype to the first one it detects.

18. **b.** False. A workgroup is a logical grouping of computers without a centralized security database. The purpose of a workgroup is to make it easier for users to identify network resources. To access these resources, a user needs a separate logon and password for each resource.

19. **a, d.** Windows 2000 supports two types of logons: SAM Account Name, which is provided for backwards compatibility with Windows NT 4, and User Principal Name, found in Windows 2000.

20. **b.** The common name, or cn, is the default Relative Distinguished Name.

Chapter 17 Solutions

1. **a.** To configure Gateway (and Client) Service for NetWare, you need to have a valid NetWare user account that is a member of the NTGATEWAY group on NetWare.

2. **b.** False. The Bindery is a standalone object. In other words, if you wanted to log on to two separate NetWare 3.12 servers, you would need a valid user

account on each server. NDS, however, is replicated and distributed among the NetWare servers on the network.

3. **d.** The Context represents the NDS location of a user's account. For example, if there is a user account called Lisa located in an OU called Marketing and it was also located in the Phoenix OU, Lisa's context would be MARKETING. PHOENIX.

4. **a, d.** To connect to a NetWare server, a Windows 2000 Professional needs to have Client Service for NetWare and NWLink installed. Client Service for NetWare permits the Windows 2000 Professional workstation to speak the same language of the NetWare servers: NCP. NWLink is the network protocol used by NetWare 3.12 servers.

5. **a.** If a NetWare 4.x or NetWare 5.x server is running with a Bindery context, you must specify the Preferred Server in Client Service for NetWare properties. A Bindery context simulates the Bindery found in NetWare 3.12.

6. **b, c.** Novell changed the default frametype following NetWare 3.11. NetWare 3.11 and earlier use Ethernet 802.3; NetWare 3.12 and later use Ethernet 802.2. Autodetect sets the frametype to the first one detected. Once set, it doesn't change "on the fly."

7. **a.** The NetWare group NTGATEWAY is given trustee assignments to NetWare resources. This allows the gateway to connect and authenticate to the NetWare resources.

8. **c.** The **net use** command can be used to map network drives and printer ports to network resources. Always remember to specify the resource's location using the UNC path: *Servername**Volumename*.

9. **b.** False. The Windows 2000 Professional workstations do not need NWLink unless that is their network's protocol. The only computer that needs NWLink installed is the Windows 2000 server that is running Gateway (and Client) Service for NetWare.

10. **a.** True. The internal network number is used for internal routing purposes; i.e., amongst the network-related processes within the computer. This is used only if you are running an application such as File and Print Services for NetWare. By default, Windows 2000 sets the internal network number to 00000000. Normally the internal network number does not need to be changed.

11. **c.** The **net use** command maps network drives to NetWare resources, much as it is used to map network drives to shares on a Microsoft network. The **net use** command uses UNC paths to locate the NetWare volume. UNC syntax is *Servername**Volume*.

12. **a.** The external network number is used for addressing and routing purposes. This is analogous to the network portion of an IP address.

13. **c.** When you are connecting to a NetWare 3.12 server, Client Service for NetWare needs to know which NetWare 3.12 server's Bindery contains the user account. Client Service for NetWare uses the Preferred Server setting to locate the NetWare 3.12 server.

14. **b.** Novell introduced NDS with NetWare 4.x. NDS is a directory service that contains all network objects such as user accounts, printers, servers, and so on.

15. **c.** The Bindery contains all user and group accounts, passwords, and trustee assignments in NetWare 3.12 and earlier.

16. **a.** Writing the Context as a typefull name means that you notate each container object with its type. For example, ou= designates that the object named is an Organizational Unit. o= designates that this is the name of the NDS tree. cn= designates the common name of the object, although that is not used in a Context. Only container objects are specified in the Context.

17. **c.** Management doesn't want Client Service for NetWare installed, so you must install a Windows 2000 server running Gateway (and Client) Service for NetWare. This setup allows existing Microsoft clients to access the NetWare servers.

18. **b.** Gateway (and Client) Service for NetWare translates CIFS requests from Microsoft clients into NCP requests that NetWare servers understand.

19. **a.** When you are using Gateway (and Client) Service for NetWare, the Windows 2000 server maps network drives to the NetWare server. These mapped drives are then turned into shares on the Windows 2000 server that Microsoft clients can connect to.

20. **c.** The **net view** command by default lists resources on a Microsoft network. By adding the switch **/network:nw**, you can also view NetWare resources.

21. **c.** Novell changed the default frametype following NetWare 3.11. NetWare 3.11 and earlier use Ethernet 802.3. NetWare 3.12 and later use Ethernet 802.2.

22. **a, d.** NetWare 5.x relies on NDS for user authentication. The Default Tree specifies the NDS tree, whereas the Context identifies the location where the user account can be found.

23. **d.** Feeling the competitive effects of the Internet, Novell redesigned NetWare 5.x to use TCP/IP as its core network protocol. Previous versions of NetWare relied on the network protocol IPX/SPX.

24. **a, c.** Objects in NDS can be either container objects or leaf objects. Container objects can contain other container objects and leaf objects. Leaf objects are objects such as user accounts, group accounts, servers, printers, and volumes.

25. **d.** NetWare 3.12 relies on the bindery for storage of user and group account information.

Chapter 18 Solutions

1. **a.** Linux is a freely distributed operating system that runs on Intel-based computers.

2. **b.** Client for NFS allows Windows NT and Windows 2000 computers to access NFS files directly. You can browse the NFS network by double-clicking NFS Network in My Network Places.

3. **b.** The statement is false. Services for Unix is an add-on package that must be purchased separately from the operating system.

4. **d.** To install Services for Unix 2, you need 60MB of free disk space.

5. **d.** NFS is a standard client/server protocol used to access files across a Unix-based network. NFS is defined in Request for Comments (RFCs) 1094 and 1813.

6. **b.** Server for NIS integrates Active Directory and NIS by allowing an Active Directory domain controller to act as a master NIS server. This permits an Active Directory administrator to create, modify, and delete user accounts in both security domains.

7. **a.** User Name Mapping provides a way to create maps between Windows and Unix user and group accounts. For example, a Windows user account is mapped to a Unix account. When a user (running either Client for NFS, Server for NFS, or Gateway for NFS) attempts to access data on a Unix server, the client contacts a User Name Mapping Server, which in turn matches the Windows account to the appropriate Unix account.

8. **c.** The Telnet Server is limited to 10 connections when installed on a Windows 2000 Professional or Windows NT Workstation 4 computer.

9. **d.** Server for NFS is not installed when performing a standard install on a Windows 2000 Professional computer. If your computer is running Windows NT Workstation 4 or Windows 2000 Professional, the following components are installed during a Standard Installation: Telnet Client, Telnet Server, Unix Shell and Utilities, and Client for NFS.

10. **d.** The Telnet Client allows a user to connect to a remote computer and execute programs. The Telnet Client uses port 23 (the Telnet protocol).

11. **a.** Server for NFS allows a Windows NT Server or a Windows 2000 Server to act as an NFS server, exporting Windows directories as NFS file systems.

12. **c.** AT&T started the development project that eventually became Unix. Sun and HP are vendors who produce two separate variations of Unix.

13. **b.** The Telnet Client command to create a new connection to a Telnet server is **open** *hostname*, where *hostname* is the name of the Telnet server.

14. **b.** The Telnet Client allows a user to connect via the Telnet protocol (port 23) to a remote computer over a TCP/IP-based network. It provides a command-line interface to execute applications remotely.

15. **a.** Server for PCNFS allows users to supply their Unix user name and password to be authenticated. Once verified, the Windows 2000 server running Server for PCNFS returns the user identifier (UID) and group identifier (GID). The user's computer then connects to the Unix server. This component is included in Services for Unix 2 to provide support for earlier Services for Unix clients.

16. **b.** The statement is false. Users accessing files on an NFS share must have a valid NIS user account.

17. **b.** If your computer is also a domain controller, Server for NFS Authentication is also installed when performing a standard install.

18. **b.** The statement is false. The Gateway for NFS component can only be installed on Windows NT Server or Windows 2000 Server computers.

19. **c.** The C programming language was adopted by the architects of Unix to enhance the operating system by introducing new capabilities, such as scripting.

20. **c.** Gateway for NFS creates connections to NFS servers and in turn hosts these connections as Windows shares. When Windows-based clients want to access NFS servers, they make a connection to the appropriate share found on the Gateway server using the native CIFS protocol.

Appendix B
Objectives for Exam 70-210

Installing Windows 2000 Professional	Chapter
Perform an attended installation of Windows 2000 Professional.	2
Perform an unattended installation of Windows 2000 Professional.	2
Install Windows 2000 Professional by using Windows 2000 Server Remote Installation Services (RIS).	2
Install Windows 2000 Professional by using the System Preparation Tool.	2
Create unattended answer files by using Setup Manager to automate the installation of Windows 2000 Professional.	2
Upgrade from a previous version of Windows to Windows 2000 Professional.	2
Apply update packs to installed software applications.	2
Prepare a computer to meet upgrade requirements.	2
Deploy service packs.	2
Troubleshoot failed installations.	2

Implementing and Conducting Administration of Resources	Chapter
Monitor, manage, and troubleshoot access to files and folders.	6
Configure, manage, and troubleshoot file compression.	6
Control access to files and folders by using permissions.	6
Optimize access to files and folders.	6
Manage and troubleshoot access to shared folders.	6
Create and remove shared folders.	6
Control access to shared folders by using permissions.	6
Connect to local and network print devices.	7
Manage printers and print jobs.	7
Control access to printers by using permissions.	7
Connect to an Internet printer.	7
Connect to a local print device.	7
Configure and manage file systems.	4
Convert from one file system to another file system.	4
Configure file systems by using NTFS, FAT32, or FAT.	4

Implementing, Managing, and Troubleshooting Hardware Devices and Drivers	Chapter
Implement, manage, and troubleshoot disk devices.	4
Install, configure, and manage DVD and CD-ROM devices.	4
Monitor and configure disks.	4
Monitor, configure, and troubleshoot volumes.	4
Monitor and configure removable media, such as tape devices.	4
Implement, manage, and troubleshoot display devices.	9

(continued)

Implementing, Managing, and Troubleshooting Hardware Devices and Drivers *(Continued)*	Chapter
Configure multiple-display support.	9
Install, configure, and troubleshoot a video adapter.	9
Implement, manage, and troubleshoot mobile computer hardware.	12
Configure Advanced Power Management (APM).	12
Configure and manage card services.	12
Implement, manage, and troubleshoot input and output (I/O) devices.	9
Monitor, configure, and troubleshoot I/O devices, such as printers, scanners, multimedia devices, mouse, keyboard, and smart card reader.	9
Monitor, configure, and troubleshoot multimedia hardware, such as cameras.	9
Install, configure, and manage modems.	9
Install, configure, and manage Infrared Data Association (IrDA) devices.	9
Install, configure, and manage wireless devices.	9
Install, configure, and manage USB devices.	9
Update drivers.	9
Monitor and configure multiple processing units.	9
Install, configure, and troubleshoot network adapters.	9

Monitoring and Optimizing System Performance and Reliability	Chapter
Manage and troubleshoot driver signing.	14
Configure, manage, and troubleshoot the Task Scheduler.	14
Manage and troubleshoot the use and synchronization of offline files.	14
Optimize and troubleshoot performance of the Windows 2000 Professional desktop.	14
Optimize and troubleshoot memory performance.	14
Optimize and troubleshoot processor utilization.	14
Optimize and troubleshoot disk performance.	14
Optimize and troubleshoot network performance.	14
Optimize and troubleshoot application performance.	5, 9, 14
Manage hardware profiles.	9
Recover systems and user data.	15
Recover systems and user data by using Windows Backup.	15
Troubleshoot system restoration by using Safe Mode.	15
Recover systems and user data by using the Recovery Console.	15

Configuring and Troubleshooting the Desktop Environment	Chapter
Configure and manage user profiles.	5
Configure support for multiple languages or multiple locations.	5
Enable multiple-language support.	5
Configure multiple-language support for users.	5
Configure local settings.	5
Configure Windows 2000 Professional for multiple locations.	5
Install applications by using Windows Installer packages.	5
Configure and troubleshoot desktop settings.	5
Configure and troubleshoot fax support.	5
Configure and troubleshoot accessibility services.	5

Implementing, Managing, and Troubleshooting Network Protocols and Services	Chapter
Configure and troubleshoot the TCP/IP protocol.	11
Connect to computers by using dial-up networking.	10
Connect to computers by using a virtual private network (VPN) connection.	10
Create a dial-up connection to connect to a remote access server.	10
Connect to the Internet by using dial-up networking.	10
Configure and troubleshoot Internet Connection Sharing.	10
Connect to shared resources on a Microsoft network.	16

Implementing, Monitoring, and Troubleshooting Security	Chapter
Encrypt data on a hard disk by using Encrypting File System (EFS).	13
Implement, configure, manage, and troubleshoot local Group Policy.	13
Implement, configure, manage, and troubleshoot local user accounts.	13
Implement, configure, manage, and troubleshoot auditing.	14
Implement, configure, manage, and troubleshoot account settings.	13
Implement, configure, manage, and troubleshoot account policy.	14
Create and manage local users and groups.	13
Implement, configure, manage, and troubleshoot user rights.	13
Implement, configure, manage, and troubleshoot local user authentication.	13
Configure and troubleshoot local user accounts.	13
Configure and troubleshoot domain user accounts.	13
Implement, configure, manage, and troubleshoot a security configuration.	13

Appendix B

Appendix C
Study Resources

Books

Microsoft Windows 2000 Professional Resource Kit, Microsoft Press, Redmond, WA, 2000. ISBN: 1-57231-808-2. This book is *the* technical resource IT professionals need to install, manage, and maintain the Windows 2000 Professional operating system. A companion CD-ROM includes tools for deploying and managing Windows 2000 Professional.

MCSE Training Kit — Microsoft Windows 2000 Professional, by Microsoft Corporation. Microsoft Press, Redmond, WA, 2000. ISBN: 1-57231-901-1. This book is the official Microsoft training kit for Exam 70-210, "Installing, Configuring, and Administering Microsoft Windows 2000 Professional." It includes many hands-on practice labs to aid in preparing for the exam.

Honeycutt, Jerry, Jr. *Introducing Microsoft Windows 2000 Professional,* Microsoft Press, Redmond, WA, 1999. ISBN: 0-7356-0662-5. This book is a great introduction to Windows 2000 Professional. It covers the new features introduced with the operating system in addition to a comparison with both Windows NT and 98.

ActiveEducation (editor). *Microsoft Windows 2000 Professional Step by Step.* Microsoft Press, Redmond, WA, 2000. ISBN 1-57231-847-3. This is a good learn at your own pace book. As with all the *Step by Step* series, this book is designed for users who need basic Windows 2000 Professional skills.

Stinson, Craig and Siechert, Carl. *Running Microsoft Windows 2000 Professional,* Microsoft Press, Redmond, WA, 2000. ISBN 1-57231-838-4. The book is well written, with detailed explanations of concepts of Windows 2000 Professional. This book is geared more toward the novice, not the power user of Windows 2000 Professional.

Periodicals

Microsoft Certified Professional Magazine, Microsoft Corporation, Irvine, CA. This monthly magazine for Windows NT experts is also a good resource for Microsoft certification information.

Windows 2000 Magazine (formerly *Windows NT Magazine*), Duke Communications, International, Loveland, CO. This magazine covers the technical aspects of Windows 2000, Windows NT, and Windows BackOffice.

Certification Magazine, MediaTec Publishing, Oakland, CA. This now-monthly magazine is slanted toward certified professionals of information technology. Certification Magazine's aim is to provide IT professionals and technical trainers with a comprehensive look at all platforms of IS/IT certification and training.

Microsoft-Approved Test Providers

➤ MeasureUp, Inc.: **www.measureup.com**

➤ Self Test Software, Inc.: **www.selftestsoftware.com**

Online Resources

http://windows.microsoft.com/windows2000/en/professional/help/ default.asp—Microsoft Windows 2000 Professional help area. This site provides Windows 2000 Professional help and documentation on the Web. Users can access the same help information that is available with the operating system.

http://support.microsoft.com—Microsoft Knowledge Base; Search the Microsoft Knowledge Base of technical support information and self-help tools for Microsoft products. This site is great for problem solving. Users can search the Microsoft knowledge base with specific questions on all of Microsoft's products.

www.microsoft.com/technet—Microsoft TechNet home page. Technet is the technical resources for Windows professionals. Technical information is provided on all of Microsoft's products.

www.windows2000experience.com—This page gives IT professionals the how-to knowledge, resources, and product information you need to evaluate and deploy Windows 2000. This site is provided by *Windows 2000 Magazine*, and it has current news on Windows 2000, reprinted articles from *Windows 2000 Magazine* and a Windows 2000 discussion forum for posted questions. This site is a good one-stop resource.

www.labmice.net/—Labmice.net prides itself on becoming "...the definitive online resource for IT Professionals who deploy, manage, and support Microsoft Windows 2000 products and services." The site consolidates information from other technical sites into one user-friendly resource. Labmice.net also has book reviews on the must-have books for keeping current with the latest technology.

www.windows2000faq.com/—Windows 2000 Frequently Asked Question resource from *Windows 2000 Magazine*. This site contains a lot of useful information about all aspects of Windows 2000. Users can search the site for specific topics. This site is updated weekly.

www.winsupersite.com/—Site provided by *Windows 2000 Magazine*; has reviews of the latest Windows products. Provides reviews of the latest Windows products. This site prides itself on being the one site you need evaluate, administer, and use Microsoft's Windows operating systems.

www.win2000mag.com—Online version of *Windows 2000 Magazine*. This is a searchable site with access to back issues of *Windows 2000 Magazine*. Detailed information is accessible only to subscribers of the hard-copy version of the magazine.

www.i386.com/win2k/—Good resource for Windows 2000 information; this site gives brief synopses of various components of Windows 2000.

www.microsoft.com/trainingandservices/default.asp—Microsoft's training and certification page; this site lists requirements for all Microsoft certifications. It also links to training resources and the latest new on training and certification for Microsoft products.

www.WindowsITLibrary.com/—This site is a free online technical-reference source on Windows NT and 2000. This site lists subjects by topic and has brief online chapters on each topic. All material is original technical content or is selected content licensed from computer book publishers.

www.microsoft.com/seminar—Microsoft Seminar Online resource center. Contains online seminars and presentations, which cover information technology (IT) topics such as product features, planning, deployment, development, and strategic assessment.

www.mcpmag.com—Online version of *Window Microsoft Certified Professional Magazine*. Very thorough site, with an MCP chat area and discussions groups. Users view current and previous issues of *MCP Magazine*. It also has salary surveys for all levels of Microsoft certification.

www.cramsession.com—Certification and training site that provides free study guides (or Cramsessions), free exam practice questions, and free information on IT topics.

www.examcram.com—The Coriolis Group's new certification site. Here, you can access training courses and materials, read the latest industry news, get study tips, find questions and answers, find out about mentor programs, join discussion groups, take real-world exam practice questions, and more.

Appendix C

www.microsoft.com/mcp—Microsoft Certification Program news and certification track requirements.

www.ittutor.com—ITTutor.com offers free online training for Windows NT and 2000. Users must download the ITT2000 applications to use the free test.

www.brainbuzz.com—BrainBuzz.com labels itself the IT Vortal (a vertical portal—a comprehensive Web site that provides information, resources, and services targeted to a specific industry). BrainBuzz.com is the vertical portal for IT career enhancement.

www.mcmcse.com—The MC MCSE certification site has three areas: (1) a certification section that contains practice exams, study notes and links; (2) a knowledge area provides links to TechTutorials.com, which is a free Web site that provides a searchable index of over 1,000 terms; and (3) an employment section that provides career advice and resources as well as access to a database of over 220,000 tech jobs.

www.mcsetutor.com—The MCSETutor.com site provides solutions for MCSE self-study needs. It has a forum area where users can post questions about various topics relating to certification. It also has book list of recommended books for Windows NT and 2000.

www.microsoft.com/DirectAccess—Microsoft Direct Access is designed to help consultants get the information they need to support Microsoft products. Listings are available for local Microsoft news and events. The Microsoft Direct Access training programs offers discounted technical training and free online courseware that allows individuals to study at your own pace. Evaluation tools and quarterly briefings are also available to help users stay up-to-date on the latest products.

http://mspress.microsoft.com—Microsoft Press is a good source for information on Microsoft products. The Mspress.Microsoft.com site is the starting point for locating Microsoft approved books, study guides and other resources for Microsoft's certification tests.

http://windows2000.about.com/compute/windows2000/—This site provides book reviews, access to forums on Windows 2000 and the latest Windows 2000 news.

Appendix D
Keyboard Shortcuts

This appendix contains 12 tables that are divided into separate areas of useful shortcuts, which you can use while working within and around Windows 2000 Professional. Table D.1 lists general keyboard shortcuts for Windows 2000.

Table D.1   Windows 2000 keyboard shortcuts.

Press	To
Ctrl+C	Copy
Ctrl+X	Cut
Ctrl+V	Paste
Ctrl+Y	Redo
Ctrl+Z	Undo
Delete	Delete
Shift+Delete	Delete selected item permanently without placing the item in the Recycle Bin
Ctrl while dragging an item	Copy selected item
Ctrl+Shift while dragging an item	Create shortcut to selected item
F2	Rename selected item
Ctrl+Right Arrow	Move the insertion point to the beginning of the next word
Ctrl+Left Arrow	Move the insertion point to the beginning of the previous word
Ctrl+Down Arrow	Move the insertion point to the beginning of the next paragraph
Ctrl+Up Arrow	Move the insertion point to the beginning of the previous paragraph
Ctrl+Shift with any arrow key	Highlight a block of text
Shift with any arrow key	Select more than one item in a window or on the desktop, or select text within a document
Ctrl+A	Select all
F3	Search for a file or folder
Ctrl+O	Open an item
Alt+Enter	View properties for the selected item
Alt+F4	Close the active item or quit the active program
Ctrl+F4	Close the active document in programs that allow you to have multiple documents open simultaneously
Alt+Tab	Switch between open items
Alt+Esc	Cycle through items in the order they were opened

(continued)

Table D.1   Windows 2000 keyboard shortcuts *(Continued)*.

Press	To
F6	Cycle through screen elements in a window or on the desktop
F4	Display the Address bar list in My Computer or Windows Explorer
Shift+F10	Display the shortcut menu for the selected item
Alt+Spacebar	Display the System menu for the active window
Ctrl+Esc	Display the Start menu
Alt+Underlined letter in a menu name	Display the corresponding menu
Underlined letter in a command name on an open menu	Carry out the corresponding command
F10	Activate the menu bar in the active program
Right Arrow	Open the next menu to the right or open a submenu
Left Arrow	Open the next menu to the left or close a submenu
F5	Refresh the active window
Backspace	View the folder one level up in My Computer or Windows Explorer
Esc	Cancel the current task
Shift when you insert a CD into the CD-ROM drive	Prevent the CD from automatically playing

Note: If StickyKeys is turned on in Accessibility Options, some keyboard shortcuts may not work.

Table D.2 lists general keyboard shortcuts for the Windows 2000 dialog boxes.

Table D.2   Dialog box keyboard shortcuts.

Press	To
Ctrl+Tab	Move forward through tabs
Ctrl+Shift+Tab	Move backward through tabs
Tab	Move forward through options
Shift+Tab	Move backward through options
Alt+Underlined letter	Carry out the corresponding command or select the corresponding option
Enter	Carry out the command for the active option or button
Spacebar	Select or clear the checkbox if the active option is a checkbox
Arrow keys	Select a button if the active option is a group of option buttons
F1	Display Help
F4	Display the items in the active list
Backspace	Open a folder one level up if a folder is selected in the Save As or Open dialog box

Table D.3 lists general keyboard shortcuts for Windows Explorer.

Table D.3   Windows Explorer keyboard shortcuts.

Press	To
End	Display the bottom of the active window
Home	Display the top of the active window
Num Lock+asterisk on numeric keypad (*)	Display all subfolders under the selected folder
Num Lock+Plus Sign on numeric keypad (+)	Display the contents of the selected folder
Num Lock+Minus Sign on numeric keypad (-)	Collapse the selected folder
Left Arrow	Collapse current selection if it's expanded, or select parent folder
Right Arrow	Display current selection if it's collapsed, or select first subfolder

Table D.4 describes keyboard shortcuts for the Windows 2000 built-in accessibility options.

Table D.4   Accessibility options keyboard shortcuts.

Press	To
Right Shift for eight seconds	Switch FilterKeys on and off
Left Alt+left Shift+Print Screen	Switch High Contrast on and off
Left Alt+left Shift+Num Lock	Switch MouseKeys on and off
Shift five times	Switch StickyKeys on and off
Num Lock for five seconds	Switch ToggleKeys on and off

Help Viewer keyboard shortcuts are useful if you prefer to use the keyboard rather than the mouse. Table D.5 lists keyboard shortcuts for the Windows 2000 Help Viewer.

Table D.5   Help Viewer keyboard shortcuts.

Press	To
Alt+Spacebar	Display the system menu
Shift+F10	Display the Help Viewer shortcut menu
Alt+Tab	Switch between the Help Viewer and other open windows
Alt+O	Display the Options menu
Alt+O, and then press T	Hide or show the navigation pane
Ctrl+Tab	Switch to the next tab in the navigation pane
Ctrl+Shift+Tab	Switch to the previous tab in the navigation pane
Up Arrow	Move up one topic in the table of contents, index, or search results list
Down Arrow	Move down one topic in the table of contents, index, or search results list
Page Up	Move up one page in the table of contents, index, or search results list
Page Down	Move down one page in the table of contents, index, or search results list

(continued)

Table D.5   Help Viewer keyboard shortcuts *(Continued).*

Press	To
F6	Switch focus between the navigation pane and the topic pane
Alt+0, and then press R	Refresh the topic that appears in the topic pane
Up Arrow or Down Arrow	Scroll through a topic
Ctrl+Home	Move to the beginning of a topic
Ctrl+End	Move to the end of a topic
Ctrl+A	Highlight all text in the topic pane
Alt+0, and then press P	Print a topic
Alt+0, and then press B	Move back to the previously viewed topic
Alt+0, and then press F	Move forward to the next (previously viewed) topic
Alt+F4	Close the Help Viewer

Table D.6 details keyboard shortcuts for the Windows 2000 Contents tab.

Table D.6   Contents tab keyboard shortcuts.

Press	To
Alt+C	Display the Contents tab
Right Arrow	Open a book
Left Arrow	Close a book
Backspace	Return to the previous open book
Up Arrow or Down Arrow	Select a topic
Enter	Display the selected topic

Table D.7 lists general keyboard shortcuts for the Windows 2000 Index tab.

Table D.7   Index tab keyboard shortcuts.

Press	To
Alt+N	Display the Index tab
Up Arrow or Down Arrow	Select a keyword in the list
Alt+D or Enter	Display the associated topic

Table D.8 lists general keyboard shortcuts for the Windows 2000 Search tab feature.

Table D.8   Search tab keyboard shortcuts.

Press	To
Alt+S	Display the Search tab
Alt+L	Start a search
Alt+D or Enter	Display the selected topic

Table D.9 lists general keyboard shortcuts for the Windows 2000 Favorites tab.

Table D.9   Favorites tab keyboard shortcuts.

Press	To
Alt+I	Display the Favorites tab
Alt+A	Add a topic to the Topics list
Alt+P	Select a topic in the Topics list
Alt+R	Remove a topic from the Topics list
Alt+D	Display a topic from the Topics list

Table D.10 lists keyboard shortcuts for the menu commands that act on the entire console or the main window of a console.

Table D.10   MMC main window keyboard shortcuts.

Press	To
Ctrl+O	Open a saved console
Ctrl+N	Open a new console
Ctrl+S	Save the open console
Ctrl+M	Add or remove a console item
Ctrl+W	Open a new window
F5	Refresh the content of all console windows
Alt+Spacebar	Display the MMC window menu
Alt+F4	Close the active console window

Note: *The Ctrl+W keyboard shortcut is available for consoles opened in author mode or user mode/full access. Other Ctrl+ shortcuts are available only for consoles opened in author mode.*

Table D.11 lists keyboard shortcuts for the menu commands that act on the active console window in a console or on the contents of a console window.

Table D.11   MMC console window keyboard shortcuts.

Press	To
Ctrl+P	Print the current page or active pane.
Alt+– (minus sign)	Display the window menu for the active console window.
Shift+F10	Display the Action shortcut menu for the selected item.
Alt+A	Display the Action menu for the active console window.
Alt+V	Display the View menu for the active console window.
Alt+F	Display the Favorites menu for the active console window.
F1	Open the Help topic, if any, for the selected item.
F5	Refresh the content of all console windows.
Ctrl+F10	Maximize the active console window.

(continued)

Appendix D

Table D.11   MMC console window keyboard shortcuts *(Continued).*

Press	To
Ctrl+F5	Restore the active console window.
Alt+Enter	Display the properties dialog box, if any, for the selected item.
F2	Rename the selected item.
Ctrl+F4	Close the active console window. When a console has only one console window, this closes the console.

You can use the keyboard shortcuts shown in Table D.12 with a Microsoft Natural Keyboard or with any other compatible keyboard that includes the Windows Logo key and the Application key.

Table D.12   Natural keyboard shortcuts.

Press	To
Application key	Display the shortcut menu for the selected item
Ctrl+Logo+F	Search for computers
Logo key	Display or hide the Start menu
Logo+Break	Display the System Properties dialog box
Logo+E	Open My Computer
Logo+M	Minimize or restore all windows
Logo+F	Search for a file or folder
Logo+F1	Display Windows 2000 Help
Logo+R	Open the Run dialog box
Logo+Tab	Switch between open items
Logo+U	Open Utility Manager

Glossary

Accelerated Graphics Port (AGP)

A dedicated bus developed by Intel, AGP allows operating systems like Windows 2000 to have high quality video and graphics. This expansion slot can only be used for AGP video cards.

Access Control Entry (ACE)

An entry in the Access Control List (ACL) for a user or group. The ACE, containing the Security Identifier (SID) along with an Access Mask, establishes which operations are allowed, denied, or audited for a particular object. See *Access Control List, Security Identifier,* and *Access Mask.*

Access Control List (ACL)

A list of ACEs that apply to a particular object and / or the object's properties. See *Access Control Entry, Security Identifier,* and *Access Mask.*

Access Mask

One of two parts of the Access Control Entry, the access mask is a 32-bit value that specifies rights that are allowed or denied for a particular object. See *Access Control Entry, Access Control List,* and *Security Identifier.*

Access Token

A security object that identifies a user to the security subsystem in Windows 2000. The access token contains security information such as the user's Security Identifier (SID) and the SIDs of all groups to which the user is a member. It also contains the user's list of privileges on the local computer. See *Access Control Entry, Access Control List, Access Mask, Privileges,* and *Security Identifier.*

Accessibility

The capability of a user interface to provide alternative methods of functionality for people with hearing, visual, and physical disabilities.

Active Directory

Directory service found in Windows 2000 that stores and distributes information about network objects. Using a single logon, users can use Active Directory to access any network object, such as printers, servers, shares, and so on. See *directory service.*

Administrator

The most powerful user object found in Windows 2000. The Administrator user object can create other objects such as users, shares, printers, and so on. The Administrator can also reconfigure and install device drivers and system files.

Advanced Configuration and Power Interface (ACPI)

An industry specification used to define power management in computers. ACPI is an open standard embraced by many hardware and software vendors, including Microsoft and Windows 2000.

Advanced Power Management (APM)

A proprietary interface developed by Microsoft and Intel used between hardware-based power management software (BIOS level) and an operating system.

Answer File

A text file used to automate the installation of a Windows 2000 computer. The answer file provides user input for questions presented by the installation routine during Setup. The default answer file in Windows 2000 is unattend.txt.

Application Programming Interface (API)

A standard set of routines that an application or operating system uses to provide basic functionality. For example, an API may contain the routines to open and write to a file. A programmer writing an application can call the API's routines to perform that operation without the need to create a new routine.

Asymmetric Digital Subscriber Line (ADSL)

ADSL is a modem technology that transforms ordinary phone lines (also known as "twisted copper pairs") into high-speed digital lines for ultra-fast Internet access.

Asynchronous Communication

A form of data communication in which the sender must notify the receiver when the transmission of data begins and ends.

Asynchronous Mode Transfer (ATM)

A connection-oriented protocol that can be used to transport many different types of network traffic, such as video, voice, and data. ATM is known for its high speed.

Attribute

For a file or directory, an attribute can be used to mark a file as read-only or hidden.

In Active Directory, an attribute can be used to describe the characteristics of an object. The schema defines which attributes an object can have.

Auditing

Used to track the activities of users or processes. Audited events are stored in the security log.

Authentication

Used to identify users and objects whether accessing the resource locally or remotely. When a user logs on, his or her username and password are checked by the security subsystem of the workstation or domain.

AutoComplete

The AutoComplete feature uses IntelliSense technology to save previous entries you've made for Web addresses, forms, and passwords. Then, when you type information in one of these fields, AutoComplete suggests a list of possible matches derived from those past entries.

Automated installation

The process of using one of several methods (Remote Installation Services, Sysprep, bootable CD) to perform an unattended setup in Windows 2000.

Automatic Private IP Addressing (APIPA)

Found in Windows 2000 and Windows 98, APIPA allows a DHCP-enabled workstation to still receive an IP address if DHCP is unavailable. The network range used for APIPA is 169.254.0.1 through 169.254.255.254, along with the subnet mask 255.255.0.0. See also *DHCP*.

Backup

A copy of data used for disaster recovery purposes.

Backup Operator

One of the built-in groups in Windows 2000 whose members have the right to backup and restore files and folders, regardless of access permissions, encryption settings, or ownership.

Backup Types

Used to determine how data is backed up. There are five backup types found in Windows 2000: normal, copy, differential, incremental, and daily.

Balloon Help

Balloon Help improves upon Tooltips, the word descriptions that appear when a user hovers the cursor over an icon. Balloon Help dialogs help users discover many of the enhancements in Windows 2000 Professional.

Basic Disk

In Windows 2000, a physical disk that contains primary partitions and/or extended partitions with logical drives. Basic disks can also contain volume sets or RAID sets.

Basic Input Output System (BIOS)

A collection of software routines used to test and startup hardware in a computer. The BIOS is stored in read-only memory (ROM). This allows the computer to be turned off without the loss of the BIOS.

Basic Volume

A volume found on a basic disk in Windows 2000.

Boot Sector

Located at sector 1 of each bootable disk, it contains the executable code to access data on the disk.

Bootable CD

Automated installation method found in Windows 2000 used to run Setup from a CD-ROM (if the BIOS supports it).

Bottleneck

A condition resulting from a poorly performing component that results in the slow performance of the entire system.

Briefcase

Briefcase is used to synchronize the files with their counterparts on a main computer. When the user reconnects their portable computer to their main computer (or insert a removable disk containing the modified files), Briefcase automatically updates the files on the main computer to the modified versions

Cable Modem

A modem used to access broadband Internet service used on Cable TV infrastructures. It operates in the range of 10Mbps to 30Mbps.

Cache

A local store of recently resolved names for remote hosts used to speed IP address resolution times. Typically, the cache is used for DNS and WINS.

Callback

A form of network security in which a remote access server calls a user back at a preset number after the user has made an initial connection and has been authenticated.

Central Processing Unit (CPU)

The heart and brain of a computer that is used to retrieve data from other hardware devices in the system. The CPU can then interpret the data and execute the required instructions.

Glossary

Certificate

A digital document used to authenticate users and their transactions. See also *Certificate Services* and *Certificate Authority*.

Certificate Services

A service found in Windows 2000 that issues certificates for a Certificate Authority (CA). See also *Certificate, Certificate Authority*.

Certificate Authority (CA)

An entity responsible for establishing and verifying the authenticity of certificates.

Challenge Handshake Authentication Protocol (CHAP)

An authentication protocol for Point-to-Point Protocol (PPP) connections.

Change Journal

Change Journal tracks modifications to NTFS 5 files over time and across system reboots. NTFS enters records into the Change Journal in streams, one record for each volume on the computer. Each record indicates the type of change (read, write, move, and so on) and the object that was changed.

Chkdsk

Creates and displays a status report for a disk, based on the file system used. Chkdsk also lists and corrects errors on the disk.

Client

A computer or program connecting to another computer or program to access resources.

COM Port

A communications or serial port used to connect peripherals such as modems, printers, and scanners.

Common Internet File System (CIFS)

A protocol used on Microsoft networks to perform file operations on a remote computer. CIFS is formerly known as Server Message Block (SMB).

Compact Disc File System (CDFS)

A file system found in Windows 2000 and Windows NT that provides access to data stored on CD-ROM drives.

Compact Disc Recordable (CD-R)

A type of CD-ROM that can be written to via a CD Recorder and read via a CD-ROM drive.

Computer Management Console

Used to manage local or remote computers from a single, consolidated desktop utility. Computer Management (an MMC snap-in) combines several Windows 2000 administrative tools into a single console tree, providing easy access to a specific computer's administrative properties.

Copy Backup

A backup type that copies the selected data to backup media but does not set the archive bit on the file. By not setting the archive bit, the file is shown as not having been backed up.

Daily Backup

A backup type that copies data that has been created or modified the day the daily backup is performed. It does not set the archive bit on the file. By not setting the archive bit, the file is shown as not having been backed up.

Data Encryption Standard(DES)

DES is an algorithm developed by the National Institute of Standards and Technology for encrypting and decrypting data.

Data Link Control (DLC)

A network protocol used for IBM mainframe computers and HP network printer connectivity.

Data Packet

A logical unit of data transmitted from one network device to another.

Decryption

The process of making encrypted data readable.

Default Gateway

The IP address of a router located on the host's local subnet.

Desktop

The screen working area where icons, menus, applications, and dialog boxes are displayed.

Device Driver

A software component that provides the operating system with routines to access a hardware device.

Device Manager

An administrative tool that you can use to manage the devices on your computer. Using Device Manager, you can view and change device properties, update device drivers, configure device settings, and uninstall devices.

Differential Backup

A backup type that copies data that has been created or modified since the last normal or incremental backup. It does not set the archive bit on the file. By not setting the archive bit, the file is shown as not having been backed up.

Digital Audio Tape (DAT)

A magnetic tape medium used to backup data as well as digital audio data.

Digital Linear Tape (DLT)

A magnetic tape medium used to backup data. DLT is known for its high storage capacity and speed.

Digital Subscriber Line (DSL)

A type of communication line used for high-speed data transfer over traditional copper telephone wires.

Digital Video Disc (DVD)

A type of optical disc storage technology. A digital video disc (DVD) looks like a CD-ROM disc, but it can store greater amounts of data. DVDs are often used to store full-length movies and other multimedia content that requires large amounts of storage space.

Direct Memory Access (DMA)

Used for data transfer directly between memory and the hardware device, without the intervention of the CPU.

DirectX

The DirectX Foundation layer contains a single set of APIs that provide improved access to the advanced features of high-performance hardware, such as 3-D graphics acceleration chips and sound cards. These APIs control low-level functions, including 2-D graphics acceleration; support for input devices such as joysticks, keyboards, and mice; and control of sound mixing and sound output.

Directory

Used to hold information about computer files (a file system) or network objects (a directory service such as Active Directory).

Directory Service

The entity or service that is used to present directory information to other objects.

Disk Cleanup

Disk Cleanup helps free up space on your hard drive. Disk Cleanup searches your drive, and then shows you temporary files, Internet cache files, and unnecessary program files that you can safely delete.

Glossary

Disk Defragmenter

Disk Defragmenter rearranges files, programs, and unused space on your computer's hard disk, so that programs run faster and files open more quickly.

Disk Management

Disk Management is a graphical tool for managing disks and volumes. It supports partitions, logical drives, new dynamic volumes, and remote disk management.

Disk Quota

The amount of disk space available to a particular user.

Distinguished Name

A method of uniquely identifying an object in a directory. This method uses the Relative Name along with the names of container objects and domains that contain the object.

Distributed File System (Dfs)

Distributed File System (or Dfs) allows Administrators to simulate a single server share environment that actually exists over several servers, basically a link to a share on another server that looks like a subdirectory of the main server. This allows a single view for all of the shares on your network.

Distribution Folder

A folder used to distribute the Windows 2000 setup files.

DNS Server

A server that responds to Domain Name System (DNS) queries from DNS clients. A DNS query is a request to resolve a host name to an IP address.

DNS Zone

A zone is an adjoining portion of the DNS namespace that is administered separately by a DNS server.

Domain

A collection of computers and resources that share a common security database.

Domain Controller

A Windows 2000 or Windows NT Server that authenticates domain logons and maintains the security database.

Domain Name System (DNS)

A service and hierarchical naming system used for locating and resolving host names on a TCP/IP based network.

Driver Signing

Windows 2000 uses a driver signing system and when a driver is signed its been tested and is known to work with Windows 2000. You should always use signed drivers where possible. If a driver is not signed and you try and use as part of an unattended installation your installation will stop and you will prompted to continue to use it, this obviously defeats the purpose of unattended so it's possible to configure the installation to ignore driver signing.

Dual Boot

The capability of a computer to boot from two or more operating systems. A dual boot computer will display an operating system selection menu upon startup.

Digital Video Disc (DVD)

A type of optical storage technology known for its high data capacity. DVDs can hold full-length movies with alternate soundtracks, scenes, and so on. It also has the capacity to contain multiple CD-ROMs.

Dynamic Disk

A physical disk that has been upgraded by Disk Management. Dynamic disks cannot contain logical drives or partitions. They can only contain dynamic volumes created by Disk Management. Dynamic disks can only be accessed by Windows 2000 computers. See *Disk Management*.

Dynamic Host Configuration Protocol (DHCP)

A protocol used on TCP/IP-based networks to supply IP configurations dynamically to TCP/IP hosts. It is used to automate and simplify the configuration of a TCP/IP network.

Dynamic Volume

A logical volume created using Disk Management and residing on a dynamic disk. Dynamic volumes can be one of the following: simple, spanned, striped, mirrored (RAID-1), and striped with parity (RAID-5).

Dynamic Link Library (DLL)

A file containing a library of executable routines used by the operating system and associated applications. These routines work together to perform a specific software function.

Electrically Erasable Programmable Read-Only Memory (EEPROM)

A user-modifiable form of read-only memory (ROM), usually a microchip, that can be erased and written to repeatedly. EEPROMs are written and erased by applying electrical voltages. Another form of EEPROM is called "flash memory", typically found in hardware devices such as routers. Flash memory is used to store the devices configuration settings.

Emergency Repair Disk (ERD)

A floppy disk that contains files necessary in the Emergency Repair Process for Windows 2000. Files from the %systemroot%\repair directory are copied to the ERD. The ERD is created using the Backup utility.

Encrypting File System (EFS)

Used to protect sensitive data on a Windows 2000 computer, EFS uses symmetric key encryption along with public key cryptography to encrypt files on an NTFS partition.

Ethernet

A networking technology that uses Carrier Sense Media Access with Collision Detection (CSMA/CD) to manage network traffic. Ethernet is used in either a bus or star topology across coaxial, twisted-pair, or fiber-optic cabling.

Export

Term used in Unix where an NFS file system is made available to network resources.

Extensible Authentication Protocol (EAP)

An update to Point-to-Point Protocol (PPP), EAP allows additional authentication mechanisms to be employed during PPP connection validation, such as Smart Cards and Secure ID.

FAT32

An enhanced version of FAT that supports smaller cluster sizes. This results in more efficient use of disk space.

Fiber Distributed Data Interface (FDDI)

A networking technology that uses fiber-optic cabling.

File Allocation Table (FAT)

One of the most universal files systems, FAT is a file system that employs a file allocation table to keep track of various portion of a disk.

File System

The method by which files and folders are named, organized, and stored on a disk.

Glossary

File Transfer Protocol (FTP)
A protocol used to transfer files from one computer to another computer on a TCP/IP-based network.

Group
A collection of users used for organizational purposes as well as to administer rights to other objects.

Group Policy
A new utility found in Windows 2000, Group Policy allows an administrator to define certain rights and capabilities for users and groups on a computer or domain.

Hardware Abstraction Layer (HAL)
Part of the modular design of Windows 2000, the HAL is comprised of many software components such as device drivers and system files. These components work together to manage and interact with the hardware components in a computer. By employing the HAL, Windows 2000 can easily be ported to other hardware platforms without the need to rewrite the entire operating system.

Hardware Compatibility List (HCL)
A list of hardware devices that have been certified by Microsoft to be used in Windows 2000. The HCL can be found on Microsoft's Web site.

Hardware Profile
A profile used to load a different set of device drivers and/or services. A hardware profile is typically used when the hardware characteristics of a computer change rather frequently. For example, a laptop used with a docking station would have two hardware profiles. One would include the hardware for the docking station and the laptop, while the other would simply be the hardware configuration of the laptop.

Hibernate
The hibernate feature saves everything in memory on disk, turns off your monitor and hard disk, and then turns off your computer. When you restart your computer, your desktop is restored exactly as you left it. It takes longer to bring your computer out of hibernation than out of standby.

Hypertext Transfer Protocol (HTTP)
A protocol used to transfer files and data between a Web server and a Web browser. HTTP is the protocol for the World Wide Web.

IEEE 1394
A type of connector that allows you to connect and disconnect high-speed serial devices. An IEEE 1394 connector can be found on the back of some computers, near the serial port or the parallel port. The IEEE 1394 bus is used primarily to connect high-end digital video and digital audio devices to your computer; however, some hard disks, printers, scanners, and DVD drives can also be connected to your computer using the IEEE 1394 connector.

Image Color Management (ICM)
Image Color Management (ICM) 2.0 is an operating system application-programming interface (API) that helps to ensure that colors will be accurately and consistently represented on all of your publishing devices.

Incremental Backup
A backup type that copies the selected data that has changed since the last normal or incremental backup-to-backup media and sets the archive bit on the file. By setting the archive bit, the file is shown as having been backed up.

Indexing Service

Indexing Service creates searchable/to query indexes of the contents and properties of documents on your local hard drive and on shared network drives.

Inherited File Permissions

Permissions on an object that are automatically inherited from its parent object. Inherited permissions cannot be modified.

Integrated Device Electronics (IDE)

A type of disk-drive interface in which the controller electronics reside on the drive itself, eliminating the need for a separate adapter card.

Integrated Services Digital Network

A type of digital phone line used for the conveyance of both voice and data communications. ISDN can operate up to 128Kbps.

Intellimirror

A new feature found in Windows 2000 used for configuration management. This feature allows a user's desktop, application, and user environments to follow them throughout the network environment.

Interactive Logon

The process of logging on to a Windows 2000 computer via that computer's keyboard.

Integrated Services Digital Network (ISDN)

A digital phone line used to provide higher bandwidth. ISDN in North America is typically available in two forms: Basic Rate Interface (BRI) consists of 2 B-channels at 64 kilobits per second (Kbps) and a D-channel at 16 Kbps; Primary Rate Interface (PRI) consists of 23 B-channels at 64 Kbps and a D-channel at 64 Kbps. An ISDN line must be installed by the phone company at both the calling site and the called site.

Internet

The TCP/IP-based network whose public infrastructure is available practically worldwide.

Internet Connection Sharing

ICS allows multiple computers in an office to access an Internet connection by using a single IP address. ICS provides *NAT* (network address translation), address allocation, and name resolution for all of the computers.

Internet Explorer

With Internet Explorer and an Internet connection, you can search for and view information on the World Wide Web. You can type the address of the Web page that you want to visit into the address bar, or click an address from your list of Favorites. Internet Explorer also lets you search the Internet for people, businesses, and information about subjects that interest you. Internet Explorer security features let you browse the Web with confidence, knowing that your computer and personal information are safe with customized security settings.

Internet Printing Protocol (IPP)

A protocol used for printing documents across the Internet. IPP uses HTTP to transfer the print jobs to printers.

Internet Protocol (IP)

A protocol that is responsible for the routing of data across a TCP/IP-based network. IP is also responsible of IP addressing and the segmenting and reassembly of IP packets.

Internet Protocol Security (IPSec)

A set of cryptography standards used to protect data transmitted using the TCP/IP protocol suite.

Glossary

Internet Service Provider (ISP)

A company that provides Internet access to individual users and organizations via either a dial-up connection, cable modem, or DSL connection.

Internetwork Packet Exchange (IPX)

A protocol that is responsible for the routing of data across an IPX/SPX-based network. More commonly known as the native protocol for Novell NetWare networks.

Interrupt Request (IRQ)

A signal sent from a hardware device to the central processing unit (CPU) to notify the CPU that the device wishes to send or receive data. Each hardware device is assigned a unique IRQ number from 0 through 15.

Intranet

A TCP/IP-based network used within an organization that employs Internet technologies such as HTTP and FTP.

IP Address

A 32-bit binary address used to identify a host on a TCP/IP-based network. Each host must have a unique IP address. IP addresses are shown in dotted decimal format, for example, 192.168.0.10.

IrDA (Infrared Data Association)

The industry organization of computer, component, and telecommunications vendors who establish the standards for infrared communication between computers and peripheral devices. IrDA standards are employed primarily in wireless infrared interfaces to more easily send data to and from portable computers and printers.

Isochronous

Time-dependant. Refers to a communication protocol based on time slices rather than handshaking. For example, a process might have 20 percent of total bus bandwidth. During its time slice, the process can stream data.

Kerberos

The default authentication protocol used for the verification of users in Windows 2000. Windows 2000 employs Kerberos version 5.

Kernel

The heart of the modular architecture of Windows 2000, this software component comprises the core software that manages basic operating system and CPU operations.

Layer 2 Tunneling Protocol (L2TP)

An industry-standard Internet tunneling protocol. Unlike Point-to-Point Tunneling Protocol (PPTP), L2TP doesn't require IP connectivity between the client workstation and the server. L2TP requires only that the tunnel medium provide packet-oriented point-to-point connectivity. The protocol can be used over media such as ATM, Frame Relay, and X.25. L2TP provides the same functionality as PPTP (when used with IPSec for encryption). Based on Layer 2 Forwarding (L2F) and PPTP specifications, L2TP allows clients to set up tunnels across intervening networks.

Local Area Network (LAN)

A network of computers located within a relatively small geographic area.

Local Computer

A computer that is accessed directly without the use of a network or a modem.

Local Group

A group that resides on the local computer or a domain-based network, resides on all domain controllers. A local group can be granted access only to resources on the local computer where the local group resides. Local groups can contain users from the local computer, and also users and global groups from trusted domains.

Logical Drive

A volume created on an extended partition of a basic disk.

Logon Script

A batch file that contains a set of commands typically used to configure a user's working environment. The logon script is executed whenever the user logs on.

Master Boot Record (MBR)

The first sector on a hard disk that is used to start the process of booting the computer. The MBR contains both the executable code for booting and the partition table for the hard disk.

Microsoft Challenge Handshake Authentication Protocol (MS-CHAP)

An authentication protocol, similar to CHAP, for Point-to-Point Protocol (PPP) connections.

Microsoft Challenge Handshake Authentication Protocol version 2(MS-CHAP v2)

An authentication protocol, similar to CHAP and MS-CHAP, for Point-to-Point Protocol (PPP) connections. MS-CHAP 2 employs stronger security mechanisms than CHAP or MS-CHAP.

Microsoft Management Console (MMC)

A software-based console used for administration. An MMC is defined by the administrative utilities, also known as Snap-ins, it contains.

Microsoft Point-to-Point Encryption (MPPE)

An 128/40-bit encryption algorithm that uses RSA RC4 for packet security between two computers employing some tunneling technologies such as.

Mirrored Volume

A volume that duplicates (or mirrors) data to two separate physical disks, resulting in fault tolerance. Also known as RAID-1.

Modem

Short for *modulator/demodulator,* a device that allows computer information to be transmitted and received over a telephone line. The transmitting modem translates digital computer data into analog signals that can be carried over a phone line. The receiving modem translates the analog signals back to digital form.

Multilink

The combination two or more physical communications links' bandwidth into a single logical link increase your remote access bandwidth and throughput by using remote access Multilink. Based on the Internet Engineering Task Force (IETF) standard RFC 1990, you can use Multilink to combine analog modem paths, ISDN B-channels, and mixed analog and digital communications links on both your client and server computers. This combining of links increases your Internet and intranet access speed and decreases the amount of time you are connected to a remote computer.

My Documents Folder

This desktop folder provides you with a convenient place to store documents, graphics, or other files you want to access quickly. When you save a file in a program such as WordPad or Paint, the file is automatically saved in My Documents, unless you choose a different folder.

Glossary

My Network Places

My Network Places displays all of the shared computers, printers, and other resources on the network to which your computer is connected. You can use the Add Network Place wizard to create shortcuts to network, Web, and FTP servers.

My Pictures Folder

The My Pictures folder is the default storage location for pictures when they are saved from a digital camera to the computer.

NetBIOS Extended User Interface (NetBEUI)

A network protocol used on small local area networks with fewer than 200 computers. It is a non-routable protocol.

NetWare

A network operating system produced by Novell.

Network Adapter

A hardware device used to connect a host to a network.

Network Basic Input Output System (NetBIOS)

Known as a network-application programming interface (API), NetBIOS is used to request lower level network services.

Network Driver Interface Specification (NDIS)

A software component that provides a common interface between network protocols and network adapters.

Network File System (NFS)

A file system found in Unix that allows computers to share files across a network.

Network Information Service (NIS)

A distributed database used in Unix that contains shared configuration files, such as password and hosts files.

Normal Backup

A type of backup that copies the selected data to backup media and sets the archive bit on the file. By setting the archive bit, the file is shown as having been backed up.

Novell Directory Services (NDS)

A distributed database that contains user, group, and network object information. NDS is found in Novell NetWare 4.x and 5.x.

NT File System (NTFS)

A file system used in Windows 2000 and Windows NT that employs transaction logging to ensure data integrity. NTFS also supports encryption and compression The Windos 2000 version is NTFS 5.

NTLM

An authentication protocol that uses a challenge/response process. It was the default authentication protocol for Windows NT 4 and earlier. Windows 2000 uses Kerberos as its default authentication protocol.

NWLink

NWLink is Microsoft's implementation of Novell's IPX/SPX protocol suite.

Offline Files

Using Offline Files, users can continue to work with network files and programs even when they are not connected to the network.

OpenType Font

Outline fonts that are rendered from line and curve commands, and can be scaled and rotated. OpenType fonts look good in all sizes and on all output devices supported by Windows 2000. OpenType is an extension of TrueType font technology. Some OpenType fonts include Arial, Courier New, Lucida Console, Times New Roman, Symbol, and Wingdings.

Page Fault
A situation in which data is requested but cannot be found in physical memory. As a result, the operating system must look in the paging file for the "missing" data.

Paging File
A file on a hard disk that Windows 2000 uses to store data and code that can either no longer fit into physical memory or has not been used recently.

Partition
The logical division of a physical disk used to organize data. A partition can be formatted only for a single file system; therefore, a single physical hard disk with multiple partitions can contain multiple file systems.

Password Authentication Protocol (PAP)
The simplest authentication protocol, PAP merely transmits the user's username and password in plaintext format.

PC Card
A removable hardware device that is placed in a Personal Computer Memory Card International Association (PCMCIA) slot. These card types are typically found in laptop computers.

PCI
PCI is an acronym for *Peripheral Component Interconnect* and is a local bus standard developed by Intel Corporation. Most modern PCs include a PCI bus in addition to a more general ISA expansion bus. PCI is a high-performance 32-bit or 64-bit bus, designed for use with devices that have high-bandwidth requirements, such as the display subsystem.

Performance Counter
A data object that is incremented according to the characteristics of the performance object with which it is associated. Performance counters can be viewed in System Monitor.

Performance Object
A logical collection of performance counters that are associated with a hardware or software resource. Performance objects can be viewed in System Monitor.

Ping
A TCP/IP utility used to verify the connection between two TCP/IP hosts.

Plug and Play
A standard set of specifications that allows a computer to automatically detect new hardware devices and install the corresponding device drivers.

Point and Print
A method of installing network printers and their associated device drivers on a computer.

Point-to-Point Protocol (PPP)
A protocol used for dial-up connections.

Primary Partition
A volume created from unallocated space on a basic disk, a primary partition is the partition used to start an operating system such as Windows 2000.

Protocol
A set of specifications used to allow two or more computers to communicate across a network.

Public Key Cryptography
One form of cryptography in which two different keys are used—one public and one private.

Quality of Service (QoS)
A method of guaranteeing bandwidth to critical or time sensitive data transmissions.

Glossary

Redundant Array of Inexpensive Disks 1 (RAID-1)

RAID-1 duplicates data to two separate physical disks to provide fault tolerance. Also known as mirroring. See *mirrored volume.*

Redundant Array of Inexpensive Disks 5 (RAID-5)

RAID-5 stripes data across three or more physical disks to provide fault tolerance. One stripe includes parity information, which allows the RAID set to continue to function even in the event of a drive failure. Also known as *striping with parity.*

Read Only Memory (ROM)

Information stored in memory (usually in a computer chip or a CD-ROM) that cannot be erased or modified.

Recovery Console

A text mode interface found in Windows 2000 that allows an administrator to troubleshoot and recover a Windows 2000 computer.

Registry

A database that contains computer configuration and user information. The registry is found in Windows 2000, Windows NT, and Windows 9x.

Remote Authentication Dial-Up Service (RADIUS)

A security authentication protocol based on clients and servers and widely used by Internet service providers (ISPs) on non-Microsoft remote servers. RADIUS is the most popular means of authenticating and authorizing dial-up and tunneled network users today.

Remote Installer Service (RIS)

The remote installation services feature simplifies the task of installing an operating system on computers throughout the organization. RIS provides the mechanics needed for computers to connect to a network server during the initial boot process, while the server controls a local installation of Windows 2000 Professional.

Router

A network device that routes packets between two or more LANs. A router can interconnect LANs of differing network technology (for example, Ethernet to Token Ring).

Router Information Protocol (RIP)

A protocol used by routers to communicate and share routing tables. RIP can be found in both IP and IPX networks.

Routing Table

A list of routes that contains network IDs and the interfaces they can be reached from.

Safe Mode

A startup option found in Windows 2000 and Windows 9x that loads a limited set of device drivers. Safe Mode is useful for troubleshooting and recovering a computer.

Secure Sockets Layer (SSL)

A protocol for secure network communications using a combination of public and private key technology. Secure Sockets Layer is also called SSL. See *Public Key Cryptography.*

Security Account Manager (SAM)

A subsystem and database that is used to store and authenticate users in Windows NT 4 and Windows 2000 Professional.

Security ID (SID)

A variable that identifies a user, group, or computer. Every SID is unique.

Server Message Block (SMB)

A protocol used for file sharing on Microsoft networks. SMB is now known as CIFS in Windows 2000.

Shared Folders

A folder on another computer that has been made available for others to use on the network.

Shiva Password Authentication Protocol (SPAP)

A proprietary authentication protocol used for dial-up connections that employ Shiva equipment.

Simple Volume

A volume consisting of disk space from a single disk. A simple volume can consist of a single region on a disk or multiple linked regions of the same disk .You can extend a simple volume within the same disk or onto additional disks. If you extend a simple volume across multiple disks, it becomes a spanned volume. You can create simple volumes only on dynamic disks. Simple volumes are not fault tolerant, but can be mirrored.

Single-Sign On

A process that allows a user with a domain account to log on to a network once, using a password or smart card, and to gain access to any computer in the domain.

Small Computer System Interface (SCSI)

A standard high-speed parallel interface defined by the American National Standards Institute (ANSI). A SCSI interface is used for connecting microcomputers to peripheral devices such as hard disks and printers, and to other computers and local area networks (LANs).

Smart Card

A device (about the size of a credit card) that is used to authenticate a user.

Spanned Volume

A volume consisting of disk space on more than one physical disk. You can add more space to a spanned volume by extending it with NTFS. You can create spanned volumes only on dynamic disks. Spanned volumes are not fault tolerant and cannot be mirrored. In Windows NT 4, a spanned volume was known as a volume set.

Subnet

A portion of a divided network.

Subnet Mask

A method of annotating the network ID portion of an IP address. It is represented by a 32-bit binary value where contiguous 1's represent the network ID.

Synchronization Manager

Using Synchronization Manager, you can control when your offline files are synchronized with files on the network.

Symmetric Multiprocessing (SMP)

Two or more similar processors connected via a high-bandwidth link and managed by one operating system, where each processor has equal access to I/O devices.

System Files

The critical files that are used to run the Windows 2000 operating system.

System Information Utility

In Windows 2000, you can use System Information in Computer Management to collect and display your system configuration data.

System Policy

A Group Policy that is used to configure user and computer settings in the registry.

System Volume

The volume that contains the files needed to boot the operating system.

Glossary

TWAIN

API for image acquisition developed by an association of industry leaders. The specification is available from **www.twain. org**. This acronym stands for "technology without an interesting name."

Transmission Control Protocol / Internet Protocol (TCP/IP)

A protocol suite used to interconnect network computers. It is the network protocol for the Internet.

TrueType Font

Fonts that are scalable and sometimes generated as bitmaps or soft fonts, depending on the capabilities of your printer. TrueType fonts are device-independent fonts that are stored as outlines. They can be sized to any height, and they can be printed exactly as they appear on screen.

Uniform Resource Locator (URL)

A standard way of specifying the location of an object, typically a Web page, on the Internet. URLs are the form of address used on the Web. They are used in HTML documents to specify the target of a hyperlink that is often another HTML document (possibly stored on another computer).

Universal Disk Format (UDF)

The Universal Disk Format, commonly abbreviated to UDF, is a superset of existing data standards used to access images by common GIS, imaging, mapping and CAD software products (i.e., you can directly access data stored in UDF format, from a wide range of software packages, without having to import the data).

Universal Naming Convention (UNC)

The full Windows 2000 name of a resource on a network. It conforms to the *servername**sharename* syntax, where *servername* is the name of the server and *sharename* is the name of the shared resource. UNC names of directories or files can also include the directory path under the share name, with the following syntax: *servername**sharename**directory**filename*.

Universal Serial Bus (USB)

An external bus that supports Plug and Play installation. Using USB, you can connect and disconnect devices without shutting down or restarting your computer. You can use a single USB port to connect up to 127 peripheral devices, including speakers, telephones, CD-ROM drives, joysticks, tape drives, keyboards, scanners, and cameras. A USB port is usually located on the back of your computer near the serial port or parallel port.

User Account

An account that contains information pertaining to a particular user, such as username, full name, password, and so on.

Virtual Memory

Also known as the paging file, a file on a hard disk that Windows 2000 uses to store data and code that can either no longer fit into physical memory or that has not been used recently.

Virtual Private Network (VPN)

A connection to a private network that employs a public network infrastructure, such as the Internet. VPNs employ tunneling protocols such as PPTP and L2TP.

Volume

A partition on a physical disk that has been formatted with a file system.

Volume Mount Points

As an alternative to assigning a drive letter to a mounted drive, Windows 2000 can assign a drive path; you are no longer limited to 26 drive letters for mounting and accessing volumes. This is made possible by NTFS volume mount points, which are new file-system objects. Placing a mount point (which is implemented as an NTFS reparse point) on a directory maps one disk volume under a directory of another volume. Because volume mount points are based on NTFS 5 reparse points, they work only on NTFS 5 volumes. Multiple volume mount points can target any volume.

Wide Area Network (WAN)

A network that consists of diverse geographic areas interconnected with routers.

Win32 Driver Model (WDM)

A Windows driver model. A driver model based on the Windows NT driver model, designed to provide a common architecture of I/O services for both Windows NT and Windows operating systems for specific classes of drivers. These driver classes include USB and IEEE 1394 buses, audio, still-image capture, video capture, and HID-compliant devices such as USB mice, keyboards, and joysticks. WDM provides a model for writing kernel-mode drivers and minidrivers, and provides extensions for Plug and Play and power management.

Windows File Protection (WFP)

A new feature found in Windows 2000 that protects system files by checking modified system files or the correct version. If the version is incorrect, the modified file is replaced.

Windows Hardware Qualify Lab (WHQL)

The purpose of Microsoft's Windows Hardware Quality Labs is to ensure the compatibility of hardware with Microsoft Operating Systems. WHQL provides test kits that are used to qualify devices, systems and servers for the Microsoft Windows logos and for inclusion on Microsoft's Hardware Compatibility List (HCL).

Windows Installer Service

The Windows Installer is a component of the Windows 2000 operating system and that simplifies the application installation and uninstallation process. Windows Installer manages the installation and removal of applications by applying a set of centrally defined setup rules during the installation process. The Windows Installer can also be considered a set of rules that developers need to follow to take full advantage of the service.

Windows Internet Naming Service (WINS)

A service found in Windows NT and Windows 2000 that resolves NetBIOS names to IP addresses.

Windows Update

An online extension of Windows 2000 that consists of a Web site that can be used to automatically locate and download updated portions of Windows 2000.

Workgroup

A grouping of computers only for identification and resource location purposes.

X.25

An X.25 network transmits data with a packet-switching protocol, bypassing potentially noisy telephone lines. This protocol relies on an elaborate worldwide network of packet-forwarding nodes that can participate in delivering an X.25 packet to its designated address.

Glossary

Index

Coriolis introduces

EXAM CRAM INSIDER™

A FREE ONLINE NEWSLETTER

Stay current with the latest certification information. Just visit ExamCram.com and sign up to receive the latest in certification and training news for Microsoft, Java, Novell, A+, and more! Read e-letters from the Publisher of the Exam Cram and Exam Prep series, Keith Weiskamp, and certification experts about future trends in IT training and education. Access valuable insider information on exam updates, new testing procedures, sample chapters, and links to other useful, online sites. Take a look at the featured program of the month, and who's in the news today. We pack all this and more into our *Exam Cram Insider* online newsletter to make sure *you* pass your next test!

To sign up for our twice monthly newsletter, go to www.ExamCram.com and click on "Become a Member" and sign up.

EXAM CRAM INSIDER – Another reason Exam Cram and Exam Prep guides are *The Smartest Way To Get Certified.*™ And it's <u>free</u>!

What's on the CD-ROM

The *MCSE Windows 2000 Professional Exam Prep*'s companion CD-ROM contains elements specifically selected to enhance the usefulness of this book, including:

➤ The testing system for this *Windows 2000 Exam Prep*, which includes 50 questions. Additional questions are available for free download from **ExamCram.com**; simply click on the Update button in the testing engine. You can choose from numerous testing formats, including Fixed-Length, Random, Test All, and Review.

➤ *RFC 826*—An Ethernet Address Resolution Protocol

➤ *RFC 950*—Internet Standard Subnetting Procedure

➤ *RFC 1034*—Domain Names–Concepts and Facilities

➤ *RFC 1035*—Domain Names, Implementation and Specification

➤ *RFC 1180*—A TCP/IP Tutorial

➤ *RFC 1219*—On the Assignment of Subnet Numbers

➤ *RFC 1518*—An Architecture for IP Address Allocation with CIDR

➤ *RFC 1519*—Classless Inter-Domain Routing (CIDR): an Address Assignment and Aggregation Strategy

➤ *RFC 1817*—CIDR and Classful Routing

➤ *RFC 1878*—Variable Length Subnet Table For IPv4

➤ *RFC 2132*—DHCP Options and BOOTP Vendor Extensions

➤ *RFC 2181*—Clarifications to the DNS Specification

System Requirements

Software

➤ Your operating system must be Windows 95, 98, NT 4 or higher. To do the Real-World Projects, however, you may need either Windows 2000 Professional and/or Windows 2000 Server.

➤ To view the practice exams, you need Internet Explorer 5.x.

Hardware

➤ An Intel (or equivalent) Pentium 100MHz processor is the minimum platform required; an Intel (or equivalent) Pentium 133MHz processor is recommended.

➤ 32MB of RAM is the minimum memory requirement.

➤ A color monitor (256 colors or better) is recommended.

➤ Available disk storage of at least 10MB is recommended.